Volume I

MANAGEMENT & CONTROL OF GROWTH

Issues • Techniques • Problems • Trends

Edited by
Randall W. Scott
with the assistance of
David J. Brower
and
Dallas D. Miner

1975

ULI

The Urban Land Institute
1200 18th Street, N.W.
Washington, D.C. 20036

About the Urban Land Institute

ULI—the Urban Land Institute is an independent, non-profit research and educational organization founded in 1936 to serve the diverse needs of those involved in land use planning, development, and management. A membership organization, ULI currently has more than 6,000 members in the United States, Canada, and 50 other countries.

ULI conducts research on environmental, legislative, administrative, and other impacts of development innovations; further, it suggests improved techniques in land use development and management, and tracks changing social and economic trends. Six councils—composed of ULI members—address major land use issues and formulate workable solutions to key problems in their respective areas of expertise.

In all of its activities, ULI has advocated a balanced approach between meeting the needs of a growing population and preserving the quality of our natural environment. Land use techniques developed by ULI have set high standards in this respect.

About the Editing of These Volumes

The Urban Land Institute's research efforts and editing of these volumes have been assisted through a research grant from the **United States Department of Housing and Urban Development**—Office of Policy Development and Research. The contents and mode of presentation do not necessarily represent any official policies or views of the U.S. Department of HUD.

Susan L. Kendall: Coordinator
Robert L. Helms: Production Manager
Sarah V. Lantz: Production Assistant
Barbara A. Taitano: Artist

Printed in the United States of America
Library of Congress Catalog Number: 74-83560
© Copyright 1975 by ULI—The Urban Land Institute

TABLE OF CONTENTS
VOLUME I

CONTENTS OF VOLUME II

CONTENTS OF VOLUME III

Foreword

The Urban Land Institute is proud to publish these books, titled *Management & Control of Growth: Issues-Techniques-Problems-Trends*. We feel that they will fulfill a necessary and vital function in the discussion of growth controls, and will prove to be valuable reference materials for several years to come.

In December of 1973, the ULI monthly magazine—*Urban Land*—ran an article covering the text of a speech I delivered several months earlier. In speaking at that point in time to the Metropolitan Washington Board of Trade, I noted that "I hope the information developed in these meetings is widely disseminated . . . and I want to offer today our willingness to cooperate; for my part, I want to assure you of the continuing interest of the Urban Land Institute in this topic—of the debate over growth."

It is now just more than a year later; in the period of approximately eleven months, this material was assembled, examined, and prepared for publication; it is an endeavor which should prove useful to planners, officials, citizens, attorneys, and others throughout the country whose communities are concerned about the issues involved in the management of growth.

The Urban Land Institute—a nonprofit research and educational organization—has consistently articulated a firm position regarding the need for quality land use planning and development practices. It has provided a national organizational focus for private individuals, corporate officers, corporations, and public officials who are concerned with the use of land and who desire to exchange ideas and support the formulation of creative, yet practical, approaches to the solution of land use problems. With over 6,000 members representing all segments of the development and planning communities, ULI has been a significant force in improving the quality of the urban environment through the sharing of experience and ideas. As a result of these interests and the efforts of its members and staff, ULI has a long record of achievement in the development of techniques for responsible and better use of land, and in promoting these techniques throughout this country and in foreign nations.

In all of its activities, ULI has advocated a balanced approach between meeting the needs of a growing population and preserving the quality of our natural environment. Land use techniques developed by ULI have set high standards in this respect; many development projects have used these standards and provide testimony to the fact that desirable and fair compromises can be made among what sometimes appear to be incompatible objectives of growth, environmental protection, and housing.

Because of the obvious and important connection between the issues discussed in this publication and the stated interests of ULI —responsible growth, environmental protection, innovations in land use management —we are pleased to have sponsored this publication. Although the material presented here is not a policy statement of ULI—the Urban Land Institute, it is our belief that the documents will be invaluable to many persons, including ULI members. As the course of events is altered

by legislation, litigation, and other policy actions, ULI will continue to participate in the
broad dissemination of information on this
and related subjects of concern.

David E. Stahl
Executive Vice President
ULI—the Urban Land Institute

The Editor

Randall W. Scott was, for a major portion of preparation of these volumes, Research Counsel for ULI—the Urban Land Institute. During 1975 he was Chief Research Attorney for the Advisory Commission on Housing and Urban Growth (of the American Bar Association). Scott holds master's degrees in planning from the London School of Economics, in governmental administration from the Wharton School, and in urban affairs from Boston University, he studied law at Harvard University.

Acknowledgements

The Editor wishes to acknowledge the significant assistance and contributions of **Mr. David J. Brower** and **Mr. Dallas D. Miner**, in collaborating on the editing of these volumes. Their efforts, aid, and advice were invaluable to the entire project.

Brower is Director of Urban Services for the Center for Urban and Regional Studies, at the University of North Carolina. A graduate of the University of Michigan as well as its Law School, he formerly was Assistant Director of the Center of Urban Affairs and Director of the Division of Community Planning at Indiana University (Bloomington). Previously, he served with the Urban Renewal Administration of the Housing and Home Finance Agency.

Miner is Director of Communications, and Environmental Analyst, at the Urban Land Institute. A graduate of the University of Wisconsin from which he also holds his master's in environmental science, he formerly was Assistant Executive Vice President of the Connecticut Conservation Association. Previously the editor of several environmental journals, he has written a number of award-winning white papers on land use and environmental-related subjects.

For their continued assistance in this undertaking, the Editor expresses his gratitude to several individuals:

> *Edward N. Reiner*, Program Analyst, Comprehensive Planning Research—HUD (a graduate of Wharton School, he holds a law degree from Syracuse University; formerly, he practiced law in New York);
>
> *Suzanne M. Wellborn*, Director, Program Coordinator/Land Use Environment, at the National Realty Committee (a graduate of the University of North Carolina, from which she also holds a master's in regional/environmental planning);
>
> *Susan L. Kendall*, Editor/Writer, Communications Division, and co-editor of *Environmental Comment* at the Urban Land Institute (she is a graduate of Azusa Pacific College).

Of importance throughout the project stages were the following persons: Donald E. Priest, Director of Research at ULI (a graduate of Stanford University, he holds a master's in city planning from Berkeley); David E. Stahl, ULI Executive Vice President (formerly Comptroller of the City of Chicago, and a graduate of Miami University); Hunter A. Hogan, the elected President of ULI (of Goodman-Segar-Hogan, Inc. of Norfolk, Virginia); and Robert L. Helms, ULI Director of Central Services (formerly with *U.S. News & World Report*, he attended Columbia Union College).

The Editor further wishes to express appreciation for the help of several federal governmental officials: James E. Hoben, Assistant Director, Comprehensive Planning Research—HUD; John J. Surmeier, Program Manager, Division of Advanced Productivity Research and Technology—National Science Foundation; and Edwin H. Clark, II, Senior Economist—Council on Environmental Quality.

Many other persons were of assistance: Katherine Sullivan, Elizabeth Jester, Ethel Hall, and others from the staffs of UNC, ULI, HUD, ABA, and the authors, publishers, and their staffs—from early solicitation of manuscripts in 1974, to completion in early 1975.

To the authors whose works appear here, the Editor expresses his appreciation for their unusual degree of willingness to allow nearly unbridled discretion regarding the method and amount of the editing undertaken. In the context of the chapters in which each appears, the material as edited should be useful to the reader and fair to the authors concerned; to the degree that there are any problems as to content or substance, the responsibility is not theirs, but that of the Editor.

Most especially, a debt is owed to Gail and to many friends who tolerated nearly unmanageable demands and uncontrolled hours in the pursuit of the elusive finé to these "managed growth" books.

INTRODUCTION FOR VOLUME I

MANAGEMENT & CONTROL OF GROWTH

The ethic of growth in America is increasingly being challenged; no longer is it being accepted unquestioningly as a premise of progress. Its effects on the quality of life are widely debated, and its management and control are seen by many as essential elements of modern land use policy.

So begins the *Executive Summary* (Chapter One) of this three-volume reference work, titled: *Management & Control of Growth: Issues— Techniques— Problems— Trends*. Containing works by over 140 authors—many of whom are renowned researchers and practioners—this anthology of material is designed to provide a convenient resource document for planners, public officials, developers, academicians, attorneys, and others who are concerned with this exceptionally complex area of public policy.

These volumes offer a cross-section of the field, just as it is beginning to develop rapidly, and as public interest is being generated across the country. Therefore, to a large degree they are intended as reference works into the managed growth topic area . . . to summarize and to bring together a number of new, often-cited, or less well-known studies and other written material in this field.

Original articles as well as reprints are contained in these volumes. Whereas some issues are treated in great depth, other sections of the books include summary versions of a series of reports: studies which local decision-makers may not have had the time to scrutinize in original form or length due to the pressures of daily operations or simply, immediate availability and convenience. Thus, the articles provide an overview of managed growth questions, while the serious researcher inevitably will be led to basic studies, to cross-references, and to more current data/information as it becomes available.

A word about the **organization of these volumes** is in order. Each text begins with a brief introduction—as with this one—which outlines the contents of that particular volume and its general relationship to the other two in the set. Each of the chapters in the books is also prefaced with an article-by-article description and comment which guides the reader to those items which may be of greatest interest by explaining the themes developed in that chapter and the central ideas of the various articles. (Finally, the three-volume set is begun, in Chapter 1, with an "Executive Summary.")

VOLUME 1 proceeds by evaluating the premise that new attitudes concerning land use controls and growth are being evidenced by a significant segment of the country's professionals, officials, and citizens . . . and that "managed growth" is an alternative which more and more communities are tending to explore. After the **Chapter 1** Executive Summary, **Chapter 2** presents a series of articles which relate to the general theme of the rise of the "new mood" regarding growth in America (see the articles by the Rockefeller Task Force and Cahn). It is pointed out that "our society is at a juncture where traditional assumptions are being tested" (in the article by Train), and this attitude is explored at some depth by other articles. This issue is being widely discussed, as several articles attest (Forbes magazine, and O'Leary); the "new mood" is also both defended (Reilly) and critiqued (Uddo) by several authors.

Chapter 3 shifts to the recognition and explanation of managed growth as a planning and management alternative (Finkler) . . . an idea whose time has come in terms of a dawning professional interest of many planners and public officials. Several organizations point out why it is essential that local communities learn about this growing debate, and deal effectively with the problems and repercussions of land use and development (the National Association of Counties, Zero Population Growth, the International City Management Association, and the Stanford Environmental Law Society; some of the policies of other organizations—as the American Society of Planning Officials, the American Institute of Planners, and the American Institute of Architects—are represented elsewhere in these volumes). The insights and the strategies incorporated in this chapter should prove to be of significant interest to the reader.

Chapter 4 represents a critique of the "traditional way of doing things," with a series of articles (Heyman, Babcock and Bosselman, Ragsdale on Siegan, Reiner, and Tarlock) outlining the system's shortcomings and the usual judicial approaches to zoning and planning. Alternative systems are examined (Sullivan and the *Fasano* case, and Fagin's introduction of the concept of development timing). At the same time, several of the reports mentioned above ("The Quiet Revolution," "The Taking Issue," and "Windfalls For Wipeouts") are presented, or are critiqued (Hagman, and more indirectly, Janis).

Chapter 5 ventures into the area of "limits to growth" . . . one of the topics which originally sparked much of the "managed growth" debate. Several of the authors present the basic thesis of "limits" (Macdonald, "The Ecologist" magazine, and the [report of the] Commission on Population Growth and the American Future), while others criticize the issues presented (Ruff and Muys). There are a number of articles which alternatively stress the risks of growth, or point out the dangers which lie in zero population/economic growth (Klein, Zeckhauser, Thompson, McKean, Peterson, Alonso, Day, Johnson, and Agelasto).

The next two chapters analyze the problems inherent in local attempts to exclude development. While most of the authors address primarily "exclusionary zoning" as it relates to low-income persons, the reader should bear in mind that many of these same arguments may be applicable to housing for a broader spectrum of income ranges and for development types and land uses other than merely residential. The traditional "exclusionary land use" challenge is examined at length in **Chapter 6**: a question which certainly will, and perhaps ought to follow the local decision-maker as he addresses issues in the managed growth area. A series of articles raise the primary issues in exclusionary land use/housing cases (Scott and Lauber), suggest alternative tactics for litigation (Williams), and evaluate the role of the judiciary in such cases (Haar & Iatridis, Furman, and Levin & Rose).

Chapter 7 completes the volume, by emphasizing the theme of regionalism and "inclusion." One article (The National Commission on Urban Problems) points out the problems and failures—with regard to exclusion and discrimination in 1968, while another article (U.S. Commission on Civil Rights) addresses the dilemmas of mid-1974. In this chapter, proposals are made for local "inclusionary controls" (the article by the Davidoffs) and for metropolitan housing allocation planning (Erber). Several other authors assess the viability of regional analysis as an "answer" for exclusionary zoning challenges (Burchell et al., point out the "pitfalls of the regional remedy").

The volume closes with the editorial observation that: "It should be stressed that we are entering an era when growth controls will affect more than racial groups and the lowest-income persons . . . . Policies on [managed] growth, if mismanaged, could strike directly at a large portion of the American public." This concern, along with the very real desire of many localities to control their rates of growth, carries over into the next volume in this set.

In **VOLUME II,** the emphasis is on examining the growth management programs and experiences of a number of communities across the country, and on exploring the legal and policy ramifications of several of the major categories of growth control techniques. Of primary importance are the two major managed growth cases of the early 1970s: those involving Ramapo, New York and Petaluma, California.

The first two chapters include articles by several of the litigators, public officials, planners, and other commentators who probe the issues and dilemmas presented in these two cases (one of which—*Petaluma*—still is being appealed through the federal court system). A third chapter analyzes a series of interrelated cases—including *Ramapo* and *Petaluma* as well as a number of others—and particularly, develops the idea of a constitutional "right to travel/mobility" as it relates to questions of equity in local and regional housing opportunities.

The next two chapters involve broad-ranging surveys of communities and their growth management tools/strategies, and includes analyses of the debates regarding such methods as interim development controls, the application of timing/phasing/ sequencing procedures in planning, long-term changes (in terms of utilizing certain types of land use controls), and the use of capital facilities to manage growth. Finally, there is a chapter outlining various methodologies for impact measurement— including fiscal analysis—of proposed land use development(s).

This set is completed with **VOLUME III**, which carries forward the discussions of the issues and techniques in growth management and then explores the roles of the various levels of government in land use-related programs. Some of the more innovative mechanisms are treated in depth in the first two chapters: environmental impact assessment and EISs, transfer of development rights, land banking, preservation of agricultural/open space, and other flexible or systematic methods.

Three chapters seek to outline and evaluate the impacts of local/regional, state, and federal programs and policies. There are surveys and articles on regionalism, state housing programs, state land use bills and a proposed model land development code, federal environmental policies, and the various inter-jurisdictional impacts of growth management schemes.

One chapter sets forth some of the reactions of the private development sector to growth controls, with analyses of "changing modes of operation," the pressures on the home-building industry, and the need for new "planning partnerships." The final two chapters of the volume include an article which explores and forecasts a number of the growth management dilemmas for the next decade, and a full research bibliography which (in conjunction with the footnote sections of many of the articles throughout the volumes) provides a valuable reference tool to the reader of these texts.

NOTE TO THE READER:

Many persons were of assistance in the preparation of these volumes—but particularly the authors, publishers, and staffs—from early solicitation of manuscripts in 1974, to publication in 1975.

To the authors whose works appear here, the Editor expresses his appreciation for the nearly unbridled discretion allowed regarding the method and amount of editing undertaken. In the context of the chapters in which each appears, the material as edited/remaining is representative of the writer's work and should be useful to the reader; to the degree that there are any problems as to content or substance, the responsibility is not that of the authors, but of the Editor.

The commentaries preceding each chapter do not necessarily represent the views or policies of either the Urban Land Institute or of the U.S. Department of Housing and Urban Development.

EXECUTIVE SUMMARY

Chapter One consists of an *Executive Summary* for this three–volume set. In an anthology such as this, the Executive Summary is designed as an "introduction" to the topic of growth management. Its basic purpose is to present an overview of the issues, techniques, problems, and trends in the managed growth field. "Capsule versions" of the chapters are not presented here, since this is accomplished in the separate introductions and critiques which preface each of the twenty chapters. (To the degree that cross-references to the individual articles and chapters are necessary there are footnotes to the text of the summary).

A large number of articles, pamphlets, and books will be appearing over the next several years in this significant area of land use planning and public policy analysis. *Management & Control of Growth* will serve as background resources current through 1974, to which elected officials, developers, practicing professionals, and other interested citizens—who are not likely to have the time individually to undertake surveys of documents, or to collect complete assortments of materials on managed growth questions—can turn for reference/research purposes; and then can build upon these three volumes with more current, detailed, or specialized information in the field.

Management & Control of Growth

An Introduction and Summary*

INTRODUCTION

The ethic of growth in America is increasingly being challenged; no longer is it being accepted unquestioningly as a premise of progress. Its effects on the quality of life are widely debated, and its management and control are seen by many as essential elements of modern land use policy.

In more and more communities across the country, the costs and benefits of continued growth are emerging as major public issues.[1] There is hesitation over accommodating further development with its attendant consequences of greater numbers of residents and higher densities, economic expansion, rapid consumption of land, and alteration of the environment. Time and again—in public hearings, in elections and bond referenda, and in the professional literature[2] as well as the press[3]—there is manifested strong resistance to unbridled growth and inadequate land use management. Misgivings have been expressed by diverse groups within society and have led, in some communities, to significant changes in public policies which affect the nature and extent of local growth.

At the same time, this trend has not been without vigorous opposition; dissent over the implications of unwise growth restrictions has been heard from various business interests, property owners, builders, and advocates for the disenfranchised:[4] the poor, minorities, the underemployed, and the aged. Frequently, the basis for opposition stems from the fact that the far-reaching repercussions of growth controls are not analyzed at length by those who are caught in the midst of public debate over alternative futures for their communities. The range of tools, systems, and methodologies—as well as the inherent legal, social, economic, and administrative questions—often are not subject to

---

*The Introduction and Summary to *Management and Control of Growth: Issues— Techniques—Problems—Trends*, 3 vols. [Washington, D. C.: Urban Land Institute 1975], was prepared principally by Randall W. Scott, American Bar Association (Wash. D.C.) with editorial collaboration by Dallas D. Miner of ULI-the Urban Land Institute.

1. Introductory subject material in this regard is contained in **Chapters 2, 3, and 5 of Volume I;** there is further elaboration in **Chapter 12 of Volume II.**
2. The depth of professional organizational interest is indicated in **Chapter 3 of Volume I,** which contains articles from the American Society of Planning Officials, the International City Management Association, the National Association of Counties, Zero Population Growth, Inc., and others. Additional organizational viewpoints are included elsewhere in these texts, from the American Institute of Architects, the Conservation Foundation, the Council of State Governments, the Mortgage Bankers Association, the National Association of Home Builders, the U.S. Department of Housing and Urban Development, the U.S. Department of the Interior, the U.S. Environmental Protection Agency, and other agencies.
3. Series of articles have appeared, for example, in the *Christian Science Monitor* (the article by Cahn is reprinted in **Chapter 2 of Volume I**); in the *New York Times* the (article by Hill, and others such as that by Klein, which is reprinted in **Chapter 5 of Volume I**); and many of the major, national, weekly magazines. Area and local newspapers typically now are more consistently covering significant growth and development-related issues (see, for example, the material by Bredemeier in **Chapter 16 of Volume III** [and additional information on the D. C. area, in the Washington Council of Governments article in **Chapter 16**]).
4. See the articles by Zeckhauser, McKean, Day, Thompson, Alonso, Johnson, and Agelasto in **Chapter 5 of Volume I;** by Scott, and Lauber, in **Chapter 6 of Volume I;** and by the National Commission on Urban Problems, and the U.S. Commission on Civil Rights, in **Chapter 7 of Volume I.**

sufficient evaluation.[5] In fact, some interest groups operate on the principle that in the midst of debate and confusion, political support can be generated through the strategic manipulation of public opinion.[6]

Solid information and resource materials can assist local governments and citizens in managed growth decision-making and can temper such other circumstances as limited staff time and expertise, and unfamiliarity with new tools and system concepts. The volume of literature dealing with these issues recently has grown to impressive proportions,[7] but too often the breadth of coverage as well as the degree of dissemination have been limited. The purpose of this three-volume publication is to respond to this need, by assembling a cross-section[8] of material on many of the basic issues in the growth management field. Intended as resource documents, the volumes provide a modest beginning as anthologies and reference works to a burgeoning subject which has significant, long-term impacts on the viability of human settlements. This Summary—which begins the volumes—serves both as an overview of the issues and as a guide to specific topic areas within the volumes. Extensive footnotes to specific topic areas appear at the bottom of each page for the convenience of the reader.

Volume I deals with the changing attitudes toward economic, population, housing and environment issues—including an examination of "managed growth" as a critical planning and land use management alternative. It includes critiques and commentaries on the "limits to growth"—problems, pitfalls, and potentials—and zoning powers and techniques, the taking issue, and windfalls for wipeouts proposals. Finally, there is treatment of social and economic equity questions, exclusionary zoning and the role of courts, and regional land use and housing approaches.

Volume II covers a number of complex areas in managed growth, including several of the major court battles such as *Ramapo* and *Petaluma* (with a series of articles by the litigants and other commentators, as well as the texts of several of the opinions). There is an examination of the many available tools and methods for controlling growth—such as interim zoning, the phasing of capital facilities, development moratoria, etc.—with several nationwide surveys by planners, local and state administrators, attorneys, and other practitioners on a variety of case experiences and techniques in growth management. The volume ends with articles on the problems and methodologies of fiscal impact analysis.

Volume III has overviews of such other land use techniques as land banking, Planned Unit Developments (PUDs), agricultural districting and open space preservation, carrying capacity analysis, Environmental Impact Statements (EISs), and Transfer Development Rights (TDRs). Other chapters examine the influence of local, state, and federal laws on growth patterns, covering such areas as the role of state housing

---

5. Regarding a series of growth management conferences in 1973, one commentator described the typical rush-for-controls over-local-growth as follows: "The halls between the meeting rooms were often filled with concerned officials looking for a few quickie, court-tested control ordinances. 'Hey buddy, can you spare an urban limit line? Well, then how about some good subdivision improvement requirements?' " Earl Finkler, "Non-growth Professionals Needed to Help Slow Things Down," *Landscape Architecture* (April 1974).
6. For operational gambits ranging from the fair to the invalid, see the articles by the Zero Population Growth and Stanford Environmental Society, in **Chapter 3 of Volume I.**
7. The reader will find cross-references to specialized literature in the bibliographies contained in various parts of these volumes. The most extensive is provided at the end of **Volume III**; brief reference sources are included as separate bibliographies or as footnote sections in many of the articles in these volumes.
8. An effort has been made in these volumes to present both operational and "theoretical" analyses and to retain a balance of the points of view and policies of diverse groups.

programs and land use laws, federal Environmental Protection Agency (EPA) regulations, and the national growth policy report. The volume concludes with views of/from the development industry, a discussion of diplomacy planning and planning partnerships, and an extensive municipal growth guidance systems bibliography.

Managed growth issues and techniques are consuming the interest of greater numbers of communities and persons in the private and public sectors. While many localities have long utilized zoning and other land use regulations in their jurisdictions, the recognition of the necessity to affirmatively guide growth in an integrated and systematic manner, is of more recent vintage.

THE SEMANTICS OF GROWTH MANAGEMENT

The rhetoric in growth management and control runs deep. Precision of meaning is often lacking, and there is a tendency to apply convenient but non-specific labels to the policies or methodologies which are being delineated.

Managed growth—for the purpose of this Summary—means the utilization by government of a variety of traditional and evolving techniques, tools, plans, and activities to purposefully guide local patterns of land use, including the manner, location, rate, and nature of development.

Ideally, *managed growth* consists of a well-integrated,[9] efficient, and affirmative system where choices or decisions are made explicitly and with full knowledge of the variables and trade-offs involved, and where the programs are coordinated in furtherance of clear community growth and land use objectives. Yet the concept of *managed growth* is often used to indicate the use of even fragmented and somewhat ineffectual governmental methods which lack comprehensiveness or goals as a basis, but which nevertheless are designed to significantly impact on a community's land use patterns and growth rate. Historically, comprehensive and explicit managed growth systems have been anomalies in the land use arena, as most controls or regulations have tended to be oriented toward a project-by-project response. Fully developed managed growth systems, therefore, merit the reader's attention and careful scrutiny. The underlying issues inevitably will consume the attention of more communities around the nation in the decades to come.[10] The tools which are incorporated will be defended and attacked in various quarters, and the principles, methods, purposes, and effects will be revisited and critiqued time and again, as is done in many of the articles in these volumes.

Other commonly seen labels such as zero growth, stop growth, and non-growth, are

---

9. Tunnel vision and dogged pursuit of singular agency-defined objectives can be severely disruptive to the effectiveness of a managed growth system. Programs for the construction of utilities, for example, can be either useful or counter-productive to the containment of development. (For the facility debate, see the questions raised by Forestell, Seeger, Ramsay, and the Hirsts in **Chapter 12 of Volume II**.) Agency policies established by state and federal governments can also raise significant issues and problems; see the lengthy discussions regarding the U.S. Environmental Protection Agency's programs in a number of articles in **Chapter 18 of Volume III**.

10. The importance of the issue is stressed in the second biennial report on national growth, submitted by President Ford to Congress in December of 1974. "In short, people want livable, safe inner city neighborhoods; more orderly, lower cost, new developments in suburban areas; and adequate, well serviced rural communities. These public preferences are the driving force behind the growth issues of the 1970s and the search by the private and public sectors for better management of the processes by which the Nation grows and develops." *National Growth and Development* (Washington, D. C.: Government Printing Office, HUD-386-CPD, December 1974), p. 19. [See also the articles by Selvaggi and Ashley in **Chapter 18 of Volume III**, regarding the growth reports.]

often used ambiguously, seemingly dependent upon the interpretations of the commentators involved. For the purposes of this Summary, such terms are differentiated from "managed growth." While a particular land use control or technique may be used both in managed growth schemes as well as in zero/stop/non-growth attempts, the latter are representative primarily of local "attitudes" and somewhat crude efforts to halt much or all of the community's growth activity. The developer who is denied an application after costly and time-consuming processing through numerous boards and agencies, may explain away the denial as an instance of "non-growth."[11] On the other hand, an environmentalist may view such a situation not as a question of growth vs. non-growth, but rather as an admirable decision to prevent despoilation of limited natural resources. Others in the community may visualize certain development proposals as threatening the quality of local education systems; the city engineer may interpret growth pressures primarily in light of facility capacities; and so forth. Thus from various points of view, the characterization of governmental attempts at growth control will differ. Certainly one is hard-pressed to decide what label, if any, to attach to most local growth management exercises.

With this caveat over terminology in mind, we can turn our attention to the rise of the still-cautious new interest in growth issues.

THE EVOLUTION OF NEW ATTITUDES

The predominant attitude in many communities long has been one of reliance on the growth ethic. Local business associations, as well as public agencies, have carried out aggressive programs of industrial and commercial expansion. Various forms of boosterism—including tax incentives, national advertising proclaiming the productivity of the local labor force and the vitality of the area's economy, and the preparation of large "industrial parks" prior to the securing of new industries — have been widespread. Local progress was, and often still is, equated with the number of jobs created and dollar-increases in local spending; such sources of local pride lent the business community and the public a degree of confidence in the future of the locality and its quality of life.

Attitudes regarding continued community growth include:

Growth stabilizes or improves the local tax situation by broadening the tax base and reducing per capita tax burdens (all other factors held constant [as inflation, new service levels demands, etc.]);

Most growth "pays its own way"[12] and, even though some growth may have costs which exceed new tax revenues, the overall benefits (as increased retail spending, etc.) counterbalance the direct costs;

New development brings a broader range of goods and services to the community through secondary and tertiary, as well as primary, growth;

Growth improves local wage levels and brings greater flexibility in job opportunities to

---

11. Yet, the perception may be quite correct at times. One developer described the process as follows: "A county commissioner bragged about his method of stopping growth, at a conference called by the governor of his state. He called it the 'pinball technique.' Just bounce the builder-developer around from one agency or department in the County to another until you wear him out and he loses interest." Jay Janis, "Managed Growth—Panel Presentation" (Speech before the National Municipal League, National Conference on Government, San Diego, November 17-19, 1974).

12. For a discussion of fiscal impact analysis, see the articles by Gruen Gruen + Associates, Ashley Economic Services, Muller, and Sternlieb & Burchell, in **Chapter 13 of Volume II.**

existing resident-workers, women not currently employed, and young persons who might otherwise leave the community for employment possibilities;

Growth brings a wider range of choice in housing types and locations; and,

Development and expansion eventually result in improved community facilities such as fire and health services, roads, schools, and so forth.

For a time therefore, growth per se was not perceived as a significant local "problem"; the net fiscal benefits to local government (gross tax revenues less public costs) of further development were, and in many instances still are, positive. Also, the then-existing facilities of the community often were able to absorb the moderate increases of gradual growth; many communities simply delayed the upgrading or expansion of inadequate facilities . . . artificially inflating "growth is good" calculations since overall costs were low. Finally, where market/demographic pressures were not overly strong, newly-arriving residents tended by self-selection to conform to the existing community "social structure."

Recently, however, there has been a swing of sentiment toward limiting the local rates of growth. Though many communities still favor expansion, many have turned sharply from active promotion of growth and residential development. Frequently, past patterns of local growth were improperly planned for, and changing social and economic conditions set the community on a course which eventually led to serious problems and a dramatic reversal in public attitudes. Where the pursuit of growth had not been carefully plotted, and where opportunities for sound land use and provision of adequate public services had been lost — the honeymoon with growth and expansion began to evaporate.[13] According to the President's Council on Environmental Quality: "Land use and growth issues are becoming increasingly important to the public, and assumptions about the inherent value of growth and change are being discarded in even the more conservative regions . . . "[14]

By the early 1970s, the backlog of demand for more adequate and improved facilities could no longer be ignored; the "catch-up" costs tended to be high, setting the stage for taxpayer reaction against increased costs, poor land use management, and further development. To these backlogged investment and tax issues were added demands for expanded public services, the costs of specialized personnel and higher pay scales, increased administrative overhead, inflation, and so forth. These items tended to edge tax loads even higher, lending credence in the public's mind to the seeming connection between growth and higher costs (as for water and sewer systems), inconvenience (as congestion on roads and highways), environmental damage (as to water supplies or recreational areas), and lower quality public service (parks, schools, etc.).

As growth accelerated and housing demand increased, "non-conforming" development was experienced. Existing residents began to perceive differing housing types, higher densities, and even some of the newcomers themselves as threats to the structure of the community, as disruptive of the status quo, and as a disturbance to existing life

---

13. Warnings as to the disadvantageous aspects of growth were being sounded by national groups in the 1960s. One prestigious organization cited a series of the consequences of "critical importance for the well-being of the nation . . . [of the] continuation of recent urbanization and economic growth trends." These included diseconomies of scale, social and psychological costs, deepening problems of the central cities, ghettoization, decline of rural areas, and acceleration of sprawl. Advisory Commission on Intergovernmental Relations, *Urban and Rural America: Policies for Future Growth* (Washington, D.C.: ACIR, 1968), p. 124.

14. Council on Environmental Quality, "Memorandum for CEQ Correspondents" (mimeographed, July 31, 1974), p. 5.

styles.[15] Of particular concern were the "problems" created for local school systems, and the perceived loss of neighborhood and small town character. Fueling this resistance to change was, and is, the dichotomy of city and suburb, the increased level of seemingly unresolvable social problems, and a growing disenchantment with major reform programs including federally subsidized housing, urban renewal, etc.

With transportation improvements that encouraged commuting, and with competitive regional shopping centers that drew shoppers from local stores, business interests in many smaller areas began to feel that the promised benefits of growth in the local economy were not likely to be experienced. Likewise, to the extent that transportation routes improved, "broad" local employment bases for mobility, job choice, and stability were less necessary (some localities even determined that existence as mere bedroom communities was quite desirable, and they adamantly resisted non-residential growth).

Time and again, the message was driven home to the public that sprawl and its consequences were accelerating,[16] with valuable land being consumed in what appeared to be a poorly guided or unplanned manner. Traditional land use controls typically were not being administered effectively or pursuant to explicit local goals regarding growth.[17] The process was viewed as failing to live up to its potential, as subject to political manipulation, and as bringing, too often, unacceptable land use patterns. A number of well-known commentators criticized existing methods, finding them subject to "games" and "dilemmas" which failed to maximize the public welfare. Such dissatisfaction began to provide an impetus for communities to wield greater use of the police power in order to restrict or limit growth.

Such local concerns were developing against the backdrop of national and world-wide attention[18] to the impacts of growth. The zero-population-growth advocates[19] stressed

15. For a discussion of exclusionary attitudes, see such articles as those by Heyman and by Babcock & Bosselman in **Chapter 4 of Volume I**, and those cited in note 4, above, regarding **Chapter 6**. See also the articles by Peterson and Raflo **(Chapter 3 of Volume I)**; the latter says that recent newcomers bring with them higher expectations of public services than might have been generated by "old-time" residents in a static community.

16. See the executive summary of the major national report—*Costs of Sprawl*—contained in **Chapter 13 of Volume II.**

17. This is the focus of several articles in **Chapter 4 of Volume I:** see the discussions by Heyman, Reiner, Tarlock, Ragsdale, Sullivan, and Babcock & Bosselman. Reference is also made to zoning hearing problems in the material by O'Leary and by *Forbes* magazine, in **Chapter 2 of Volume I**. The "classic" works in this regard are: Richard F. Babcock, *The Zoning Game* (Madison: University of Wisconsin Press, 1966); and Daniel R. Mandelker, *The Zoning Dilemma* (The Bobbs-Merrill Company, Inc., 1971).

18. In terms of popular literature which enjoyed widespread circulation, some of the following material has significant public impact relative to "growth limitations": "Blueprint for Survival," *The Ecologist* 2 (January 1972):22; Kenneth E. Boulding, "The Economics of the Coming Spaceship Earth," in Henry Jarrett, ed., *Environmental Quality in a Growing Economy* (Baltimore: Johns Hopkins Press, 1966); Rachel Carson, *Silent Spring* (Boston: Houghton Mifflin Company, 1962); Commission on Population Growth and the American Future, *Population and the American Future* (Washington, D. C.: Government Printing Office, 1972); Paul R. Ehrlich, *The Population Bomb* (New York: Ballantine Books, 1971); Jay W. Forrester, *World Dynamics* (Cambridge: Wright Allen, 1971); John Maddox, *The Doomsday Syndrome* (New York: McGraw Hill, 1972); Donella H. Meadows, Dennis L. Meadows, et al., *The Limits to Growth* (New York: Universe Books, 1972); E. J. Mishan, *The Costs of Economic Growth* (London: Staples Press, 1967); E. J. Mishan, *Technology and Growth: The Price We Pay* (New York: Praeger, 1970); and Barbara Ward and Rene Dubos, *Care and Maintenance of a Small Planet: Only One Earth* (New York: W. W. Norton, 1972).

Several recent books in this area are Kan Chen and Karl F. Lagler, eds., *Growth Policy: Population, Environment, and Beyond* (Ann Arbor: University of Michigan Press, 1974); Robert L. Heilbroner, *An Inquiry Into the Human Prospect* (New York: W. W. Norton & Company, Inc. 1974); Lester R. Brown, *In the Human Interest* (New York: W. W. Norton & Company, Inc., 1974); and the excellent survey in "The No-Growth Society," *Daedalus* 102 (Fall 1973, special issue).

19. See the article by ZPG in **Chapter 3 of Volume I.**

the dangers of increased populations.[20] A number of renowned economists voiced strenuous opposition to pursuit of the ethic of growth which, they claimed, transfixed the attention of national governments. This tended to cause a failure to calculate the "real" costs of growth diverting national energies from the resolution of major social, environmental, and economic problems; specifically those of limited global food supplies and dwindling resources and energy.[21] But the zero-growthers call did not escape criticism.[22] Critics saw many of the projections of doom as overstated, illogical,[23] or lacking in understanding of the capability of technology, government, and other social processes to accomplish needed change. Some felt that an economy geared toward zero-growth could lead to instability, social injustice, and even international disharmony.[24]

Perhaps equally persuasive to the general public were the alarms sounded by environmentalists and conservationists who viewed the growth orientation of society as inflicting serious wounds to the environment. The problems cited ran the gamut from the loss of scenic wilderness, to the major dangers imposed by heavy concentrations of pollutants in air, water, food, and other life support systems. Thus, the "new environmentalism" movement gained strength on the local as well as the global levels. Many localities formed conservation commissions and citizen environmental advisory or review boards, adopted special regulatory procedures such as the designation of critical areas, or established on-going environmental assessment procedures,[25] including carrying capacity

---

20. Given the current composition of the United States population, some experts suggest that it will take approximately 75 years before the population stabilizes at a fixed [theoretical] level. (This assumes a 2.1 replacement fertility rate constant for all years through 2050, and with no international in-migration.)

    In 1970, the total resident population of the U.S., including members of the armed forces stationed abroad, was 204,335,000. [This total represents the Census figures of 203,235,000 plus 1,100,000.]

    Using a "zero population growth rate"—defined more accurately as a replacement fertility rate—of 2.1 births per woman, and using the Census Bureau's projection of a July 1, 1972 base-population figure of 208,872,000 . . . the population in Year 2020 would be 297,756,000. (This figure includes the addition of persons through legal immigration at a constant annual estimated rate of 400,000. [This is a ten-year average of immigration figures used by the Census; it compares with an average of 384,671 persons on the average during the years 1970-1974.])

    Prior to 1972, the fertility rate exceeded the 2.1 figure. In 1972, it had fallen and remained below that level, and continued to decline to the 1974 level of 1.9. (Some doubts have been expressed as to whether this low rate will continue, due to the young age composition of the population and the possibility that childbearing decisions may have accounted for only a temporary delay . . . and thus an artificially depressed rate.)

    The Census Bureau, using three alternative fertility rates—1.8, 2.5, and 2.8—projects population figures for the year 2020 as 264,564,000, 351,368,000, and 392,030,000 respectively. These represent increases over the 1972 base of 27 percent, 68 percent, and 88 percent. The 2.1 figure (including in-migration, and thus not true ZPG) of 297,746,000 in Year 2020 would result in a 43 percent increase.
21. This is the theme of several articles in **Chapter 5 of Volume I**; see particularly the materials by Macdonald, and in The Ecologist.
22. See the critiques by Ruff and Muys, and the general analyses by Zeckhauser, McKean, Thompson, and Alonso—in **Chapter 5 of Volume I.**
23. Ruff, in **Chapter 5 of Volume I**, sets forth major problems which he has with the analysis in the well-known The Limits to Growth (note 18, above).
24. See the observations of Klein, in **Chapter 5 of Volume I**. It has been suggested that national and international zero economic growth can restrict the social and economic mobility of certain groups, freezing their current (relative) status. A number of writers also believe that with ZEG (if there were no welfare or redistribution programs in effect to mitigate the disadvantages—see the articles by Zeckhauser and Johnson in **Chapter 5 of Volume I**), the foundations of society would be shaken, (on the other hand, the report of the Commission on Population Growth and the American Future makes findings to the contrary; see **Chapter 5 of Volume I.**) a "poverty of the spirit" might set in (per McKean's article, in **Chapter 5 of Volume I**), and there might be stagnation in place of the former growth/work/productivity ethic—and all that it portends—in this country. Day, however, evidences hesitation over any firm guesstimates about long-range ZEG demographic trends; see **Chapter 5 of Volume I.**
25. For analysis of environmental impact assessment methods, see **Chapter 15 of Volume III** and the articles by Gladstone and Witherspoon, Andrews, Twiss, Tremaine, and Leopold et al. (Developers particularly see some of the concepts as they have been instituted as unnecessarily greatly increasing time, costs, and risks: for example, environmental review procedures when they are poorly integrated with other land use decision-making processes [see **Chapter 19 of Volume III**, for views from the private sector].)

analysis.[26] The state and federal governments also adopted various land use control and management-assistance programs to help lead this effort.

These, then, are some of the concerns which have played a part in the increased antipathy toward growth and which have helped lead to what one report has labeled the "new mood."[27] Such a change in the American consciousness regarding land use and development has been multi-faceted in origin; admirable goals have played their role, but so have less noble motives.[28]

Today there is evidence that "managed growth" is well on its way to becoming a predominant trend in community land use decision-making. As this attitude or movement matures, there will be increasingly sophisticated consideration of growth alternatives and of the techniques or systems to achieve sound land use.

EVALUATING GROWTH RESTRICTIONS

Nearly all land use controls and planning activities impact on growth and development patterns. It is important to recognize that such governmental controls and policies not only have great potential for serving the public, they also have significant potential for abuse. It is important that decision-makers appreciate how different available land use guidance techniques[29] (see Appendix I) can be used to achieve managed growth goals. Following are six evaluative factors[30] that local officials can utilize in selecting the appropriate guidance techniques to achieve their land use objectives.

Quantity   How can the amount of growth and development be guided by a community?

These considerations can be affected by: (a) The *densities* permitted under current comprehensive plans and zoning; (b) The various *types* of uses permitted; (c) The response of the private sector in proceeding with construction and the zoning changes, if any, which occur as a result of private and public sector interface and, (d) The demands placed on the commu-

---

26. Carrying-capacity analysis is dealt with by Odell in **Chapter 14**, and Godschalk in **Chapter 17 of Volume III**.

27. The new mood is dealt with in **Chapter 2 of Volume I**, in the articles by the Rockefeller Brothers' Fund Task Force, Cahn, and Uddo (the last two being reviews of *The Use of Land* report); **Chapter 3 of Volume I**, in the articles by the ICMA, NACO, and Finkler; **Chapter 4 of Volume I** (see the "Quiet Revolution"), and **Chapter 16 of Volume III** (the article by Lamm).

28. See, for example, note 17 above; moreover, spurious environmental determinations also have been used as rationalizations for refusing to accept further growth and development (distinguishing between solid, well-motivated planning or land use decisions and those which are based on questionable or badly-analyzed assumptions is a difficult problem).

   Concern has been expressed by the Administrator of the U.S. Environmental Protection Agency, that environmental regulations can be abused. "I want, at this point, to express my dismay over the fact that environmental and ecological values have at times been invoked as excuses for blocking the construction of low– and moderate–income housing. Communities who have never displayed much concern for sewage capacity or open space needs—as long as the 'right' kind of development for the 'right' kind of people was involved—have suddenly 'got religion' when somebody proposed to build within their boundaries some low–or–moderate income housing. I can think of few greater tragedies than to allow 'environment' and 'ecology' to become code words for economic and racial exclusion—for efforts that in intention or in effect, deny or diminish housing opportunities to Americans of modest means." Russell Train, "Remarks before the Middle-West Regional Conference [of the Council on Environmental Quality and the Conservation Foundation]" (March 15, 1974). Also, see the article by Train in **Chapter 2 of Volume I**.

29. Techniques in general are discussed primarily in **Chapters 11 and 12 of Volume II**, and in **Chapters 14 and 15 of Volume III**.

30. Methods of evaluation—and the major issues to be spotted—are stressed throughout these volumes. Of particular importance methodologically are the fiscal techniques (**Chapter 13 of Volume II**), environmental assessment (**Chapter 15 of Volume III**), and the legal and equity issues (in **Chapters 6 and 7 of Volume I**, and **Chapters 8 through 12 of Volume II**).

nity by non-residents, commuters, and so forth.

Type   What are the methods by which a community can guide the types of growth it will accommodate?

Such methods could include: (a) Direct public restrictions, zoning, and regulatory measures such as prohibitions against the construction of multi-family units, etc.; (b) Indirect effects, as in building codes, which can effectively increase the costs of residential development; and, (c) Special incentives, as tax abatement, used to recruit desired industry and other types of employers.

Cost   In what ways can the costs to both the public and private sectors be minimized by the growth management policies adopted by a community?

The costs are affected by: (a) The degree to which market supply is repressed by planning and zoning restrictions; (b) Directly-levied costs imposed by the public sector; (c) Indirect costs as large-lot zoning and; (d) The manner in which land use and facility planning affects the public service costs of local governments.

Location What are the factors which can determine the location and direction of growth?

Of primary concern are: (a) Traditional use-determinations contained in local zoning ordinances and maps; and, (b) Publicly-created market effects, as the construction of mass transit facilities or government employment centers.

Timing   In what ways can government phase/time the (re)development of land?

Such methods include: (a) A combination of pre-planning of land uses by a municipality with the approach of "wait-and-see" zoning; and, (b) Via the utilization of more sophisticated controls such as the phasing of the provision/extension of vital public services or facilities.

Quality How can levels of quality be affected by local public policies?

Quality may be influenced in part, by: (a) Manipulation of the costs and the types of development [above]; (b) Negotiation with developers during approval stages; (c) Use of flexible land use control tools such as density bonus systems; and, (d) Selective recruitment of certain types of growth.

Furthermore, the local policy maker should analyze growth control(s) or managed growth systems in terms of "cumulative" impacts, including:[31]

The distortion-effect on local and regional demographic and market trends. The primary issue is the degree to which municipal controls measurably affect the land use and development patterns which would otherwise occur if the market and demographic pressures were relatively undistorted by public regulation/determinants.[32]

The extra-jurisdictional or externality effects. If the techniques utilized by a com-

31. The problem inevitably relates to what constitutes sound regional planning, and, secondarily, whether a non-binding regional plan—which too often is lacking—should be given policy weight and legal effect. This issue is reiterated throughout these volumes; it is an underlying theme of **Chapters 6 and 7 of Volume I,** of **Chapter 8, 9, and 10 in Volume II,** and of **Chapter 16 of Volume III.**
32. See the problems in such analysis, as discussed by several authors in the *Petaluma* litigation (**Chapter 9 of Volume II**), and by Burchell, et al. (in **Chapter 7 of Volume I**).

munity are pervasive, the impacts may measurably affect neighboring jurisdictions and therefore the general welfare of the region as a whole. (The analysis of this issue is particularly difficult, as various experts oftentimes isolate inconsistent variables and present contradictory results.) Instead of concentrating merely on local changes, this type of analysis should ask such questions as: what strain if any does the technique or plan place on the region as a whole; what regional inequities (cost and taxation loads) or inefficiencies (as sprawl) may result?[33]

The external effects on the social/economic system. With local controls affecting the quantity, timing, costs, etc. of growth, a significant issue is the extent of the impact on housing opportunities, employment possibilities, etc., and specifically—the ways in which various groups of persons throughout the region are affected.[34]

Community motivation or intent. While the major issues deal with the effect(s) rather than the "intent" of a locality in pursuing growth-limiting alternatives, nevertheless the motivation is important (such as in court challenges) if it can be shown that there is arbitrariness, unreasonableness, capriciousness, or purposeful avoidance of municipal responsibilities.[35]

The approval[36] of proper managed growth systems is primarily the responsibility of local elected officials and major administrative officers in the communities concerned. The burden of the work of designing and supervising the propriety, equity, and rationality of growth guidance systems falls first on public planners, city managers, and attorneys, who must study and then recommend to elected officials the use of selected techniques. Yet a number of factors can also interfere with such "professionalism,"[37] for instance, accountability to the elected official—whose interests are primarily local; a day-to-day orientation toward the perspective of the local unit of government; and, an attitude of proceeding to maximize local control over growth, even at the expense of the

---

33. Regional "externalities" are a problem inherent, by definition, in a fragmented governmental system. It is desirable to minimize undesired externalities to the extent feasible, but ultimately it is an issue of not having the "proper jurisdiction" over the factor which is generating the disadvantageous side-effects. The former chairman of the President's Council on Environmental Quality identified this dilemma as "an intractable institutional problem. It is not possible to design institutions that are optimal both in terms of the geographical area they cover and in terms of the environmental problems they are concerned with." Russell E. Train, "Remarks Before the 'Massachusetts Tomorrow' Conference" (December 5, 1972).

34. This is the focus of the last several articles in **Chapter 5**, as well as much of **Chapter 6 and 7 in Volume I**. For a discussion of the difficulty of valid cause-effect analysis regarding land use controls and housing costs, see the article by Bergman in **Chapter 19 of Volume III**.

35. See **Chapters 6 and 7 in Volume I,** as the question relates to exclusion; also, **Chapter 4 of Volume I** as it deals with failures of traditional zoning.

36. Growth may be considered incrementally, in terms of project-by-project approvals (see note 17) or by the adoption of general growth management ordinances, and regulatory methods, and comprehensive plans (see the experience of Petaluma, in **Chapter 9 of Volume II**).

37. The planning profession has struggled with the problem of ethics for some time. The question of the responsibility of the planner has been debated at length in the literature, from the early article by Melvin M. Webber, "Comprehensive Planning and Social Responsibility: Toward an AIP Consensus on the Professions' Roles and Purposes," *AIP Journal* 29 (November 1963): 232; and Michael P. Brooks, *Social Planning and City Planning: PAS Report 261* (Washington, D. C. : American Society of Planning Officials, 1970) [see this report for a good bibliography]; to more recent statements by study groups and task forces of the American Institute of Planners. The issues, unfortunately, except for bland platitudes, remain relatively unresolved.

region and other interests.[38] It is critical therefore that decision-makers have an under-standing of how such methods of restricting growth may disadvantageously affect the citizens of the community and of the region.

It is also important to consider that growth control and its effects can be perceived from quite different perspectives. At the local or "micro" level, the prohibition or severe restriction of growth is viewed as a possible alternative since the demographic and market pressures can be deflected to other jurisdictions, where development can be more freely accommodated due to fewer restrictions and comparatively more attractive mar-kets. However, at the "macro" level—regional and national—the perspective changes abruptly; here, severely restricting growth is not a viable alternative,[39] since the demands of an expanding population cannot be as easily ignored. Thus an enlightened public policy regarding growth recognizes that it is a matter not of "whether" further population growth should be accommodated,[40] but "where" that growth should be guided. In other words, growth management on the macro scale, at the very least, is an issue of distribution and location.

This macro view of restricting growth as an "alternative" illustrates the inherent irrationality of allowing communities to unilaterally stop their growth without regard to regional effects. Yet our governmental system has given local governments the responsi-bility to govern land use and planning—a role which they may not pursue properly, unless their policies are supervised and purposefully made to coincide with the greater general welfare (of the region and of the state).

State and national governmental units have traditionally shied away from using what potential or actual powers they may have in this regard and those few which have been designed to consider overall growth questions have tended to have only marginal effect.[41]

While severe growth restrictions may appear at least superficially to be an excellent alternative in terms of the self-interest of the community,[42] local "solutions" are a regional dilemma. Unilaterally-determined growth policies may seem to "make sense" to

---

38. For a discussion of the role of regionalism in planning, see the sources cited in note 31, supra, as well as the following: Constance Curtis, *Home Free? New Vistas in Regional Housing*, (Washington, D.C.: National Committee Against Discrimination in Housing, 1974); Feiler, "Metropolitanization and Land-Use Parochialism: Toward a Judicial Attitude," 69 MICH. L. REV. 655 (1971); Hammer, Greene, Siler Associates, *Regional Housing Planning: A Technical Guide* [prepared for American Institute of Planners] (Washington, D.C.: AIP, 1972); Keeler, "*Recent California Planning Statutes and Mountain Area Subdivisions: The Need for Regional Land Use Control*," 3 ECOL. L. Q. 107 (1973); Mandelker, *The Role of Zoning in Housing and Metropolitan Development*, from Papers Submitted to Subcommittee on Housing Panels, Committee on Banking and Currency, U.S. House of Representatives, 92nd Congress, 1st Session (1971); "Report of the ICMA Management Policy Committee on Regionalism," *ICMA Committee Reports* (Washington, D. C.: International City Management Association, 1974); Weinberg, "Regional Land-Use Control: Prerequisite for Rational Planning," 46 N.Y.U. L. REV. 786 (1971). *See also* the studies by the Advisory Commission on Intergovernmental Relations, titled, "Substate Regionalism and the Federal System, Volume I (Washington, D.C.: Government Printing Office, 1973).

39. Non-growth in terms of zero *economic* growth is a different matter.

40. Urban areas particularly face nearly inevitable population growth. Of the 1970 Census figure for resident population and members of the armed forces overseas, 149,324,930 (or 73.5 percent) were urban residents, defined as ". . . all persons living in urbanized areas and places of 25,000 inhabitants or more outside urbanized areas." (*Demographic Projections of U.S.*, U.S. Bureau of the Census, Report P-25-493, December 1972.) In 1974, the number of SMASs had risen to 265 (from 246 in 1970). Some projections hold that the percentage of urban residents will increase to 84 percent by 2020.

41. See, however, the article by Brussat, in **Chapter 16 of Volume III**. Moreover, regional or state review is usually triggered only on major projects.

42. The need for regional approaches to growth management is stressed in the article by Parker in **Chapter 16 of Volume III**. See also the materials cited in notes 31 and 38.

local decision-makers; the cost-benefit equations seemingly support such reasoning[43] (since many of the "true" or avoided costs are left hidden). These include externalities which are imposed on the surrounding jurisdictions and citizens, but which "disappear" into non-costed inefficiencies, environmental burdens, loss of opportunities, poor quality development and land use, etc.; also thereby not counted are costs which are indirectly "absorbed" in terms of inconvenience, transportation problems, and the "forcing out" of potential or actual residents (such as low-income wage earners) and industry.

If local growth policies significantly interfere with demographic and market trends, this may inequitably shift the burdens of growth absorption to surrounding jurisdictions. One commentator has labelled this "the meanest form of mercantilism."[44] Such pawning off of growth on neighboring jurisdictions can cause overloads on their facilities (as sewers); if those facilities in turn are inadequate, the regional capacity for growth may be unduly limited.[45] The net result of course, is either that some jurisdictions are pressured into ever-higher facility/taxation levels because of the policies of their neighbors, or else ultimately there is an "artificially"-limited regional housing capability. Optimally, growth would be viewed in light of regional natural capacities/limits, and then adequate facilities could be scheduled for construction—where and when appropriate, and with a regional-cost allocation method for sharing costs.

Unless the growth which is displaced by local growth-avoidance policies is accidentally well-located to regionally-optimal sites, regional inefficiencies will result. Such a "redistribution" of growth can only exacerbate the problems of improper land use. Sprawl, for example, is especially likely if the jurisdiction which is engaging in unilateral stop-growth is one which is "close in" to the region's core; this may force growth outward,[46] where the service infrastructure is weak and where large-lot zoning[47] may help accelerate inefficient land use patterns.

If there are not only local, but region-wide growth limitations, other effects may be observed. The economic health of the central city may be effected, and the flight-to-outer suburbia may be aggravated.[48] Second, the prices of new and existing housing may be unduly inflated,[49] rental housing may decrease in supply and increase in effective rent; with fewer units coming into the mainstream, the "filter-down" effect may nearly cease.[50] Third, financial pressures may be experienced by existing residents, whose assessments can be adversely affected. The major losers are those who can't afford to purchase housing as well as those property owners on fixed or limited incomes. Fourth, growth restrictions

43. See note 81; moreover, prolonged non-growth which restricts the housing supply may have the "beneficial" side-effect of inflating the sales prices of local residents' homes (upon resale).
44. See the article by Alonso, in **Chapter 5 of Volume I.**
45. Curiously, the overwhelming of a community which has inadequate treatment facilities may in turn provide an "environmental" justification for stopping further development.
46. Some commentators have argued the reverse: that developers will return to the central cities, where rehabilitation activities will be stimulated. But, see the two articles by Priest, et al., in **Chapter 16 of Volume III.**
47. Some jurisdictions purposefully utilize large-lot zoning. While avoiding immediate cost burdens, it may generate others (it helps "control" growth, but encourages sprawl; it supposedly protects environmentally sensitive areas, and yet it may eventually cause even greater damage [as with the deterioration of septic and other sytems over a period of time, etc.]).
48. See the articles by the Davidoffs in **Chapter 7 of Volume I**; by Priest in **Chapter 19 of Volume III**; and articles in James Smith (ed.), Environmental Quality and Social Justice in Urban America (Washington, D. C.: Conservation Foundation, 1974).
49. Housing cost problems are widespread in some non-growth jurisdictions, and repercussions can be felt as well by the mid-spectrum of wage earners. See the articles by Bredemeier, and others, in **Chapter 16 of Volume III**, and by Gruen in **Chapter 9 of Volume II.**
50. See the article by Gruen, and the Petaluma case decision itself, in **Chapter 9 of Volume II.**

can force increased separation between place of residence and primary employment centers, thereby increasing commuting costs and foreclosing various job opportunities for persons unable to absorb the higher costs or to utilize alternative transportation modes. Fifth, the supplier of housing—the residential construction industry—may experience a major squeeze,[51] slowing the construction of new units for an extended period.

Another major problem is that too often, managed growth decisions are made solely on the basis of fiscal issues, with growth being rejected because of direct "costs," etc.; such an emphasis can lead to a distortion in proper land use management. One expert has pointed out: "There has been an unduly great importance attached to the fiscal effects of growth based on the premise that taxes and the quality of public services are the main issues. As noted previously, social, and in some cases environmental, concerns are the basis for much of the opposition to development, although economic effects are the ones brought forward in public hearings and in other forums."[52]

A final, and often-repeated, criticism is that localities are not the "logical" jurisdictions for growth limitations (even though they have inherited the power to do so from the states) both for the reasons already expressed regarding regional inefficiencies and inequities, and because communities are not necessarily rational, ecological planning units. Nor in some cases do they have the required expertise.[53]

Compounding the search for effective and fair procedures for managed growth is the dilemma that equity issues tend to lack effective "constituencies." While the "stop growthers" have had their clarion call supported by diverse groups, too frequently there is no real constituency for monitoring the potential abuses of growth restrictions. To some extent, the development sector has assisted in this regard, but only to the degree that the market encourages it to do so. Thus the "unrepresented constituency" is seldom accounted for, and there seems to be little to behoove the average locality to plan for growth and housing which it does not want. Likewise, the complaints of neighboring jurisdictions generally do not carry much weight; the interests of the region as a whole too often are ineptly considered.

The above, then, summarize a number of the generic, socioeconomic concerns of the managed growth movement. (Specific legal challenges are detailed in a later section of this Summary.) It must be re-emphasized that in evaluating and designing an appropriate managed growth system, a community should undertake to analyze such effects and criticisms as those outlined above. Moreover, affirmative programs, such as adequate housing planning and program implementation, should then be undertaken to ameliorate the difficulties which are identified as a result of this type of policy analysis.

BASIC LEGAL ISSUES IN MANAGED GROWTH

Inexorably many of the problematic issues involved in the management and control of growth find their way to state and federal courts. Some observers have questioned the "appropriateness" of having the judicial branch resolve these complex land use dilem-

---

51. See the articles by Drachman, Epstein, Watson, Chamberlin, Larson, and Searles in **Chapter 19 of Volume III.**

52. Thomas Muller, "Public Resists Private Development Due to High Costs," *Mortgage Banker* 34 (September 1974): 70. (By the same token, fiscal analysis can be used to sway opinion such that development is rejected, even though there are social and other reasons for its acceptance in the community concerned.)

53. Higher-level planning—including that undertaken by states—is analyzed in **Chapters 15 through 18 of Volume III.** But for a dissent as to the escalation of land use regulation to higher units of government as part of the fever-pitch of "liberalism," see the article by Frank J. Popper, "Land Use Reform: Illusion or Reality," *Planning,* The ASPO Magazine 40 (September 1974):14.

mas and thus "interfere" with legislatively-determined/supervised public policies. Perhaps more correctly, it has been suggested that "in a rational, democratic world, these questions would be resolved by political compromise and accommodation in the legislature. However. . .as long as the legislature defaults in its obligation, the judiciary will be required to respond as best it can. . . [T]he courts will continue to be faced with the unpromising task of attempting to reconcile antithetical goals of competing segments of our society."[54]

The search for answers through litigation is a less than optimal (and often traumatic) course. For the litigants involved, particularly private property owners, the process can be frustrating, time-consuming, costly, and ineffective.[55] For the public official, court battles may be disruptive of effective regulatory processes. By having public actions continually subjected to challenges, administrators may experience uncertainty and inefficiency; significant staff and monetary costs may be involved; and occasionally, havoc may be wreaked on the local controls schema. Some communities unfortunately exhibit timidity,[56] in the sense that rigorous planning and controls are unnecessarily avoided in order to avert legal challenges — in turn reducing the likelihood that effective or rational managed growth systems that would better serve the public interests will be adopted. It is advisable therefore for planners and local administrators to consult competent local counsel during the early stages of regulatory and plan formulation, as to the legal parameters and repercussions of the various tools and systems which are being proposed.[57]

The most frequent litigants in land use cases include: the neighbor or abutting property owner who is challenging a variance, rezoning, or other decision which favors another parcel of land; the owner or developer who is unable to obtain the rezoning or the use-permissions needed; interest groups which allege that the local controls are in some way detrimental[58] (as civil rights groups alleging exclusion, or environmental organizations seeking to reverse or promote the enforcement of certain governmental actions); the community itself and other governmental units (an example being the litigation brought by federal environmental agencies against state and local actions). A type of plaintiff

---

54. Jerome G. Rose, "Should the Courts Control Growth?" *Planning* 41 (November 1974): 18. For further information on judicial review and the scope of remedies, see: Rose, *The Courts and The Balanced Community*, 39 AIP J. 265 (1973); as well as: Feiler, *Zoning: A Guide to Judicial Review*, J. URBAN L. 319 (1969); Hartman, *Beyond Invalidation: The Judicial Power to Zone*, 9 URBAN L. ANN.___ (1975); Plager, *Judicial Review 1970*, 37 AIP J. 1974 (1971); and, Ruttger, *Judicial Remedial Action in Zoning Cases: An Emerging Standard for Review*, 7 URBAN L. ANN 191 (1973).

55. For example, a private party may litigate, win the court decision, and still "lose" due to delays or still other regulations. Moreover, adequate remedies may not be imposed or supervised (see the articles by Haar and Iatridis, by Levin and Rose, and by Furman, in **Chapter 6 of Volume I**).

56. As to observations relating to "too much caution" (relative to the taking issue problem), see **Chapter 4 of Volume I.** As to successful challenges potentially undermining the entire land use machinery of a community, see the articles on the *Petaluma* case (by Hart, Gray, and others in **Chapter 9 of Volume II**) and on the *Oakwood at Madison* case (by Furman, in **Chapter 6 of Volume I**).

57. See Chris Oynes, "Get Legal Advice Before, Not After," *County News* (Washington, D.C.: National Association of Counties, September 30, 1974):12; as well as the articles by the International City Management Association, in **Chapter 3 of Volume I.**

58. Among various groups there is extensive information exchange regarding ways in which "effective" lawsuits can and are being brought. Most noteworthy in this regard are the National Committee against Discrimination in Housing as well as the Metropolitan Clearinghouse of the Potomac Institute (both of which hold sessions and publish frequent litigation-oriented reports and analyses); the National Association of Home Builders (which has annual litigation conferences and regional sessions, and maintains a sizeable "sensible growth" litigation fund); the several national, environmental organizations (such as the Sierra Club, the Environmental Defense Fund, etc.); civil rights groups (such as ACLU); the Lawyers Committee for Civil Rights Under Law: and others handling such managed growth-related issues as local property taxation inequities and the unequal provision of equal municipal services.

conspicuously absent is the community which is being impacted unfairly by externalities such as environmental damage generated by a neighboring municipality; both the state of the "law" and evaluative methodologies are weak in this regard and thus, such cases are difficult to carry forward.

The total amount of court activity is indicated by the fact that during the last 75 years of zoning and land use management, there have been more than 10,000 reported case decisions.[59] (Such a total would be significantly larger if there were added the cases dropped, compromised, or otherwise averted, and the large number of controversies settled prior to court actions actually having been undertaken.) Thus the American law of zoning in large part has developed not only from legislative and administrative decisions, but from the differing judicial interpretations which have been based on a seemingly endless disarray of legal and fact situations.

For several years, courts increasingly have been drawn into the managed growth thicket. Sensitive jurisprudence questions — as issues of the extent, propriety, and method of judicial "interference" — are constantly raised. Yet, since the validation of zoning by the U.S. Supreme Court (in *Village of Euclid* v. *Ambler Realty Co.*, in 1926), the predominant trend has been one of allowing significant latitude in the scope and use of local governmental powers.[60] Among the primary assumptions adopted by the courts is that local "legislative" determinations are given a presumption of validity, based in part on the concept of the separation of powers and on the notion that zoning changes and land use decisions in general are imbued with a legislative character.

Thus local governments have been able to operate under an effectively "expanded" range of police powers in furtherance of what they individually conceive as promoting the public health, safety, morals, and welfare. Their policies and programs typically have been seen by the judiciary as most appropriately addressed by legislative bodies (as social and political contingencies might require, within certain bounds). Reinforcing this predilection has been the argument that the courts should avoid active policy definition roles: that instead they should assume a posture of relatively circumscribed review, intervening only where there are clear abuses of legislative discretion.[61] By and large, absent clear showings of constitutional or statutory invalidity, communities therefore have not been obliged to "justify" the rationality or desirability of ordinances, etc.; if on balance the questions have been seen as fairly debatable, the courts have found the public actions or ordinances to be valid.

In taking this posture of "respect" for the policy and decision-making powers of legislatures, the judicial branch has left local governments with relatively free rein in much of their land use decision-making. But a number of commentators have pointed to the need for courts to take far more positive roles in major land use and managed growth issues and especially, those with significant regional (general welfare) impacts. They argue that the traditional presumption of validity ought to be lessened, in that communities should be required to assume heavier burdens of justification or proof where the regional effects are undesirable, where the local planning is shown to be inadequate, or where exclusionary effects are evident.

---

59. Norman Williams, *American Planning Law: Land Use and the Police Power*, 5 vols. (Chicago: Callaghan Co. 1974 and 1975). Another major reference work is that by Robert M. Anderson, *The American Law of Zoning*, 4 vols. (2nd ed. forthcoming 1976).
60. See the articles by Reiner, and Babcock & Bosselman, in **Chapter 4 of Volume I.** (Discussion of some more specific doctrine is contained in a number of the articles in **Chapters 6 through 12, in Volumes I and II.)**

Introduction and Summary

A number of the legal hurdles and tests which are involved in cases dealing with managed growth are listed in the discussion which follows. While each question has been the subject of intensive commentary in the professional literature,[62] the coverage below is in the nature of a brief outline of major points with which the reader should be familiar. Public officials must be particularly concerned with these types of issues if their programs are to withstand potential legal scrutiny and challenge.

Police Power (In General). The police power is an inherent characteristic of sovereign governments, and is exercised in pursuance of protecting, enhancing, and promoting the public health, safety, morals, and general welfare; in turn, it is delegated in part to the creatures of the State: the local governments. It is this power which serves as the primary basis by which zoning and other land use controls are exercised without the necessity of paying compensation to affected property owners.

The term "police power" is ambiguous, without sharp delineation as to meaning or import; moreover, the concepts it encompasses are in constant flux due to amendments to or changing interpretations of statutory, constitutional, and case law. It is this dynamic nature of the law which has buttressed government's broadened regulatory controls and policies allowing it to keep pace with changing societal needs. Yet this very lack of precision in the law has also led to confusion in both the public and the private sectors. The property owner often is uncertain as to his "rights," and the public official must carefully ascertain whether the managed growth techniques are safely within the scope of the police power.

One of the major problems which may or may not face local officials in the future, as they deal with police power questions, is the potential issue of *regional general welfare* and the degree of responsibility which a community may have to its surrounding region.[63] The basic question is: can the police power, which is delegated by the state, be exercised solely for the benefit of the residents of the locality and with minimal regard to the housing and other needs of the citizens in the larger region? Or, is there a "regional context" to the local use of police powers? These types of questions must be thought through by public officials; some may form the basis of political and judicial challenges.

If in fact there is such an inherent regional duty, does it require: (a) that the community merely refrain from inflicting a significant detriment to the interest of the region as a whole, or (b) does it require that planning be performed in a regional perspective and that programs be enacted in order to help meet a "share" of identifiable regional needs? The answers to questions such as these can be pervasive in their effects on managed growth systems. The New Jersey courts have advanced this doctrine farthest, in the *Oakwood at Madison,*[64] and the *Mount Laurel* cases, the latter of which is of particular significance for

---

61. But for a brief discussion of active judicial scrutiny, see generally the articles by Franklin in **Chapters 8 and 10 of Volume II,** by Williams in **Chapter 6 of Volume I,** by Sullivan in **Chapter 4 of Volume I,** and by several of the authors in **Chapters 6 and 7 in Volume I.**

62. The various "legal topics" in this section are not dealt with at length here. The reader might wish to make use of the *Index to Legal Periodicals* (available in any major law library) which lists articles—by subject—which appear in the major legal publications. For a useful desk reference (in addition to the several books mentioned in notes 17, 59, above), see Donald Hagman, *Urban Planning and Land Development Control Law* (St. Paul: West Publishing Co. [Hornbook Series], 1971).

63. This is discussed in various articles in these volumes, including those sources cited in notes 31 and 38, above. See the materials in **Chapters 8 through 10 of Volume II,** relative to *Petaluma* and *Ramapo.*

64. See the article by Furman, in **Chapter 6 of Volume I.** The New Jersey Supreme Court in midspring 1975, heard oral arguments in the case after its remand to and decision by Judge Furman.

Introduction and Summary

its broad implications for land use and housing.[65]

Enabling Legislation. Another initial question pertinent to any managed growth scheme is whether the regulation or ordinance is within the ambit of state enabling legislation. Some courts require that there be a "specific" grant of power — relatively precise language in the relevant state enabling legislation — relating to such regulations, and particularly if the controls are innovative or if the case precedent is weak. Other courts are satisfied with "general" grants of power and even imprecise statutory or constitutional language. In this regard, the status of the municipality may be a telling factor, with charter or home rule cities typically being viewed as having wider latitude.

A similar type of enabling legislation challenge arises when it is alleged that an agency is enforcing land use regulations where it is debatable as to whether there is adequate authorization in the local ordinances themselves. Finally, a local government may be challenged on the basis that although it has the necessary authority and capability to undertake a particular function, it is failing to fulfill its statutorily-mandated responsibilities.

Improper Delegation. An issue related to enabling legislation questions is whether there has been an over-broad or improper delegation of authority to non-legislative agencies and their administrators. While the abdication of legislative responsibility is frowned upon [in theory], the courts usually are amenable to being shown that in the particular situations involved there has been sufficient retention of (partial) authority by the legislature or that sufficient standards have been provided to the administrative agency, such that invalidation of the legislation is not necessitated. (Significant administrative discretion or flexibility may be permitted as long as the legislative guidelines are adequate and explicit.)

Vagueness. Plaintiffs frequently argue that an ordinance as drafted is ambiguous, unclear, or relatively uninterpretable, and that its enforcement or application would therefore be inequitable. If this claim is determined to be well-founded, the court may prohibit the application of the regulation in the specific instance involved, or alternatively it may make a broader finding that the ordinance per se is fatally defective. Legislative draftsmen should balance the need for the use of broad phrases to convey maximum/general scope of power to local governments, with the need for precise language in order that such challenges of ambiguity or uncertainty may be avoided.

Restricted or Preempted Powers. Occasionally the issue arises as to whether a governmental unit is exercising powers reserved or preempted by higher levels of government — regardless of whether or not the locality has passed its own supposedly valid legislation suggesting otherwise. This type of challenge may arise where a field of regulation has been preempted in part or in toto by state or federal statutes, or where a local ordinance is alleged to be invalid due to specific constitutional or statutory restrictions. Such preemption or restriction occurs most frequently in relation to the taxing power and to environmental regulation.

Abuse of Discretion. One of the most frequent complaints in the litany of litigation challenges is that the governmental unit has abused its discretion by acting in an arbitrary, unreasonable, or capricious manner. Unless interference with fundamental constitutional rights can also be shown, the plaintiff's burden of proof is a heavy one. He

---

65. This case decision was handed down by the Supreme Court of New Jersey in Spring 1975. *Southern Burlington County NAACP v. Township of Mount Laurel,_____ A.2d_____ (1975).*

must show that administrative discretion was exceeded or exercised in a manner which was non-uniform in application and which effected an intentional detriment; furthermore, the action must bear no reasonable or rational relationship to police power objectives, and it must have been undertaken or administered in a manner which was not reasonably founded in law or fact.

A related complaint is that of "special treatment": in effect a combination of claims that a governmental unit, by granting or denying special treatment to one party, has abused its discretion, has acted in an arbitrary or capricious manner, and has exceeded its authority. (This typically arises relative to "neighbors' " challenges regarding [spot] rezonings granted to third parties. Some of the more innovative growth management techniques, such as TDRs, may be especially susceptible to such a challenge.)

Equal Protection. Probably the single most pervasive legal challenge to be used against land use regulations, is the denial of equal protection. There are two basic sets of equal protection challenges. The first involves allegations that the application of a regulation, or the regulation itself, bears no reasonable relation to a permissible governmental objective and that it has been unequally, unreasonably, or inequitably administered. The second is whether a suspect classification or a fundamental interest is involved. Those areas identified as "fundamental" usually do not involve land use questions, whereas the "suspect" classification issue[66] generally is one of racial discrimination.[67]

In the 1960s, some observers felt that the courts might eventually move in the direction of expanding equal protection guarantees by elevating economic discrimination to a status equivalent to racial discrimination — as a suspect classification. To date however, such an expansion of doctrine — to the chagrin of the anti-exclusionists — has been almost totally unsuccessful; this is the case, even though the majority of the class discriminated against — the poor — consists primarily of racial minorities in most fact situations. An equally disappointing defeat for the anti-exclusionary movement was that decent housing was deemed not to be a "fundamental interest" by the federal courts.

Reliance and Estoppel. Plaintiff property owners and developers frequently attempt to allege that a community is, in effect, "estopped" from prohibiting continuation of an activity once permission already has been granted. A determining issue in this regard is whether the challenger in good faith has proceeded to take actions and has incurred substantial expenses in reliance thereof, thus acquiring a "vested right." Courts differ widely as to what constitutes such a right: from mere contractual "arrangements," to actual starts on construction.

---

66. If the plaintiff shows that the control involves a suspect classification and is discriminatory on its face or in intent, or has the overriding effect of being discriminatory, the court will undertake "strict scrutiny" of the challenged regulation. The governmental unit must then bear a "heavy burden of proof" to show that the regulation or classification concerned nevertheless is necessary to promote a "compelling" state interest. Moreover, it must be shown that the alternative chosen to accomplish this compelling state interest is the "least intrusive" means. Thus the situation is quite different from one in which the plaintiff must bear the burden of proof that the classification is in fact "arbitrary," etc.; instead, the government must go significantly beyond the mere showing that the controls are "reasonably or rationally related" to "permissible" public purposes or objectives.

   For a discussion of least intrusive means analysis relative to the *Petaluma* case, see **Chapter 9 of Volume II**, as well as the article by Franklin in **Chapter 10 of Volume II**. This test is one which may ultimately prove to be one of the most troubling to local governments, as it requires that a community not pursue merely "convenient" or "politically palatable" courses of action where equal protection is denied.

67. For a bibliography on exclusionary land use in general, see Scott in **Chapter 6 of Volume I**. (Available, free on request, is the full 72-page publication, *Fair Housing & Exclusionary Land Use* (Washington, D.C.: ULI—the Urban Land Institute, 1974).

Introduction and Summary

Travel/Mobility/Settlement. One of the more recent constitutional challenges in terms of application to land use management is whether a particular control interferes with the "right to travel,"[68] which may or may not encompass (according to various commentators) inter- and intra-state mobility and the right to settle or reside in a chosen locale.[69] The right to travel is viewed by some as "inherent" in the U.S. Constitution, and a personal liberty included under the right not to be deprived of life, liberty, or property without due process of law. Interpreted as constituting a "fundamental liberty", the right to travel is accorded a degree of judicial scrutiny similar to that in other fundamental interest challenges, with such tests as those classification challenges, where there are tests of a compelling state interest and least intrusive means. If such a "right" is sustained as a major new standard by which all land use regulation and planning can or should be judged in the future, it might become one of the most potent tools[70] in the exclusionary land use challenger's arsenal, and therefore be a highly important issue to public officials in designing managed growth systems. Other observers believe the question is of only minimal value or application to most land use questions.

The Taking Issue. An area of significant debate and interest to public sector decision-makers is what has been popularly called the "taking issue":[71] the question of what/when governmental regulations so interfere with the use and enjoyment of private property that there is necessitated a public payment of just compensation to the owner, due to a "taking". As nearly all public activities in one way or another interfere with the exercise of private property rights, the question is one of degree: of when the taking "line" is crossed. Inconsistent case precedents have developed, along with a number of legal "tests" and such phrases as the balancing test, abatement of nuisances, (degree of) diminution of value, and inverse condemnations and constructive takings (regulatory actions which are judicially construed as amounting to takings).

Since before the inception of zoning, some writers have claimed a "vital connection" between liberty and man's right to the highest and best use of his property, short of inflicting a nuisance. Others have argued that a virtual physical possession or confiscation of use is necessary in order for there to be a governmental taking: that absent such a level of interference, public regulations are valid and compensation is not required. Recently evolving concepts of the appropriate role of governmental regulation — including what constitutes a "reasonable" use of land, the need to protect environmentally sensitive areas, a broader interpretation of the general welfare/public interest, and in-

---

68. See the lengthy discussions relating to travel in the articles by Fielding, Franklin, and Bosselman, and in the *Boulder* case decision, in **Chapter 10 of Volume II.** Moreover, the articles on *Petaluma* (**Chapter 9 of Volume II**) deal with the problem extensively. A number of pre-*Petaluma* decision articles have discussed the concept, including: Note "The Right to Travel and Its Application to Restrictive Housing Laws," 66 N. W. U. L. REV. 635 (1971); Note, "The Right to Travel: Another Constitutional Safeguard for Local Land Use Regulation?" 30 U. CHI L. REV. 62 (1972); Note, "Shapiro v. Thompson: Travel, Welfare and the Constitution," 44 N. Y. U. L. REV. 989 (1969); and Thompson, "The Right to Travel—Its Protection and Application Under The Constitution," 40 U.M.K.C. L. REV. 66 (1971).

69. There is major debate as to whether or not—even assuming some sort of "right to travel"—this includes the "right" to actually be housed in the community of one's choice at the "end of one's travel/mobility." (See the articles by Misuraca, and the brief by Attorneys for the Appellants, in **Chapter 9 of Volume II.**)

70. For opinions relating this thesis, see the articles by Hart and by Fielding in **Chapters 9 and 10** respectively **of Volume II.**

71. The taking issue is discussed at length in the articles by Hagman and by Bosselman, Callies, and Banta, in **Chapter 4 of Volume I;** the problem is mentioned in the material by the Rockefeller Task Force and by Reilly, in **Chapter 2 of Volume I;** moreover, it is a consistently repeated theme throughout the legal issue discussions in these three volumes. The reader may also wish to refer to a concise layman's version, titled, "The Law and Land Use Regulation" [**Chapter 4**] of the Council on Environmental Quality, *Environmental Quality: The Fourth Annual Report of the CEQ* (Washington, D.C.: Government Printing Office, 1973), pp. 121-53.

novative techniques as compensable regulations[72] — suggest to many observers that the courts are becoming more lenient as to whether takings are a "problem" regarding most public regulations or programs. This is particularly the case as the environmental ethic and the complexities of growth management are recognized by the judiciary, and as local and state governments gain greater sophistication in the subtleties of legislative draftsmanship and the proper design and operation of land use controls.

Due Process. A classic constitutional challenge is that an ordinance, decision, or other governmental action constitutes a violation of federal or state guarantees of due process. Historically, due process has been seen from two perspectives: the right to "procedural" due process, and "substantive" due process review by the judiciary.[73]

Procedural due process is most commonly violated when the local government body fails to give adequate notice to all affected parties or ignores the requirements of fair hearings such as the right to be heard and to present evidence. Other problems include the making of decisions on the basis on material not properly before it or on the record, or ignoring procedural requirements specified in the enabling legislation, ordinances, or the city charter. The due process question may become even more important if the courts adopt the theory that re-zonings, as well as variances, etc., are not legislative but are quasi-judicial or administrative in nature;[74] this characterization would tend to emphasize procedural concerns and the integrity of the process by which rezoning decisions are made.

Comprehensive Planning. Finally, a policy area closely related to legal issues per se (including planning for and defining the regional general welfare) is the relationship and role of the comprehensive plan to the utilization of local land use controls.[75] Debates have raged as to precisely what constitutes adequate comprehensive planning and whether regulatory actions must be "in accordance" with such plans; or, whether the plan is

---

72. See Bosselman and Hagman (note 71), as well as mention of the technique in **Chapter 14 of Volume III.**

73. Substantive due process—"content analysis" and a weighing/balancing of the validity of the regulation itself—is a somewhat questionable theory of constitutional interpretation, suggesting, in effect, a review of the inherent validity of a decision/regulation in certain circumstances (even absent assertions of problems of equal protection, etc.), and the "balancing" of various substantive considerations by the judiciary. This in turn involves the problems of jurisprudence noted earlier [in the text to notes 54 to 62]. (See some mention of the theory, in Babcock & Bosselman: **Chapter 4 of Volume I.**)

74. The procedural practices of many communities are relatively lax; if the *Fasano* precedent (see the article by Sullivan in **Chapter 4 of Volume I**) were to take hold, much more stringent application of due process would be required, and in turn would lead to major reforms in this decision-making sphere. (For a recent case akin to *Fasano,* see the opinions in *Kropf v. Sterling Heights,* 391 Mich. 139 (1974). *See also* Sullivan, "From Kroner to Fasano: An Analysis of Judicial Review of Land Use Regulation in Oregon," 10 WILL. L. J. 353 (1974).

75. The concept of the comprehensive plan is dealt with in some detail in several of the books and articles cited above. See the arguments developed by Reiner and Sullivan in **Chapter 4 of Volume I,** and also the discussions in: Edward Bassett, *The Master Plan* (New York: Russell Sage Foundation, 1938); William I. Goodman and Eric C. Freund, eds., *Principles and Practice of Urban Planning* (Washington, D.C. International City Management Association, 1968); Haar, *In Accordance With a Comprehensive Plan,* 68 HARV. L. REV. 1154 (1955); Haar, *The Master Plan: An Impermanent Constitution,* 20 LAW & CONTEMP. PROB. 353 (1955); Heyman, *Innovative Land Regulation and Comprehensive Planning,* 13 SANTA CLARA LAW. 183 (1972); T. J. Kent, Jr., *The Urban General Plan,* (San Francisco: Chandler Publishing Co., 1964); Norman Marcus and Marilyn W. Groves, eds., *The New Zoning* (New York: Praeger, 1970); Plager, *The Planning/ Land-Use Control Relationship,* 3 LAND USE CON. Q. 26 (1969); Raymond, *How Effective the Master Plan?,* 2 J. ENVIRON. SYS. 225 (1972); Sullivan & Kressel, *Twenty Years After—Renewed Significance of the Comprehensive Plan Requirement,* to be published in a forthcoming issue of the URBAN LAW ANNUAL; Tarlock, *Not in Accordance with a Comprehensive Plan . . .* 2 URBAN L. ANN. 133 (1969); Webber, *Comprehensive Planning and Social Responsibility: Toward an AIP Consensus on the Profession's Roles and Purposes,* 29 AIP J. 232 (1963); Comment, *The Local General Plan in California,* 9 SAN DIEGO L. REV. 1 (1971); Comment, *Zoning Shall be Consistent with the General Plan—A Help or a Hindrance to Planning?,* 10 SAN DIEGO L. REV. 901 (1973); See also the discussion of comprehensive plans in Article 3 of the ALI *Model Land Development Code,* Proposed Official Draft No. 2 (1975).

merely an advisory "guidance document" for policy makers, to be accorded no real legal effect by the courts. These knotty problems have been raised recently in a number of cases,[76] and will be central to law and planning issues for years to come. The tension between substantial, long-range planning and fragmentary, incremental policy-making inevitably will increase; this particularly will be the case as more localities enact stronger growth management measures and seek to defend them against legal challenges.[77]

The above material thus outlines some of the issues in the law which are most frequently encountered when parties dispute the validity, operation, or effects of managed growth techniques and systems.[78] At the same time, there are few clearcut standards in the legal doctrine; the various state and federal courts consistently exercise their prerogatives to shape the case law in ways which differ significantly among the various state and federal jurisdictions.[79] Moreover, the diverse legislation of the different state and local governments often leads to jurisdiction-specific interpretations. The result is that much legal doctrine is not "ready-mixed" for inter-jurisdictional "transfer"; attorneys, planners, and laymen quite understandably are frequently confused by the complex and even contradictory strands of legal thought.

In summary, it may be noted that many professionals are now beginning to see the need for legal doctrine to move beyond the more traditional basis of nuisance theory and property law to much broader jurisprudence. This includes a recognition of the importance of having communities exercise their police power in ways which lead to the effective, affirmative management and control of growth — but within the context of a firm responsibility to the regional general welfare. This requires the active evaluation and balancing of the social, economic, physical, and environmental needs of the community with those of the region as a whole.

---

76. In addition to the material cited in notes 63 and 75, above, see particularly the articles by Furman and by Levin and Rose, in **Chapter 6 of Volume I**; and by Sullivan, in **Chapter 4 of Volume I.**

77. The furtherance of legitimate goals may come under closer scrutiny by the courts, as they seek to find growth planning as more than mere ideas sketchily handed down in the "minds of men" and the "folklore" of the city [per Judge Neighbors, in the *Boulder* case: see **Chapter 10 of Volume II**]. But see the problems addressed above in the text to note 75.

78. A number of other legal-planning dilemmas not mentioned here remain to be solved. For example, there is the question of what duty exists for a municipality to furnish services within its "sphere of influence" to guide growth, when no other reasonable method of securing such services is available. (See the *Boulder* case in **Chapter 10 of Volume II**, as well as the discussion by Franklin in his two articles [in **Chapters 8 and 10 of Volume II**].) Another series of questions revolves around exclusionary land use controls cases (discussed at length, from Agelasto and Johnson in **Chapter 5 of Volume I**, through **Chapters 6 and 7 in Volume I**, to **Chapters 8 through 10, Volume II**). One example is the "purposeful avoidance of additional burdens" issue; this was addressed as early as 1965, when the Pennsylvania Supreme Court said: "A zoning ordinance whose primary purpose is to prevent the entrance of newcomers in order to avoid future burdens, economic and otherwise, upon the administration of public services and facilities cannot be held valid." *National Land and Investment Company v. Kohn*, 419 Pa. 504, 215 A.2d 597, 612 (1965).

79. The role of state and federal programs is discussed primarily in **Chapters 16 through 18 of Volume III** (as well as Clawson and Perloff, in **Chapter 14 of Volume III**). See particularly: Brussat on A-95 review procedures—in **Chapter 16**; the Pattons on state growth policies, Godschalk on carrying capacity, Stegman on state housing finance agencies, and the Council of State Governments on housing programs—in **Chapter 17**; Widner on state and federal policies, Ashley on the 1972 federal growth policy report, Selvaggi on the 1974 and future reports, Mields on new communities, Marston on federal land use programs, both Kirk and Mack on federal environmental programs, the Environmental Protection Agency on the land use implications of EPA regulations and activities, and the American Institute of Architects on national strategies—in **Chapter 18**. (See also the material from the private sector, as well as public participation ideas by Rivkin, Artemel et al., and Hodges— in **Chapter 19**.)

CONCLUDING NOTE

Over the course of this past century, the Nation has sought and has gradually devised means by which it could guide the use of its land and the course of its growth and development. With increased concern over the management of land resources, public planning and regulation has increased at a nearly Malthusian rate with the addition of new methods and innovative schemes to conventional control formats.

At this juncture, communities have run the gamut from early theories of zoning based on nuisance to far more sophisticated phasing techniques, and from single purpose and uni-jurisdictional planning to the consideration of needs in a regional general welfare context. Over the last decade, there has erupted an awareness among public and private sector participants of the need for proper planning for land use, growth, and the environment. The widespread nature of such attitudes indeed has been somewhat revolutionary.

It is essential to reiterate the comment made by numerous observers that in attempting to design managed growth systems, the governmental units concerned must strive to understand and account for the diverse impacts of their actions: from economic efficiencies to effects on styles of life, and from the utilization of scarce resources to the protection of individual rights. The potential costs and benefits of such programs loom large; the field demands that in adopting new strategies, there be a search for methods which fully evaluate and explicitly analyze the "externalities" of managed growth decision-making and policy formulation.

The planning-for-managed-growth process should assure that regions are treated as more than mere collections of individual local governments. The potential detriments to the "public interest" of purely parochial approaches are too high a price to be paid merely to preserve local, unilateral prerogatives. We must, for example, establish the means to understand and plan for the needs of entire regions — their environmental capacities, appropriate land uses, housing requirements, and so forth — and then provide the mechanisms and methods to insure rational trade-offs.

At the same time, elected and appointed officials must begin to assume a greater measure of responsibility in guiding growth decision-making away from response-oriented, incremental methodologies. Medium- and long-range growth planning and programming must be actively pursued, on a basis which reaches beyond particularized interests of local jurisdictions, in order to achieve and to promote equitable public objectives.

To the extent that the "ethic of growth" of years past has been replaced by an Ethos of Managed Growth, the mood and the effort are to be applauded. But the rationality of such an approach must not obscure the fact that complex systems often have untoward consequences . . . and that, as a result, the repercussions of our failures and of our attempts at managing and controlling growth must come under far more careful scrutiny than before.

APPENDIX I

A SUMMARY OF TECHNIQUES FOR MANAGED GROWTH

The following material lists some of the techniques which individually and in concert comprise the tools of managed growth. But as pointed out repeatedly by several authors:[80] (a) fragmented use of tools in an ill-coordinated manner falls far short of the goal of having well-integrated managed growth systems; (b) growth controls have many side effects which should be, but often are not, carefully examined prior to implementation; and, (c) managed growth can be a cover for exclusion[81] and an excuse for escaping fiscal burdens: practices which must be addressed by responsible citizens and professionals and by the legislatures and courts in their supervisory roles, if the greater public interest and general welfare are to be served.

With each of the tools and techniques noted below, the local official or citizen must apply considerations of legal, social, economic/fiscal, and administrative factors. Are the techniques defensible, and from which points of view? Or, has the decision-making process at least made these elements an explicit part of the analysis, before arriving at policy trade-offs and conclusions? And finally, has the community made a conscious effort to deal systematically — versus ad hoc control-by-control adoption — with the tools that are currently and prospectively available to it?[82]

Action Planning: this systematic approach, as set forth by the League of California Cities, calls for area-wide identification of problems, regional analysis and carefully supervised expansion of local powers.[83] **Administrative Delays:** delays may be intentionally pursued or result from administrative inefficiencies; they may have the effect of discouraging development and also of increasing the overall costs of the housing produced. **Aesthetic Controls:** used for regulating exterior appearances and design, this technique is occasionally utilized by some communities to reject or otherwise control development proposals according to perceived levels of "desirability."[84] **Agricultural Zoning:** this involves the designation of whole land areas or districts for agricultural use in order to preserve such activity, to maintain open space, and to limit land speculation and development.[85]

ALI Proposals: The ALI Code has a number of provisions relating to land use and managed growth which are noteworthy as reform proposals for local and state regulatory

---

80. See the quotations from several articles in the Introductions to **Chapters 11 and 12 in Volume II,** as well as the articles themselves by Einsweiler et al., Carter et al., and Freilich.
81. There are persons not adequately represented in managed growth questions and, thus, their interests are not supported by an effective constitutency. It is important to consistently refer to the potential exclusionary effects of many managed growth systems, which intentionally or in effect are discriminatory to the ill-housed, the poor, or the under-employed. Few localities strive to undertake any real programs to ameliorate disadvantageous and inequitable side-effects. (In regard to such programs, see the articles by the Davidoffs, Erber, and two national commissions, in **Chapter 7 of Volume I.**)
82. Descriptions of various communities' approaches are cited in many of the articles throughout these volumes. The primary articles for this purpose are by Einsweiler, et al., and Carter, et al., in **Chapter 11 of Volume II,** and the International City Management Association in **Chapter 16 of Volume III.**
83. *Environment Control and Land Use Element: Action Plan for the Future of California Cities* (League of California Cities, October 1974), 16 pp.
84. The difficulty of course is that this supposedly "scientific" method becomes a question of debatable aesthetics. (See the manner in which Petaluma, California proceeded to rate proposals via a point system, as discussed generally throughout **Chapter 9 of Volume II.**)
85. See the articles by Miner, and Isberg, in **Chapter 14 of Volume III.** (This method usually is coordinated with certain financial incentives: reduced tax assessments, etc.)

procedures and processes.[86] **Amenities Requirements:** communities may, by ordinance or negotiation, impose requirements for extensive provision of amenities; while encouraging higher "quality," this may significantly affect the costs of housing construction. **Annexation Policies:** annexation may be used to secure jurisdiction over outlying areas that may not otherwise be in accord with the community's plans or overall growth management strategy.

Building Codes: housing costs may be impacted by unrealistic code standards; also, some types of units can be effectively excluded due to, for example, material-specifications (as prefab or mobile homes). **Building Permits:** formal or unofficial restrictions on the location, type, or total amount of permits can restrict residential construction and housing opportunities in a given area.[87] **Capital Budget:** the budgetary process, when used to reduce the level of improvements or expansion of public facilities, can cause a lowering of the capacity to absorb growth.[88] **Capital Programming:** the long-term programming of public facilities in accordance with comprehensive plans, can guide and even restrict the location, timing, and quantity of development which may be accommodated.[89]

Carrying Capacities: this analytical concept can aid in determining the "natural" ecological limitations of the land, and can provide a basis by which development proposals can be evaluated.[90] **Compensable Regulations:** this method, proposed as a means to avoid the taking problem, compensates the property owner for those rights which are severely restricted by the imposition of regulations.[91] **Comprehensive Planning:** adequate comprehensive planning can aid in providing coordinated policy guidance, in substantiating and validating local controls, and in making explicit community growth decisions.[92] **Conditional Zoning:** this technique, invalidated in some states, amounts to a method of "negotiation" whereby developers make concessions in order to obtain their requested rezonings (there is no "contract" to rezone, however [see below]).

Conservation Zoning: akin to "Critical Areas" protection [below], such zoning limits growth in areas which are specially designated due to their fragile nature or unique value (as wildlife preserves). **Construction Taxes:** special taxes are often imposed on develop-

---

86. See the article by Dunham, in **Chapter 17 of Volume III.** The reader is well-advised to read ALI Model Land Development Code Proposed Official Draft Number 2 (1975). (For a discussion of a number of the early drafts of the ALI Code, see the 116 pages of materials in David G. Heeter and Frank S. Bangs, eds., *ASPO Land Use Controls Annual 1971* [Chicago: American Society of Planning Officials, 1972].) See also the article by Bagne, in **Chapter 17 of Volume III,** on drafting state land use legislation.

87. Building permit restrictions are the subject of discussion in an article by Allen, as well as several other authors, in **Chapter 12 of Volume II.** The process, if formalized, runs the risk of being challenged in the courts as arbitrary and capricious, denying equal protection, being uncertain and ambiguous, etc.

88. For an example of how the budget can affect planning of facilities and limit the use of land, see the article by Emanuel in **Chapter 16 of Volume III.**

89. Less obvious is the "failure" of a community's officials to affirmatively plan for the accommodation of growth, thereby not making the facility-capacity question an explicit public policy question at all. The Hirsts in **Chapter 12 of Volume II,** also make the point that the public is rarely excited into any real concern with facility questions; yet it is this public investment decision which may be one of the primary growth determinants. (Note the methodology used by the Township of Ramapo, as described in **Chapter 8 of Volume II.**)

90. See the articles cited in note 26.

91. See the materials in note 71.

92. See note 75 for references.

ers (per the total amount of land area, volume of new units, etc.), to obtain revenues, discourage construction, or recapture publicly-generated benefits.[93] **Contract Zoning:** this method, also frequently invalidated, is an agreement by the government to rezone property, in turn for which the developer is often required to incorporate restrictions in the deeds to the land. **Covenants/Restrictions:** a public agency can obtain voluntary deed restrictions or covenants (via tax incentives, etc., or otherwise negotiate and acquire such limitations) on the private ownership and use of land.

Critical Areas: land areas of particularly sensitive nature — as wetlands, aquifer recharge areas, etc. — may be protected from development via special zoning classifications, environmental reviews, higher standards, and so forth. **Dedication/Fees:** land (with or without improvements) and/or fees in lieu may be required of the developer — either mandatory or "voluntary" — to cover public costs of new development.[94] **Development Rights Transfer:** also commonly known as TDRs, "development rights" are severed from other property rights by public action, for exchange in the open marketplace.[95] **Districts — "Tiered":** this method is one which emphasizes having development occur in certain "zones" prior to others: a staging or phasing technique usually used in conjunction with other tools.[96]

Down-Zoning: this approach, where the minimum lot size requirements for parcels are increased, lowers overall density-potential and often increases housing costs.[97] **Easements:** rights to property may be obtained by a public agency in order to assure, temporarily or in perpetuity, certain types of uses or non-use of land. **Eminent Domain:** public agencies can acquire (through the inherent right of the sovereign to take property, with compensation) fee simple or other interests in land for facilities, for various public uses, or to, in effect, contain or guide growth. **Energy Siting:** communities and states may significantly impact on development patterns by their decisions regarding the siting of new energy generation or transmission facilities.

Environmental Controls: the major environmental controls are those dealing with air and water quality, noise, flood controls, etc. (the federal government being the primary promulgator[98]). **Environmental Reviews:** environmental assessment procedures consti-

---

93. Various contribution and "recovery" methods are discussed by Hagman and Tarlock, in **Chapter 4 of Volume I.** Janis presents (also in **Chapter 4**) the builder's point of view: the unfairness and invalidity of such schemes.
94. *Ibid.*, and note 71. Moreover, the levying of excessive impact/permit fees or development "taxes," and stringent mandatory dedication requirements can affect housing prices, mortgage payments, down-payment requirements, and the marketability of housing in that locale.
95. See the articles by Costonis, Schnidman, and Chavooshian, et al., in **Chapter 14 of Volume III.**
96. Such zones have been labelled: urban, urban transition, and urban reserve; or urban area, urban growth area, urban frontier area, and urban reserve area; or in terms of Tucson's planning: areas of peripheral expansion, activity centers, contained growth (areas), and satellite cities. A state which is using this concept to some degree, is Hawaii.
97. See Bergman, in **Chapter 19 of Volume III.**
98. See the articles by Kirk, Mack, EPA, and others in **Chapter 18 of Volume III;** and by Epstein and Chamberlin in **Chapter 19 of Volume III.**

tute a development impact analysis tool (as the EIS[99]); exorbitant time or expense may limit or "allow" only selective growth. **Environmental Standards:** standards may be incorporated into local ordinances and other regulations to prevent building in areas with steep slopes, floodplains, and the like. **Excess Condemnation:** additional land — more than is necessary for the immediate purpose concerned — may be obtained for scenic or other reasons at the time of original acquisition by the governmental agency involved.

Exclusive Districts: by zoning for exclusive, rather than cumulative, uses within particular districts (as commercial areas, etc.), a locality may restrict residential development potential. **Extraterritorial Powers:** a local government may seek to utilize its authority to exercise extraterritorial planning and zoning powers outside of its boundaries but within its "sphere of influence."[100] **Facility Adequacy:** by informal public policies or ordinance requirements, development may be conditioned on the adequacy and availability[101] of public services and facilities. **Fair Share:** this concept, most commonly used with regard to dispersal of low- and moderate-income housing, is applicable in terms of planning and programming to other regional growth problems, as well.

Federal Taxation: federal taxes have macro-effects on development (on a purchase of new housing, on commercial investment, etc.), but only limited "micro" growth-guidance use.[102] **Fiscal Analysis:** this approach is primarily methodological (rather than the growth control technique per se); its purpose is the evaluation of impacts and as an aid in planning decision-making.[103] **Floating Zones:** this type of zone — as planned unit development[104] — allows both flexibility and negotiability in application; the exact future sites are not indicated, thereby encouraging wait-and-see zoning. **Greenbelts:** open space zones may be formed via the use of conservation zoning, condemnations, easements, etc.; such greenbelts or buffer areas tend to constrain the location and amount of development.

Height Restrictions: this type of restriction serves to limit highrise and multifamily development, to reduce densities, and to "protect" aesthetic and property values. **Highway/Roads:** highways, roads, and other modes of transportation are major growth determinants. **Historic Districts:** development may be restricted in areas about to experience growth pressures by designating some as strictly-controlled historic preservation districts. **Holding Zones:** this general method (including agricultural and large-lot zoning, and the designation of areas for uses which, in fact, are unlikely in the long term) is another wait-and-see zoning approach.

---

99. The environmental impact statement (EIS) is an example of a procedure with admirable intentions but often mixed consequences. See the treatment of EISs in **Chapter 15 of Volume III**, and the general reactions to regulation by developers (Epstein, Chamberlin, and others) in **Chapter 19 of Volume III**. Information on environmental impact statements may be found in the material in **Chapter 15 of Volume III**. Additionally, the reader should refer to: Frederick A. Anderson, NEPA In the Courts: A Legal Analysis of the National Environmental Policy Act (Washington, D. C.: Resources for the Future, 1973); Bowie, Maryland Commission for Environmental Quality, The Role of Environmental Impact Statements in Local Government Decision Making, 6 URB. LAW. 95 (1974); Robert Burchell and David Listokin, eds., The Environmental Impact Handbook (New Brunswick: Rutgers University, forthcoming); Greis, The Environmental Impact Statement: A Small Step Instead of a Giant Leap, 5 URB. LAW. 264 (1973) Hagman, NEPA's Progeny Inhabit the States—Were the Genes Defective? 1974 URB. L. ANN. 3 (1974); and Levine and Colgan, The Effect of Environmental Impact Statements on the Real Estate Investment Trust Industry, 6 URB. LAW. 1 (1974).
100. See note 83.
101. Ramapo used this methodology; see **Chapter 8 and 10 of Volume II**. But note the issues raised by the Hirsts, and Ramsay, in **Chapter 12 of Volume II**.
102. Federal taxation has little intra-jurisdictional, fine-tuning effect. Theoretically, however, it could be of benefit in terms of the core city problems, by encouraging certain types of investment and rehabilitation.
103. Fiscal analysis is detailed in the articles in **Chapter 13 of Volume II**.
104. See the article by Mandelker, in **Chapter 14 of Volume III**.

Impact Zoning: this methodological approach, utilized to scrutinize the full range of development impacts, is an analytical tool for understanding the prospective effects of growth.[105] **Incentive Zoning:** land may be so zoned or regulated that builders may apply for higher densities or other incentives, but can receive same only by meeting special additional construction or development requirements.[106] **Industrial Recruitment:** the type of industry deliberately planned for a community tends to influence the employment base, housing needs, rate of growth, etc., in that locality.

Initiative Method: the initiative and referendum processes are often used by citizens to reverse or force actions by local legislative bodies; frequently, rezonings and low-income projects are denied by these methods. **Land Banking:** this technique consists of the acquisition of land by a public body in advance of actual need in order to control the location and rate of development, to reduce speculation, etc.[107] **Large-Lot Zoning:** land may be zoned so as to preserve open space, or to encourage somewhat costly single-family dwellings and thus slow growth or limit the overall potential densities in and around the locality.[108] **Mandatory Housing Requirements:** mandatory low- and moderate-income housing requirements can be used to provide new housing opportunities to low-income persons; at the same time, this can also so burden subdivision development as to discourage building. **Maximum Bedrooms:** restrictions on the maximum number of bedrooms permitted (on the average or per unit), can reduce the likelihood for large families to establish local residence.[109] **Minimum Floor Space:** by placing a minimum on permissible unit square footage, a locality can restrict the type and cost of housing built; lower-cost housing may become prohibitively expensive. **Mobile Homes:** some communities restrict or prohibit mobile homes due to their lower tax bases and (sometimes) their school loads; the effect tends to be exclusionary.

Moratoria—Building/Planning: Moratoria may be instituted on subdivision requests, building permits, rezoning proposals, and variances; the purpose usually is to allow a "pause" for land use and facility planning.[110] **Moratoria — Sewers:** a legitimate type of sewer moratorium usually results from inadequate sewer facilities, combined with an

---

105. See the articles by Schaenman and Muller, and by Hysom, et al., in **Chapter 13 of Volume II;** as well as several articles in **Chapter 15 of Volume III,** including those by Tremaine, Andrews, and Twiss (these latter articles particularly refer to environmental impacts).
106. An outgrowth of incentive zoning, but more sophisticated, is the special purpose district (best exemplified by the Special Greenwich Street District and others, including Fifth Avenue and Battery Park, in New York City).
107. See the articles by Fishman, and Kamm, in **Chapter 14 of Volume III** (extensive references are also included).
108. This method is one of the oldest challenges in exclusionary land use controls cases; see **Chapters 6 and 7 of Volume I.** In the absence of substantial environmental justification, such zoning may be invalidated.
109. See the estimate of children and costs by family size and housing type, in Sternlieb and Burchell, in **Chapter 13 of Volume II.**
110. For a discussion of the uses and abuses of interim zoning or planning moratoria, see the articles by Freilich and by Heeter, in **Chapter 12 of Volume II.** A moratorium is often judged in terms of time (whether limited), legitimacy of purpose, and demonstrated public action to seek resolution of the underlying problems, (such as inadequate local comprehensive plans). Challengers will suggest that there ought to be a heavy burden of proof placed upon a community when it institutes this type of process—and most especially, where the moratorium is for "planning purposes," or where facility inadequacy has been created by the community itself. (See note 101, and the article by Franklin in **Chapter 10 of Volume II.**)

actual or imminent threat to public health and safety, or to the environment.[111] **Multifamily Prohibitions:** some communities strictly prohibit or otherwise limit the building of or zoning for multifamily units; exclusion is resultant. **Negotiation — Administrative:** one of the most frequently-used "regulatory tools" is the art of informal negotiation and compromise among developers and local governmental staff/officials.[112]

Official Maps: the official map sets forth the projected locations of roads and other public facilities so as to guide private and public sector decisions and to reduce the need for condemnations. **Open Space:** through acquisition zoning or other regulatory powers (incentives, donation, easements, etc.) a locality can preserve open space and recreational areas, as well as maintain low densities. **Over-Zoning:** by this technique, land is zoned for "inappropriate" uses or for uses not expected in the long term (as industrial), thereby preventing immediate residential building. **Parking Requirements:** unreasonable parking requirements or limitations can increase overall building costs and discourage marketability of some types of units.

Performance Standards: performance criteria are concerned with levels of effects, leaving "flexible" the determination by developers and public administrators of means/use/material adequacy. **Permit Review:** the administrative permit review process is typically used to exert considerable pressure for informal accommodation of development to community/plan objectives. **Point Systems:** points may be "awarded" developers' projects according to evaluation systems set forth in the ordinances; high thresholds can, in effect, limit the type and number of permits.[113] **Pollution Regulations:** air, water, and sewer requirements — and especially those established at the federal level — can affect overall regional capacities[114] [see "Environmental Controls"].

Population Caps: ceilings on the total local population to be accommodated are at least implicit in most zoning; "caps" are formal restrictions in ordinances and plans, to which facilities/capacities, etc., must conform.[115] **Preferential Assessment:** this may take the form of assessment/tax favoritism (as for agricultural lands). **Preferred Use:** this consists

---

111. Sewer moratoria are specifically discussed in the articles by Rivkin, Freilich, and the Hirsts in **Chapter 12 of Volume II.** It is a subject previously referenced (in note 101, and 110). See also: Donald A. Downing, *The Role of Water and Sewer Extension Financing in Guiding Urban Residential Growth* (Water Resources Center of the University of Tennessee, June 1972).
   According to The Council on Environmental Quality: "The difficulties of sewer moratoria are succinctly stated in a report of the County Executive's staff in Montgomery County: 'The results [of the moratorium] have been disappointing. The increase in sewage flows has not tapered off. The residential construction rate has actually increased . . . The price of housing, both rental and sale, has risen extraordinarily in recent years, making it increasingly difficult for people in lower and moderate income ranges to obtain housing in the county. The end result is that both water quality and socioeconomic problems have gotten worse.' " CEQ, *Environmental Quality—1974: The Fifth Annual Report of the Council on Environmental Quality* (Washington, D. C.: Government Printing Office, December 1974), p. 62.
112. This "flexibility" is useful to both sides, but is often abused—as stated at length by the Rockefeller Task Force **(Chapter 2 of Volume I)**, and in a number of the critiques of traditional systems (in **Chapter 4 of Volume I**).
113. "Point-system" limiting devices were used in several different ways in *Ramapo* and *Petaluma* **(Chapters 8 and 9, as well as 10, of Volume II)**.
114. See the materials in note 79.
115. A more subtle means is the population "ceiling" which is implicit under the existing planning/zoning, or the population "goal" or "range" which is expressed in general terms (and which may be nearly as effective as an absolute population limit if it is "informally" observed. The point is, that these tend to be more difficult to challenge in the courts). Such caps are most pronounced and questionable if the ostensible population limits are markedly less than local and regional demographic pressures or needs otherwise suggest; this is particularly the case if there are no significant environmental problems which justify the limitations. An analysis of this line of argument is found in **Chapter 9 of Volume II**, where the *Petaluma* litigation is analyzed at length. (See particularly the articles by Gruen, Misuraca, the Attorneys for Appellants, and the District Court decision itself.) Reference is also made to the case by Franklin in **Chapter 10 of Volume II**.

of special procedures for the consolidation and approval of certain types of development proposals (as for low- and moderate-income housing). **Ramapo System:** this approach to growth management by means of special permits, point systems, phasing of capital facilities, down-zoning, etc., is analyzed at length in these volumes.[116] **Rationing Methods:** rationing consists of a range of methods: from restricting building permits to the limiting of sewer capacities for certain types of development.[117]

Regional Taxation: this method may be utilized to collect, pool, and redistribute on a regional basis portions of the local property taxes in order to reduce disparities and misallocations.[118] **Rezonings:** the rezoning of land to increase, decrease, or "hold" densities and to alter types of land uses is a major control tool; "cyclical rezoning" can be further used to limit development.[119] **School Capacity:** a controlling factor in many communities is the capacity of the educational system; towns frequently use this "method" to deny growth or to encourage developer-provided school sites.

Service Areas: certain sectors of the locality may be designated for public service levels which for extended periods can effectively limit the density/type of land use which is accommodated.[120] **Sewer Facilities:** sewer capacity is one of the critical "facility adequacy" issues (noted previously); public investment decisions in this regard are one of the most effective managed growth techniques available.[121] **Social Analysis:** as with environmental assessment, this is a methodological approach; it can be used to examine both developer's proposals as well as the impacts of public actions and programs. **Special Districts:** the formation of special districts allows for "unequal" provision of services and "nonuniform" taxation, where deemed desirable by the community or by the district itself.

Special Permits: this method, rather than allowing development as a matter of right, offers the opportunity for intensive administrative review;[122] particularly for the purposes of limiting residential construction. **State planning:** certain land use planning activities, data collection, review functions, and controls may be exercised at the state level[123] for effective growth management. **State Assistance:** financial and planning assistance can be provided to communities to assist their growth planning; financial aid can also help alleviate special tax burdens such as low-cost housing. **Subdivision Control:** subdivision controls are one of the long-standing methods of reviewing and controlling development.[124] **Taxation Methods:** there are numerous taxation incentive and disincentive alternatives which can be utilized by the several levels of government to meet

---

116. See notes 113 and 126, and the articles in **Chapter 10 of Volume II,** and **Chapter 16 of Volume III.**
117. Rationing development as to types of uses or as to location (sectors of the city), raises novel legal dilemmas—particularly if this is done in pursuit of "good planning" but where there is not real problem with sewer/water capacities.
118. A recent Minnesota Supreme Court case on point, which upheld a regional tax reallocation scheme, is the *Village of Burnsville v. Onischuk,* 222 N.W. 2d 523 (1974).
119. Discussions of cyclical rezoning involve the idea of allowing all or various geographic sectors of the community to be eligible or to be considered for rezoning only periodically; prior requests may be held over until the next scheduled consideration/hearing period for that area.
120. This is a phasing or sequencing technique; see also "Districts—'Tiered'."
121. See note 114 for references.
122. The treatment of the *Ramapo* case in several of the articles in **Chapter 8 of Volume II,** questions the validity of this residential classification.
123. See note 99.
124. One text is Richard M. Yearwood, *Land Subdivision Regulation* (New York: Praeger, 1971).

managed growth goals.[125]

Timing/Phasing: one of the most valuable methods available to localities is the "sequencing" of facilities, zoning, permits, etc. in order to "time" the absorption of appropriate increments of growth.[126] **Urban Renewal/Rehab:** central-city revitalization techniques cannot only alter the growth-and-decline patterns of the urban core, but affect the viability and functioning of the entire region.[127] **User Fees:** as a method of taxation often dicussed, user fees can be structured so as to discourage development in outlying areas, as well as types and rates of facility usage. **Zoning:** one of the most traditional of tools, zoning affects the type, cost, location, timing, quantity, and quality of growth; it can be supplemented by the other techniques outlined briefly in this Introduction and Summary.

---

125. For a good overview on taxation and managed growth, see Zimmerman, "Tax Planning for Land Use Control," 5 URB. LAW. 639 (1973). "This article will therefore attempt a thorough discussion of the range of possible tax mechanisms that might be available to local communities to achieve certain planned development goals and will also suggest a comprehensive approach to the use of such devices and a mechanism to make such a tax program a part of an overall community program for growth." See also: Mitchell, "The Use of Special Districts in Financing and Facilitating Urban Growth," 5 URB. LAW. 185 (1973); and "Symposium on Local Government Finance," 6 URB. LAW. 325 (1974). Another major source of information is the Advisory Commission on Inter-governmental Relations—which has produced a number of excellent state/local fiscal and tax studies.

126. The phasing technique is discussed by a number of authors in **Chapter 12 of Volume II** (most especially, by Urbanczyk); see also Fagin in **Chapter 4 of Volume I.** The *Ramapo* phasing methodology of sequencing is analyzed in **Chapter 8 of Volume II** (and occasionally by other authors throughout these volumes); see particularly the articles by Stollman, Silverman, O'Keefe, Franklin, Bosselman, and the Court.

127. See the several articles in **Chapter 16 of Volume III,** dealing with the central city, and the concluding article in **Chapter 19 of Volume III.**

Appendix II

AREAS FOR RESEARCH: A GENERAL DISCUSSION

The managed growth field is one which will command the attention of numerous governments and agencies over the coming decade. As an important area of public policy analysis, research proposals will abound; thus national organizations and agencies, as well as local and state groups, will need to structure their research priorities carefully. It is therefore useful to note some of the potential research areas, as listed in the material below.

One of the primary difficulties for both researchers and funding sources will be to assure that the work undertaken does not take too narrow a view by failing to scrutinize the full implications or repercussions of the methods being advocated. (For example, research cannot merely emphasize the advantages of particular tools without analysing system-wide economic and social externalities, equity problems, legal entanglements, administrative difficulties, or the need for integration with other portions of the locality's growth guidance system.)

In the paragraphs below, major topics requiring further policy research attention are outlined.

Pre- and In-Service Education. Given the increased emphasis on managed growth concepts, what additional courses of instruction might be appropriate for professional curricula? In what ways are the current courses lacking both in subject coverage and in interdisciplinary considerations (constitutional and land use law for planners, regional economic and impact analysis, etc.)? What programs might be carried out in order to acquaint practicing professionals with managed growth concepts? How should these programs be structured (state-of-the-art seminars, problem solving workshops, etc.), and how should they be organized (through local/state chapters of professional societies — AIP, ASPO, ICMA, NACO, etc. — or integrated, multi-organizational conferences)?

Information/Communication. What types of materials should be prepared and disseminated to local government officials and others? How can joint organizational sponsorship be encouraged to maximize the impact on the respective professions, to avoid repetition, to coordinate research, and to encourage more in-depth analyses? How can decision-makers gain increased access to existing and new reference materials? How can the organization of material (cross-reference, annotation, synopsis) be improved to maximize ease of identification and study? Are there means by which a central clearinghouse can be effectively operated?

National Programs and Policies. How can the Congressionally-mandated national growth report be made into a more effective policy guidance document? Given the report's current level of influence on other governmental agencies, how might both the report preparation and the "implementation" processes better reflect and assist in domestic strategies and national growth programs? (See the articles by Ashley and Selvaggi in Chapter 18.) What national programs and activities are often ignored as to their growth/land use impacts? How can identifiable "national goals" (housing, social equity, environmental enhancement, etc.) be fully integrated with growth/land use policies? How can the dysfunctional aspects of certain national programs (as federal highway planning if it in fact interferes with local managed growth plans) be minimized?

Introduction and Summary

Housing and Land Use Acts. What is the probability that the 1974 Housing Act will encourage adequate local managed growth systems, and the meeting of the housing needs of low- and moderate-income families? What type of monitoring of the Act is essential? Is meaningful federal review and enforcement of local community assistance likely? How should federal land use legislation be designed to encourage localities and states to undertake comprehensive managed growth programs? How might the programs be administered, and with what degree of review and enforcement? How can a strong linkage with national growth policy and housing programs be forged?

EPA/Environmental Activities. What are the land use implications of federal (and state) environmental regulations? In what ways do the specific programs of EPA conflict with the policies and programs of other federal agencies? How do such programs affect both the amount and type of growth within regions and communities? To what degree are some growth "decisions" largely pre-empted by environmental regulations? How must local planning be adjusted to properly acommodate these requirements? To what degree/effect are there inadequacies (as inadequate protection of special areas) or disadvantageous side-effects of current programs (as interference with the market, costs, etc.)?

State Programs. What state level programs are often ignored as to their growth/housing/land use impacts? What programs of information, incentives, and assistance to communities might serve to foster adequate managed growth planning? How should states assist the private sector, in order to encourage sound development patterns? What are other areas of potential reform (as property taxation for educational purposes, for redressing urban vs. suburban fiscal dichotomies, etc.)?

State Policies and Planning. How can states be encouraged to engage in the preparation of state growth policies, similar in concept to the national report? What are the means by which states also can pursue such planning on a multi-jurisdictional basis (as was done by the Commission on the Future of the South)? What are the various methods and options for states to become involved in land use decision-making? With what procedures, standards and criteria for local "conformance"? How is hierarchial review best lodged (example: should sub-state growth planning districts be established, and with what powers)? Should there be higher level review of local comprehensive plans and land use regulations? Should such review require conformance with regional and state land use plans?

Regionalism. Are there operationally effective regional review mechanisms which could affirmatively provide more adequate and coordinated growth guidance? What federal program precursors might be useful in this regard? Would such procedures reduce parochialism and exclusionary effects? Is the idea of regional planning of growth and land use a viable concept.? What are effective planning "areas," given the fact that political jurisdictions rarely coincide with geographical units (as in watershed management)?

Comprehensive Planning. What is the policy-guidance role of the local comprehensive plan? Should such plans be required by state statute? What measures might be applied to judge their adequacy? What weight, if any, should courts attach to such plans? Should the administration of certain land use and managed growth controls be conditioned on the existence of acceptable local comprehensive plans?

Housing Strategies and Social Planning. Should housing elements be required of all local comprehensive plans, and what should be their content? How can the evaluation of the social effects of land use and growth systems be institutionalized into on-going planning? Should socio-economic analysis requirements also be established (similar in concept to EIS procedures)? What local/state programs, regulations, or incentives might be designed to increase the supply of housing for low- and moderate-income families, particularly in the absence of full-scale, federally-subsidized housing programs? At the same time, what diseconomies could potentially result from the stringent application of mandatory "inclusionary" systems?

Procedural Reform. What are the possible procedural reforms for the land use management processes? What are the costs and benefits to the public and the private sectors for each of the proposed institutional arrangements (as hearing examiners and the ALI code), including "political accountability," equity, optimality, and so forth? What could be done with respect to integrating fragmented local, state, and federal review procedures (e.g., "one-stop permit" procedures)?

Impact Analysis and Monitoring. What methodologies — carrying capacity analyses, fiscal evaluations, etc. — are effective and accurate for evaluating the impact of further growth and development? What variables should be considered, what measures used, and how should balancing of interests take place? How can such analyses be effectively incorporated into the local decision-making process? What are the costs and disadvantageous side-effects of such policies? What types of data should communities gather relative to land use, carrying capacities, etc., as an ongoing planning function and prior to the actual submission of project proposal data by developers? What is the best form of such information; how might the data be used or retrieved by different user-sectors? How might this reduce the cost and delay problems in most development, and yet aid in promoting sound land use patterns? What techniques or systems are available to localities to monitor current land uses and to project alternative futures based upon incremental growth and development proposals (see Chapter 13 of Volume II)?

Growth Management Techniques. For each of the techniques, what are the social and legal implications, the administrative costs and needs, and the side-effects? How are they best used in tandem with other methods? Where have such techniques met with success and failure (case studies), and what were the causes of same? Which techniques deserve special research emphasis, as the role of utilities in controlling growth, taxation methodologies, the preservation of environmentally sensitive land, development impact taxes or fees, etc.? Is it possible to develop "model" policies and ordinances, for use by local decision-makers?

Legal Issues. What are the basic constitutional, statutory, and legal questions involved in managed growth techniques? What special problems are being encountered? What are the alternative doctrinal interpretations, and how might they be developed differently (as the taking issue, the travel/mobility concept, etc.)? How might this information best be disseminated to governmental administrators? What is the "appropriate" role of the courts in dealing with managed growth issues? What remedies and devices are utilizable, as special masters or court advisers? What informational materials might be developed that would be particularly beneficial for the courts, in dealing with complex managed growth cases?

Central City. How is the central city affected by various managed growth strategies throughout the region? What programs can be designed to bring the development sector into renewed commercial and residential building in central areas? What public and private sector, as well as individual property owner, incentives are available for central city revitalization?

Rural Areas/Open Space. What unique problems of some rural areas (as stagnating economies, population decline, and the disappearance of prime agricultural land) often fail to be considered in local and state growth policies? What measures could be taken to arrest or reverse these land use and housing patterns? What methods are available to preserve agriculture land and open space? What are the social/economic/legal implications of the various techniques? What are the unique problems relating to the sale of "raw land" for second-home development or recreational purposes? What failures in regulation and management have been experienced in this regard, and how can these problems be rectified? What state and federal review is necessary; which should be the responsible lead agency?

Centrifugal Forces. What forces encourage the continuation of inefficient energy and land use and development practices? What programs might be developed to discourage these types of land use patterns and building practices? Can the continuation of urban sprawl be controlled, absent enormous public investment in large-scale development? To what degree will inefficient land use practices be influenced by economic/energy-availability considerations?

Other Factors. What are the growth impacts of the siting of governmental facilities (including transportation arteries and public buildings)? What should be the responsibility for ascertaining actual and prospective availability of adequate local housing in relation to proposed facilities; (likewise, with regard to the secondary and tertiary development which will be generated)? What special problems arise in regions where growth pressures are exceptionally strong, such as in areas where local governments are faced with extra-jurisdictional growth due to resource-harvesting industries (coal, oil, iron, and so forth)?

Managed/Zero Growth Issues. What are the long-term demographic and consumption trends of economic and population growth? What are the potentially de-stabilizing social and political influences which accompany zero growth? What adjustments in land use, housing, welfare, etc., programs could ameliorate these effects? How are locally-imposed managed growth trends likely to change the nature of the development industry: its risk venture decisions, types of development, and the scope and method of operations? What governmental incentives might be utilized to bring about desired patterns if current where market forces appear too weak to accomplish public objectives?

This list could be expanded at length to deal with such questions as: What are the psychological and other normally "non-costed" effects of alternative growth patterns; what is the concept of "optimum size"; what are the means by which the public can become meaningfully and yet not inappropriately involved in the growth management process; how might an adequate social-indicators system be developed; ad infinitum. The reader who is interested in research needs would do well to examine the gaps identified by professional organizations, national advisory groups, and representatives of the private sector, as well as background materials prepared for the Policy Development and Research Division of the U.S. Department of Housing and Urban Development, the President's Council on Environmental Quality, the U.S. Environmental Protection Agency, the U.S. Department of the Interior, the Library of Congress, the National Science Foundation, and the National Academy of Sciences.

These sources can help to stimulate analysis of the policy dilemmas and research needs facing citizens and professionals in the decades to come.

CHAPTER TWO

GROWTH AND CONTROLS: NEW ATTITUDES

Attention is being focused on an increasingly widespread national phenomenon—the growing public concern with growth management, land use controls, and the quality of urban, suburban, and rural life. There can be little doubt that much of the American public has been experiencing at least a dawning awareness of the side-effects of inadequate control of growth and urban sprawl. Significant discussions have been initiated in a number of communities and in some, planning/programming changes have begun to be made which have the potential for more effectively guiding local growth.

Seldom, however, are the debates designed to fully disclose the various available alternatives and the depth of the problems involved. More often than not, pressure groups in a jurisdiction will attempt to lead the deliberations into pre-formulated directions; as a result, the debates may in turn structure non-optimal frameworks in which analyses are undertaken, as well as tend to distort the nature of the recommendations and policies which are eventually adopted by the community.

As an example, an advocate for protecting civil rights and for expanding housing opportunities (or for that matter, the developer and his desire to maximize benefits through increased densities and homes priced at levels which appeal to as large as possible a segment of the market), is likely to cast his arguments quite differently than those of say, an ardent open space enthusiast or a local farmer who wishes to protect his land for agricultural uses. The voices which appear early in most growth-control debates tend to be those of the strident minority . . . the dissenters who are bent on a policy of preserving the status quo of the community, based on their perceived self-interests, and often regardless of equity considerations [as any exclusionary effects]. The more moderate voices must struggle, through the art of political compromise, to reach "sensible" or "rational" solutions. [The problem is, of course, that managed growth questions are steeped in grand rhetoric; the observer is forced to sift through the phraseology to the real proposals for changes that lie below . . . if he is to gain any appreciation of the reality of what is being said.]

One voice of reason—and a person with impeccable conservationist credentials—is that of **Russell Train**, Administrator of the United States Environmental Protection Agency. Noting that the growth debate is one which will rage for some time, he states: "It is important that we recognize the wide diversity of values and concerns involved. We should avoid dogmatic, categorical approaches. We are in a period of evolution of values and we should respect and encourage wide diversity of views. . . . Beware of insistent voices that categorically tell us what our values should be."

These remarks appear in the first article of this volume, the basic substance of which was presented in two speeches in 1973 and 1974. Train states that for a long period of time, the idea of growth and expanding opportunity "was as unquestioned as gravity itself." But now it appears that "our society is at a juncture where traditional assumptions are being tested by new aspirations, new priorities, and new values." The debate centers around the question: "is more [growth] necessarily better?"

EPA itself has begun to strike out boldly [some would say, too boldly] to provide some answers, in such areas as regulations regarding air quality and water quality . . . regulations which if strictly and broadly enforced, may profoundly affect the land use decisions of governments across the country over the next several decades. [See Volume III for EPA's proposed land use policy statement.] Train himself notes that this new emphasis which has been placed on clean air "has run head-on into the value of personal transportation freedom—or at least sideswiped it. . . . The howl tends to vary in intensity in different parts of the country." [The reader will wish to refer to Chapter 18 in Volume III, for further commentary on the effects of federal environmental regulation on land use patterns and life styles.] The author feels there is good reason to believe that solid decisions will be made only if we—the American public—"develop institutions and processes that provide truly effective means for public participation and choice [and] . . . develop, as rapidly as possible, effective democratic institutions on the state and regional level to direct and regulate growth. As long as we fail to do so [develop such effective state and regional mechanisms], then communities . . . that are engaged in what appear to be thoughtful efforts to manage their growth will find themselves increasingly thwarted."

The second article—by **James O'Leary**—is included in part to illustrate the very point Train made in his speeches, that: "Once sedate zoning and permit hearings have become noisy, crowded battlefields where developers and their teams of architects, planners and lawyers match wits, and often verbal abuse, with a formidable array of 'concerned' citizens supported by their lawyers, environmentalists, and sociologists." Proposals are being turned down in a growing "list of casualties, succumbing to a widespread malady known among builders and developers as the no-growth syndrome."

O'Leary also points to the fact that "confrontations over individual projects are now giving way to an even more ominous approach . . . moratoriums on all development." In a somewhat pro-builder article, the author correctly notes that there is a "lack of accepted guidelines for determining what kind and rate of growth is best for a given community," and, that the trend of conflict seems to be setting a course such that "if the picture appears bleak, rest assured, it is."

The **Forbes** article—excerpted from a mid-1971 publication—traces some of the old and the new attitudes about growth, and thus is one of the first national, popular magazines to signal the "new mood" or "new trend." " 'Welcome, Stranger,' the typical American attitude, is fast changing to that of 'Stranger, Get Lost.' . . . People are banding together to fight pollution, to fight industry, to fight more people."

But a *caveat* is posed. "Certainly, it is commendable that Americans want to protect their families and their communities from pollution; to preserve open spaces; to curb urban sprawl; to count other than economic blessings. The problem is this: because there is no overall, national plan for use of our resources and land, individual states and counties must struggle alone to protect and improve their quality of life. If they succeed, surely they are going to attract outside industry and people, which may threaten that very quality of life. So keep-out policies are formulated. Thus, the country is in danger of becoming compartmentalized, of breaking up into territorial and ecological have and have-nots."

". . . As things stand, the no-trespassing signs just keep going up and up. And business is increasingly caught in the middle. . . . And there is another issue, a very thorny one. It is this: the ecology and no-trespassing movements have a middle-class character."

Approximately three years following this article—on May 15, 1974—Forbes ran another commentary on the continuing confrontation in growth attitudes, stating that "there is much good in all the excitement [and debate over growth]. The critics of growth have forced economists and politicians to think about the possible consequences of a heedless consumption of resources and endless destruction of the environment. Neither the romantic no-growthers nor the laissez-faire pro-growthers have the argument all their way." The article also pointed to the debate among the various factions, quoting one portrayal [an unfortunately typical perception] of for-growthers versus anti-growthers; one economist bewails the seeming identification of a person who is against growth as "a granola-eating, backpacking, transcendental-meditating, canoe freak." [This perhaps matches well with the miscellaneous cross-complaints of the little-old-ladies-in-tennis-shoes stereotype, and the rapacious-profiteering-land-destructive-developers syndrome . . . a trap of *argumentum ad hominem* into which much public discussion too often falls.]

An often-quoted series of articles titled "Where Do We Grow From Here?" was written in 1973 by **Robert Cahn** for the *Christian Science Monitor* shortly after the release of *The Use of Land* report [the next article in this chapter]. Cahn covers much of the same territory as the report . . . selecting major points and elaborating on them, or noting recent examples and discussions of the issues. His articles serve to show that nation-wide, the issues of growth and development increasingly are being debated, and often with little in the way of satisfactory resolution.

Cahn states that "this new growth-limiting mood has a number of hidden time bombs that now are exploding into controversies and lawsuits around the country." Property owners and other allegedly aggrieved or interested parties are fighting some restrictions which have been imposed upon them by the public sector. [Examples of some of these growth-limiting controls—such as the down-zoning of 'critical' areas—are discussed in Chapters 4 and 6 of Volume I, Chapter 12 of Volume II, and Chapter 14 of Volume III.] "The results of those lawsuits and the precedents they set may play a large role in determining where, and in what setting, future Americans will live." "Intense controversy," claims the author, will continue for some time among the various parties and in different localities, and will strain the institutions that are attempting to regulate and/or balance interests in land.

Generally, Cahn's material provides a salutory summary of the report . . . prepared as it was for journalistic consumption; as such, it is worth reading in conjunction with the article which follows [and then—if the opportunity permits—with the full version of the Task Force report].

"There is a new mood in America." So starts the report of the **Rockefeller Task Force,** titled, *The Use of Land.* "The repeated questioning of what was once generally unquestioned—that growth is good, that growth is inevitable—is so widespread that it seems to us to signal a remarkable change in this nation." Finding "unrestrained, piecemeal urbanization" and non-rational use of land—along with a rise of the new mood—the Task Force believes that there is a need to seek "balance" among various "public interests." The report suggests that the old institutional procedures and the traditional ways in which "compromise" is reached, promises in the future only to perpetrate upon the public, more of the same problems and the same dilemmas. This report seeks in effect, to issue a clarion call to public reconsideration of the use of land, and to new, more effective programs and regulatory actions.

The Task Force began in mid- 1972 to investigate the experiences and efforts of a number of communities to control growth . . . especially in Florida, New York, California, and Colorado. [Description of the field studies is contained in the full report; however, a few commentators have observed that the material does not fully analyze the local situations . . . as in the case of Ramapo, New York. The reader might also turn to the discussion of Ramapo and other localities, as contained in Chapters 8, 9, 11, and 12 of Volume II, and in Chapter 16 of Volume III.]

Hoping to tap the "broad, popular concern for planning and regulating land use," the Task Force sets forth a series of recommendations which supposedly favor "the re-arrangement of processes and the redesign of incentives to get the system working for, not against, quality urban development." These include provision for, acquisition of, and incentives regarding open space; historic preservation programs and activities; and adaptation and interpretations of the "takings clause" to fit new regulatory circumstances (to counter the now "exaggerated fear that restrictive actions will be declared unconstitutional"), including a proposal for U.S. Supreme Court re-examination of precedent, to [now] state that "a mere loss in land value is no justification for invalidating the regulation of land use"; modernization of development regulations, including passage of more extensive environmental laws and requirements for environmental impact statements; the offering of incentives and flexible procedures for better "quality development," and the elimination of exclusionary land use practices; restrictions on certain raw land/lot sales practices in rural areas; and finally, analysis of the role of the citizen in the planning and zoning processes.

Many of the statements made in *The Use of Land* certainly would not elicit universal agreement. Many property owners and other persons who are not imbued with magnanimous public spirit, might easily find significant room for disagreement. Similarly, developers might accept some recommendations as potentially useful, but would find other conclusions blocking their attempts to keep the cost of housing within the reach of the majority of the market . . . or as being simplistic and non-understanding of the delicate nature of the development process [of time, cost, and risk constraints]. On the other hand, many environmentalists have criticized the report as "giving away too much," and as failing to take a firm stance where they might otherwise deem environmental values to be "paramount."

For the full flavor of potential areas and issues of disagreement—and in the case of the planner or public official who is interested in pursuing any of these issues further—the full Report should be read. [Certain other topics—as "The Taking Issue"—are analyzed separately and in greater detail in Chapter 4, Volume I . . . in the articles by Fred Bosselman, et al., and Donald Hagman.]

In his article, **William Reilly** reiterates a number of the points which were made both implicitly and explicitly in *The Use of Land* report, for which he acted as staff director. Believing that the country can capitalize well on the "new mood" in America, he states: "It is important to be clear about what is happening, and why. Otherwise we might well botch an opportunity [to work within the new mood] the like of which has not existed in the fifty years since states began enacting their first basic zoning enabling laws." Seeing various groups as "subscribing to different myths" (as he calls them) the author elaborates on why six such myths are inaccurate or invalid.

Claiming that the groundswell for managed growth is not "darkly fearsome" or "anti-American," Reilly nonetheless understands that it appears almost inevitably easier for citizens to "take a negative rather than a positive turn; . . . that is a consequence of the fact that citizens are more often able to block what they don't want than they are consulted about what they do want." In the second myth, the author dispatches the idea that no-growth is a possible option nation-wide, given the current demographic trends. On the local level, he finds that such efforts will "not survive attacks in the courts unless . . . [they are] based upon demonstrated ecological or health considerations, or unless . . . part of a regional scheme which included a method for accommodating reasonable growth needs somewhere else."

In what the reader might find at first to be a curious dilemma, the article finds that citizens distrust flexibility and discretion in the zoning process because of past abuses of the system, but still contends that controls must be flexible in order to obtain quality development. He makes a valid set of points: "Nevertheless the answer is not to impose more onerous restraints on development, or to tighten minimum standards. Rather the means must be found to improve the incentives for good development, to reward builders who do the right thing. Eventually, I believe that public intervention will be necessary to assist developers to assemble land, to provide help with sewer and other infrastructure, possibly to award density increases when developments are particularly responsive to community land conservation or social policies."

At the same time, the article insists that "we must move away from purely demand-oriented, to resource-oriented, planning." A call with which a number of planners would agree, and others would debate vehemently as to application [see Petaluma, in Chapter 9 of Volume III]. The article's concluding statement that communities "have their tolerances" leaves the reader interested, but the discussion unfortunately makes no attempt to take the idea further: a problem of course with much of the planning literature, which is good in concept but low on methodology which might be uniform or acceptable. It is a problem that a number of organizations, such as the author's [the Conservation Foundation] will be dealing with in the next several years.

The last article, by **Basile Uddo,** is a review of *The Use of Land.* The article originally appeared in the *Harvard Journal on Legislation.* Uddo sees the report as "often naive in its recommendations and analysis. Although its objective—a more pleasing human environment—is appealing, the report is inadequate in terms of recommended implementation." Uddo also complains of a lack of analysis of "proximate causes and the possible obstacles to implementation," and a tendency to lose "sight of the practical problems to implementing proposed solutions."

The report is scored on several counts, for "the authors' reliance upon local control [that] rests on an unduly optimistic view of the local desire to significantly control development." Furthermore, too much of the "new mood" (in terms of anti-growth concern) is explained away in the report as "humanistic"—when other objectives, as exclusion, may more adequately describe the motivations involved.

Thus, Uddo emphasizes a significant point that: "despite its emphasis on humanism, the report clearly lacks sufficient consideration of the problems and needs of low income and minority groups. . . . [and] it offers no solutions. Recognizing that the new mood is thought to be tailored to white middle class interests, the reporters imply this criticism is unjustified, but never say why or what should be done about it." The author therefore concludes that "until a commonality of perspective as to what constitutes humanistic land use can be achieved, the report's suggested growth policy will not, indeed, should not, be readily accepted."

Other recommendations of the report are reviewed and critiqued. As to the taking/compensation question (with regard to private property rights), it is seen that "the Task Force has substituted naive generalities where it might have suggested manageable standards. This leaves the taking issue as confused as ever." Overall, Uddo finds that the report "is generally useful, but [only] in a very limited sense. . . . Perhaps its chief value as a policy guide is that it may heighten public awareness of the problems and issues of land use."

With the above series of articles for Chapter 2, the "new mood" or the "new attitude" stage has been set and described in some detail—as to ideas and the most visible manifestations across the country. The second set of articles [Chapter 3] addresses the "managed growth" syndrome in terms of its possibilities as a local land use and planning system. Later in this volume, we will also look at the questions of limits to growth, and analyses of what the other end of the spectrum—no-growth, or zero-growth—might mean to society's current resources and values.

—RWS

Growth With Environmental Quality

Russell E. Train

Russell Train is Administrator of the United States Environmental Protection Agency. Formerly, he was chairman of the Council on Environmental Quality [CEQ]; president of the non-profit Conservation Foundation; and, Under-Secretary of the U.S. Department of the Interior. Mr. Train is a graduate of Princeton University, and Columbia University Law School.

This article is adapted from a speech delivered at the National Forum on Growth With Environmental Quality, in Tulsa, Oklahoma, in September 1973.

Is More Better?

The issue of growth with environmental quality has vital implications for our nation and the world. And yet it is important that we recognize the wide diversity of values and concerns involved. We should avoid dogmatic, categorical approaches. We are in a period of evolution of values and we should respect and encourage wide diversity of views.

Different social and economic groups will inevitably have different perceptions of the costs and benefits of different kinds of growth—or the lack of it. Different geographic areas will, likewise, differ in their perceptions of these questions. Again, this is as it should be. Beware of insistent voices that categorically tell us what our values should be. We should adhere firmly to our own values and never hesitate to speak up for them. But we should also be tolerant and understanding of the values of others.

During the last four years this Nation has begun a broad, concerted, and conscientious effort to clean up its environment. We have moved swiftly to reduce air and water pollution, control pesticides, abate noise, dispose of solid waste, protect wildlife, and regulate ocean dumping. We have given strong leadership to international cooperation in some of these same areas. Most of these are relatively simple, preliminary tasks. Cleaning up pollution and managing our wastes is mostly just plain good housekeeping.

The subject of growth is an entirely different matter. Growth has been associated for over 100 years with prosperity, expanding opportunity, and social progress. It has produced so many benefits, both apparent and real, that for a long time it was as unquestioned as gravity itself.

But throughout the developed world that attitude is fading fast. Many are beginning to ask whether we should continue to regard growth of population, technology, and affluence as the primary measure of progress. Stated simply, *is more necessarily better?*

Of course, this question has no useful answer unless we also ask: *"More of what?"* This is another way of suggesting the question of growth is not one of absolutes. The really meaningful questions go to the kinds and the directions of growth or, indeed, to the rates of growth.

Quality of Life

In the broad sense, concern over the growth issue is closely related to concern over the *quality of life*, and I am convinced that this issue is emerging as the issue for the rest of the century. Our society is at a juncture where traditional assumptions are being tested by new aspirations, new priorities, and new values.

Growth issues are being hotly debated all across the country in the context of real life concerns—energy needs, environmental protection, land use regulation, etc. It is in such terms that the issue really comes to life. It seems to me that questions of growth, both how much and what kind, can only be addressed practically within the context of a value system. Thus, the question of whether we should have more or less highways can only be addressed usefully in relation to the values we attach to mobility, landscape impacts, traffic congestion, pollution, etc. The way we perceive and apply such values must usually be in the framework of actual choices among real alternatives, not as abstractions.

There is no useful way to address the question of whether to have more or less energy, except in terms of the positive and negative value impacts of the various choices. Thus, as our society has come to attach a steadily higher value to clean, healthy air, it has imposed steadily higher controls on sulfur oxide emissions from fossil fuel power generation. Obviously, such controls, and the underlying values, have important implications for growth in terms of power plant location and investment patterns.

Each day society is addressing growth questions locally and nationally, in our homes and communities as well as in the Congress and federal agencies. Transportation control plans proposed by the Environmental Protection Agency are a case in point. Growing land use controls, at the community and state level, are another. *Both reflect the new priorities and new values which are rapidly evolving within our society.*

Evolution in Priorities

It is important to emphasize the evolutionary nature of these changes in national priorities. They are real but there is still no necessary national consensus on many of the growth issues because there is still considerable uncertainty over what it is we really want, and because our newer values have not yet been fully tested. We are rapidly entering the period of such testing.

For example, it is fair to say that there is a national consensus in favor of clean air. There is really no argument over the overall objective of air quality. At the same time, when transportation control plans for urban areas are proposed in order to meet the primary, health related, ambient air quality standards by 1975—and those plans call for drastic reductions in automobile driving—there may be real howls. Plainly, the value of clean air has run head-on into the value of personal transportation freedom—or at least sideswiped it! It is also instructive to note that the howl tends to vary in intensity in different parts of the country—once again attesting to the diversity of value perceptions.

I see the democratic, political process as a critical element in the way we deal with growth questions. Societal values cannot be altered by fiat but only through a complex, evolutionary process of social interaction. This fact underlines the critical importance of fully involving our citizens in decision-making in this area.

Again, I would emphasize that we are dealing with choices which should be based upon a careful analysis of the costs and benefits involved and influenced by value judgments. *The economic cost of sprawl and other forms of poor development are usually very real.*

Rational Planning Is Essential

In this connection, a growing phenomenon around the country is the local "no-growth" or "controlled-growth" ordinance which, through a variety of mechanisms, seeks to put a lid on further growth. Such ordinances are coming under strong attack in the courts and the legal issues are still to be resolved.

To some people these ordinances represent a sort of absolutist, all-or-nothing response to a complex problem, involving the very kind of rigidity which we should avoid in dealing with social values. On the other hand, such community responses are arising, in my view, for the very reason that land use planning and regulation in this country as a whole have not been the subject of an orderly process which has afforded anything approaching true choice. What many communities have experienced is controlled, undirected growth, without plan or purpose; a process in which permanent choices are made without community involvement. In the absence of a more rational process, it is small wonder that many communities are simply shouting, "Stop!" This is one reason why it is so important that Congress complete action soon on national land use policy legislation. It is essential that we develop rapidly at the state and local level orderly and effective mechanisms for making rational land use choices.

I have been asked whether I was for or against off-shore oil development, deep water ports, and similar facilities. The answer, of course, is that there are certain places where we should probably not undertake such developments, and we should never push them down the throats of communities which are adamantly opposed to the developments. At the same time, there are places where such development can be undertaken and in ways which will do minimal harm to environmental and community values and which will also provide substantial benefits to our society. It is a matter of careful analysis of costs and benefits, and of the trade-offs. It is basically a matter of making rational, orderly choices.

Public opposition to such development is sometimes described as emotional and unreasoning. We have seldom presented the public with any rational process for participating in the choices involved. As in the cases of uncontrolled, "willy-nilly" community growth, these kinds of development have just happened and the public has been confronted with decisions that have already been made. If we are to avoid emotional responses, I think it necessary we develop institutions and processes that provide truly effective means for public participation and choice.

Power plant and refinery siting are other cases in point. Some feel public participation in such matters can only lead to delay. However, these individuals tend to be the same ones who describe public response in such cases as emotional. We cannot have it both ways. We need an orderly process for making choices, not confrontation. For these reasons, like national land use legislation, we need power plant siting legislation at an early date.

Overall, we need to create a sense of public confidence in the ability of the private citizen to influence the process of decision-making, to bring about meaningful change within the framework of our institutions. The National Environmental Policy Act provides a major reform in this direction. The Act's provision for environmental impact statements is essentially a full disclosure requirement. To an extent unprecedented in our history, government plans are made available *in advance* for public examination and comment. Whatever inconvenience and discomfort this process may occasionally cause government, these are far outweighed by the inherent value of public involvement in decision-making. Environmental programs and concerns touch almost every facet of our life. They provide a major opportunity to build a new confidence in the governmental process and bring new vitality and a new sense of responsibility to our citizens—both individual and corporate—in the business of public decision making. I might add that the impact statement requirement applies to EPA's major determinant of growth patterns. I am determined that EPA do a better job than we have in the past in preparing such statements.

Environment as Whipping Boy

As you know, I am concerned that we do not permit our environmental priorities to become the "whipping boy" for our energy problems. Environmental considerations are a part of our energy difficulties, but only a part. Other factors include poor planning by both government and industry, oil import quotas, price regulation, gas curtailment, international considerations, and failure to make adequate investments for research in new energy sources and technologies. Hopefully, we are making major improvements in these areas. It will ill-serve our real energy needs, if we permit them to distract us from effective action to meet our equally real environmental needs. The environmental problems associated with energy production will not go away by weakening or slowing our commitment to their solutions. They will only be solved as we make the investments, do the research, and install the technologies required.

We have all heard it suggested that environmental programs will stop or slow down economic growth. It is pollution, not its control, that limits growth. The American people will not, and cannot, tolerate unrestrained activities adversely affecting public health and welfare. Thus, the real anti-growth forces are those who oppose environmental progress.

This point has, I believe, profound implications for any consideration of the interrelationships between growth and environmental quality. The sooner we minimize or eliminate adverse environmental effects, the sooner this country can direct its energies positively and creatively.

Looking Ahead

We must develop better measurements of social progress and quality of life than we now have. The much-maligned GNP was never designed for such a purpose and is grossly inadequate to the job. We need to do far more research on the economic aspects of growth questions, including studies of economic and other impacts of reduced rates of population growth and of a stable population.

We need to develop institutions in both public and private sectors to address growth issues. We need a focal point in the federal government for the identification and analysis of long-range trends and their implications for the quality of life. The Council on Environmental Quality would represent an appropriate institution for such a task.

We need to address the global implications of growth issues and open an active dialogue with other nations and regions, both developed and developing. World population trends, agricultural production, and resource utilization must be examined in their totality. We should give some thought to the intense pressures growing world demand for food will place on our own agriculture, and the stresses on our own environment that will thereby result. We cannot disassociate ourselves on growth issues from the rest of the world.

Finally, we need individually and as a society to develop a clearer vision of what kind of world it is we really want. In its absence, the hard choices may only lead to confusion. We need greater certainty as to the values we believe in. From such confidence will come the strength of purpose that will direct growth to the ultimate service of the quality of life.

The Quality of Growth

[Editor's Note: The following material is excerpted from a February 25, 1974, speech titled "The Quality of Growth" by Russell Train, before the annual meeting of the American Association for the Advancement of Science.]

Our growing environmental concerns, and most recently the energy crisis, have combined with gathering force to make us understand that we do not have unlimited room or resources. We are starting to see that our energy and environmental ills stem, essentially, from the same source: from patterns of growth and development that waste our energy resources just as liberally as they lay waste our natural environment.

We no longer live in a time when we were few and the land was wide and waiting for us. We have reached the point where we can no longer insulate ourselves from the punishment and pollution we visit upon the earth and the atmosphere, and where the natural resources we once regarded as so endlessly available and expendable are becoming increasingly hard to get.

Perhaps our most enduring changes must come in our patterns of urban growth, in the way we organize our activities in our urban areas. We hear it said, often, that most of our urban ills are the result of overcrowding and congestion. There are just too many people, we are told, jammed together in much too small a space. Yet what creates the sense of overcrowding and congestion is not simply the number of people who live and work in our urban areas, but rather the fact that their jobs, homes, shopping centers, recreation areas are strewn like debris across the length and breadth of the landscape.

It seems quite clear, for example, that we could take the city of Los Angeles—with the precise number of people, schools, airports, power stations that it now contains—and by arranging these differently achieve a hundredfold improvement in the quality of life and save, in the process, considerable amounts of energy, money and time. The streets would be less congested; open spaces and recreation areas more open and easily accessible; the air would be cleaner; far more of the services people need and the activities they seek to enjoy would be only a few minutes away by foot, by bicycle, by bus or by train; and life would be far brighter and far more bearable.

The spread patterns of settlement and development that characterize our urban areas are the unfortunate legacy of our old illusion that we had endless acres of land to build on and unlimited energy to burn. Unlike the cities of Europe, where land was scarce and small, our cities did not grow up—they grew out. They became what Wilfred Owen has called "accidental cities," which put "a premium on moving" because they "offer so little in the way of living." We have, as a result, become a country in which licensed drivers outnumber registered voters, in which for every baby born more than two cars roll off Detroit's assembly lines, in which—according to one estimate—the average commuter spends a month of daylight hours every year driving to and from work.

We need to bring our cities back together and reduce all the unnecessary travel and travail that, in Wilfred Owen's words, result "from the inconvenience of having things located in the wrong places." More compact forms of urban settlement and growth would be far more conservative of both energy and environment, and far more conducive to the "good life" that we so ardently seek.

We could make changes to reduce our demands upon our resources and our environment while, in many respects, improving the quality of our life. If we use a little imagination and innovation in making these changes, they would not require reductions in the level of economic activity, but it should be emphasized that such changes would be far easier to accomplish—and the benefits of these changes secured—if we move more rapidly toward population stability. In my view, we should—as a matter of explicit national policy—do whatever is possible and practicable to hasten the achievement of population stability, and we should take all appropriate steps to provide leadership in achieving global population stability. But we should not deceive ourselves into believing that population stability—even if it were to occur tomorrow—would free us from the necessity of making the kinds of changes I have described.

For, the energy and environmental ills that afflict us, along with a great many other aggravations that seem so inseparable a part of modern life, are in large measure the result—not simply of how much and how fast we grow—but of *how* we grow, of the character and composition and quality of growth.

Institutions and Leaders

At precisely the point when the institutions and processes of government and politics are becoming absolutely essential if we are to resolve the intricate and interrelated issues before us, the citizens of this country are becoming more and more alienated and indifferent to those institutions and processes, which seem as ineffective as they are unresponsive. At precisely the point when the discoveries and achievements of our various sciences seem to bear most directly upon so many of our most pressing public problems, the gap between what the scientist knows and what the citizen understands has grown increasingly wider.

If we are to come to grips with the issues that I have touched upon—with what might be called the problems of growth—we are going to have to find ways of diminishing the distance between scientific knowledge and public understanding, and between the public and the processes of public decision-making.

To begin with, we are going to have to find new kinds of political leaders—leaders who understand that the fundamental issues before us are not always the isolated and immediate ones, but the interrelated and the long-range ones; leaders who understand that, in an age of growing scarcities, the ancient and honored practice of promising more of everything, of guaranteeing two chickens in every pot and two cars in every garage, is neither relevant nor responsible; leaders, in short, who understand that less is often better.

At all levels of government, we need *first*, to strengthen our ability to assess problems and programs not simply in isolation, but in their interrelationships; not simply over the short-term, but over the longer span of ten or twenty or thirty years; and *second*, to devise ways of keeping citizens abreast and involved in these longer-range analyses and, on the basis of these, in developing and deciding upon basic plans and priorities as well as strategies for achieving them.

Americans, more than most people, have failed to take good care of the things that belong to all of us together: air, water, land, cities, regions, neighborhoods. Yet unless we start taking care of these things that belong to nobody in particular and everybody in general, we are going to find ourselves faced not only with a narrower range of individual choices than before, but with individual choices that are less worth making.

These common choices must be made through political processes and institutions that are both democratic and effective, that are large enough to encompass the problems and small enough to reflect and respond to the needs and desires of the citizens concerned. Most of these common choices involve problems that simply cannot be contained within any single local jurisdiction. Local governments are too feeble and too fragmented to cope with an increasing range of problems such as transportation, air and water quality, and above all the problems of growth—of the patterns and pace of development, of the way in which housing, jobs, schools, recreation and similar activities are distributed within a given area.

Citizens within each separate jurisdiction are deeply and directly affected by decisions made within other jurisdictions; yet they have no say in those decisions. Each jurisdiction pushes and pulls against the other. And the citizens of each watch helplessly as their region assumes shapes and directions that are determined by forces they do not understand and cannot influence.

If the citizens of this country are going to have the chance to make intelligent, effective decisions about the patterns and problems of growth—if they are to exercise any real control over those patterns that so deeply affect and influence their lives—then we are going to have to develop, as rapidly as possible, effective democratic governmental institutions on the state and regional level to direct and regulate growth. As long as we fail to do so, then communities like Petaluma and others across the country that are engaged in what appear to be thoughtful efforts to manage their growth will find themselves increasingly thwarted.

Growth vs. No-Growth:

The Suburban Dilemma

James M. O'Leary

James O'Leary is the head of the firm of O'Leary Writing & Design. He was previously the information director for the National Association of Building Manufacturers, and was editor of Land: Recreation & Leisure *published by ULI—the Urban Land Institute. Mr. O'Leary is a graduate of the University of Illinois.*

This article appeared in and is reprinted with permission from the Washington Building Congress Bulletin, *1211 Connecticut Avenue, N.W., Washington, D.C. 20036. June 1973 issue.*

Introduction

Packed . . . the hearing room was filled to overflowing; tempers flared; boisterous shouts interrupted speakers at the microphones; beads of sweat dotted foreheads throughout the room as the air-conditioning faltered under the load; yet a certain air of confidence characterized the onlookers, everyone knew what would happen . . . the outcome was predictable.

"It's a damned good development plan. The board's refusal to grant the necessary zoning has absolutely no rational basis," agonized the construction firm's senior vice president, as he left the hearing. The company's project proposal had just become another in a long list of casualties, succumbing to a widespread malady known among builders and developers as the no-growth syndrome.

The no-growth syndrome, practically unheard of a few years ago, is rapidly spreading through suburban communities across the country. In previous years any reasonably good developer could enter a zoning or permit hearing, confident that, if his project was well-planned, he would get anything he needed in the way of zoning modifications, sewer permits, and other special requirements. Local governments were more than happy to remove any potential roadblocks in the name of encouraging progress.

Today, the picture is quite different. Zoning commissions, county councils, community supervisory boards and other governing bodies are delaying or rejecting proposed development projects in wholesale numbers. Once sedate zoning and permit hearings have become noisy, crowded battlefields where developers and their teams of architects, planners and lawyers match wits, and often verbal abuse, with a formidable array of "concerned" citizens supported by their lawyers, environmentalists, and sociologists.

Confrontations over individual projects are now giving way to an even more ominous approach . . . moratoriums on all development. Sewer moratoriums, rezoning moratoriums and other similar deterrents to overall growth are becoming the most popular tactics of no-growth advocates in the Washington, D.C. metropolitan area.

Many moratorium supporters call themselves controlled growth advocates and regard such actions as necessary in order to provide time to create a coherent and workable set of criteria for controlling future development. Unfortunately, in attempting to halt such a vital function in the well-being of a community, they run a heavy risk of killing the patient they are attempting to cure.

The lack of accepted guidelines for determining what kind and rate of growth is best for a given community, the wide divergence of opinion between the developer and the no-growth proponents, and the highly emotional questions involved have, inevitably, given many recent hearings the flavor of an old-fashioned public hanging, with the developer on the destructive end of the rope.

In such confrontations, the local officials sit uncomfortably between the opponents. They are expected to summon the wisdom of Solomon (who never had to worry about re-election) in evaluating and ruling on the advisability of development vs. no development. Painfully aware that any acquiescence to the developer's point of view must be accompanied by the strongest possible justification in terms of environmental as well as economic good (lest they also be placed in the noose), elected officials often opt for the moratorium approach.

Therefore, proponents of growth who haven't developed a modicum of citizen support and a portfolio of valid reasons for continuing development before entering a public hearing on a moratorium proposal can hold little hope of gaining any sort of acceptable compromise.

If the picture appears bleak, rest assured, it is. Perhaps a look at the pressures for and against growth will aid in providing the necessary background for analyzing and developing solutions to the conflict.

Pressures for Growth

Growth is dictated not only by new families moving into an area but also by new family formations within the population already residing in the locality. About half the new families seeking housing in the Washington area already live here.

The post-war baby boom, advances in medical science and the continuing growth of the federal government and its related industries have guaranteed that the Washington metropolitan area will continue to experience a great deal of growth pressure throughout the rest of the century. The problem of where to house, educate and employ these people is not going to disappear.

As one developer pointed out recently, all of the people who are going to create pressure for growth in this area during the remainder of this century are alive today. Moratoriums on building can only serve to increase the already strong pressures for growth. All a moratorium can hope to do is briefly hold back growth until the demand for new shelter forces a breaking point. Then, everything the no-growth advocate is striving to attain will be swept aside in the pell-mell atmosphere of unchecked development which must certainly follow.

Supporters of growth agree that new development should proceed under some sort of overall control but believe the pressure for growth must continue to be absorbed while the control mechanisms are being created and implemented.

Pressures Against Growth

The ranks of the no-growth advocates are populated by a diverse cross-section of people with one overwhelming common bond . . . frustration. It is frustration with a system which encourages them to make a long-term commitment to purchasing a home, then doesn't see to it that they are provided with adequate public facilities and services, despite the fact that they have paid for the services when purchasing the home.

For the suburban dweller in a growth area, just getting to work in the morning becomes a monumental task. The largely rural road system which usually forms their only link with the inner city employment centers cannot handle the volume of traffic the new developments generate. The result is massive traffic jams.

As the horde from the newer developments wends its way by older suburban sections, more combatants must join the battle for position on the road. They do so with the memory of their once pleasant trip into town fading rapidly.

Schools present another source of frustration. Families who buy homes in new developments hear promises of the new school to be located just two blocks away, which the community plans to build soon. Years later the school site is still a vacant field and their children are contributing to overcrowded conditions in an older more established section of the community.

With incidents such as these widespread in our suburban areas, can the homeowners, both new and old, be blamed for venting their frustration, anger and mistrust by advocating an end to further growth?

Who Is To Blame?

Most of the righteous anger expressed by the anti-growth groups is focused on the builder or developer, because it was his representatives who first promised the new roads, schools, firehouses and other community facilities which haven't materialized.

Certainly, accusing fingers can be pointed at some unscrupulous builders who improperly develop an area through various means and without regard for the future well-being of the community. However, the greatest majority of the businessmen involved in the construction industry are very concerned about maintaining a high quality of life throughout the community in which they build. Not only do they usually live in the community, but their business investment in the area is normally a long-term one.

In most cases, the developer is locating his projects in accordance with an overall community development plan. Sometimes this is a largely informal, loosely defined plan for growth; while in other instances, it is a highly formalized and expertly developed master plan. Fairfax County provides an excellent example of this latter situation.

During the Sixties, the Fairfax County Planning Commission received approval from the county government on carefully laid out master plans for development within the entire county. Areas of high, low and medium density were outlined, as well as proposed sites for the necessary community facilities needed to support the expected population in a given area. The plans even called for a system of interconnecting roadways, designed to easily handle traffic flow throughout the county.

The plans were widely acclaimed and subsequent development largely followed their dictates. Unfortunately, a time phase scheduled for private and public development was never created and implemented. As a result, residential and commercial development progressed at a rapid rate while public development of the necessary facilities lagged far behind.

What caused the delay in building community facilities needed to serve the newly developed areas? Recent studies have shown that county revenues from new residential and commercial developments more than offset the costs of providing the services and facilities called for in the master plan.

One can only surmise that the funds were used to upgrade community services and facilities in older, more established sections of the county, as well as to add new social programs at the expense of the new developed areas. Occurrences of this nature are not unusual, since elected officials naturally place a high priority on meeting the needs of constituents in areas where they feel their support is strongest. In essence, the residents wanted the highest possible quality in community social services and facilities, but didn't want a higher tax rate to support the upgrading program. The elected officials gave them exactly what they wanted. Now, everyone is paying for it.

Who is to blame? The builders who took the county government at its word, and didn't bother to make certain that the county could and would keep pace with private development? The elected officials who chose to heed the wishes of the established electorate, as opposed to meeting the needs of the newcomers? The people themselves, who refused to realize that first class schools, and other community facilities and services require increased tax rates? All must share the burden of responsibility.

Fairfax County isn't alone in this predicament. Other suburban communities in the Washington area are facing situations which are very similar. The causes may be quite different in each instance, but the result is the same. Groups of frustrated residents blindly trying to halt inevitable growth, instead of working to accommodate it in a fashion that will benefit the entire community.

Possible Solutions

The no-growth syndrome has reached critical proportions in most Washington area suburban communities and, unless some concerted action is taken to fully explain the hazards involved in such a course of action, development will all but cease in most jurisdictions within a matter of months.

Perhaps the no-growth problem would not have reached today's monstrous proportions had members of the construction industry assumed an active role in focusing public attention on the real causes of environmental decline in their respective areas.

No-growth is a community-wide problem and must be solved by efforts involving all who have a stake in the future of the community. Builders and developers are not the only ones who must act. Building materials and services suppliers, financial institutions, labor organizations, and a wide range of other construction-related industries must join with other progressively minded businessmen to encourage a realistic attitude toward growth throughout the areas involved, and foster sensible programs for meeting these growth needs.

Community education, political action, and legal recourse provide three major channels which can lead to elimination of the no-growth syndrome. The degree of success in ending this problem will depend largely on how well proponents of sound development policies use these channels.

Community Education. Factual explanations, outlining basic causes of the apparent degeneration in quality of life which most suburban communities are experiencing, can go a long way toward dispelling the pall of mistrust and anger which now covers the construction industry. These facts, coupled with a comprehensive look at the detrimental effects of a no-growth policy and supported by a number of workable alternatives, can be very effective in gaining community support for sensible growth solutions.

Political Action. Political action represents a strong force in quickly putting a community back on the right course. Elected officials readily respond to identifiable pressure groups, and the no-growth advocates have been exceptionally well-versed in the art of political pressure. It is essential that the proponents of growth become just as effective in this area. Until now, pro-growth forces haven't taken full advantage of this means to convince local politicians that moves toward no-growth are not based on sound principles and, in many instances, could be construed as extremely irresponsible.

Legal Recourse. Where moratoriums are instituted on a highly questionable or grossly unfair basis, the courts offer an effective means of recourse. Court action should always be considered and used when necessary.

Fellow Americans—
Keep Out!

Forbes

This article originally appeared under the same title in Forbes *magazine; as such, it was one of the first popular magazine articles to signal the "new trend." It is reprinted here by permission of* Forbes *magazine (June 15, 1971 issue).*

Introduction

No Growth. Slow Growth. Ecology. They all mean parts of the U.S. are solving their problems in ways that may make things worse for the rest of the country.

Go West, Young Man. Go to the Big City, Farm Boy. Make It Big. The Fastest-Growing Little Town in Wannabagga County. Growth Is Good. Such for two centuries was the prevailing American ethic: The bigger, the better. The welcome mat was nearly always out, because more people meant more money, more business, more growth. Make our own state (county, town) grow. So welcome. Bring money. Bring markets.

Oh yes, there were dissenters. Thomas Jefferson believed that industrialization was dangerous to democracy. Henry David Thoreau took to the woods. The "Know-Nothing" party fought immigration. Cattlemen battled the homesteaders for the West's wide-open spaces. Theodore Roosevelt railed at the greedy interests despoiling the nation. But, prominent as they are in the history books, these men's ideas did not prevail.

"The two sides have always existed in this country," says Robert Douglas of the University of Pennsylvania's Regional Science Research Institute. "Those who felt they could make money off economic expansion, and those who felt it was going to ruin an environment they loved. What is changing is that the power in communities is not so centralized as it was in the hands of those who benefit from the growth. The rest of the population is getting more vocal."

As a result, the no-trespassing signs are going up. Though a number of states and localities still assiduously seek new industry, sometimes even they meet new resistance. Many others are becoming choosey, and some are flatly hostile to growth. It's not just "Keep the Smokestacks Out." "Welcome, Stranger," the typical American attitude, is fast changing to that of "Stranger Get Lost."

Oregon's Governor Tom McCall, a strapping six-foot-six Republican, likes to invite tourists back for another visit but adds: "Just don't come here to live." Delaware Governor Russell W. Peterson, a Republican and former Du Pont executive, has just turned away a $360-million chemical complex from his state. California's Santa Clara County—growth was once its middle name—has dramatically reversed gears. Boulder, Colo., nervous about losing its small-city convenience and character, is talking about a 100,000 population ceiling. In many rural spots, from the Far West to New England, Boise Cascade and other real estate developers are running into serious roadblocks in plans to build vacation-home communities.

What Price Growth?

Ecology? Pollution? Are these the driving forces behind the new regional exclusionism? In large part, yes. In the last three years, pollution control has become a hot issue nearly everywhere. In the almost forgotten tradition of Jefferson and Thoreau, Americans are asking: What price our growing economy?

But there is more than ecology to these first few signs of regional isolationism. Sociology plays a part. So does anthropology. For example, in his best-selling book, *The Territorial Imperative* (1966), Robert Ardrey wrote: "If we defend the title to our land . . . we do it for reasons no different, no less innate, no less ineradicable, than do lower animals. The dog barking at you from behind his master's fence acts for a motive indistinguishable from that of his master when the fence was built."

In short, a good many parts of the country are fighting to keep their elbowroom, to defend their turf against growing pressure from the teeming, troubled parts of the country. "Don't crowd us," they're saying.

Such a basic human urge may well lie beneath a good deal of the outcry over pollution. It certainly motivates the suburbanite who resists tooth-and-nail the encroachment of urban people and urban problems.

And so people are banding together to fight pollution, to fight industry, to fight more people. Dozens of local groups have sprung up: BAG (Beach Alliance Group) in San Diego County; GASP (Group Against Smelter Pollution) in Phoenix, Ariz.; SODA (Stop Ocean Dumping Association) in Wildwood, N.J., to mention only a few. Meanwhile, the memberships of national organizations grow to record levels: San Francisco-based Sierra Club, 130,000 members; Washington-based Nature Conservancy, 26,000 members; New York-based Audubon Society, 38,000 members; Zero Population Growth of Los Altos, Calif., 40,000 members; San Francisco-based Friends of the Earth, 22,000 members.

All this happens at a crucial point in U.S. history. For centuries Americans spread out and filled the open spaces. Then, with the agricultural depression of the Twenties, Americans began deserting the countryside for the cities. And the population concentrated again. Whereas 49% of the population lived in rural areas in 1920, only 37% did in 1960. Farm centers in the Midwest became ghost towns. In New England, once-thriving mill towns nearly disappeared.

Now, because of the rising costs and tensions of the overcrowded cities, the U.S. seems in the early stages of spreading out—again. The urban dweller buying an abandoned farm for weekending is in the vanguard. So is the corporation moving to the suburbs or building a plant in an underdeveloped area; the whole industrial development of the South is part of this phenomenon.

But this new wave of spreading out is in trouble. Today it is nearly impossible to build an electric power plant, a jet airport, an open-pit mine or a resort community without strong protest from keep-out forces. Even tourism, once considered the ideal "clean" industry, has run afoul of the no-trespassing mood in places.

Certainly, it is commendable that Americans want to protect their families and their communities from pollution; to preserve open spaces; to curb urban sprawl; to count other than economic blessings. The problem is this: Because there is no overall, national plan for use of our resources and land, individual states and counties must struggle alone to protect and improve their quality of life. If they succeed, surely they are going to attract outside industry and people, which may threaten that quality of life. So keep-out policies are formulated. Thus, the country is in danger of becoming compartmentalized, of breaking up into territorial and ecological haves and have-nots.

The New Border Guards

During the Great Depression of the Thirties, border guards in California turned away Okies and Arkies, the dispossessed tenant farmers from Oklahoma and Arkansas. The border guards were, in the end, declared unconstitutional. But today, zoning and pollution laws and court decisions do a similar job, on a national and local level, of keeping out people and industries. Legal briefs have replaced border guards.

On the federal level are the National Environmental Policy Act of 1969, which requires all federal agencies to consider the environmental effects of their decisions, and the amended Clean Air Act, which gives local air pollution control districts great, though as yet untested, power. Also important is the River & Harbor Act of 1899, which lay nearly moribund until resurrected by the Administration in a crackdown on polluters. On state and local levels, tougher pollution and zoning laws are going into effect or being considered. The intent is clear: A pleasant environment is at least as important as industrial expansion. Maybe more so.

The no-trespassing mood is strongest, as might be expected, in the more scenic areas. Take Oregon, again. State Treasurer Robert Straub echoes Governor McCall: "We have a slow rate of growth right now," he says, "and personally I'm very happy with it. I'm not interested in industry for industry's sake, or payroll for payroll's sake, or population just for more population's sake."

A lot of Oregonians agree. The cities of Astoria, Eugene, and Portland have recently frozen or restricted various kinds of development. A strong statewide zoning bill is being considered by the Oregon legislature. Straub is pushing for an antipollution tax—"a use fee on air and water," he explains—that would eventually ban pollution-producing companies from the state. And many motorists display a bumper sticker: "Save Oregon for the Oregonians."

In West Virginia, a poor state heavily dependent on coal mining, Governor Arch Moore recently cancelled a strip-mining project and warned industry: "We are not going to sell our environment for industrial development." Florida's Governor Reubin Askew takes a similar stand. "We are tightening up our restrictions for commercial development. We want to make sure that we are not simply attempting to grow for growth's sake."

That kind of rethinking is now being done at the county and city levels, too. Look at Santa Clara County, at the southern tip of San Francisco Bay. For years it was one of the country's fastest-growing areas, zooming in population from 290,000 in 1950 to just over a million in 1970.

Now county officials are applying the brakes. "We feel that we should stop, or at least slow down, so we can take care of the major problems we have," says Victor Calvo, chairman of the board of supervisors. Zoning is being tightened up to prevent both high density and sprawl. The county has cut in half its Chamber of Commerce budget and has told the Chamber to spend that money on local studies, not national advertising.

Voters in San Jose, the once expansion-minded county seat, have elected go-slow councilmen. Nearby Palo Alto is considering buying a large area of land rather than permitting it to be developed. Explains Calvo: "They discovered that if they expanded into the foothills, by the time they extended services like roads and schools and police and fire protection, it would actually cost the city money despite the new tax revenue. They would come out ahead if they purchased the land and left it open space."

In Loudoun County, Va.—a state long dominated by pro-expansion interests—county commissioners refused the final permits for a 4,200-home Levittown on 1,200 acres. The

Levittown application came just as Boise Cascade was opening the first houses of its Sugarland Run project, which required the usual county services and prompted a reassessment of property in the county. "The property tax bills had risen for many of our big farm owners," explains County Planning Director Bruce Drenning, "and they were mad. So when Levitt came along with a proposal to double the growth rate without paying its own way in taxes, the commissioners just said no."

Even in Los Angeles County there are signs of change. The city of Los Angeles, now with 2.8 million people, is considering a new zoning plan that calls for no more than 5 million, vs. the 10 million allowed under the old plan. One catalyst has been Lesser Los Angeles, founded by Los Angeles *Times* columnist Art Seidenbaum in 1969. Seidenbaum feels the bumper-sticker-and-button outfit influenced the city to make the population study. "We enabled the Establishment to understand that there are a lot of people here who do not favor an enlarged city," he says. Lesser Los Angeles was inspired by Lesser Seattle, a bumper-sticker group formed in 1962, and it in turn inspired several other Lesser groups, including Lesser San Diego, known by its initials.

Ban the Skyscraper

Perhaps nowhere have the keep-out forces had as much impact as in San Francisco. A year ago U.S. Steel and others were busy planning new skyscrapers there; today, the U.S. Steel building, a 550-foot-high, $200-million office-hotel complex on the waterfront, has been killed by the board of supervisors, and an anti-high-rise referendum, which would ban buildings taller than six stories unless approved by the voters, is scheduled for November balloting.

The anti-skyscraper forces are led by a businessman and based on business reasons. "The Establishment says we need these buildings to bring in money for the city," says Alvin Duskin, a San Francisco-born dress manufacturer. "But just what does the city make on high-rise buildings? Nobody has been able to show me."

Roger Boas, a member of San Francisco's board of supervisors, voted against the U.S. Steel building because he thought it should be in the financial district, not on the waterfront. But he is well aware of the new wave of keep-out sentiment. "Developers have been just too darned greedy in the past, and have neglected esthetics, air space and the like," he says. "People across the state, across the country, feel they've got to do something to stop this promiscuous growth." Boas himself led the fight against freeways in San Francisco in 1964-65, and since then the construction of freeways there has practically ground to a halt.

In Boulder, Colo. the no-trespassing signs are going up. "The city is going to examine the whole growth issue," says Community Development Director William Lamont. "Boulder has always had a strong attachment to its natural setting and I think most people, as they come here, say let's shut the door and let nobody else in." One proposal: Rezone the remaining undeveloped industrial land. "If you are going to control growth," explains Lamont, "you should begin by discouraging employment centers rather than housing, which is a by-product."

Listen to David P. Lim, city planning director of Tucson, Arizona's second largest city, with about 260,000 people: "Since the latter part of last year," he says, "there have been more, shall I say, grumblings: 'Why do we have to grow? Why do we have this many people?' Tucson was known many years ago as the power structure that didn't want industry, that didn't want this, that didn't want that. Perhaps this feeling is coming back."

"There's Just No Place . . ."

There is an economic price in all this, of course. Consolidated Edison Co. of New York, for example, has vainly tried to construct a pumped-storage project at Storm King Mountain on the Hudson River 50 miles north of New York City for ten years. A local group, the Scenic Hudson Preservation Conference, has so far blocked the project, is growing in power and expects to win. Meanwhile the metropolitan area faces growing power shortages.

Southern California Edison Co. has had similar problems. The people of little Victorville, on the edge of the Mojave Desert 90 miles northeast of Los Angeles, blocked construction of a new coal plant, while to the south, Orange County officials are fighting the expansion of an old gas-oil plant. "It's getting to the point," says Edward A. Hummel, an assistant director of the National Park Service, "where there's just no place the power companies can put up a plant."

In states like Montana and Arizona, the big mining companies are the basis of the economy. In past times, they could do just about anything they wanted. But now the keep-out forces have won some big victories. In Montana, Anaconda's proposed copper-molybdenum open-pit mine at Heddleston was stopped. So was its plan to mine copper at the site of a former chromium mine on government land.

New Montana air-pollution standards could close down Anaconda's Columbia Falls aluminum smelter, which pours fluorides into the air that have caused damage estimated as high as $1 billion to the surrounding forests. "If the state adheres to the law and will give us no variance," says Anaconda Director of Technology George Wunder, "then I presume they will shut the plant down."

Wunder says that if the new pollution standards of Montana and Arizona go into effect, the price of copper, now at 52 cents a pound, will increase by about 6 cents a pound. Already American Smelting & Refining Co. has had to cut production in Arizona by 15% to meet that state's current standards, and Anaconda is now selling some ore concentrates that went to Arizona to the Japanese instead—at a lower price and hence for a smaller profit.

An $11-Million Loss

Boise Cascade has repeatedly run afoul of the keep-out forces. Its resort projects in California, Nevada, Washington and Connecticut have been harshly criticized by conservation groups and government officials. Unit Six at its Incline Village development at Lake Tahoe, Nev. was blocked by local authorities, who are considering a ban on all further development there. In New Hampshire, Governor Walter Peterson has warned Boise Cascade that he will closely monitor its project and not allow his state to be plundered by irresponsible out-of-state developers.

Indeed, tougher local building regulations were a big reason Boise Cascade's recreational community subsidiary lost $11 million in 1970, vs. an $11-million profit in 1969.

The fate of Disney's Mineral King ski resort project is now before the Supreme Court. The Cross-Florida Barge Canal, hale and hearty just months ago, has been cancelled by President Nixon. The giant jetport under construction next to the Florida Everglades has been cancelled. And in New York, the Port Authority, after vainly battling keep-out forces in New Jersey and Long Island for a decade, had to settle for a remote former Air Force base 65 miles north of the city as the site of its fourth jetport. But a keep-out movement is building rapidly in nearby Newburgh, even though the new jetport would replace some revenues lost when Stewart Air Force base was closed.

To a large degree, the no-trespassing phenomenon is very much part of the save-the-environment movement. As former Sierra Club President Phillip S. Berry says: "The key issue for conservationists is open space; there can't be any more growth at the expense of our open space or prime scenic areas." Virtually all environmentalists would agree with him, and that's why they are so quick to call for keep-out laws.

Of course, one way of lessening pollution and preserving natural beauty and amenities appears to be through a no-growth economy. Though there is increasing talk about a "steady state" economy, few people take this theory seriously: Population pressures and the demand for higher living standards are irresistible. Moreover, thoughtful environmentalists believe that in order to clean up the environment, more economic growth will be needed. The economists are refining their measurements of growth: A new steel mill is not growth if the pollution it causes equals the value of the steel it produces.

Nonetheless, without subscribing to the no-growth theory, the keep-off-our-turf forces and ecologists are in a stronger position than ever to restrict economic growth. Take, for example, the 1970 amendments to the Clean Air Act. "These amendments give us rather vague but I think wide power in land use controls and population densities," says Victor Calvo of Santa Clara County, who also is head of the San Francisco Bay Area pollution control district. "It may very well be that air pollution will be the one criterion that can be readily applied to the problems of land use and density." In other words, an air pollution control district may be able to simply forbid construction.

Faintly reminiscent of the border guards that kept off the Okies of the Thirties is a proposed state plan prepared by California Tomorrow, a respected citizens' group. "Our plan," President Alfred Heller says, "recommends that each state be authorized to establish a capital investment fee of $1,000 that would be charged to each new resident and collected in installments as part of the state income tax process." No-trespassing spelled with dollar signs.

Some Long-Range Questions

But what about the 60 million to 100 million new Americans expected in the next 30 years? Where are they going to live? Where are they going to work? And play? What about the growing numbers of people taking longer vacations and finding increasing resistance to tourists? Will only the rich be able to afford grass and trees? Will population growth choke instead of fuel economic expansion?

And there is another issue, a very thorny one. It is this: The ecology and no-trespassing movements have a middle-class character. For the poor, the disadvantaged, jobs are still what count. The Kentucky Commissioner of Commerce points out that for a backward state, jobs may be relatively more important than clean air. Interestingly, the battle to keep BASF out of South Carolina was led by the wealthy citizens of Hilton Head—many of them out-of-staters. Reports from the area indicate that most of the poorer residents favored the plant, pollution or not.

Thought of in this way, no growth or slow growth can take on an anti-Negro, anti-poor character.

Unfortunately, questions like these have been largely avoided by both the government and the public. It is a situation where typical American individualism and regionalism no longer provide the answers. What is needed is a balanced approach, reconciling the need for economic growth with the equally compelling—but no more so—need for clean air and open spaces. Such planning, to be effective, must be at least statewide—probably nationwide eventually. As things stand, the no-trespassing signs just keep going up and up. And business is increasingly caught in the middle.

Note: Jobs at Any Price

[On a previous page], we quote a University of Pennsylvania professor as saying that real political power is no longer the near monopoly of industrial interests; hence voices against indiscriminate growth are increasingly heard. But in the Deep South, where political and economic power remain relatively concentrated, there seems less opposition to all-out industrialization. Billy Jo Camp of Alabama Governor George Wallace's staff hinted to *Forbes* that his state wasn't going to be zealous about anti-pollution standards: "Alabama," he said, "will not be at a competitive disadvantage with her sister states. We will abide by these new federal water standards but we aren't going to be more extreme than the other states."

Fred G. Kessner, director of Virginia's Department of International Trade and Development, says: "If a steel company wanted to build a $20-million plant in Virginia, would I tell them to go away? I would not." An aide adds: "A large majority of our new industry has been nonpollutant, electronics and the like, but it hasn't been by design, I can tell you."

You find the same attitude in some border states. Paul Grubbs, Kentucky's able Commissioner of Commerce, is quite frank: "We don't have resistance to growth in our state like they do in some. We have phased environmental impact into all our programs [but] we still maintain an industrial location should be 95% economic.

"With us, meat on the table is a bigger issue than 100% clean air. We don't want to continue poor. We want to be a rich state."

But even the poorer states are beginning to think twice about growth for growth's sake. Senator Strom Thurmond, the powerful South Carolina Republican, boasted about his role in getting tax breaks for German chemical giant BASF, which planned a $200-million petrochemical plant at Port Victoria, S.C. that would provide 650 jobs in a poor area. He ended up with egg on his face.

What happened was this: Port Victoria is just eight miles from the resort of Hilton Head. Resort owners and shrimp fishermen objected to the big plant. Vociferously. BASF backed out, and the state government is the embarrassed owner of a 1,500-acre tract assembled for the project. The resort owners propose using the land for an agricultural cooperative. The State Development Board reportedly is still thinking of building a deep-water port there.

Remember when the high school band—not pickets—met those visiting industrial delegations?

Note: The Case for Selectivity

Delaware's Republican Governor Russell W. Peterson is a politician, birdwatcher and businessman. As a Du Pont executive for 26 years, he knows what it means to meet a payroll. Drawing on that background, Peterson made a thorough analysis of industrial development, and one result was that he coolly turned away a proposed $360-million oil-coal-steel complex on Delaware Bay.

"Twenty years ago," he explains, "a state would think Delaware Bay was a gift of God because you could get industry. And I probably would have been promoting industrial development there myself. But a couple of things in America have changed. We are getting much more sophisticated in our analysis of all the factors involved, which is a great thing for the quality of life."

That's the nub of Peterson's argument. He's well aware that Delaware Bay, perhaps the best deep-water port in the East, is ideal for supertankers, oil refineries, coal docks and steel mills. But he also knows what those would do to the bay's relatively undeveloped coastline. "Fly over that assembly of industrial facilities from Philadelphia down to Delaware City," he says. "Then fly over the open country from there south. If anybody doesn't get the message I'm talking about, there's something wrong with him."

But what about the demand for industrial output? "Yes, we have an obligation relative to the need for oil and steel and paper and so on," he says. "But we also have an obligation to provide recreation facilities for the whole East Coast region. So although industrial development is one big opportunity for Delaware Bay, another is recreation and tourism. We have to make a choice."

Peterson's choice has brought howls of anguish from the companies involved, especially Shell Oil, which wants to build a $200-million refinery. They argue, for example, that oil industry economics dictates the use of supertankers, and only Delaware Bay can handle them. "Why do you start with the idea that you need big tankers?" Peterson asks. "If there are no ports for big vessels, then big vessels are not economic, are they?" True, but then the price of petroleum might go up. "Maybe there are worse things than high-priced oil," answers Peterson.

Shell also argues that it owns the land—a big tract near Smyrna zoned for industry. Peterson's response is to push for statewide coastal zoning laws and more money to buy coastal lands from private owners.

Peterson is not against all development; he just wants "corporate headquarters, research labs, assembly plants—high-salaried jobs, considerable jobs per acre," he says. "A high quality of life and recreational opportunities can be our best selling points in getting good jobs to Delaware. The refinery complex would do the opposite."

Peterson's message is clear: If your company fouls the air, pollutes the water or despoils the landscape, keep out of Delaware.

Where Do We Grow From Here?

Robert Cahn

Robert Cahn is presently writer in residence, Conservation Foundation, Washington, D.C. Formerly, he was Environment Editor for The Chrisian Science Monitor. *He served on the President's Council on Environmental Quality from 1970-1972; in 1969, he received the Pulitizer Prize in journalism for a series on the national parks. Mr. Cahn is a graduate of the University of Washington.*

Reprinted by permission of The Christian Science Monitor. © *1973 The Christian Science Publishing Society. All rights reserved. Bulk prices for the 31-page brochure: 1-499 (35¢); 500-2,999 (30¢); 3,000-5,999 (25¢); 6,000-9,999 (20¢); 10,000+ (15¢).*

Mr. Developer, someone is watching you—1

Frustrated by traffic jams, shocked at urban sprawl, choked by pollution, citizens and local governments across the United States are rebelling against unrestrained growth. This, the first of six articles, tells how concern for the quality of life is replacing America's "growth mystique."

As you drive south out of Santa Fe toward Albuquerque, N.M., on Interstate 25, a lone billboard irresistibly draws your attention with its bold, one-word message:

"UNDEVELOP!"

The mural portrays what the highway traveler would see were there no billboard at all—the volcanic beauty of Black Mesa and the Rio Grande Valley. Carefully lettered in the lower righthand corner is the name of the billboard's sponsor: New Mexico Undevelopment Commission. It is not entirely a gag. Although no such "commission" exists in governmental circles, this unofficial undevelopment commission has immeasurable gadfly influence throughout the state. Its founder, a young, articulate newspaper publisher, Mark Acuff, who writes a watchdog column in his weekly *New Mexico Independent*, has issued more than 500 commission membership cards and has sold 5,000 "UNDEVELOP!" bumper stickers. In these ways the "commission" keeps the advocates of unchecked development off balance with the knowledge that someone is watching.

Like their counterparts in many parts of the nation, New Mexico's self-appointed undevelopers are riding the spreading wave of national sentiment which questions what was heretofore unquestionable—the star-spangled theme of chambers of commerce from coast to coast:

"Grow!" "Grow!" "Grow!"

The just-released report by the Task Force on Land Use and Urban Growth, headed by Laurance S. Rockefeller, says this questioning of growth is a "new mood" that is sweeping the nation. Its opponents refer to it as "anti-growth," "no-growth," or "zero growth," while advocates generally call it "controlled growth," "limited growth," or "quality growth."

Where Do We Grow From Here

No growth outlook dim. The privately funded Rockefeller report, commissioned by President Nixon's Citizen Advisory Committee on Environmental Quality, arrives at the conclusion that absolute "no growth" is not a viable option in the near future. Population will grow. People will improve their status and seek more desirable living areas. A policy that would discriminate on individual freedom of mobility would be both legally and morally wrong.

Yet the report traces the pervasive opposition to uncontrolled growth throughout the nation. It points out that this opposition is motivated in part by concern for the quality of life. The report suggests that new institutions and procedures are needed to find ways of controlling the excesses that have resulted from the often unplanned or ill-planned development that has occurred in cities, suburbs, and countryside.

The anti-growth mood has been evident to me in travels around the country the last few years investigating environmental activities. According to the Rockefeller report and to urbanologists and planners, however, the mood is not being created by far-out environmentalists. Many citizens are conscious that new development carries potential economic hardships as well as harmful environmental effects. The ready assumption of city or county officials that new growth automatically brings more jobs and more tax benefits has been sharply questioned in studies and in the personal experience of many taxpayers who find that the services required to accommodate the new growth can be more costly than the tax benefits derived therefrom.

But mostly, the new mood is just a feeling that creeps up on one as increased traffic extends commuting time or crowds impede shopping. Or the citizen finds new and often inappropriate buildings cluttering former open spaces or scenic landmarks. Or the signs of air, water, noise, and solid-waste pollution suddenly appear "next door" instead of being something to read about in the papers.

Exclusionary reaction involved. In some areas, the new mood, consciously or unconsciously, rightly or wrongly, may be an exclusionary reaction of the citizen who likes things as they are and doesn't want others, and especially others who may have differing standards of living, to enter his city or neighborhood or block. This kind of reaction can come from the pioneer resident, or from the newest arrival all too ready to block the road behind him to others.

What is "new" about this many-faceted movement or mood opposing growth is that it has surfaced in action, instead of just in grumblings and letters to the editor. New restrictive laws, zoning actions, moratoriums on building permits, density limitations, size or height limitations, or bans or septic tanks, are sprouting all over. They are accompanied by citizen lawsuits to prevent development. Once-tranquil city council or county commission meetings have become arenas of protest, overflowing with citizens seeking to block new subdivisions or factories or amusement parks. In New Mexico, before Mark Acuff started the New Mexico Undevelopment Commission, citizens had raised such loud and vigorous protests over a proposal to locate a Kraft paper mill near Albuquerque that the company finally gave up and settled elsewhere.

Development held down. Most of the state is still relatively undeveloped. The average New Mexican wants to keep it that way. Albuquerque, with its snowballing population and physical growth over the past two decades, and a crime rate that last year was the highest in the nation, no longer seeks new residents.

1. The Albuquerque City Commission, with a new antidevelopment majority, voted a temporary moratorium on providing sewage disposal, water, and utilities to new areas outside the city.

2. The once-enthusiastic Greater Albuquerque Chamber of Commerce last September adopted a policy statement recommending "a moderate growth policy . . . geared to preservation of the quality of life."

3. The State Legislature, with a wary eye on the horde of second-home subdividers who are crosshatching the hinterland with roads and house lots, voted to require each county to establish regulations for subdivisions.

A decade ago, citizens of Oregon were developing an anti-growth attitude, even though their then governor (now senator), Mark O. Hatfield, was trying to bring in new industry to help the state's depressed economy. But among Oregonians, many of whom had recently migrated to the state for wartime jobs, the Hatfield industrial push met with resistance. There were already too many people and too much polluting industry, the people said. The current governor, Tom McCall, has gone the opposite route. "Come, but don't stay," he told Oregon visitors two years ago. Then last year he suggested maybe they shouldn't come at all. This year he has requested the Legislature to slash the "Come to Oregon" travel advertising budget by 30 percent. The Legislature may reduce it another 30 percent.

Adequate planning encouraged. Governor McCall believes some growth is inevitable. But he wants adequate planning for it. He is pushing strongly for a state land-use law with provisions to protect environmentally critical areas. A few months ago, he used the public-health laws of the state to force a booming coastal county to issue a moratorium on all new building permits until plans are devised for adequate sewage disposal and water supply. His latest move is a request to the Legislature to raise camping fees for out-of-state cars at state parks.

Florida and California, states that traditionally have vied with each other to attract visitors and industry, now are seeking to outdo each other in growth-control measures. Florida has only recently awakened to a need for stemming the tide of growth. Its extensive advertising of sunshine and the good life had increased population by almost 2 million, or 40 percent, from 1960 to 1970. But by 1970, a combination of new and old causes suddenly made the citizens aware that there were already too many people jammed into urban areas. Added to the normal influx of tourists and retirees, thousands of Cuban refugees moved into southern Florida. Disney World brought a massive surge of unplanned growth to central Florida. And installment-land-sales companies increased their promotions to bring potential buyers to the state.

Under the immediate pressure of a severe drought, Governor Reubin Askew in 1971 called a conference of 150 experts in science, government, agriculture, and conservation to deal with the state's growth problems. Led by Profs. John DeGrove of Florida Atlantic University and Arthur R. Marshall of the University of Miami, the conference proposed remedies and formed teams to draft new legislation. After continuing efforts by these citizen leaders, the State Legislature in 1972 passed four key planning and water conservation laws. This was despite opposition from forces of growth and development who succeeded in softening some of the measures but could not stop them. "We have had a total and sudden shift in state policy from expansion to no-growth, from a pro-business climate to an attack on private enterprise," said one Tallahassee lobbyist in a speech to industry people.

New controls enacted. The most vital new law, the Environmental Land and Water Management Act, provides the necessary land-planning control to protect areas designated to be of critical environmental concern. It also provides control over areas that are to have developments of regional impact. And last fall Florida voters, by a large majority, approved a $240 million bond issue for the purchase of environmentally endangered lands.

At the same election, the city of Boca Raton, north of Miami, became the first city in the nation to vote a population maximum by adopting a city charter law to limit to 40,000 the total number of dwelling units to be allowed within the city limits. City commissioners in nearby Hallandale and Hollywood have also passed ordinances lowering the density of future growth. Dade County (Miami), faced with overcrowding, air and water pollution, and inadequate sewage treatment, had a citizen revolution. This saw three commissioners recalled. A new mayor and two new commissioners were elected on a platform that called for a moratorium on development-oriented rezoning whenever the water supply, sewage treatment facilities, or road capacity, were found to be inadequate.

Palm Beach and Martin Counties on the Atlantic Coast, Collier County on the Gulf of Mexico, and the St. Petersburg-Tampa area have recently adopted building moratoriums or density limitations. New dredge-and-fill operations throughout the state have been drastically curtailed. The state is even forbidding dredge-and-fill actions on state-owned land it had sold to developers for development purposes.

Preservation priorities pushed. Other evidences of the new mood in Florida are the efforts to preserve the Big Cypress Swamp and to protect Everglades National Park against development intrusions and water shortages; Governor Askew's appointment of Professors DeGrove and Marshall to the board of directors of the powerful and development-biased Central and Southern Florida Flood Control District, and an awakening by townspeople in central Florida that Disney World may eventually bring more troubles than profits. Disney World adopted some environmental protections for its own site. But it did nothing to help the many nearby towns that now are overrun with traffic, are sprouting new motel and tourist service facilities, and are faced with demands for water, sewage treatment, and electricity that far exceed supplies. Many of these central Florida towns are considering growth limitations.

At a recent conference sponsored by the Florida Defenders of Wildlife 65 of the state's top scientists, educators, conservationists, economists, land planners, and urban experts spent two days discussing the effects of growth on the ability of nature to serve man, on the ability of government to serve man, and on the cost of living. The conference concluded that, as a consequence of unchecked growth, the state is misusing its water supply, outdoor recreation will deteriorate, and inequitable economic effects will occur.

Increases in population that raise the cost of services are devastating to those citizens with fixed incomes. Benefits that seem to accrue to the middle-income range of the population from increased salaries are largely illusory because of the increase in the cost of living and the environmental debt incurred by not paying the full costs of growth in the past.

In-migration discouraged. Among other things, the conference recommended that the state discourage all in-migration "until we know what areas can accommodate growth"; limit commercial development and divert in-migration from areas known to be overloaded; produce an economic analysis that will clearly show the costs as well as the benefits of growth, and take strong steps to discourage land speculation, such as providing a tax on land sales.

California's anti-growth activities started earlier than those in Florida. In some ways they are more sweeping. Through statewide vote, the entire coastline is being protected for 1,000 yards inland. State and regional commissions have been established to control coastal development. A state environmental policy act, stronger than the national law, requires environmental impact statements for most commercial development as well as for state actions. A powerful citizen group, California Tomorrow, has produced a comprehensive state plan for conservation and development. This explores alternatives for immediate actions and implications of these actions. It makes projections to the year 2000.

Citizens of Livermore and Pleasanton, cities 50 miles east of San Francisco, passed an initiative limiting issuance of new building permits until school, sewage-treatment, and water facilities exist to serve new populations. The San Francisco Bay Area Governments Association adopted a regional policy to halt the area's population growth at 5.5 million by 1980, only a million more than at present.

Compliance demanded. San Diego has acted to deny services to developers who do not comply with provisions for needed services. And last November the city voted a height limitation on shoreline buildings, which will stop the growth of skyscraper condominiums. Meanwhile, the San Francisco Bay Area Conservation and Development Commission is effectively curtailing deterioration of the bay and preventing damaging commercial development along the shoreline.

Among other areas in which the new mood has been translated into action and controversy are Colorado, Long Island and other Metropolitan New York areas, the suburban areas in Virginia and Maryland surrounding Washington, D.C., and a number of towns in New England.

This new growth-limiting mood has a number of hidden time bombs that now are exploding into controversies and lawsuits around the country. Whenever planning to restrict further growth occurs, an inevitable result is to forestall some property owners from developing their land. Popular attitudes call for more restrictions and laws that will sustain these actions. Present property laws and court interpretations, however, seem inadequate to serve the common interest and at the same time protect the property owner against inequities. The institutions that are calling for regulation and restrictions are thus drawn into intense controversy.

Thwarted developers are taking the Fifth—2

The U.S. Constitution's Fifth Amendment doesn't deal with just self-incrimination. It also states that private property shall not be taken for public uses without just compensation. Increasingly, as would-be land developers fetch up against environmental restrictions, they are taking to the courts. Decisions stemming from these court actions could determine where and in what setting future Americans live.

A Connecticut firm wants to build an industrial complex on 277 acres it has owned for 20 years in Stratford's Great Salt Meadow. The development would bring jobs and tax revenues to the area. But the state has denied the application because of projected environmental damage.

A man who, 12 years ago, bought 22 acres in the Palo Alto, Calif., foothills has been refused permission to subdivide his plot into small lots. The city has classified the foothills area as open space with 10-acre minimum zoning.

On the western shore of Lake Tahoe, a developer seeks to put 60 vacation condominium units on a 17-acre tract that was formerly a retreat for Henry J. Kaiser. The application has been blocked by low-density restrictions of the Tahoe Regional Planning Agency, a joint California-Nevada entity.

All of these thwarted landowners now are in court trying either to invalidate the restrictive regulations or to get compensation for the full development value of their property. All assert their constitutional rights have been violated because the actions of government constitute a "taking" without compensation. These claims are based on the Fifth Amendment provision that "private property" shall not be taken for public purposes "without just compensation." This provision is applicable to the states through the Fourteenth Amendment's provision that property shall not be taken "without due process of law."

Controls challenged. The adoption by state and local agencies of laws and regulations to control the consequences of unplanned growth, to restrict development of environmentally critical lands, and to control pollution has caused many citizens to challenge the actions in court. They allege violation of their property rights. The results of these lawsuits and the precedents they set may play a large role in determining where, and in what setting, future Americans will live.

Public attention is being focused on these issues by a report on land use and urban growth issued by a citizen task force headed by Laurance S. Rockefeller. The task force points out that a new mood of limiting or controlling development and growth is sweeping the nation. When cities expand or suburban areas sprout new developments, natural features and open space that have been serving a common interest are threatened. Wetlands supporting the fish-bird-mammal food cycles, aquifer recharge areas (water-bearing beds of rock, sand, or gravel), coastal dunes, forests that reduce floods or prevent erosion of productive agricultural land or cherished scenic meadows—all are jeopardized.

The law has never allowed owners to do entirely as they please with their land. Regulation, however, has always brought owner resistance. Years ago, landowners attacked single-family zoning as a taking of property rights without compensation. But a wide variety of restrictions have evolved and been recognized as allowable regulatory activity within the public interest and not requiring compensation.

Regulations upheld. While various legal formulas are offered to explain just when compensation is required, courts traditionally uphold regulations designed to protect the public interest as long as some "reasonable use" is left to the property owner. Thus, the mere fact that a property owner cannot make the most personally beneficial use of his property, or is unable to realize speculative investment gains, does not mean that he must be compensated. The crunch seems to come when regulations do not leave the owner with any economic use of his land at all. If development is the only possible use for the private owner, as is claimed, for instance, in the Great Salt Meadow Case, then it may be argued that an agency which restricts such development should be required to pay compensation.

But if governments are forced to pay full development value for all such areas of critical public interest, this could be so expensive it would inhibit protective legislation entirely. In the Great Salt Meadow Case, the plaintiffs are demanding $77.7 million compensation. More than $200 million in claims have already been filed by landowners against the Lake Tahoe Regional Authority. "The takings issue is at the heart of the planning problem," says William K. Reilly, staff director of the Rockefeller task force. "If the public cannot compel landowners to maintain critical environmental property in present use without being required to pay compensation, then you can forget about preserving much of what we value in this country."

Conscious choice urged. "It is important to recognize that a vast amount of property will remain in present use for decades to come even without strong public controls," Mr. Reilly adds. "But without these controls the market will decide which land gets developed and which remains as it is. What the task force is recommending is that a process of conscious public choice is a better way to make these decisions, so that development is steered away from the wetlands and beaches, the unique farmlands, and steep mountain slopes."

In a significant recommendation, the Rockefeller task force urges the U.S. Supreme Court to reexamine decisions made in an earlier era before land was recognized as an irreplaceable natural resource instead of as a commodity to be considered for its maximum market value. In tracing court decisions on the takings issue, the report notes how the U.S. Supreme Court has apparently adapted constitutional language to meet what the court saw as society's contemporary needs. Of particular importance has been a 1922 decision—*Pennsylvania Coal Company v. Mahon.* Pennsylvania had passed legislation forbidding coal mining that would cause the surface of land to subside under homes or public buildings. The mining company, in this case, argued that the law was an unconstitutional taking of property by the state because it interfered with the right to pursue mining on their property even if it disturbed other landowners nearby.

The Holmes decision. In the court's opinion favoring the coal company, Justice Oliver Wendell Holmes said that "the general rule at least, is that while property may be regulated to a certain extent, if regulation goes too far it will be recognized as a taking . . . we are in danger of forgetting that a strong public desire to improve the public condition is not enough to warrant achieving the desire by a shorter cut than the constitutional way of paying for the change."

In dissent, Justice Louis Brandeis argued that compensation should not be required where the facts demonstrated an important public need. A restriction upon the use of property which deprives the owner of some right theretofore enjoyed is not a taking when the restriction is imposed to protect the public health, safety, or morals from threatened dangers, Mr. Brandeis said. "The property so restricted remains in the possession of its owner," wrote Justice Brandeis. "The state does not appropriate it or make any use of it. The state merely prevents the owner from making a use which interferes with the paramount rights of the public."

A more recent (1962) Supreme Court decision, *Goldblatt v. Hempstead*, upheld state prohibitions for a gravel pit operation in an urban area and did not provide compensation for resulting economic loss. It may have given state courts a signal that they should be moving in this direction.

Few cases accepted. In the last half century, however, the Supreme Court has only rarely taken cases involving the regulation of land. It has preferred to leave the subject to state courts. Recently, courts in California, Wisconsin, Maine, and Maryland have sustained state land-use controls against owner challenges.

The Rockefeller report says that, at the time of earlier cases, such as *Pennsylvania Coal*, there was little knowledge of the interrelationships of land uses and their political environmental impacts. "It would be inconsistent with our constitutional tradition to adhere blindly to these past precedents now that we have better information," the report says, recognizing that courts respond to basic change in society. Lawmakers in states and localities are warned in the report not to be intimidated by older court decisions. The report urges them to "adopt stringent planning and regulatory legislation whenever they believe it fair and necessary to achieve a land-use objective."

The task force also recommends that courts presume that any change in existing natural ecosystems is likely to have adverse consequences that are difficult to foresee. The proponent of the change should therefore be required to demonstrate, as clearly as possible, the nature and extent of any changes that will result.

Historic sites disputed. Another area of dispute over the "takings" question has developed as a result of recently adopted historic-site preservation laws. While some courts have indicated concern over whether aesthetic preservation is as important as the regulation of safety and health, other courts have upheld efforts to prevent activities that would deface or destroy places of historic or cultural significance. Since property subject to historic-preservation requirements generally still has some economically reasonable use, preservationists argue that the mere fact that more profit might be made by destroying a historic structure or altering a site does not necessarily justify doing this.

A major case now awaiting decision in the New York County Supreme Court tests the relevance of this rationale as applied to Grand Central Terminal, one of the nation's classic railroad stations. The present owner, who prefers to use the space for a 59-story office building, has challenged New York City's Landmark Preservation Law. Under this law, the station has been declared a historic landmark. The city has turned down the application for the skyscraper. The owner is asking $8 million a year in compensation.

Court role involved. The growth and development of the country will thus be greatly affected by the courts as they seek to determine the adjustments in property rights required in the general public interest. In a recent U.S. Court of Appeals decision, which denied a developer's complaint and upheld six-acre minimum lot zoning in Sanbornton, N.H., Chief Judge Albert W. Coffin summarized the view from the bench:

> This court, like other federal and state courts throughout the country, finds itself caught up in the environmental revolution. Difficult and novel legal and factual questions are posed which require the resolution of conflicting economic, environmental, and human values. The problem inherent in quantifying a way of life, the beauty of an unspoiled mountain, may never be solvable with any degree of certitude.
>
> Thus basic value judgments will be made by legislatures and voters which courts can review in most instances, not on the basis of the wisdom of these decisions, but rather only to determine whether they are permissible within the relevant statutory and constitutional framework.

Where the (court) action is.

1. Great Salt Meadow, Stratford, Conn. The Rykar Industrial Corporation seeks to develop an industrial facility and fill the 277 acres it has owned for more than 20 years in Great Salt Meadow. Local zoning regulations have permitted industrial development in the area since 1927. Development would benefit the area with new jobs and an increased property tax base. The Rykar application to fill the marsh has been denied by the Commissioner of Environmental Protection under recent state legislation to protect coastal wetlands. Rykar alleges this action constitutes a "taking." It wants $77.7 million compensation from the state. The Commissioner of Environmental Protection says the Rykar property is part of a tidal wetland subject to flooding, hurricanes, and other natural disasters and that dredging would destroy shellfish grounds. At local hearings, residents warned of dangers to adjoining Long Beach, if dredging is permitted. They argued that the meadow's use as a wildlife area would be damaged by development. The case now is before the Superior Court of Hartford County, Conn.

2. Fleur du Lac, Lake Tahoe, Calif. Owners of Fleur du Lac, a 17-acre site on the western shore of Lake Tahoe, seek to build 60 second-home condominium units. The land, once a vacation retreat for Henry J. Kaiser, is heavily wooded. It has 12 or 13 old buildings and was zoned for medium density. The developer's plan would give maximum protection to trees and other vegetation. But the application has been

denied by the Tahoe Regional Planning Agency. The developer says this constitutes a "taking" and asks $4.5 million in compensation. The case is awaiting trial. The Tahoe agency, required by an interstate compact to deal with development pressures, has lowered the allowable density for Fleur du Lac to one unit per acre. The agency made engineering studies to determine the classification of the land. But it also made its rulings on the basis of reducing maximum use of the entire Lake Tahoe basin to preserve the ecology of the area.

3. Grand Central Station, New York. In August, 1967, the New York City Landmarks Preservation Commission designated Grand Central Terminal a "landmark." Penn Central Railroad, which owns the terminal, and UGP Properties, Inc., lessee of the air rights over the terminal, plan a 59-story structure that would demolish all but the main concourse. The landmarks preservation commission has turned down the plan. Under the landmarks ordinance, which protects only the exterior of the building, the commission is empowered to help the owner find alternative paying uses for an uneconomic landmark. The New York City Planning Commission's suggestion of alternative sites for the floor area that could be developed at Grand Central was not implemented. The owner and lessee alleged a "taking" and are asking $8 million a year in damages. The case, already tried, is awaiting decision by the Supreme Court, New York County.

4. Palo Alto foothills, Calif. Much of the 7,500 acres composing the foothills behind Palo Alto is suitable for subdivision development. Water and sewage lines were extended to the area after it was annexed by the city. The owner of one 22-acre parcel in the meadows of the upper foothills applied for subdivision approval. This was denied. He claims he purchased the land in 1961 expecting to subdivide and that new low-density zoning comprises a "taking." He asks $445,000 compensation from the city. Palo Alto, on the basis of a study showing that costs for services would substantially exceed revenues from development of the foothills, adopted an open space ordinance for the entire area, with 10-acre minimum parcel size. The ordinance recognized that open space is a land use equal in importance to the traditional residential and commercial categories.

Stop growth here, and it will pop up there—3

Halting runaway growth will take more than zoning and other legal restrictions, warns a presidential task force. Across America, communities wonder how to cope with a problem that springs from the basic fact that people are not going to go away.

Is "no growth" a realistic answer to the overcrowding of the land and environmental decay that threaten many American communities today? Citizens of some cities, such as Boca Raton, Fla., or Boulder, Colo., have so strong an anti-growth sentiment that they are trying to close their gates. Other cities, caught up in the new mood, are taking such steps as enacting zoning restrictions, denying sewer permits, or imposing building moratoriums to limit growth and development.

These actions appear to be needed and plausible, especially to the citizens living within a threatened area. However, a new report by a prestigious citizen group points out dangers in trying to stop growth on a piecemeal, city-by-city basis. Nationwide, it must be recognized that, by the end of the century, an additional 54 million people will need living space. "Stop growth here, and it will pop up there; slow it down over there and it will speed up somewhere else, because people are not going to go away," states the report of the Task Force on Land Use and Urban Growth, chaired by Laurance S. Rockefeller.

Migrations expected to continue. The study, commissioned by President Nixon's Citizens Advisory Committee on Environmental Quality, notes that even with zero population growth (the rate at which we simply replace ourselves), population would not actually level off for about 75 years. The migrations from rural to urban areas and from inner city to outlying suburban areas are expected to continue for some time. This concentration of population in regional urban constellations will result in five-sixths of the people living in large urban regions by the year 2000. Adding to the housing demand is the increase in the number of both young and old living apart from their families. During the 1960's, while total population increased about 11 percent, the number of households increased by 17 percent. Each new household takes up living space and requires services. From now until 1985, over 27,000 new households—as many as in a city the size of Kalamazoo, Mich.—will be established each week.

Exclusive motive rejected. Members of the Rockefeller task force warned that while limiting growth and development may be justifiable in order to protect the physical and social environment, restrictions should not be imposed purely for exclusiveness or economic reasons. Growth-limiting measures cannot be applied indiscriminately on a wide scale without affecting the aspirations of millions of Americans who may later seek to exercise their rights of mobility.

Options available for dealing with growth problems are expanding as communities seek their own solutions. The movement is so new that it is not yet clear which of the plans will eventually work out, and which may be unfair or unduly restrictive. Some of the current efforts, however, warrant careful analysis. Take Boca Raton, Fla., for instance. This community of 41,000, north of Miami, composed mostly of middle-to-upper-income residents, voted last November to establish a ceiling on growth. The city was started as a wealthy private club. It had only 7,000 residents in 1960. But by 1970 it had grown to 28,500. With new oceanfront condominiums attracting retirees from the North, and with an expanding Florida Atlantic University drawing other residents, the city was becoming more crowded than its residents desired. Many of the loudest complainers were the newest arrivals.

Dwelling units limited. At the polls last November, Boca Raton voted a "population cap." This limits to 40,000 the number of dwelling units—both houses and multiple dwellings such as apartments and condominiums—that can ever be built. With an average of 2.5 people per unit, this would mean an ultimate ceiling of 100,000. After that total is reached, the city could deny any more housing-construction permits. The city already has imposed a moratorium on new building permits in order to prevent a rush of development before the new controls are clamped down. Some developers with building permits, and homeowners desiring to sell, will immediately benefit from the increase of demand over supply. But the law will impose hardships on land owners who expected to develop in the future. The law will undoubtedly be challenged at some time on whether this arbitrary ceiling is in fact exclusionary and goes beyond the constitutional powers of a municipality.

Voters in Boulder, Colo., narrowly defeated a maximum-population limit in November, 1971. The city, 22 miles northwest of Denver, has been one of the leaders in anti-growth sentiment, however, and is doing something about it. A recent report by the American Society of Planning Officials says Boulder is "probably the farthest along of any city in the country when it comes to a public consciousness that growth can be controlled or significantly affected as a matter of public policy."

Green-belt plan adopted. Boulder adopted one of the nation's first locally financed green-belt programs in 1967, voted a sales tax to help support open-space purchase, and has already bought or optioned more than 2,700 acres. With the population jumping from 37,000 to 67,000 between 1960 and 1970, citizens became alarmed with the results of a comprehensive plan that predicted the population of the city and nearby county area would double again in 20 years. In the same election, when the voters turned down the population ceiling, they adopted a 55-foot height limit on downtown buildings and approved a resolution directing that the local government "take all steps necessary to hold the rate of growth in the Boulder valley to a level substantially below that of the 1960's." A study supported partly by the federal government is seeking to determine the physical, social, and economic effects of different growth strategies. And the city council in February, 1972, voted to discourage new primary employment centers from locating in the valley. Although Boulder's planning may, in effect, work to exclude low-income residents, the city is the only one in the Denver area to have a public-housing program.

Ramapo system studied. Meanwhile, a number of communities across the nation have expressed an interest in what has been called the "Ramapo plan," based on the actions of Ramapo, N.Y., in prosperous Rockland County about 35 miles from New York City. Ramapo, which had doubled its population from 1960 to 1970, adopted a time-controlled zoning ordinance in 1969 for the unincorporated 60 square miles of the township.

Land for new housing in Ramapo can be developed only after the owner receives a "special permit." This is granted if the land is located in an area served by a minimum level of community facilities. These facilities—sewerage, drainage, parks and recreation areas, roads, and firehouses—are scheduled to be installed in accordance with an 18-year, capital-improvement program. In order to build, an applicant must have a minimum number of points (15) based on so many points for each of the services. He can speed up the schedule only by installing enough of the services himself to gain his required number of points.

Discrimination charged. This "development timing" plan was taken to court by a developer. But the New York Court of Appeals upheld it last year. Under the new ordinance, the building rate has been cut from approximately 1,000 new dwelling units a year to about 350 a year. Critics claim that the development-timing regulations work to exclude minority groups. The town had banned any more apartment building. And, it is claimed, at the end of the 18 years, all new residential building could be denied. This would make the plan a measure for establishing a maximum population.

Palo Alto, Calif., throws yet another light on the growth issue. The city's 56,000 residents live within half of the town's acreage. The other half is undeveloped foothills. At one point, the city had been planning 3,480 dwelling units in the lower foothills. It had extended water and sewer lines to the area. But as part of an overall development study for the Palo Alto area, a startling discovery was made. It would actually be cheaper for the city to buy the foothills outright than to allow them to be developed. The study by the San Francisco planning firm of Livingston & Blaney showed that the cost of schools, roads, police, fire, and other services would far exceed projected tax revenues. The city council used $4 million from its budget to start foothills acquisition. And to prevent development, the city then voted to reduce zoning density in the foothills from one unit per acre to one unit per 10 acres. It also voted to allow a variety of land uses such as golf courses, educational or research institutions, or farms that were consistent with open-space requirements.

Conclusions verified. While the costs versus tax revenue estimates are frequently disputed, other studies have verified the Palo Alto conclusions. It is rare these days for a city council or county board of supervisors to accept without questioning a developer's argument that his additional new homes or development will be economically beneficial to an area.

In 1972, the Urban Institute, Washington, D.C., studied 800 residential units and 30 acres of commercial development in a new area surrounding the city of Charlottesville, Va. It found that county expenditures associated with the proposed development would exceed county revenues by $101,000 per year. And a 1970 Stanford Law School study of a 690-acre tract in the city of Half Moon Bay, Calif., showed that the property and other local taxes would fail to pay for the cost of new schools, fire and police protection, and other services. By the time of the development's projected completion in 1982, the population of Half Moon Bay would be increased by 85 percent. The net loss (over tax revenues) to the city for providing services would come to $400,000 a year.

Need for services calculated. Another projection has been provided by Albert Veri, associate director of the Division of Applied Ecology at the University of Miami. Dr. Veri calculated costs for replacing 20 single-family units with a multiple-family apartment complex which would increase the population to 270 families. The 270 families would, Dr. Veri calculates, generate a need for 12 acres of public land for open space and recreation, three acres for service industry, four acres for retail stores, 11 more classrooms, 400 more cars, 120,000 more gallons of water per day, and for disposal of 100,000 more gallons of effluent and wastes per day. They would also need two more firemen plus $8,100 per year more equipment, 12 more teachers plus $12,900 per year for facilities, 1,600 more library books, and two miles more of improved streets. An additional $39,000 would be required each year for health services, $4,160 for recreation, and $69,000 for other services.

Full challenge ahead. While courts are beginning to support communities that seek to limit growth, the full dimensions of the challenge have yet to be confronted. No city or town, by itself, can deal with what is essentially a regional, indeed a national, problem.

As an antigrowth measure, the small town of Sanbornton, N.H. (population 1,000), adopted six-acre minimum zoning for the remote sections of the town. This new zoning effectively blocked the plans of a developer who expected to put about 500 family units on his 510 acres, mostly "second homes" for people from nearby metropolitan areas. In the resulting lawsuit by the developer, U.S. Court of Appeals Judge Albert W. Coffin upheld the zoning as being reasonable to protect the general welfare. He held that the town could consider that hundreds of new homes would have an irreversible effect on the area's ecological balance. They would destroy scenic values, decrease open space, significantly change the rural character of this small town, pose substantial financial burdens for services, and open the way for tides of weekend "visitors" who would own second homes. If the federal government, Judge Coffin said, can require environmental concerns to be considered in its actions, he did not see why Sanbornton could not consider such values in its zoning ordinance.

Judge voiced reservations. But Judge Coffin warned in his decision that the town had accomplished its zoning in a most crude manner. He noted that no professional or scientific study was made showing why six-acre zoning rather than four, or eight, is the right way to protect the values cherished by the town. And, although the ordinance may be a legitimate stopgap measure, "Where there is natural population growth, it has to go somewhere, unwelcome as it may be, and in that case we do not think it should be channeled by the happenstance of what town gets its veto in first," said Judge Coffin. The Sanbornton action typifies the present dilemma—how to prevent the separate actions of the individual communities from being exclusionary and, at the same time, protect the natural values and maintain a livable environment. Statewide land-use controls for critical areas and for placement of major developments, as well as regional planning, are needed, says the Rockefeller task-force report.

People or land—which 1st?—4

"Now would be the worst possible time to declare that America is going to rest in place, or that everyone will stay where they are until environmental dangers are dealt with," commented one speaker at the conference to discuss recommendations of a new citizen task force on land use and urban growth. "The buffalo hunter mentality of development that is threatening the great reservoir of natural land in the nation must be stopped," said another speaker.

The first comment, made by Ronald H. Brown, general counsel of the Urban League, reflected the viewpoint of those who view the current national trend toward limiting growth in urban areas as being restrictive on the poor and minority groups. They are skeptical of the motives of some who would limit urban growth. "A concern for the environment and for proper land use can never be accepted as a cover for efforts to exclude people on racial or class grounds from living in a community," said Mr. Brown.

Top priority seen. But to Oregon's articulate and forceful Governor, Tom McCall, who spoke of the "buffalo-hunter mentality," protection of the land is the No. 1 priority. Encouraged by word he had just received from Salem that a tough state land-use control law he had been pushing for several years had just passed the Oregon Legislature, Governor McCall stressed that while population was increasing, no more land would ever be available. And he warned of activities such as a proposal to put 2,100 houses on a small rural hillside near the Oregon coast, where the land could not support such development without being ruined.

Most of the comments during the conference of 250 public officials and citizen leaders in environment and urban affairs, however, agreed with the task force chairman, Laurance S. Rockefeller, on his summary of the intent of the citizen report: that the massive urban growth foreseeable by the end of the century must be managed without destroying neighborhoods or nature, but also must be managed so that opportunities are not shut off to any segment of the population.

Study completed. The 12-member citizen task force set up by President Nixon's Citizens Advisory Committee on Environmental Quality has just completed an eight-month, privately funded study of land-use problems associated with urban growth. The study reported on a "new mood" gathering strength in the nation to limit or stop urban growth that is perceived as destructive to established communities and to the environment. The study also emphasized the need to reevaluate traditional attitudes that accept automatically every property owner's right to develop his land to its highest economic potential. Mr. Rockefeller, although characterizing the report as "hopeful," said that "the task before us consists of learning to do what we have not yet successfully accomplished on any scale: the creation of communities that are socially open and environmentally sound."

Extremes called threat. The time is propitious for exacting higher standards of development, he added, "because only now have the forces of conservation acquired sufficient strength to be taken seriously by traditional spokesmen for development."

The need for compatibility of economic and environmental demands is threatened by extreme positions, said Sen. Henry M. Jackson (D) of Washington. "The no-growth philosophy encourages rather than mitigates confrontations between the 'haves' and the 'have-nots' and denies to our society the very wealth and technological advancements which we must have if we are to cleanse and improve the environment," he said. Equally harmful, the Senator said, are the charges of "those who make predictions of ruin should the laws of the free market be amended, or of those who claim that public planning and implementation of policies for protection of the environment invade constitutionally protected rights."

Inviting mobility. The deputy chairman of the task force, Paul N. Ylvisaker, dean of Harvard's Graduate School of Education, said that "when we talk about opening new land to quality growth we are inviting mobility of a population that land-use controls, tax powers, and so on have really imprisoned within the central city." Dr. Ylvisaker said he hoped that a future task force would deal with "how as we open the city to the flight of even those prisoned within it, we also anticipate the conservation and regrowth of these areas."

Dr. Ylvisaker and several other conference participants stressed that land-use issues involve a social as well as a physical dimension. "We can't just think in physical terms," Dr. Ylvisaker said. "We have to think in human terms as well. Sometimes to go too quickly in the direction of physical salvation may take you to human destruction."

Rethinking choices? Russell E. Train, chairman of the Council on Environmental Quality, said that "it may well be time to rethink our ways of dealing with growth. The limitations of local home rule and the owner's right to develop property may need to be adjusted to new needs." The problem of determining how society can best allocate resources so as to serve the broader community "may entail frank acknowledgment that some individual choices may not be accommodated," Mr. Train added. "It may be better not to build a highway if it is only likely to induce more sprawl and more pollution. It may be better to restrict automobile access to parts of cities if letting them in destroys neighborhood tranquillity and pedestrian freedom."

Another challenge for rethinking was given by William K. Reilly, staff director of the Rockefeller task force, who said that the report suggested it is time to try to reinvigorate the processes for people getting along with each other.

Running away cited. "Much of the urban-growth experience in the United States over the past quarter-century has consisted of people running away—from other people in the older cities, now even from the suburbs to the mountains and the seas. Now it is dawning on us that there is not really any place to run to.

"Clustering, green belts, new communities with a full mix of uses, more inclusive decisionmaking processes—all of these involve higher levels of social interaction and cooperation than we usually have achieved," Mr. Reilly said.

Former Interior Secretary Stewart L. Udall praised the report, but he criticized the acceptance as inevitable the trends toward decentralization and enlargement of urban regions.

Auto's importance. The study should have taken up critical energy problems and the need for ending the "automobile culture" which has caused the sprawl and unplanned growth of metropolitan areas, Mr. Udall said. The present energy crisis, he said, which will grow more serious, will actually prove an ally to the environment because the decline of the automobile will force a move to more compact cluster living and thus save much of the land from development.

How much should Uncle Sam let out his green belt?—5

As the American population expands, so does the demand for living room. And the resulting pressure on the nation's open spaces poses a growing threat to the quality of the environment. A presidential task force suggests alternatives to an unplanned, wall-to-wall megalopolis.

By the year 2000, say those who project present statistics into the future, five-sixths of the American population will be housed in vast urban regions. What the statisticians do not yet know, however, is whether these megalopolises will be huge sprawls the length of Atlantic, Pacific, and Gulf Coasts, around the Great Lakes, blanketing Florida, and radiating out from a few other centers.

An alternative would be distinctive communities set in open farmland and countryside, the nearby mountains and seashores protected and retaining their distinctiveness and integrity. Abundant parks and accessible waterfronts along unpolluted waterways would grace the inner cities. Such an alternative is possible, according to a report by the Task Force on Land Use and Urban Growth, headed by Laurance S. Rockefeller. But the report, done for the President's Citizens Advisory Committee on Environmental Quality, warns that the alternative will not be available without basic reforms in attitudes and institutions controlling the use of land.

It is also now becoming clear that open space, long valued for esthetic and recreation purposes, can have a very powerful influence on the growth and shaping of cities and urban regions if it is well planned.

Visual relief offered. Some of the open spaces—aquifer recharge areas (water-bearing beds of sand, stone, or gravel), coastal dunes, highly productive agricultural areas, forests that reduce floods, and wetlands which start the biological food chain—must be preserved for the essential part they play in ecology. Green spaces that give visual relief also provide recreational opportunity for the expanding population. They also keep cities and neighborhoods from merging into a solid mass. Without open space, qualities that made the areas desirable places in which to settle are lost. Although some communities are making progress, the nation as a whole is doing a grossly inadequate job of making wise use of open space and green space, say urban experts and conservation leaders. The best available studies also estimate that from 500,000 to 750,000 acres of rural open space are lost each year in the urbanization process.

Combined action urged. To deal with the problems of green space, the Rockefeller report recommends a combination of governmental and private actions. The task force seeks to have higher levels of government working to guide development, but with decisions being made locally. The report suggests that land kept open for purposes other than recreation is best left in private hands and regulated to prohibit uses inconsistent with the conservation of scenic characteristics or ecological processes. It also recommends that vacant areas within urban regions—most often the unwanted leftovers of development—be preserved and grouped where they can do the most good.

Where Do We Grow From Here

Millions of acres already have been set aside by federal and state governments for permanent preservation of natural lands as national and state parks, wildlife refuges, national forests, and other designated public areas. Most of the national areas, however, are far away from population centers. For years the federal government—primarily through the Land and Water Conservation Fund of $300 million a year (cut to $55 million for fiscal 1974 for Nixon administration budgetary reasons)—has been buying up land for national parks and forests and wildlife refuges and giving matching funds to states for purchase of park and wildlife areas.

Price keeps spiraling. However, private lands within the boundaries of national park areas still remaining to be purchased would require $250 million, at present land prices—and going up in price 10 percent each year. The price tag on the projected acquisition of Florida's Big Cypress swamp, needed to protect Everglades National Park's water supply, is $170 million.

Several states have voted legislation protecting certain types of natural areas. Hawaii has a statewide plan for classification of all land, with special designation of agricultural or conservation lands which are given some protection from development and tax benefits. Florida last year passed a land-use law setting up a system for protecting critical natural areas. The state's voters then passed a $240 million bond issue, most of it to be used for purchase of designated critical areas. New York State also passed a $1.15 billion environmental bond issue, including $175 million for parks and open-space acquisition.

Regulations needed. Land purchase by government agencies can satisfy only a small part of the open-space requirements, although as seed money it at present serves a vital purpose. The larger need is for protective regulation and full cooperation from those engaged in the private development process.

"If the open space determination is framed for the public in terms of 'buy it or lose it,' we would surely lose most of our scenic countryside," says William K. Reilly, staff director of the Task Force on Land Use and Urban Growth. "The answer has to be a mix of solutions that involves primary reliance on regulations, backed by property-tax assessments that reflect present use value. Sewer systems and roads, which attract housing, for instance, should be planned in such a way as to steer growth away from the lands that need to be protected from development."

Attempts by local governments to maintain green space by adopting town or county plans are often unsuccessful. Some citizens are led to believe their town's conservation and open-space needs are met because planners show maps with substantial areas marked in green. When the plans are checked against the zoning, however, citizens may find that the so-called conservation areas are zoned for two-acre lots.

Vermont's permit plan. Vermont has a new land-use law which requires permits before development projects are started. Permits can be denied unless the developer can show that his project: will meet a number of strict environmental criteria; will not have an unduly adverse effect on the natural beauty of the area; and is in conformance with a local or state land-use plan.

Two California counties have taken noteworthy steps. In 1965, Marin County placed two-thirds of its 300,000 acres in an agriculture preserve. One of these thirds has since been placed under preservation contract, with local governments authorized to reduce property-tax assessments. In 1971, the county rezoned land in the agricultural preserve from one dwelling per 3 acres to larger parcels, the majority of which are now zoned for 60-acre-minimum lots. Monterey County now has about one-third of its land zoned for 40-acre lots. New York State's recently legislated plan for keeping the 3.7 million acres of private land in the Adirondacks Park permanently protected will provide for an average of only one building for each 42 acres on more than half of the private land, industrial development will be largely confined to areas already built up, and large second-home developments will be curbed by the low-density zoning.

Unfair application seen. Agricultural zoning, by which property owners are allowed reduced taxes for maintaining their land undeveloped, has not been generally satisfactory in maintaining open space in most states where it has been tried, and has been subject to unfair application and windfalls for many landowners. The Rockefeller task force recommends that existing programs be redesigned to apply two principles to agricultural zoning laws: (a) that benefits apply only to farmland located where it needs to be preserved; (b) that some permanent protections be provided so that the owner cannot use the subsidy and then sell off to developers at a large profit after five years.

One of the major recommendations of the Rockefeller task force calls for a federally assisted green-space program which would give permanent protection to green belts around cities and buffer zones between urban regions and within the regions. A "national lands trust" with federal funding of $200 million annually is advocated. It would be made available on a matching basis (75 percent federal) to assist state and local land-use agencies in the designation, planning, and conservation of extensive green spaces in and around areas that are becoming urbanized. The federal government could make funds available for partial interests in strategically located lands.

Other means such as purchase of development rights along highways or waterfronts and the use of police powers for noncompensatory conservation zoning are also recommended.

Clusters permitted. Local governments already can regulate development and preservation of open space by requiring developers to set aside for open space or park use a portion of any proposed subdivision. The developer may be allowed to cluster units in one part of the subdivision in order to leave larger sections in open space and still maintain an average density that can meet regulations. But inasmuch as this type of regulation does not cover the small developer, the Rockefeller task force has recommended that in newly developing areas, local governments require that all developers contribute open space, or cash to be used to acquire open space, sufficient to satisfy the reasonable needs of the residents in their developments.

Another potential for providing green space is by voluntary donations from citizens. This activity has been aided by federal income-tax provisions. These generally permit income-tax deduction of such charitable gifts for five years and exclude appreciation of the value of the donated property.

45-year accomplishment. The Nature Conservancy, largest of many nonprofit land trusts around the country seeking to assist in preservation of natural land, has helped save 972 areas involving 377,055 acres over the past 20 years in 45 states and the Virgin Islands. In addition to making purchases and receiving land gifts from private citizens or corporations, the Nature Conservancy can option or buy an area threatened by development, but sought by a government agency which does not have purchase funds immediately available. The Nature Conservancy can then hold the land until the agency has funds appropriated for purchase.

A new organization, the nonprofit Trust for Public Land (TPL), has recently been formed to help save threatened key urban-oriented natural lands. Most land trusts deal principally in rural natural areas. The TPL's founders, Huey Johnson, formerly western director of the Nature Conservancy, and Greg Archbald, a former Nature Conservancy lawyer, feel that while it is important to save wild and remote natural areas for the escaping urban dweller, it is equally or even more important to preserve urban open space.

Wooded ranch saved. One of the TPL's first ventures was to assist in preserving a 672-acre ranch in Granada Hills, within the Los Angeles city limits. The ranch—with woods, cliffs, and streams—is situated at the edge of suburbia. As such it was a prime target of subdividers. The land had been held by a family for many years, and the sale price was just over $1 million. The TPL was contacted by the owner, who hoped to have the ranch kept intact, possibly as a park, and was willing to make part of it a charitable contribution. On the last day of 1972, Mr. Johnson and Mr. Archbald put together a package to buy half of the ranch, provided the owner would donate the other half if the whole area could be preserved. The TPL then turned over the entire 672 acres to the City of Los Angeles for $450,000, and it has become the city's second-largest park. The owner has the satisfaction of seeing the ranch preserved, receives income-tax deductions, and is able to make a charitable gift to society.

Developers' aid essential. The use of regulations and governmental purchase or incentives in setting aside of open space must be balanced with getting the development process of the private sector to move on its own. This is being done most effectively by the developers of new towns. For the most part they operate on a scale where open space helps to form neighborhoods and causes the value of the developed areas to appreciate. By planning the whole project as a unit, the new-town developer can have some development of high density, and yet keep flood plains, wooded areas, steep slopes free from development. New towns remote from urban areas are not seen as a long-term solution to the need for absorbing population growth because of the reluctance of most people to stray far from the attractions of large cities.

The developer, who claims to be starting a new community, but is basically selling raw land on an installment basis with little building—the traditional "second home" investment scheme—is perhaps the worst enemy of the wise use of open space. When this remote and frequently environmentally critical land has been divided into uniform small lots, it is most difficult to plan for clustering or common open spaces. Reassembling the land for protection as open space, if the proposed new town never becomes a reality, is almost an impossibility because of the many landowners involved.

Plan phased out. Another form of open space even more difficult to preserve is land within the center city which may play a major part in making urban environment livable. A highly publicized but never adequately implemented "open space" program for acquisition of land for parks and green space in cities now has been phased out in favor of revenue sharing. It is doubtful that cities, on their own, will be willing to give a high enough priority to open-space land acquisition once it must compete with more pressing demands for the revenue-sharing dollar.

Some planners believe that one effect of the new national mood of challenging unrestricted growth will be to change the methods used to assist decaying inner-city neighborhoods. Instead of trying to replace these neighborhoods with higher-intensity development, a more logical solution, say some experts, might be to construct townhouses, and small buildings, and seek to reshape neighborhoods through open spaces. The use of urban waterfronts, now in decay in many cities, can play a role in rebuilding vitality into core areas. And industrial waterfront property might be replaced with parks and low-density housing. With many of the nation's rivers now in the process of being cleaned up, urban waterfronts will grow in economic value.

Court decisions important. The preservation of open space may depend largely on obtaining more liberal attitudes and court opinions relative to the rights of development that go along with ownership of land. Most land-use regulations have been viewed as restrictions on each landowner's preexisting rights, rather than as grants of rights he did not have before.

The Rockefeller task force concluded that it was likely that the traditional assumption of urbanization rights arising from the land itself will be gradually abandoned in the future. "What is needed is a changed attitude toward land, not simply a growing awareness of the importance of stewardship, but a separation of commodity rights from urbanization rights," the report said.

Willy-nilly suburban overspill can be tempered—6

As in many other "bedroom" communities near major cities, citizens in Virginia's Fairfax County realized a few years ago that uncontrolled growth was heading their county toward a crisis. In this 400-square-mile area a half-hour from downtown Washington, schools were jammed, sewage treatment plants were overloaded, and traffic clogged the roads. The county had grown from 22,000 in 1920 to 98,000 in 1950 and to 453,000 in 1970. It was run by a board of supervisors whose majority still believed in growth at all costs. Taxes were skyrocketing as costs of additional schools and county-provided services exceeded revenue from new residents.

Then the citizens organized to do something. Only 10 percent of the county residents lived in incorporated towns and cities. Those in the vast unincorporated areas had little identification with county government. But there was a federation of 130 neighborhood civic associations. In 1969 it turned its attention toward controlling growth.

Building moratorium adopted. As a result of this new citizen interest in growth, Fairfax County voters elected a slate of candidates pledged to control growth. This changed the balance of power on the board of supervisors. A moratorium against further building was adopted by the new board for most of the county on the basis of inadequate sewage treatment. In April 1973 the supervisors held a two-day citizen workshop to discuss methods of controlling growth. Last month an all-day planning session of the entire board was televised throughout the county on public TV. And next week the board will hold a public hearing to discuss plans for further moratoriums on development, for controlled growth that would link future development to availability of services, a "land banking" policy in which the county would buy up key developable areas to control land use, and establishing a requirement for environmental impact statements on all proposed major public and private development.

Not that all of this has been without controversy. Developers are still winning some fights. And 37 lawsuits have been filed against the supervisors by landowners who claim the county has illegally denied them the right to develop their property.

Politics upstages homemaking. Here, then, is an archetypal case of the rise of citizen resistance to uncontrolled growth. The Fairfax Board of Supervisors chairman, Jean R. Packard, set aside her homemaking chores to enter politics last November. She won on a controlled-growth platform. She says that active citizen participation—attending hearings, making studies of growth cost vs. tax revenues, spending time informing others, and voting in local elections—is the only means for accomplishing change. "If we can keep local government going the way the citizens want it to go," she says, "then we don't have to rely too heavily on the restraining powers of the federal or state government over which the citizens have far less direct control."

Citizen concern, however, can make itself felt in state government, too. In Oregon, for example, citizens started opposing new industrial expansion and growth more than a decade ago. Despite this sentiment, Gov. Tom McCall had been frustrated in efforts to get a recalcitrant Legislature to pass a state land-use control bill.

Citizens support organized. Then last November, Governor McCall sponsored a symposium on land use. Conservationists, business and labor leaders, bankers, farmers, builders and developers, and about one-fifth of the state Legislature met for three days to discuss the issues. Six hundred-strong, opponents and proponents, they met in small groups for debate, then reassembled to hear reports. This basis of citizen support has continued during the current session of the Oregon Legislature. Late in May 1973 a strong land-use law was voted which listed 10 priority areas in which controls should be exercised to preserve land. It established a state land commission and a standing joint legislative land-use committee and set in motion a process for identifying statewide land-use goals. The law also sets up a state citizen advisory committee on land use and requires each county to state how it is going to involve citizens in the planning program.

Fairfax County and Oregon illustrate the point that citizen involvement is the key ingredient of the anti-growth "new mood" that the report by the Task Force on Land Use and Urban Growth found to be sweeping the country.

Traditional processes protested. "Increasingly, citizens are . . . questioning the way relatively unconstrained, piecemeal urbanization is changing their communities and are rebelling against the traditional processes of government and the marketplace which, they believe, have inadequately guided development in the past," states the Laurance S. Rockefeller-headed citizen task force that made its study for President Nixon's Advisory Committee on Environmental Quality.

What, specifically, is the role of the citizen who desires a change in land-use and urban growth policies?

1. Organization. Citizens have found that the first hurdle confronting them is organization. In community after community the average citizen showing up for a meeting discovers that he does not have the necessary resources and staying power to fight well-equipped developers. Many find strength in numbers when they look around at a hearing and see similarly concerned neighbors giving up an evening to protest a development proposal or rezoning. Citizens have provided new issues for already existing citizen organizations, or have formed ad hoc groups to meet specific problems.

2. Donations of land or development rights. A growing number of environmentally oriented landowners are voluntarily giving up their development rights, sometimes in concert with neighbors. Or they are donating land outright to public agencies or nonprofit land trusts. Typically well off and deeply committed, they want these natural areas or historic sites permanently protected against development or alteration. Their gifts usually can be used as income-tax deductions.

3. The ballot box. Ultimately, citizen strength must translate into electoral power. Citizens must not only keep informed on the issues but must actively work for candidates whose views they share. They can also write or wire their representatives and senators in Congress on issues such as the land-use policy act being considered now. Or they can write or wire the President or federal officials on environmental and urban issues concerning growth. Last November's election proved the voter strength controlling land use and growth. In Colorado, voters barred the use of state and Denver city funds

to bring the 1976 Olympic winter games to Colorado, after a campaign in which unwanted growth and environmental damage were the main issues. Florida voters approved a $240 million bond issue to purchase environmentally endangered lands, in accord with a new state land-use act previously voted. Californians adopted a law to control development within 1,000 yards of the entire coastal shoreline, and voters in three counties approved major open-space purchases. And in Boca Raton, Fla., voters took the unprecedented action of setting a maximum on the number of housing units that could be built in a city, establishing, in effect, a population growth limit.

4. Changing policies. Initially citizens concerned about growth tend to be more clear about what they are against than what they are for. But they soon learn that, to have any lasting impact, they will have to develop their own program. To help citizens identify possible needs in their communities, the Rockefeller task force includes in its study a series of specific questions to which citizens should be seeking answers: The Rockefeller report, "The Use of Land: A Citizens' Policy Guide to Urban Growth," published by Thomas Y. Crowell.

How You Voted

This survey, "How You Voted," appeared in The Christian Science Monitor, *and accompanied the preceding series of articles written by Robert Cahn. It is reprinted by permission from* The Christian Science Monitor. © 1973 *The Christian Science Publishing Society. All rights reserved.*

Local Population and Growth Limits

In one community after another across the United States, citizens are beginning to equate unrestrained growth with a deteriorated quality of life.

1. Each community, through democratic process, should determine its own population limit, and when and where development should occur, even if that may limit the opportunity of others to move into the community. 47 responded.
2. Communities should be willing to surrender the prerogative of population limit to a higher level of government, one which can ensure that area development needs are met while at the same time provide that the "undesirable" aspects of growth (airports, power plants, etc.) are shared equally. 30 responded.
3. Communities that impose population or density limits should first be required to support their action with an analysis of potential environmental damage from the additional growth. 30 responded.
4. Each community would phase growth at a pace that its citizens are willing to support with sewers, schools, and other services. 39 responded.
5. Growth should occur at its own pace. There should be no limitations on the landowner's "right" to develop. One responded.

To Purchase or to Regulate?

Historically, laws have tended to favor private development of critical environmental areas—wetlands, steep slopes, dunes, historic sites—when economic benefits outweighed intangible environmental benefits. Yet today more than ever we are beginning

to understand the importance of these areas to the overall ecological system, or in the case of historic sites, to our heritage. I believe that:

1. Where public benefits are demonstrable, such as in the case of areas of critical environmental concern, an appropriate level of government should be allowed to exercise increased regulatory powers over development, even to the point of prohibiting development outright. 77 responded.
2. An appropriate level of government would be expected to honor developers' "rights" by purchase of lands or payment of just compensation to landowners affected by new regulations to protect critical environmental areas, even if this means increased taxes where funds on hand are inadequate or allowing uninhibited development of critical areas if funds for such compensation cannot be raised. 15 responded.
3. When government compensates landowners affected by new regulations it should be required to pay only the value of the land in present use, not its potential value for development. 58 responded.
4. When government compensates landowners affected by new regulations, it should be required to pay the landowner what he would get if he could develop the property. 8 responded.
5. The government should not be allowed to abridge the "rights" of property owners even in critical environmental areas. In the final analysis, it is the marketplace that should determine which lands are worthy of preservation. 2 responded.

The Automobile Culture

Millions of people have apparently chosen the suburban way of life. Generally speaking, this means lower land development densities, extensive use of the automobile on large networks of roads and freeways, regional shopping centers as the focal point of a sprawling urban region. Critics say these patterns are wasteful of land and costly in providing services and place special burdens on those who cannot afford this style of living—the poor, the elderly, the handicapped, and the young.

1. All levels of government should continue to facilitate low-density suburban patterns of development, as this is what people want. 5 responded.
2. Governments should intervene in some areas to provide for more compact urban settlements, more townhouses and apartments, mass transit, and shopping within walking distance of homes. 49 responded.
3. New communities that can be planned from the beginning so that a full range of public services and facilities are available, along with large amounts of community open space, should receive the financial support of the federal government. 44 responded.
4. Government should use all practical means to steer growth into new communities that are separated from existing urbanized areas by green spaces, and that include the full range of public services, clustered housing, parks, and an industrial base for local employment. 49 responded.

Open Space

Many people in urban areas complain that new subdivisions tend to grow into one another without any provision for preserving farmland, woods, and other open areas. This has led some authorities to propose that governments classify certain private lands as green spaces and regulate their use so that they will be permanently preserved. Also, open space within inner cities is often inadequate to serve the needs of large numbers of people in older or higher-density neighborhoods.

1. Governments should classify some private lands outside urban areas as extensive green spaces to be kept free from development permanently. 65 responded.
2. Developers of subdivisions and new towns should be required to reserve enough parkland and open space to serve the needs of the residents of their projects. 74 responded.
3. Governments should acquire prime recreation land on urban waterfronts before water-pollution cleanup results in raising the value of such lands. 49 responded.
4. All levels of government should encourage donations of ecologically significant land through tax benefits. They should also have institutions that actively solicit gifts of land by explaining public needs to landowners and advising them on the tax advantages of donation. 61 responded.
5. Statistics indicate that, even in the year 2000, plenty of open space will still be undeveloped. The fact that these areas will be far from cities is no justification for interfering with the way the real estate market works in and around cities. 2 responded.

Citizen Participation

Citizens complain that many decisions affecting growth of cities are made by a few public officials, sometimes at closed meetings, or with inadequate public hearings and information. Before any city council or county commission makes decisions affecting major zoning changes or supplying of services or limiting or of expanding density, the public officials should:

1. Require public hearings be held in advance of any zoning change or growth control decision. 74 responded.
2. Require an environmental analysis of the impact of the proposed development or zoning change or other activity being considered, together with economic data to show relationship of costs of increased services vs. added tax revenue. 75 responded.
3. Open to the public all meetings in which such decisions are made. 67 responded.
4. Disqualify themselves from voting on any matter in which they, their family, or professional or business associates have a financial interest. They should disclose their real estate holdings located within the jurisdiction for which they are making decisions. 73 responded.

My Community—for Better or Worse

1. Do you believe that additional urban development is desirable in your community? 29 responded "Yes"; 71 responded "No."
2. Do you believe that zoning and other land-use decisions in your community are fairly arrived at? 38 responded "Yes"; 62 responded "No."
3. Which, if any, of the following do you think developers of large tracts should be required to install or provide for at their own expense?

	Yes	No
Roads	92	8
Sewers	93	7
Water connections	94	6
Open space	98	2
Sidewalks	89	11
School land	80	20
School buildings	32	68
Community recreation	68	32
Community health clinic	27	73

Ranking Your Community (Town, City, or County)

How would you rank your community on a scale of 1 (very poor) to 10 (excellent) in the following categories?
Adequacy of parks. 6
Public access to waterfronts. 5
Adequate and enforced policies to protect established neighborhoods from incompatible new development. 5
Integrity of officials responsible for zoning and land-use permits. 5
Adequacy of off-street parking. 5
Mass-transit services. 3

Th(
of L**␣␣**␣.

A Citizens' Policy Guide
to Urban Growth

**A Task Force Report Sponsored by
The Rockefeller Brothers Fund**

William Reilly is president of the Conservation Foundation in Washington, D.C.: a nonprofit, environmental, research and education organization. Previously, Mr. Reilly was the executive director of the Task Force, and prior to that—a senior staff member at CEQ. He is a graduate of Yale College and Harvard Law School, and holds a master's in urban planning from Columbia University.

Introduction

There is a new mood in America. Increasingly, citizens are asking what urban growth will add to the quality of their lives. They are questioning the way relatively unconstrained, piecemeal urbanization is changing their communities and are rebelling against the traditional processes of government and the marketplace which, they believe, have inadequately guided development in the past. They are measuring new development proposals by the extent to which environmental criteria are satisfied—by what new housing or business will generate in terms of additional traffic, pollution of air and water, erosion, and scenic disturbance.

This mood defies easy generalization because it springs from a melange of concerns—many that are unselfish and legitimate, some that are selfish and not so legitimate. The mood is both optimistic and expansive in its expectations of the future, and pessimistic and untrusting about inevitable change, even (perhaps especially), in places where change is the only constant. Its demands range from managed growth to no growth, from "stop-til-we-plan" to "stop," period.

There have been isolated instances of such reactions before, of course. But today, the repeated questioning of what was once generally unquestioned—that growth is good, that growth is inevitable—is so widespread that it seems to us to signal a remarkable change in attitudes in this nation.

Once, citizens automatically accepted the idea that growth—in numbers of people, in jobs, in industries—would ease the public burden by increasing the tax rolls and spreading per capita costs. Now they have doubts. They seem to be expressing the belief that larger size means not only lesser quality but also higher costs. Pressed by inflation, they listen carefully to arguments about the hidden costs of growth.

The new mood reflects a burgeoning sophistication on the part of citizens about the overall, long-term economic impact of development. Immediate economic gains from job creation, land purchases, and the construction of new facilities are being set against the public costs of schools, roads, water-treatment plants, sewers, and the services new residents require.

But the new attitude toward growth is not exclusively motivated by economics. It appears to be part of a rising emphasis on humanism, on the preservation of natural and cultural characteristics that make for a humanly satisfying living environment.

This is a hopeful report, one that acknowledges the political constraints in our cities, states, and federal government, one that tries to assess realistically what we can and cannot influence, one that sets out a selective strategy for improving the way in which our cities, suburbs, and even some remote areas are physically developed and redeveloped.

Our central concern has been with the use of land as it affects other conditions of life: what happens to the environment we rely on and enjoy, where we live and shop and work, who our neighbors and our children's classmates are.

We have looked for the point of leverage at which public policy might improve circumstances and free private energies to contribute to, not work against, the broader public interests.

The Situation

On the one hand, unrestrained, piecemeal urbanization—supported by a value system that has traditionally equated growth with the good life—has produced too many dreary, environmentally destructive suburbs of a single lifestyle; too many bland, indistinct city centers; extensive mismanagement of the earth's resources; and rising popular discontent. (In many areas experiencing especially rapid growth, citizens are questioning the desirability of more growth. People concerned about urbanization tend to be against high-density development and to sanctify the single-family home. They challenge rezonings that would accommodate more growth, propose studies of optimum population, and approve height limitations on buildings. Often, they seem to be viewing development itself as the enemy, as a kind of pollution that causes congestion and destroys views.)

On the other hand, the needs of the American population, existing and projected, can be met only through continuing development. (The fertility rate would have to stay at the low replacement level for about seventy-five years before population growth would stop. The number of U.S. households is increasing even more sharply than the number of people: from now until 1985 more than 27,000 new households are anticipated every week, equal to a city the size of Kalamazoo, Michigan. This increased household formation rate is one-third greater than the rate from 1960 to 1970. With high incomes have come high levels of consumption—automobile ownership, recreation, travel, the purchase of bigger homes and even second homes, with the result that people are spreading out farther over the land. As a consequence, urban land area is increasing far faster than the size of the urban population or the number of urban households.)

The Problem

How shall we organize, control, and coordinate the process of urban development so as to protect what we most value in the environmental, cultural, and aesthetic characteristics of the land while meeting the essential needs of the changing U.S. population for new housing, roads, power plants, shopping centers, parks, businesses, and industrial facilities?

Main Obstacles to a Solution

Historically, public opinion has favored development almost irrespective of the cost to the environment. Our laws and institutions, many of which evolved during a time when growth was a national ideal, reflect a pro-development bias.

Although public opinion is now changing and agencies that play by the old rules are increasingly coming under attack, new rules have yet to be formulated and accepted.

Processes that allow for sensitive accommodations and balances—that assure protection of critical open spaces and historic buildings, but also assure that essential development needs are met—are not yet in effect in most areas.

Many citizens lack confidence in official land-use plans. They distrust the way zoning decisions are made.

Landowners expect to be able to develop their property as they choose, even at the expense of scenic, ecological, and cultural assets treasured by the public.

Most developers lack the opportunity to significantly improve the quality of projects. The small scale of their operations, or the restrictive policies of local government, work against variety, protection of important open spaces and other environmental lands, and the accommodation of low-income people and mixed lifestyles in many areas.

Developers are increasingly having difficulty getting land in sufficiently large parcels and with zoning and sewerage adequate to permit large-scale development. The land market is a large part of the problem; so, in some areas, are anti-growth attitudes.

Incentives created by the local property tax and the small size of many local governments lead them in some growing suburban areas to resist essential urban development, to exclude the poor, and to make decisions that will not raise property taxes or visit change on established residents. The same incentives can sometimes lead them to permit development in the wrong places.

Our Working Assumptions

The United States has institutions and policies for solving the problems of air and water pollution. We have neither adequate institutional processes nor the necessary legal doctrine to solve the problems of urban growth.

We have not yet learned to build communities that are environmentally sound and socially open.

We are in a period of great ferment when citizens' groups, the courts, a number of state governments, the national administration, and congressional committees have begun to consider fundamental reforms in the way state and local responsibilities for land-use control are distributed. At the heart of this ferment is recognition that states must have the responsibility to control land-use decisions that affect the interests of people beyond local boundaries if critical environmental lands are to be protected and if development needed by a regional population is not to be blocked by local governments.

Public land acquisition cannot, need not, be the whole answer to the problem of open space protection or historic preservation. With private property rights go obligations that society can define and property owners should respect.

It is not enough to think only of conserving what we have. Conservation must be part of a larger effort to create what we want. In a time of massive change, the task must be to maintain a creative balance between the forces of conservation and the forces of development. Only recently and in selected areas where people are applying new high standards to development is this balance becoming possible.

Our Conviction

There is no need for people or their governments to accept a future of blanketing urbanization in which individuals and communities lose their identities.

Nor is there need to put up with some of the suburban barriers that limit the mobility of people with low and moderate incomes.

Nor is there need to accept development stretching endlessly along the edges of roads and sprawling across scenic hills and valleys, forests and farms.

There is opportunity, in short, to have urban regions that contain natural beauty, to have new and renewed urbanized areas more varied and satisfying than those we are familiar with.

Our Approach

Before we came to our conclusions: we surveyed the major reports on land use and urban growth of the past five years; we examined significant state and national legislation, pending and enacted; and we conducted field studies in:

1. **Florida** ("Paradise in Peril"), which attracts 4,300 new residents each week, 550 to Dade County (Miami) alone; which includes three of the fastest growing metropolitan regions in the nation (South Florida, Tampa-St. Petersburg, and Orlando); which from 1950 to 1969 lost 169,000 acres of estuarine habitat to dredging and filling; which in April 1972 passed one of the strongest set of state land and water management laws.

2. **Long Island, New York,** where 2.6 million people are concentrated in two counties fragmented into 110 taxing jurisdictions; which in ten years (1954-64) lost 29 percent of its coastal wetlands; where the NAACP is suing Oyster Bay on charges that zoning has been used to keep out poor and black people; where environmentalists now form more than a hundred diverse groups.

3. **Colorado**, where in November 1972 voters barred the use of city and state funds to support the 1976 Winter Olympic Games, pulling in a welcome mat that had been out for twenty years; where, in Boulder, citizens considered (but defeated) the first referendum in the nation to limit population size but approved a city study of ways to reduce population growth to a level "substantially below" that of the 1960s; where longtime U.S. Representative Wayne Aspinall was defeated in the 1972 primary by a law professor running as an environmentalist; where a statewide land-use plan is due to be completed by December 1972.

4. **California**, probably the only state where concerned private citizens have produced a comprehensive plan to provide alternatives to the development proposals of federal, state, and local agencies; where environmental impact statements are required for significant private as well as public developments; where a powerful independent regulatory agency has been authorized to control all development along the shores of San Francisco Bay; where voters have now empowered the state to take a similar approach to regulating all development along the California coastline and, in most instances, 1,000 yards inland.

Conclusions

A new mood in America has emerged that questions traditional assumptions about the desirability of urban development. The motivation is not exclusively economic. It appears to be a part of a rising emphasis on human values, on the preservation of natural and cultural characteristics that make for a humanly satisfying living environment.

This new mood represents a force of great energy. On the one hand it presents opportunity; finally, a broad, popular concern for planning and regulating land use has emerged that can be offset against the one-sided, purely economic values that have characterized much development pressure. On the other hand, it presents a challenge, for it encompasses a range of negative attitudes that are sometimes confused and even hostile to the needs of our society for new development.

Nevertheless, this new mood is the most hopeful portent we see. Although it expresses a range of anxieties and discontents, it can be used as a lever to achieve the changes in land-use planning and control that will make possible a qualitatively different future for us and for American generations to follow.

The most serious charge against the new attitudes is that public policies developed in response to them would necessarily impose their heaviest burdens on the least advantaged members of society. It must be recognized that the disadvantaged have legitimate needs that only development can meet—and that a measure of urban growth is inevitable in our lifetimes, for the poor and for nearly everyone else.

No growth is simply not a viable option for the country in the remainder of this century. The case for more development is not based simply on demography—on the fact that we must house the people who are already around or whose birth is foreseeable—nor even on projections of economic growth. There is also an ideal involved, that of respecting the free choices of Americans to move in search of a better job or a better life. Mobility has been a traditional road to opportunity in America. Wholesale growth restrictions, imposed by many communities, could block that road for the many who still want to travel it.

Efforts to divert growth away from metropolitan areas and into "lagging" areas or to small towns have had little success. The likelihood, in the absence of major changes in attitudes, is for continuation of metropolitan concentration.

The urban region is a fact of life. The vast majority of Americans will live, not predominantly in cities as we have known them, but in suburbs and exurbs that will be contiguous in many areas. The issue is not whether there will be urban regions—that is, regional constellations of urban centers and their hinterlands as opposed to single super cities—but what form these urban areas will take.

High-density or highrise living are not the only alternatives to sprawl. Even with low densities, utilities and services can be provided economically and substantial open spaces conserved.

In most instances, we have favored the rearrangement of processes and the redesign of incentives to get the system working for, not against, quality urban development. We have consciously focused less on negative compulsion than on creating positive inducements, less on increasing public expenditures than on making sure that the governmental entity with the proper perspective is the one responsible for dealing with a particular issue, less with tilting the balance toward environmental groups or development interests than in trying to see that a newly emerging balance between these forces is maintained.

Although we recommend a number of measures to inject higher levels of government *into the development guidance process, we think that the broad base of regulations should be established by local decisions.*

Findings and Recommendations

Open Space. We believe there is an enormous opportunity for the federal government to encourage open space protection by formulating, mapping, and publicizing a set of advisory national open space classifications for consultation by federal agencies in the planning of development projects, for use in support of state and local plans and regulations, and for consultation by private land buyers and sellers.

Especially in newly urbanizing areas, we see both recreation and social needs best served by establishing as public policy that the limited natural supply of prime recreational open spaces, particularly beaches and other waterfront areas, should, to the maximum feasible extent, be acquired by government, preserved, and made publicly accessible.

Federal spending for open space acquisition should be maintained at levels commensurate with needs. We see particular merit in continuing to extend the network of parks, seashores, and lakeshores that are owned and managed by the federal government itself. States, many of which are currently enjoying budgetary surpluses, should also adjust open space acquisition plans to rising needs, particularly with respect to areas where urban growth is anticipated and where waterfront land is beginning to appreciate as a result of pollution-control activities.

Since no combination of federal, state, and local land purchases is likely to acquire enough open spaces to satisfy demand, other techniques must be used as well.

State and local governments should assert and protect often neglected public rights in beaches and other recreation land. Similarly, the federal government should exploit its full range of powers, including its permit authority and public works activities, so as to promote protection, public access, and use.

Federal estate tax laws and regulations should be amended to permit the transfer to the federal government of land determined by the Secretary of the Interior to be of national significance, with the fair market value of the land offset against federal estate tax liabilities.

Governments at all levels should actively solicit open space donations and should facilitate the work of responsible private organizations, such as the Nature Conservancy, by granting them charitable status for real estate tax purposes.

Mandatory dedication requirements (imposed on developers) can be an equitable and inexpensive way to provide essential urban open space. We believe the requirements should be used even more widely than they already are.

In newly developing areas, developers should contribute open space or cash for the purchase of open space, sufficient at least to satisfy the reasonable needs of the residents of their developments. Local governments should adopt regulations requiring such contributions, preferably in connection with "cluster" provisions. States should authorize and encourage the adoption of these local regulations or should adopt similar state regulations.

State legislation and local regulations should assure that adequate public accessways exist before allowing the subdivision or development of private property adjacent to public beaches and waterfronts.

To protect public open space against diversion to other public use, states should, at a minimum, provide that: (a) alternatives to the diversion of parkland be formulated with full opportunity for public comment; (b) any open space taken be replaced by other open space that will, wherever possible, meet similar public needs; (c) additional procedural protections be established to ensure careful evaluation of proposals by one agency to condemn open space under the jurisdiction of another agency; and (d) methods for determining the value of open space be improved so that any open space may be replaced by land of at least comparable monetary value.

Since it is neither feasible nor acceptable for governments to acquire the vast agricultural and natural areas that ought to be conserved within future urban regions, mechanisms to protect privately held open space are essential. Without such mechanisms, even moderate objectives of protection programs are unlikely to be achieved.

The land market, as it operates today, is the principal obstacle to effective protection of private open space.

To achieve permanent protection, open spaces should be insulated as completely as possible from the market forces that now inexorably press them into development. One way to accomplish this objective is for owners of open spaces to give up or sell part of their property rights. Another is for local or state governments to regulate development of open spaces, requiring owners to maintain them as they are.

State as well as local governments should establish protective regulations to prevent development that would be incompatible with open space needs in critical agricultural and environmental areas. Where protected areas are carefully selected through comprehensive planning, states should authorize and encourage, in appropriate cases, very low density zoning, including, for example, requirements for 50 or more acres per dwelling unit. Enactment of pending national land-use policy legislation is urgently recommended as a means to encourage state and local regulation in a balanced framework that is respectful both of conservation and development priorities.

Decisions to construct sewers and to provide other public services should be taken only after careful consideration of whether these decisions will stimulate or discourage the development of designated open spaces. Plans for the location of federally assisted sewers should be consistent with state, regional, and local plans.

Governments and charitable organizations have a significant opportunity to preserve open space by providing owners with a just and convenient method of donating urbanization rights and then persuading owners to use it. In time, we believe, ownership of open spaces without urbanization rights should become as commonplace as ownership of land without mineral rights.

Incentives are often needed to encourage protection and to back up regulations. Because incentives involve a trade-off—offering the landowner something in return for a desired response—care must be taken to assure that public benefits are commensurate with public costs.

Measures that grant partial relief from real estate taxes on farms in urbanizing areas, in force in about half the states, should be re-examined to assure that the public benefit in open space protection warrants the substantial expense reduced taxes entail. Provisions that grant reductions in the absence of permanent restrictions should be regarded as half-way measures, justified only when permanent restrictions are politically unacceptable.

We are persuaded that a mix of techniques, including public acquisition of land and of development rights in strategic land parcels (those located along highways, directly adjoining urbanized areas, and along waterfronts) but with primary reliance on federally supported, state-administered, non-compensatory regulations appears to present the only realistic hope of achieving the permanent protection of critical open spaces, including buffer zones between urbanized areas.

We see the need for a National Lands Trust to be established either within the Interior Department or by federal charter to assist public bodies, particularly state land-use agencies, in the designation, planning, and conservation of extensive greenspaces in and around major urbanizing areas. The National Lands Trust would advise on regulatory and acquisition measures and make funds available for acquisition of full or partial interests in strategically located lands within greenspaces. For this purpose, federal funding of $200 million should be made available annually on a matching basis with a 75 percent federal share.

A changed attitude toward land—a separation of ownership of the land itself from ownership of urbanization rights—is essential.

Historically, Americans have thought of urbanization rights as coming from the land itself, "up from the bottom" like minerals or crops. It is equally possible to view them as coming "down from the top," as being created by society and allocated by it to each land parcel. We think it highly likely that in forthcoming decades Americans will gradually abandon the traditional assumption that urbanization rights arise from the land itself. Development potential, on any land and in any community, results largely from the actions of society (especially the construction of public facilities). Other free societies, notably Great Britain, have abandoned the old assumption in their legal systems and now treat development rights as created and allocated to the land by society.

Historic Preservation. Historic areas need protection, too. Many communities have important or unusual historic buildings or whole streets and neighborhoods with historic integrity, where the buildings, by their age, design, and scale, form a unit of visual continuity and character. Such areas may already be registered historic districts, as in Charleston, Boston, and Santa Fe, or they may be stylistically varied areas lacking any significant single buildings but forming units of pleasing proportion and providing a sense of the past. Such historic properties are vulnerable to the same threats as open space, and their preservation often poses the same buy-it-or-lose-it dilemma to local authorities. We see historic districts and buildings benefiting from the approach and many of the techniques we recommend for protecting privately owned open space, an approach based primarily on regulation, not purchase.

We need broadened classifications for historic areas. Present criteria for listing in The National Register of Historic Places are that the area possess integrity of location, design, setting, materials, workmanship, feeling, and associations and represent a significant and distinguishable entity. These criteria discriminate against areas with a stylistic mixture, areas that can often support a varied rent structure and provide a refreshing diversity of uses and people. We urge that urban neighborhoods characterized by a mix of uses, a vitality of street life, and a physical integrity be recognized on the National Register as "conservation areas."

For historic preservation, as for open space protection, the first requisite is a framework for regulation, preferably a statewide system for registration of historic districts and properties and a clear policy favoring preservation. States should enact appropriate legislation to implement the Model State Guidelines for Historic Preservation recommended by the Council of State Governments among its 1972 suggested legislative proposals. Such legislation would establish a state institutional structure for review and regulation of historic sites, structures, and districts and would enable local governments to protect the integrity of historic areas.

The Use of Land

Adapting Old Laws to New Values. To protect critical environmental and cultural areas, tough restrictions will have to be placed on the use of privately owned land. These restrictions will be little more than delaying actions if the courts do not uphold them as reasonable measures to protect the public interest, in short, as restrictions that landowners may fairly be required to bear without payment by the government. The interpretation of the "takings clause" (which has sometimes been construed to prohibit governmental restrictions on the use of privately owned land as, in effect, "takings" of the land itself for which landowners must be compensated) is therefore a crucial matter for future land-use planning and regulatory programs (The so-called takings clause in the Fifth Amendment to the U.S. Constitution: ". . . nor shall private property be taken for public use, without just compensation.").

Many judicial precedents (including some from the U.S. Supreme Court) date from a time when attitudes toward land, natural processes, and planning were different than they are today. Many precedents are anachronistic now that land is coming to be regarded as a basic natural resource to be protected and conserved and urban development is seen as a process needing careful public guidance and control.

Ignorance of what regulations higher courts have been willing to sustain against landowner claims that a restriction amounted to a "taking" has created an exaggerated fear that restrictive actions will be declared unconstitutional. Such uncertainty has forestalled countless regulatory actions and induced numerous bad compromises. The popular impression of the takings clause may be even more out of date than some court opinions.

Extensive case preparation is necessary to demonstrate the constitutional validity and public benefit of land-use regulations. To facilitate that preparation, the trend toward "environmental divisions" within the offices of state attorneys general and county and municipal attorneys should continue, and attorneys in these divisions are urged to devote a substantial share of their efforts to land-use regulation.

Existing nonprofit organizations should be supported and appropriate additional organizations established that will provide governmental attorneys with the expert testimony, research assistance, and skilled tactical advice needed to prepare for important land-use cases.

State and local legislative bodies should continue to adopt stringent planning and regulatory measures whenever they believe them fair and necessary to protect natural, cultural, and aesthetic values. This legislation, in addition to its direct benefits, can help create a climate of opinion in which lawmakers and judges will regard strong, needed restrictions as a proper exercise of governmental power.

The courts should "presume" that any change in existing natural ecosystems is likely to have adverse consequences difficult to foresee. The proponent of the change should therefore be required to demonstrate, as well as possible, the nature and extent of any changes that will result. Such a presumption would build into common law a requirement that a prospective developer who wishes to challenge a governmental regulation prepare a statement similar to the environmental impact statements now required of public agencies under federal programs.

It is time that the U.S. Supreme Court re-examine its precedents that seem to require a balancing of public benefit against land value loss in every case and declare that, when the protection of natural, cultural, or aesthetic resources or the assurance of orderly development are involved, a mere loss in land value is no justification for invalidating the regulation of land use.

The Use of Land

Development: Regulations. The mechanisms used to regulate development need improvement. Under present laws, localities can take many—probably most—of the regulatory steps needed to control development. To do so, however, localities must often distort their regulatory process to fit a mold established by half-century-old state legislation. The distortion—particularly the overemphasis on detailed preregulation and underemphasis on flexible response to what is actually taking place—often obscures how development is guided (even to decision-makers), seriously misleads the public, and deprives landowners of essential procedural safeguards. We look forward to completion and release (scheduled for the spring of 1974) of the American Law Institute's model land development code, which promises to furnish invaluable aid in the modernization of out-of-date state enabling acts.

Except for small projects with limited impact, discretionary review should be at the heart of development guidance.

The best regulatory mechanism so far for development review is environmental impact analysis. The great benefits of the process are its focus on proposed development, its consideration of feasible alternatives, and its replacement of the "minimum standards" concept with a concept of seeking among feasible alternatives what is best for the public interest. In the long run, the greatest importance of the environmental impact analysis process may lie in its establishment of a higher standard of conduct for development agencies, requiring them to publicly evaluate opportunities within a broad spectrum of public objectives. States should enact legislation, modeled on federal environmental law, requiring environmental impact statements in connection with major state, local, and private actions that significantly affect the environment.

For the convenience of all concerned—builders, neighbors, administrators, the general public—a convenient, nondiscretionary mechanism must be provided so that the mass of small projects can proceed without elaborate review—a mechanism resembling today's nondiscretionary building permit.

As agencies gain experience with environmental impact statement requirements, they should seek increasingly refined ways to identify the actions and issues important enough to warrant such review. Plans, minimum standards, or other criteria that assure some alternative form of control over the less important actions may prove most acceptable.

For power plants and other critical development, project review procedures should be modified so that disapproval of one development proposal must be accompanied, in the same proceeding, by approval of an alternative (or abandonment of the project if need cannot be satisfactorily demonstrated). A much more thorough planning process is needed for this purpose as well as review agencies with larger geographical jurisdictions. Passage of the proposed power plant siting legislation would be an important step toward fulfilling this need.

Every element of the regulatory process, including deliberations, advisory recommendations, and final decisions, should take place at advertised meetings open to the public. Local and state laws should establish open meeting requirements for all governmental agencies responsible for land-use regulations.

To reduce the reality or appearance of conflicts of interest, state and local laws should disqualify local and state officials from voting or otherwise participating in any regulatory decision whose outcome could confer financial benefit, or could appear to the public to confer financial benefit, to themselves, their families, or their business or professional associates. All persons having any responsibility for land-use regulation, including elected and appointed officials and employees, should also be required by law to make periodic public disclosure of their financial interests and real estate holdings within the jurisdiction over which they exercise responsibility.

Citizen suits appealing from local regulatory decisions should be permitted by any local resident or civic organization in the public interest, without regard to property ownership or other financial interest. Citizen suits to enforce ordinance requirements should also be permitted. Safeguards against premature or frivolous litigation may be necessary to guard against abuse.

Local officials and citizens should periodically try to identify aspects of local procedures that may give rise to citizen mistrust. Insofar as practical, measures that cause mistrust, whether or not the resulting suspicions are in fact warranted, should be changed.

Fairness alone is not enough. The regulatory process will not merit public trust and respect unless decisions are based on consistent policies and plans. A process of planning and policy-making far superior to the one now found in most localities is essential. Such a process will include clear protection policies and plans for existing neighborhoods and critical land areas as well as frank acknowledgment of uncertainty about the nature of unforeseeable new development.

Development: Incentives and Opportunities. Even though communities must be more effectively protected against inappropriate development, additional protection is not the most pressing need at the community level. The greater need is to remold the development process—not only the regulatory process but also the methods by which land and utilities are made available—in order to foster quality development.

Important development should be regulated by governments that represent all the people whose lives are likely to be affected by it, including those who could benefit from it as well as those who could be harmed by it. Where a regulatory decision significantly affects people in more than one locality, state, regional, or even federal action is necessary.

Congress should enact a national land-use policy act authorizing federal funding for states to assert control over land use of state or regional impact and concern. Such legislation should include incentives in the form of federal financial aid and sanctions in the form of reduced highway, airport, and open space funds.

Just as state governments are intervening to provide more protection in some areas, so must they intervene for more development, particularly the sort that local governments often exclude.

State legislation should deprive local governments of the power to establish minimum-floor-area requirements for dwellings in excess of a statewide minimum established by statute.

The continuing efforts of civil rights groups and other litigants to obtain court decrees invalidating exclusionary regulations are encouraged as essential steps toward achieving the state legislation and administrative action that are ultimately necessary to safeguard fundamental rights and assure needed development.

Economic self-interest often leads local governments to concentrate less on achieving quality than on prohibiting development altogether. To discourage excessive reliance on local cost-revenue criteria as the basis for evaluating the acceptability of new development, and to increase public acceptance of state responsibility for guiding locally excluded development, we encourage the states to enact measures that would reduce the impact of new development on local tax rates.

The Use of Land

Revisions to existing federal housing assistance programs, particularly those introduced by the Housing Act of 1968, should concentrate on a restructuring of incentives to encourage private investors to take a long-term interest in their investments. Expanding the options of assisted persons through housing allowances should be considered in designing new housing programs.

The small scale of most development remains a major obstacle to quality development. Although an increase in scale does not guarantee higher quality, it significantly increases the developer's opportunity to achieve quality. To promote large-scale development, communities should adopt planned unit development (PUD) regulations that permit flexibility in project design, subject to overall design review. The community, as well as the developer, should have the power to require that significant projects be reviewed under PUD procedures. A part of the review should be patterned after environmental impact statements.

Governments should use all acceptable means to channel development into new communities or, to the extent that these are unachievable, into "growth units" of 500 or more dwellings with related services, as recommended by the American Institute of Architects. The success of this policy will rest on overcoming the obstacles that now keep developers from operating at larger scales.

Density bonuses are one way to encourage larger scale development. Even though few localities have yet been willing to grant sizable bonuses, and despite the risks in awarding vastly increased density (and thus vastly increased land value, which raises the risk of corruption), we believe that large density bonuses should be authorized, in appropriate cases and after careful design review, to new communities and other sizable projects.

The federal government now guarantees bonds issued by developers to finance new communities that meet the social, environmental, and other criteria set out in Title VII of the Urban Growth and New Community Development Act of 1970. The aggregate of loan guarantees now available under the act should be increased and the guarantees made available for developments as small as 500 housing units together with related facilities.

The states should establish governmental entities, comparable to New York's Urban Development Corporation, responsible for assisting and when necessary directly undertaking large-scale projects. These entities should have the full range of powers, including the power of eminent domain, the power to override local land-use regulations, and the power to control the provision of public utilities, when necessary, to overcome the barriers that now prevent most developers from operating at the larger scales that the public interest requires.

The development process should, insofar as possible, be shaped by planning and regulatory bodies, lenders, accountants, appraisers, and other participants so that developers, home-buyers, and other consumers come to perceive the maintenance and enhancement of quality as the key to profitability. Divergence between quality and profitability should be minimized.

Lot Sales in Rural Areas. An estimated 95,000 second homes were started in 1971—up from an estimated average of 20,000 per year in the 1940s, 40,000 per year in the 1950s, and 75,000 per year in the 1960s. Second home starts are expected to reach 150,000 annually during the 1970s.

Nevertheless, rural lots are being created far faster than second homes. For the nation as a whole, at least six recreational lots were sold in 1971 for each second home started. Much of the excess of lots sales over second-home starts is the result of demand artificially inflated by high-pressure sales practices. Many buyers are encouraged to think of the lots as speculative investments rather than as building sites to someday use and enjoy.

The Use of Land

There should be no effort to discourage the creation of bonafide recreation communities. In the absence of specific problems, such as consumer victimization or environmental damage, there is nothing wrong with second homes. The over-all goal should be to encourage the creation of livable, enjoyable, and ecologically sound recreation communities and to prevent lot sales where such communities seem unlikely to come into being.

Recreational home developments should be required to satisfy the same environmental and land-use policy standards that ought to apply to first-home developments. This does not mean that such communities need have curbings or sidewalks any more than communities for first homes in every case require such facilities. It does mean that local governments should establish subdivision requirements sufficient to assure that all subdivisions, whether for first or second homes, will attain acceptable development standards. Adequate public facilities, including water supply and sewage disposal facilities (installed or bonded) should be required as a condition of subdivision approval.

Although strong local controls are essential, states should establish their own regulations to assure that planning expertise is applied, that adequate facilities are required, and that inappropriate subdivision is prohibited, even in remote areas.

Every effort should be made to bar lot sales projects in which management and sales practices encourage sellers to disregard the suitability of projects as places to live and to enjoy. Particular attention should be given to projects in which the manner of the seller's operation enables him to make substantial profit—or to show a substantial profit on his corporate books—before he installs water supply and sewage disposal facilities and the other rudimentary essentials of community existence.

To reduce opportunities for high-pressure salesmanship, the federal and state laws requiring full disclosure of lot sales information to protect lot buyers should be amended to give buyers of lots (in projects governed by the acts) a nonwaivable cooling-off period of 30 days instead of the present 48 hours. The cooling-off period should be granted to all buyers including those who have seen the land before they buy. The acts should also be amended so that projects containing more than 50 lots are covered, irrespective of the acreage contained in each lot.

Congress should amend federal securities legislation so that the sale of lots in any project containing more than 50 lots will, unless all obligations of the seller are performed before any payments by the buyer, be regarded as a securities transaction subject to the prospectus and other requirements of the Securities and Exchange Commission.

The Securities and Exchange Commission should require that descriptions of development programs be made available in conjunction with financial statements of land sales corporations, including pertinent information concerning the types and scheduling of promised community facilities.

For the inexperienced buyers likely to be purchasing unimproved lots, the protection afforded by disclosure requirements is insufficient. We believe that a warranty is needed as well. Federal and state legislation should obligate the sellers of lots (in projects containing 50 or more lots) to guarantee to each buyer that his lot will, for one year after the date on which he is scheduled to obtain title, and again for one year after the date on which the contract obligates the seller to complete all improvements, be fit for construction of a dwelling (or for any commercial or industrial use specified in the sales contract). Fitness for use should be defined, by statute or regulation, to include suitable water supply, the availability of lawful sewage disposal facilities, and safety elements (such as that the land is not subject to flooding). The warranty should be unwaivable and breach of warranty should entitle the buyer to return of all his payments, with interest and damages, up to the date of breach.

We recommend that careful consideration be given to requiring that a portion of the lot buyers' payments be deposited in escrow until the seller has fulfilled his obligations to the buyers. Escrow accounts could be held by banks and released to the sellers as facilities are completed. If promised improvements are not made, escrow money could be applied to construction costs.

The Role of the Citizen. The vastness of the work ahead does not mean we should leave it to the experts. We believe that civic organizations can make an important contribution to the quality of life in their areas by helping to decide what should be protected and preserved in their localities and how and where essential development needs are to be met and by helping to assess systematically the adequacy of local plans, laws, regulations, and procedures affecting urban growth. The 1976 bicentennial year would be an appropriate time to complete the first phase of such an assessment. We urge that federal assistance be made available for these citizen efforts as part of the bicentennial program.

Appendix

Members of the Task Force on Land Use and Urban Growth

Chairman, Laurance S. Rockefeller, New York, New York

Deputy Chairman, Paul N. Ylvisaker, Dean, Graduate School of Education, Harvard University, Cambridge, Massachusetts

John F. Collins, Consulting Professor of Urban Affairs, Massachusetts Institute of Technology, Cambridge, Massachusetts

John R. Crowley, Chairman, Colorado Land Use Commission, Denver, Colorado

Henry L. Diamond, Commissioner, New York State Department of Environmental Conservation, Albany, New York

Walter E. Hoadley, Executive Vice President and Chief Economist, Bank of America National Trust and Savings Association, San Francisco, California

A. Wesley Hodge, Lawyer, Hodge, Dahlgren & Hillis, Seattle, Washington

Vernon E. Jordan, Jr., Executive Director, National Urban League, New York, New York

Virginia Nugent, Chairman, National Land Use Committee, League of Women Voters, Washington, D.C.

John R. Price, Jr., Vice President, Manufacturers Hanover Trust, New York, New York

James W. Rouse, Chairman of the Board and Chief Executive Officer, The Rouse Company, Columbia, Maryland

Pete Wilson, Mayor of San Diego, San Diego, California

Task Force Staff

Executive Director, William K. Reilly

Senior Staff, John H. Noble, Thomas A. Barrington, Gordon Binder, Phyllis Myers, Michael Rawson, Sara M. Mazie

Report Staff, Jo Tunstall, Elizabeth Arensberg

Support Staff, Barbara N. Gray, Josephine Haley

Other Individuals

Many individuals have helped us with advice, analysis, and encouragement. We wish to thank particularly those who made oral presentations or wrote papers for task force meetings, including: Fred P. Bosselman, David Callies, and John Banta of the Chicago, Illinois, law firm of Ross, Hardies, O'Keefe, Babcock and Parsons; Lois Craig of the Federal Architecture Project; Herbert M. Franklin of the Washington, D.C., law firm of Frosh, Lane and Edson;

The Use of Land

Robert H. McNulty of the National Endowment for the Arts; C. Willis Ritter of the Washington, D.C., law firm of Haynes and Miller; and Don Detisch and James Goff of the San Diego city government. We are also grateful for the papers prepared by Stan Ross and Michael Feinstein of Kenneth Leventhal and Company, Los Angeles, California; Roy Mann Associates, Cambridge, Massachusetts; and Ecology and Environment, Inc., of Buffalo, New York, and for the interviews conducted and photographs provided by Janet Mendelsohn of Cambridge, Massachusetts. Helpful advice, information, verification, and critiques of drafts were provided by many agencies and individuals. We wish to acknowledge particularly the comments and advice of Stanley D. Heckman of New York City; Frank Beal of the American Society of Planning Officials; Lawrence N. Stevens, executive director of the Citizens' Advisory Committee on Environmental Quality and G. Merrill Ware of the committee staff; Boyd Gibbons, Timothy Atkeson, and Philip Soper of the Council on Environmental Quality; Randall Scott of ULI-The Urban Land Institute (formerly of the National Association of Home Builders); Robert Cahn of the *Christian Science Monitor*; Ralph Field of Westport, Connecticut; Art Davis and William Duddleson of the Conservation Foundation; Huey Johnson and Greg Archbald of the Trust for Public Land; Robert Stipe of the Institute of Government and Jonathan Howes of the Center for Urban and Regional Studies, University of North Carolina; Steven Weitz of the Department of Housing and Urban Development; William H. Whyte, New York, New York; Fred Anderson of the Environmental Law Institute; Edward J. Logue, Steven Lefkowitz, and D. David Brandon of the Urban Development Corporation of New York State; Richard Wiebe of the New York State Office of Planning Services; and Calvin Kytle and Don Lief of Washington, D.C. William Dietel and Marilyn Levy of the Rockefeller Brothers Fund provided encouragement and assistance that went beyond the financial. We would also like to acknowledge the helpful comments and data provided by the following agencies: the U.S. Bureau of the Census; the Tri-State Regional Planning Commission and the Regional Plan Association, New York; the Southeastern Wisconsin Regional Planning Commission, Wisconsin; the Metropolitan Washington Council of Governments, Washington, D.C.; the Division of State Planning, Florida; the Metropolitan Areas Planning Council, Massachusetts; and the Division of Planning Coordination, Office of the Governor, Texas. And we would like to thank the firm of Parsons, Brinckerhoff, Quade and Douglas, who loaned us Thomas Barrington. Finally, we are greatful to the hundreds of citizens in New York, Florida, California, and Colorado who freely shared their views on urban growth. Our assessment of their attitudes leads us to believe that many of the far-reaching proposals we have made are realistic, timely, and most important of all, responsive to the emerging concerns and values of Americans.

Six Myths—

About Land Use in the United States

William K. Reilly

William Reilly is president of the Conservation Foundation: an environmental [nonprofit] research and educational organization. He previously was the executive director of the Rockefeller Task Force (The Use of Land), and was a senior staff member at CEQ. Mr. Reilly is a graduate of Yale, holds a master's in planning from Columbia, and has a law degree from Harvard.

Introduction

"Real estate," as one dealer recently remarked, "is the last frontier. Only now people are thinking about getting up a posse."

Citizens have been getting up posses all across the country—from Hawaii to Vermont, from Wisconsin to Florida, in places like Sanbornton, N.H., Petaluma, Cal., Fairfax, Va., Boca Raton, Fla., and Ramapo, N.Y. The circumstances and the specific issues differ from place to place, court case to court case. But the basic concern of citizen movements to affect land use is similar in many parts of the country: more and more people are concluding that there is something wrong with the way we are using our land and guiding urban growth. And they are increasingly saying to officials responsible for urban development, "stop," "enough," or at least, "stop til we plan, *really* plan."

Citizen concern about urban growth has brought about more changes in state and local land use laws during the past four years than had occurred in the previous four decades. As interest in land use has spread well beyond the narrow band of professional observers and plain scolds [the people who used to fascinate one another with monographs decrying America's lack of an "urban tradition"], the prospect for substantial improvement in our land use guidance systems has arisen. Now, as we embark on an era of unprecedented reforms, it is important to be clear about what is happening, and why. Otherwise we might well botch an opportunity the like of which has not existed in the fifty years since states began enacting their first basic zoning enabling laws.

There are a number of myths about land use, many of them unspoken. Different groups and interests tend to subscribe to different myths, and the result is sometimes an obstacle to communication, a failure to acknowledge basic facts. I propose a brief look at the following six myths.

Six Myths

Myth No. 1: *The groundswell against unplanned, unmanaged urban growth is something irrational and darkly fearsome, an un-American, anti-progressive mood, a kind of mass hysteria.*

Certainly there are obstructionists, Luddites, and even racists fighting development projects. But no one who stops to think about it will seriously contend that they ac ⌐⌐ted for the passage of the coastal zone referendum in California, the two-to-one vote in favor of a $1.15 billion environmental bond issue in New York, the overwhelming voter endorsement of a $240 million bond issue for the purchase of critical lands in Florida, or for scores of other protection-oriented county and local votes on land use matters.

In-depth interviews conducted by the Rockefeller Task Force on Land Use and Urban Growth in New York, Florida, Colorado and California [and reported in *The Use of Land: A Citizens' Policy Guide to Urban Growth,"* published by Thomas Y. Crowell Co., New York] confirmed the existence of a "new mood in America . . . that questions traditional assumptions about the desirability of urban development." According to the Task Force:

> [t]he motivation is not exclusively economic. It appears to be a part of a rising emphasis on human values, on the preservation of natural and cultural characteristics that make for a humanly satisfying living environment.

Popular attitudes reflect a dissatisfaction both with the way in which land use decisions have been made, and I suspect also (though this is more difficult to prove) a discontent with the quality of much of the urban development that the nation has experienced since World War II. People are unhappy about a growth process that in many communities has freely overrun stunning countryside and valued natural areas, disrupted established neighborhoods with large and intrusive projects and shown little or no regard for the unique and distinctive—in buildings, topography, or setting. And if citizen concerns seem more often to take a negative than a positive turn—"this we don't want," coming through more loudly and frequently than "this is how we want it to be"—well, that is a consequence of the fact that citizens are more often able to block what they *don't* want than they are consulted about what they *do* want. The sooner that all parties in the urban development process acknowledge that there *is* something wrong with plans and regulations that fail to conserve open spaces in and around urbanizing areas, where we need them most; that there *is* something odd and defective about the ease with which "recreational" land subdividers are allowed to wreak gigantic ecological havoc from California hills to New Mexico desert to Florida swamp and coastline to Virginia and Pennsylvania mountains; that the edges of our great cities *are* disturbingly formless and life there overly dependent upon the automobile—the sooner we can move on to constructive reforms in the processes for guiding future urbanization. It is wrong to analogize development to pollution. It is also possible to appreciate how the misunderstanding has arisen.

Myth No. 2: *No-growth (i.e. urban growth) is possible for the country.*

It isn't. Even a fertility level at or slightly below replacement does not appreciably reduce the high rate of household formation projected through the remainder of the 20th century. The United States is currently experiencing the creation of 27,000 new households per week: up sharply from the average rate experienced during the 1960s. Short of making people move in with their mothers-in-law, this household formation rate must be built for—with houses, stores, power plants, airports and all the other supporting systems of an urbanized society.

Moreover, it is doubtful that the tools could effect a no-growth solution for any sizable geographic area. Sewer and other public facility moratoriums must be regarded as temporary. Land use controls such as zoning and other density control mechanisms, if applied over a large area so as to reduce very sharply new development, would probably not survive attacks in the courts unless they were based upon demonstrated ecological or health considerations, or unless they were part of a regional scheme which included a method for accommodating reasonable growth needs somewhere else. This leads me to myth number 3.

Myth No. 3: *State and local governments cannot substantially restrict land use unless they are prepared to buy the lands they wish to protect from development.*

If valuable natural areas are to be conserved, prime farmlands and attractive rural areas to be kept free of urbanization, established neighborhoods to be kept as they are—all desired by a growing number of Americans—then substantial rollbacks in permitted densities may be necessary.

Often citizens and elected officials who consult their city and county attorneys about implementing more protective land use regulations are told that what they wish to achieve is unlawful or even unconstitutional, unless they are willing to pay the owners of land to which the low density limits are to be applied. Sometimes the lawyers' views accurately reflect the state of the law in their jurisdiction. But the extent to which the public may allocate development where it wishes, and deter it in areas where it is deemed contrary to planning objectives, is by no means a settled area of the law. Indeed, recent decisions of the highest courts of California, Wisconsin, New York, Maine and Maryland, and in the U.S. Court of Appeals (1st Circuit), indicate a growing acceptance on the part of the judiciary of plans and regulations aimed at protecting critical land resources against impairment. The Wisconsin Supreme Court has given succinct expression to a growing judicial attitude. Confronted with a challenge by a property owner to the constitutionality of a shoreland zoning ordinance that placed wetlands in a conservancy district, essentially limiting uses to those consistent with the natural character of the swampland, the Wisconsin high court declared:

> An owner of land has no absolute and unlimited right to change the essential character of his land so as to use it for a purpose for which it was unsuited in its natural state and which injures the rights of others . . . [We] think it is not an unreasonable exercise of [the police power in zoning] to prevent harm to public rights by limiting the use of private property to its natural uses.

Myth No. 4: *There is nothing wrong with the land use planning process that enforcement of plans—insistence upon implementation—wouldn't cure.*

This is a myth subscribed to even by many of the experts. There is more than a small measure of truth in it.

However, it is not only that plans fail to be respected. Plans are often conceived in an atmosphere of unreality. Zoning, for example, and other techniques of pre-regulation invite officials to pretend to be able to predict precisely how areas will be developed ten, twenty, thirty years hence. When economic circumstances and housing demand change, so must the rigid plans. However, citizens who bought land believing in the future charted on a land use map feel deceived when changes occur, and frequently allege fraud on the part of public officials who acquiesce in the changes.

The real problem is often a lack of sufficient flexibility and discretion in the procedure for evaluating development proposals. Such techniques as planned unit development ordinances and environmental impact analysis allow a community to review site plans and development schemes comprehensively, considering impacts and alternatives and encouraging variety in designs. However, an essential feature of such approaches is flexibility and discretion, which citizens upset about past urban development are increasingly unwilling to entrust with public officials. Not until conflicts of interest and corruption are severely dealt with in state and local laws governing land use decision-making will popular suspicions of flexible controls abate. Cynicism about the motives and interests of decision-makers has more than a little to do with demands in some quarters for rigid prohibitions on further growth. Those who have come to believe that the engine of development can run on only one track want to rip up the track.

Nevertheless, the answer is not to impose more onerous restraints on development, or to tighten minimum standards. Rather, means must be found to improve the incentives for good development, to reward builders who do the right thing. Eventually I believe that public intervention will be necessary to assist developers to assemble land, to provide help with sewer and other infrastructure, possibly to award density increases when developments are particularly responsive to community land conservation or social policies.

Whatever the techniques, citizens must be honestly included in land use decision-making. The great reform of the environmental revolution is the achievement of formal processes for consulting people about issues that touch closely on their lives. In a world where bureaucracies are often big and sometimes arrogant and unconcerned, public hearing requirements, provisions for citizen comments on plans, and citizen access to courts are necessary safeguards: guarantors that single-minded agencies do not ignore broader responsibilities for social and environmental impacts and secondary effects. Environmental impact analysis required by the National Environmental Policy Act for major federal actions significantly affecting the environment, and backed up by court review and enforcement, has introduced a more open and inclusive style of federal planning. Nearly a score of states have required some form of environmental impact statement for various types of actions. The requirement should be implemented for important land use decisions at the local government level also, where its public exposure of the rationale behind proposed decisions, its focus on alternatives, and its inclusion of non-development as well as public works agencies, would respond to real defects in the more conventional decision-making processes.

Myth No. 5: *The essence of sound planning is to assess the level of facilities and services people want before they will "need" it, and then provide it in time to meet demand.*

This is a difficult-to-shed carryover from a time when resources appeared unlimited, and when we did not understand that satisfaction of some wants—such as the desire to drive to work in the morning—can impede the satisfaction of others—the achievement of clean air, uncongested roads, cities pleasant to walk in.

One of the great insights of the late 1960s is that we must move away from purely demand-oriented, to resource-oriented, planning. We cannot meet all demands—not even in America, and those we choose to meet must be selected with full knowledge that their selection makes others impossible. Natural systems have their tolerances, and so do communities.

Myth No. 6: *The energy crisis will solve our land use problems, stimulate a recentralization of development, a revitalization of older cities.*

Remember the energy crisis?

To a large extent, land use configurations have exacerbated our energy problems. But we should not be sanguine about the new concern with energy conservation leading to a solution to the sprawl problem. People will continue to exercise choices—planners are not simply going to decide where to put them—and people who have a range of options are not going to move to neighborhoods where the streets are congested and crime-stricken, the schools inferior or dangerous, the air foul, and the open spaces given over to parking lots. We are going to have to take a series of steps to improve the urban environment, social as well as natural, and to concentrate development so that dependence on the automobile is reduced and shopping facilities are more accessible to residential areas by a means other than driving.

A recent report of the New York Regional Plan Association spoke well to the issue:

> To reduce energy demand, in addition to the use of smaller cars, a change in the pattern of residential development is imperative. That means governmental action to inhibit free-standing shopping centers, strip-highway commerce, isolated office and educational campuses, and other such elements of Spread City. With respect to housing, we will have to go back to homes on smaller lots, substituting siting and landscaping for space and more of our apartments will have to be clustered around commercial, office and public facility centers, instead of wherever a crack in a community's zoning pattern can be found.

Conclusion

All things considered, the challenges to those who would improve land use policies are great but the opportunities for making constructive changes are real, thanks to the effective insistence of concerned "new mooders." In the field of land use and urban growth, the task is even more complex than in pollution control. For there is no standard of pure air or clean water to guide us: only a cacaphony of deeply felt, but divergent, voices raised by people with very different preferences—to live close together or far apart, in highrises or on five-acre lots, to walk, drive or ride a bus to work, to live among their own income or ethnic group or to mix in a melting pot neighborhood. None of these desires is necessarily illegitimate and, thus, planning for future land use and urban development will require that we make our peace with pluralism, and construct a system capable of making the sensitive accommodations and balances a diverse society requires.

A friend who visited the country parks and greenbelts of England returned enthusiastic about what he had seen and announced "I have seen the past, and it *works*."

There is a very real prospect that, in the field of land use and urban growth, the future could work better than the past.

The Use of Land:

A Review*

Basile J. Uddo

Basile Uddo is an associate with Liskow and Lewis of New Orleans. Formerly he was an instructor at Boston University School of Law. Mr. Uddo is a graduate of Loyola, has a law degree from Tulane, and holds an LL.M. from Harvard Law School.

This article originally appeared as a book review in 11 Harvard Journal on Legislation 539 (1974), and is reprinted here with permission.

In the summer of 1972 the Citizen's Advisory Committee on Environmental Quality created its blue-ribbon Task Force on Land Use and Urban Growth. The Task Force brought together an impressive array of able participants from various disciplines.[1] Unfortunately, despite the expertise of the authors and the commonsense approach adopted in identifying the problems of land use, the Task Force's report, The Use of Land, is often naive in its recommendations and analysis. Although its objective—a more pleasing human environment—is appealing, the report is inadequate in terms of recommended implementation. The reader is first presented with a catalogue of evils that have emerged in American land use. Then the report turns optimistically to possible solutions. The intervening questions of proximate causes and the possible obstacles to implementation generally are not considered.

The report's chief value is as a nontechnical, thought-provoking work to stimulate the layman's awareness of land use problems. A chief defect is that, despite the report's claim to the contrary,[2] it loses sight of the practical problems in implementing proposed solutions.[3] The report begins with the admirable assumption that Americans must begin to view land as a resource, as limited as minerals, water, and clean air (pp. 7, 15-16, 24). A more realistic assumption would be that nothing short of a full-scale land crisis will so drastically restructure the American attitude toward land.[4] In fact, even a crisis is no guarantee that this salutary attitude will emerge. For example, the energy crisis has recently been responded to with popular skepticism and selfishness, precluding effective voluntary remedial controls.[5] Thus one notes at the outset that the authors display a probably unjustified optimism.

The report recommends balancing rational development and such values as environmental protection, a middle ground approach which is hardly novel and offers no unique insights.[6] It entrusts the ultimate responsibility for the balancing to local authorities.[7] Though the authors admit the need for state and federal involvement, they feel that the municipalities must be the ones to enact and enforce workable land use regulations (p. 19). The optimism inherent in this suggestion may be warranted for a few areas (notably those used as reported examples), but hardly for the many areas that will have to cooperate if rational land use is to become a national reality. The reporters seem to overlook the fact that many municipal governments are strongly influenced by development interests.[8] Even if innate conservatism were not motive enough to shun meaningful regulations, dependence upon continued development is.

The body of the report deals with a list of specific findings and suggestions related to the problem at hand. Generally, these findings are informative and merit some individual consideration. High on the Task Force's list of priorities is the preservation of open spaces (p. 103). The reporters betray an initial premise of the study, the commitment to local regulation, by relying heavily upon federal (and sometimes state) involvement to secure effective open space preservation (p. 106). Federal tools are varied in form and highly effective since they generally appeal to economic considerations via the tax system (pp. 112-13). The Task Force recognizes this and recommends encouragement of estate tax breaks[9] and extension of charitable status to land preservation groups (p. 113).[10]

On the state and local level, the report suggests acquiring green space by noncompensatory means (p. 135).[11] The problems in implementing this proposal would be enormous. The reporters' idea that land development rights will some day be viewed in the same light as separable mineral rights not only is counter to the American philosophy,[12] but also overlooks implementation problems that might well produce unrecoverable social costs in excess of the ultimate benefit.[13] The Task Force feels, however, that many urban areas would benefit by division of property rights through the planned unit development (P.U.D.)[14] and transferable development rights[15] (pp. 138-39). The report admits that no substantial use has been made of these techniques and that public and legal attitudes toward them have not yet reached a consensus.[16]

Even if PUDs and transfers of development rights can withstand judicial scrutiny, the report suggests no way to motivate local authorities to enact the firmer development regulations necessary to ensure that developers make use of them. Today developers know that soft zoning and planning laws (and boards) allow them sufficient freedom without requiring some amenity (i.e., open space) as a quid pro quo for the right to develop. Without stricter regulations, PUDs and development transfers are emasculated. Therefore, we return to the earlier criticism that the authors' reliance upon local control rests on an unduly optimistic view of the local desire to significantly control development.

The report suggests that municipalities create the atmosphere necessary to divide up property rights by changing the view from "bottom up" to "top down" (p. 22). That is, governments should no longer allow land owners to feel that ownership of land brings with it ownership of development rights, but rather that society sends down to the landowner those circumscribed rights that it decides to grant. Perhaps creation of this view of land ownership is possible, but it does represent a significant departure from traditional American attitudes toward property.[17]

Other specific recommendations in the report also depend upon certain philosophical attitudes toward growth which should be understood. As a prerequisite to its specific plans, the report suggests that the country adopt a new growth policy. This new policy is similar to the Task Force's suggested transformation of attitudes toward property rights and suffers from the same deficiency.

The reporters sense an amorphous "new mood" (p. 33) that seriously questions the traditional growth orientation of American cities.[18] They say this new mood springs in part from humanistic concerns.[19] As examples the writers cite several recent political or quasi-political occurrences (p. 35). However, as they point out,[20] these occurrences could also be explained by reference to justifications other than humanism. For example, Colorado's rejection of the Olympic games was often justified in economic terms.[21] And certainly the Boca Raton growth ceiling ordinance is as much a case of exclusionism as it is one of humanism.[22] Thus the Task Force may again err on the side of optimism by defining a major element of the new mood in terms of humanistic concerns.[23]

Despite its emphasis on humanism, the report clearly lacks sufficient consideration of the problems and needs of low income and minority groups. Thus the "public policies" which the report says should be developed in response to these new attitudes "would impose their heaviest burden on the least advantaged members of society" (p. 53). While the report highlights the problems of discrimination and exclusion, it offers no solutions. Recognizing that the new mood is thought to be tailored to white middle class interests (pp. 53-54), the reporters imply this criticism is unjustified, but never say why or what should be done about it. As it is presently constituted the new mood is an illustration of the haves protecting what they have to the exclusion of the have-nots.[24] This image will not be shed until the purported humanism incorporates the concerns of the disadvantaged. Therefore, until a commonality of perspective as to what constitutes humanistic land use can be achieved, the report's suggested growth policy will not, indeed, should not, be readily accepted.[25]

Understanding these basic philosophical weaknesses, one can examine more closely other specific proposals of the report. The writers suggest that "state and local legislative bodies adopt stringent planning and regulatory legislation whenever they believe it fair and necessary to achieve land-use objectives" (p. 173). To protect this tougher legislation the Task Force proposes that the courts relax the compensation requirement and allow these enactments to be upheld as merely regulatory (pp. 173-75).

The report further recommends an increase in the resources available to government attorneys who must argue in favor of these anticipated regulations.[26] It recommends that private and governmental groups mobilize their forces to support government attorneys with man hours and expertise (pp. 172-75). This, the report asserts, would balance the disparity of legal power that now favors the affluent developer when issues of responsible regulation versus confiscation are raised. This partial measure makes sense because, presumably, the judicial process functions with greater fairness when both sides wield commensurate legal resources.[27]

This, however, does not create workable standards for defining the limits of a taking. The mere fact that government can become more persuasive in assessing and presenting the social costs which argue against invalidating a land use regulation does not necessarily enable a court to decide how these intangible considerations should be weighed against raw property values.

In answer the authors state that along with this buttressing of legal capability the courts should reassess their method of examining land use regulations (p. 174). First, a presumption should be created that any change in an existing ecosystem will have adverse consequences difficult to foresee. This they assert would "build into common law a requirement that a prospective developer who wishes to challenge a governmental regulation prepare a statement similar to the environmental impact statements now required of public agencies under federal programs" (p. 174). But increasing the bureaucratic requirements for developers may serve only to make the final outcome more costly, for in the final analysis the determination will be a contest of experts not unlike present courtroom battles.[28] In contrast, if standards and guidelines were provided, use of the impact statement would create an effective superstructure for resolving the taking issue.[29]

The second suggestion for reexamining the judicial attitude toward land use regulations goes to the heart of the economics of land ownership. In the words of the report:

> It is time that the U.S. Supreme Court re-examine its earlier precedents that seem to require a balancing of public benefit against land value lost in every case and declare that when the protection of natural, cultural, or aesthetic resources or the assurance of orderly development are involved, a mere loss in land value will *never* be justification for invalidating the regulation of land use (p. 175) (emphasis added).

As a legal standard this is deficient since there is no theory upon which the Court could issue a mandate to ignore diminution of property values, especially to protect such things as "aesthetic resources," since it is difficult, if not impossible, to secure agreement as to what these are.[30] The report is saying in effect that we shall balance the interests but the developer shall have no interests to balance since mere land value is not a valid concern. Here again, the Task Force has substituted naive generalities where it might have suggested manageable standards. This leaves the taking issue as confused as ever.[31]

The Task Force also examined the use of incentives to encourage the kind of development needed for America's future growth. Generally, the report's suggestions in this area are somewhat more realistic and offer at least minimal guidelines for implementation. The analysis begins by recognizing that the local control initially recommended by the report may be used in too exclusionary a manner to achieve the desired growth pattern (pp. 223-25). Local areas have historically established themselves as the guardians and spokesmen of those who were there first (p. 225). This produces an inclination to exclude what will adversely affect (in a real or imagined way) the "natives." As a threshold solution the reporters turned to the federal government to establish a national land use policy that would be the foundation for state legislation directed at standardizing land use regulations throughout the country (p. 240).

Implicit in this federal and state involvement is an active role for the courts. The report proffers a rule of moderation between the courts' role as protector of minority and low income groups and its role as protector of valid community interests (p. 243). This ideal may never be achieved since it relies on case-by-case vigilance rather than permanent changes in the system that would better protect *both* sides. The authors suggest that grassroots watchdogging may serve the function of counterbalancing development powers that threaten the disadvantaged:

> The continuing efforts of civil rights groups and other litigants to obtain court decrees invalidating exclusionary regulations are encouraged as essential steps toward achieving the state legislation and administrative action that are ultimately necessary to safeguard fundamental rights and assure needed development (p. 243).

The Task Force does go on to suggest some specific incentives to encourage acceptable development. For this it relies on the large scale unit development (usually a PUD) (p. 250). The writers adequately describe the use and benefits of the PUD, but they mention without suggested solutions several difficult obstacles to its practical implementation (pp. 250-54).

The authors predicate use of the PUD upon local acceptance of the concept as evidenced by a proper regulation or ordinance. The report seems to assume that localities can be readily encouraged to enact such ordinances (pp. 27-29). However, it is likely that some communities will find opposition from development interests. Though this opposition may vary in kind and intensity, one must consider the possibility that significant pressure can be asserted against the PUD.[32]

Developer opposition arises for two reasons. First, developers in many areas have traditionally enjoyed a free hand in what they do and may find the PUD an example of giving more than they get. Under classical multilot subdivision practice, developers generally can (or may believe they can) develop land more profitably without regard for open spaces, recreation facilities, or other amenities. Even where they face large minimum lot sizes and other zoning restrictions they may have greater success with rezoning, variances, and exceptions than the community would like to admit.[33] Under these circumstances developers would hardly welcome a concept that would put them under the greater scrutiny of PUD plan review and possibly cause them to sacrifice large amounts of land for amenities in order to gain final approval.

Second, small developers would seem particularly opposed since, as the Task Force admits, PUD's work best for large-scale developments. In fact the report recommends local encouragement of only large-scale projects (pp. 248-54) because the costs of PUD's could only be borne by large (often corporate) developers. The small-scale developer would face not only the disparity of size and economic power, but also the eventual antipathy of local government catering only to large-scale projects. This poses a significant threat to the small developer—a threat that is not thoroughly addressed by the report (pp. 251-254). Further, the report goes on to suggest a state participation that would essentially assure the large developer high-level assistance:

> The states should establish government entities, comparable to New York's Urban Development Corporation, responsible for assisting and when necessary directly undertaking large-scale projects.
>
> These entities should have the full range of powers, including the power of eminent domain, the power to override local land-use regulations, and the power to control the provision of public utilities, when necessary, to overcome the barriers that now prevent most developers from operating at the larger scales that the public interest requires (p. 261).

In essence, the report suggests the concentration of not only economic power but also the full array of governmental power in the hands of a few large developers. As bigness has not proven itself synonymous with quality or human concern, another source of opposition to the report's proposal may well be suspicious citizens.[34]

All this is not to say that the PUD is a bad approach to development. Indeed PUDs do offer an important avenue for rational, high quality residential development.[35] These issues are raised merely to point out the report's chief weakness—failure to fully recognize the source and nature of opposition to its suggestions.

The Task Force report is generally useful, but in a very limited sense. It impressively highlights the major problems facing future rational land use. But in producing a commonsense view of the problem it often oversimplifies, exhibits excessive optimism, and recommends inadequate strategies for implementation. Perhaps its chief value as a policy guide is that it may heighten public awareness of the problems and issues of land use.

Footnotes

*The Use of Land: A Citizen's Policy Guide to Urban Growth. By The Rockefeller Brothers Fund, New York: Thomas Y. Crowell Co., 1973, Pp. 318, index. $3.95.

1. The Task Force prided itself on its balanced, interdisciplinary complexion. Representatives were included from banking, law, planning, government, education, and civil rights and citizen action groups (pp. 1-2).
2. The report claims to be "one that acknowledges the political constraints in our cities, states, and federal government, one that realistically assesses what we can and cannot influence . . . ." (p. 5).
3. The failure to consider these practical problems will be treated in this review. Generally, they concern the report's failure to recognize that private interest pressures will greatly affect local government attitudes toward land use regulations.
4. For a further discussion of this attitude see B. Siegan, Land Use Without Zoning 222-234 (1972); Dunham, Property, City Planning, and Liberty, in Law and Land 28 (C. Haar ed. 1964). See also J. Cribbet, W. Fritz & C. Johnson, Cases and Materials on Property ch. 1 (2d ed. 1966) (discussing the development of property as a legal institution). The traditional American attitude toward property largely relies upon statements like this:

The Use of Land

There is nothing which so generally strikes the imagination, and engages the affections of mankind, as the right of property; or that sole and despotic dominion which one man claims and exercises over the external things of the world, in total exclusion of the right of any other individual in the universe.
21 W. Blackstone, Commentaries *2.

5. For examples see Time, Feb. 25, 1974, at 26; U.S. News & World Rep., Feb. 25, 1974, at 13.

6. Other authors have already taken this position. ALI Model Land Development Code (Tent. Draft No. 2, 1970); S. 3354, 91st Cong., 2d Sess. § 401 et seq. (1970); Law and Land (C. Haar ed. 1964).

7. "Although we recommend a number of measures to inject higher levels of government into the development guidance process, we think that the broad base of regulations should be established by local decisions" (p. 19).

8. See generally Comment, Land Use Control in Metropolitan Areas: The Failure of Zoning and a Proposed Alternative, 45 S. Cal. L. Rev. 335 (1972) (discussion of the weaknesses of zoning and zoning boards under pressure from private interests).

9. To facilitate the acquisition of open spaces by the federal government the reporters make one particularly interesting suggestion—payment of federal estate taxes by transfers of land to the government. The fair market value of the land would be offset against the estate's federal tax liability (p. 113).

10. The report fails to note a possible complexity in such a system. Presumably these groups would wish to influence legislation. Since this is proscribed activity for charitable organizations, separate foundations would have to be formed to perform this function. Int. Rev. Code of 1954, § 501(c)(3), Treas. Reg. § 1.501(c)(3)-1(c)(3) (1974).

11. The reporters allude to the English Town and Country Planning Act (1947) as an example of what can be done to effectuate this type of land use regulation (p. 133). However, the American reaction probably will be that the British are more likely to accept this socialized view on property rights. This comment is not intended to discourage such regulation but to point out a likely public response not anticipated by the report. Additionally, the report fails to recognize that the 1947 version of the Act has been widely recognized as deficient:
    In spite of hopes and best intentions of planners and legislators, it is generally conceded that the system [the 1947 Act] did not work well in practice . . . . Consequently, Parliament abolished the development charge [one aspect of the system] in the Town and Country Planning Acts of 1953 and 1954.
    Rose, A Proposal for the Separation and Marketability of Development Rights as a Technique to Preserve Open Space, 2 Real Estate L.J. 635, 644-45 (1974).

12. See note 4 supra.

13. For a discussion of the implementation problems, see Rose, supra note 11, at 644-45. For a discussion of the mitigation of these problems, see Costonis, Development Rights Transfer: An Exploratory Essay, 83 Yale L.J. 75, 122-23 (1973).

14. The PUD (also sometimes known as cluster zoning) is a land use regulation device allowing a developer to deviate from traditional single use, lot-by-lot subdivisions to create a more flexible mixed use development. In return for the suspension of traditional zoning regulations, the developer provides certain predetermined amenities, i.e., open spaces, municipal facilities, school buildings, recreational facilities. For further explanation of PUDs, see U.S. Advisory Comm'n on Intergovernmental Relations, State Legislative Programs 5 (Cum. Supp. 1970). See also Babcock, Krasnowiecki & McBride, Planned Unit Development, Model State Statute, 114 U. Pa. L. Rev. 140 (1965).

15. Development rights transfers can be used to relax economic pressures on open spaces and historical landmarks. These land uses are generally less economically productive than would be allowable under the prevailing zoning provisions. To encourage their preservation the municipality could provide for sale of the unused right to develop the land. This compensates the owner for not fully exploiting the land. The rights would be salable on the open market to developers who could then increase their intensity of development at some other site beyond zoning maximums. See Elliot & Marcus, From Euclid to Ramapo: New Directions in Land Development Controls, 1 Hofstra L. Rev. 56, 72 (1973); Costonis, Development Rights Transfer: An Exploratory Essay, 83 Yale L.J. 75, 85-86 (1973).

16. The lack of judicial authority and resulting speculation on the legal basis of development rights transfers is discussed in Costonis, The Chicago Plan: Incentive Zoning and the Preservation of Urban Landmarks, 85 Harv. L. Rev. 574, 602 (1972). For attitudes on PUDs, see Orinda Homeowners Comm. v. Board of Supervisors, 11 Cal. App. 3d 768, 90 Cal. Rptr. 88 (1970); Eves v. Zoning Bd. of Adjustment, 401 Pa. 211, 164 A.2d 7 (1960). See also Krasnowiecki, Planned Unit Development: A Challenge to Established Theory and Practice of Land Use Control, 114 U. Pa. L. Rev. 47 (1965); Mandelker, Reflections on the American System of Planning Controls and a Response to Professor Krasnowiecki, 114 U. Pa. L. Rev. 98 (1965); Craig, Planned Unit Development as Seen from City Hall, 114 U. Pa. L. Rev. 127 (1965); Annot., 43 A.L.R.3d 888 (1972).

17. See note 4 supra. The taking issues this suggestion raises are considered in the text following note 25 infra.

18. The report describes the mood on page 33:
    This mood defies easy generalization because it springs from a melange of concerns—many that are unselfish and legitimate, some that are selfish and not so legitimate. The mood is both optimistic and expansive in its expectations of the future, and pessimistic and untrusting about inevitable change, even (perhaps especially), in places where change is the constant. Its demands range from managed growth to no growth, from "stop-til-we-plan" to "stop," period.

19. "But the new attitude toward growth is not exclusively motivated by economics. It appears to be part of a rising emphasis on humanism, on the preservation of natural and cultural characteristics that make for a humanly satisfying living environment" (p. 34).

20. *See* note 18 *supra.*
21. The report itself points out the economic concerns of Coloradans: "Other citizens, concerned about rising property taxes, joined with the environmentalists in opposition. They insisted that, on balance, the *costs in public dollars* alone would far outweigh whatever revenues were generated" (p. 44) (emphasis added).
22. "This was El Camino Real, or the King's Highway, which led to the Mizner principality of Boca Raton, the most snobbish of all the Florida real estate subdivisions." A. Johnston, The Legendary Mizners 235 (1953), quoted in C. Haar, Land-Use Planning (2d ed. 1971).
23. If humanism, as it is commonly understood, were really a major component of the new mood, would the report have to note the concern of low income groups that decent, affordable housing will be the victim of post-new mood development (pp. 53-55)?
24. The report acknowledges this exclusionary aspect (p. 53):
    If Boulder or Boca Raton takes measures to limit its population, for example, the price of land and homes may be driven up, thereby pricing out the poor, and probably many of the middle class. . . .
    . . . [I]f large tracts of open spaces or wooded areas are to be preserved, a possible effect, whether intended or not, could be to close off potential housing sites.
25. For example, the view taken by Claire Stern of the Long Island Environmental Council is hardly what we commonly think of as humanistic; however, it is consistent with the approach suggested by the report:
    Although she believes blacks need more housing opportunities on the Island, she says that "until better land-use decisions are made, I'll stand in opposition to density development, although my gut feeling is that this is arbitrary and wrong" (p. 55).
26. "The government has a more difficult task [than the developer]. It must show the value to society of limiting development on a land area or saving a historic building . . . .
    All too often, however, government attorneys cannot spare the time for the extensive preparation required" (p. 172).
27. For a further discussion of this point see F. Bosselman, D. Callies & J. Banta, The Taking Issue 284-302 (1973).
28. The difference will be one of degree, *i.e.*, the government's case will be better prepared. The difficult judicial determination of regulation versus taking must still rely upon imprecise guidelines.
29. Presumably, the impact statement would produce the information needed to apply the standards and guidelines most effectively.
30. *See* Masotti & Selfon, *Aesthetic Zoning and the Police Power,* 46 J. Urban L. 773 (1969); Note, *Aesthetic Zoning: A Current Evaluation of the Law,* 18 U. Fla. L. Rev. 430 (1965). *But see* Note, *Beyond the Eye of the Beholder: Aesthetics and Objectivity,* 71 Mich. L. Rev. 1438 (1973).
31. For a discussion of the complex taking issue, see B. Siegan, Land Use Without Zoning 224-27 (1973). *See generally* F. Bosselman, D. Callies, & J. Banta, The Taking Issue (1973).
32. *See* Lloyd, *A Developer Looks at Planned Unit Development,* 114 U. Pa. L. Rev. 3, 4 (1965); Krasnowiecki, *supra* note 16, at 78-97.
33. *See* note 8 *supra.*
34. *See* Lloyd, *supra* note 32, at 6; Krasnowiecki, *supra* note 16, at 65-78.
35. *See* Lloyd, *supra* note 32, at 3-14; Mandelker, *supra* note 16, at 98-105.

CHAPTER THREE

CONTROL OF GROWTH: A MANAGEMENT ALTERNATIVE?

The concept of "the new mood" regarding land use and growth problems was popularized in 1972 and 1973 by such groups as the American Society of Planning Officials and the Rockefeller Task Force *(The Use of Land)* . . . as discussed at length in Chapter 2 of Volume I. In 1973 and 1974, still other organizations began to more fully treat these subjects in their professional journals. Some attempted to give serious guidance to local officials regarding the techniques and policy options for adequate growth management; but most articles tended, and still have the predilection, to dwell on general discussions of "there is a new mood" without offering much in the way of *substantive* tools and methodologies to local officials and planners.

One of the first persons to help initiate national scrutiny of this general field was **Earl Finkler,** whose two publications appear as the first (combined) article in this chapter. As explained on the third page of his discussion, it was in the Spring of 1972 that a last-minute informal session on "non-growth" was held at the American Society of Planning Officials' conference in Detroit, and was attended by a surprising number of persons. [Earl Finkler has also recently published a book regarding growth controls, titled *Nongrowth Planning Strategies* (Praeger, 1974).]

Finkler's central theme is to "reexamine the planner's traditional orientation toward growth and to explore theory and practice which might lead to much more than merely redistributing growth . . . [and] to strike some sparks of creativity or imagination as the planning profession starts to confront the important question of nongrowth." The author also states that although most planners see that it would be most appropriate for growth policies to emanate from the state or regional level, "few communities . . . are willing to wait." There consequently was evidenced a keen desire and need for information in most of the local jurisdictions which he contacted in assembling data for his study.

Touching on non-growth as an alternative, the author is also concerned with the increasingly problematic cross-currents expressed by advocates of "social justice." Apparently genuinely perturbed by this conflict, the author nonetheless states time and again that a continuation of historical patterns of "unchecked growth will not guarantee integration, social justice, or economic uplifting of the disadvantaged in the future any more than it has in the past." Moreover, the claim is made that the legal questions of nongrowth tend to be "overshadowed by the courts' reactions to overt cases of exclusionary zoning and related policies." [See Chapters 6 and 7 in Volume I, for legal and planning issues relating to exclusion.]

The difficulty with this type of analysis, is that it perhaps too easily brushes aside the equity dilemma by almost leading the reader into the conclusion that "if it was unsolvable then, [exclusion] probably remains so now . . . so why not proceed with controlling growth problems anyway." A more difficult type of analysis indeed would be (once the above types of observations are made) to address explicitly and at length various methods on the local level by which equity and social justice problems can be solved *in concert* with on-going managed growth policies. One such analysis could include an exhaustive tracing of "inclusionary"—rather than exclusionary—techniques. [See Chapter 7 of Volume I.]

The article correctly points out: "The planner should remember to be comprehensive, cool, and logical when approaching nongrowth, lest some person or group's civil liberties or social welfare get trampled in the process." It can be argued however that the responsibility goes beyond this mere problem-avoidance approach. The question is; what *affirmative* planning can the locality undertake to assure that such equity issues are properly handled during the pursuit of other objectives, such as growth management?

Finkler then ventures into several concepts, such as optimal city size and cost-benefit analysis. [In the original report he spends 33 pages on case studies and selected readings . . . material which is omitted from the article as it appears here. See Chapter 11 of Volume II for 1974 case study material, from a National Science Foundation-sponsored study.]

In the fall of 1973, the **International City Management Association** published the report of one of its Municipal Management Policy Committees which considered the area of "managing growth." The central conclusion of that committee is: "It is recommended that the professionals work with their administrations and governing bodies to assess community growth needs and adopt a community growth policy. Desirable levels of growth should be defined in terms of both the timing of growth and the area to be covered by future populations."

The committee throughout its report suggests a series of actionable steps, including the basic idea that: "In developing growth programs, managers should explore the available techniques for land use control, recognize the importance of capital projects as part of growth programs, create within the municipal attorney's office a division dealing with land use and other growth-related issues, pay close attention to policies that cause land developers to pay the secondary costs of development, and ensure that growth policies do not create *de facto* racial or economic segregation." The article notes that although many of the tools for growth management have been available to localities for some time, such techniques generally have not been handled on a coordinated basis or in an integrated fashion . . . a management problem which local administrators will have to tackle if they are to deal with local growth issues at all effectively.

Furthermore, the committee castigates a series of national "task force" reports from 1968 through 1973 for failing to recognize "the cornerstone role of local government in managing growth. None explored growth as would a local administrator responsible for dealing with local and federal programs related to growth. . . . At the same time that groups such as AIA ignore or seek to abolish a meaningful role for local government, they claim to value highly individuals' freedom of choice with regard to where and how they live."

These comments validly criticize most reports for not dealing with an appropriate range of local techniques and alternatives for growth management. But the criticism of "freedom of choice" is based on the rather curious conclusion of ICMA that "when decisions are made [at other than the local levels] . . . people necessarily will be saddled with more uniformity and less freedom of choice." [For specific arguments to the contrary, see Chapters 9 and 10 of Volume II.]

ICMA then turns to the failure of local comprehensive planning: lack of communication between departments; nonconversion of policies into zoning ordinances; nonrealistic political assumptions; non-integration of planning into local public programs; and so forth. A series of recommendations is then made—recommendations which offer programmatic guidance to local planners and government officials. These include: the setting of community goals, directives, and objectives; the need to carefully sequence and time the provision of various services (rather than merely making lump-sum, futuristic aggregate demand projections); proper capital programming; expansion of professional staff skills (especially, the city attorney's office); managerial integration of local departments' programs and controls; identification of secondary costs of development, etc.

The report concludes that "ICMA must redouble its efforts to collect information on growth programs nationally and to make the information widely available through its information sources." [Similarly, this important need for further information was identified by the U.S. Department of Housing and Urban Development, which funded the basic editing of these volumes on the *Management and Control of Growth*.]

The third article includes a series of commentaries on the roles of *counties* in growth management issues. As **Bernard Hillenbrand,** executive director of the National Association of Counties, states: "While counties have traditionally been thought of as only providing basic services such as election administration, court administration and tax collection, their increasing population and the needs of that population have expanded the county role to include many services and powers which affect and are directly affected by growth management." In a set of statements endorsing effective comprehensive planning, Hillenbrand reiterates the official NAC position: "the comprehensive planning process is essential to all counties . . . as a means for providing the management framework; [it] should be comprehensive in area and participation as well as in content; . . . counties must recognize the planning needs of multi-county regions and encourage all governmental units within such regions to cooperate and participate in a comprehensive regional planning program."

Hillenbrand's welcome endorsement of area-wide comprehensive planning runs into the same predicament of much discussion-in-principle, where statements of the desirable are made without the accompaniment of a thorough exploration of pragmatic mechanisms. Policy-wise, it is interesting to read presentations such as that above (or the two which follow); the question is how is the proposal to be achieved or realized? How, for example, can the following be done? "Since county government is the only areawide government at the local level, it must accept the responsibility and exercise initiative in the development of a comprehensive planning program for the entire county area. . . . County governments, through their elected officials, should accept the responsibility for and exercise the initiative in the organization and operation of institutions and mechanisms for voluntary solution of regional problems."

Francois, in his article, stresses that development must pay its own way ("in some jurisdictions, contributions are now exacted to buy parkland and build schools . . ."). As the author admits, such ideas, which more and more localities are utilizing, tend to drive up the cost of housing, reduce the ability of some consumers to purchase housing, and so forth. The reader might also observe that such fees may run into any number of challenges, such as those noted by Janis in Chapter 4 of Volume I.

Francois further urges that communities, when they enter the growth management arena, should plan for the housing needs of low– and moderate–income families. Such affirmative planning and program formulation may in part help ameliorate some of the disadvantageous side-effects of various growth management tools, as impact fees and increased costs. (Left in the middle, nevertheless, is the potential middle-income home purchaser, who cannot escape cost pressures unless he directly attacks the fee system in the courts.)

The article by **Harman** basically consists of a quick checklist of considerations which local officials might use in structuring the necessary "systematic programs to link development levels with coherent plans and programs." The final article in the series-—by **Raflo**—is included here because it succinctly restates the attitudinal resistance to mounting growth pressures in many rural-but-urbanizing communities and counties around the country.

The next article—a policy statement by **Zero Population Growth**—is particularly intriguing for its nearly Machiavellian approach to using various tactics and arguments to achieve the broader limits-to-growth goals of ZPG—namely: "achieving the population stabilization objectives already held by ZPG. . . . Where efforts at controlling local growth have been organized, those people will probably be more receptive to the population/resources message. . . . The student is attentive and the message will probably be absorbed . . . [and they] can be developed into proponents for regional and state controls on land use and urban growth."

The basic goals of the ZPG slow-growth program are summarized, and the methods for broadening support for slow-growth and planned-growth policies are set forth. [The reader should note some of the nearly incredible assumptions contained in this advice, part of which is reprinted below.] "Relate high taxes to exponentially increased costs of public services. . . . Relate increased food costs to the one million acres of land which is lost to urban growth each year; and to fouled or filled estuaries. Relate costly housing and shoddy construction to land boom development. Link brown-outs, traffic snarls, fuel shortages, and dirty air to population growth, poor urban planning, and short term energy policies. . . . Relate social problems such as poverty, mental illness, crime, drug abuse, lack of concern for the aged, and urban decay to unrestricted growth."

Objectives for local action include: freezing local re-zoning actions; opposing bond issuances; eliminating "boosterism"; securing publicity; preparing court suits; encouraging political activism for selected candidates; and so forth. In spite of these ideas, for the anti-exclusionist there is one bright spot in the report: "Limited-growth and optimum-growth activities shall be assisted when the objective is to ensure a quality environment; slow-growth or non-growth efforts which are based on racial or economic discrimination shall not be assisted. . . . If the 'control local growth' movement is to gain full steam across the nation, we must have such policies [equity to the poor] as a matter of basic justice."

Following the general line of intonations of Zero Population Growth, the **Stanford Environmental Law Society's** article further expands upon this chapter's coverage of available tactics and strategies for the citizen-activist re slow-growth. The article claims: "Knowledge of various techniques for local growth control is clearly valueless without some grasp of methods of implementation." The authors see the use of establishing a "central group" to keep an "eye to the overall picture," while utilizing expanded participation of other citizens for special issues or to "effectively block an undesirable growth project."

One tactic is to attack "cost/benefit analyses put out by pro-growth advocates. . . . Such statements are perfect targets for well-aimed attacks by growth control advocates." Other methods discussed are: publicizing the anti-growth positions through the local media; fund-raising; effective lobbying with the local planning department, zoning board, and city council; use of the referendum and the initiative to reverse, or encourage the passage of, certain decisions and ordinances; the election of "responsive" officials; and if necessary, the use of the courts and law suits as a growth control device.

The astuteness of this article is further displayed in this unfortunately bald, unqualified set of statements: "Lawsuits have a number of advantages. First of all there is obviously a chance of winning the suit. However, the mere threat of a suit can also be an impressive political tactic, expressing acute citizen displeasure with the activities of the incumbent government. And finally, suits can be an effective delaying tactic in order to force compromises. Developers may want to postpone their project until the court has closed their status, or the court itself may issue an injunction or temporary restraining order. Extensive delay may even force the developer to abandon his plans due to financial difficulties."

The articles in this chapter clearly illustrate that various national organizations are sending forth messages to be informed about growth controls; with some even issuing a call to arms for their members to seek firmer control over the local decision-making processes. Whereas the first two chapters of this volume concentrate on the new mood regarding growth, with an examination of non-growth as a management alternative, the more in-depth analyses of specific growth land use planning techniques are covered in Volume II and in parts of Volume III. [For issues of equity and social justice, see Chapter 6 and 7; for views of/from the private sector, see Chapter 19.]

The next set of articles looks in detail at the partial failure of current planning and zoning systems, with an overview of several recent studies including the so-called "quiet revolution" in land use controls.

—RWS

Nongrowth as A Planning Alternative:

A Preliminary Examination of an Emerging Issue

Earl Finkler

Earl Finkler is the Principal Planner for the Comprehensive Planning Program at the City Planning Department of Tucson, Arizona, where he is supervising the formulation of growth alternatives for the city. He was a senior research associate for the American Society of Planning Officials from 1970-1973. Mr. Finkler is a graduate of the School of Journalism at Marquette University, and holds a master's from the Department of Urban Affairs, University of Wisconsin–Milwaukee.

This article is reprinted with the permission of the American Society of Planning Officials. It is a digest of an extensive, 65-page publication by the same title, published as an ASPO Planning Advisory Service Report, Number 283–September 1972. The full report, which includes expanded materials, case studies, etc., is available for $6.00, prepaid, from ASPO; 1313 East Sixtieth Street; Chicago, Illinois 60637.

Introduction

The title of this report, *Nongrowth As a Planning Alternative*, could mean many things to many different planners. Some might automatically think of population distribution, greenbelts, etc. Others might see the report as a planner's introduction to the Zero Population Growth and/or stationary-state economics movements. The report, which is quite fluid in definitions and distinctions, covers most of these concerns and many others. Population growth is perhaps emphasized more than economic growth, but both forms of growth are considered to be related. The central theme is to reexamine the planner's traditional orientation toward growth and to explore theory and practice which might lead to much more than merely redistributing growth.

The rate of growth and the absolute amounts of growth are emphasized over the distribution of growth. The latter is a major and complex topic on its own and, by itself, does little to help resolve the dilemma of growth versus nongrowth. Many communities in this country are experiencing nongrowth or decline as a natural fact, instead of through some public policy. While this is another important topic, time and space limits ruled out the necessarily lengthy analysis this topic would require.

Some might argue that realistically the term in the title should be "limited growth" or "growth control," rather than "nongrowth." In a number of instances, especially in the case studies, this is probably true. But the term "nongrowth" implies a rather unre-

Nongrowth As A Planning Alternative

strained intellectual and pragmatic inquiry into the heart of the growth issue. No one expects to stop all forms of growth overnight, even if this were deemed desirable. But the complex and deeply rooted growth ethic in this country—accepted by much of the planning profession—cannot really be analyzed, corrected, thrown out, or even endorsed until it is subject to much more skepticism and weighed against possible alternatives.

This report is a preliminary effort on a relatively new item of planning concern. The main purpose of the report is to strike some sparks of creativity or imagination as the planning profession starts to confront the important question of nongrowth. It is dangerous to state conclusions at the beginning of a long and wide-ranging report such as this. Often it is only the conclusions, and not the content, which find their way into reviews and discussions. In spite of this risk, it was decided to list a few conclusions, if only to prevent readers from becoming lost. There are points to be made by this report, but they should be made primarily by readers who think for themselves and weigh the material as it is presented. The following conclusions will be presented in this report:

1. Nongrowth (in addition to logical, limited, planned, and other forms of growth) should be studied by planners and blended into planning considerations. The topic should be relevant in most communities facing growth, regardless of size or type of jurisdiction. It can be a mistake to deal only with the results of growth, while automatically eliminating growth as a factor in itself.
2. Nongrowth is presently a dangerous and controversial topic for planners, one which can threaten their job security and professional standing. On the other hand, ignorance or apathy toward this planning alternative can also be dangerous as a community's environmental awareness develops.
3. There are not a lot of hard data presently available to back up local policies and decisions regarding growth versus nongrowth. A number of local and regional studies were started in 1971 and 1972, but many questions are still unanswered, especially in terms which planners would accept. Even though the information is scarce, the planner should consider temporary nongrowth measures, if only to buy time for an improved planning effort or a stabilization of local conditions which will allow citizens to plan for the future instead of reacting to the past.
4. The appropriate jurisdiction for nongrowth is ultimately the world. While there are increasing national problems with growth, it is presently the local communities which are identifying the problems and seeking the solutions. The author found few local communities which are willing to wait for appropriate policies to emerge at the state or national level, despite the almost unanimous opinion that these are the most appropriate jurisdictions. An environmentally contained region, such as the Lake Tahoe basin between California and Nevada, has been frequently cited as an appropriate jurisdiction, but studies of the population-carrying capacities of such regions and interfaces with adjacent regions have been slow to surface.
5. Contrary to popular belief, there are some legitimate economists who believe that this nation would not go down the drain if we stopped growing, both in terms of population and gross national product. The concept of net stability of population and the economy has received much less attention at the regional level, but it may be related to these theories which have been emerging at the national level.
6. The legal environment for nongrowth is cloudy, having generally been overshadowed by the courts' reactions to overt cases of exclusionary zoning and related policies. But there are lawyers (and even some judges) who are starting to make some distinctions.

The legal situation is not an automatic dead end or an insurmountable obstacle for nongrowth.

Overview of Growth and Nongrowth—A Journey to the Center of the Planner's Mind

Alvin Toffler points out in *Future Shock* that "acceleration is one of the most important and least understood of all social forces." He also notes that "the increased rate at which situations flow past us vastly complicates the entire structure of life, multiplying the number of roles we must play and the number of choices we are forced to make."[1]

The planner contemplating nongrowth, whether favorably or unfavorably, should be aware that acceleration and growth are sort of compound problems, somewhat like McLuhan's "medium and the message." Not only is growth, especially population and economic growth, being perceived as a problem by a "growing" number of publications, people, and communities, but the pace of the recognition, definition, and even the proposed solution of the problem is extremely rapid. In the first three months of 1972, two major studies of the dangers of growth, one at the world level[2] and one at the national level,[3] were released. Within the past year or so, there has been extensive media coverage of nongrowth or limited growth ideas and strategies in such publications as the *New York Times*, *Newsweek*, the *New Republic*, *Science*, and *Business Week*.

An ad-hoc session on "Nongrowth As a Planning Alternative," held during the 1972 ASPO National Planning Conference in Detroit, attracted some 150 planners and interested persons, despite the fact that it wasn't listed on the formal program. As the case studies and listings presented later in the report will show, an increasing number of planners are initiating or being drawn into local growth-nongrowth controversies. Many planners no longer have to be told that they (and many others) came up short in the 1960s with regard to plans for the black community and other general social concerns. In the 1970s, the planner is being told to be extra careful of a deteriorating environment. Planners like Paul Davidoff appear to be concentrating on the exclusionary zoning issues, with less emphasis on environmental matters.

Planners who see some benefits in population control and family planning have heard accusations from some black leaders that they are trying to "legitimatize vicious extermination" and "conjure up the specter of genocide."[4] Every planner knows one of the most apparent objections to the concept of nongrowth—the present and continuing gaps in this country between rich and poor, white and black, etc. Planners have been trained to be comprehensive and a comprehensive approach to nongrowth dictates that all races, income groups, etc., come along for the ride. The planner notes that black ghetto areas have some of the worst environmental problems: noise and air pollution from passing automobiles (many of which belong to commuting suburbanites), pesticides, lead poisoning from paint, etc. The planner might also want to stress greater political sophistication and economic power for disadvantaged groups so that all can share in future decisions regarding growth or nongrowth.

The apparent crosscurrents between nongrowth and black power, between environmental concern and social justice, have been and should be stressed. But the theme which this report will explore is that such concerns are not mutually exclusive, that unchecked growth will not guarantee integration, social justice, or economic uplifting of the disadvantaged in the future anymore than it has in the past. (For example, Orange County,

Nongrowth As A Planning Alternative

California, one of the fastest growing areas in the country, went from 1.2 per cent nonwhite in 1950 to only 2.7 per cent nonwhite in 1970.)

Traditional economists have been quick to knock down any emerging stationary-state or equilibrium economic thrusts by saying that growth is the only way in which America will ever reduce poverty.[5] Other motherhood items on the national agenda, such as curbing pollution, are also deemed possible only through economic growth. But planners who don't tune out at this point might become concerned about some of the people cutting off debate on nongrowth in the name of social justice and by the extreme nature of their views. For example, economist Henry C. Wallich wrote that: "Growth is a substitute for equality of income. So long as there is growth, there is hope, and that makes large income differentials tolerable."[6]

Mobil Oil Company reprinted part of a paper published by Anthony Crosland, a Labor member of the British Parliament, in a recent advertisement in the *New York Times*. Mr. Crosland characterized nongrowth advocates in the following terms:

> Their approach is hostile to growth in principle and indifferent to the needs of ordinary people. It has a manifest class bias and reflects a set of middle- and upper-class value judgments. Its champions are often kindly and dedicated people. But they are affluent; and fundamentally, though of course not consciously, they want to kick the ladder down behind them.[7]

Such arguments certainly should be considered. But the planner should read on, lest the thought emerges that more suburban tract housing, four gas stations to a corner, and three cars in every garage are the only way to solve the critical problems in our black ghettos. The U.S. riot commission report said in 1968 that the relative economic deprivation of blacks was increasing:

> Although it is growing, Negro family income is not keeping pace with white family income growth. In constant 1965 dollars, median nonwhite income in 1947 was $2,174 lower than median white income. By 1966, the gap had grown to $3,036.[8]

If planners and economists want to discuss some very necessary redistribution of income, housing resources, etc., such discussion is long overdue. But there is some emerging evidence or contention that such talk need not automatically be couched in terms of unlimited population and infinite economic growth. Anthony Lewis noted that:

> It is true . . . that America's postwar growth has given more money to those at the bottom of the income ladder. But it has done so at a terrible social cost.
>
> The emphasis on private enrichment has so degraded the public sector that life in cities is nasty and brutish at any but the highest income levels. Moreover, there is a growing consciousness of economic inequality—of unfairness in the system—that shows up now in the populist appeal of George Wallace. Anyone who thinks the American pattern of economic growth is a path to social justice could not have lifted his eyes from a textbook for years.[9]

Economist Herman E. Daly put some of what Lewis said in more specific economic terms as he talked about a stationary-state economy:

> For several reasons, the important issue of the stationary state will be distribution, not production. The problem of relative shares can no longer be avoided by appeals to growth. . . . It is hard to see how ethical appeals to equal shares can be countered. Also, even though physical stocks remain constant, increased income in the form of leisure will result from technological improvements. How will it be distributed, if not according to some ethical norm of equality? The stationary state would make fewer demands on our environmental resources, but much greater demands on our moral resources.[10]

The planner appears to be caught in a cross fire of serious and immediate concerns expressed by environmental and social justice advocates.

The planner thus has to "deal with" or "cope with" growth which has both statisical and cultural momentum, but not necessarily any permanence or guaranteed infallibility. If growth is to be slowed by public policy at any or all planning jurisdiction levels, the time for study and action is now. The longer we wait, the more difficult it could become. For example, the Rockefeller Commission projections show that 100 years from now, the two-child family would result in population of about 350 million persons, while the three-child family would produce a total of nearly a billion.

Risks of Nongrowth Planning. There are other considerations which should preface the main body of this report, however. For one thing, the planner himself may become an endangered species by trying to take a leadership role in nongrowth or limited growth. Many planners have just begun to convince hostile or apathetic commissions and political leaders that planning can mean economic gain, industrial development, commercial rejuvenation, and more federal money. It is probably no accident that a number of state and other planning jurisdictions include the words "economic development" in their agency titles.

The April 1, 1972, issue of TAB, ASPO's jobs in planning periodical, contained the following advertisement which is certainly not atypical of those from many other smaller communities:

> *Planner* City desires person interested in community development, attracting new industry, maintaining city's eligibility for federal programs, and keeping city aware of federal aid available. Must be a mature individual with not less than two years' responsible planning experience. Salary open, depending on qualifications. Apply to City Clerk, 619 16th St., Moline, IL 61265.

Population Projections and Growth Stimulants. The notion that growth is good, or at least inevitable, has been ingrained in much of the planning profession, at least up until recently. One of the classic planning texts, F. Stuart Chapin, Jr.'s *Urban Land Use Planning*, devotes 39 pages to population studies and never once suggests nongrowth as a possible planning alternative. The major theme of the section is that the planner should strive for greater and greater accuracy in his or her population projections. The planner is urged to start with the projection and accommodate the growth with various categories and amounts of land use, rather than first analyzing environmental, social, or economic optimums and then recommending a population limit. Chapin does note that sudden growth can cause problems, but these are defined as methodological to a great extent:

> . . . areas in the throes of a spectacular and particularly a sudden growth cycle present more difficult problems than those experiencing growth at a slower pace. At the same time, this rapidity of change makes the necessity of a population forecast more pressing.[11]

Chapin also advises the planner to err on the high side:

> For land use planning purposes, a single estimate is generally used, with the choice being made with a bias more to the high than the low side. This is based on the reasoning that it is better to err on the high than on the low side in the estimation of space needs for housing, industry, and other land uses.[12]

Now some planners are beginning to wonder whether inflated projections and capital expenditures and projects to meet the projections are not actually causes of growth in themselves. Professor Sanford Farness of the Michigan State University School of Urban Planning noted that:

> Projection theory of population, a method utilized for urban and metropolitan highways, and other types of planning, ignores the fact that population growth should be a deliberate policy made by the particular community or the governmental unit. Consider the case of the Chicago region: I can flatly state that unless additional public facilities and services are created here in the future little population or economic growth can take place . . . . But this is precisely the

122

critical public policy question that is ignored and glossed over in population and economic studies. Instead, most planning agencies derive past population trends through a variety of mathematical methods, producing a future growth estimate to some decade in the future which then becomes a benchmark for defining what are called future "needs" for various kinds of public investment and public facilities. . . . Thus hidden policy decisions made by technicians regarding the future public expense and future levels of taxation are never brought to public awareness or made explicit.[13]

Some planners might object to Professor Farness' criticism of their methods by saying that they are merely being realistic. But others have also accused planners of stimulating or encouraging undesirable growth. The charge has been heard that planners who have advocated urban renewal programs or extensive bonding for capital improvements have contributed to an understandable, but sometimes unrealistic, growth ethic in certain communities which struggle for many years to pay off obligations from an undersized tax base.

How many times have we planners recommended favorable action on new annexations "because some other jurisdiction will get the area if we don't"? How many of us have recommended capital improvements programs on the generalized theme that "it's better to build now than later"? How many have recommended that our jurisdictions apply for federal funds primarily because "the money is there now, but who knows how soon it will dry up"? This is not meant to put undeserved blame on planners or their motives. However, since we planners are charged to deal in the future, we should theoretically at least be able to take a longer view on potentially undesirable growth than others.

Professional Pride and Coping with Growth. One reason the planning profession may be in for some "future shock" is that one of its prime missions has been to "tame" growth, to channel and direct it into a pattern which one hopes is beneficial to the particular residents of the planner's jurisdiction and to the public interest in general. There is a basic feeling among some planners that almost any amount of growth can be handled, given the proper planning influence and controls. As one recent Los Angeles planning report said:

> The mere addition of people has not caused problems in Los Angeles. Problems have been caused by the uncontrolled and undirected growth. The addition of people has not been matched with proper constraints and public services designed to insure the highest possible quality of life for the entire citizenry.[14]

But given the theoretical ability of planning to cope with growth, even the most objective observer would be hard pressed to explain some of the major environmental and social problems which have developed in some communities, such as those in California, which had professional planners on hand during most if not all of their history.

One recent study of San Jose, prepared by the Stanford Environmental Law Society, made the following two conclusions about local planning: ". . . first, the General Plan is inadequate in itself; second, it has been largely ignored in government decision making."[15] Some planners might prefer to dwell on the second reason while ignoring the first and also ignoring the basic question of the wages of rapid growth. The Stanford study charged that local planners and other city officials have almost daily contact with people who represent development interests, but much less with other relevant interests:

> Advocates of the public interest are rarely seen. Thus . . . the innumerable individual decisions made over the years that have helped developers may be due to neutral or even laudable motives. But the results are nonetheless unfortunate.[16]

The planner at times appears to be on a long strip of linoleum. He or she moves rapidly ahead, trying to spread out planning techniques as fast as possible to accommodate growth. The planner tends to forget to look to the rear where, in many cases, the linoleum is rolling right back up behind him. Some planners now seem to feel that the process of accommodating or dealing with growth can sap most of the planning effort. As one member of a planning commission who wrote ASPO on nongrowth noted:

> Planning Commissions such as ours spend the bulk of the time on annexations, subdivisions, planned developments, and rezoning to more intense land usage. Little, if any, time is available to plan for those already living in our community. Our professional planning staff is burdened by the daily investigative task associated with recommendations on growth stimulated petitions. Comprehensive planning too often receives the leftover staff time.[17]

It appears to some segments of our society that environmental, economic, social, and governmental problems have gotten so far out of hand that planning as we know it can no longer "cope with growth." The planner can dismiss this as rhetoric, or he or she can react by taking a new look at nongrowth or more limited growth as a planning alternative, or as a local plea for more lead time and a national growth policy. This report will examine more local problems and alternatives in subsequent sections.

Some experts are saying that our knowledge of how to "deal with" growth has not kept up with growth itself. The handwriting is on the wall, according to some sources. The theme, which will be expanded in the sections on technology and population, is that we haven't done that great a job handling growth up to this point and that the exponential or geometric acceleration of future growth will make things worse.

Make No Big Plans—Quality Versus Mere Survival. One fairly recent article in the *Journal of the American Institute of Planners* asked planners to limit the scope of our actions and adopt a more boundary-oriented view of the world, in part to ensure that unexpected and disastrous consequences be minimized:

> This is turning things around 180 degrees, but we feel this is the only way to proceed. Success has given us freeways, urban renewal, and public housing projects. We must reduce the size of our institutions to ensure their flexibility and respect for the system of which they are a small interacting part.[18]

As another report noted:

> Under the best of conditions and governmental organizations, the population growth of the next few decades will be difficult to accommodate, particularly if the public demands that environmental conditions not be permitted to deteriorate but insists that they be somewhat improved over present conditions.[19]

There seems to be some sentiment in planning and related professions that one way to get a handle on things is to slow down population and other forms of growth. This would allow more lead time to catch up with the problems we have and, at the same time, devote more attention to the concept of amenity as opposed to mere survival dominated by a "coping with growth."

A message is that rapid population and industrial growth force upon us slowly perceived, but often irreversible, changes in our life style or basic living environment. Few planners would be naive enough to suggest that all changes should cease once a certain agreeable (and often prosperous) life style has been achieved. After all, even the basic world environment has changed over relatively long periods of time, with man arriving on the scene extremely late. But many planners might agree that their clients should have some fair notice about the potential changes in life style which might result from or with growth. As the Rockefeller Commission report noted:

> Imbedded in our traditions as to what constitutes the American way of life is freedom from public regulation—virtually free use of water; access to uncongested unregulated roadways;

freedom to do as we please with what we own; freedom from permits, licenses, fees, red tape, and bureaucrats; and freedom to fish, swim, and camp when we will. Clearly, we do not live this way now. Maybe we never did. But everything is relative. The population of 2020 may look back with envy on what, from their vantage point, appears to be our relatively unfettered way of life.[20]

Given the present population, Constitution, traditions, etc., in the U.S., it is most likely that there will continue to be many constraints on human freedom of one sort or another and considerable change, whether we cut back on population growth or not. But one thing seems certain, at least for people who are fairly satisfied with their socio-economic position—an indefinite expansion of growth will certainly not result in any more personal freedom or general stability.

Planner Reactions to Upcoming Hysteria. The planner should become more aware of the costs and implications of growth, but he or she should not rush off in some extreme reaction if it becomes apparent to him or her that growth is not an automatic good. The planner should remember to be comprehensive, cool, and logical when approaching nongrowth, lest some person or group's civil liberties or social welfare get trampled in the process.

The subject of the traditional and constitutional American right to travel and migrate is also explored in the section on nongrowth at the national level. But a few evidences of possibly dangerous trends are mentioned here.

For example, the *California Tomorrow Plan* recommended that a $1,000 fee be collected from new residents from out of state as part of the state income tax process to help "pay for the improvements and services which are provided for all new residents of California and discourage excessive in-migration."[21]

Not to be outdone, various environmental and zero population groups in Colorado are looking westward with apprehension as California residents become disillusioned with overcrowding and pollution. Apparently the second choice of such Californians is to move to Colorado. "This would not be in Colorado's interest," one unpublished report on Colorado's future said. There is also the oft-quoted statement by Oregon's Governor Tom McCall, "Come and visit us again, but for heaven's sake don't come here to live." Others take a more subtle approach: "If you don't want immigrants, don't brag about the place," a Sierra Club representative told a San Francisco Bay Area population growth symposium last March.

The accelerating influences of population and economic growth and the possibility that technology and planning techniques may be growing at a slower rate should be the cause of more concern or at least some informed dialogues. Simple solutions to simplified problems can be viewed with valid skepticism by the planning profession. But the planner should not "tune out" at this point—and let others grab and hold the center stage. It is possible that planners, economists, and other experts have been boxed-in too long with the traditional notions that growth is good. Breaking out of the box may reveal a complex new world, a place of danger, frustration, uncertainty, and numerous blind alleys. But the potential rewards in terms of the environment and individual dignity may justify the risks.

Some Aspects of Nongrowth

This is a wide-ranging section in which issues and problems relating to nongrowth are discussed. Some topics, such as optimum city size and cost/benefit concepts, are covered in detail because this seems to be the initial approach taken by planners and others who challenge growth. Others, such as the biological perspective on growth, are included merely to broaden the perspective. The section starts out with some economic and legal perspectives which are far from definitive, but which attempt to make the point that continued growth is not an axiom in these fields.

Economic—The Stationary-State Economy. A number of traditional economic concerns, such as those of infinite wants and unlimited economic growth, are now being challenged—even by some economists. It is impossible to go into much detail on the new economic offshoots or older economic discards which have again resurfaced as nongrowth, and stationary states become somewhat more respectable. This section will merely skim off some of the highlights and provide a reading list for those who wish to go on further.

Economists such as Herman Daly, Kenneth Boulding, E. J. Mishan, Walter A. Weisskopf, and John Kenneth Galbraith have all questioned and criticized the view that economic growth means progress.

[Report material omitted.]

Legal. Some planners might be more inclined to show an interest in nongrowth as an alternative policy if they thought the idea had any legal foundation. It is not possible to provide any real conclusive legal analysis in this report. The budget did not allow for outside legal consultants, and the general legal environment for nongrowth seems to be intertwined with that of exclusionary zoning and other planning policies which attempt to keep people out of a community because of their race or income level. Some might even say that exclusionary zoning cases have overshadowed some of the more legitimate attempts by communities aimed at environmental protection and stability along with social justice.

The building interests have been quick to remind planners about the legal pitfalls of nongrowth. As one recent publication on planned unit development noted:

> In 1966 the Pennsylvania Supreme Court, in a landmark decision, ruled that a certain suburban town could not zone a large portion of its undeveloped area for four-acre lots. Since then, several other state supreme court decisions have upheld the same principle: zoning cannot be used to hold down a town's population growth. Other more recent court decisions have ruled out zoning as a device to exclude lower income people.
>
> In other words, what . . . concerned residents consider an important part of their town's defense against an engulfing wave of new development might well be overturned if a builder chose to take it to court.[22] [Note: apparently the case mentioned is *National Land and Investment Co. v. Kohn*, 419 Pa. 504, 215 A.2d 597 (1965).]

The environmental movement, however, has apparently started to drive a wedge into the general legal position that all forms of nongrowth are illegal. Some foundation for such a wedge might be found in two dissents in the Mineral King Valley, California, case which reached the U.S. Supreme Court in April 1972. In this case, the court ruled 4-3 against the Sierra Club on a single procedural issue. The Sierra Club was attempting to stop a Walt Disney complex in the secluded wilderness area in the Sierra Nevadas. One dissenter in this case was Justice William O. Douglas who put forth the concept that environmental issues should be litigated "in the name of the inanimate object about to be despoiled, defaced, or invaded by roads and bulldozers and where injury is the subject of public outrage." This would seem to indicate that since a corporation has a legal personality in corporate law, a valley or a river might also have a legal personality for the purposes of environmental law. The dissent by Justice Harry Blackmun might be even more appropriate to the subject of this report:

> Must our law be so rigid and our procedural concepts so inflexible that we render ourselves

helpless when the existing methods and the traditional concepts do not quite fit and do not prove to be entirely adequate for new issues?

In a more specific legal challenge to a community's power to regulate its growth, the town of Ramapo, New York, found its zoning ordinance, which attempts to phase development according to the availability of public facilities, upheld in May 1972 by the highest court in the state, the Court of Appeals.[23] The ordinance applies to the unincorporated area of the town, which contains about 45,000 residents.

One emerging legal issue is likely to be how far the government can go in separating development rights from the traditional rights associated with property ownership. One attempt in this direction is reflected in Senate Bill No. 254 introduced in the 1972 session of the Maryland State Senate. The bill called for a new set of property interests, to be called "developmental rights."

The concepts of social justice and a regional approach seem to be some of the major legal keystones to a successful growth limitation policy. As one unpublished report generally favorable to nongrowth, which was prepared by Richard D. Lamm, who is a lawyer and Colorado legislator, and Steve Davison, said:

> Municipal communities do not exist in a vacuum, and growth restrictions obviously must be part of a regional plan. Local governments must also begin to coordinate their zoning ordinances and subdivision regulations on a regional basis so that industrial development and location and construction of housing units are designed to achieve regional goals. It may be the regional policy, for instance, to make population density uniform throughout a region. Each community in a region should then cooperate with each other to adopt uniform zoning ordinances and subdivision regulations designed to implement this policy, or it may be the regional decision to concentrate growth in one area and leave other areas agricultural, open space, or green belt. . . .
>
> . . . The courts would likely approve such cooperation and coordination by local governments. Local governments have been allowed to "provide cooperatively for the needs of neighboring communities as well as their own," (Andrews v. Board of Adjustment, 30 N.J. 245, 251, 152 A.2d 580, 583 (1959) and have even been required to give due consideration to the needs and conditions of surrounding communities (Borough of Cresskill v. Borough of Dumont, 15 N.J. 238, 104 A.2d 441 (1954). See Haar, Regionalism and Realism in Land-Use Planning, 105 U. Pa. L. Rev. 515 (1957); Note, Zoning Against the Public Welfare: Judicial Limitations on Municipal Parochialism, 71 Yale L. J. 720 (1962). See also River Vale Township v. Town of Orangetown, 403 F.2d 684 (2 Cir. 1968). Through such coordination and cooperation, local communities would not have to allow every use within their boundaries (Cf. Fanale v. Borough of Hasbrouck Heights, 26 N.J. 320, 325, 139 A.2d 749, 752 (1958), provided that an excluded industry—which could not be prohibited in every community as a nuisance—could be located in nearby communities (See Duffcon Concrete Products, Inc., v. Borough of Cresskill, 1 N.J. 509, 64 A.2d 347 (1949).[24]

Obviously, Lamm and Davison's regional strategies seem designed more to redistribute growth around a region than to stop it cold. Nevertheless, the connection of growth limitation to regional cooperation should not be ignored.

However, given the general lack of cooperation and effective planning in many regions, what are some possible parameters for an individual community to consider regarding nongrowth? Winton Woods, a professor of law at the University of Arizona in Tucson, made the following observations:

> No one would argue that a city faced with a limited supply of water could not prohibit all future growth in order to preserve the public health. On the other hand, modern judicial opinion holds that a community cannot intentionally exclude "undesirables" from its midst. But between these extremes lies a broad group of de facto exclusions that may one day be upheld in order to preserve the basic characteristics of a given community.

Nongrowth As A Planning Alternative

After citing the basic rights of freedom of movement which have been upheld by the U.S. Supreme Court on a number of occasions, Woods noted:

> Against such a background, any governmental attempt to influence or control the pattern of interstate migration must meet a heavy burden of justification. Any policy intended to exclude the poor, the nonwhite, or the unpopular would, regardless of rationalization, be unconstitutionally discriminatory and void under the Fourteenth Amendment's equal protection clause. But what of a nondiscriminatory policy intended to preserve and protect basic environmental quality?
>
> . . . One man's right to move to the city may infringe upon the right of those already there to preserve the amenities that brought them in the first place. Must Santa Barbara become Los Angeles? Or may it act to stop "progress" that would alter if not destroy its unique balance of land, sea, and city? Must the state of Vermont stand mute while the inexorable pressure of population turns it from its past towards New York's most pleasant bedroom community? Clearly, the answer to these questions must be negative.[25]

It is rather obvious to the author after talking to lawyers such as Woods and Lamm that the nonexclusionary part of nongrowth must be more than lip service. The legal and moral form of nongrowth which emerges for a local community is close to a sort of net figure resulting from dynamic in-migration which balances or relates to the out-migration. Every effort should be made to include a variety of races, income groups, etc., in the in-migration. With regard to the natural increase from births, the community will have to analyze how many young people are naturally leaving the community, whether this rate is too low or too high, and what altering the rate means in terms of growth, public facilities, etc.

But while it seems to be accepted that communities should be diverse, it remains open to question whether they all have to become some form of Los Angeles to satisfy some interpretation of social justice. It is interesting to note the new "strange bedfellows" of homebuilders' associations (representing some of the interests involved in building high-cost housing in exclusionary suburbs) and civil rights and antiexclusionary groups that are apparently in common cause to fight nongrowth efforts by communities.

Energy and Resources. Planners have always prided themselves on being comprehensive, but perhaps they have not been comprehensive enough to realize all the apparent results of growth. The energy crisis is a case in point.

[Report material omitted.]

Optimum City Size—Costs and Benefits. One reaction to a controversial topic such as nongrowth is to relate it to some rather universal population figure which indicates optimum city size. It is easier to advocate a halt to growth if one can show that a community is coming up near the optimum figure. Once a community has passed the optimum, however, it becomes necessary to either write it off or else advocate some form of decentralization or dispersal (hopefully voluntary).

With the emergence of nongrowth sentiment in some communities, there has been a sort of revival of the old optimum city size idea with a few new twists. While there have been a few attempts to determine an optimum based on the physical environment's carrying capacity (such as the one prepared by the Lake Tahoe Regional Planning Agency), such studies are complex, expensive, and time-consuming. Also, the jurisdiction of many planners does not fit the description of a closed or independent environmental system such as a valley or basin.

Information on items of extreme community concern such as taxes and crime is easier to obtain and present. Whether a narrow emphasis on economic cost-revenue and/or crime rate data is really desirable or to the point, such studies have taken place in some early attempts to justify nongrowth. Therefore, it is the purpose of this section to look at these parameters, along with some others which, in total at least, might ultimately provide some sound basis for growth limitation policies.

One rather persistent current of thought in the planning profession has held that there is an optimum size of city which is something less than a megalopolis.

. . . In summary, it appears that the beauty of many past optimum city concepts has often been in the eye of the beholder. Various analysts approached the optimum with preconceptions which were then realized. In more recent works, the optimum concept has usually been in economic terms, especially the public economics related to the costs and benefits of municipal services. However, it is important to note a sort of historical paradox in America. Our cities became progressively larger and more people lived in them, but there was always a general undertone favoring the rural, small town atmosphere.

With such a perplexing American history regarding growth and optimum city size, and with people tending to view optimums to serve a wide range of perceived and often subjective goods, it should surprise no one that we still have no clear notion of the optimum size for a city, or even what factors to consider or how to rank them.

More recent years have witnessed a confusion of estimates, even when the studies are almost purely economic. Parentheses and question marks abound as economists throw out figures.

. . . Some analysts have produced arguments that favored the consolidation of cities too small to realize net economies of scale in public production, while others have called for fragmenting or splitting the metropolitan area into a number of smaller cities to improve urban efficiency and provide a greater spatial differentiation in the supply of urban public services.

It can be seen that optimums have been discussed in both maximum and minimum terms. However, the planner who looks for a good simple optimum based on some concept of economic efficiency in the public sector is going to be disappointed. There is nothing comparable to the definitive standards planners have come to depend upon in other areas of their work. An optimum figure for the most efficient city size can fall almost anywhere.

The primitive state of the art has not prevented planners and other experts from concocting seemingly authoritative efficiency models for their clients. For example, the ACIR report, *Urban and Rural America: Policies for Future Growth*, included a regression analysis to isolate the population factor from other factors that might influence per capita government costs—population, density, rate of population growth, and population size. The fact that no one seems to know what the optimum size of a city should be, or how to establish and interpret economic criteria related to an efficient and optimum city, should not necessarily stop planners from moving in this direction. The basic point of this ASPO report is that they should do so in an objective and comprehensive manner.

Even some relatively good work in this area can be subject to distortion or misinterpretation. For example, Barton-Aschman Associates, a national planning consultant firm, prepared a cost-revenue analysis of various land uses for Barrington, a distant suburban area northwest of Chicago.[26] School expenditures in the Barrington area account for over 70 per cent of all local governmental expenditures. The study found that "more expensive homes ($100,000 range) are likely to exhibit modest net (school) tax deficits," while "homes in lower price brackets will be capable of producing substantial net (school) tax deficits." The report concludes "Unless developments of this type are accompanied by sufficient nonresidential development, additional tax burdens will be placed upon existing property owners." Apartments were found to generate high school costs, but produce even larger tax revenues. The results were reported in newspaper stories with headlines such as "Low Cost Housing Can Hurt Tax Base." In one newspaper article, the authors of the report said their conclusions were directed to the factual situation in Barrington. But an Urban Land Institute spokesman was reported as saying that the report would apply, at least in broad outline, to much of the nation.

In a 14-page follow-up article in *Urban Land*,[27] the authors of the Barrington cost-revenue study noted on the last page that cost-revenue comparisons can be regarded only as approximations, that environmental health and environmental conservation "externalities" may sometimes be much more important than any pertinent numerical cost-revenue comparisons. The authors also said that any expected impact upon broader environmental considerations—including "traffic patterns, zoning, housing choice, aesthetics, and balanced urban growth—will often be of overriding importance."

Planners will have to consider both the public and the private economy in their optimal size deliberations. The private economic benefits of concentration of substantial amounts of production in one location have to be considered, along with the economies of size with relation to exchanges in the production of goods and services. Private income levels in various-sized cities should be considered. Studies which discuss only the per capita cost of urban public services apparently assume that per capita gross income is a constant. Some studies have shown a tendency for such income to increase with city size.[28] Planners will have to evaluate the economies of the competition of more market entrants in larger communties with the near monopoly array of various commercial services in smaller communities. Trade-offs are certainly possible, depending on the views of the citizens and their concept of the broad public interest, but planners should better identify the trade-offs.

The planner should range beyond economic parameters in drawing up city size optimums. This may be the only route to success in a very difficult assignment. Dr. Otis Dudley Duncan, a University of Michigan Professor of Sociology and a member of the Commission on Population Growth and the American Future, back in 1956 listed a host of factors that might be relevant to determination of an optimum:

> . . . accessibility, health, crime and safety, educational facilities, leisure and recreational activities, social institutions, community and family ties, psychological and mental health hazards, and the desire for political participation.[29]

The planner should be familiar with people's desire for the "best of both worlds." But he or she should also know from past experience on other topics that this is seldom possible and that trade-offs are frequently involved. The planner should try and make some informed recommendations on these trade-offs. The question at this point is how planners can start on the right road to develop a notion of optimum city size and chart the costs and benefits of growth. Some new beginnings are needed, based on some broader base than traditional economics.

The preoccupation with economics has diverted some attention away from environmental parameters on city size. These, along with social and psychological factors, may be much more important in future meaningful optimum city estimates. Economists still are not in agreement on which considerations are "external" and which are "internal" to the concept of an efficient city. They have trouble with pollution, which some call the "major externality." The economic quantification of pollution costs in terms of human health, plant and animal life, and building and property damage has been slow to develop.

Nongrowth As A Planning Alternative

Somewhere between Plato and Aristotle and the present, or even between medieval city builders and the present, man may have forgotten the full range of factors which should shape (and maybe stop) the growth of cities. The relatively recent acceleration of environmental concern, counter-cultures, and amenity rights have prompted the question to come up again, but we are devoid of answers.

Growth presents problems not only in representation, but in administrative complexity and bureaucracy. As a community grows, its management direction and planning become more complex. There are methods which planners and other officials can use to restructure their functions to cope with the greater complexity, but these usually involve some costs. These costs can involve increased impersonality, more committees, greater specialization, and less attention to the needs of the community as a whole. Effective coordination can also become more difficult, both internally and externally.

This is a complex issue which could vary from community to community. There appear to be some advantages in having a planning operation and jurisdiction which are large enough to handle the real problems. But there is probably a delicate balance between "large enough" and "too large."

[The section concludes with an examination of other elements, as social factors, and other views: census, biological, national, and world; material omitted.]

Case Studies and Local Examples

In the three basic cases described below and on the following pages, ASPO research was done in person by the author. Following these cases, there are two California cases where information was supplied to ASPO by a local planner or planners, primarily in response to a list of specific questions. Finally, there are several instances cited in which most of the information was obtained by letters, newspaper clippings, and various other secondary sources. The cases, especially those directly researched by ASPO, get to the meat of some key nongrowth questions. Of special interest is the role of the planner as a local nongrowth issue germinates and develops. The comments and experiences of local, county, and regional planners involved in these specific cases should be helpful to a great many of their professional colleagues.

The first three cases which follow—Boulder, Colorado; Orange County, California; and the Willamette Valley in Oregon—represent the only detailed field research performed in connection with this report. Most of the material presented was gained through field trips by the author in April and early May of 1972. The major emphasis in the case studies, especially the first three, will be on the "why" of the issues and not on the "how." One reason for this will be the fact that no city has discovered the ultimate, legal, and socially responsible way to stop its growth as a matter of public policy. Some growth studies will be mentioned in the case studies and other local examples, but most of these were in their early stages as this report was prepared. Another reason is the basic contention of this report that some fundamental changes in attitudes of both planners and clients are needed before serious progress can be made in the treatment of growth as a critical variable which can be affected by public policies. When it comes to attitude analysis, especially in something as new as nongrowth, the "why" may be of more critical importance than the "how." The list of cases and examples is far from exhaustive, but the major cases are presented in some depth.

[This material is omitted; there are 33 pages of case studies, selected readings, and appendices in the original ASPO PAS Report No. 283.]

Footnotes

1. Alvin Toffler, *Future Shock* (New York: Bantam Books, Inc., 1971), pp. 32-34.
2. Donella H. Meadows, Dennis L. Meadows, Jorgen Randers, and William W. Behrens III., *The Limits to Growth* (New York: Universe Books, 1972).
3. *Population and the American Future: The Report of the U.S. Commission on Population Growth and the American Future* (New York: Signet Books, The New American Library, Inc., 1972).
4. "A Blast at Planned Parenthood," (a report on a speech by the vice-president for academic affairs at Howard University), *San Francisco Chronicle*, October 27, 1971, p. 2.
5. See, for example, "Don't Knock the $2-Trillion Economy," by Columbia University economists Peter Passel and Leonard Ross in the *New York Times Magazine*, March 5, 1972.
6. Henry C. Wallich, "Zero Growth," *Newsweek*, January 24, 1972, p. 62.
7. "Growth is Not a Four-Letter Word," *New York Times*, February 17, 1972, p. 37.
8. *Report of the National Advisory Commission on Civil Disorders* (New York: Bantam Books, Inc., 1968), p. 251.
9. Anthony Lewis, "Ecology and Politics," *New York Times*, March 6, 1971, p. 31.
10. Herman E. Daly, "Towards a Stationary-State Economy," in *Comprehensive Planning Process for Wayne County: Planning and the Environment*, Wayne County Planning Commission, Detroit, MI 48216, 1971, pp. 133-134.
11. F. Stuart Chapin, Jr., *Urban Land Use Planning* (Urbana, Ill.: University of Illinois Press, 1965), p. 197.
12. *Ibid.*, p. 202.
13. Sanford S. Farness, "The Democratic Choice of Ecologically Determined Regional Population," *ECHO Brochure Number 1*, Defenders of the Fox River, Inc., 9 Otis Road, Barrington, IL 60010, March 23, 1970, pp. 3-4.
14. *Population and Zoning Issues Raised by the Concept Portion of the General Plan*, a report from the Los Angeles Department of City Planning to the City Planning Commission, January 20, 1971, p. 1.
15. Stanford Environmental Law Society, *San Jose: Sprawling City* (Stanford, Calif.: Stanford Law School, 1971), p. 2.
16. *Ibid.*, p. 24.
17. Letter from Howard T. Bonnett, Planning Commissioner, City of Eugene, Oregon, March 14, 1972.
18. C. S. Holling and M. A. Goldberg, "Ecology and Planning," *Journal of the American Institute of Planners*, July 1971, p. 229.
19. "Is Dispersal the Answer to Urban Overgrowth?" *Urban Land*, January 1970, pp. 9-10.
20. *Population and the American Future*, p. 73.
21. *Ibid.*, p. 15.
22. Maxwell C. Huntoon, Jr. "PUD—A Better Way for the Suburbs" (Washington, D.C.: The Urban Land Institute, 1971), p. 16.
23. See the ASPO magazine, *Planning*, July 1972, pp. 108-113, for a detailed discussion of the Ramapo case and relevant passages from the zoning ordinance.
24. Richard D. Lamm and Steven A. G. Davison, "Legal Control of Growth" (unpublished), November 1971. (This paper subsequently was revised and published in the *Denver Law Journal*, Vol. 49, No. 1, 1972.) Those interested may contact Lamm in care of the University of Denver, 200 W. 14th Avenue, Denver, CO 80204.
25. Winton D. Woods, Jr., "Control of Migration and the Urban Crisis" (unpublished draft), April 2, 1971, University of Arizona, College of Law, Tucson, AZ 85721, pp. 9-10.
26. Barton-Aschman Associates, Inc., *The Barrington, Illinois, Area–Cost-Revenue Analysis of Land-Use Alternatives* (Chicago, Ill.: 1970).
27. Darwin G. Stuart and Robert B. Teska, "Who Pays For What? A Cost-Revenue Analysis of Suburban Land Use Alternatives," *Urban Land*, March 1971.
28. Baum, *Issues in Optimal City Size*, (Los Angeles: University of California, Graduate School of Management, 1971), p. 28.
29. Otis Dudley Duncan, "Optimum Size of Cities," in *Demographic Analysis*, eds., Joseph J. Spengler and Otis Dudley Duncan (Glencoe, Ill., 1956), pp. 372-385.

A Review of the Literature

The following materials are reprinted with the permission of the American Society of Planning Officials. The listing below is a digest of an 18-page annotated bibliography by Earl Finkler, titled "Nongrowth: A Review of the Literature". Published as an ASPO Planning Advisory Service Report—PAS No. 289, March 1973—it is available only to PAS subscribers for $5.00, prepaid, from ASPO; 1313 East Sixtieth Street; Chicago, Illinois 60637.

Nongrowth As A Planning Alternative

Introduction

This bibliography is a follow-up to ASPO's previous Planning Advisory Service report entitled *Nongrowth as a Planning Alternative*. The subtitle of the original report was "A Preliminary Examination of an Emerging Issue." The issue of growth versus nongrowth is emerging rapidly and unmistakably as illustrated by the number of reports noted here which have been published recently.

Local reports are emphasized in this bibliography because, in the opinion of the author, this is where the real action is taking place on the nongrowth issue. Notices were placed in the ASPO job bulletin *TAB* that we were looking for local planning reports dealing with growth versus nongrowth for listing in a bibliography. The response was good and information was received from many areas of the country. This bibliography is generally annotated, and it stresses reports which are both recent and available for public distribution. The notes about the reports are intended to provide both an overview and some useful information to those unable to obtain a copy. There are 25 local reports annotated. These came from eight states in almost every geographic region of the country, although California led the list with eight sources. The selected list of reports, both local and general, is not comprehensive or all-inclusive, but it should give the planner a view as to recent contributions to the growth-nongrowth debate.

Some who read these reports, especially those from the local agencies, might be disappointed in their quality and grasp of the complex problems surrounding growth versus nongrowth. Some might not get beyond the overly simple and rather convenient conclusion that all forms of nongrowth are merely a sham to cover up exclusion and racial prejudice. These responses, in the opinion of the author, fail to grasp the idea that calls for nongrowth might signal a basic feeling of alienation and frustration in this country. Planners perhaps are being asked to respond with new value sets, guidelines for changing life styles and greatly improved and more innovative recommendations. Some are calling for basic redistribution of resources, rather than continued reliance on the filtering down of supposed benefits from rapid growth. A "business-as-usual" approach with a few cosmetic references to growth and the environment might not be good enough anymore in many jurisdictions. On the other hand, the planner might go through a long and exhaustive set of meetings, reports, and exchanges with citizens and political leaders and discover that now the majority of citizens really want to implement the old open space plan the planner proposed 10 years ago.

The big need at this point is for a free exchange of information and for planners to be able to think out loud about possible innovations, including nongrowth. It is hoped that this bibliography will be a small contribution to this process.

Local Reports

1. *Expanding the Environmental Responsibility of Local Government-Claremont's Environmental Task Force and Its Recommendations.* Available from the Center for California Public Affairs, Claremont Colleges, Claremont, CA 91711. Sept. 1972. 172 pp. $4.50.

2. *Garden Grove General Plan—Growth Policy Element.* Garden Grove, Urban Development Department, 11391 Acacia Parkway, Garden Grove, CA 92640. 46 pp. (Working document; final report in preparation as of February 1973.)

3. *Open Space vs. Development.* Livingston and Blayney, City and Regional Planners. Available from the City of Palo Alto, Civic Center, Palo Alto, CA 94301. 1971. 194 pp. $4.

4. *Pleasanton General Plan Review—Alternate Growth Policies.* Prepared by Livingston and Blayney, City and Regional Planners, 40 Gold St., San Francisco, CA 94133. Oct. 1972. 16 pp., plus appendices and tables. (Availability unknown.) For more information, contact Ricardo Castro, Director of Community Development, City of Pleasanton, Drawer C, Pleasanton, CA 94566.

5. *Economic Analysis Project—The Economics of Urbanization; Phase-1 Final Report: San Diego Joint City/County Task Force report.* Available from San Diego County Environmental Development Agency, 1600 Pacific Highway, San Diego, CA 92101. Feb. 1973. 128 pp. Free; supply limited.

6. *Urban Growth Policy for the San Francisco Bay Region.* Issue Paper No. 1. Feb. 1972. 6 pp. Free.

7. *Formulation of Regional Growth Policy for the San Francisco Bay Region.* Issue Paper No. 2. Nov. 1972. 11 pp. Free.

8. *Zoning and Growth in the San Francisco Bay Area.* Issue Paper No. 3. March, 1973. 8 pp. Free.

9. *Santa Rosa Optimum Growth Study.* Prepared by Livingston and Blayney, City and Regional Planners (see previous listing for Palo Alto and Pleasanton). Available from Santa Rosa City Planning Commission, Box 1678, Santa Rosa, CA 95403. Jan. 1973. 137 pp. $5 to $10, depending on source and location of request. The higher rates are for individuals and government units outside of California.

10. *The Costs and Benefits of Alternative Open Space Policies: A Report to the City Council and the City of Thousand Oaks and the Conejo Recreation and Park District.* Gruen Gruen and Associates. Available from the City of Thousand Oaks Planning Department, P.O. Box 1496, Thousand Oaks, CA 91360. Feb. 1973. 155 pp. $15.

11. *A Report on Population Growth in the City of Aurora.* Department of Planning and Community Development, Aurora, CO 80010. March 1973. 76 pp. No information on availability.

12. *OPUG—A Growth Policy for Manatee County, Florida.* Manatee County Planning Department, 212 Sixth Ave. East, Bradenton, FL 33505. May 1973, 45 pp. Free.

13. *Growth Policies and Projections for the Chicago-Northwestern Indiana Standard Consolidated Area.* Walter Vissotski. June 28, 1972, 53 pp.

14. *Forecast Decisions Facing the Chicago-Northwestern Indiana Standard Consolidated Area 1972-2020.* December 1972. 11 pp.

15. *Components of Demographic and Economic Growth of the Chicago-Northwestern Indiana Standard Consolidated Area.* Mary Deming and William Dieber. Jan. 12, 1973. 49 pp.

16. *Regional Growth Policy and Governmental Powers.* Walter Vissotski. Feb. 5, 1973. 16 pp.

17. *Alternative Demographic and Employment Forecasts for the Chicago-Northwestern Indiana Standard Consolidated Area.* Mary Deming and William Dieber. April 25, 1973. 44 pp. (plus tables).

18. *Final Report of the Select Committee on Goals for Amherst.* January 1973. 127 pp. Available in very limited quantities from Town Planner, James Cope, Town Hall, Amherst, MA 01002 for $3.50 (prepaid). A 16-page summary is available in greater numbers for 40 cents per copy (prepaid).

19. *Rapid Growth: A General Discussion of Problems and Solutions for the Old Colony Planning Council Area.* Old Colony Planning Council, 232 Main St., Brockton, MA 02401. April, 1973. 54 pp. $3.

20. *The Ann Arbor Growth Study.* Ann Arbor City Planning Department. Available from the City Clerk, Box 647, Ann Arbor, MI 48107. Oct. 1972. 435 pp. $10 (prepaid).

21. *Santa Fe Growth Impact Study.* City of Santa Fe Planning Department, P.O. Box 909, Santa Fe, NM 87501. June 1973. $2. An accompanying technical report is also available for $2.

22. *Land-Use Plan Alternatives for Dane County, Wisconsin.* Dane County Regional Planning Commission, Room 312, City-County Building, Madison, WI 53709. Oct. 1972. 100 pp. $2.

23. *Citizen Response to Land-Use Plan Alternatives, Part I: Report and Analysis of Community Meetings, Questionnaire Returns and Regional Conference Working Paper.* Jan. 1973. 67 pp. 50 cents.

24. *Citizen Response to Land-Use Plan Alternatives, Part II: Complete Transcript of Written Comments Submitted by Organizations and Individuals.* Jan. 1973. $1. (Only a handful of copies were left as this report was being prepared. The Dane County planners said they might reprint it if several requests came in.)

25. *More Is Less.* Capital Community Citizens, 114 N. Carroll St., Madison, WI 53703. March 1973. 76 pp. $2.25.

General National Reports

26. *Demographic and Social Aspects of Population Growth.* Commission on Population Growth and the American Future. Charles F. Westoff and Robert Parke, Jr., Editors. Vol. I of Commission research reports. Available from Superintendent of Documents, U.S.G.P.O., Washington, DC 20402. 1972. 674 pp. $5.55.

27. *Population, Resources, and the Environment.* Commission on Population Growth and the American Future. Ronald G. Ridker, Editor. Vol. III of Commission research reports. Available from Superintendent of Documents, U.S.G.P.O., Washington, DC 20402. 1972. 377 pp. $4.25.

28. *Population Movements and the Shape of Urban Growth: Implications for Public Policy.* Prepared for the Commission on Population Growth and the American Future by Peter A. Morrison of the Rand Corporation. Available from the Publications Department, The Rand Corporation, 1700 Main Street, Santa Monica, CA 90406. Aug. 1972. 71 pp. $3.

29. *The Use of Land: The Citizens' Policy Guide to Urban Growth.* June 1973. Task Force on Land Utilization and Urban Growth, Laurance S. Rockefeller, Chairman. Available from Thomas Y. Crowell Co., New York. June 1973, 384 pp. $10; $3.95 (paperback).

30. *Toward a Steady-State Economy.* Herman E. Daly, Editor. W. H. Freeman and Co., 660 Market St., San Francisco, CA 94104. 1973. 332 pp. $8.95; $3.95 (paperback).

31. *No-Growth and the Poor—Equity Considerations in Controlled Growth Policies.* (Unpublished paper.) M. Agelasto, Department of City and Regional Planning, University of California at Berkeley. March 1973. (Availability unknown.)

Legal Reports

32. *Controlling Urban Growth—But for Whom? The Social Implications of Development Timing Controls.* Herbert M. Franklin. Available from the Potomac Institute, Inc., 1501 18th St., N.W., Washington, DC 20036. March 1973. 41 pp. 75 cents (quantity prices on request).

33. "The Right To Travel: Another Constitutional Standard for Local Land-Use Regulations?" By Richard Fielding in *University of Chicago Law Review,* Vol. 39 (1972), pp. 612-638.

34. *A Beginning Acquaintance: Planning and the Right To Travel.* Sue Goldsmith. Available from the Tucson Planning Department, P.O. Box 5547, Tucson, AZ 85703. Dec. 1972. 19 pp. (There may be a slight charge for reproduction of this unpublished paper.)

35. "Proposed Development Rights Legislation Can Change the Name of the Land Investment Game." By Jerome Rose in *Real Estate Law Journal,* Winter 1973.

36. *Legal and Political Aspects of Reducing the Rate of Urban Growth: A Study of Vista, California.* Bruce W. Oliver, 8309 E. Beverly Drive, San Gabriel, CA 91775. Spring 1973. 33 pp. (Availability unknown.)

ASPO Conference Tapes

Tapes of the sessions on Growth Controls at the ASPO National Planning Conference in Los Angeles. April 9, 1973. The following cassettes are available from On-the-Spot Duplicators, Inc., 13356 Sherman Way, North Hollywood, CA 91605 at a cost of $4.95 each.

37. *Growth Controls I—Cost-Revenue Approaches to Growth*

This session featured John Blayney, the consultant who prepared the Palo Alto development-versus-open-space study; Bill Lamont, the planning director and acting city manager of Boulder, Colorado; Professor Hyung C. Chung of the University of Bridgeport, who did a cost-revenue study for Ramapo, New York; John Goldberg of the Sacramento County planning department; and Bill Toner, an economist on the planning staff of Orange County, California. There was also audience participation, generally focused on the effects of growth controls on the price of housing. (When ordering cassettes, ask for session no. 6.)

38. *Growth Controls II—Luncheon Session*

The featured speakers at the luncheon session were Mayor Pete Wilson of San Diego, who discussed his city's attempts to limit and direct growth, and Robert Wood, president of the University of Massachusetts, who spoke about the report of the Rockefeller Commission on Population Growth and the American Future and the response by the Nixon administration to urban problems. (When ordering cassette, ask for session no. 10.)

39. *Growth Controls III—Legal Devices and Related Issues*

This might be the best of the three tapes. The session featured attorney Herbert Franklin of the Potomac Institute Metropolitan Housing Project; Professor Winton Woods of the College of Law at the University of Arizona in Tucson; Al Bell, the director of the Orange County, California, Growth Study Policy Team; Bill Lamont of Boulder; and David Peterson, a planning and economic consultant from California, who wound up with a superb overview of the nongrowth issue in California. (When ordering cassette, ask for session no. 15.)

The author served as moderator of sessions I and III and wrote a short review entitled "Toward a Planning Philosophy of Nongrowth." This is available free of charge from the Defenders of the Fox River Incorporated, 94 Otis Road, Barrington Hills, IL 60010.

Managing Growth:

Report of the ICMA Committee on Growth and the Environment

International City Management Association

This article originally appeared in the September 1973 issue of Public Management, and is reprinted with permission © 1973; PM is a monthly magazine of the International City Management Association; 1140 Connecticut Avenue, N.W.; Washington, D.C. 20036.

This is one of five reports of the ICMA 1973 Municipal Management Policy Committees—as explained by Laurence Rutter, National Policy Coordinator, in the footnotes section of this article.

The Report in Brief

Although both growth and the environment are extremely important concerns of government today, and highly interrelated, this report will focus primarily on the problem of managing growth. The report deals with the problem of excessive population growth, its impact at the local level, and local programs for dealing with growth.

The problem of excessive growth has received much attention in recent years, with great public concern, national action, and intensive study. Most attention has tended to ignore or play down the role of local government in managing such growth. Thus, this report deals primarily with that role.

Every level of government (federal, state, and local) has a role to play in dealing with growth. But, because localities are heavily involved in land use and other growth-related services and programs, and because of their ability to maximize citizens' freedom of choice on where and how they live, and because unless they act they may lose the initiative to states and other entities, localities should exercise leadership in controlling excessive population growth.

There will be a number of constraints upon local government if it attempts to assume the leadership in dealing with growth. Many federal programs inadvertently undermine local efforts to control growth. At least one prospective federal program will cause local government to work in greater concert with both states and the federal government. Also, localities will find themselves constrained by the ineffectiveness of traditional local programs for dealing with growth, such as zoning and comprehensive planning.

In view of the importance of excessive population growth, the unique ability of local government to deal with growth, and the constraints on local government in managing growth, it is recommended that the professionals work with their administrations and governing bodies to assess community growth needs and adopt a community growth policy. Desirable levels of growth should be defined in terms of both the timing of growth and the area to be covered by future populations.

Managing Growth

In developing growth programs, managers should explore the available techniques for land use control, recognize the importance of capital projects as part of growth programs, create within the municipal attorney's office a division dealing with land use and other growth-related issues, pay close attention to policies that cause land developers to pay the secondary costs of development, and ensure that growth policies do not create de facto racial or economic segregation.

Umbrella regional organizations should seek to coordinate local growth policies and provide localities with information and technical assistance that will enable them to make informed and rational growth decisions.

The role of states should be one of protecting the overall interests of citizens with regard to land use, conservation of resources, and protection of the environment. Coordination and development of growth policies in urban areas, however, should be left to umbrella regional bodies. States should provide funds for the management and planning of local growth programs, and should enact legislation that permits localities to assume a strong role in land use regulation.

National concerns related to growth should be cared for through federal programs, but these programs should be consistent with the efforts of localities to manage growth. Funds for assisting the local planning and management of growth should be available.

ICMA should provide the membership with information and technical assistance related to growth, encourage state associations of managers to work for appropriate state enabling legislation on growth, work closely with the other associations representing local and state government in seeking appropriate congressional and administrative actions, and report to the membership at the 1974 Annual Business Meeting on the progress made on implementing recommendations of the committee adopted by the membership.

Introduction

Growth and the environment are two areas of concern to municipal management that are extraordinarily broad. They also are highly interrelated and often overlapping. A very lengthy report would be necessary to do justice to both areas of policy. In spite of the interrelationships and overlapping concerns, the focus of the study and report of this committee must be narrowed to just one of these extremely important policy areas.

This report will focus on the problem of growth in the hope that a committee of ICMA will examine the management of the environment in the near future. It will look at policies and programs that are most relevant to growth, but by necessity will deal also with programs, policies, and problems that are related to the environment.

Excessive growth and local government. There are a variety of dimensions to growth and a number of perspectives from which to examine growth. However, this report looks at excessive population growth from the perspective of local government.

Rapid population increase and its potential consequences on the quality of life are aspects of growth that are both novel and pressing today. Recently, people have begun to realize that a growing nation eventually begins to use up its natural resources faster than they can be replenished. Vacant land and clean air and water have become increasingly scarce in the last half of the 20th century.

Decades of growth for which we have been unprepared have produced highly wasteful, inefficient, ineffective, and unsightly urban sprawl across the nation. Commuting times in even smaller metropolitan areas have become enormous. Congestion has produced air and water pollution almost everywhere in North America. Vital energy sources are being depleted rapidly. Never before has the United States had to deal with these problems on so large a scale.

Population growth and its consequences can be addressed through a variety of programs by local government. The programs include land use regulation (zoning, subdivision control, open space, and comprehensive planning), regulation of capital projects both public and private, sewer and water programs, transportation, environmental controls, and building and housing codes.

Many of these programs have been carried out routinely by local governments. Some have not. But, few local governments have handled these programs in a coordinated fashion, with their consequences for growth clearly in mind.

Because of the novel and pressing nature of growth, and the need for unprecedented coordination of growth-related programs and policies, this report will concentrate on the problem of excessive population growth.

A major result of the concern over excessive growth has been the increasing demands being made on government to begin to effectively manage, or at least guide, growth and its consequences. The demands have resulted in several tentative national growth programs. For example, Title VII of the Housing Act of 1970 called upon the President to prepare a biennial report on national growth policy.

Currently before the Congress are a number of alternative federal proposals for managing land use. At the same time, there has been what has been called a "quiet revolution" in land use controls, with many states assuming the powers and prerogatives once left solely to local government.

Also, in response to these demands, a number of studies and recommendations have been made for further initiatives. They have been made by organizations such as: the Advisory Commission on Intergovernmental Relations (Urban and Rural America: Policies for Future Growth, 1968); the Douglas Commission (Building the American City, 1968), and the American Institute of Architects (A Plan for Urban Growth, 1972). They have come from the President (Report on National Growth, 1972), and the Task Force on Land Use and Urban Growth of the Citizens' Advisory Committee on Environmental Quality (Land Use and Urban Growth).

But, none of the studies recognized the cornerstone role of local government in managing growth. None explored growth as would a local administrator responsible for dealing with local and federal programs related to growth.

This report does. It examines local management of growth, assesses local growth management needs, and makes recommendations believed to be responsive to the needs.

Report: Local Leadership

Growth problems are the responsibility of all levels of government in this country. Anyone inquiring into how all levels should deal with growth is faced with the questions: How should that responsibility be apportioned? Who should take the lead? Who should follow?

The basic conclusion of this committee is that growth should be managed nationally through a system in which local government assumes the primary responsibility for making growth decisions, and in which regional organizations, states, and the federal government support local government and set broad guidelines within which local government may work. Such a system is not radically different from the present system.

Managing Growth

The major change is in the role of local government. Although local government has a major responsibility for dealing with growth, few cities or counties have fully assumed that responsibility. The result is the manifest failure of the present system. The committee, therefore, recommends that local government take the initiative where the problem of excessive growth is significant and develop plans and programs for dealing with growth and its potential consequences.

Why should local government assume the leadership? There are a number of reasons. Local government is best suited for the role. Only by participating in, and relying upon, local government can people be guaranteed the greatest freedom of choice in deciding where they live and how they live. Also, changes are taking place in the roles of states with regard to growth which may mean that local government can lose the initiative for dealing with growth unless it takes the initiative now.

Best equipped. Local government is best suited, among all levels of government, for taking the lead in controlling growth. It has the authority to regulate land, water and sewer construction, transportation, the environment, and other areas, in most states. It provides the major services that influence growth: schools, police and fire services, solid waste collection, and similar services. In the area of land use, for instance, all but a few states have left the responsibility for regulation to local government.

Secondly, the nature of growth problems varies so drastically between localities that any blanket federal or state policies would be unrealistic and unworkable. The density, dispersion, and socio-economic status of the population differ widely between jurisdictions; so too do the age and condition of the housing stock and infrastructure. State and federal policies that recognize the vast diversity must leave final decisions and implementation of policy to local government.

A number of formal proposals for dealing with growth nationally have left virtually no role for local government to play. Such is the case, for instance, in the proposals of the American Institute of Architects (A Plan for Urban Growth), which otherwise are well reasoned, articulate, and highly imaginative proposals. At the same time that groups such as AIA ignore or seek to abolish a meaningful role for local government, they claim to value very highly individuals' freedom of choice with regard to where and how they live. Indeed, it is expressly the basic tenet of the AIA proposals. They believe—and this committee concurs—that all policies to regulate growth should seek to maximize the freedom of choice.

But, freedom of choice is not maximized when the essential policy decisions are not made by local government. It is minimized. When decisions are made by regional governments, states, or the federal government about where and how people will live, people necessarily will be saddled with more uniformity and less freedom of choice.

Freedom of choice is greatest when local governments can choose the array of living arrangements, services, and controls that best fit their respective citizens' needs—without encroaching on the basic requirement of equal access to resources and amenities of life without racial, economic, or other forms of discrimination. To put it another way, freedom of choice is greatest when the choices available to everyone are greatest. And, the choice is greatest when localities basically are free to be unique. For this reason, too, it is recommended that local government assume the major responsibility for dealing with the problem of excessive growth.

"The Quiet Revolution." Local governments must assume the initiative, also, because unless they do, it will be assumed by states. States increasingly are assuming major responsibility for land use decisions that affect entire states. This already has resulted in state encroachment on traditionally local prerogatives.

Managing Growth

What has been called "The quiet revolution in land use control," has taken place in states such as Hawaii and Vermont. In these states and others, the state has reasserted its constitutional right to regulate land use, leaving a much smaller role for local government. There is a role for states in controlling growth through programs of land use. The role should be one of setting standards and coordinating development planning in metropolitan areas, and seeing that state-wide needs for recreation, natural resources, open space, and so on are met in nonmetropolitan areas. This role should not increase to the point where local government loses its ability to take the initiative to deal with the problems associated with growth.

The need to take the initiative in dealing with growth problems, therefore, is predicated on the challenge of state domination of land use regulation, the inherent ability of local government to deal with the problems of growth, and the ability of local government to maximize freedom of choice as it deals with growth.

Constraints on local government. Although best suited to take major responsibility in dealing with growth, local government has a number of constraints upon it that must be recognized. The first constraint is largely a product of federal government activities and decisions. Current federal policies that impact upon growth are wasteful, ineffective, and contribute to the problems of growth. The current policies often nullify, even reverse, the efforts of local governments to deal with problems of growth.

For example, a study by the Rand Corporation for San Jose, Calif., as reported by its mayor before the Subcommittee on Housing and Urban Development of the U.S. House of Representatives, underlines the constraints that federal growth programs put upon his city. The problem is the accidental, rather than deliberate, impact of federal programs on cities. According to the mayor, the study showed that there is an "inadvertent national urban policy, made up of elements like mortgage insurance, tax loopholes, and interstate highway construction." For example, it has been the policy of the Federal Housing Administration (FHA) to favor mortgage insurance for new homes in suburbs over existing homes in core cities. The result of this policy, it has been argued, is to completely nullify the massive urban renewal and modest housing programs for core cities financed with local and federal funds in the past 25 years.

The second constraint is federal, but it is prospective at this time, and probably supportive of a system of dealing with growth where local government held major responsibilities. The constraint is federal land use policy and planning programs, for which legislation is pending before the Congress. The result of such a program, if adopted, would be to provide local government even greater incentives for taking aggressive action in land use planning. Of course, this action would have to take place within a framework created by state policy and the federal grant program. At present, the precise nature of such a framework is unknown.

A third constraint upon local government as it takes the lead in dealing with growth problems is the failure, or inadequacy, of current local growth-related programs. Zoning, for instance, often has proven to be an ineffective tool for channeling growth, especially where large scale development is concerned. It has been found to exclude the poor in many communities, for example. It often has been weak in the face of pressures for further development. It seldom is found to be coordinated in any sense with ongoing local comprehensive planning. It often is out of date. And, recently courts have ruled against zoning that produces de facto imbalances in local services (e.g. Serrano v. Priest).

Housing and building code enforcement is another traditional means of dealing with land use. But, it also has been the subject of some criticism, especially in older urban areas. In many cases, enforcement tends to increase the cost of maintaining subsistence housing, leading to abandonment rather than improvement.

Construction of water and sewer facilities and roads has been found to be a major determinant of where people live, and the density of population. But, many communities have failed to take this into account in their water, sewer, and road construction programs. Also, many communities have failed to recognize that since population tends to follow water, sewers, and roads, when these facilities are built they create the need for additional municipal services. Sewers attract homes, which require schools, police, fire, trash, and other costly municipal services. Many localities have failed to anticipate the consequences of the construction of water and sewer systems and transportation facilities.

One of the most well known failures of local government in dealing with growth has been in the area of comprehensive land use planning. Many large communities have prepared comprehensive land use plans, costing themselves or the federal government tens of thousands of dollars, resulting in massive tomes with many colorful renderings—only to have the plans lie on the shelf and gather dust. The reasons for the failure of comprehensive land use planning are many. One is the lack of communication between management and planning agencies in local government. Another is the failure of councils to convert plans into zoning ordinances and other enforcement programs. Still another is the failure of planners to make realistic assumptions about the political system, or to make plans which relate to specific concerns of on-going programs.

Failure in this and other areas—zoning, code enforcement, coordination of planning with capital programs, and comprehensive land use planning—acts as a constraint upon a unit of local government as it seeks to assess and regulate its growth.

Recommendations

The importance of growth, the key role to be played by local government, and the constraints placed on local government in managing growth all lead to the following recommendations.

To the profession:

1. Managers and administrators should work with their governing bodies in assessing their communities' growth needs, and in adopting a community growth program which includes a set of goals, directives, and objectives and a set of companion environmental standards. Assessment of needs should include peoples' attitudes toward the desirability of various levels of population growth, as well as population projections, and the present and future capacities of city and county services and infrastructure (e.g., sewer and water systems, solid waste disposal facilities, transportation systems, recreational facilities, etc.).

   Assessment also should include the cost of anticipated future growth in terms of higher levels of services and improvements of physical facilities. Further, assessment should consider peoples' physical and psychological tolerances for congestion and technical developments designed to cope with pollution. From the assessment, managers should guide their councils in the adoption of a community growth program. The program should include desirable levels and rates of growth, ways to guide growth to those levels, and programs for meeting the cost of further growth.

2. Managers should see that desirable levels of growth are defined in terms of both the timing of growth and the area to be covered by future development. Community

comprehensive plans often are expressed in terms of the population levels and land to be used at a given point in time, for instance the year 2000. Few plans explain how a community gets to year 2000. Few plans are timed or staged in any sense. Few say what the population and land use will, or should, be in 1975 . . . or 1980, 1985, and so on.

Managers should ensure that in the process of setting growth goals the goals are expressed first in terms of the timing of growth—the levels desired in 1975, 1980, 1985, and so on. Managers also should see that growth goals are expressed in more than aggregate numbers, but also in terms of the specific land on which the additional population and industry will be located. Specific areas for future growth also should be timed.

Without carefully specifying the timing and area for growth, it is difficult, in fact impossible, to coordinate a growth program among various city and county departments. If a sewer department does not know where and when development will occur, it cannot build a sewer system. On the other hand, if it makes the determination of where and when a sewer system may be needed, this may not correspond with where the police department thinks a sub-station will be necessary, or where a new fire station will be needed.

3. In preparing community growth programs, managers should thoroughly investigate and utilize the available techniques of land use control or create new ones as tools for limiting growth.

   In recent years, a number of techniques have been developed for the control of growth through land use. These techniques in many cases are simply refinements of localities' zoning powers. The legality of these techniques, however, has not been fully tested in every state. Down zoning is one such technique, which takes land out of development. It retards growth by limiting the land available for residential and commercial development. In many cases, down zoning is accompanied by some form of compensation for the owners of the land, such as a reduction in property taxes.

   Land banking is another land-use technique for discouraging development. Under such a program, a locality acquires a substantial part of its undeveloped land, and holds it in the public name. The land acquired helps influence development patterns and controls land prices.

   A controlled growth ordinance has been used successfully in Ramapo, N.Y. Although it involves more than simple land use considerations, the ordinance results in controlling the use of land. Under the Ramapo system, residential development can take place only if the developer obtains a special permit. The permit, however, is issued only if the land is qualified. Qualification is obtained through a point system, computed on the basis of the availability of five kinds of facilities or services: sewers and other sanitary facilities; drainage; improved parks; roads, and firehouses. Complementing the point system is a capital improvement program which extends for 18 years into the future, phasing the creation of these same facilities or services.

   There are a great many other land use techniques available to local governments which should be explored by managers when helping prepare community growth programs.

4. Managers and administrators should recognize the critical interrelationship between capital projects and growth in communities. People follow sewers, roads, and other community facilities. The existence and location of these facilities should be an integral part of any growth program. The absence of water and sewer facilities, for

instance, will greatly retard growth, especially high density growth where septic tanks are ineffective.

Growth programs should not end with land use plans; they should be accompanied by capital programs and plans, which extend for at least five years and, if possible, longer. And, they should specify the phased development of capital facilities within a locality.

Many communities have found that without a capital plan and program coordinated with land use controls, it is difficult to enforce the controls. Courts are more reluctant to uphold land use systems that retard growth that are not based upon a reasonable capital program.

5. Managers should create within the municipal attorney's office a division devoted to land use, the environment, and other growth related issues.

Perhaps the greatest barrier to dealing effectively with growth at any level has been the reluctance of the nation's courts to rule in favor of government policies that treat land as a resource rather than as a commodity. Courts have tended to favor the interests of individual land holders, even when the individuals' use of the land may not be in the public interest.

However, there appears to be more of an opportunity for reversing judicial precedents on land use than was once the case. "Ignorance of what higher courts have actually been willing to sustain," reports the Task Force on Land Use and Urban Growth of the Citizens' Advisory Committee on Environmental Quality, "has created an exaggerated fear that restrictive actions will be declared unconstitutional." The result is that many local governments have not gone as far as they might in regulation of land to control growth.

An office of the municipal attorney responsible for exploring germane rulings of the higher courts, and for informing the manager and council of the realistic limitations to land regulation, could be an important part of any ongoing growth program.

6. Managers should propose policies that cause local land developers to pay the secondary costs of their development and construction.

One of the greatest consequences of rapid development for many local governments has been the additional burdens that development puts on the taxpayer in other parts of the community. Housing subdivisions mean that roads, water and sewer facilities, schools, etc., will have to be built to accommodate the new residents. The cost of the individual house includes these facilities—even though they often are not paid by the owner or developer, but by the community at large. If land use is to be realistic, it must make certain that the secondary costs of development are identified and apportioned correctly.

Programs which facilitate correct identification and apportionment of secondary growth costs include: (a) growth impact statements much like (but not necessarily as extensive in smaller communities) environmental impact statements, prepared by developers and city officials before construction is approved to determine secondary costs and effects; (b) public education programs to create greater awareness of the real cost as well as benefit of growth and development; (c) planned unit developments, an especially effective concept that requires inclusion of infrastructure as well as open space costs along with land use planning in new developments; (d) use privilege charges for utility tap-ins, to assure that new developments pay their fair share of the costs of existing and future community infrastructure; and (e) construction taxation on new buildings, as a percent of the cost of buildings, designed to reimburse cities and counties for secondary costs.

7. It is the responsibility of administrators to see that programs directed toward controlling or influencing growth do not erect barriers to equal access to community resources and amenities because of economic status, race, ethnic origin, or religion.

   One of the greatest objections to local control of growth policy nationally has been that land use controls and other growth control programs tend to discriminate against persons because of race or economic status. Zoning ordinances have been struck down by the courts for this reason.

   If local government is to remain in the driver's seat in determining its own growth patterns, it will have to be especially alert to this criticism and avoid policies that discriminate, even if inadvertently. As the ICMA statement on "Managing for Social and Economic Opportunity" and the report of the ICMA Committee on Human Resource Development in this issue of **PM** make clear, it is the responsibility of managers to see that growth programs are nondiscriminatory.

To regional organizations:

8. In order to deal with growth, it is especially important that regional bodies be constituted as umbrella, multijurisdictional organizations, made up of at least a majority of locally elected officials, as recommended by the ICMA Committee on the Problems of Regionalism. The emphasis on multifunctional, multijurisdictional, locally controlled regional bodies permits local officials to have a major role in regional decision-making, not only in land use, but in many other areas related to growth regionally.

   It is important that regional planning organizations encompass entire urbanized areas and their surrounding corridors for possible growth. Any smaller region will tend to diminish the effectiveness of regional planning and the input of local officials. In nonmetropolitan areas, it is anticipated that local officials will be working more closely with state officials in making growth-related decisions because of the greater state interest in the recreation facilities, roads, natural resources, and other statewide land uses in rural areas.

9. Regional bodies should seek to coordinate area development and local policies and programs related to growth and land use that have regional significance. Coordination should include determination of the implications of development in a given locality for the whole region, and the ability to recommend or reject such development depending upon its impact on the region. Coordination also should extend to the uniformity of utility service charges.

   With the increased state activity in land use, it is especially important that local officials recognize that for them to maintain a strong role in land use control they must act in concert decisively at the regional level. The only alternative to state domination of land use in many areas is a strong regional approach controlled by local officials.

10. Regional organizations should provide local governments with information and technical assistance that will enable them to make informed and rational growth decisions. Many localities are unaware of the impact of their actions on other localities, and vice versa. More important, they often are unable to assess the impact of their actions on themselves in the future. It is the job of regional planning and

policy development organizations to help provide the information and expertise necessary for wise local decision-making.

To states:

11. States should act to protect the overall interests of citizens in the state with regard to land use, conservation of resources, and protection of the environment by the issuance of standards and guidelines for land use development and other aspects of growth.

    With the increase in the scale of population settlements, the necessity for state involvement in land use and growth decisions becomes both inevitable and desirable. States can set standards and guidelines that relate to the overall needs of the state, and in general outline the ways in which the needs are to be met. Major locational decisions will have to be made by states, such as the location of parks and wilderness areas to be preserved and public access to beaches and other important natural assets. States also will be more involved in the regulation of "complex sources" of environmental pollution, such as shopping centers, large office buildings, and housing subdivisions. The regulation of "complex sources" is being thrust on states and localities by actions of the federal Environmental Protection Agency. Although states may make the major locational decisions for many kinds of land uses, the basic and specific locational decisions should be left to regional organizations and their constituent local governments.

12. States should delegate growth policy coordination and development in urban regions to the umbrella, multijurisdictional organizations charged with land use and growth planning and policy development in the region. In urban areas, the major locational decisions of concern to states have either been made or are precluded because the land is already used. The remaining land use decisions relate to the use of the small amount of land available for development and the improvement of existing structures on the land. These decisions should be left to local determination with regional coordination.

13. States should provide local government with funds for planning and management, technical assistance, and information relevant to growth. The role of states should be one of overall guidance and support for essentially local decisions. Perhaps the most important forms of support are funds and technical assistance that help make possible intelligent and informed local decisions. As in many areas, local funds are too scarce to be used for long-range planning and policy development because there are too many demands for immediately pressing needs.

14. States should enact legislation that permits local government to assume a strong role in land use regulation. In many states, the failure of local government to control growth is due in part to a dearth of authority to act. Land use and taxation laws are too restrictive to permit local innovation. It is important that states provide local governments with maximum flexibility in terms of legislation to control growth effectively and in an innovative fashion.

To the federal government:

15. National concerns related to growth should be cared for through federal growth programs. Many needs are national when it comes to growth policies and the needs should be dealt with nationally. The need to ensure that discrimination does not take place as a consequence of local growth policies is a federal prerogative, as is the preservation of certain unique local environments.

16. Existing and future federal programs should be consistent with the efforts of local

145

officials to manage growth. The inadvertent national growth policies, expressed through mortgage guarantees, transportation networks, environmental protection, and tax laws, must be reviewed seriously to remove their undesirable effect on local growth. If the federal government is to impose national growth priorities, as mentioned above, it also must impose priorities upon itself. If not, the federal government will continue to frustrate local efforts at growth management.

17. Funds should be provided to assist local planning and management of growth policy. The role of providing overall direction and support extends to the federal government as well as to the states. In this role, the federal government must seek to direct its funds to support local growth planning and implementation.

ICMA should:

18. The membership should be provided with information and technical assistance about new approaches to local growth programs. One of the greatest weaknesses of the present system of running growth policy locally has been the absence of effective new approaches to land use and related growth programs. In cases where new programs have been developed successfully, another weakness is their failure to be widely disseminated.

    ICMA must redouble its efforts to collect information on growth programs nationally and to make the information widely available through its information services. Kits of alternative growth programs based upon experiences of other localities should be prepared. Also, ICMA must seek to develop training programs and seminars which address growth management.

19. State land use and growth programs that are most responsive to local needs should be encouraged by state associations of municipal administrators, working closely with state leagues of municipalities. There is a need for a grassroots participation of the membership in developing effective growth policies at the state level. State associations should ensure that professional input is made to legislatures through municipal leagues for strengthening the local base of the pyramid.

20. ICMA should work closely with the other national associations of local and state government officials as well as with the federal government to seek adoption of the recommendations here on growth management and to provide members with information on programs relevant to local growth. ICMA should open up a two-way dialogue with federal officials on managing growth. On the one hand, the work of this committee should be made available to the Congress and the federal agencies. On the other hand, information on federal programs and policies relevant to local officials should be made available to the membership.

21. A report should be made to the membership at the 1974 Annual Business Meeting on the progress made on the implementation of the recommendations of this committee. If ICMA's municipal management policy is to have any effect on the local management of growth, it is necessary that the membership be informed of developments in the area and the impact of their recommendations on changing the existing system.

Committee on Growth and the Environment

John Witherspoon, Chairman (County Manager—Guilford County, N.C.), Joseph Baker (City Manager—Burbank, Calif.), Osmond Bonsey (City Manager—Falmouth, Me.), Don Bown (City Manager—Bartlesville, Okla.), James Chandler (Deputy City Manager—Hollywood, Fla), Jorene Coffay (Administrative Assistant—New Castle County, Del.), Larry Coons (City Manager—Richland, Wash), Lindsay Cox (Executive Director—Piedmont Triad COG, Greensboro, N.C.), Norman Cravens (Assistant to the Mayor—Phoenix, Ariz.), William H. Edgar (City Manager

—Pleasanton, Calif.), James Eide (City Manager—Ketchikan, Alas.), Howard Gary (Chief Administrative Assistant—Newark, N.J.), James K. Giese (City Manager—Greenbelt, Md.), Richard N. Gray (City Manager —Norman, Okla.), Lloyd Harrell, Jr. (City Manager—Nevada, Mo.), Don W. Hataway (City Manager—Loveland, Colo.), James King (Director, Intgov't. Affairs—San Jose, Calif.), John T. McHugh (Township Manager —Willingboro, N.J.), Don McIntyre (City Manager—Pasadena, Calif.), Simon Melendez (City Manager—Norco, Calif.), Gifford Miller (City Manager—Orange, Calif.), Robert S. Moore (City Manager—Salem, Ore.), Richard Pearson (Executive Director—Mid-Columbia Econ. Develop. Dist., The Dalles, Ore.), David H. Pence (City Manager—Poplar Bluff, Mo.), Ray Remy (Executive Director—So. Calif. Assn. of Govt's, Los Angeles, Calif.), Ray Riley (City Administrator—Ft. Smith, Ariz.), John Salisbury (Executive Director—Maine Municipal League, Hallowell, Me.), George Schrader (City Manager—Dallas, Texas), Gerald Schwerm (Village Manager—Brown Deer, Wis.), George Sipel (City Manager—Palo Alto, Calif.), James C. Smith (City Manager—New Carlisle, Ohio), Daniel E. Stone (City Manager—Riverside, Calif.), Lyle Sumek (Assistant Professor—Northern Illinois University, DeKalb, Ill.), Ted Tedesco (City Manager—San Jose, Calif.), and Allen L. Torrey (City Manager—Amherst, Mass.).

Note on the Reports

Laurence Rutter, National Policy Coordinator—ICMA, introduced the five reports [(a) Managing Growth; (b) Managing Human Resources; (c) Achieving Quality Local Government; (d) Regionalism and Municipal Management; and, (e) The Federal Block Grant and Community Development] as follows: "The reports of the five ICMA Municipal Management Policy Committees that are the focus of this issue of *Public Management* have important features of which readers should take note. Each report is preceded by a summary of its major findings and recommendations. Each report then follows with a statement of the major findings in the respective areas of concern that emerged from the work of the committees. Each then presents and discusses the recommendations that followed from the findings. The recommendations are addressed to the profession, state and federal governments, and ICMA. The reports were submitted to the Executive Board for consideration at its July meeting. The Board's actions are reported in the preceding article. The key Board action is a request for membership reaction to the reports. . . . (ICMA's reports are limited expressly to those areas which the membership selected—at the recommendation of the Executive Board and the 170-member Regional Policy Advisory Groups—as the highest priority policy areas for the profession) . . . "

"The result of this intensive work by the committees was intended to be a consensus statement for guiding the profession. Each report reflects, at a minimum, a majority opinion of the committee. At many points, the reports are based upon unanimous agreements. But, it should be emphasized that not all members of any committee were in agreement on all the points contained in the committee's report. Each report's findings and recommendations, if adopted by the membership of ICMA in whole or in part, are intended to serve also merely as guides to the profession. If adopted, they will in no sense bind the membership to any course of action."

Growth: The Roles for Counties:

A Series of Four Articles

Bernard F. Hillenbrand (with the assistance of Eileen Hirsch); Francis B. Francois; Douglas Harman; and, Frank Raflo

Bernard F. Hillenbrand is executive director of the National Association of Counties. He was previously the assistant director of the American Municipal Association, and formerly was the deputy director of Municipal Research for Syracuse, New York. He serves as the editor of the weekly newspaper County News, has written numerous articles on local government for national publications, and has taught special courses in local government at American University and Cornell University Extension Division. Mr. Hillenbrand is a graduate of Syracuse University, from which he also holds a master's in public administration.

Eileen Hirsch is a student of the University of Virginia Law School. She was previously the assistant to the public affairs director of the National Association of Counties, and formerly was a reporter for the Faribault, Minnesota Daily News. She is a graduate of the University of Wisconsin.

Francis Francois is chairman of the Prince George's County [Maryland] Council, and a member of the NACo board. He is also a patent attorney with the law firm, Bacon & Thomas. Mr. Francois is a graduate of Iowa State, and holds a law degree from George Washington University.

Douglas Harman is deputy county executive of Fairfax County [Virginia]. He formerly was director of Fairfax's Office of Research and Statistics, was previously with ICMA, and had been an associate professor at American University. Dr. Harman is a graduate of Nebraska Wesleyan, and holds both a master's and a Ph.D. from American University.

Frank Raflo is a member of the Loudoun County Board of Supervisors, and is second vice-president of the Virginia Association of Counties. He was previously mayor of Leesburg, Virginia. Mr. Raflo is a graduate of the College of William and Mary.

Several of these articles also appeared in the September 1974 issue of Outlook, and are reprinted here with permission of the National Association of Counties (1735 New York Avenue, N.W., Washington, D.C. 20006).

Counties as Leaders in Growth Management—By B. Hillenbrand

Growth management has been a common topic of public debate and attention during recent years. Thousands of pages have been written and millions of words have been spoken about controlling and managing growth. Experts have emerged from every corner of the nation.

But when one looks for the leaders in growth management—the people who are actively managing growth—the picture is that of local government officials who are confronted daily with tough decisions which affect community growth, environment, and quality of life.

As people have outgrown city boundaries, suburbia and even exurbia is becoming a new way of life. The tremendous pressures of soaring populations have taken place outside the city, in counties throughout the nation. A 1970 U.S. Census Report indicates that in the nation's Standard Metropolitan Statistical Areas (SMSAs) central city populations increased by 6.4 percent from 1960 to 1970, but suburban populations increased by 26.8 percent.[1] The expansion in population has been accompanied by a rapid expansion in county services and facilities. General county government expenditures increased from $12,933 million in 1966-67, to $24,410 million in 1971-72, an increase of 89 percent.[2]

While counties have traditionally been thought of as only providing basic services such as election administration, court administration and tax collection, their increasing population and the needs of that population have expanded the county role to include many services and powers which affect and are directly affected by growth management. A 1970 survey of counties of more than 100,000 population suggests the importance of the county growth management role: 76 percent are responsible for comprehensive planning, 78 percent for roads and highways, 55 percent for zoning, 51 percent for subdivision control, 42 percent for code enforcement, 33 percent for sewerage facilities, 38 percent for schools, 37 percent for solid waste disposal, and 31 percent for fire protection.[3] Where county governments do not handle these functions, they are often the responsibility of a quasi-public agency or special district. In addition, county government functions include those related less directly to growth management, but are nevertheless important: police protection, parks and recreation, welfare and social services, public health care, public housing and soil conservation are examples.

In each of these areas, county government is involved legislatively—through county board action on ordinances, and administratively—through management decisions and planning. The decisions made by county officials are often necessitated by pressure for growth, and each decision may have a significant impact on the future growth of the county. Growth management to county officials, then, is not only a topic of discussion and study. It is a recurring problem, always requiring decisions and action. Just a few examples of county growth management action illustrate the extent of local experimentation with new growth control techniques and new ways of using old techniques.

Prince George's County, Maryland—a part of the rapidly growing metropolitan Washington, D.C. area—experienced an 85 percent population growth between 1960 and 1970. As the county population continues to cope with rapid growth, officials have inaugurated a growth control program based on the county's role as a provider of water and sewerage facilities, capital improvements, and public services; their power to regulate zoning, subdivisions and building permits; and their responsibility for planning economic development. Through coordinated legislative and administrative action, the county is controlling the type, timing, and location of development.

Although *San Diego County*, California, has long been aware of the problems of growth management and has effectively used several tools and techniques to cope with the problem, the county government has recently adopted an overall growth management policy. The policy identifies factors which should be considered in determining the amount, type, and location of growth—such as the existing capacity of public services and utilities; whether the county's socio-economic balance would be improved or impaired; natural hazards; and preservation of natural resources. Additionally, the policy provides a simplified approach for utilizing these factors in determining whether development should be encouraged, discouraged, or avoided in a particular area.

Suffolk County, New York—a highly urbanized county on Long Island—is using an innovative approach to preserve its rich productive agricultural land. The county is buying and holding development rights on farm land, thus lowering farmers' taxes so they can continue to farm, and preserving the open space the farmland provides for citizens in more urban areas of the county.

Broward County, Florida—which experienced a growth of 85,000 people in 1973 alone—has combined modern technology and bold political initiatives to improve its growth management. Each of the county's 29 municipal jurisdictions has traditionally done its own planning, resulting in a fragmented approach to growth management. The county is now putting together a comprehensive county planning and zoning process, utilizing an advanced computer system. With data gathered by many county departments, the computer will help planners analyze the impact of development proposals on transportation, utilities, pollution, drainage, employment, education, governmental services, and the county's tax base. The system is scheduled to be fully operational in November, 1974.

As these examples indicate, counties have placed themselves on the firing line with innovative, progressive growth management techniques. Although they have, are, and will probably continue to make a few mistakes as they forge ahead, they are clearing a path which will impact on future development of the nation.

As the only organization which represents county government in the United States, the National Association of Counties (NACo) has developed a position on land use planning which reflects the growth management philosophy of NACo's more than 1,200 member counties:

- NACo recognizes that the comprehensive planning process is essential to all counties, whether they are urban or rural, as a means for providing the management framework within which necessary, efficient, economic and satisfying decisions can be made and implemented. . .

- The planning process should be comprehensive in area and participation as well as in content, and involve all areas, agencies and jurisdictions which have a community of interest in the subject matters involved in the planning process. Since county government is the only areawide government at the local level, it must accept the responsibility and exercise initiative in the development of a comprehensive planning program for the entire county area.

- Counties must recognize the planning needs of multi-county regions and encourage all governmental units within such regions to cooperate and participate in a comprehensive regional planning program. County governments, through their elected officials, should accept the responsibility for and exercise the initiative in the organization and operation of institutions and mechanisms for the voluntary solution of regional problems.

As that policy statement indicates, counties recognize the need for truly comprehensive land use planning. In many cases, a single county is the appropriate region for comprehensive planning—as evidenced by the fact that 127 U.S. Census Bureau Standard Metropolitan Statistical Areas (SMSAs) are single county areas. Comprehensive planning for single county areas is also appropriate in rural areas where county geographical size may be very large.

But county officials recognize that multi-county or regional cooperation is necessary for sound growth management in some areas. In those cases, counties agree that the regional organizations must be voluntary. While NACo policy urges county officials to support regional councils or government, it also states that regional councils should not become yet another layer of government. This is especially important as counties deal with the issue of growth management, because it is a controversial political issue, as well as a technical challenge. Growth management policies must be determined by people who are politically accountable to the citizens who must live with those policies.

To help counties with growth management, NACo co-sponsored a "growth management conference" in May, 1974, which brought together city and county elected officials, planners, attorneys, and managers/administrators for intense discussions about the practical problems of growth management. From that conference, NACo has created a *Growth Management Task Force*, charged with writing and recommending a nation-wide county policy on growth management for NACo members. The Task Force, which is just beginning its work, includes county officials who serve on NACo's environment and energy, land use, transportation, and community development policy-recommending committees. The Task Force also hopes to focus attention on the progressive growth management policies of county government throughout the nation.

Footnotes

1. U.S. Bureau of Census, U.S. Census of the Population 1970, "Number of Inhabitants, U.S. Summary," Washington, D.C., 1971.
2. 1972 Census of Governments, Volume 4, County Finances, No. 3, *Finances of County Government*, Washington, D.C.
3. United States Advisory Commission on Intergovernmental Relations, *Profile of County Governments*, Washington, D.C., 1971: Herbert S. Duncombe, *County Government in America*, 1966.

Putting the Costs "Up Front"
—By F. Francois

The Growth Gospel

County governments across the nation, and in particular those in suburban locations near large central cities, have become aware in the past several years that uncontrolled growth is not the panacea it was once thought to be.

There was a time when county officials bought the developer philosophy that says "any growth is good growth," and believed that the way to lower the tax rate was to build more housing to thereby bring in more taxpayers. But when we found that after building the housing and adding the taxpayers to our rolls the tax rate continued to climb, elected officials and the citizens we represent started to question the growth gospel.

When local governments analyzed why their tax needs kept climbing in the face of new growth, they found many causes. In some instances the development practices of builders had caused physical problems that government then had to correct—for example, the practice of stripping bare a piece of ground months or years before building was to commence resulted in heavy siltation that would fill in a stream, causing flooding that in turn required dredging of the stream and possibly building dikes and other runoff control structures. It became evident that the flood control work would have been unnecessary if there had been no development, or if the development had occurred properly. The cost of the corrections could therefore be directly attributed to the builder—but nevertheless the taxpayers had to pay the bill.

In many jurisdictions years ago, the developer built the houses—but not the roads, or the water lines or the storm and sanitary sewers. It was up to the county to put in these public facilities: again, at public cost. The same has been true of schools, where the taxpayers generally have had to pay for the schools to educate the children generated from new housing construction. Also, over the years the cost for furnishing park and recreation facilities generally has been charged against the taxpayers, and not just the new development that created the need.

Costs Up Front

Once these economic facts were understood, steps were taken by many local governments to put the cost of development more on the specific new development project itself than on the taxpayers generally. Grading and other development controls were created that require the builder to operate in an ecologically sound manner—thereby avoiding the past rapes of the land that ultimately cost public money to correct. Builders were required to pay for their own roads, sewers and water lines, and in some jurisdictions contributions are now exacted to buy parkland and build schools. The whole effort is to have development pay its way.

There is an old cigarette commercial that goes, "it's what's up front that counts." Today, many county governments are applying that slogan to growth and development, by insisting that the old hidden costs of development be put "up front" for all to view. The result, of course, is that the sales price of housing has been driven sharply upward, much to the unhappiness of many builders and prospective home buyers.

The builders ultimately pass on the increased costs to the buyer, in nearly every case. The buyer has no choice but to pay the bill or go without housing. In a sense, in this era of consumer protection, this is more fair to the buyer than past approaches—for in the old days he still paid the bill, but later on in the form of the higher real estate taxes (that he then complained no one had warned him about). On the other hand though, the initial higher costs for housing now limit the ability of many to acquire it.

In our efforts to control growth we have used many tools, including: large lot zoning; water and sewer moratoriums or stretch-out programming; the use of planned urban development techniques; adequate public facility laws; and, the sophisticated point-system building permits of the Ramapo type. To a great extent these have been successful in slowing and controlling growth in our jurisdictions, thereby solving what has been a prime concern for many county governments: bringing rising tax rates under control.

New Problems/Challenges

At the same time though, as is so often true, growth management techniques can create new problems. First is the need to expand the governmental work force with the skilled personnel needed to operate a sophisticated growth management system. Good, well-trained people are often hard to find, especially as the demand for them increases with more and more governments entering the growth management field.

Within the development community a like demand for new talent is created, and must be satisfied. Further, lending institutions must come to understand the new requirements for development and, in particular, the greater planning expenses and longer lead times before building can commence.

The issues of fairness to those who want to develop become more complex, too, with growth management. In the old days anyone could build, anywhere. Today, priorities must be set by the county government, in a way that will meet Constitutional tests of fairness. Inevitably, law suits must be expected, and the local government will need the legal talent to defend its actions in this complex area of the law.

Beyond these more or less technical problems lie some philosophical challenges. If we are going to put the cost of development "up front," and thereby increase the sales price of ownership and rental housing, then what are we going to do to meet the housing needs of middle and lower income residents? If we do nothing, these individuals will simply be forced out of the jurisdiction to somewhere else—if there is a somewhere else. This can mean that our senior citizens, our children getting married and about to start a new household, and minorities on low incomes will no longer be able to live in the county. A policy decision will need to be made as to whether this is what is wanted, or if it is acceptable.

The effects of high cost housing on efforts to attract industry will aslo need to be analyzed. If a new industry cannot find housing for its workers, then usually they will not locate in a jurisdiction.

What all this means is that with the "up front" cost approach to development in general and housing in particular, it may also be necessary to devise a strategy for meeting community needs for moderate and low income housing. This makes the whole picture more complex, and calls for still more effective county planning and action programming.

Fortunately for the 80 some, large, urban counties—the ones faced most directly with both the need for growth management and the need for moderate and low income housing—the new Housing and Community Development Act of 1974 has been enacted into law. It allows the urban counties to create their own community development plans: ones that can take into account growth management and housing needs. The new federal monies made available under the law come just in time to help us meet the twin goals of stabilizing tax rates, while at the same time ensuring an adequate supply of housing for our needs.

In summary, growth management is a complex field. County officials need to be aware of that fact, and look ten or twenty years into the future at the goals and objectives of the community. Only then can we hope to produce a comprehensive program designed to give the kind of governmental services we want at a cost we can afford, and at the same time satisfy the legitimate housing aspirations of the whole community.

County Strategies for Growth Management——By D. Harman

[Editor's Note: this is a digest of the original article (less the introductory material).]

Key Issues About Growth Management

The extent of local authority. Under the Dillon's Rule system of government, what is the extent of local government's capacity to influence growth? Local governments long have exercised basic powers which facilitate growth, but they seldom have acted to constrain or redirect development. When growth was encouraged by local actions, few questioned this function of local governments. When powers are used to restrict or channel new development, a strong challenge is raised about the legal authority of local government. Each state necessarily must be a separate arena for this question with the local officials, legislators, judges, interest groups, and citizens seeking agreement or resolution on the extent of local powers.

Approaches to growth management. Can local governments effectively influence growth and development? It is not yet resolved whether local governments can meaningfully influence growth through positive planning mechanisms. The challenge before local governments is whether they can mount systematic programs to link development levels with coherent plans and programs.

Exclusionary effect. Is growth control a fancy term for exclusionary policies? The purpose of the controls is to exclude additional housing and businesses until they fit into rational development patterns. The important question is whether this exclusion impacts unfairly on people as a result of race, religion or national origin. Key court cases have found certain local planning measures to be unconstitutional because of their exclusionary nature. This is not the likely result where the local program includes special provisions for low and moderate income housing. Local officials must evaluate their desired plans carefully in light of possible exclusionary effects.

Economic impact. Will attempts to manage growth have a negative impact on the local economy? This is a great concern strongly expressed by the many interests involved in the construction industry. Undoubtedly the impact would be great if a local government sought to stop all development. However, the basic thrust of the growth management trend is not to halt all growth, but rather to redirect and phase it into rational patterns. It must be recognized that many other factors influence the local level of development, including the money market, availability of labor, and supply and demand. The danger is that any local attempt to manage growth rationally may take full blame for any setbacks in the complex development economy.

The resolution of these and related questions represents a significant challenge to county officials.

Implementation Strategies

Political commitment. An essential ingredient for growth management is political commitment. Without it, a program has no chance of success. Political commitment must emerge from the locality's experiences with urban development and an understanding of the complex issues associated with it.

The program design. No county should attempt to initiate a growth management program without an overall program design which has been subjected to thorough debate. It is at this point that the community dialogue must be translated into specific objectives, management approaches, legal strategies, and manpower allocations.

The revitalization of planning. The planning function long has suffered from many problems brought on by its own practices and procedures as well as management's misuse of its potentials. Planning has been too concerned with both idealized 20-year future plans and day-to-day zoning decisions. The often-heard jokes about plans gathering dust in municipal closets are painfully true. Yet, managers seldom have taken the initiative to revitalize planning.

Legal approaches. In this field, it is imperative to have creative legal talent available to the government. In too many communities, the local government's legal staff is almost exclusively reactive: assigned a role of defending the government in court. In growth management, the lawyers must be part of the management team making the important decisions. The precise legal approach taken must reflect the needs of the community and the opportunities allowed under state law and local charter. There are many approaches which draw upon different legal strategies. These include: (a) innovative zoning controls; (b) special development permits; (c) adequate public facilities ordinances; (d) population limits; (e) urban service boundaries; (f) environmental impact assessments; (g) land banking; and, (h) largelot and agricultural zoning and other legal tools.

Team management. Growth management exemplifies the necessity for team approaches in local government. Growth cannot be affected without the coordinated involvement of many key departments. The discussion about legal strategy (above) indicates that lawyers, planners, and top management must work closely together. The participation cannot stop there—particularly in large governments with numerous relevant programs.

Analytical tools. Growth management requires the use of the most advanced analytical tools available. The seat-of-the-pants methodologies of traditional planning will not suffice today in an age which requires advanced mathematics and computers to analyze complex environmental issues, such as air quality and drainage.

Community participation. The tendency is for complex efforts to pay lip service to community participation. There is serious danger in a rationalization for minimal public involvement. The extent of community feelings on the growth issues will be reflected in the political support for government action. Administrative officials need a sensitive ear to learn those feelings because programs cannot extend too far beyond the general community consensus without running the risk of rejection.

Fairfax County—through its Planning Land Use System (PLUS)—is deeply involved in each of these areas. Since February 1973, the county has devoted great energies to the complex issues of growth management. Each county government must fashion its own programs and strategies to achieve successful growth management systems.

Critical Issues for the Future

Is "growth management" here to stay as a major concern of local governments? Other terms may be used in future years, but there can be little doubt that the nation has reached a critical point in its attention to the quality of new urbanization. This new point in the evolution of land use controls and the "new mood" on the part of citizens will remain an important part of the country in the coming years.

There are specific key issues which will influence growth management trends. The legal battles over phased growth methods will be extremely important. Because of the complexities of state legal systems, there will be 50 legal arenas in which these cases will be argued. However, the trend seems certain: local governments will gain increasing powers to plan sequential growth in accord with environmental constraints. New land use control approaches will be formulated which will make future development a positive planning system rather than a game for land speculators.

The greatest responsibilities will rest on the thousands of county officials with growth problems. They must fashion their own approaches and implement growth management programs. Great political judgment and planning perspective will be required. Local officials must be willing to "bite the bullet" on development decisions, even when contrary to vocal groups. They must address emotional issues about life style changes in suburbia where the single family detached home is becoming too expensive for middle income America. The tasks before these local officials are enormous.

Citizens, community groups, and business groups have important roles to play, too. They must be part of the process for it to be successful. The time and dedication required for such planning efforts is frightening, but it is the price which must be paid. Achieving sound participation in growth management programs demands much attention and understanding on everyone's part.

The national scene is important as well. The federal government has enormous resources which should be brought to bear on growth management issues. The National Association of Counties and the other public and professional interest groups have vital roles to play in helping to maximize national resources on the local level. State governments must also assume positive roles on growth problems in the coming years.

Growth management is a term for making the institutions of government strong, positive partners in shaping our future urban America. It reflects both the need to make old planning tools work better and the necessity for new tools to achieve more satisfactory phasing of growth patterns. It rests on the shoulders of court officials and citizens to make growth management a reality and this can only be achieved through tireless efforts to improve and strengthen the basic planning and implementation process of city and county governments.

Cows or Condos: Values in Conflict
—By F. Raflo

To even the unobservant, it is obvious that Loudoun is a county of many faces: geographic, economic, and sociological—each presenting a firm point of personal view. Is a consensus—a reconciliation of obvious conflicts—possible that will permit the county not only to survive, but to have a positive direction to move forward?

Growth: The Roles for Counties

- Where do the young people find a place to live?
- Will the fertile farmland continue to produce food or be turned into squared-off, closely-mowed, small, front and backyard tracts for the wealthy to plant their grass and flowers and try to pay the taxes?
- Is Loudoun to be only a county of the past?
- Will this county in its efforts to preserve what many feel is its "way of life," fall off the cliff, stepping ever backwards . . . or will the uncharted push into a totally developed future shove it into an expensive future of too much, too soon?
- What part should government play in setting forth the directions? What part new industry? What part the young? What part the senior citizens? How important is history and heritage?
- Shall we judge our course solely on what has up to now been a successful experience or do we just make this past record one item to be fed into the computer along with self-fulfilling population projections for the consulting purveyors of expertise to take only a small percentage of, as they print out a demographic model of not so much what we are, but what we must be like to adjust to our future?
- If there is to be governmental direction, will it emanate from the "closest to the people" decisions of local government, or will the acceptance of federal funding relegate the local officials to "tenders of the grass around the Courthouse green" while the major movements come from the federal bureaucracy in Washington.

Actually, before one attempts to answer these questions, there must first be the designation of who will frame the questions themselves, because, from our first example, it is clear that the very wording of the questions affect the answers. Words are words, but meanings vary.

Whether the farmers in the west trying to hold on to their land or the suburbanites in the east, pressing for more county service, realize it or not, they all will be a part of that tug of war, trying to tilt the decision to their philosophy. Not to be overlooked is the possibility that the very tugging and pulling might snap the rope in two and leave a county in total irresolvable conflict.

The odds at the outset favor those forces which first overcome a lack of knowledge about the county and then replace it with willingness to act affirmatively on what is now a prevailing apathy among the majority of the citizens to not do anything that does not touch them directly. If for no other reason than longer years of residence, first let us look at the county from the point of view of the west.

There is certainly no unanimity here. An ever decreasing amount of the land is held by those whose roots go deep into this land and its productions of grain, milk, cattle and horses. As a boy, I recall that all requests for geographic directions always ended with the explanation that it is up route (—): the "old (———) place." In most cases, the farm in question has been the old (———) place for many years—passed down to the next generation, a generation that continued to farm it, but did so with much greater efficiency of method, production, and generally profit.

As these farming methods and directives for better crops, fatter cattle, and faster horses were distributed through state and county and farm agencies with VPI providing much of the basic source information, the farm prosperity continued to grow.

There was little open admission that things would ever change—only get better. Intense growth was something that was happening somewhere else. The basic battle was, and to some extent still is, "keep down the real estate taxes": the repeatedly pictured threat to farm survival.

The "it was good enough for grandpa, look how well he made out" answer was offered as the excuse for opposition to the most obvious improvements in education and social services that would cost the county money. Federal subsidy of crops was accepted begrudgingly at first, but never objected to quite as much as federal money, and with it federal guidelines for programs aimed at upgrading education for all and broadening the general well-being of the county as a whole.

Yet, there was a certain inevitable realization by many in this class that tomorrow would be different than today. Change was coming. For some, change represented a profitable sell out to development that paid off in real dollars for the years of tilling the soil despite flood or drought, trying to make it. With those who held on, and many are still doing this, one eye remains cocked over the left shoulder—looking not at the future way ahead, but the next year of more taxes and less profit from farming—scanning the horizon while trying to find adequate farm help and finally agreeing that maybe the young sons nurtured by the soil of the farms and educated from its profit no longer were willing to stay with the land.

The comment most heard is, "I can't get anyone to work anymore. I want to protect my land but then what will my kids do when I am gone? I didn't work all of these years just for nothing. I want to be able to leave them something for all of this effort, and I am getting too old to keep at it like it has been."

Land Use Tax—the opportunity which permits farms to pay a much lower real estate tax than the fair market value as long as the use of the land does not change—offers real help to some, but again here the suspicion that it is just some kind of gimmick that is not for real, plagues the uncertain. Some signed up, some are waiting to "see how it works out."

For the Loudoun pictured here, there is much nostalgia. It is a continuing case of retreating to new positions of defense, new lines from which there can be no further retreat without selling out altogether. As each neighbor down the road or across the hill makes the firm break with the past and gives up, the decision as to what to do becomes more uncertain for those who remain.

In one section of west Round Hill, good farmland zoned for agriculture with no developments even on the horizon, a check shows that more than half of the land is already in the hands of absentee owners who wait for the change in use to come, to provide then for sure profit bonanza for themselves or their heirs.

In the above context there is much "one to one" worrying about what to do, but not too much willingness to get behind a single course of action. Ten-acre zoning was made available as a possible solution, but it has up to the fall of 1974 brought on nothing but ten-acre tract development, which, at best, will not create an overwhelming cost for new schools and at worst is a shameful waste of the land.

Old established western Loudoun waits. The complaints about money spent for county schools and services diminish and most everyone defines his position as "conservative" . . . but does so with a great reluctance to explain exactly what is meant by the word.

That is one part of the west. The other part is considerably different. Expansion, progress, development, certainly up to recent months, has been the watchword of the incorporated towns who realize that to continue to exist and to provide additional public services, they must have an ever increasing number of service users to help pay the bill. Stuck in between the towns and the older farms, are the new one to three acre owners who, starting in the sixties and multiplying swiftly in the early seventies, came to Loudoun to acquire that "place they have always wanted in the country."

Largely not dependent on the production of the land to sustain their economic well-being, they clan together to support causes and corrections about which they openly ask, "why was this not done before?"

In bringing moderate change, however, in the land and its use, many immediately after being permanently ensconsed in their location, recognize that if their numbers increase too swiftly the very thing they came to Loudoun for in the first place will be diluted. Theirs is not a preservation of the past, but a determination not to have the present which they, themselves, changed into its "now" shape, move on to something else.

Among these two points of view there is much in common and mutual support, but there is also existent, if hidden under the surface, the charge that "the newcomers seem to want to do it all."

Growth: The Roles for Counties

It must be stated that to charge this new group with being the holders of the "last one in" philosophy—determined that they shall let no one else in—is not fair. Indeed, the survival of the west in total has been greatly solidified by the new people, the new ideas, the new money, and the new willingness to bring support, conciliation, and confidence to the entire county.

The struggle to keep the old farm and to farm it, is not exactly the same as the struggle to not pave the narrow road so there won't be so many cars going by "our new place," but, in confrontation with the much more intensive development that came to the east—because the east had the sewers to take care of many, many more people—the west stands united uneasily in its unseen division, if such a contradictory position is possible.

Unfortunately to still a large number of Loudouners, the west is the county. The east is the land of newcomers who bring only problems, demands, and higher taxes. Even though as the west grumbles, the east, certainly in sheer numbers, is fast becoming "the county."

Those in the east also came looking for a place in the country—but for different reasons: money, job, travel time, or the unwillingness to care for a horse and three acres, they settled in a more intensified section which in a decade grew to the capacity of its available sewers.

No longer can the east of Goose Creek be called the new. The numbers there out count the west. The enthusiasm and drive for things called progressive and good, for schools and recreation and leisure time, for police protection and fire service, all thrust into the county seat in Leesburg everyday. As the numbers grow, the requests grow. Slowly also comes the growing self-realization that the east no longer must come cup in hand to the county seat and ask. Sufficient in number, confident in their contribution of money, material and new intellectualism, the east now begins to compete from a position of strength.

Here, there is little fear of federal intrusion. The oft-cried directive that "this was the way grandpa did it," is no stone around the neck of young families with children who look at the balance of county as a misty opposing conglomerate across the creek. The need for more teachers, swimming pools, parks and ever increasing social services, for them, has been unfilled too long.

"Tell us what the bill will be for the things we know we need" is the oft-heard plea, and the follow-up is quickly added, "and we will pay the bill." "We don't have enough police; our little league fields are so crowded there is no place to practice; above all we need recreational facilities and parks."

"You really can't mean that," is their response to those from the west who proclaim, "all of Loudoun is a park?" "For whom to use?" is their immediate responding question.

The experts on family behavior attribute many family squabbles to money. Money, or where it comes from, may indeed be the root of the contention in Loudoun.

The west—certainly, the tied-to-the-land west—pays its taxes directly to the county in real estate assessments, but enjoys many of the tax deduction benefits of being a farmer when it comes to federal payments. The citizens in the east are now paying an ever-increasing real estate tax also to the county, but they make their major contribution to the federal government.

Under such circumstances, it is not hard to understand their reluctance to object to federal assistance to the people of the county in any form whatsoever. "If we are paying it, should we at least get our fair share back," is their position and it is a firm one, allowing little compromise.

At this point, one must ask: are the differences that severe in Loudoun, and the conflicts so great, for any movement to the middle? The answer is, each month (fortunately) coming into sharper focus. The west's unaltering refusal to spend for new county needs is being nudged into the positive, while those from the east having the desire to make changes at any price are slowing down considerably. The man in the west complains about what paving his dirt road will do to his county atmosphere, and the new settler in the east sees that despite a four lane highway, he must spend longer and longer periods of time getting to his central city job.

Growth—its size, shape, form, and magnitude, how much, and when—is hovering over both east and west now in the form of a continuingly more brilliant and piercing light more easily identified. The 'what to do about it' still brings contradictory answers, but the problem in its broadest context seems mutually to be recognized.

Where then stands the middle—the central county: the evolving towns with their hard to be paid for public service needs? Where do I stand, rooted as a native in the past, while at the same time proud of having amassed a record for supporting continuing expansion of the vital public services?

Is the reconciliation between cows and condominiums possible? The answer can be a tentative yes. Why the optimism? Largely because of the aforementioned mutual recognition of the problem.

My answer is tied to what I so repeatedly have called "affordability": the spending of the resources of land, money, and environment at a rate that can be absorbed. The reconciliation emerges through a concerted joint effort to make the county and its government function. Provide for growth, for citizens of all economic levels—but don't pave all of the beautiful countryside. After all, the children of residents living in a condominium also want at least to go out and look at a cow.

Set up a schedule for the provision of public service improvements. Don't play catch up football with schools, but build and pay for what is needed, when they are needed. Don't over-build and then go searching for developers to bring in children to fill up the empty seats. Make it clear to the county level and the town level governments that they are now probably having their last chance to do the job. In so doing, in so providing the needed local services at an affordable level, the dangling apple of federal money and federal control, need not appear quite so enticing.

Above all this, the county of Loudoun must look both east and west, asking from both directions: what do you want, what are you willing to pay for? What are you willing to do without? How many neighbors do you really want?

Of great relative importance to all of this schedule for the future, is the provision for commerce and industry in the county. For too long, Loudoun has been only a place where our young brains and talent came from, as they went elsewhere to prosper. While seeking means to maintain at least basic farm industry, efforts should constantly go forward to encourage industrial and commercial development that will provide jobs and business opportunity for a reasonable and affordable growth.

The way to all of this is reasonable judgments and discretion in all decisions. Too much, in too small a place, is not the answer for Loudoun or is "no growth."

The pressures on all levels will continue in Loudoun. If the pressures are the outgrowth of real citizen concern, such as sprung up over-night in the Taylorstown water impoundment fight; if the people continue to try to find out as much as they can about the county in which they live; if the best of the past can be meshed without too much grinding of the gears with the new hopes and enthusiasms of the present; and if above all, a genuine feeling of concern for one's fellow man can prevade the thinking, and the praying of Loudoun—then the future may well continue to hold a workable combination of cows and condominiums.

Footnotes

At a recent session by management systems experts to train mid-level executives, the coordinator started off by saying: "Now I am going to give you a simple instruction. It is, Clean the room."

"In the next four minutes," he continued, "I want all of you to write down specifically what I said to do."

Four minutes later, he picked up the slips of paper. No two answers were alike. For some, "Cleaning the room" involved washing and waxing the floor; for others, the floor was not to be touched, but the furniture was to be polished; for still others, the list ran short or long, but above all varied.

The obvious conclusion then is that communication and description is not just getting out the words, but getting across what the words mean, the interpretation.

If I asked people living in Loudoun to describe their county, where it has been, and where it is likely to go, chances are that the answers would be so varied that the name, "LOUDOUN" might seem not to tie to any of the answers.

In defining our county, I speak in the hope that the words and descriptions which I attribute to the various groups will not bring too often the response, "He certainly did not speak for me." With this apology in advance, that the words I offer from the mouths of others are only as it seems to me, let me describe Loudoun . . . as I see it.

Policy Statement
On Local Growth

Zero Population Growth

Zero Population Growth, Inc. (ZPG) is a national organization headquartered at 1346 Connecticut Avenue, N.W., Washington, D.C. ZPG believes that the present population of the United States exceeds the optimum level for the continued well-being of its citizens and that a reduction in its current rate of population growth is necessary. The 150 local chapters throughout the country have been active in increasing public awareness of population and environmental problems and in lobbying for laws related to family planning services and land use planning [see the "footnote section" for a further explanation of ZPG's goals].

Background

In New Mexico, Oregon, California, Florida and New England—areas in which environmental and fiscal resources are already overloaded—and in other parts of the country where such overloads are seen as imminent, people are beginning to rise up in opposition to uncontrolled and unplanned growth at the local level.

Citizens are realizing that new development carries potential economic hardship as well as harmful environmental effects. More people usually mean more pollution, more traffic jams, more crime, and higher taxes. The traditional assumption by city and county officials that new growth automatically brings more jobs and more tax benefits is now being questioned. Numerous studies and the personal experience of taxpayers across the country show that the services required to accommodate the new growth usually cost more than the taxes contributed by this new growth.

The Task Force on Land Use and Urban Growth, headed by Laurence S. Rockefeller, examined the motivations behind the mounting sentiment for controlling urban growth. It concluded that the movement is *not* primarily motivated by environmental extremists, economic considerations, or the desire to exclude minority interests. Rather, the report stressed, "It appears to be a part of a rising emphasis on human values, on the preservation of natural and cultural characteristics which make for a humanly satisfying living environment."

What is "new" about this many-faceted movement is that it has surfaced in action, instead of just in grumblings and letters to the editor. New restrictive laws, zoning actions, moratoriums on building permits, density limitations, size or height limitations, and bans on septic tanks, are sprouting up all over. They are accompanied by citizen lawsuits to prevent development. Once tranquil city council or county commission meetings have become arenas of protest, overflowing with citizens seeking to block new subdivisions, shopping centers, factories, or amusement parks.

These "new" activists are the PTA joiners, the Boy and Girl Scout leaders, the garden clubbers, and the Little Leaguers. To defend their neighborhoods from what they see as undesirable development, and to gain a greater control over the future of their communities, they are willing to form and found opposition groups, often in the form of homeowners associations. The objectives of these groups are generally quite narrow—to prevent the intrusion of new apartment buildings, sewage treatment plants, expressways, or airports in their immediate area. It is important that these groups start now to relate their neighborhood goals to those of the total community and region of which they are a part. Too often their attitude is summarized by the cliche, "Anywhere but here."

Why ZPG Is Involved in the "Slow Local Growth" Movement

1. The nationwide sentiment is mustering large amounts of energy, money, and votes for achieving the population stabilization objectives already held by ZPG.
2. Where efforts at controlling local growth have been organized, those people will probably be more receptive to the population/resources message. Because the lesson plan in this "learning laboratory" deals specifically with the quality of one's own backyard and the personal, out-of-pocket costs needed to maintain a desirable quality, the student is attentive and the message will probably be absorbed. A great many people who are becoming involved have had no previous commitment to environmental or social goals.
3. Once people have become sensitized to the need for controlling growth in order to achieve a satisfactory *local* environment, they can be developed into proponents for regional and state controls on land use and urban growth.
4. Through their efforts to challenge irresponsible growth, private citizens and groups will have the opportunity to present to politicians, planners and builders, information on the economic and social ramifications of alternative growth policies which has been developed by the U.S. Population Commission, the national Task Force on Land Use, and other organizations.
5. Each successful effort by citizens to control the development and future of their community, will spawn new efforts in the same community or in ones nearby. Such efforts must sooner or later provide the political leverage necessary for long-term change. Where areas have administrative structures for dealing with large metropolitan areas containing several independent political entities, the citizen groups can effect adoption of comprehensive development plans. If such superstructures are needed, the coalition can help bring them into being.
6. At the same time that communities are being saved from the bankruptcy of unwise development, it will be possible to reallocate financial and planning resources to begin ecologically sound and socially just redevelopment of decaying inner cities.

Goals of ZPG's "Slow Local Growth" Program

1. To direct growth away from sensitive areas such as floodplains, marshes, estuaries, beaches, wildernesses, and open space which are needed for farmland, ground water recharge, and other processes needed to support the life of our citizens.
2. To distribute population so as to avoid concentrations of populations which overload the environmental, economic, social, or psychological resources of an area.
3. To reduce the intolerable demands of our life style—on resource consumption; on the pollution of air, land, and water; and on the generation of wastes.
4. To bring about urban environments which are healthy, safe, and enriching for every member of society, including the poor.
5. To move a broader segment of the public to insist on state and national land use policies which are based on population and resource realities.

Policy Statement On Local Growth

Methods for broadening support for slow-growth and planned-growth policies:

1. Tap the energies and political weight of those sectors of the community who wish to limit or redirect growth at the local level;
2. Relate objections to local growth to the underlying causes—too many people to be accommodated in too short a time (too many people being defined as any situation where delivery of public services has not kept pace with growth, for whatever reason);
3. Relate high taxes to exponentially increased costs of public services for population loads which exceed the optimum for per unit cost savings;
4. Relate increased food costs to the one million acres of land (much of it prime farm land) which is lost to urban growth each year, and to fouled or filled estuaries;
5. Relate costly housing and shoddy construction to land boom development;
6. Identify and support low-income housing proposals and economic opportunities for the disadvantaged which are environmentally sound;
7. Increase understanding of the need for environmentally-sound and socially-just land use planning at a regional and national level, as a prerequisite for the solution of many growth problems at the local level;
8. Emphasize the immediate health hazard of unmanaged wastes;
9. Emphasize the looming hazard of nuclear power plants pressed into service without adequate testing or provision for the safe long-term storage of radioactive wastes;
10. Link brown-outs, traffic snarls, fuel shortages, and dirty air to population growth, poor urban planning, and short-term energy policies which dictate automobile dependency; and,
11. Relate social problems such as poverty, mental illness, crime, drug abuse, lack of concern for the aged, and urban decay to unrestricted growth.

Strategy

Land use and urban growth policies are being debated and resolved at many levels: local, state, national, and regional (may be entirely within one state as with southeast Florida's Goldcoast, or may encompass several states as with the Regional Plan Association's tri-state area of New York, New Jersey, and Connecticut).

To a large extent, the "growth vs. non-growth" battle can be viewed as involving three distinct camps: (a) pro-growthers—primarily businessmen and real estate brokers who stand to make a profit from growth; (b) non-growthers—environmentalists and just plain folks who are striving to create a more human environment; and (c) the poor and minorities—who are primarily just trying to better their own conditions. They have been on the sidelines of the action for the most part, but are being seduced by the businessmen's rhetoric that "it's either jobs or the environment, you can't have both."

Since the "new mood/new activist" energy is focused primarily at the local level, much of ZPG's energies will be directed there while anticipating the spin-off benefits that will accrue to the higher level goals.

Local. Where citizens are in revolt over a local situation, ZPG chapters and individuals can provide assistance by (a) serving as a catalyst to forge coalitions; (b) helping to define immediate, short, and long range objectives; and (c) providing resource materials and case studies of other groups which have faced similar problems. Homeowners associations, conservation groups, organized social workers and landscape architects, welfare and tenants' rights organizations are likely possibilities for such coalitions.

1. *Immediate objectives* might include one or more of the following: (a) freeze rezoning

or work for downzoning in a specific area; (b) oppose bond issues that will finance new or wider roads, schools, sewer and water line expansion, expressways, jetports; (c) eliminate "boosterism" advertising from a city budget; (d) convince newspapers and TV stations to run a poll on citizens' reactions to growth. Or sell city officials on mailing one out with the tax or garbage bills. This would be a good job for the League of Women Voters. Questionnaires have been prepared by several communities which can be used as models. Tabulation of responses can be done by computer centers of local colleges or cooperative business corporations; (e) secure publicity in the local media for cost/benefit studies which have been done in other communities; and, (f) find an up-to-date lawyer to prepare a suit challenging zoning or planning decisions which do not protect the health, safety, and welfare of the community.

2. *Short-range objectives* might include: (a) prepare a cost/benefit study for the total community or for a particular development project; (b) pressure the zoning board or the city commission to maintain stringent controls on agricultural and general use zoning to inhibit sprawl (such as a ¾ affirmative vote of the body, not the quorum, to intensify usage); (c) encourage new activists to nominate each other for appointments to zoning boards, sewer boards, and planning commissions; and, (d) propose innovative taxation and financial programs to encourage redevelopment of inner city areas rather than development of open spaces.

3. *Long-range objectives* might include: (a) election of knowledgeable population/resource candidates at all levels; (b) development of zoning maps which conform to comprehensive city or regional plans which have been based on criteria which are environmentally sound and socially just; (c) coalescence of political support for regional and state land use legislation providing balanced, integrated transportation systems; (d) support for initiatives when necessary to set limits on population size; and, (e) passage of sufficient appropriations bills to meet the needs for housing and health care for the poor.

Regional/State. Efforts to deal with land use and urban growth at the regional and state level will continue to be quarterbacked and hustled primarily by environmental organizations. During the fall of 1973, it is highly likely that federal land use legislation will be passed which will require that states develop statewide land use plans. Federal funding to develop such plans will probably be in the neighborhood of one billion dollars.

ZPG chapters and federations can be instrumental in arranging seminars for representatives of environmental organizations and others that have shown an interest. Appropriate topics for such seminars include model land use plans, creative real estate taxation, and guidelines for distributing population growth. ZPG's national office presently maintains a clearinghouse for information in these areas. Adoption of some measures for support by a conservation/professional planners' coalition could mark the beginning of serious lobbying and pressure for ZPG's larger goals.

ZPG intends to work with other organizations in developing specific policies geared to slowing growth at the local level, which are also equitable to the poor. If the "control local growth" movement is to gain full steam across the nation, we must have such policies as a matter of basic justice. Furthermore, if such policies are not developed, those working on behalf of the poor and civil liberties will provide substantial opposition to efforts to control or slow local growth.

National. Zero Population Growth's Washington lobbying office has worked for the passage of land use planning legislation at the national level, which contains adequate sanctions. Legislation presently under consideration would provide $1 billion over eight years to states and Indian tribes for the development of land use plans and regulations. Once such legislation has been passed, ZPG intends to continue its efforts to ensure that appropriations come through at the level approved.

Policy Guidelines

ZPG's program to help local communities control their population growth is carried out within the following policy framework:

1. Limited-growth and optimum-growth activists shall be assisted when the objective is to ensure a quality environment; slow-growth or non-growth efforts which are based on racial or economic discrimination shall not be assisted.
2. The expertise of ecologists, economists, political scientists and other specialists will be actively solicited to ensure sound environmental and economic benefits from successful control activities.
3. The participation of inner city residents shall be actively solicited, to ensure recognition of the needs and preferences of workers, minorities, and the elderly.

ZPG's Controlled-Growth Program

ZPG presently maintains a nationwide clearinghouse in the area of "controlling local growth," and provides assistance to individuals, local organizations, and others, who are interested in slowing or stopping growth in their area. Materials which have been developed to assist local activists include: a bibliography of cost/revenue studies on new residential development; a "Population Poll Package" to assist citizens and groups in polling the population and environmental attitudes of the members of their community; a Non-Growth Bibliography, which covers a wide variety of information geared to activists; and two issues of ZPG's quarterly magazine *Equilibrium*, which have been devoted entirely to the subject of local growth. For information on these materials, direct queries to the "ZPG Task Force on Local Growth" at ZPG's national office.

Statement of Goals

[*Editors Note: the following has been published by ZPG as "A Statement of the Goals of Zero Population Growth, Inc.*]

The long-term survival of the human species is dependent upon the establishment of an equilibrium between human demands and the carrying capacity of nature. The earth and its resources of land, air, water, and minerals are finite, and therefore there are limits to the cumulative demands which can be placed upon them. In addition, the earth and its resources and the users of those resources comprise a series of intricately complex ecological systems. No demand or action can be considered in isolation; all things are interconnected.

Foremost among the pressures on the boundaries of finity and ecological balance is the strain of a growing human population now numbering in the billions. The number of human beings that the earth can support is a function of the per capita demands of those individuals. It is preferable to support a smaller number of human beings at an equitable and sufficient standard of living than a greater number at a lesser level.

Zero Population Growth, Inc. (ZPG) concerns itself primarily with the United States, but these principles are universal.

ZPG has adopted a limited number of broad goals to guide its activities:

1. ZPG believes that the present population of the United States exceeds the optimum level for the continued well-being of its citizens. ZPG therefore advocates the achievement, by voluntary means, of an end to U.S. population growth by 1990, and a reduction in U.S. population size thereafter. Among the conditions necessary to achieve this goal, ZPG stresses: freedom of access for every person to all means of voluntary birth control; a major research effort to develop safer and more effective means of birth control; complete equality of opportunity for all women and men; and removal of all legal and societal pro-natalist pressures. The population size

Policy Statement On Local Growth

should stabilize at a substantially reduced level which will maximize diversity, freedom of choice, and the quality of life for all.

2. ZPG believes that land is a resource too important to human survival to be subjected to misuse. Ecological land use planning is essential in determining the appropriate patterns of distribution of people on the land, and of migration between states and regions. Thoughtful land use planning at all levels of government is necessary to assure the long-range stewardship of the land and well-being of mankind.

3. ZPG believes that human activities are causing the rapid depletion of the world's available stock of mineral resources. Simultaneously those activities are resulting in increased pollution of land, air and water resources. ZPG therefore recommends 1) reduction in the rate of growth and eventual stabilization of United States consumption of non-renewable resources; and 2) rapid stabilization of total national energy consumption at least until environmentally sound sources are developed.

ZPG recognizes that none of its goals can be justified unless concurrently with their achievement adequate levels of income, health care, and educational opportunity are assured to all persons.

Citizen Tactics:

Pressure, Power, & the Courts

Stanford Environmental
Law Society

The "Acknowledgements" Section of A Handbook for Controlling Local Growth—by Mary Cranston, Bryant Garth, Robert Plattner, and Jay Varon—states:

"This handbook was compiled during the summer of 1973 by members of the Stanford Environmental Law Society, a student organization at Stanford Law School. Our work was made possible by grants from the Alamo Foundation, the Wallace A. Gerbode Foundation and the Nicholas B. Ottaway Foundation."

Reprinted with permission of the Stanford Environmental Law Society, © 1973 by the Board of Trustees of the Leland Stanford Junior University.

Preface

The purpose of this book is to direct the attention of local communities and their citizens and governments toward the issue of controlling their growth. As its title indicates, this book will suggest a number of techniques by which such a policy may be effectuated.

While our analysis is largely focused on California, most of it is of a general nature and is equally valuable to communities across the nation. In those places where the discussion is particularly detailed, it is primarily designed to function by way of example. Specific differences from California law or procedure are readily discernible by examining the relevant case or statutory materials.

This book is divided into several chapters. . . . Chapter V presents a list of tactics which can best implement the techniques. . . . [Editor's Note: the "Tactics" chapter is reproduced here.]

Knowledge of various techniques for local growth control is clearly valueless without some grasp of methods of implementation. This section will briefly outline approaches for transforming theory into action.[1]

Citizen Pressure

Politicians are influenced by citizen opinion, but those opinions must be made clear to officials in order to effectuate results. The following techniques all have such clarification as their primary goal.

1. Organize a Group of Concerned Citizens. Groups have more environmental clout and credibility than an individual, and obviously more manpower to do a more thorough job of presenting a cogent growth control plan. Unfortunately, controlled growth proponents often lack "an issue"—such as the proposed building of an eyesore of thirty stories in a peaceful suburb—around which to rally support. Their goals are more long range and they must slowly build up a dedicated corps of workers. This core group may then organize less involved citizens for specific campaigns as they arise. The remainder of the section will deal primarily with the management of more short term campaigns, but the importance of an ongoing central group with an eye to the overall picture cannot be over-emphasized.

2. As a Group, Become Informed About Growth Control and Formulate Goals and a Plan. In a general sense, the group should be familiar with the make-up of the community, including the persuasions of the elected officials, the structure of governmental bodies and agencies, relevant federal, state and local statutes and ordinances, and basic demographic factors. Additional and more specific information will be required for particular campaigns, whether the purpose is to stop excessive development or to urge adoption of positive growth control devices.

In order to effectively block an undesirable growth project, the group must know three things: what the proposal ostensibly consists of, what the developers really intend to do, and what the effects of the proposed development will be.[2] The city planning department can usually provide the details set forth by the developers for public consumption. The real picture may be harder to uncover. Visiting the site may reveal inconsistencies between what the developers claim they are going to do and what they are in fact planning. Checking public records for ownership may reveal conflicts of interest on the part of city or county officials in favor of the development. Sympathetic expert testimony should also be garnered; names of experts such as soil engineers may usually be obtained from large environmental groups.

A more difficult investigative task is posed when the group desires to advocate a positive proposal for controlling growth. If the city planners are sympathetic, their expertise can be an invaluable source. Extensive statistics should be compiled: present growth rate, employment capacity of the area at the present stage of industrial development, capacity of utilities, and any other relevant figures. The political climate of the community must be gauged: is the area ready for a total plan, or are smaller steps indicated? What action has been taken in the past? Finally, the group must merge these factors into a well-documented and workable proposal.

One increasingly popular method of documenting growth control proposals is through the use of cost/revenue and cost/benefit analyses. A study sponsored by growth control groups, however, could be suspect, particularly since many local officials are aware of the probability of a range of outcomes from such studies depending on the factors considered in the analysis. Growth control groups would probably be more successful if they attacked cost/benefit analyses put out by pro-growth advocates, and used to their advantage any objective reports sponsored by public or private agencies. Developers will often glibly argue for growth in terms of increased revenues to the area, creation of new jobs, and meeting the needs of the areas' projected growth, concluding with a tidy total of monetary benefit to the community. Such proposals fail to account for long range maintenance costs, economic effects on other parts of the area, or environmental deterioration. They ignore the well-documented fact that preparing to meet projected growth ensures at least that level of development, and increases pressure for further development. Finally, they fail to discuss the housing crunch which may result from the increased jobs. Such statements are perfect targets for well-aimed attacks by growth control advocates.

This cautionary note about cost/benefit and cost/revenue analyses is not to discourage persuasive statements in support of a campaign position, such as "This project will put a severe strain on our already overcrowded schools," or "Increasing the amount of water available to our county will open the door to high density development." The group may also profitably urge an organization with unimpeached credibility to undertake a detailed study. Our point here is simply to note the precariousness of announcing a comprehensive study producing *the best* result.

3. Publicize Your Position. *(a) Advertisement:* Paid advertisements which are imaginative and eye-catching are expensive but have an effective initial impact on citizens and their elected officials. The ad should include an address or phone number of local government to which citizens may send their expressions of concern.

(b) The Press: Newspapers will generally find growth control activities newsworthy, and if they are behind the group's goals may do away with the need for paid advertisements. Get to know the reporters and editors covering areas related to growth control and explain clearly the group's goals and objectives. Ask for editorial support as well as coverage in the news columns. It is important to maintain credibility with the press: 1) Always make sure that remarks are accurate and if possible hand out a press release to avoid damaging misquotes. 2) Don't hold a press conference or pass out a news release unless the group has something new and significant to say. 3) Don't "tell" the press what to say, or argue about lack of coverage. These grievances should be handled privately. However, if the group has an honest disagreement with an editorial policy of the paper, these views should be presented in a letter to the editor.

(c) Television and Radio: Contact radio and television stations which broadcast news and supply them with press releases. In addition, the FCC requires commercial radio and television stations to make available a certain amount of free time to community organizations and causes, which may be available to growth control groups. Local daily talk shows are another possibility. To get on radio and television, organize a few definite program ideas, visit the station's manager or program director, and present your position.

(d) Enlist the Support of Outside Groups: Excellent sources of manpower for specific issue campaigns are often organized groups whose primary focus may not be growth control, but who are sympathetic to environmental aims; Boy Scouts, League of Women Voters, Taxpayers Associations, tenants unions and other powerful lobby groups, including at times developers, can be persuaded to assist in the effort by showing them that a project is adverse to their best interests.

(e) Public Meetings: A general meeting of citizens supporting the growth control side of a specific issue may be the next step—politicians will be impressed with a sizeable turnout. Choose an easily accessible and inexpensive meeting hall, such as a church or high school, geared to the size of the turnout expected. The meeting should be short, organized and confined to issues at hand. Dealing with specific problems rather than general issues usually creates a more interested audience. Use this meeting to collect names and commitments from additional volunteer workers to help on specifically outlined portions of the campaign.

4. While Publicizing the Growth Control Position, the Group Must Concurrently Raise Funds for the Campaign Effort. Realistically, most of the money for the campaign will come from the pockets of concerned citizens. Appeals for donations in conjunction with other publicity and mail-outs to members of local environmental groups are two ways to contact potential donors. Beware of "events" such as picnics to raise money: the profit is often low and the amount of work required to organize may drain manpower from more effective modes of campaigning.

5. Arguing the Case to City Government. *(a) Planning Department:* As mentioned previously, the planning department should be approached first. Planners are experts and will be more receptive to arguments based on concrete environmental and economic effects rather than aesthetics. While planners rarely hold official hearings, they are often willing to discuss issues with citizens; (b) *Approaching the City Council:* The main thrust of most campaigns will be to influence the votes of the final decision maker: the city council, county board of supervisors, LAFCO, or the equivalent.

One effective approach is lobbying. This entails a direct contact with each individual decision-maker armed with the argument most likely to influence that official to vote the preferred way. For example, if the key vote on rezoning a parcel for more intensive use is held by a councilman who has no interest in conserving open space but who opposes development which will increase the local property tax load, he ideally should be approached with tax-related arguments.

Testifying at hearings is a particularly critical means of influencing the votes of decision makers, not only because of what is actually said at the meeting but also as a clearcut expression of citizen concern. The group must be careful to be informed of the requisite procedure; some cities require pre-hearing registration while others allow the audience to express their views. Activists who have had experience in "hearing strategies" emphasize the desirability of bringing large numbers of people, especially local voters, to the meetings. A large turnout, in contrast to the usual sparse attendance at city council meetings, graphically informs the decision-makers of strong citizen support or protest. The group should present well-researched testimony by engineers, lawyers, housewives and others, thus presenting a spectrum of arguments.

Letters and phone calls are other effective methods of demonstrating opinion. People rarely write or call their councilmen or mayor, and local officials have come to expect apathy on most issues; fifty or sixty such communications may have a tremendous impact on officials' conclusions. Form letters and petitions are less effective because they indicate a well-organized lobby group which may have little real support.

Citizen Voting Power

If the local government fails to respond to the pressure for controlled growth, more sympathetic local officials must be elected, or the citizens must work for adequate law outside the normal channels of the city council or board of supervisors. [*Editor's Note: this discussion is in the context of California law.*]

1. Overriding the Policies of Elected Officials—the Referendum. The referendum gives citizens the power to veto legislation at the polls. Our discussion here will focus on the general law city referendum procedure, but charter city provisions are similar,[4] and referendums are also possible at the county and state levels with some procedural modifications.[5]

Most laws adopted by local governments become effective thirty days after passage. During this waiting period, the effective date of the law may be suspended if ten per cent of the local voters protest by signing petitions filed with the city clerk.[6] (It is better to try to collect twenty per cent of the voters' signatures as a cushion against the invalidation of some signatures.) After the filing of the petition, the city council, or whatever local body is involved, has the option of either submitting the ordinance to the voters at an election or repealing the law. Generally the council places the issue on the ballot of the next general election (to save the expense of a special election), and the law is dormant until the election. The opponents of the law may have a statement of their views mailed with the sample ballot. If a majority of the voters fails to approve the ordinance, the ordinance is void and may not be reenacted for one year. If a majority of the voters approves the measure, the proposal becomes law.

2. **Citizen Proposal of a Growth Control Ordinance—the Initiative.** The initiative allows voters to completely bypass the local government in enacting ordinances.

(a) *Procedure:* Again we note that while we will be discussing general law city procedures,[7] somewhat similar rules are applicable in charter cities, and at other governmental levels.[8] Proponents have 180 days in which to obtain fifteen percent of the signatures of the city's voters. If they are successful the city council must either adopt the proposed ordinance or submit it to the voters at a special election. If the proponents have only collected ten per cent of these signatures of voters, the council must adopt the ordinance or submit it to the voters at the next general election.[9] Again proponents may have a statement of their position mailed out with the sample ballot. The proposal becomes city law if it is approved by a majority of the voters.

(b) *Current Limitation on the Use of the Initiative:* Unfortunately, California courts have seen fit to curtail the availability of the initiative in general law cities, particularly with regard to zoning initiatives, perhaps the most critical tool of growth control. General law cities must follow zoning procedures specified by state statute, and the courts have held that the initiative process is not compatible with those procedures.[10] Charter cities, on the other hand, need not follow state-prescribed procedures. Thus the California courts have held that unless the charter provides otherwise, a zoning ordinance can be adopted by initiative in a charter city.[11] In the landmark case of *Bayless v. Limber,* which upheld an initiative zoning ordinance prohibiting the drilling of oil wells in a residential neighborhood, the court gave a liberal interpretation to the initiative power in the city charter:

> The initiative power reserved to the people of a city by its charter must be liberally construed . . . . It is the duty of the courts to guard jealously this power of the people . . . the reservation of this power within the charter is not expressly limited in its coverage over municipal affairs in any manner at all.[12]

The court went on to note that the initiative process was a fair and equitable method of creating an ordinance and thus did not violate the Constitution, either state or federal. The distinction between the two types of cities with regard to the use of the initiative seems somewhat arbitrary—only in general law cities is the initiative zoning ordinance considered to be violative of due process of law. Several traditional general law cases are on appeal now, and it would appear worthwhile for growth control proponents to continue to test these cases. The major obstacle to compliance with procedural due process in the general law cities appears to be the state statutory provision for notice and hearing in the zoning process.[13] There are two possible approaches to this problem:[14] First, it can be argued that Sections 65800 and 65801 of the Government Code of California enacted in 1965 play a critical role in determining the validity of zoning initiatives. Section 65800 shifted the power over zoning from the state government to local government while Section 65801 barred any procedural error as grounds for invalidating any legislative action unless that error was shown to have prejudiced the outcome. Growth control proponents can present the theory that Section 65801 implicitly provides that an election may constitute hearing and notice such that only prejudicial damage as a result of the initiative may void the zoning ordinance. Secondly, growth control advocates can argue that an election *does* provide adequate notice and hearing as required by Sections 65351 and 65355 of the Government Code. (A positive court decision on this second theory would provide support for the first argument by showing that an election is *not* a defective form of hearing and notice.) Some courts have held that an election is not an effective substitute for notice and hearing, and Section 65801 was not intended to "bypass" the zoning procedure sections of the statute.[15] However, some courts have adopted a more reasonable approach and viewed Section 65801 as "modifying" rather than "bypassing" the procedural requirements. One court, for example, interpreted Section 65801 as manifesting a legislative intent to prescribe any reasonable form of notice which accomplishes its purpose.[16] The test for adequate notice should be what common experience can expect to be reasonably adequate notice to all.

(c) *Further Uses of the Initiative in Charter Cities:* The initiative does not necessarily have to be a zoning ordinance. It may, for example, freeze the existing zoning while changes are being studied.[17] Furthermore, if the charter provisions do limit the availability of the initiative, citizens can place an amendment to the charter itself on the ballot by gathering the signatures of fifteen per cent of the city's voters.[18]

3. Election of Responsive Officials. The expense as well as the statutory and court decreed limitations on the initiative and referendum processes reduce the practicality of these methods as ongoing forces shaping growth control policies. A sympathetic city council is thus crucial to a truly effective program. There are essentially two ways of achieving a voting majority on a city council or county board of supervisors: recall and the general election.

(a) *Recall:* The power of voting citizens to oust an irresponsible legislator can be an essential tool in forging a positive growth control plan.[19] The general law recall process begins by notification of the challenged official and the city clerk of the proposed recall by the concerned voters. These voters must also publish the information that a recall is sought. If these voters can gather the signatures of twenty-five per cent of the city's voters within sixty days, the city council must call a special election in which candidates nominated to succeed the challenged official also run. If a majority of the voters approve the recall, the candidate receiving the most votes takes the seat on the council. Hopefully, a growth control group well-enough organized to oust an incumbent can also poll enough votes to elect its candidate as the successor.

(b) *General Elections:* The general election is normally the easiest time to elect concerned councilmen. The election suggestions below have proved successful in the past and apply to initiative, referendum, and recall elections as well as general elections.

(c) *Organization:* Early planning and thorough organization are crucial to success. Other projects should be temporarily set aside to concentrate fully on the election. City Hall should be contacted for information concerning election filing dates. Activists in the area should then get together to prepare an inventory of questions for candidates. These early meetings should also plan the basic strategy: should the group nominate a candidate or endorse the best of those already running? Running a candidate allows concentrated energy in a single campaign, and may be the only choice available if none of the other candidates is suitable. The endorsement approach, on the other hand, has the advantages of allowing participation in more than one race and of lending to the endorsed candidate the prestige of support from an outside group. Local conditions should dictate the strategy chosen, but only an early start will allow a choice.

(d) *Choosing Candidates to Run as Growth Control Candidates:* The line of least resistance is the education of an incumbent through a showing of political support and lucid argument. If the incumbents are beyond redemption, they must be unseated, even though this is a somewhat difficult undertaking. Consideration should be given to candidates who support growth control but whose primary focus may be elsewhere. Other possibilities include selecting a prominent local environmentalist or running an "unknown" from the growth control group. It is important that any candidate chosen have electable and strong views on matters other than growth control.

(e) *Evaluating Candidates Already Running for Possible Endorsement:* One possible method is to send questionnaires to all those declared for the race, informing the candidates that the group will support those qualified. Consider supporting those who showed concern for growth control in their responses but beware of candidates who skirted the difficult issues while eloquently advocating lesser solutions. On the other hand, the group must also be alert to the possibility of educating candidates with an initially wishy-washy commitment. The questionnaire should be followed up with personal interviews of those candidates showing any promise of effective advocacy of growth control. This provides an opportunity to probe views more thoroughly, and to note any possible conflicts of interest on important issues. It is also helpful in assessing the effectiveness of the candidate as a legislator.

(f) *Running an Endorsement Campaign:* A press conference with the candidates and the growth control group is often an effective beginning, particularly if the newspapers in the area are endorsing other candidates. Brochures should be distributed door to door and in shopping centers. When the day of the election approaches, concentrate on areas where support is likely. At that point, getting out the positive vote is more likely to produce the desired result than trying to change any minds.

(g) *Running a Campaign for a Growth Control Candidate:* After a candidate is chosen, the first step is the organization of a volunteer staff for precinct work, phone calls, and literature distribution. The core group of the growth control organization can be useful in recruiting people. Possible sources of labor include the mailing lists of environmental organizations and the pools of people who have attended various related public hearings. The campaign organization must then begin contacting the voters to increase awareness and support for the growth control candidate. Voter registration lists are public records available from the election clerk. Avoid antagonizing those who oppose the candidate since such behavior will encourage these voters to go to the polls. Concentrate on getting supporters to the polls with such aids as car pools and baby sitting facilities.

Courts and Law Suits

Courts have recently demonstrated an increased willingness to interfere with local land use decisions. The primary motivation for this trend is the clear expression of the state and federal legislatures that the environment is a concern of high priority. Because local governments are often susceptible to development pressures, the courts will often have to encourage them to perform their proper function.

1. Advantages of a Lawsuit. Lawsuits have a number of advantages. First of all there is obviously a chance of winning the suit. However, the mere threat of a suit can also be an impressive political tactic, expressing acute citizen displeasure with the activities of the incumbent government. And finally, suits can be an effective delaying tactic in order to force compromises. Developers may want to postpone their project until the court has cleared their status, or the court itself may issue an injunction or temporary restraining order. Extensive delay may even force the developer to abandon his plans due to financing difficulties.

2. Standing, or the Right to Sue. Not everyone can bring any given suit. The courts have limited the right to sue to those who have been affected or aggrieved by the activity against which the suit is brought. The limitations on standing in environmental litigation are presently somewhat unclear. However, recent court opinions have indicated that the standing requirements will be fairly liberal.[20] Currently, if a growth control group member lives in an affected neighborhood, a suit could probably be brought in his name, with the growth control group "intervening" as a "friend of the court."

3. Traditional Litigation—Methods of Challenging Governmental Decisions. The following tools are available to courts to correct illegal governmental decisions and activities.

(a) *Ordinary Mandamus:* One method of judicial review of local laws is called the "writ of mandate." Mandamus is the power of the court to compel the performance of a duty which the law requires. Mandamus cannot be used where the legislature or agency has been granted discretionary power, and so has been ineffective in the past for controlling zoning and open space acquisition activities. However, new state laws[21] requiring zoning ordinances to comply with the general plan of the city and to provide open space may put some force into the concept.

(b) *Administrative Mandamus:* Administrative decisions are also reviewable by the courts through a procedure known as administrative mandamus. According to California law, administrative decisions such as variances and use permits can be overruled by the court if the administrative agency abuses its discretion in a way that affects the outcome of the decision. The criteria for showing abuse are: 1) a showing that the agency has not proceeded in the manner required by law; 2) a demonstration that the decision of the agency is not supported by its findings of fact; or, 3) a showing that the findings are not supported by the evidence.[22] California courts have recently begun to effectively utilize this power to review such decisions. For example, the courts have overturned variances where the planning commission report set out detailed findings which were inadequate.[23] In addition, the new open-space legislation makes clear the state legislative intent to reduce abuses of variance process.[24] This recent expression of legislative intent may produce further court readiness to closely examine the granting of variances and use permits. Procedural challenges to local land use decisions are difficult to maintain in California. The statute requires a showing that a "different result would have been probable if such error had not occurred."[25] Furthermore, even successful challenges are only temporary victories since the local government can reinstate the ordinance by following the proper procedure.

(c) *Injunctions:* Courts have started to use injunctions more frequently in sustaining complaints that local governments have not followed state zoning law. An injunction forbids the local government from continuing whatever activity is found to be objectionable, and may be permanent or temporary. Before going to court to seek an injunction, however, the challengers must have appealed the decision to the highest administrative level possible.

4. Modern Environmental Litigation. The foregoing legal remedies can be used to stop any kind of governmental abuse, and are not concerned exclusively with land regulation. For the above tools to be most effective, therefore, it is critical that the law itself be environmentally sympathetic so that rampant pro-growth activities of local government will be more clearly an "abuse." The following statutes not only strengthen existing judicial remedies, but provide some new causes of action of their own.

(a) *NEPA and CEQA:* The National Environmental Policy Act (NEPA) bestows high national priority on environmental concerns and requires federal agencies to examine ecological factors before undertaking projects that might affect the environment. While the courts have generally required the federal agencies to comply with the requirement of submitting a report concerning environmental impact, the courts have split on the issue of whether the agency must do anything about the results of its study.[26] The California Environmental Quality Act (CEQA) is the state's version of NEPA. The statute requires an Environmental Impact Statement (EIS) for development projects ordered by local governments or any level of government within the state. The California Supreme Court recently read the statute to encompass projects public or *private* which require governmental use permits in order to be carried out.[27] The actual effect of this decision remains to be clarified in further court action. CEQA will apparently be a powerful delaying tactic in the instance where the developer has failed to submit an EIS or has submitted an inadequate EIS. However, once such statement has been prepared there is at present no requirement for evaluating its quality, so the impact statement requirement can currently have no permanent disqualifying effect.[28]

(b) *Open Space Planning:* As has been mentioned elsewhere, California has recently passed legislation requiring all cities and counties to include an open space element in their general plans by June 30, 1973.

5. Get a Lawyer. This section has not presented anything approaching the in-depth knowledge necessary to bring a successful suit. The first step for any growth control group contemplating court action is to obtain a competent attorney. Realistically, a lawyer is the only person in a position to estimate the chances of success of the suit, and to make the strategic decisions which are important to the ultimate success of a legal claim.

Getting a lawyer for environmental litigation is at times a difficult proposition since law suits are expensive and there are rarely funds to reimburse even the legal costs of the attorney. However, the Ninth Circuit Court of Appeals recently awarded court and attorney fees in the case of *La Raza Unida.*[29] Only time will indicate whether this is a trend of the future.

How do you find a good lawyer? This is a new field, and the problem is complicated by the fact that expert firms such as the Environmental Defense Fund prefer to tackle cases of national or statewide significance, rather than little cases which are important only to the local community. Nonetheless, it does not hurt to approach these firms. Perhaps the case presents an important legal question in a desirable factual setting. And even if the case is refused, environmental firms or clubs are the best place to be referred to a lawyer who will take the case. These organizations usually have a list or at least some names of private attorneys who know the field.

Footnotes

1. Much of this information has been previously set out in the *California Land Use Primer* also published by the Stanford Environmental Law Society; however, there has been some variation in techniques due to the substantive differences between growth control and the topic of the *Primer.*
2. *California Land Use Primer,* Stanford Environmental Law Society, 1972, p. 52.
3. The Livingston and Blaney study is discussed more fully in the Palo Alto Case Study.
4. Cal. Elections Code, 4050-4057 sets out the general law city referendum procedures.
5. County referendum procedures are found in Cal. Elections Code, 3750-3754; special district procedures in Cal. Elections Code, 5200-5203; state procedures in Cal. Const., art. 4, 23, and Cal. Elections Code, 3500-3508.
6. A petition in a city of 1000 or fewer voters must be signed by 25 percent of the voters or 100 voters whichever is fewer. Cal. Elections Code, 4051.
7. General law city initiative procedures are found in Cal. Elections Code, 4000-4023.
8. The state legislature, however, does not have the local governments' option of adopting the measure itself, but must submit all initiated proposals to the voters. Cal. Const., art. 4, 22; Cal. Elections Code, 3500-3508; county procedures: Cal. Elections Code, 3700-3721; special district procedures: Cal. Elections Code, 5150-5162.
9. Once again, the signature requirement is different in cities of 1000 or fewer voters. Cal. Elections Code, 4011-4012.
10. Hurst v. Burlingame, 207 C. 134, 227 P. 308 (1929); Johnson v. City of Claremont, 49 C.2d 826, 323 P.2d 71 (1958).
11. Dwyer v. City Council of Berkeley, 200 C.505, 253 P.932 (1927); Bayless v. Limber, 26 C.A.3rd 463, 102 Cal. Rptr. 647, petition denied by the Calif. Sup. Ct., September 7, 1972; Duran v. Cassidy, 28 C.A.3rd 574, 104 Cal. Rptr. 793 (1972).
12. Bayless v. Limber, 102 Cal. Rptr. 647, 649 (1972).
13. Cal. Govt. Code, 65350 et. seq.
14. Chien, *Limitation of City Size: Whither the Initiative?,* unpublished article, University of San Diego Law School, 1973.
15. City of Escondido v. Desert Outdoor Advertising, Inc., 8 C.3rd 785 (1973); Tascher v. City Council of Laguna Beach, 4 Civil 12090, Superior Court No. M-1838, Ct. of App., 4th D., March 8, 1973.
16. City of Sausalito v. County of Marin, 12 C.A.3rd 550, 90 Cal. Rptr. 843 (1970).
17. Fletcher v. Porter, 203 C.A.2nd 313, 21 Cal. Rptr. 452 (1962).
18. Cal. Const., art. 6, 8; Cal. Elections Code, 4080-4085.

Citizen Tactics

19. General law city recall procedures are found in Cal. Elections Code, 27500-27521; county recall procedures in Cal. Elections Code 27200-27216.
20. Association of Data Processing Service Organizations v. Camp, 397 U.S. 150 (1970); Sierra Club v. Morton 405 U.S. 727 (1972) is generally seen as primarily a pleading decision and not a step backwards from Association of Data Processing.
21. Cal. Govt. Code, 65860.
22. Cal. Code of Civ. Pro., 1094.5(b).
23. Broadway, Laguna, Vallejo Ass'n. v. Board of Permit Appeals, 66 C.2d 767, 59 Cal. Rptr. 146 (1967); Hamilton v. Superior Court, 269 C.A.2d 64, 75 Cal. Rptr. 106 (1969); Cow Hollow Improvement Club v. DiBene, 245 C.A.2d 160, 53 Cal. Rptr. 610 (1966).
24. Cal. Govt. Code, 65911.
25. Cal. Govt. Code, 65801.
26. For examples of the majority view that an agency must make an adequate study of the environment but doesn't necessarily have to act on any resultant recommendations, see E.D.F. v. Corps of Engineers, 325 F. Supp. 728, 342 F. Supp. 1211 (E.D. Ark.), aff'd 470 F.2d 289 (8th Cir. 1972); Wilderness Society v. Hickel, 325 F. Supp. 422, sub nom, Wilderness Society v. Morton, 463 F.2d 121 (D.C. Cir. 1972), F. Supp., rev'd F.2d (D.C. Cir. 1973). Some cases have seemed to require stricter consideration of environmental factors revealed in environmental studies and include: Calvert Cliffs Coordinating Committee, Inc. v. AEC, 449 F.2d 463 (D.C. Cir. 1971); Green County Planning Board v. F.P.C., 455 F.2d 412 (2d Cir. 1972). The strongest view not yet adopted by the courts that NEPA 101 creates justifiable standards of administrative conduct is found in Justice Douglas's dissent from the denial of certiorari in Scenic Hudson II, 407 U.S. 926 (1972).
27. Friends of Mammoth v. Mono County, 8 C.3rd 247, 104 Cal. Rptr. 161, 502 P.2d 1049 (1972).
28. Further technical details on environmental litigation: California Environmental Quality Act Developments, California Continuing Education of the Bar, Program Material, March, 1973.
29. La Raza Unida v. Volpe, 57 F.R.D. 94 (1972).

CHAPTER FOUR

TRADITIONAL SYSTEMS: ISSUES & DILEMMAS

The complaint has been often heard that the traditional planning and zoning systems have been subject to abuse, misinformation, and poor guidance . . . with the result that a significant part of the citizenry feels either disenfranchised by the land use controls system (as those excluded from suburban communities) or that the current system cannot adequately manage growth.

Commentators such as Richard Babcock and Daniel Mandelker have viewed the system variously as the "zoning game" and the "zoning dilemma," while one attorney who often represents developers, titled his 1971 article: "Discretionary Land-Use Controls: The Iron Whim of the Public." Needless to say, few embrace the system wholeheartedly; but on the other hand, to paraphrase one observation on government: "Our traditional zoning and land use controls may not be admirable or even particularly workable, but at present they may comprise the best system that we have."

The authors in this chapter analyze and dissect zoning, point out its major shortcomings, and propose alterations to the system . . . some of them modest changes, and others, sweeping reforms.

Ira Heyman mentions the three main objectives of land use regulation as they were originally conceived: segregation of inconsistent uses; prevention of congestion; and economic public service provision. But more importantly, he says the original system was built upon five "crucial assumptions . . . . First, a simplistic segregation of uses would result in a quality urban environment. Second, it would be possible, in drawing the zoning map, to formulate an intelligent all-at-once decision to which the market would conform. Third, the governors of the system would rarely change the rules. Fourth, nonconforming uses would go away. Fifth, municipal power would accomplish the goals." [Of course, as Heyman proceeds to point out, these assumptions have generally proven to be wrong; day-to-day changes and the playing of the "zoning game" have taken their toll.]

Failing to achieve many of its goals, and tending to buttress exclusion in many instances, zoning has come under attack by six major groups because "it has been fairly successful as an exclusionary tool." The "assaulters" of zoning are "the environmentalists, the lawyers, the market, the manifold proponents of open housing (especially the civil rights movement), state governments, and the federal government." Heyman speculates on the types of attacks which might be launched by open housing advocates: equal protection, the supremacy doctrine, and substantive due process. [Some commentators do not look kindly upon the last legal assault, but the author points out that state court judges may seize the opportunity whereas the federal courts are less likely to do so. This of course requires judges to step heavily into the area of what was once seen as the "legislative prerogative," and to substitute their judgement for that of the legislators in some instances. For further development of this theme, see Chapter 6 and 7.]

The author sees a "powerful stimulant" to the regionalization of land use regulation as being the "environmental movement." While much of this higher-echelon decision-making or review may be desirable, Heyman makes the exceptionally important observation (that will be repeated time and again in these volumes), "The environmental movement will produce agencies that will slow down development and make it more expensive—thus increasing the exclusionary effects of present local land-use regulations . . . . [N]ewly created state and regional agencies are likely to exercise their negative powers to prevent development that would have adverse physical environmental effects . . . . If rulings are based upon environmental considerations alone and social goals are ignored, development will become more expensive, thus heightening exclusionary impacts."

The article by **Babcock and Bosselman** comes from their book, titled *Exclusionary Zoning: Land Use Regulation and Housing in the 1970s.* They see the challenges brought in the courts over land use regulations as having "given rise to a see-saw battle in which the courts have experienced major shifts of emphasis and attitude in deciding how the balance of competing interests should be struck."

The ways in which the courts have dealt with these issues are divided into three eras: pre-*Nectow* (1928), post-*Nectow*, and post-Watts (1965). The early regulations are seen as having been tightly drawn and relatively limited in scope. The courts in turn found the zoning approach to be valid, laying down three basic principles: that the "scope of the police power is elastic"; that "diminution in value" of property as a result of regulation, would not necessarily invalidate the zoning concerned; and, that zoning enactments should be accorded a "presumption of validity."

During the second period, the courts did little to intervene with the now rapidly-expanding scope of local regulation. Several observers pointed out that zoning was having unfortunate social side-effects . . . but as the article states "the contention that the 'general' welfare served by zoning is not circumscribed by local boundaries, but extends to the region as well, fell on unresponsive ears." Only one judge (Justice Hall of New Jersey) spoke clearly to this issue.

The article then reviews the most recent period, when a series of court cases and "novel" challenges were initially successful in overturning certain exclusionary regulations in some states. But it was not long before still other case decisions somewhat dampened the litigation attacks (as in *Valtierra*, and in *Lindsey v. Normet*).

It is interesting to note several statements in the article, which talk to the role of the judiciary in zoning challenges. The authors probably correctly note that "judicial action is a heavy tool with which to fix the intricate clockwork on the land use controls system. The impact of judicial reexamination may break the machine rather than repair it. All but the most intransigent . . . would do well to reform the present system . . . to avoid the disarray of major judicial overhaul." Yet this apparently clear denunciation of too much judicial activism is partially countered by the authors' conclusion that "all the cluck-clucking by the purists to the contrary notwithstanding, the judge in the United States has been in the van [guard] of the forces that have led to the restructuring of our institutions and reappraisal of national policies. In our fractured society a good case can be made for such a circumstance with all its attendant disarray."

The article quite properly reaches the conclusion that as ineffective as the courts may often be, they can "act as a predicate to legislative reform . . . [and] can dramatize the absurdities and inequities in a fractured system of governmental regulation designed for a quieter era . . . ."

Edward Reiner traces the development of traditional zoning, and asks whether in fact the process is a failure or is approaching obsolescence. The question he addresses is the "alleged failure of the traditional zoning process to manage the land development process . . . ." He suggests that in part, this perception of zoning has led to the emergence of the managed growth philosophy.

He first looks at the inception of zoning in the early 1900s, at the adoption by states and localities of zoning ordinances, enabling legislation, and at the *Euclid* case (it is here, he points out, that the Court, in endorsing zoning as a valid exercise of the police power, tangentially commented on the necessity of zoning serving the general welfare, and more than merely local needs). But, the author points out, the history of zoning is marked by local governments proceeding to adopt ordinances and regulations often with little or no connection with adequate local comprehensive planning. He states, "This too-rapid adoption of zoning legislation by communities throughout the nation . . . was marked by the appearance of several trends whose ultimate effects have wrecked a costly havoc —economically, socially, and environmentally—on our society. The first trend is the shortcut approach adopted by numerous local governments [not to engage in comprehensive planning] . . . . The second is a consistent failure on the part of an overly acquiescent or unschooled . . . judiciary to uphold or enforce . . . the mandates of state enabling legislation, i.e. that zoning regulations shall be drawn 'in accordance with a comprehensive plan' . . . ."

Reiner cites the costs of this attitude: minimal regard for regionalism, environmental dysfunctions, lack of planning for social and housing needs, and so forth. Attempts have been made to address these problems through litigation (such as the exclusionary zoning suits of the 1960s and 1970s). But, he asserts, the need remains . . . to fill the gap; both judicial and legislative responses are long overdue.

Interestingly, the author claims that zoning has not been a "failure," since it has tended to achieve many of its original [limited] objectives. The problem is that perhaps too much has been asked of the zoning technique per se . . . that the expectations that it would adequately handle the many problems of land use, were and are unwarranted. What is needed is proper planning, the use of supplementary tools and techniques in some instances, and perhaps a few basic changes in the process [as outlined elsewhere in this chapter and in these volumes] . . . if the system is to "work" regarding society's burgeoning growth problems.

One suggestion made repeatedly by a number of authors is that the current system of zoning must be reformed; Bernard Siegan develops this theme in his book, *Land Use Without Zoning*—which is reviewed here by **John Ragsdale**. Ragsdale summarizes Siegan's basic complaints as follows: "He sees the overall attempt to effectuate planning as an artificial restriction on market forces, a position reflected in his book's title which, unlike many other recent works, does not couple the concept of land use with that of planning . . . . The foaming denouncement of zoning as an inherent infringement on property rights is a conclusive tipoff that Siegan, unlike many of his contemporaries, is not interested in reforming zoning . . . . Siegan's solution to the zoning problem is to throw the rascal out, and he selects for his prototype, zoneless Nirvana, the city of Houston . . . ."

Supposedly, Siegan's premise is that "economic forces will produce a natural separation of land uses," with builders and developers being able to "accurately assess the housing demand and supply it, without artificial restraints and unnecessary land price increments." Ragsdale then proceeds to point out that Houston has a number of land use regulations and controls which "help along" the allocation of land uses, even in the absence of formal zoning. Further, he suggests that Siegan's type of system tends to "gloss over several critical issues such as aesthetics, open space and conservation of scenic and agricultural resources." [Since many of these criticisms may appear harsh in the absence of the reader having had the opportunity to analyze Siegan's thesis directly, those interested further in the concept would do well to turn to the author's text, which was published in 1972 (see the Footnotes section to Ragsdale's article).]

In the next article, **Dan Tarlock** sets forth to "explore the reasons, in light of the historical origins of American city planning and zoning, that a satisfactory relationship between land-market operation and public intervention has failed to develop." The author then postulates that "contemporary zoning should be conceptualized as a system of joint ownership between the public entity and the regulated private owner." [In taking this lead from welfare economics, Tarlock in effect is redefining the concept of property . . . running head on at least superficially into a long legal tradition which is not attuned to making decisions under these system precepts.]

Tarlock believes that in society's struggle to redefine property as a "less-than-absolute concept" by nearly eliminating the hurdle of what constitutes a "taking" under the police power . . . "the result has been an uncritical acceptance of the need for public action and a lessening of interest in methods of improving markets or in simulating their operation through decentralized allocation systems." The courts have been tossed into the battle to define "what is and what is not in the public interest," with the consequence that this tends to "frustrate most principles of resource allocation . . . ." According to the author, the zoning system has been turned into an especially inefficient allocation system. Moreover, it has "become a burdensome licensing process for land developers which increasingly neither (1) performs its original justification of minimizing the externalities of land-use patterns nor (2) provides a demonstrably superior pattern of land allocation."

Tarlock examines both traditional and welfare economics-related rationales for land allocation through public regulation (he finds the former as "very costly and produces doubtful efficiency gains") both in developed areas and in the undeveloped fringe. With respect to his discussion of undeveloped areas, the author discusses the "recapturing" of value by the public when it zones and rezones land [a topic dealt with at length later in this chapter, by Hagman]. But Tarlock sees this proposal as allowing the regulatory body to appropriate "the benefits of ownership for itself, but [unfortunately] not the responsibilities" and he is not convinced that it "will produce a superior allocation of land."

He concludes by sketching a more efficient allocation system utilizing his principles of allocation, some conventional techniques, the public purchase of land, and the establishment of a market in development rights. [Regarding the last item, see the extensive treatment of the transfer of development rights concept in Chapter 14 of Volume III.]

A change in the way the zoning dilemma is being handled—a "quiet revolution" of sorts which occurred as a result of litigation—is explained by **Edward Sullivan**, who litigated the *Fasano* case that he discusses. As in many states, he points out, the "status of land use law in Oregon . . . is best described as chaotic. It seemed to change with the exigencies of the moment . . . [and] a substantial departure from the present system was required." The author notes that "little in the way of procedural fairness in zoning hearings" was required in the past, and they generally were deemed "legislative in character." The legal fiction of the "presumption of validity" grew up around zoning determinations, and judicial review tended to be quite limited. "The result was to play one fiction against the other to achieve a desired result . . . . It was against the background of this unacceptable state of affairs that the case of *Fasano* was decided."

Sullivan writes that "the Oregon Supreme Court undertook to abandon previous fictions utilized in the review of local land use decisions . . . . [T]he court went out of its way to emphasize the primacy of the comprehensive plan as the major standard by which local land use decisions were to be judged." [This has long been a matter of confusion to courts, many of which tend to regard virtually any governmental representation as constituting a "comprehensive plan" . . . including the zoning maps of the town, planning studies, or scattered program goal statements, and so forth. What constitutes an adequate comprehensive plan continues to be the subject of much debate.]

Two other revolutionary aspects of the decision are commented upon by the author. The first consists of the court's opinion that any requested rezoning of land must fulfill a "public need," and that alternative property should also be evaluated. [This constitutes a problem of interpretation for many localities in Oregon. It smacks in part of a NEPA-like analysis (see Chapter 15 of Volume III.] The second noteworthy change was the decision that "the nature of the rezoning process (and other permit-granting functions)" partakes more of a adjudicatory procedure than a legislative process. [This determination that certain functions are "quasijudicial" rather than "legislative" (with all the old shibboleths of "presumptions of validity," etc.) shakes the very foundations of the traditional zoning process. As the author notes, there now are a whole series of procedural requirements which must be met in such hearings. The case (as well as the accompanying explanation of the Oregon *Frankland* case) may be one which other jurisdictions will adopt in the future, either through judicial interpretation or legislative action . . . to reform at least in part the zoning process.]

One of the most well-known reports of recent years, was that prepared by **Bosselman and Callies**, titled *The Quiet Revolution*, and issued by the Council on Environmental Quality in late 1971. [The article as it appears here consists basically of two chapters and the postscript of the full report, and should serve to introduce the reader to the themes of that report.] The authors found the country "in the midst of a revolution in the way we regulate the use of land . . . . The *ancien regime* being overthrown is the feudal system under which the entire pattern of land development has been controlled by thousands of individual local governments, each seeking to maximize its tax base and minimize its social problems, and caring less what happens to all the others."

The so-called quiet revolution, disorganized and fragmented in its attempts, has as its tools "new laws taking a wide variety of forms but each sharing a common theme—the need to provide some degree of state or regional participation in the major decisions that affect the use of our increasingly limited supply of land." The article (and better, the full report) proceeds to examine the laws of several states, and to point to new and desirable threads of legislative action.

In line with the other articles of this chapter, the authors find that "local zoning . . . has proved woefully inadequate to combat a host of problems," and this has helped initiate the quiet revolution addressed here. Taking a "broad perspective," Bosselman and Callies identify six major issues: a changing concept of land (both a resource and a commodity); new roles for the states (in decisions regarding developments of significant impact); the role of local governments and the unfortunate tendency for duplicative procedures imposed by some states; the need for regulation and planning (the necessity for the integration of sophisticated planning and balancing of needs, in the regulatory process); the choice of the appropriate state agency tracing the various alternatives as to which state agency is best suited to administer the programs; and, the issues of constitutional limitations. Here the primary concern is with the taking issue, a subject which resulted in the authors undertaking another study for CEQ. Since the issuance of *The Quiet Revolution*, a number of organizations have produced periodic reports surveying the status and experience of land use legislation around the country. Some of that material is referenced in the articles in Chapter 17 of Volume III. Various reporting services have also been keeping tabs on legislative and administrative activity . . . particularly during the period that many persons believed the passage of a national land use bill was eminent (during 1974).

The next article—by **Bosselman, Callies, and Banta**—develops one of the themes highlighted in *The Quiet Revolution*. This article consists of several chapters from the full 1973 report, titled *The Taking Issue: A Study of the Constitutional Limits of Governmental Authority to Regulate the Use of Privately-owned Land Without Paying Compensation to the Owners*. The title, in effect, states the basic theme of the article—which is based on the premise that: "all over the country . . . attempts to solve environmental problems through land use regulation are threatened by the fear that they will be challenged in court as an unconstitutional taking of property without compensation."

The authors review the long history of the taking issue, which is rooted in English law; they analyze the state of the current law as it has been interpreted and legislated over the past half century; and, they look to a series of strategies for dealing with the taking issue. (The article admits to being "impressed with the profound logic" found in the legal periodicals over the years, and states that what was not needed was "one more analytically good, true and beautiful solution to the taking problem.")

The strategies proposed vary from paying compensation to foreclose legal attacks, to the drafting of new legislative standards regarding when compensation is required, to the presentation of sound factual data/rationales for governmental actions (with an estimate that the probability of a court still declaring that compensation is necessary, is indeed low). But the most often-quoted strategy is that contained in Chapter 12 of the full report, where the authors present "the argument that the courts should discard the idea that a regulation of the use of land can constitute a 'taking' . . . ([since] the idea of a regulatory taking was a judicial fiction of the early 1900s, wholly inconsistent with the tradition of the founding fathers)."

Donald Hagman reviews *The Taking Issue* in his article, and points out a number of fears, in addition to that of a "taking," which the authors did not cover but which are on the minds of many local decision-makers when they consider more extensive land use regulation(s). After summarizing the contents of the report and commenting occasionally on the applicability and reasoning of the various parts of the report, Hagman concentrates on the "five governmental strategies" presented in the report's Chapters 12-16. He does not find the logic particularly convincing when the authors discuss the test (of which they disapprove) developed in the *Mahon* case, and he states that the authors' "strict construction strategy is also deficient in that it is not something we can do by just deciding to do so." [This also is the section of the taking issue with which most landowners and developers find reason to "take issue" . . . as evidenced by numerous reviews published concerning the report over the past two years.]

Hagman then admits his own fascination with "compensable regulations"; moreover, he points out that some attention should be paid to the "density transfers" system proposed by John Costonis [see the article on TDRs in Chapter 14 of Volume III], and notes that his study on "Windfalls For Wipeouts" will touch on many of these same issues when it is completed in 1975.

At the 1974 American Society of Planning Officials conference, **Hagman** presented a preliminary paper on his *Windfalls For Wipeouts* project . . . the theme of which he characterizes as an "ageless conundrum of equity—should the owners of real estate be able to keep increases in values caused by society rather than by themselves? And, on the other hand, should society be able to impose losses on the owners of real estate without paying damages?" The author sees that "fairness" may require a redistribution as between "windfallers" and "wipeoutees"; but the determination of causation—whether government-caused or not—is a difficult matter in many circumstances. In addition, increasingly tough environmental regulation (such as that suggested in the report on *The Quiet Revolution*) is leading to a "synergistic nightmare . . . the market is so confused with the numerous signals that it doesn't know where to jump."

The author feels that a "planning system which does not address the windfall and wipeout problem is perceived as basically inequitable and no planning so conceived can survive." [The difficulty with this assessment perhaps, is that the "system" has managed to limp along for some time without restoring equity among the various windfalled/wipedout land owners; optimistic forecasts of change rising out of current, certainly problematic planning and zoning systems may be unwarranted. One instead is led to believe that it is more likely that communities will be interesting in "taxing the newcomer" to the community in order to reduce public investment and service costs upon his entry, than they will be in instituting some sort of overall windfalls-for-wipeouts system.] With regard to what he calls "horsetrading" over exactions on development permissions, Hagman himself states, "The chances that such a system can be administered with fairness are remote to the point of nonexistence." Yet the various devices to do so are the ones Hagman first deals with. Moreover, regarding the principles involved, he asks, "And why not?"[An attempt at answering this question is made by Jay Janis, in the next article.]

The Hagman article outlines a number of the techniques (which the author is investigating in his multi-continent study) for the recapture of windfalls, the avoidance of wipeouts, and the design of integrated systems of windfalls for wipeouts. However, as to discussion of "criteria for a workable . . . system," he suggests that as yet the research work has not progressed to the stage where conclusions are possible. [Most communities will be interested in the study by Hagman once it is completed; it may be expected that a great number will pass various measures which they find particularly attractive and suitable to the local situation. Several have already begun to experiment with "impact fees/taxes"].

The next author—**Jay Janis**—takes the impact fee approach to task; he states that while such taxes may have "good intentions," they are "unfair" and perhaps illegal; to assess this possibility, he suggests that three questions should be asked. Who should pay for the costs of growth? Where should the funds be used? On what basis should the tax be assessed?

Janis finds the use of the impact tax as a means to "make up for past[service and facility] deficiencies" as "grossly unfair"; that the "old residents" were not similarly charged a "move-in" fee; that the tax raises the cost of housing; that it has an exclusionary effect; that there are better legal methods to levy special taxes; and that the tax is inequitable when it benefits the community as a whole, rather than just the project so taxed (the original "justification" for levying the fee being the costs and the need for services resulting from that particular project).

The article concludes with a lengthy footnote section which sets forth two major items: first, the basic challenges brought by Janis' firm in a lower state court action against Broward County, Florida; and second, selected portions of the decision of Judge Arthur Franza in that case. [The reader should note that this case obviously is not dispositive of the issue of impact fees; it is presented here as a useful discussion for the local decision-maker as he considers such fees or methods.] Franza did not like what he saw, and in occasionally terse language, stated: "Paper walls of ordinances around any city cannot endure. . . . Laws that command one group of people to pay for a benefit inuring to all the people must be rejected. Every incidence that encroaches on our individual liberty or right must be struck down."

The final article in this chapter—by **Henry Fagin**—returns us to one of the underlying themes of these volumes, for he discusses the concept of regulating the timing of urban development. (Moreover, what makes the article especially interesting, is that it appeared in 1955; at least a decade and a half before much of the planning profession had even begun to seriously study the techniques of phasing/sequencing/timing growth. Fagin states that planning involves *space* and *time*. "Effective urban planning demands a simultaneous attention to both."

The author points out that time coordination consists of regulating the tempo (rate of development) and sequence (the where/when). He then explores five planning bases for timing control—which are as valid now as they were in the 1950s. He then ventures a prediction which still holds true today: "It is my belief that until the science of planning invents greatly improved methods for regulating the timing of urban development, many attempts at space coordination must continue to fail—master plans remaining un-realized, zoning ordinances ineffectual and rapidly obsolescing. Static space coordina-tion is not merely inferior, it is impossible in a dynamic world."

In the conclusion therefore, this chapter examines the growing dissatisfaction of the public and the professions with the ways in which traditional planning and zoning systems have reacted to development pressures and competing uses of the land. Some of this concern of course has been in response to a new awareness of environmental and resource limitations; such "limits to growth" and the corresponding criticisms of zero-/no-growth policies, are dealt with at greater length in the next chapter of this volume.

—**RWS**

Legal Assaults–

On Municipal Regulation

Ira M. Heyman

Ira Heyman is vice-chancellor at the University of California, Berkeley. He is a legal consultant to numerous government agencies, including the Tahoe Regional Planning Agency; formerly, he was professor of law and city planning at the University of California, Berkeley, and a visiting professor of law at Stanford Law School, Stanford, California. Mr. Heyman is a graduate of Dartmouth College, and holds a law degree from Yale Law School.

This article is a digest to approximately one-half of the original, which appeared under the title "Legal Assaults on Municipal Land Use Regulation" in The Urban Lawyer, *copyright 1973. Reprinted from the Winter, 1973 issue of* The Urban Lawyer *(Volume 5, No. 1), published by the American Bar Association Section of Local Government Law.*

For good or ill, the institution of land use regulation is far from being a dead letter. I firmly believe that we are, or will be, relying more heavily on regulation as time progresses[1] especially to protect environmental goals. But a major trend away from the municipal monopoly on the land-use regulatory powers has emerged and there are strong tendencies towards the reorganization of governments at the state and local levels and the assignment of land-use regulatory powers to higher echelons. This trend should have important impacts on future land development processes.

A Brief History

Zoning and subdivision regulation on any real scale came into being in the United States during the first quarter of the twentieth century. The objectives were relatively benign, and the assumptions were simplistic.[2] The most important objectives were threefold: to segregate inconsistent uses; to prevent congestion; and to provide for the economical provision of public services. To accomplish these, within the then conceived limitations of governmental structure and constitutional prohibitions, zones would be established at the municipal level within which certain uses (with attendant bulk and yard requirements) would be permitted as "of right," that is, without need for individualized administrative treatment and merely by proof of compliance with the stated law. Zones would be cumulative from single family homes to relatively unrestricted use. They would also be few in number and large in size. A minimum of legislative and administrative flexibility was envisioned. Amendments, especially boundary changes, would occur when conditions changed, but only on an extraordinary vote in the case of protest. An individualized administrative variance might be issued, but only for unique hardship cases.

There were at least five crucial assumptions upon which the original system was built. First, a simplistic segregation of uses would result in a quality urban environment.

Second, it would be possible, in drawing the zoning map, to formulate an intelligent all-at-once decision to which the market would conform. Third, the governors of the system would rarely change the rules. Fourth, nonconforming uses would go away. Fifth, municipal power would accomplish the goals. Most of these have proved to be wrong.

Undoubtedly, land-use control at the municipal level has had some beneficent effects, especially as it has become much more sophisticated. It has reduced some situations of potential land use conflicts and has thus aided certainty of expectations and marketability of property—especially residential property. It has permitted somewhat better planning for the provision of public services. It has been increasingly useful for various environmental ends. It has permitted a local neighborhood majority to act in concert in situations where one or two landowners could destroy neighborhood values. It has helped to maintain the special character of selected areas, such as ones of historic importance. It has provided a vehicle for shifting some public costs to development, especially through subdivision exactions.

But land-use control at the municipal level has largely failed to accomplish many of the original and emerging goals. It has not been able to withstand pressures created by an active market. The extraordinary congestion in downtown Manhattan and San Francisco attests to this. It has not been able to withstand inter-municipal competition for tax revenues and business activity. Shortages of strategically placed open spaces in metropolitan areas are the result. A host of other examples could be mentioned.

Perhaps one of the principal effects of land-use control at the municipal level has been to buttress exclusionary tendencies. This objective was undoubtedly unintended, at least consciously, by the fathers of land-use control. But it was not wholly unanticipated. It is instructive to recall the words of the District Judge in the famous *Euclid* case who, as we know, was reversed in the United States Supreme Court:

> The plain truth is that the true object of the ordinance in question is to place all the property in an undeveloped area of 16 square miles in a straitjacket. The purpose to be accomplished is really to regulate the mode of living of persons who may hereafter inhabit it. In the last analysis, the result to be accomplished is to classify population and segregate them according to their income or situation in life.[3]

It seems safe to say that a great many people prefer to live in the midst of cultural homogeneity. The typology of homogeneity is difficult to state. In its simplistic forms: many whites want to live apart from blacks, or at least low-income blacks; many blacks want to live apart from whites; many middle- and upper-income people want to live apart from lower-income people; ethnic enclaves have a tendency to persist, for both inclusionary and exclusionary reasons.

Presuming that the generalization is roughly true, how do groups of relatively homogeneous people seek to assure relative cultural isolation? The very wealthy can often buy exclusivity in large estates protected by restrictive covenants. Those who reject mainstream values can depart for rural communes. But the middle class, especially the white middle class, does not have these options. It seeks to rely on governmental, quasi-governmental, and private institutions.

The most accessible governmental institutions are local ones. And the ones most amenable to such use are the rich profusion of suburban general purpose municipal governments that abound, and can still be created, in our metropolitan regions. And, as previously stated, it is to these governments that we have heretofore entrusted general jurisdiction over land-use controls.

We should not be surprised, therefore, that land-use controls, together with a number of other manipulations of legal institutions at the local level (such as the refusal to create a public housing authority) have played an important part in barring low-income persons, especially members of minority groups, from access to many suburban areas.

The sum result has been that while municipal land regulation has been far from a total success in accomplishing many of its more benign objectives, as Robert Weaver reports,[4] and as the National Commission on Urban Problems (Douglas Commission) suggested earlier,[5] it has been fairly successful as an exclusionary tool.

Attacks on Municipal Land-Use Regulation

Six of the major sources of assault on municipal land-use regulation are explored in this paper: the environmentalists, the lawyers, the market, the manifold proponents of open housing (especially the civil rights movement), state governments, and the federal government.

The Environmentalists. The Council on Environmental Quality recently published *The Quiet Revolution in Land-Use Control,*[6] in which the authors review nine new innovative land-use regulatory systems, most of which have been fashioned and adopted to protect physical environmental values. The striking feature of all of them is that they interfere, often substantially, with the municipal land-use control monopoly.

The systems are premised on the realization that a municipality cannot provide rational treatment for ecological systems that transcend local boundaries. Moreover, many of the systems reflect the evident fact that a local jurisdiction, because of perceived self-interest will take actions that are harmful to the combined interests of a larger constituency. [*Editor's Note: materials (examples) omitted.*]

The lesson of this trend line is clear. Municipal governments will increasingly be shorn of significant land-use control powers in order to protect environmental values.

The Lawyers. Another assault on municipal land use regulation is coming from the legal fraternity through one of its most prestigious (and conservative) institutions—the American Law Institute [ALI]. The Institute, which has been the sponsor of a variety of restatements of the law and of model and uniform statutes that have had considerable impact, has been struggling with a Model Land Development Code for nearly [four] years.[14] There is a good reason to believe that the effort will produce a product that is acceptable to the Institute membership and that will be adopted in the near future. Whether or not this occurs, the draft sections already circulated are affecting lawyers' attitudes and are providing bases for new legislation in a number of states. Three major sets of provisions contained in the circulated drafts of the Code are of importance to the subject of this paper.

First, the draft Code's planning section, which replaces the old Standard Planning Enabling Act, calls for what might be called an impact statement relating to social concerns.[15] The Code provides for long-range planning and short-run programming, with emphasis on the latter. In both instances, the Code suggests (although perhaps it should require) text analyzing the probable social and economic consequences of provisions of a proposed plan or program, including the impact on population distribution by characteristics (such as race and income) and an evaluation of the consequences of alternative plans and programs. While this direction is addressed to local governments, the identification of these outcomes could have powerful influences upon extra-municipal review, and internal municipal politics.

The second set of provisions of particular relevance appears in the section on land-use regulation and represents an attempt to "legalize" land-use control, which as practiced, consists largely of *ad hoc* or piecemeal decision-making despite the facade of prestated standards and certainty.[16] These provisions therefore, impose explicit and detailed procedures for making rules and for granting permits. The latter provisions require records as well as hearings and written findings. Again, these sections are directed at local governments, but the disclosure of the actual reasons for local decisions is intended to facilitate extra-local review.

Finally, and of most importance, the Code provides the detailed machinery for state planning, state regulation, and state administrative review of local land-use decisions.[17] [*Editor's Note: material omitted re critical areas, etc.*]

The Market. A third assault on municipal land-use regulation will predictably come from the new participants in the land development market. Richard Babcock has pointed out that in the past fifteen years the "housing industry has undergone evulsive change" with "corporations, national in scope, immense in capital, and diversified in market ambitions, announcing . . . entry into the housing field by acquisition or by internal expansion. . . . These sophisticated aggregates are chagrined to discover that village codes are a major barrier to marketing their dwelling-related products,"[23] many of which, for various reasons, consist of all or component parts of low-income housing. [*Editor's Note: material omitted.*]

Babcock concludes that "the impact of this change in the housing industry on the allocation of governmental power can be profound."[28] This conclusion seems warranted. First, these new participants can effectively seek state and federal legislative and administrative intervention to override municipal bars to their products. A good example is the recent spate of legislation creating state boards to license prefabricated housing, thus overriding inconsistent local code provisions.[29]

Second, well-capitalized industrial entities are in a position to invoke judicial review of local exclusionary regulations and to test their validity. They can finance the delay, especially if big projects are involved. This will create opportunities for repetitive judicial reflections on the rationality of local regulations that are inconsistent with regional needs.[30]

The Use of the Courts by Proponents of Open Housing. A fourth attack on municipal land-use regulation has come from litigation by proponents of open housing. Dan Fessler's presentation at the RFF Conference addresses the legal questions raised in the vast number of lawsuits brought mainly by lawyers deeply involved in the civil rights movement. Some noteworthy battles have been won. If federal or state courts could be convinced to adopt legal theories that should be easily relied upon to strike down municipal land-use regulations that operated to exclude low-income persons from residency, the utility and impact of municipal land regulation would be seriously undercut. It seems somewhat doubtful at this point in time, however, that doctrines with such sweeping impact will be embraced by the judiciary.

Fessler discusses three potential bases for federal court negation of local regulations such as large lot zoning, exclusion of multiple dwellings, and prohibition of mobile homes: equal protection, supremacy, and substantive due process.

A successful equal protection attack might proceed from a judicial determination:
1. That the purpose of a particular regulation was to exclude members of racial minorities;
2. That a regulation that produces such an effect, regardless of purpose, is invalid; or, more broadly:

3. That a regulation having the effect of discriminating on the basis of wealth is invalid. Judicial acceptance of the third proposition would seriously weaken the validity of much zoning, especially in the suburbs. And the cases would not be difficult to litigate because the factual basis could be proved statistically. But, for the reasons Fessler indicates, it is highly doubtful that the federal courts (or state courts) will embrace this view. Similarly, it is doubtful that the courts will adopt the second position, although there is some arguable precedent for it.[31] More likely, the federal courts will only interdict local regulation on the basis of equal protection when it is shown that the locality adopted or perpetuated a regulation for the purpose of excluding (or ghettoizing) a racial minority.[32] Such a judicial position would require individualized proofs of a difficult order in each case and would seriously blunt the efficacy of the judiciary as a tool for achieving open housing.

The supremacy doctrine—that state and local laws that are inconsistent with federal law based on express powers (in this case, the Thirteenth Amendment) are invalid —offers an attractive opportunity, as Fessler establishes, to the federal executive and legislature to sweep away a variety of local regulations that exclude disadvantaged minorities. But the judiciary alone will not do this, it will require the action of the political arms of government.[33]

Finally, Fessler investigates the doctrine of substantive due process. This doctrine essentially asks the judges to substitute their value judgments for those of the legislature on matters not treated directly in constitutions (i.e., matters other than speech, religion, search and seizure, and criminal procedure). The judges are importuned to rule that a particular regulation is invalid, usually as applied, because it does not accomplish a particularly important purpose and/or it unreasonably interferes with other values. Thus, for instance, a litigant attacking a zoning ordinance that completely excludes mobile homes entirely from a town might argue seriatim that the exclusion serves no useful purpose, that the exclusion is inconsistent with other town regulations (permitting, for instance, semi-permanent occupation of motel units), that the exclusion is inconsistent with the regional need for locations for lower-income residents, and that the regulation thus arbitrarily interferes with the rights of the owner to use his property.[34]

Fessler concludes, properly in my view, that it is unlikely that federal courts will make free use of the substantive due process approach in reviewing local regulation.[35] On the other hand, as Fessler argues, it is much more likely that state judges will be willing to find local regulations with exclusionary impacts "unreasonable," especially if the state constitution, or state legislation, contains language leading generally in that direction. Some recent cases might indicate a trend line.[36]

What the foregoing indicates is that judicial attack on municipal land-use regulation will most likely continue to exert a pressure towards either regionalization of the low income access problem or at least selected judicial vetoes of particular municipal policy decisions that operate to deny access to low income residents. The frequency of such suits will increase as the new participants in the market find such grounds effective. But judicial attack will not produce rapid across-the-board change, because the courts appear unwilling to premise decisions on sweeping doctrinal grounds.

State Governments. The environmental movement is largely responsible for the creation of a number of state (and regional) agencies that are playing an increasingly important role in land regulation. These agencies have usually been given negative powers and can do no more than veto land-uses and development licensed by local governments. But we are beginning to witness the evolution of state agencies that function positively. The state planning agency proposed in the ALI Model Land Development Code, for instance, is given power to override local development vetoes in selected cases. And developments in New York provide a good example of state efforts with the potential for positive action.[39] [Editor's Note: material omitted.]

Federal Stimulants. From the great variety of federal programs ranging from planning grants to river basin commissions, I have selected only a few prominent undertakings, or prospects, that bear particularly on the continued vitality of municipal land use regulation.

There are two especially noteworthy programs that have been adopted and one prospective program, that if adopted, will further erode the municipal monopoly over land use controls: metropolitan clearing house A-95 type review; and HUD policy regarding the distribution of subsidy funds for housing,[46] and pending measures involving a national land-use policy.

The Office of Management and Budget Circular A-95, Title IV of the Intergovernmental Cooperation Act of 1968, provides for review of applications for assistance under more than 100 federal grant and loan programs by state, regional and metropolitan clearinghouses.[47] The reviews, which are advisory only, seek to identify the relationship of the proposed project to area comprehensive plans. The review requirements, originally established for metropolitan areas by a 1966 statute,[48] have stimulated the creation of numerous councils of government and the preparation of regional and metropolitan plans.

A-95 review, as practiced, will obviously not regionalize land-use regulation. But it does provide an evolutionary base, for negotiation between a regional agency and local governments regarding municipal exclusion of developments of regional consequence. The experience of the Dayton, Ohio, area exemplifies this possible trend.[49] There, the Miami Valley Regional Planning Commission devised a plan "to disperse in four years 14,000 units of federally subsidized housing throughout the Dayton, Ohio, Metropolitan area on a 'fair share' basis, computed on the basis of both community needs and capacities—in other words, a plan to build low- and moderate-income housing, including public housing, in white suburbs."[50] The plan was unanimously adopted in 1970 by the local elected officials who constitute the Commission, and its chances of success appear substantial.[51] A-95 type review was one of the levers for Commission implementation, but, more important, it appears to have been the prime stimulant for the creation of the regional commission that provided the crucial framework for building a metropolitan consensus. [Editor's Note: material on housing programs and land use legislation omitted.]

Speculations on the Future

What are the probable land development consequences of today's broad trend toward regionalization? At the outset two points should be noted. First, various sources of pressure towards change have different goals and strengths. The environmental movement, for instance, is not centrally concerned with the dispersion of low-income persons throughout a metropolitan area, as is the civil rights movement. Second, it is considered less of an invasion of local prerogatives. In addition, to create a regional or state agency that can veto a development licensed by a local government is characteristically perceived as less of an invasion than to empower such an agency to license a development that local government has traditionally had authority to veto.[62] Therefore, objectives that can be accomplished through a system that reviews local determinations, and weeds out unacceptable development, stand a better chance for implementation than objectives that require imposing a regionally important development on unwilling localities.

The seemingly most powerful stimulant towards regionalization of land-use regulation is the environmental movement. Four chief reasons support this assertion.

1. First, the conditions it opposes are concretely perceived as ones requiring extra-local control: air and water pollution, loss of open space, disappearance of undeveloped shoreline, and freeway traffic.
2. Second, these conditions are part of everday life and not visited primarily on deprived classes or racial groups.
3. Third, a large constituency of politically able and influential persons are interested in these problems.
4. Finally, for many people the costs of environmental quality do not enter into the calculus of decision-making because the trade-offs involved are remote or the added costs as distributed do not seem consequential. There are few persons, for instance, who consider the probable increase in electricity rates occasioned by regulations prohibiting the use of low-grade fuel oil with a high sulfur content. Similarly, there has been very little public concern with the cost consequences of the automobile emission standards promulgated under the Clean Air Act of 1970.

If the recent past evidences what is likely to occur in the near future, we can predict the creation of numerous regional and state agencies empowered to veto locally licensed development.[63] The veto power will take the form of both zoning-type regulations (such as the Hawaii state conservation zone where urban development is prohibited in advance) and performance standards (such as the regulations of the Tahoe Regional Planning Commission requiring elaborate mechanical systems to preclude siltation otherwise produced by land development). Such regulations will almost invariably render development more expensive by internalizing costs that previously were externalized. Thus in the Tahoe example, for instance, the developer and his buyers will have to pay the cost of cleaning up storm runoff rather than having discharged wastes cause pollution that is harmful to other users of the Lake. And the probabilities are substantial that the regulations will be considerably more onerous than at present, especially as the regulating agencies will, at the outset at least, be devoted to the single goal of environmental protection and will not be charged with responsibility for solving associated social problems, such as housing and employment.

If these predictions are correct, the environmental movement will produce agencies that will slow down development and make it more expensive—thus increasing the exclusionary effects of present local land-use regulations. (Low- and moderate-income housing projects, for instance, will have to satisfy two reviews, not the single local one as at present.) Local government resistance to regional edicts involving these subjects will not be intense because the local constituencies, at least in the suburbs, will generally agree with the regional goals. Agreement, in fact, will be easy because the regional regulations will operate primarily to the disadvantage of nonresidents who might like to move in; existing homes and business will be largely unaffected. The acceptability of tough regional environmental regulations will be even more pronounced where courts embrace the *Serrano v. Priest* doctrine. For if the states assume a larger share of fiscal responsibility for schools and other local services, suburban governments will find it less necessary to attract industry (and provide housing for workers) to solve their fiscal problems.

Four of the other pressures for change will act at variance with the environmental stimulant, in form and, to an extent, in goals.

1. Open housing proponents are seeking to emasculate local veto powers.
2. Market pressures operate similarly.
3. State efforts of the sort exemplified in New York and provided for in the ALI Model Land Development Code authorize state licensing of regionally important development over local objection.
4. Federal policy is conflicting, but HUD dispersion policies and metropolitan clearing-houses for federal subsidies seek to overcome the potency of local opposition to development of regional importance. [Editor's Note: further discussion of the above omitted.]

Conclusion

We are witnessing a substantial transfer of land-use control from the local to regional and state levels. Professionals, both lawyers and planners, have long called for this move, and lawyers, as well as the planners, are now beginning to act institutionally to achieve it. More important, however, there are new participants in the process, and the groups exerting the greatest contemporary pressure are involved in the environmental movement. As power moves upward in response to this pressure, newly created state and regional agencies are likely to exercise their negative powers to prevent development that would have adverse physical environmental impacts. The strongest exercise of these powers will probably restrict the actions of land owners far more than zoning does now. If rulings are based upon environmental considerations alone and social goals are ignored, development will become more expensive, thus heightening exclusionary impacts.

The new agencies will provide a governmental framework which could be used to achieve social outcomes. Whether they will be so used will depend upon the vitality of the new participants in the housing market and the proponents of open housing. The ability of the housing groups to secure state and federal interventions which override local development vetoes will determine the substantive outcome of the movement of land regulation power upward.

Footnotes

*This paper was prepared as a speech intended to provoke discussion among the participants of an RFF conference held in March, 1972. Thus, many of the ideas are not fully worked out and the author cautions the reader that the purpose of the exercise is to paint a relatively broad picture and discern probable major trend lines. The investigation is far from definitive.

1. Ira Michael Heyman, *Innovative Regulation and Comprehensive Planning, The New Zoning,* (1971) spells out the reasons for this.
2. This matter is reviewed and analyzed at much greater length in Heyman, *Innovative Regulations supra* note 1.
3. 297 F. 307, 318 (N.D. Ohio 1924), *rev'd.* 272 U.S. 365 (1926).
4. Robert Weaver, Housing and Associated Problems of Minorities.
5. Building the American City, 211, 217 (House Doc. No. 91-34, December 12, 1968).
6. Fred Bosselman and David Callies, *The Quiet Revolution in Land-Use Control* (Council on Environmental Quality, December 15, 1971) (hereafter *The Quiet Revolution*).
14. American Law Institute, *A Model Land Development Code.* Tentative Draft No. 1 (4-24-68); Tentative Draft No. 2 (4-24-70); Tentative Draft No. 3 (4-22-71). Citations below are at Tentative drafts No. 2 and No. 3 (hereinafter ALI draft 2 and ALI Draft 3).
15. ALI Draft 2, §§ 3-102(5); 3-103(2); 3-104(2); 3-105(2)(e).
16. *Id.* at §§ 2-303-2-305.
17. ALI Draft 3, Articles 7 and 8.
23. Richard Babcock, *The Courts Enter the Land Development Market,* 5 City 58 (1971).

28. *Supra*, note 23.
29. *See*, Automation in Housing, 42-43 (Sept. 1971) reporting the adoption of such acts in nineteen states, and consideration of such acts in nearly every other state. *See also*, Note, *An Analysis of the Probable Impact of the California Factory-Built Housing Law*, 23 Stan. L. Rev. 978 (1971).
30. *See e.g., In re* Kit Mar Builders, 439 Pa. 466, 268 A.2d 765 (1970); *In re* Girsh, 437 Pa. 237, 263 A.2d 395 (1970).
31. Dailey v. City of Lawton, 425 F.2d 1037 (10th Cir. 1970); Kennedy Park Homes v. City of Lackawanna, 436 F.2d 108 (2nd Cir. 1971); *But see*, James v. Valtierra, 91 S. Ct. 1331 (1971) where "motive" or "purpose" was not found, and despite "effect" of racial exclusion the local regulation was upheld.
32. Dailey v. City of Lawton; *supra*, note 31; Kennedy Park Homes v. City of Lackawanna, *supra*, note 31; Crow v. Brown, 332 F. Supp. 382 (N.D. Ga. 1971).
33. In Shannon v. HUD, 436 F.2d 809 (3rd Cir. 1970), the court read the history of housing and civil rights legislation to create a national policy requiring HUD to take into account racial concentration in dispersing federal housing subsidies. It is quite doubtful, however, that a federal court on supremacy grounds would invalidate local laws that exclude without a direct and bold congressional statement to that end. The probabilities for such legislation do not seem high.
34. *See, e.g.*, Judge Hall's classic dissent in Vickers v. Gloucester Township, 37 N.J. 232, 251, 181 A.2d 129, 148 (1962).
35. *But see*, Southern Alameda Spanish Speaking Organization v. City of Union City, 424 F.2d 291 (9th Cir. 1970) and the district court's subsequent determination, No. 41490 Memo. of Decision by Sweigert, J. filed July 31, 1970.
36. *E.G., In re* Girsh, 437 Pa. 237, 263 A.2d 395 (1970); *In re* Kit Mar Builders, 439 Pa. 466, 268 A.2d 765 (1970); Board of County Comm. v. Casper, 200 Va. 653, 107 S.E. 2d 390 (1959).
39. This text is based largely on Vincent I. Moore, *Politics, Planning and Power in New York State—The Path from Theory to Reality*, 37 J. Am. Instit. Planners, 66 (March 1971).
46. Revenue sharing, with payments directly to local governments, if it comes to pass, will exert a contrary pressure.
47. William Brussat, *Realizing the Potentials of A-95*, Planning 1971 (ASPO 1971); Vincent Smith, The Intergovernmental Cooperation Act of 1968; Opportunity for State Government, *id.* at 61.
48. Section 204, Demonstration Cities and Metropolitan Development Act of 1966, Pub. L. No. 89-754, 80 Stat. 1255.
49. Lois Craig, *The Dayton Area's "Fair Share" Housing Plan Enters the Implementation Phase*, 6 City 50 (1972).
50. *Id.*
51. *Id.*
62. This statement excludes, of course, subject matters that traditionally have been administered at the state level; such as highway location and construction.
63. Nearly every environmental agency studied by Callies and Bosselman exercises this type of authority.

Land Use Controls:

History and Legal Status

Richard F. Babcock
and Fred P. Bosselman

Richard Babcock is a member of the law firm of Ross, Hardies, O'Keefe, Babcock & Parsons; Chicago, Illinois. He specializes in land use law, is the author of The Zoning Game *and numerous other articles, and has served as president of the American Society of Planning Officials. He is an adjunct professor at the University of Illinois, and is chairman of the Advisory Committee for the American Law Institute's Model Land Development Code.*

Fred Bosselman is a partner in the firm of Ross, Hardies, O'Keefe, Babcock & Parsons; Chicago, Illinois. He is the associate reporter for the American Law Institute's Model Land Development Code, director of the Metropolitan Housing and Planning Council of Chicago, co-author of the Quiet Revolution in Land Use Control *and* The Taking Issue, *and has served as a consultant to the President's Council on Environmental Quality, the U.S. Environmental Protection Agency, the States of Florida and Virginia, and the National Commission on Urban Problems. Mr. Bosselman is a graduate of the University of Colorado and of Harvard Law Schol.*

This article consists of an edited version of Chapter 2, "The History and Legal Status of Land Use Controls," which appeared in a book [Babcock & Bosselman] titled: Exclusionary Zoning: Land Use Regulation and Housing in the 1970s *(New York: Praeger, 1973), and published in cooperation with the American Society of Planning Officials.*

Introduction

The next few pages provide a backdrop, mostly legal, to the current scene. If it occasionally seems to drag, the reader is free to pass on at his peril.

Throughout U.S. history the courts have played a key role in resolving tough political issues. The independent bench can resolve conflicting interests that may paralyze the traditional political process. As the courts become increasingly aware that the debate over land use controls reflects a conflict between the local government and the state or nation, they may be more ready to sanction an erosion of the local power formerly sanctioned by earlier courts. The courts' willingness in recent years to reconsider the validity of such entrenched institutions as segregated schools and legislative malapportionment should make local governments realize that their present predominance in land-use matters is not carved in marble.

Judicial action is a heavy tool with which to fix the intricate clockwork of the land use controls system. The impact of judicial reexamination may break the machine rather than repair it. All but the most intransigent of the beneficiaries of the present system would do well to reform the present system of land use controls through legislative and administrative channels to avoid the disarray of major judicial overhaul.

Land use regulations have been the target of numerous constitutional and statutory challenges from their initial appearance in the United States in the first part of the twentieth century. These challenges will multiply during the remainder of the century.

Three groups in particular have contended and will continue to contend for constitutional recognition and protection of their respective interests.

1. The first is composed of landowners or developers whose land use options are restricted by the regulations.
2. The second encompasses the present residents of communities themselves who seek, by their regulations, to promote and protect their own version of desirable development.
3. The third group is drawn from the region and actually includes two subgroups: surrounding communities and potential residents. The former are properly concerned with local land use determinations that threaten to have adverse regional consequences. The potential residents, of course, have an interest in securing decent housing in the community. Most frequently today, the potential resident is a city dweller who wishes to exchange the hardships of life in an overcrowded, deteriorating environment for the benefits of adequate housing, improved educational opportunities, and expanding job opportunities found in the suburbs of the metropolitan region. His hopes will not fare well in the face of local land use regulations that impose stringent limitations on population density or that aim at the maintenance of social, economic, and racial homogeneity.

The vigorous efforts of each of the foregoing groups to promote their particular set of interests have given rise to a see-saw battle in which the courts have experienced major shifts of emphasis and attitude in deciding how the balance of competing interests should be struck. In the attempt to assay the future attitudes of the courts toward exclusionary land use regulations, it is useful to examine these shifting attitudes for clues concerning the likely path of future legal developments. The remainder of this chapter is divided into three sections that correspond in time with the three periods that have witnessed the most emphatic shifts in constitutional protection of the above interests:

1. The early 1900s to the decision of the United States Supreme Court in the *Nectow* case;[1]
2. The post-*Nectow* period to the middle 1960s; and,
3. The post-Watts period.

This admittedly somewhat artificial time framework offers a convenient basis of discussion because the interests of landowners, communities, and regions, in that order, have received their greatest constitutional recognition during each of these successive periods. During the first three decades of this century, even for the decade following the courts' acceptance of zoning in principle, the property owner remained king. The judiciary remained suspicious of municipal efforts to restrain development. After World War II the courts became increasingly tolerant of local regulations that severely impaired both private property rights and regional interests. The third period, which is still in its infancy, will see the courts increasingly presented with challenges based on regional interests and the interests of potential residents in equal housing opportunities.

Early 1900s To Nectow

The early 1900s was not an auspicious time for the introduction of land use regulations of any kind, exclusionary or not. Significant restrictions upon rights in private property were not favored in a land-rich country strongly committed to laissez-faire economic and social philosophy. Persuasive arguments favoring such restrictions were not easily found because the complex problems of contemporary urban life were not a significant factor in the national consciousness. Most of the nation's population lived in rural areas, moreover, and land was plentiful near urban areas.

The draftsmen of the early zoning acts were fully aware of the obstacles they faced in obtaining judicial approval of their efforts. Having ruled out the payment of compensation to affected landowners as too costly, they were required, under established constitutional doctrine, to insure that the acts fell within the state police power. The latter, according to the stock judicial formula, embraces measures that further the "health, safety, and general welfare" of the community. Such measures receive the sanction of the courts, even if they tend to impair private property rights.

The early zoners also knew that to pass judicial muster their enactments must meet three additional, settled, constitutional tests:
1. They must be reasonably calculated to achieve the purposes for which they were designed.
2. They must not single out individuals for unusually harsh burdens.
3. They must treat similar properties in a like manner.

The early zoning acts reflected the caution of their draftsmen. They were lean documents, whose use, area, and height provisions were designed to separate houses, commerce, and industry. Vacant land was left unzoned. All provisions operated prospectively. Fine distinctions among uses, building types, and area requirements were avoided. Minimum lot, setback, and other quantitative standards were modestly drawn and usually incorporated the prevailing patterns of existing development within each district. In brief, the draftsmen endeavored to include in their acts only "hard" requirements that bore a demonstrable relationship to community health and safety or, if these categories were not meaningfully involved, to a tightly drawn concept of the general welfare.[2]

The constitutionality of zoning was not brought before the United States Supreme Court until 1926. In the meantime, it traveled a rocky road in the state courts in spite of the cautions of its advocates. As one commentator observed:

> Prior to 1926, the struggle for legal recognition of zoning was being fought in the state courts and it was a "near thing." The judiciary was reluctant to sanction this invasion of traditional property rights, and some states felt required to pass constitutional amendments to remove any doubts about the validity of zoning. There was always a lurking suspicion that the whole scheme was unconstitutional . . . and that some day the Supreme Court would invalidate all of the acts or ordinances and plans.[3]

In 1926 the United States Supreme Court decided the celebrated *Euclid* case.[4] The charge was that the zoning ordinance of the Village of Euclid severely impaired the value of a tract that was being held for speculative sale. The Ambler Realty Company leveled a frontal attack on the very concept of zoning itself as outside the ambit of the police power and therefore a "taking" of property proscribed by the due process clause of the Fourteenth Amendment. Although successful in the trial court and, initially, before the Supreme Court, Ambler's claim was rejected on rehearing in an opinion that, together with the *Nectow* opinion two years later, established the framework within which subsequent constitutional challenges to zoning have been conducted. The Court agreed with the applicability of the police power test, but narrowly construed the purpose of the ordinance as the separation of incompatible uses, a purpose that, in the Court's view, demonstrably furthered the Village's health, safety, and general welfare.

Land Use Controls

The Court found that the ordinance, like the common law concept of nuisance, sought to prevent property owners from using their land in a manner that adversely affected neighboring lands. The Court experienced little difficulty applying the analogy to the exclusion from single-family residence districts of industrial and commercial uses. It recognized that the analogy was less apt respecting the exclusion of multifamily housing from such zones—an exclusion based on building type rather than use—but likened apartment houses to "mere parasites" that feed upon the light, fresh air, and open space of the single-family district.[5]

The opinion laid down three principles that have shaped all subsequent zoning litigation.

1. First, the Court emphasized that the scope of the police power is elastic and capable of expansion to meet the complex needs of an urbanizing society. Measures that would have been rejected in earlier times might now be accepted as a reasonable response to these needs.
2. Second, challenges based upon dollar loss in property values would not be sustained on that ground alone. Diminution in value would henceforth be considered as only one factor in a calculus that weighed the community's interest in orderly development against the landowner's claim to unrestricted property use.
3. Finally, the Court extended to zoning enactments a presumption of validity that it had not formerly received.

These principles tipped the scales in zoning litigation in favor of local governments and against landowners and, as subsequent developments indicated, against regional interests as well. Health, safety, and general welfare are crude tools for evaluating land use regulations. Few such regulations can be conceived that do not further these values for the class benefited by the measure. The knotty problem that the Court left unresolved is to determine which of the unlimited number of measures that meet these general criteria are nevertheless invalid because they encroach on other constitutionally protected interests. The Court's deflation of the economic loss test, of course, reduced the utility of what had theretofore been the most potent weapon in challenging land use regulations. Finally, the presumption of validity to zoning enactments erected a formidable barrier to successful challenge.

The *Nectow* case, decided two years later, differed from *Euclid* because the landowner-challenger conceded the validity of zoning as a governmental function. He alleged that the ordinance, as applied to his property, deprived him of any reasonable use and thus constituted an uncompensated "taking." The court ruled that the ordinance, which placed the westerly 100 feet of a 29,000-square-foot industrial tract in a residential zone, failed to "promote the health, convenience, and general welfare of the inhabitants of the part of the city affected."[6]

Nectow added to the principles enunciated in *Euclid* the rule that the unreasonableness—on substantive planning grounds—of an ordinance as applied to a specific parcel is a permissible ground for constitutional challenge. But general constitutional doctrine and most state zoning enabling acts made the standing of persons seeking to challenge local measures turn on whether the latter had suffered some injury—usually pecuniary—different than that suffered by members of the community generally. In practice this requirement limited standing to affected landowners and, in the case of approval of a zoning change, to abutting landowners who seek to challenge the proposed use.

Nectow to the Late 1960s

Alfred Bettman, one of the zoning pioneers, described the *Euclid* decision as a "most important and joyous event."[7] The *Euclid* ordinance, as seen by the Supreme Court, pursued a distinct, modest objective: separation of incompatible uses through proper districting of the community. Or, as Seymour Toll has described it, a "fixed, developmental pecking order for every square inch of city land . . . "[8] The decision sparked the adoption of ordinances by hundreds of communities that had earlier been dissuaded by hostile state court opinions on the subject.

Judge Westenhaver, the trial judge in the *Euclid* case, had ruled in favor of the plaintiff and held zoning unconstitutional, concluding that "in the last analysis the result to be accomplished is to classify the population and segregate them according to their income or situation in life."[9] In retrospect it seems likely that the Supreme Court reversed not because it disagreed with the trial judge's conclusion that zoning would create economic segregation, but because it thought economic segregation was not all that bad. In the 1920s the idea of orderliness had a great appeal, while the dangers of segregation had received little public attention.

After deciding *Nectow* in 1928, the Supreme Court turned the subject of zoning back to the state courts, refusing all petitions to review cases dealing with the subject. The fears voiced by Judge Westenhaver were almost forgotten in the clamor of cities rushing to adopt the new technique. The state courts contented themselves with determining whether the loss of the landowner's property values was sufficiently great to bring him under *Nectow* rather than *Euclid*.

The Supreme Court had, however, left the door open just a crack. Responding to the plaintiff's argument that the cumulative effect of all the municipalities' desires to segregate various land uses would create serious hardships, the court said:

> It is not meant by this [decision] to exclude the possibility of cases where the general public interest would so far outweigh the interest of the municipality that the municipality would not be allowed to stand in the way.[10]

As zoning matured from a novelty to an accepted institution, a few critics sought to reopen the argument that Judge Westenhaver had lost in 1926. In the mid-1950s, Charles Haar and Norman Williams each wrote pioneering articles calling attention to the social consequences of zoning's system of economic segregation.[11] A few imaginative litigants tried to raise these arguments in the state courts, most frequently in two types of cases: objections to the zoning of property for large minimum lot sizes, and objections based on the impact of zoning on the surrounding region.

Large-Lot Zoning. A community that adopts a minimum lot requirement on the order of two to five acres may give any number of justifications. It may seek to protect public health and safety because soil conditions and lack of sewer facilities mandate large lots to prevent contamination of drinking water. It may argue that the increased open space and general amenity are "necessary" to promote health and safety, or to preserve its physical character as a rural township. Or the community may seek to regulate the tempo and location of development. Finally, the community may view its provision as an effective form of fiscal zoning designed to exclude development that will demand more in public services than it returns in taxes.[12]

Despite the unique circumstances of each large-lot controversy, dominant trends can be detected in the court opinions during the post-*Nectow* period. The parties in interest are deemed to be the landowner/developer and the community; the former's interest in greater densities is pitted against the latter's concern for maintenance of the status quo; and the former is saddled with the burden of setting aside the presumption of validity of the ordinance.

In deciding a given case, courts almost invariably examine whether the acreage requirement is consistent with the character of the surrounding neighborhood and with the other residential sections of the community and surrounding communities.[13] Significantly, the existence of smaller lots in the neighborhood may cause the court to conclude that the requirement is discriminatory or unsupported by sound planning considerations.[14] Minimum standards that are compelled by a demonstrable relation to health and safety factors such as water contamination are often upheld, but the opinions are notoriously uneven on what constitutes a "demonstrable relation."[15] Finally, the courts often seek to measure the economic harm suffered by the challenger by hearing evidence concerning both the nature of the market for dwellings constructed on lots of the required size and the difference in return likely under the desired as against the existing zoning, but opinions differ on the degree of economic loss that they will tolerate.[16]

Cases in which large-lot zoning has been employed for fiscal objectives or to regulate the tempo of development also reflect a mix of judicial attitudes. Some courts hold that neither are permissible purposes of zoning.[17] More will approve such ordinances if these objectives are "incidental" to the more traditional zoning goals.[18] A third group expressly approves fiscal and development timing objectives providing that they are accomplished through reasonable regulation that does not substantially deprive the landowner of his investment.[19]

No case decided during the post-*Nectow* period expressly holds that large-lot zoning is unconstitutional on the ground that it fails to take account of the housing needs of potential residents or adjoining communities. Judicial uneasiness over this consequence can be detected from time to time in the opinions.[20]

The most striking feature of the large-lot decisions is the absence of serious judicial examination of their exclusionary consequences. With the exception of scattered dicta the issue has not even been posed in these cases. This is the legacy of the *Euclid-Nectow* framework. The assumption that large-lot litigation is only a dispute between the developer and the community tends to foreclose examination of the broader issue.

The presumption of validity that the courts attached to local zoning also makes it difficult to challenge large-lot zoning successfully. It forces the plaintiff to bear the burden of showing that the zoning could not have had a valid purpose. It diverts the courts from looking beyond the challenged technique to its ultimate purposes or effects.

Regionalism and the Courts. Speaking to the role of regionalism in the decisions of the post-*Euclid* courts, Robert Anderson has commented:

> The cases are rare which expressly require that the zoning municipality consider the extraterritorial effect of a zoning restriction . . . . Most courts have respected the power of each municipality to seek its own solutions, to fashion its own character, and to prescribe its own exclusions, without regard (or with very small regard) to the needs of its neighbors of its larger community.[21]

Duffcon Concrete Prods. v. Borough of Cresskill,[22] a case usually cited enthusiastically by proponents of regional zoning, is in point. The petitioner, wishing to construct a concrete plant in Cresskill, N.J., challenged the borough's zoning ordinance on the ground that it excluded all industrial uses from its boundaries. The court's opinion reads like a paean to regional interests and expresses the view that "the effective development of a region should not and cannot be made to depend on the adventitious location of municipal boundaries . . . "[23] The result: The court concluded that Cresskill could *exclude* industrial uses, reasoning that alternative, more "advantageous" sites could be found elsewhere in the region.

Other courts have used a rationale similar to that in *Duffcon* to sustain ordinances that excluded trailer parks, apartment houses, gravel pits, and other disfavored uses from municipal boundaries.[24] With few exceptions, no court during the second period adopted the converse of the *Duffcon* position—namely that regional considerations mandate the *inclusion* of uses within a community. The contention that the "general" welfare served by zoning is not circumscribed by local boundaries, but extends to the region as well, fell on unresponsive ears.[25]

A more significant development is the refusal of a few courts to permit communities to exclude on aesthetic or fiscal grounds socially useful institutions such as hospitals, asylums, delinquent children's centers, and the like. Some courts have concluded that a community's exclusion of this type of institution is invalid in the absence of compelling reasons, because the exclusion of a socially beneficial use is inimical to the public health, safety, and welfare of the people of the entire region.[26]

The Vickers Case. Toward the end of the second period a remarkably prescient dissenting opinion challenged the *Euclid-Nectow* framework in a number of important respects. The dissenting opinion was filed by Justice Frederick Hall of the New Jersey Supreme Court in *Vickers v. Township Committee of Gloucester Township*,[27] a case in which the majority upheld the regulation of a New Jersey township excluding trailer parks within its borders. His arguments have had great influence on the courts of the 1970s.

Justice Hall rejected the view that a challenge to exclusionary regulations is just a duel between the community and the developer. Instead, he insisted that the balance to be struck in such controversies is not simply one between private profit and orderly community growth. Justice Hall proposed the unlikely notion that the community's interests must be weighed against the interests of potential residents in decent housing and of surrounding communities in an equitable distribution of socially useful, if inconvenient, development.[28] Justice Hall also proposed that judicial review not stop at the stated purposes of the ordinance, but extend to its unstated but intended purposes and to its effects, whether or not intended. Applying this prescription in *Vickers* itself, he concluded that the township's claim that the antitrailer provision merely furthered statutory zoning purposes was a sham:

> I submit that [the statutory purposes of zoning] are perverted from their intended application when used to justify Chinese walls of exclusion on the borders of roomy or developing municipalities for the *actual* purpose of keeping out all but the "right kind" of people or those who will live in a certain kind and cost of dwelling. What restrictions like minimum house size requirements, overly large-lot area regulations and complete limitation of dwellings to single family units *really* do is bring about community-wide economic segregation.[29]

Justice Hall deplored the failure of the judiciary to devise meaningful tests for determining whether challenged measures advance the "general welfare." Noting the broad construction given the phrase by the post-*Euclid* courts, he observed that "one could hardly conceive of any land use regulation which would not fulfill [the general welfare], especially when the governing body's determination is so controlling."[30]

The Post-Watts Period

Today most of these early decisions involving regional issues seem from another planet. In August 1965 the blacks burned Watts (a section of Los Angeles) and brought everything down to this earth. White citizens became painfully aware that the nation was becoming divided geographically into "a white society principally located in the suburb, in smaller central cities, and in the peripheral parts of large central cities; and a Negro society largely concentrated within large central cities."[31] The racial confrontations of the late 1960s aborted the placid view of suburban life. The exclusiveness of the suburbs became a major social issue of our time.

As the 1960s ended, civil rights organizations began to mount a concerted attack on "exclusionary zoning," asking the courts to reexamine in sharper focus the true implications of our system of land use controls. It would be overstepping to assert that these attacks have anything more in common than a dislike for the status quo. In this book we will sketch the general outlines of the various arguments raised by those who seek to overturn local zoning practices, and review some of the initial court decisions. It is too early to discern the outlines of a new world at the end of the judicial road, but some landmarks along the way are worth noting.

The Scope of the Police Power. Virtually all zoning litigation has been brought in the state courts. These courts tested local actions against the requirement of state law that any exercise of the police power must promote the public health, safety, and general welfare.[32] This judicial handle offers the skimpiest of criteria for influencing social policy, as Justice Hall lamented in his *Vickers* dissent.[33]

The Supreme Court of Pennsylvania has recently grappled with the problem of devising such criteria, but the very complexity of the undertaking suggests that an ideal solution falls beyond the capabilities of the judiciary alone. In a recent decision invalidating large-lot zoning of a specific parcel on exclusionary grounds, the Pennsylvania Supreme Court appears to have conceded as much, noting:

> We fully realize that the overall solution to these problems lies with greater regional planning, but until the time comes that we have such a system we must confront the situation as it is. The power currently resides in the hands of each local governmental unit, and we will not tolerate their abusing that power in attempting to zone out growth at the expense of neighboring communities.[34]

Nevertheless, the recent decisions in Pennsylvania show that at least one court is willing to use the scope of the police power as a basis for invalidating large-lot zoning and the exclusion of apartments.[35]

Regardless of what happens in the federal courts, the state courts will undoubtedly continue to exercise their power to determine the wisdom of local zoning decisions according to their own view of the general welfare.[36] Norman Williams has expressed distress that "the prevailing intellectual equipment . . . is merely vague, and . . . practically leaves it up to judge's preferences to choose his presumptions and decide on the validity of public regulations."[37] But those who have been taught that the "substantive due process" type of reasoning was "unjudicious" when it was used to void the social experiments of the New Deal should remember that, whether jurisprudentially sloppy or not, it was effective. All the cluck-clucking by the purists to the contrary notwithstanding, the judge in the United States has been in the van of the forces that have led to the restructuring of our institutions and reappraisal of national policies. In our fractured society a good case can be made for such a circumstance with all its attendant disarray.

Racial Discrimination. The United States Supreme Court first invalidated a zoning ordinance specifically prohibiting occupation of housing by "persons of color" in 1917.[38]

It based its decision on "the fundamental law enacted in the Fourteenth Amendment of the Constitution preventing state interference with property rights except by due process of law."[39] In other words the court was concerned about the loss in value to the landowner because of this restriction on his market.

In subsequent years the Court has changed its focus on racial discrimination from the property rights of the landowner to the civil rights of the excluded minority. It has invalidated a wide series of state and local measures designed to further racial segregation, using as a basis the equal protection clause of the Fourteenth Amendment.[40]

Since 1917 the Supreme Court has not faced a zoning decision based on racial motivations. The federal circuit courts have invalidated such decisions, however, in two important cases: The Tenth Circuit ordered the City of Lawton, Oklahoma, to rezone property for a low- and moderate-income housing project when it found the refusal to rezone motivated by a desire to maintain racial segregation;[41] the Second Circuit has overturned the refusal of the City of Lackawanna, New York, to permit the construction of a low- and moderate-income housing project where the refusal was clearly attributable to the fear that the project would introduce blacks into an all-white area.[42]

In 1971 President Nixon instructed the Department of Justice to bring legal proceedings in appropriate circumstances where changes in land use regulations are made for what turns out to be a racially discriminatory purpose. There seems little doubt that such cases can be won, but proof of racial motivation tends to be difficult and expensive, and the volume of government-initiated litigation has not been extensive.[43]

Economic Discrimination. Because of the difficulty of proving racial discrimination, civil rights groups have sought to establish the principle that local regulations that preclude the construction of low- or moderate-income housing are invalid because they discriminate against the poor.

The argument that discrimination against poor persons creates a presumptive violation of the equal protection clause of the Fourteenth Amendment is of relatively recent origin, and based on the substantial broadening of the equal protection clause by the Supreme Court in recent years.[44] The court struck down state laws imposing poll taxes[45] and requiring criminal defendants to pay for their own transcripts,[46] in each case indicating that classification on the basis of wealth would be considered "suspect," and would require "special scrutiny." In effect this meant that such classifications would be held invalid unless their supporters could show compelling reasons for their existence.

The use of the equal protection clause to attack economic discrimination added a major new weapon to the civil rights lawyer's arsenal. The reasoning of these cases was sufficiently sweeping that commentators suggested that zoning that affected the poor adversely could be brought under the wing of the "new" equal protection.[47] The suggestion was frankly based on the apparent desire of the Court to effectuate broad social change rather than on any inherent logic in the reasoning of the decisions.[48] Lawrence Sager conceded that the doctrine contained "the possibility of . . . leading the judiciary beyond all reasonable restraint," but hoped that the Court would apply the doctrine to remove "severe inhibitions to social mobility and opportunity."[49]

The Second Circuit Court of Appeals had relied in part on the right of the poor to equal protection when it enjoined the City of Norwalk, Connecticut, from operating its urban renewal program in a manner that had the effect of forcing poor people to leave the city.[50] The Ninth Circuit in the "*Sasso*" case extended this rationale to a city that faced a substantial reduction of its low-income housing supply because of highway and transit takings and general deterioration. The court suggested that Union City, California, must have a plan to meet the housing needs of the persons facing displacement from its declining stock of low-income housing if it is to deny applications for zoning permits to build new, low-income housing.[51]

The optimism of backers of the "new equal protection" received a severe setback with the Supreme Court's decision in *James v. Valtierra*.[52] The Court upheld the validity of a California requirement that each public housing project be preceded by a referendum. Responding to the plaintiff's argument that the referendum constitutes unconstitutional discrimination because it hampers persons desiring public housing from achieving their objective when no such roadblock faces other groups, the court observed that "a lawmaking procedure that 'disadvantages' a particular group does not always deny equal protection," and declared itself unwilling to determine whether each state or local practice "is likely to 'disadvantage' any of the diverse and shifting groups that make up the American people."[53]

To the dissenting judges the majority opinion seems to deny that discrimination against the poor requires the "special scrutiny" with which the court has examined actions that discriminate on the basis of race.[54] The majority gave further support to the dissenters' interpretation in *Lindsey v. Normet*,[55] in which the court upheld the constitutionality of an Oregon statute authorizing swift eviction procedures for residential tenants who fall behind in their rent. The court found that the selection of "residential tenants" as a category to whom special judicial procedures would be applied was justified because "speedy adjudication is desirable to prevent subjecting the landlord to undeserved economic loss and the tenant to unmerited harassment . . . Therefore the court found that the statute had a rational basis. The court did not stop there, however, but went on to reject explicitly the idea that there is 'any constitutional guarantee of access to dwellings of a particular quality' . . . "[56] So much for housing as a "fundamental interest."[57]

Whatever interpretation future courts may choose to give *Valtierra* may be less important than its immediate effect, which, as Professor George Lefcoe has pointed out, has been to discourage developers of both public housing and other subsidized housing from seeking sites outside existing areas of minority concentration.[58] The threat of a referendum chills all but the most determined developer. Moreover, the increased willingness of the federal courts to grant standing to neighbors who wish to challenge any housing project offers a significant deterrent to developers who might have considered venturing into unpopular areas.[59]

The Right to Travel. While equal protection is in its post-*Valtierra* limbo, civil rights strategists will be dusting off a variety of half-forgotten constitutional clauses to be trotted before the courts. (Ever since the Supreme Court found that private residential segregation violated the constitution's prohibition against *slavery*, the boys in the back rooms have been straining their eyes reading that constitutional fine print.)

The right to travel, a constitutional principle recently reemphasized by the Supreme Court in a variety of contexts, offers intriguing possibilities.[60] The basic nature of the right to travel from state to state was described by Chief Justice Taney many years ago:

> For all the great purposes for which the Federal government was formed, we are one people, with one common country. We are all citizens of the United States; and, as members of the same community, must have the right to pass and repass through every part of it without interruption, as freely as in our own states.[61]

The case of *Edwards v. California*[62] involved the attempt by California in the 1930s to prevent the migration of "Okies" to the state by stationing guards at the border and preventing the entry of any person who could not show he had an existing source of employment in the state. The court held that this exclusion could not be constitutionally maintained. The applicability of this rationale to exclusionary zoning has attracted considerable attention. Frank Aloi and Arthur Abba Goldberg summarized the argument:

> It is evident that exclusionary zoning ordinances deny a specific class of citizens the right to enter a community with the hope of bettering their lives in terms of housing and education, among other things. If the right to enter and abide is a constitutionally permissible goal, then certainly exclusion of any citizen by a community violates his constitutional rights.[63]

Although to the uninitiated the phrase "right to travel" might carry connotations of tourists and vacations, the Supreme Court cases in which the term has been used justify the interpretation of it as a right "to enter and abide." And surely the right extends throughout each state, and cannot be satisfied by laws that permit people to enter the state only if they remain in restricted locations within it.

The fact that the Court has devoted renewed attention to the right to travel, citing it in a number of cases where the Warren court would probably have relied on other grounds, indicates that arguments based on the right to travel may find receptive ears.

Other Constitutional Issues. Peter Weiner has suggested that the use of zoning by people already living in a community to keep others from moving in discriminates against those excluded because it denies them a vote on the decision made to exclude them:

> [Exclusionary action] by communities which control large amounts of vacant land seriously affects unrepresented nonresidents, . . . since individual mobility is thereby greatly curtailed and change in land use patterns is stifled. Any change in policy which might be expected to flow from the suburb's internal political process is hampered by the exclusion from the community . . . of citizens who would be likely to work for change. In such situations, where the political structure is immune from internal challenge, courts have even more reason to force a restructuring of the political system. Since the state cannot here assert a compelling interest in delegation, and since individual voting rights are seriously compromised, acts delegating control over vacant land to local political units should be held unconstitutional.[64]

A final possible line of attack on exclusionary zoning is the Ninth Amendment to the U.S. Constitution which refers to other unspecified rights retained by the people. The Ninth Amendment is usually the last hope of frustrated constitutional litigants, but the Colorado Supreme Court did declare residential segregation invalid on that basis.[65] Other even mustier clauses may be repolished as the ingenuity of the bar is focused on finding a rationale for attacking local zoning policies.

The Future Role of the Courts

No one would venture to predict the ultimate outcome of the current debate about the constitutionality of local land use practices. Even if the United States Supreme Court will accept a case that squarely raises the issue, and even if it condemns exclusionary zoning with the most sweeping language, the contest is not over. One case involving one municipality and one parcel of land will have been settled. The decision in *Euclid* sustained the validity of zoning—in principle—but was soon followed by *Nectow* in which the Supreme Court established the right of a landowner to obtain judicial relief from particular applications of that valid principle. Since *Nectow*, innumerable zoning cases have demonstrated that where land and municipal planning are involved there is little in the way of first principles except that each case is unique.

The most important role of the courts, however, is to act as a predicate to legislative reform. The courts can dramatize the absurdities and inequities in a fractured system of governmental regulation designed for a quieter era, and create real pressure for reform.[66] But in the long run it is the legislators who must get about the business of realigning some of the decision-making power and redefining the criteria by which the public regulation of land use is to be measured.

Summary and Recommendations

1. An understanding of how the law of zoning developed is a necessary predicate to an evaluation of the probable results of the current unrest with the system.
2. Zoning is a relatively recent concept in American land use law and it can be somewhat arbitrarily divided into three stages: (a) A struggle in the early decades of the twentieth century to persuade the courts that comprehensive public regulation of the use of private land was not an unconstitutional interference with a person's right to do much as he wished with his property. (b) A period of about 35 years until the middle of the 1960s when the courts showed increasing sympathy with municipal regulation, and municipalities were encouraged to extend the concept of "public health, safety, morals, and general welfare" to embrace more sophisticated and complex methods of regulation of the use of private land. (c) A period just under way and too young to categorize by any clear trend, but marked by challenges to municipal preeminence in zoning.
3. It is recommended that municipalities request their legal counsel to make his own review of the law as it is developing in their particular state and provide them with his evaluation of the trends with respect to the impact of local land use laws on moderate- and low-income housing.

Footnotes

1. Nectow v. City of Cambridge, 277 U.S. 183 (1928).
2. For a comprehensive account of the efforts of early zoning draftsmen to develop regulations that would meet with the approval of the courts, see Edward Bassett, Zoning, 1st ed. (New York: Russel Sage Foundation, 1936), and Seymour Toll, Zoned American (New York: Grossman, 1969).
3. John Cribbet, "Changing Concepts in the Law of Land Use," 50 Iowa L. Rev. 257 (1967). See Richard Babcock and Fred Bosselman, "Suburban Zoning and the Apartment Boom," 111 U. Pa. L. Rev. 1040, 1047-48 (1963).
4. Village of Euclid v. Ambler Realty Co., 272 U.S. 365 (1926).
5. Id., p. 394.
6. Nectow v. City of Cambridge, 277 U.S. 183 (1928).
7. Alfred Bettman, "The Decision of the Supreme Court of the United States in the Euclid Village Zoning Case," 1 Cinc. U.L. Rev. 184 (1927).
8. Toll, Zoned American, p. 183.
9. Ambler Realty Co. v. Village of Euclid, 297 Fed. 307, 316 (N.D. Ohio 1924) rev'd 272 U.S. 365 (1926).
10. Village of Euclid v. Ambler Realty Co., 272 U.S. 365, 390 (1926). Compare this quote from the trial court's opinion, reported in Amber Realty Co. v. Village of Euclid, 297 Fed. 307, 316 (1924).
11. Charles Haar, "Zoning for Minimum Standards: The Wayne Township Case," 66 Harv. L. Rev. 1051 (1953); Norman Williams, "Planning Law and Democratic Living," 20 Law & Contemp. Prob. 317 (1955).
12. Cf. Babcock and Bosselman, "Suburban Zoning and the Apartment Boom," pp. 1062-72.
13. See, e.g., State v. Kiefaber, 181 N.E.2d 905 (Ohio 1960); Senior v. Zoning Commission of Town of New Canaan, 153 A.2d 415 (Conn. 1959); Fischer v. Bedminster Township, 93 A.2d 378 (N.J. 1952).
14. See Lasalle National Bank v. City of Highland Park, 189 N.E.2d 302 (Ill. 1963); Bismark v. Incorporated Village of Bayville, 267 N.Y.S.2d 1002 (1962). Grant v. Washington Township, 203 N.E.2d 857 (Ohio, 1963).

15. Compare *Appeal of Medinger*, 104 A.2d 118 (Pa. 1954); *Hitchman v. Oakland Township*, 45 N.W.2d 306 (Mich. 1951); *Elizabeth Lake Estate v. Waterford Township*, 26 N.W.2d 788 (Mich. 1947) [all disapproving the challenged minima] with *Lionshead Lake, Inc. v. Wayne Township*, 89 A.2d 693 (N.J. 1952); *Thompson v. City of Carrollton Township*, 211 S.W.2d 970 (Tex. 1948); *Dundee Realty Co. v. City of Omaha*, 13 N.W. 2d 634 (Neb. 1944) [all sustaining the challenged minima]. Special characteristics of the community—such as the predominance of large tracts in single ownership, the presence of historic sites or buildings, an extremely high amenity level reflecting the wealth of the residents or a rural location outside of the path of metropolitan expansion —may persuade the court of the reasonableness of the requirement. See *County Commissioners of Queen Anne's County v. Miles*, 228 A.2d 450 (Md. 1967); *Fischer v. Bedminster Township*, 93 A.2d 378 (N.J. 1952); *Zygmont v. Planning and Zoning Commission of Town of Greenwich*, 210 A.2d 172 (Conn. 1965); *Senior v. Zoning Commission of New Canaan*, 153 A.2d 415 (Conn. 1959); *Flora Realty and Investment Co. v. City of Ladue*, 246 S.W.2d 771 (Mo. 1952); *County Commissioners of Queen Anne's County v. Miles*, 228 A.2d 450 (Md. 1967).
16. Compare *Senior v. Zoning Commission of New Canaan*, 153 A.2d 415 (Conn. 1959); *Honeck v. County of Cook*, 146 N.E.2d 35 (Ill. 1957) [permitting severe deprivation of value] with *Aronson v. Town of Sharon*, 195 N.E.2d 341 (Mass. 1964); *Grant v. Washington Township*, 203 N.E. 2d 857 (Ohio 1963); *Christine Bldg. Co. v. City of Troy*, 116 N.W.2d 816 (Mich. 1962) [opposing deprivation of value].
17. See, e.g., *Board of County Supervisors of Fairfax County v. Carper*, 107 S.E.2d 390 (Va. 1959); cf. *Albrecht Realty Co. v. Town of New Castle*, 167 N.Y.S.2d 843 (1957).
18. See, e.g., *Rockaway Estates v. Rockaway Township*, 119 A.2d 461 (N.J. 1955).
19. See, e.g., *Josephs v. Town of Clarkstown*, 198 N.Y.S.2d 695 (1960).
20. See *Board of County Supervisors of Fairfax County v. Carper*, 107 S.E.2d 390, 396; *Gignoun v. Village of Kings Point*, 99 N.Y.S.2d 280, 284 (1950); *Simon v. Town of Needham*, 42 N.E.2d 516, 519 (Mass. 1942).
21. Robert Anderson, "Provincialism and the Public Interest," in *Federation Planning Information Report* (N.J. Federation of Planning Officials 1970), p. 405. See Robert Walsh, "Are Local Zoning Bodies Required by the Constitution to Consider Regional Needs," 3 *Conn. L. Rev.* 244 (1971).
22. 64 A.2d 347 (N.J. 1949).
23. Id., p. 350.
24. *Vickers v. Township Committee of Gloucester Township*, 181 A.2d 129 (N.J. 1962), cert. den., 371 U.S. 233 (1963) (trailer parks). *Fanale v. Hasbrouck Heights*, 139 A.2d 749 (N.J. 1958) (apartments). *Valley View Village, Inc. v. Priffett*, 221 F.2d 412 (1955) (gravel pits).
25. See, generally, Richard Babcock, *The Zoning Game* (Madison: University of Wisconsin Press, 1966), pp. 178-80.
    Judicial treatment of the zoning of tracts that adjoin the boundaries of other municipalities can hardly be called an exception to this attitude. A number of courts have permitted evidence to be taken that related to the alleged compatiblity or incompatibility of the challenged designation with existing and abutting development in an adjoining municipality. See, e.g., *Gartland v. Maywood*, 131 A.2d 529 (N.J. 1957); *Borough of Cresskill v. Borough of Dumont*, 104 A.2d 441 (N.J. 1954); *LaSalle National Bank v. City of Chicago*, 122 N.E.2d 558 (Ill. 1968). Some have even interpreted the standing requirements of local or state laws sufficiently broadly to allow the adjoining municipality or its residents, or both, to litigate the offending provisions. See, e.g., *Koppel v. City of Fairway*, 371 P.2d 113 (Kansas 1962); *Borough of Leonia v. Borough of Fort Lee*, 151 A.2d 540 (N.J. 1959); *Hamelin v. Zoning Board*, 117 A.2d 86 (Conn. 1955). But see *Town of Huntington v. Town Board of Oyster Bay*, 293 N.Y.S.2d 558 (1968). These cases do not signal judicial concern for the regional consequences of municipal zoning. They differ from the run-of-the-mill neighborhood controversy only because the abutting property happens to be across the line in an adjoining municipality.
26. For a collection of cases, see Annotations in 27 A.L.R.3d 1022 (1969) and 36 A.L.R.2d 653 (1954), and in Note, "Zoning Against the Public Welfare: Judicial Limitations on Municipal Parochialism," 71 *Yale L.J.* 720 (1962). Among the factors considered by the courts are the necessity that the institution be located in a specific physical environment and a specific community; the class of persons served by the institution; the existence of state policies favoring the use; the extent to which the inconvenience caused by the use exceeds that generally created by uses of the same type; the number of similar uses already found within the community; and the actual or likely resistence to the use on the part of other communities within the region.
27. 181 A.2d 129, 140 (1962), cert. den. 371 U.S. 233 (1963).
28. See also Justice Hall's opinion in *Rutgers v. Piluso*, 60 N.J. 142, 286 A.2d 796 (1972). The response of courts to the zoning out of socially beneficial institutional uses (see text accompanying note 26) reflects many of the considerations that Hall thought significant.
29. 181 A.2d 147 (Emphasis added).
30. Id., p. 146.
31. Report of the National Advisory Commission on Civil Disorders 407 (1968).
32. See, e.g., *Bilbar Constr. Co. v. Easttown Township Board of Adjustment*, 393 Pa. 62, 141 A.2d 851 (1958). This concept of a government of limited powers, so familiar to state court judges, is new ground to many civil rights advocates familiar with federal doctrine that requires infringement of some specific constitutional right to invalidate most governmental enactments. See Lawrence Sager, "Tight Little Islands: Exclusionary Zoning, Equal Protection, and the Indigent," 21 *Stan. L. Rev.* 767, 783-84 (1969).

33. See note 30, *supra*.
34. *Appeal of Kit-Mar Builders*, 268 A.2d 765 (1970). It took a bizarre union of diverse views among the justices to produce the conclusion that the township had erred. See, Richard Babcock, "The Courts Enter the Land Development Market-Place," *City* (January/February, 1971), pp. 58, 60-61.
35. Other recent Pennsylvania cases include *Appeal of Girsh* 263 A.2d 395 (1970) (exclusion of multifamily dwellings held unconstitutional) and *National Land and Investment Co. v. Kohn*, 215 A.2d 597 (1965). Compare the discussion of these cases in Frank Aloi and Arthur Abba Goldberg, "Racial and Economic Exclusionary Zoning," *Urban Law Annual* (1971), pp. 9, 38-47, with Norman Williams, Jr. and Thomas Norman, "Exclusionary Land Use Controls: The Case of Northeastern New Jersey," 22 *Syracuse L. Rev.* 475, 498-99 (1971). See also *Oakwood at Madison, Inc. v. Township of Madison*, 117 N.J. Super. 11, 283 A.2d 353 (1971).
36. For a more pessimistic evaluation of this prospect, see the testimony of David Trubek before the U.S. Commission on Civil Rights, June 15, 1971.
37. Norman Williams, "Planning Law and the Supreme Court," *Zoning Digest* 13 (1961): 57, 64. Williams does believe that state courts may include low-income housing in the category of regional institutions given judicial preference. See, e.g., *Wiltwyck School for Boys, Inc. v. Hill*, 11 N.Y.2d 182, 227 N.Y.S.2d 655, 182 N.E.2d 268 (1962); *Appeal of Gilden*, 406 Pa. 484 (1961).
38. *Buchanan v. Warley*, 245 U.S. 60 (1971).
39. Id., p. 82. See Norman Williams, *The Structure of Urban Zoning* (New York: Buttenheim Publishing Corp., 1966), p. 94.
40. See, e.g., *Reitman v. Mulkey*, 387 U.S. 369 (1967); *Jones v. Alfred H. Mayer Co.*, 392 U.S. 409 (1968).
41. *Dailey v. City of Lawton*, 425 F.2d 1037 (1970).
42. *Kennedy Park Homes Ass'n Incorporated v. City of Lackawanna*, 436 F. 2d 108 (1970); *cert. den.* 91 S. Ct. 1256 (1971). See also *Crow v. Brown*, 332 F. Supp. 382 (N.D. Ga., 1971).
43. Equal Housing Opportunity Statement, p. 6 (June 11, 1971). The courts will infer racial motivation without proof of actual intent if there is a continuing pattern of discriminatory results, but proving such a pattern can require extensive investigation. See *Hawkins v. Town of Shaw*, 437 F. 2d 1286 (5th Cir., 1971), *aff'd on reh'g en banc*, 461 F. 2d 1171 (1972).
44. For a general discussion of the Warren court's expansion of the equal protection clause, see Note, "Developments in the Law—Equal Protection," 82 *Harv. L. Rev.* 1065 (1969).
45. *Harper v. Virginia Board of Elections*, 383 U.S. 663 (1966). Compare *McDonald v. Board of Election Commissioners*, 394 U.S. 802 (1969).
46. *Griffin v. Illinois*, 351 U.S. 12 (1956). See also *Douglas v. California*, 372 U.S. 353 (1963).
47. Sager, "Tight Little Islands," p. 767; Aloi and Goldberg, "Racial and Economic Exclusionary Zoning," pp. 16-21.
48. See Frank Michelman, "On Protecting the Poor Through the Fourteenth Amendment," 83 *Harv. L. Rev.* 7 (1969).
49. Sager, "Tight Little Islands," pp. 767, 790, 800.
50. *Norwalk CORE v Norwalk Redevelopment Agency*, 395 F. 2d 920 (1968). Cf. *Western Addition Community Organization v. Weaver*, 294 F. Supp. 433 (N.D. Cal., 1968).
51. *Southern Alameda Spanish Speaking Organization v. City of Union City*, 424 F. 2d 291 (1970). See also *Kennedy Park Homes Association Incorporated v. City of Lackawanna*, 318 F. Supp. 669, 697 (W.D. N.Y. 1970). Aff'd on other grounds, 436 F. 2d 108 (2d Cir., 1971); see note 42, *supra*.
52. 402 U.S. 137 (1971). See George Lefcoe, "Public Housing Referendum Case, Zoning, and the Supreme Court," 59 *Calif. L. Rev.* 1384 (1971); Note, 81 *Yale L. J.* 61 (1971).
53. See *English v. Town of Huntington*, 448 F. 2d 319, 324, 327 (1971).
54. See also *Townsend v. Swank*, 92 S. Ct. 502, 508 (1971), in which the court treated a case of alleged discrimination against needy children under the "rational basis" test rather than under the "new" equal protection.
55. 92 S. Ct. 862 (1972).
56. Id., p. 874. The court distinguished the poll tax and welfare residency cases as "classifications burdening or infringing constitutionally protected rights," the right to vote and the right to travel. Compare F. W. Roisman, "The Right to Public Housing," 39 *Geo. Wash. L. Rev.* 691 (1971).
57. See Note, 81 *Yale L. J.* 61, 81 (1971); Comment, 40 *U.M.K.C. Rev.* 24, 45 (1971).
58. George Lefcoe, "From Capitol Hill: The Impact of Civil Rights Litigation on HUD Policy," *Urban Lawyer* 4 (1972): 112, 118.
59. See *Fletcher v. Romney*, 323 F. Supp. 189 (1971).
60. *Griffin v. Breckenridge*, 29 L. Ed. 338, 350-51 (1971); *Shapiro v. Thompson*, 394 U.S. 618 (1968); *U.S. v. Guest*, 383, 745 (1966). See *Graham v. Richardson*, 91 S. Ct. 1848, 1854 (1971).
61. *Passenger Cases*, 7 How. (48 U.S.) 283, 492 (1849).
62. 314 U.S. 160 (1941).
63. Aloi and Goldberg, "Racial and Economic Exclusionary Zoning," pp. 9, 24. See Comment, "The Right to Travel and Its Application to Restrictive Housing Laws," 66 *Nw.U.L. Rev.* 635 (1971). Donald Hagman, "Urban Planning and Development—Race and Poverty—Past, Present and Future," *Utah L. Rev.* 46, 65-66 (1971); Note,

40 *U.M.K.C.L.* Rev. 66 (1971).
64. Note, "The Constitutionality of Local Zoning," 79 *Yale L.J.* 896, 923 (1970).
65. *Colorado Anti-Discrimination Commission v. Case,* 151 Colo. 235, 380 P. 2d 34, 40 (1962).
66. See Mary Brooks, *Exclusionary Zoning* (American Society of Planning Officials, 1970), p. 27.

Traditional Zoning:

Precursor to Managed Growth

Edward N. Reiner

Edward Reiner is a program analyst in Policy Development and Research–HUD. He formerly practiced law in New York City, and was an instructor at NYU Graduate School of Business. Mr. Reiner holds his undergraduate degree from Wharton School, and has a law degree from Syracuse University.

Introduction

The recent emergence and national recognition of "managed growth" as the latest progeny of community development/land use control philosophy has been acclaimed by some as undeniable proof of the validity of two related theories:

(1) That our urban *society will be unable to perpetuate its accustomed mode of living,* promote sound community development, and at the same time, conserve and protect its natural resources and environmental concerns *without adopting some form of managed growth techniques;* and,

(2) That the *traditional zoning process has failed* to perform these critical functions — resulting in spiraling housing costs, overloaded sewage treatment plants, inadequate transportation systems, prohibitive property taxes, overcrowded educational facilities, and a downgraded environment characterized by diminishing open land and national resource reserves.

Reasons advanced for the alleged failure of zoning to effectively manage land development are legion. Included among them are: its relative inflexibility; its inability to regulate the timing of development; its often cited practice of promoting economic and racial exclusion; and its emphasis on local control of land use by a vast array of local jurisdictions unable and/or unwilling to consider regional and statewide interests while in pursuit of their characteristically parochial goals.[1]

This article takes issue with the "zoning has failed" hypothesis. In retort, it proposes that the zoning function in the United States has generally fulfilled its historic role; that such a role was never allowed to encompass or accomplish the broad and multifaceted objectives of contemporary managed growth programs; and that the newly emerging concepts of growth management—sequential growth, timed development, population "caps," no-growth, non-growth, etc.—whose precursor was traditional zoning, constitute evolutionary steps in a land development process shaped by interactions between political, economic, and environmental concerns.

The first part of this article focuses on the factors which led to the development of comprehensive zoning in the United States, with an emphasis on the objectives to be attained by such legislation. The second part examines a critical legal doctrine—the "presumption of validity" traditionally accorded legislative action—and considers how early governmental and judicial treatment of this principle severely constrained the potential effectiveness of comprehensive zoning, then and in the future.

Origin of the Zoning Species

The development of the first comprehensive zoning ordinance in the United States was begun in New York City in 1913, in anticipation of a delegation of authority by the state legislature to the city to zone. Neither the concept nor the ordinance itself sprang forth full-blown in an historic or evolutionary vacuum. Zoning had been employed as a "useful" tool in California by the late nineteenth century—primarily as an exclusionary discriminatory device against Chinese settlers. Modesto, California, in 1885, passed an ordinance making it:

> . . . unlawful for any person to establish, maintain, or carry on the business of a public laundry
> . . . within the city of Modesto, except that part of the city which lies west of the railroad track
> and south of G street.[2]

In effect, this ordinance placed a great number of Chinese immigrants in violation of the law, inasmuch as virtually all of them lived and worked on the wrong side of the tracks.

The desire for land use controls was based on other more equitable motives by the turn of the century. Federal decontrol policy had succeeded in transferring over one-half of its public land holdings into state or private ownership. Our western frontiers were no longer boundless, and to the dismay of the ever-increasing population of our burgeoning cities, land was becoming a scarce commodity. Growth pressures, transportation inadequacies, and unchecked development patterns in the cities were creating health and safety problems. These dilemmas, which additionally threatened to devalue the price of land, could not be alleviated in a meaningful way by the common law of nuisance, which for years had provided the rural citizen with a legitimate method of restraining outside interference with his property interests. As a result of the inability of private remedies[3] to curtail growing urban problems, citizens began to look to their local governments to fill the regulatory void. The response of urban officialdom was a profusion of police power enactments calculated to protect the public interest in private land use decisions.

By the time Edward Bassett was named chairman of the New York City Advisory Commission on the Height of Buildings in 1973,[4] numerous cities had already legislated at least minimal height control restrictions on development with a fair degree of success.[5] Public control of private land use through exercise of the police power (by regulating under the rubric of the public, safety and welfare) was already a well-recognized practice.[6] Clearly, a broad range of methodologies and experience was available to the first comprehensive zoners to help shape their thoughts and legislation. To better understand the pressures that led to the advent of comprehensive zoning, a closer look at pre-zoning land use controls is warranted.

Land Use Control Devices Antedating Comprehensive Zoning

The common law of nuisance gave legal effect to the ancient maxim "sic utere tuo ut alienum non laedus," that enjoined a property owner to use his land in such a manner as not to injure the property of another. This legal doctrine, when properly invoked, prevented a property owner from using his land without regard for the possible deleterious effects that such use might have on other property. Although nuisance law legitimatized the major premise of comprehensive zoning—the recognition that certain land uses are "incompatible with others and that the rights of all landowners will be diminished unless the rights of all are subject to reasonable restraints"[7]—two basic weaknesses limited the effectiveness and utilization potential of the law. First, the burden of proof imposed on a complainant required showing that the use complained of was not only unreasonable but also substantially destroyed the use value of his property. The necessity of proving substantial reduction of value often presented an insurmountable evidentiary barrier in cases involving aesthetics and the senses of sight and smell, as opposed to claims averring actual physical injury to a plaintiff's property.[8] Secondly, nuisance theory had been primarily a remedy for the private, negatively-impacted citizen; a local government has little initiative or opportunity to invoke the process as a regulatory device of the land development process. Nuisance doctrine is a process uniquely geared to respond to individual property conflicts on a case-by-case basis, and is not readily adaptable as a community-wide land use management device.

Sophisticated landowners—and some not so sophisticated but who had learned by experience—recognized that an adjacent landowner could downgrade surrounding properties often without causing the "substantial injury" required by nuisance doctrine. Furthermore, they sought a technique that would prohibit uses potentially injurious to property rather than having to await "substantial injury" before invoking legal process. Thus there evolved the restrictive covenant: a device which, when incorporated into a deed, proscribes certain land uses for the benefit of other landowners. There covenants contractually limited, initially on a mutual basis, a landowner's[9] use of land as long as the proscription was reasonable in its relationship to the development of the properties enjoying the benefits of the restrictions. Restrictive covenants—powerful tools when fully utilized—were again a basic tool of the private landowner, and offered minimal assistance to local governments attempting to control private development and land use.

Municipal invocation of its most powerful talisman, police power prerogatives, however, represented a land use control device which was very much a "public" tool. The power to legislate the conduct of citizens in the name of the public health, safety, welfare, or morals requires no direct public expenditures to indemnify landowners for proscribed uses. If the police power is properly invoked, losses sustained by landowners as a result of limitations on land use are borne by the individual landowners.

Before comprehensive zoning began in earnest, many ordinances were adopted in the name of the public health or safety of a community; and these ordinances were upheld on such basis. Additionally, the ordinances did not constitute a "taking" by the government.[10]

The power to legislate in the name of the public welfare was to provide the primary cornerstone to comprehensive zoning legitimacy. In *Hadacheck* v. *Sebastian*,[11] the Supreme Court dealt with a Los Angeles, California ordinance which prohibited the manufacture of bricks in a developing residential area where a brick kiln had already been in operation for some time. Although the property in question was admittedly being utilized for its most productive land use, and prohibition of brick manufacture would reduce its value from $800,000 to $60,000, the Court nevertheless upheld the ordinance as a reasonable restriction protecting the health and welfare of the community. A similar result was reached in *Reinman* v. *Little Rock*[12]—another 1915 decision in which the Court approved an ordinance excluding stables from a commercial district.

Landowners in both instances were required to absorb the substantial diminution in value of their property without compensation. These Supreme Court decisions, and others from state forums marked the early peripheries of police power [in terms of judicial approval]. Whereas a court might consider the regulation of a slaughterhouse[13] to be within the police power, prohibition of billboards[14] was not to be countenanced. Pre-comprehensive zoning courts used as a rule of measure whether the regulated use bore a reasonable relationship to any common law nuisances. The greater the resemblance to a "nuisance," the greater the likelihood that a court would murmur the magic words: "This is a proper exercise of police power." Thus the courts, in evaluating ordinances supposedly passed in the name of public health, safety and welfare, exhibited a marked tendency to judge the legislation by standards similar to those used in deciding common law nuisance cases. This conservative attitude necessarily limited the initiative of communities to adopt broader or pervasive land use control legislation.

The Birth of Comprehensive Zoning

All of the aforementioned land use control devices, when measured against the almost unrestricted power to develop property, were insufficient to protect urban areas from the social, economic, aesthetic, and environmental problems whose growth seemed to parallel that of their major progenitor, the skyscraper.[15] There was a rising clamor for new and more restrictive methods of land use control. Problems of overcrowding, transportation dysfunctions, creeping blight and decay which were threatening urban communities could not be halted by the assortment of policy power regulations, codes, and laws which were generally aimed at the lesser goals of excluding hazardous or noxious land uses. The situation is well summarized by John Delafons who states:

> The arrival of the skyscraper forced New York to take the lead in instigating land-use controls. By 1913 there were over fifty buildings in Manhattan of more than twenty stories and nine above thirty stories. The highest was fifty-five stories. The concentration of tall buildings downtown, shutting off light and air from many older properties, caused growing concern and resentment. For example, the Equitable Building at 120 Broadway, which covered a solid city block to the height of thirty-eight stories, cast its shadow over seven acres of adjacent property. Something had to be done if property values in New York were not to be concentrated in a bunch of skyscraper office buildings below which all was darkness.[16]

It was within this legal and historic context that New York City in 1916 adopted the nation's first comprehensive zoning ordinance. As the Commission on Building Districts and Restrictions stated in its preliminary report, released in March 1916:

> New York City has . . . reached a point beyond which continued unplanned growth cannot take place without inviting social and economic disaster. [I]nterests involved are too great to permit the continuance of the laissez faire methods of earlier days. There is too much at stake to permit a habit of thought as to private property rights to stand in the way of a plan that is essential to the health, order and welfare of the entire city and to the conservation of property values.[17]

The words of the Commission were weighty indeed, and to a casual observer bespoke of a major impending effort to manage the urban growth process through planning. Despite such language, however, these lofty goals were apparently not intended and most certainly were not carried out after zoning became law in New York City on July 25, 1916. According to the *New York Times:*

> [t]he plan is practical, not ideal . . . it recognizes existing conditions, does not require the removal of inappropriate buildings and uses, does not seek to restore depressed districts, and, in a word, does not sacrifice vested rights . . . of the individual for the creation of the City Beautiful, or even of districts.[18]

The major promise of the ordinance was its limitation of high rise buildings in the future: a planning feature already in limited use in other cities, but here extended to include commercial as well as residential structures.

Two basic constraints limited the drafter's freedom to innovate in this first comprehensive ordinance, such that the land use reforms finally incorporated into the regulations were neither as far-reaching or as restrictive as originally contemplated when work began in 1913. The first curb was epitomized by the emphasis on law over planning in the preparation of the ordinance. A majority of the Commission members, including Bassett, were attorneys; operating as they were in a new theatre of the law, the specter of "unconstitutionality" constantly clouded their vision and acted as a restraint on broad land use reform notions. An overriding concern with what the courts would "accept" outweighed planning innovations calculated to effectively manage the urban development process. The drafters wanted this legislation to pass judicial muster. Consequently there was often an emphasis on "legal form" over "substance" in the drafting—resulting in carefully drawn regulations expected to pass safely through the gauntlet of judicial scrutiny.

The second major constraint limiting reform was the traditional notion of individual "property rights." It is important to note that the greatest impetus for the New York City ordinance was provided by the efforts of Fifth Avenue businessmen to protect their fashionable street from further encroachment by the amoeba-like growth of the garment district. A major objective of the law therefore, became preservation of the status quo:

> [and] at the very outset zoning's control over urban development was essentially a holding operation rather than an apparatus for resolving such problems as chaotic land uses or implementing plans for future development.[19]

Nonconforming uses became institutionalized because the Commission feared the legal implications of adopting restrictive/prohibitive planning powers similar to those that had been studied in urban areas of Germany. This occurred despite the Supreme Court rulings in *Hadacheck* and *Reinman*, which authorized retroactive termination of uses incompatible with current law.

In further pursuit of "property rights" objectives, the ordinance was geared towards the stabilization and protection of property investment. Care was to be exercised to safeguard assessed valuations. Businesses were to be kept out of residential areas, and industrial uses were to be excluded from business districts. Stability was of primary concern to a Commission that was trying to successfully juggle property rights, business interests, and urban land use requirements under an uncertain legal umbrella: a goal pursued even today. As the committee report on the Land Use Policy and Planning Assistance Act of 1973 states in its section critiquing early land use controls in the United States:

> The varied and complex land use controls in use today by some 10,000 local governments are, to a large extent, merely refinements upon the land use controls developed and validated in the first third of this century. These controls enabled local governments for the first time to place significant restrictions on private land use to protect the larger public interest. Yet in keeping with the traditional concept of land, for the most part the larger public interest was and is interpreted to be protection of property values and the economic value of land. The dependency of most cities on property taxes, which in turn are dependent on property values serves to reinforce this prevailing purpose of land use controls.[20]

On balance, the comprehensive zoning ordinance was a major step forward. The creation and legislative formalization of distinct zoning districts (residential, business and unrestricted) with accompanying bulk and height regulations represented important advances when comprehensively applied. Inconsistent land uses could thereby be segregated; more efficient public service facilities provided; and the congestion and transportation dysfunctions created by untrammeled growth mitigated. By 1923, two hundred and ninety-two cities had promulgated zoning regulations—most of them using New York City as their model. The city's original ordinance, though amended several thousand times, remained in effect until 1961.

Under the circumstances, it is difficult to conceive of comprehensive zoning as an initial failure. True, it emphasized the conservation of existing property values more than the guidance of future development, but the zoning mechanism cannot be blamed for failing to address concerns that were never incorporated into remedial legislation by the drafters. Too much has been asked of traditional zoning by modern-day managed growth enthusiasts. The ordinance was not intended to conquer the many problems of land use; it was operating in a climate where the "police power" was still relatively undefined and the planning community had little direct impact in the shaping of major reform legislation. Comprehensive zoning was a step forward: a systematized method whereby government could exercise greater and broader control over land use than had previously been possible with such limited devices as restrictive covenants, nuisance law, and eminent domain. It represented a major evolutionary step in the land development process, and ought to be judged in that context.

Legal Constraints on the Zoning Process

Critics of the zoning process are on stronger grounds when they challenge the effectiveness and goal orientation of comprehensive zoning as it developed after 1924. Bassett, the foremost zoning authority of his time, felt that regulations:

Must be reasonable . . . and have a substantial relation to the health, safety, comfort and convenience of the community . . . Land similarly situated must be zoned alike.[21]

He believed that zoning should be based on a comprehensive plan, and that judicial approval of zoning should be bedrocked in the ability to show such comprehensiveness.

The power to zone is a power of state government. Consequently cities, counties, etc., cannot exercise this formalized extension of the police power without state enabling legislation or a specific grant of power. In 1924, the first model Standard State Zoning Enabling Act was published and distributed to states and municipalities. It was the product of a three year study of an Advisory Committee on Zoning chaired by then-Secretary of Commerce, Herbert Hoover. The act, when adopted by a state, lawfully delegated to cities and municipalities the power to zone land. Nineteen states quickly adopted such legislation before amended model legislation was made public in 1926. Sections 1 and 3 of the model act state as follows:

Section 1, GRANT OF POWER—*For the purpose of promoting health, safety, morals, or the general welfare of the community,* the legislative body of cities and incorporated villages is hereby empowered to regulate and restrict the height, number of stories, and size of buildings and other structures, the percentage of lot that may be occupied, the size of yards, courts, and other open spaces, the density of population, and the location and use of buildings, structures and land for trade, industry, residence, or other purposes. [Emphasis added.]

Section 3, PURPOSES IN VIEW—*Such regulations shall be made in accordance with a comprehensive plan* and designed to lessen congestion in the streets; to secure safety from fire, panic, and other dangers; to promote health and general welfare; to provide adequate light and air; to prevent the overcrowding of land; to avoid undue concentration of population; to facilitate the adequate provision of transportation, water, sewerage, schools, parks, and other public requirements. Such regulations shall be made with reasonable consideration, among other things, to the character of the district and its peculiar suitability for particular uses, and with a view to conserving the value of buildings and encouraging the most appropriate use of land throughout such municipality.[22] [Emphasis added.]

The importance of the act is demonstrated by the fact that by 1930, 35 states modeled their enabling legislation after it. Today, all 50 states and the District of Columbia have passed zoning enabling legislation.[23]

The most critical language of the model act required that "such regulations [zoning] shall be made in accordance with a comprehensive plan . . ." and be "for the purpose of promoting . . . the general welfare of the community. . . ." There was no room for doubt, or was there? The language appeared to constitute a legislative mandate and an affirmation of Bassett's beliefs. However, such was not the meaning of the language either in the eyes of numerous municipalities adopting zoning regulations, or of a significant number of courts weighing the validity of these ordinances.

As indicated in Section 1 of the Standard State Zoning Enabling Act, zoning is concerned with protection of the public welfare through police power prerogatives. This concern has traditionally been expressed through legislation calculated to maximize self-interest on a local level, whether that level be a city, village, etc. Local governments for the most part saw no reason to change their habitual stance based upon the language of state enabling legislation. In drafting zoning legislation, optimization of parochial goals remained the primary concern.

As a result of these attitudes, basic legal interpretative debates were kindled as to the definition of the phrases "general welfare," and "in accordance with a comprehensive plan." Whose "general welfare" did the enabling act refer to—that of the community adopting zoning legislation, or was there a greater interest: a regional or state consideration? Was there a legal requirement for a written comprehensive plan? If so, was such plan to be adopted antecedent to, or simultaneously with, the zoning legislation?

These basic issues, and others in a similar vein, questioned the very legitimacy of comprehensive zoning as it progressed from its fledgling status in New York City in 1916 to its dominant position as the primary land use control device in the nation. At the heart of these issues was the status of the "presumption of validity," the judicial stamp of approval generally accorded legislative acts. How these questions were resolved by legislators and the judiciary have heavily impacted the land development process for over fifty years (and have contributed significantly to the claims that the zoning process has failed to control land use development adequately).

The Presumption of Validity

A basic tenet of American law is that the legislative act of a properly constituted government is presumed to be constitutional and valid. Comprehensive zoning constitutes such a legislative function; the enabling statutes specifically empower local governments to "regulate and restrict" land use and development for the purpose of "promoting the general welfare of the community."

> Zoning represents a legislative judgment as to how particular land should be classified, where zoning boundaries should be drawn, and the nature and extent of the restrictions which should be imposed.[24]

Consequently, a zoning ordinance is entitled to a presumption of validity if it is promulgated in pursuance of state enabling legislation, and is not arbitrary or unreasonable in its operation. Whether or not an ordinance is in compliance with the statutory requirement that it "promote the general welfare of the community" is therefore of critical importance to its validity and its potential longevity.

This proper doctrinal analysis was clearly recognized, emphatically endorsed, and relied upon by many local governments drafting their first comprehensive ordinance. They did not feel that their traditional objective of maximizing the general welfare within the boundaries of their particular community in any way conflicted with the statutory requirement that zoning "promote the general welfare." In fact, a highly rational syllogistic argument could be presented to any reviewing court, demonstrating the logic of this view. It went as follows:

(a) the interest sought to be protected by the "general welfare" requirement was the public interest of the constituency of the particular governmental unit;

(b) a local government that pursued that goal through legislation, parochial in nature, was acting in accord with enabling legislation mandates;

(c) such local legislation was therefore entitled to a "presumption of validity."

The success of this contention is illustrated by the decision of the Supreme Court in *Village of Euclid* v. *Ambler Realty Company*, in which the principle of comprehensive zoning was upheld for the first time.

It must be said before the ordinance can be declared unconstitutional, that such provisions are clearly arbitrary and unreasonable, having no substantial relation to the public health, safety, morals, or general welfare.[25]

Thus the highest judicial forum recognized the "presumption of validity" regarding local zoning.

An important reinforcing principle that served to strengthen the presumption of validity concept is the separation of powers doctrine that is an inherent part of our republican form of government. Courts are loathe to interfere with what are traditionally considered to be legislative functions. As the Supreme Court of Ohio has stated:

The legislative, not the judicial authority is charged with the duty of determining the wisdom of zoning regulations, and *the judicial judgment is not to be substituted for the legislative judgment* in any case in which the issue or matter is fairly debatable." [Emphasis added.][26]

As a result of these judicial statements, the burden of proof immutably was placed on the complainants who attacked the validity of zoning regulations. (Although the presumption was rebuttable, a litigant first had to overcome the substantial evidentiary burden of proving that the ordinance was arbitrary and unreasonable.)

The question can be raised though, and reasonably so, that despite the fact that a zoning ordinance is a legislative act, it should not always be entitled to such a constitutional presumption. In the instance of zoning legislation, the propositions advanced by localities that the "general welfare" is defined on the local interest level; that municipalities engaging in the zoning process need not consider the context of surrounding communities; and that regional (and possibly statewide) interests are irrelevant to local decisionmaking processes have never been endorsed by the Supreme Court. Even in *Euclid*, the Court recognized (albeit tangentially) that the "general welfare" was composed of more than local perspectives.

It is not meant by this, however, to exclude the possibility of cases where the general public interest would so far outweigh the interest of the municipality that the municipality would not be allowed to stand in the way.[27]

The *Euclid* decision could have explicitly required that local governments preparing to zone give serious consideration to the possible regional impacts of their proposed regulations. In this manner, it would have been made abundantly clear that the "general public interest" was a concern of which the "interests of the municipality" were but a major part. The Court did not utilize this approach; instead it merely indicated that under different circumstances it might rule against a municipality.

This was the Supreme Court's first decision regarding comprehensive zoning, and it therefore had high precedent value.[28] In addition to approving the creation of use districts, the Court went so far as to indicate that certain uses could reasonably be prohibited in a district, despite the fact that they were neither hazardous nor offensive. [29]

A powerful new land use control such as this—which previously was thought to be confiscatory in nature—should have been tempered by precautionary language. Perhaps the reason for the Court's only passing reference to the "possibility" of a "greater public interest" was the fact that in most comprehensive zoning of the 1920s (and certainly in *Euclid*) there was no greater public interest to consider than that of the locality. No significant regional housing inequities were at issue, and environmental consequences of local ordinances were for the most part just that, *local*. Communities could therefore pursue their insular objectives of preserving the status quo and protecting property values without negatively influencing the surrounding environment—socially, economically, or otherwise.

However unclear the Court's intent may have been, the results of its actions have been reported in the decisions of state and federal courts ever since. Local governments continued to apply their overly-insular definitions of the general welfare concept to zoning legislation—even as society became more mobile, economically and in terms of transportation. Massive redistributions of population began to take place as the process of "urban sprawl" accelerated. Communities on the periphery of settled urban cores began to experience the pressures and problems of unplanned development: a legacy of past failures to include proper planning considerations in the drafting of zoning ordinances.

The reaction of many communities was entirely predictable. In an attempt to perpetuate the status quo and freeze out unwanted development (such as housing demands generated by unwanted income, ethnic, and racial groups), various exclusionary zoning techniques were utilized—hopefully hidden behind the cloak of the "presumption of validity." Large lot zoning,[30] minimum floor space and building size[31] requirements, moratoria and the exclusion of high-rise, multi-family, or mobile home dwellings were just some of the devices employed by local governments to protect what they considered to be their interests.[32]

Not until the late 1950s—fully a generation after *Euclid*—did courts begin to pierce zoning's "corporate veil" of validity and examine the relationship of particular proscribed uses to the general welfare of the community. The negative effects of these exclusions were twofold. These were: the hardships imposed on the individual through deprivation of housing and employment opportunities; and the multiple effect, whereby pervasive adoption by local governments of legislation designed to restrict legitimate housing and/or employment opportunities resulted in widespread regional exclusions and dislocations.

Today, the courts are exhibiting a new awareness of the scope of the term "general welfare." Increasingly, decisions have been emphasizing the "dangers inherent in each municipality determining land use policy without regard to the needs of the region of which it is a part."[33] Recent cases such as *Oakwood at Madison, Inc. v. Township of Madison,*[34] *In re Appeal of Joseph Girsh,*[35] *In re Appeal of Kit-Mar Builders,*[36] *Construction Industry Association of Sonoma County, v. City of Petaluma,*[37] and *Golden v. Town Planning Board of Ramapo,*[38] are significant indicators of the current imperative that regional needs are a proper and necessary consideration in local zoning. As the the court so clearly enunciated in *Oakwood at Madison,*

> . . . a municipality must not ignore housing needs, that is, its fair proportion of the obligation to meet the housing needs of its own population and of the region.[39]

These cases indicate the new attitude on the part of the judiciary: a willingness to abandon old habits whereby zoning ordinances were upheld on a *pro forma* basis, and to look behind the "presumption of validity" to see if enabling legislation mandates have actually been complied with.

Is the Zoning Ordinance "In Accordance with a Comprehensive Plan?"

Just as an ordinance must promote the general welfare, so must it also be in accordance with a comprehensive plan if it is to comply with enabling legislation, and thereby be entitled to a presumption of validity. The previous section [of this article] clearly made the point, however, that definition of statutory terms has proven to be a task incapable of resolution by consensus. In the instance of comprehensive planning, differing viewpoints,[40] the abundance of jurisdictions deciding the same issue, and the virtual race of diligence pursued by hundreds of communities in adopting comprehensive zoning without planning led to the development of numerous judicial interpretations of the phrase "in accordance with a comprehensive plan." The only real consensus achieved was the end result—near unanimous judicial approval of comprehensive zoning despite the absence of a formal comprehensive plan or a reasonable facsimile thereof.

As stated by an acknowledged expert in the field, Charles Haar:

> For the most part . . . zoning has preceded planning in the communities which now provide for the latter activity, and indeed, nearly one half the cities with comprehensive zoning ordinances have not adopted master plans at all.

> As a result, there appears to have been a judicial tendency to interpret the statutory directive that zoning ordinances shall be "in accordance with a comprehensive plan" as meaning nothing more than that zoning ordinances shall be comprehensive—that is to say, uniform and broad in scope of coverage. The lack of a master plan is deemed irrelevant to the validity of zoning measures.[41]

In New Jersey, it has been held that the zoning ordinance itself may contain the comprehensive plan. "There need be no extrinsic guide."[42]

> The absence of a land use plan other than the plan which is implicit in the ordinance has been held not to invalidate a zoning ordinance. Indeed, where a community has developed and adopted a master plan, the legislative body is not required to follow it.[43]

Those cases that have negated a comprehensive zoning ordinance have usually done so on the grounds that the ordinance is not truly "comprehensive" in nature (such as where the entire territory of a community is not zoned).[44]

In 40 states, the zoning enabling legislation reiterates the exact language of the model act. Other states use the phrase "a well-considered plan."[45] The requirement that zoning be "in accordance with a comprehensive plan" is logically founded on the supposition that a zoning ordinance is the implementing device to carry out community developmental plans.

As is often the case with new concepts, however, debate and diversity attended the "comprehensive plan" requirement of the standard enabling act. Zoners and planners of the 1920s differed on the amount of planning that should precede comprehensive zoning. The amended 1926 version of the Standard State Zoning Enabling Act, commenting on the phrase "with a comprehensive plan," stated:

> This will prevent haphazard or piecemeal zoning. No zoning should be done without such a comprehensive study.[46]

But beyond mandating the need for *study*, the act made no *explicit* provision for the preparation of a written plan. Whether it be the result of poor legislative draftmanship or by design, state courts were left with the ultimate responsibility of defining the phrase "in accordance with a comprehensive plan."

Although the reasons underlying approval varied, the end result—judicial sanction—was inevitable in light of the overall recognition by the courts that invalidation would probably increase the harm that unplanned development had already caused. Local governments successfully managed a *fait accompli*, by elaborating to the courts the parade of urban horrors that would ensue if their often ill-considered actions were not upheld.

Yet perhaps the most detrimental effect of this plethora of legal and governmental activity was the precedent-setting nature of the judicial process. The courts were dealing not only with a particular ordinance, but were defining the law for years to come. In 1953, of 791 cities over 10,000 in population, only 434 had adopted master plans. The trend was set in the 1920s and since then "zoning has preceded planning in the communities which now provide for the latter activity." Unplanned land use activities have led to burdensome and uneconomic sprawl, insufficient or inadequate municipal facilities, blight, noxious air, water, and noise pollution, municipal financing problems, and a serious diminishing of natural resources.

As the Senate Committee on Interior and Insular Affairs stated in its report concerning the Land Use Policy and Planning Assistance Act of 1973:

> In the absence of State concern or guidance the cities (and, for that matter, the courts) came to treat the decidedly negative local land use regulations as though they embodied whatever planning was considered necessary. Thus, rather than guiding planned development, land use controls have lent protection to virtually unplanned development. As a result, whether land use decisions have been left entirely to the market place or to local regulations absent a planning base, inefficient, unsightly, and often costly land use patterns have developed. For example, open spaces valuable for recreation, greenbelts or just a break in the carpet of urbanization have succumbed to private development catering to the one-acre recreational homesite dreams of our nation's city-dwellers. Land uniquely suitable for certain uses, such as major airports, has been preempted for other uses which possess far less demanding criteria. And unwanted but essential projects, such as powerplants, have met with wasteful delays and been sited finally in locations of least public and political resistance, but often without consideration for sound developmental and environmental needs.[47]

Conclusion

Can the traditional zoning process be held accountable for our current land use and development problems? Perhaps not. Once the ice had been broken by adoption of the New York City ordinance in 1916, the history of zoning was marked by too-rapid adoption of zoning legislation by communities throughout the nation. Our zoning history thereby was marked by the appearance of several trends whose ultimate effects have wrecked a costly havoc—economically, socially, and environmentally—on our society.

The first trend is the short-cut approach adopted by numerous local governments of not engaging in comprehensive planning. The second trend is a consistent failure on the part of an overly acquiescent or unschooled state and federal judiciary to uphold or enforce the mandates of state enabling legislation in the early years of zoning, i.e., that zoning regulations shall be drawn "in accordance with a comprehensive plan" and promote the "general welfare of the community."

Detractors of comprehensive zoning too often fail to realize that its relative success or failure must be measured against the yardstick of the original objectives legislated by local governments, rather than the perceived needs of today's perspectives. Zoning for fifty years substantially achieved its main objectives: segregation of inconsistent uses, provision of public services, and preservation of property values. It has thereby served a particular regulatory/protectionary role in the chronology of the land development process. Unfortunately, the parochial emphasis which historically marked the zoning process has left some scars: a minimal regard for regional needs; environmental dysfunctions; lack of planning for social and housing needs; and exclusion of minorities from fair housing and job markets.

What is needed today is a return to the original mandates of the enabling statutes—proper planning and consideration of the needs of all sectors and interests impacted by zoning legislation. The newly emerging concepts of managed growth possess the potential for placing zoning in the context of extensive comprehensive planning and capital facilities programming. At the same time however, exclusionary proclivities continue to exist on the local governmental level. A great degree of care will have to be exercised by both the courts and local officials if managed growth is to reach the objectives that comprehensive zoning did not achieve: the promotion of sound community development and land use planning practices.

Footnotes

1. See generally, R. Babcock, *The Zoning Game* (University of Wisconsin Press 1966); D. Mandelker, *The Zoning Dilemma* (Bobbs-Merrill 1971).
2. See J. Delafons, *Land Use Controls in the United States* (Joint Center for Urban Studies 1962), p. 19.
3. Other remedies of the private landowner not discussed here include the use of restrictive covenants (discussed later in this article) and the law of trespass. For an examination of trespass doctrine, see Prosser, *Law of Torts*, Chapter 3 (Third Edition 1964).
4. Pressure from Fifth Avenue businessmen, concerned with unsettling urban conditions in New York City, led to the formation of this commission whose report was instrumental in the formulation of the first comprehensive zoning ordinance.
5. In 1889, Washington, D.C. passed the first height control regulations, and in 1909 the United States Supreme Court upheld as reasonable similar height controls enacted by the city of Boston, Massachusetts.
6. By 1908 New York, New Jersey, Connecticut, and Pennsylvania had passed laws limiting tenement lot coverage. The cities of Cleveland, Boston and Chicago followed suit with similar legislation.
7. R. Anderson, 1 *American Law of Zoning* 37 (Lawyer's Co-op. 1968), §2.03.
8. *Wade v. Miller*, 188 Mass 6, 73 N.E. 849 (1905); see generally, Anderson, 1 *American Law of Zoning*, §7.14.
9. These contractual limitations normally extend to any and all future owner and/or users of the property as well.
10. The Fifth Amendment of the United States Constitution provides: "nor shall private property be taken for public use without just compensation." When a land use restriction is so arbitrary and unreasonable in its effect that private property is essentially being used for public purpose without just compensation, a "taking" has occurred. For a history of this issue, see F. Bosselman, et al., *The Taking Issue*, Council (U.S. Superintendent of Documents, No. 4111-00017), 1973. The "taking" issue should not be confused with the power of eminent domain which was a governmental technique for restricting land use that specifically provided for payment to injured property owners. Eminent domain was a short-lived tool in the early 1900s due to its prohibitive cost and lengthy administrative procedures.
11. 239 U.S. 394 (1915).
12. 237 U.S. 171 (1915).
13. *Albany v. Newhof*, 230 App Div 687, 246 NYS 100 (1930), aff'd 256 NY 661.
14. *Varney and Green v. Williams*, 155 Cal 318, 100 P 867 (1909).
15. For a complete study of the historical development of comprehensive zoning, see S. Toll, *Zoned American* (Grossman Publishers 1969).
16. Delafons, *supra* note 2, at 20.
17. Report of the Building Districts and Restrictions Commission (1916) p.6.
18. New York Times, March 12, 1916, Sec. I, p. 18, col. 2.
19. Toll, *supra* note 15, p. at 179.
20. Report of the Committee on Interior and Insular Affairs, United States Senate Report No. 93-197, p. 75 (1973).
21. E. Bassett, *Zoning* (2nd Edition 1940), p.9.
22. United States Department of Commerce (1926).

23. R. Anderson and B. Roswig, *Planning Zoning and Subdivision: A Summary of Statutory Law in the 50 States* (New York State Federation of Official Planning Organizations 1966).
24. Anderson, *supra* note 7, at 65-66.
25. 272 U.S. 365, 395 (1926).
26. *Willott* v. *Beachwood*, 175 Ohio St. 557, 197 N.E.2d 201 (1964). See also, *Zahn* v. *Board of Public Works*, 274 U.S. 325 (1927).
27. *Supra* note 25, at 390.
28. The fact that the Supreme Court historically sidestepped zoning cases for approximately forty years lent additional strength to the precedent-setting nature of this decision.
29. *Supra* note 25, at 388.
30. N. Williams and T. Norman, *Exclusionary Land Use Controls: The Case of North-Eastern New Jersey*, 15 Syracuse Law Review 475 (1971).
31. Note: *Snob Zoning—A Look at the Economic and Social Impact of Low Density Zoning*, 15 Syracuse Law Review 507 (1964).
32. See generally, *Fair Housing and Exclusionary Land Use* (National Committee Against Discrimination in Housing and ULI—the Urban Land Institute, 1974).
33. Id. at 50.
34. 117 N.J. Super. 11, 283 A.2d 353 (1971).
35. 437 Pa. 237, 263 A.2d 395 (1970).
36. 439 Pa. 466, 268 A.2d 765 (1970).
37. C-73-0663-LHB (N.D. Cal. Jan. 17, 1974).
38. 30 N.Y.2d 359 (1972), cert. den. 93 S.Ct. 440 (1972).
39. *Supra* note 34.
40. See Haar & Mytelka, *Planning and Zoning*, 13 Zoning Digest 33 (1961) for their argument pro statutes that require planning as a prerequisite to zoning; see McBride & Babcock, *The Master Plan—A Statutory Prerequisite to a Zoning Ordinance?*, 12 Zoning Digest 353 (1960) for a less adamant position.
41. C. Haar, *In Accordance with a Comprehensive Plan*, 68 Harvard Law Review 1154, 1157 (1955).
42. *Ward* v. *Montgomery Tp.*, 28 N.J. 529, 147 A.2d 248 (1959).
43. Anderson, *supra* note 7, at 234.
44. Anderson, *supra* note 7, at 272-75; Haar, *supra* note 41, at 1158.
45. Anderson and Roswig, *supra* note 23.
46. Department of Commerce, *supra* note 22, at n.22.
47. United States Senate Report, *supra* note 20.

Land Use Without Zoning:

A Review*

John W. Ragsdale, Jr.

John W. Ragsdale is assistant professor of law, University of Missouri, Kansas City, Missouri. He was formerly an associate in the Denver law firm of Humphrey and Wood, and was law clerk for the Tenth Circuit Court of Appeals. Mr. Ragsdale is a graduate of Middlebury College; he holds a law degree from the University of Colorado and an LL.M. from the University of Missouri, Kansas City.

Copyright 1973. Reprinted from the Fall, 1973 issue of The Urban Lawyer (Volume 5, Number 4) published by the American Bar Association Section of Local Government Law.

Background

In how many ways does Bernard H. Siegan detest zoning? His new book, Land Use Without Zoning, helps us count the ways.

Using a basically deductive format throughout the book (although his conclusions never appear in doubt), Siegan first itemizes the failures of the land use planning process. He feels that planning, as reflected in the comprehensive zoning ordinance, bears an attenuated relation to actual land economics. Planners are, too often, influenced by political pressures, being primarily responsible to the city council that employs them. The council is, in turn, influenced more by vocal interest groups and graft than by legitimate land use considerations. Siegan completes his indictment of planning by questioning the ability of any planners, politics aside, to forecast future economic, social and physical influences on the land use pattern, and to fix use districts and regulations accordingly. He sees the overall attempt to effectuate planning as an artificial restriction on market forces, a position reflected in his book's title which, unlike many other recent works,[1] does not couple the concept of land use with that of planning.

Switching without apparent discomfort to the role of civil libertarian and social engineer, Siegan joins the general outcry that has, in recent years, been raised against zoning for exclusionary purposes. Siegan vilifies suburban controls which, by excluding certain uses such as apartments and trailers and by mandatorily increasing the minimum size of lots and houses, have limited the supply and raised the cost of new housing. The effect, he asserts, is to lock the poor and racial minorities in the central city where the pressure for better housing leads to doubling up in apartments, racial tension and increasing blight and decay.

It is, however, the discussion on property rights that is most revealing of Siegan's deepest feelings. In contrast to his earlier, dispassionate economic analysis, Siegan, a real estate lawyer, lets it all out when portraying the infringement of zoning on the basic, inalienable rights of property.

> I submit that zoning is not entitled to constitutional protection. It is not necessary; it is not desirable; it is detrimental. It has no relationship to public health, safety, and welfare except on the whole, an adverse one. It is regulation almost solely for the sake of regulation.[2]
>
> (Zoning laws) . . . are an anomaly in the law of property, contrary to significant meanings and values in the society.[3]

The foaming denouncement of zoning as an inherent infringement on property rights is a conclusive tipoff that Siegan, unlike many of his contemporaries, is not interested in reforming zoning. Rather, he examines reform attempts with a jaundiced eye, stating that flexibility devices such as PUD, floating zones and special permits merely point up the basic planning failures of zoning. In addition, they could actually make matters worse by increasing the concentration of legislative power, as well as opportunities for arbitrariness and graft. He further feels that current efforts to check zoning parochialism, with controls at regional and state levels, are unacceptable. Such controls will contrive to artificially restrict land use productivity and will spread the power around on three levels instead of one.

Siegan's solution to the zoning problem is to throw the rascal out, and he selects for his prototype, zoneless Nirvana, the city of Houston, sixth largest city in the United States and never defiled by the heavy hand of zoning. Siegan sees Houston (and several other Texas cities) as conclusive proof that zoning is not needed to guarantee use separation and residential protection. Rather, economic forces will produce a natural separation with industrial, commercial and residential uses each tending to congregate with its own. Residential land owners can increase this level of natural selection through the use of restrictive covenants. He notes that Houston's 8,000 or so individual subdivisions are controlled internally by vast networks of these covenants, which are enforced by the city as well as privately.

Houston is not devoid of formal controls. Subdivision regulations control minimum lot size, house size, setbacks—in short, most of the items regulated by traditional zoning. However, as Siegan points out, the fundamental difference lies in the scope of regulation. Subdivision controls, as well as covenants, affect the land within the subdivision—and no more. Undeveloped land is not artificially restricted to a pre-determined use.

In addition to subdivision regulations, Houston land use controls include building codes, housing codes, health and safety ordinances, and a capital budget controlling municipal improvements such as parks, sewers, roads and buildings. Siegan does not denigrate all government attempts at planning and regulation—only the comprehensive zoning ordinance which, as he continuously reiterates, artificially and unproductively restricts the natural market mechanism.

Siegan feels that land use in an unzoned city will be a product of market-determined supply and demand. Builders and developers can accurately assess the housing demand and supply it, without artificial restraints and unnecessary land price increments. The result, he feels, will be more new housing of varying types and in various price ranges; and more used housing made available through the filtration process. There will be, incidentally of course, more profits for the developers. Homeowners, meanwhile, can be adequately protected from discordant uses through the mechanism of restrictive covenants.

Critique

Siegan's book is a most interesting contribution to planning literature, but, in taking an extreme position, he, inevitably, opens himself to some criticism. By necessity, he has examined a limited number of non-zoned cities and, with this sample, he makes rather limited comparisions—focusing primarily on Dallas and occasionally on Chicago. It is open to question whether his narrow sample or his chosen economic determinants support his sweeping conclusions. It may be premature to isolate zoning as the universal housing cost culprit, to assert that its demise would lead to housing for the poor or to generalize that nonzoning is the ultimate land use approach for the nation as a whole.

Siegan's veneration of natural economic forces causes him to gloss over several critical issues such as aesthetics, open space and conservation of scenic and agricultural resources. He dismisses aesthetics as something not reducible to general standards, not susceptible to regulation, and therefore, something not to be pursued other than as a factor of natural economic selection. Likewise, he sees land conservation as a counterproductive effort, in the face of unmet housing demands.

Americans have ignored their environmental responsibilities for far too long. Many of our cities have become undesirable places to live because of a lack of environmental concern; our rivers and skies are polluted and, indeed, the entire ecological balance is threatened. These abuses have long been justified by economic apologists who assert that immediate financial incentives are necessary for progress and the economy, that regulation is counter-productive, and who ignore the ultimate transcending disaster that inevitably awaits a society that continually flouts the natural balances. Environmental factors are often not reducible to economic calculation and, thus, they may require both affirmative consideration and protection from a central body. Therefore, it would seem that Siegan's approach would perpetuate or even accelerate unplanned growth and land misuse.

In a similar sense, Siegan seems too ready to denounce land reform efforts as merely more layers of unjustified, counter-productive restrictions on top of the unacceptable old layer. It is submitted that parochialism is one of the most obvious problems with current land use regulation, and a factor responsible for many of the abuses cited by Siegan, such as incomplete planning, political influence and exclusion. Regionalizing critical zoning and planning decisions would alleviate many of these abuses. Planning would be comprehensive, local competitions reduced, and exclusion of poor and racial minorities prevented. In addition, a regional body would be better able to control growth and new development, and assure more orderly service provisions, better use balance, and less unnecessary intrusions on the ecology.[4]

Finally, Siegan too readily passes over the substantial role that zoning can and does play in the planning of public facilities, and in the timing and control of new development. The Ramapo experience has shown that zoning, in accord with capital budgeting, can allow a municipality to control the where and when of new development, and to plan its municipal installations accordingly.[5] Again, it is possible that Siegan's anti-regulation bias prompts him to consider such techniques as unconstitutional takings of property. However, it is noteworthy that other jurisdictions are experimenting with methods such as benefit assessment[6] and development rights transfers[7] which could alleviate the burden on the restricted landowner.

A book cannot, obviously, be all things to all people. The omissions or de-emphasized material in Siegan's book cannot detract from its uniqueness, its provocativeness, or from the fact that it will undoubtedly be a benchmark in the realm of possible land use policies.

Footnotes

*Land Use Without Zoning. By Bernard H. Siegan, Lexington, Massachusetts: D. C. Heath & Co. 1972. $12.50 (hardcover).

1. Haar, Land Use Planning (1971); Hagman, Urban Planning and Land Development Control Law (1971); Roberts, Land Use Planning (1971).
2. Land Use Without Zoning at 221.
3. *Id.* at 227.
4. Senate Bill 238, now before the House, offers financial inducements to the states to centralize their land use planning processes and control development in areas of critical environmental importance.
5. The plan was sustained in Golden v. Planning Bd. of Ramapo, 30 N.Y.2d 359 (1972), *appeal dismissed,* —U.S.—, 93 S. Ct. 440 (1972), against a claim that a possible 18-year delay in building permission, pending completion of capital improvements, was a taking.
6. Kansas City v. Kindle, 446 S.W.2d 807 (Mo. 1969).
7. See 1 Land Use Planning Rep. No. 12, at 8 (Aug. 13, 1973).

Toward A Revised Theory of Zoning

A. Dan Tarlock

A. Dan Tarlock is a professor of law at Indiana University, Bloomington, Indiana, and is a visiting professor of law for the academic year 1974-1975 at the University of Pennsylvania Law School. He was an assistant professor of law at the University of Kentucky and an instructor in law at the University of California, Los Angeles. Mr. Tarlock is a graduate of Stanford University, from which he also holds a law degree.

This article originally appeared in 1972 Land Use Controls Annual 141 (1972), and is reprinted with permission from the American Society of Planning Officials (ASPO).

Introduction

This paper proposes a revision of one of the major methods of controlling land-development decisions—zoning. Zoning has been increasingly transformed from a technique to remedy a limited class of market defects to a potential system of administrative allocation of land-development opportunities, but in the process we have failed to develop an adequate rationale for contemporary (and more importantly, proposed) uses of zoning. Substantial evidence is accumulating that in many cases zoning decisions either duplicate the market or do not produce an efficient allocation of land.

In this paper, I trace briefly the decline in the reliance on property systems as a method of allocating resources. In addition, I will explore the reasons, in light of the historical origins of American city planning and zoning, that a satisfactory relationship between land-market operation and public intervention has failed to develop. I argue that efficiency rather than redistribution is the proper objective of land-use regulation in order to pose the question: as between a property rights system and administration allocation, which produces superior information on which efficiency calculations can be made? Finally, I suggest a method of market allocation for land-development opportunities.

Starting With A New View of Land Ownership

The development of an adequate theory of zoning should start from recent developments in welfare economics regarding property rights theory. In that light, contemporary zoning should be conceptualized as a system of joint ownership between the public entity and the regulated private owner. It is a form of joint ownership in which the owner of the fee retains possession and the right to manage subject to a veto by a co-manager, the public entity. A private resource holder constantly faces a series of decisions about future value in deciding the use which he should make of his property, and more importantly he must bear the responsibility in the form of foregone gains if his calculations are wrong. But a public entity, in deciding whether to veto a private management decision, bears none of the responsibility of ownership, and thus the chances that the resource will be used efficiently are decreased. My hope is that by viewing the powers of private owners and public entities in common terms, it will be possible to examine more clearly the rationale for collective action in the form of publicly imposed zoning ordinances.

Legal vs. Economic Thought: Some Theoretical Crosscurrents

In their analysis of the ownership and use of land, legal scholars have traditionally followed a jurisprudential approach which begins by asking the question: what is property? This ignores the more fruitful direction taken by economists who ask: what is the function of a property rights system in allocating scarce resources?[1] Recent scholarship by economists such as Allen Kneese, Otto Davis, E. J. Mishan, to name a few, establishes that resources shared by all (air, for example) are over-used because a private property regime does not exist for resources which are appropriated in the process of producing and using other resources. Thus, a river basin or airshed is polluted because it is currently treated as a common property resource. No market institutions exist which set a price for clean air or water (or, conversely, the cost of pollution), because no single user can be excluded from enjoying their benefits.

The same problem exists with the use of land. In most significant zoning controversies, a development is opposed because it appropriates neighborhood or area amenities others wish to preserve. Just as no one owns an airshed or river basin, no one owns a resource labeled "amenity level of the area," and thus it is allocated first on the basis of prior use and then on the basis of *ad hoc* legislative decisions. The proposed remedies of economists such as standards or shadow prices[2] are efforts to impose a property regime over a common property resource, so that a market which takes into account the adverse side effects of single users' decisions can operate to promote efficiency.

Lawyers have viewed property as a set of relationships between an individual and either a physical object or an artificial construct such as a security interest and therefore found it difficult to define except in descriptive terms.[3] It is a tautology to stop with Bentham's dictum (often misunderstood) that property is what the legislature says it is. The problem of defining property is made more difficult because historic property theory has either been so abstract as to be of little operative value or because a definition has been seen as a means toward a broader objective. This latter characteristic is not objectionable since it applies to most abstract philosophical concepts. What is troublesome is that for the past fifty years or so, the majority of legal scholars has not been interested in defining the positive aspects of a system of property rights. Bentham made the question of whether society should defer to individual decision making with respect to the use of property an empirical one, depending on whether the recognition of rights is useful to the community as a whole.[4] However, in accepting the principle, it seems clear that we have been unable to develop concepts or institutions capable of undertaking the accounting. As Harold Demsetz has reminded us: "The primary problem of the government is the estimation problem."[5]

The Substitution of Public Interest for Market Allocation

Scholarly energy has been directed toward establishing the principle that property is a flexible, less-than-absolute concept.[6] By lowering the hurdle posed by the argument that any government action which runs counter to the holder's expectations generally recognized by the market is a taking without due process of law, the way has been cleared for much public regulation. But, as a consequence, today there is a lack of consensus about the reasons for which one creates a system of property rights. Much modern property scholarship is coming to accept, almost as a conclusive presumption, the principle that properly organized markets are unable to deal with complex externality problems. This scholarship also seems to reject the utility of the concept of simulated markets.

The result has been an uncritical acceptance of the need for public action and a lessening of interest in methods of improving markets or in simulating their operation through decentralized allocation systems. In the process the concept of property as a maximization of individual discretion with respect to resources has been subordinated to the notion that it is possible to define the general welfare by public action. Courts have begun to accept the notion that in cases where there is a conflict over who has a property right, abstract notions of public welfare provide standards to resolve the conflict.

Nowhere is this type of judicial thinking illustrated better than in a 1967 California Supreme Court decision *Joslin v. Marin County Municipal Water District*,[7] which involved a conflict between a downstream riparian landowner who depended on the flow of the stream for the replenishment of a gravel supply and an upstream municipal appropriator who dammed the stream. The court denied the gravel company's claim for compensation, observing that they could find no public interest in gravel and that the California statutes were replete with sections manifesting a public interest in municipal water supply. Such reasoning robs property rights of their most important element: security. The notion that public allocative decisions are superior to private ones is implicit in much of the modern law, though seldom displayed as blatantly as in *Joslin*.

Judicial review of public resource allocation decisions starts from the presumption that the regulatory action is reasonable. The protesting private holder has a heavy burden to overcome this presumption in order to obtain compensation for his loss. In far too many cases it is not clear whether this form of reasoning produces either a superior allocation or *distribution* of resources over that which would be provided by the market. The basic deficiency in this form of analysis is that judicial pronouncements such as *Joslin* of what is and what is not in the public interest frustrate most principles of resource allocation because the regulator is relieved of the burden of calculating the costs of his decision.

Zoning: An Unsatisfactory Technique in Search of a Rationale

The tension between the choice of use an owner proposes to make and that allowed by a zoning ordinance is as great today as it was when zoning was developed. This is so, not because there is any doubt as to whether zoning is constitutionally permissible, but because it has become a burdensome licensing process for land developers which increasingly neither (1) performs its original justification of minimizing the externalities of land-use patterns nor (2) provides a demonstrably superior pattern of land allocation. Therefore, there is a need to define with greater rigor the reasons for government intervention.

The basic reasons for the failure to develop a satisfactory theory lie, in part, in the history of zoning. Theoretically, zoning was to be a tool to implement a series of decisions made by planners about the desirable allocation of land. Planners argued that city planning was "objective and 99 per cent technical."[8] Value judgments and the necessity of making political choices were largely ignored. City planning commissions were not conceived of as dispute-adjudicating agencies, but as a means of educating the public to accept the obvious benefits of planning.

However, the wide-scale application of zoning outpaced any theory,[9] and city planning commissions by and large have gone the way of many administrative agencies: they have been captured by the regulated or at least have become oriented to the needs of their most vocal client, the land developer. Zoning is much too important to leave to disinterested citizens. As a result, there is remarkably little consensus about why zoning is necessary. Due to their modern tendency to loosely define property rights and deference to government discretion, lawyers have had little inclination to reexamine the rationale for zoning. The lack of a satisfactory rationale is especially crucial today because planners and courts have gone beyond the original constitutional justification for zoning adopted by the Supreme Court in *Village of Euclid v. Ambler Realty Co.* — the prevention of nuisances in advance of their occurrence. Today the vaguest of all rationales, advancement of the public welfare, serves as a basis for a wide variety of nonnuisance regulations.

It has been loosely assumed that the welfare economics concept of externalities—the costs of an activity which are not borne by the decision maker[10]—provides a sufficient justification for zoning. The existence of externalities blocks the efficient allocation of resources because persons undertaking an activity do not bear the full cost of their activity. The market system does not, therefore, accurately register how much of a use of the resource is demanded because the real social profitability of alternative uses of the resources is not considered. The traditional solution has been to force the internalization of the costs through taxes or regulation.

However, the case for public regulation can no longer be assumed in light of Professor Ronald Coase's seminal article, "The Problem of Social Cost."[11] Coase argues that in an ideal economic world in which there are no transaction costs,[12] the market will produce an efficient allocation of resources because those whose enjoyment of their property is reduced by another's activity will bribe[13] the actor to cease or modify his activity if the expected gains exceed the bribe's cost. Conversely, if the actor is made liable, he will either modify his activity or bribe those claiming injury to modify their activity, move or accept the payment of damages depending on which alternative is cheaper. In short, the efficient allocation of resources, assuming no transaction costs, is independent of the initial assignment of liability or assignment of property rights. All that is required is that property rights be made certain. A recent study of Houston, which has no zoning but extensively uses restrictive covenants, asserts that land development in Houston is no better or worse than other comparable American cities with zoning[14] and thus lends empirical support to Coase's argument.

A Theory For Regulation in Developed Areas

The search for the rationale for zoning must start from the question: why is collective action through government regulation necessary to control land-use development? When land uses affect the use and enjoyment of surrounding land by foreclosing or increasing the cost of a desired use and the transaction costs of accomplishing a market solution are too great, there is, of course, a case for collective action although not necessarily for government regulation. Zoning can be initially justified on the grounds that private collective action fails to provide sufficient quantities of a desired public good, in this case amenity levels. As Mancur Olson argues, public goods will be provided by an individual only so long as "his personal gain from having the collective good exceeds the total cost of providing some amount of that collective good."[15] The incentive for an individual or group of individuals to provide the good decreases as the group increases "since an individual member thus gets only part of the benefit of any expenditure he makes to obtain more of the collective good. . . ."[16]

Applied to land development it can be argued that private collective action through a scheme of restrictive covenants will not produce a sufficient level of amenity because small groups of individuals who enter into a covenant scheme produce benefits for nonjoining surrounding landowners. The danger exists that surrounding landowners will hold out either by refusing to join the scheme or by requiring a large bribe to secure their compliance. For example, covenant schemes are most successful when a single developer has control of a large tract and imposes a scheme on all purchasers.

Thus, government may intervene through a zoning ordinance to simulate the result that would have been accomplished had the initial landowners but for high transaction costs been able to impose a covenant scheme on surrounding landowners. This should be successful because the effects of land-use changes are generally "highly concentrated in some distribution around the sites of changes."[17] This is, in effect, applying a doctrine of prior appropriation to zoning. The first users appropriate the amenity level, and subsequent users must buy their way in. This is consistent with the principle that economic efficiency will be furthered if property rights are assigned so that the transaction costs associated with the initiation of negotiations will be minimized.[18] Assigning property rights to existing users rather than to those who wish to initiate a new use will minimize the costs of forming a coalition.

This would be especially so if the existing users took some sort of collective action to bind themselves to a bargain such as a voting procedure or the creation of a board to act for them. This is illustrated by Professor Thomas Crocker's study of phosphate manufacturers, who emitted fluorides, and citrus and cattle industries in Polk County, Florida, who were injured by the emissions. Negotiations were stimulated after the citrus and cattle industries were assigned the rights to be free from certain levels of fluoride emissions when the local air pollution control district told the phosphate companies to buy up lands subject to pollution damages or face the possibility of regulations which would reduce emissions to the minimum technologically feasible level. Crocker found that as a result the receptors no longer had to bear the informational, contractual, and policing costs

> involved in searching out the causes of damages, identifying perpetrators, and obtaining participation by other receptors who would benefit from emission reduction. Nor did they have to consider in deciding on a proposed bargain, the expected costs of policing adherence to the bargain . . . . Emitter . . . costs, in addition to the usual property transfer fees, now consisted of arriving at an agreement among themselves as to what combination of receptor land purchases and emission cutbacks each would make and identification of polluted areas and the receptors within it.[19]

New land users would face similarly reduced transaction costs as they would not have to organize a coalition of existing users as a prerequisite to instituting negotiations.

Under the existing zoning system subsequent users who wish to deviate from the surrounding land-use pattern must "buy" their way in through the political process. Majority approval from an appointed commission or elected local legislative body is required. The process, I have argued, is very costly and produces doubtful efficiency gains. Arguably the costs of administering a zoning system would be decreased and efficiency gains more certain if entrants had to bargain directly with surrounding landowners. The function of the government would be to impose an initial covenant scheme and then let the market or a close proxy determine subsequent reallocations of land.

Professor Nicolaus Tideman of Harvard has proposed an administered compensation scheme to determine if land-use changes will be allowed. The area affected by the proposed change, which is likely to be small, would be defined, and the person initiating the change would propose a compensation plan related to projected impact on surrounding property within the defined area:

> Compensation will be directly proportional to property value and inversely proportional to some empirically estimated function describing the way that direct effects fall off with distance from the site whose use has changed. A person proposing a change in land use of a type thought to have significant direct effects would propose a constant of proportionality for the compensation function. A vote would be held over the area where effects would be greater than 0.1 percent of the property value, with votes weighted by estimated effects, and if a majority approved, the change would be permitted.[20]

The benefit of this scheme is that it combines flexibility with fairness to surrounding landowners. The scheme allows property owners to respond to shifts in markets demands but only so long as they are willing to compensate surrounding property owners for the loss in value caused by the new use. This solution promotes the efficient use of resources because it ensures that in every case the full social costs of an activity will be part of its costs. The large number of spot-zoning cases litigated confirm that this is not true of the present zoning system.

A Theory For the Undeveloped Fringe

The theory described above does not apply so readily to undeveloped land on the fringes of the city. The standard planning response to this problem is the adoption of a comprehensive community land-use plan which according to Charles Haar:

> . . . takes cognizance of the future; it explores it to isolate and identify the economic, social, and physical forces at work in the shaping of the community—changes in technology, in resources, in regional and national influences. Having identified these trends and appraised them in terms of impact and probability, the plan is itself a conscious master strategy to optimize the future of the community. It orients public policy in a predictable way. It endeavors to liquidate the caprice of circumstance and thus provides Businessman X, his competitors, the public, and property owners with a rational framework within which each can pursue his interests, protected to some extent from the attrition of the unexpected—certainly so far as public policy is concerned.[21]

To control development on the urban fringe, planners have generally recommended the creation of low-density holding zones in order to defer decisions on more permanent classifications until a sufficient number of requests for rezoning are made, but the resulting tension between a current owner's development plans and the local government's projected use for the area is often the cause of the plan's failure to exert a consistent influence on future development. The essence of planning is discrimination among land uses. However, planning commissions and local legislative bodies as well as courts have conceived their function as guaranteeing equal protection to development applicants. Thus, these bodies have focused less on communitywide and fiscal effects and more on the compatibility of the proposed use with surrounding uses. More recent planning theory argues that public authorities should be able to predetermine the use of this undeveloped land and implement their choice by denying petitions for rezoning which they consider would result in underutilization of the land. Professor Daniel R. Mandelker makes this argument in his new book, The Zoning Dilemma:

> [D]ifficult problems in zoning control arise in those situations in which an intensive land use has been indicated by the comprehensive plan or zoning ordinance, but the market is not yet ready to respond to the planning or zoning proposal at that level of development. For example, suppose that the planning agency decides that an optimum place for apartment development is a highway interchange area on the edge of its metropolitan area. It is also clear that this area is not yet ready for such development . . . it is in the community interest to forego development at a

lower intensity now in the expectation of a more intensive development later. Unfortunately, at least in the apartment development context, the municipality is rarely permitted to make this decision. Given a taste preference at the peak, and resultant zoning schemes which usually assume that single-family development is always a permitted, residual use, the zoning agency may not be able to defer single-family development in anticipation of a more intensive (and more desirable) multifamily use. It may do so, of course, if it adopts a strategy of large-lot zoning as a device for deferring any development in a substantial segment of its jurisdiction. But zoning of this kind is suspect and so far has not been heavily tested. A more straight-forward approach is simply to use the zoning process to reject an applicant on the ground that the area is more suitable for a more intensive use. In economic terms, the municipality simply decides that the discounted value of the future use is at present more valuable to the municipality than the present value of the use for which a zoning change has been requested. What the municipality has on its hands is a developer with a high discount rate who cannot afford to wait out the uncertainty of the future return. My argument is that the municipality is entitled to say that the developer's discount rate should be lower![22]

The rationale is that cities ought to be able to prevent diseconomies which arise from land use and to capture the economies which it creates by the exercise of its zoning power. The problem with this analysis is that the city (or other regulatory body) has appropriated the benefits of ownership for itself, but not the responsibilities. If zoning authorities can deny rezonings to control the timing of development and prevent the underutilization of land, they have, in effect, an option on the property which allows them to veto its development until a suitable user is found. The city does not have to sacrifice any resources to acquire the option. I have a great deal of doubt that granting broader powers, such as Professor Mandelker advocates, will produce a superior allocation of land. Because the city does not have to calculate the opportunity costs[23] of nondevelopment, there is a danger that the city will not develop adequate information on which proper efficiency calculations can be made. As Harold Demsetz has argued:

> The costs and benefits of a prospective change in resource allocation cannot be treated as given datum. The marginal cost and benefit curves associated with a prospective realignment of resources are not known by the government. Each affected individual knows his benefit or cost, and, in the absence of high exchange cost, this information would be transmitted to others in the form of market negotiations.[24]

One logical answer to this problem would be to have cities enter the market directly by giving them the power to buy undeveloped land, as some Canadian cities are doing, and grant it by fee simple or long-term lease to an appropriate developer. However, I suggest that the criticisms of Professor Mandelker's proposals apply equally to land banking.

These comments regarding Professor Mandelker's argument do not exclude public controls on the fringe but suggest a more precise role for regulation. Zoning should perform the same function it does in more intensely developed areas—the internalization of serious side-effects which stem from market imperfections. On the fringe one cannot expect the market to perform this function because often those who will be affected over time by proposed uses such as a shopping center or apartment complex do not yet own surrounding land. Therefore, no fixed amenity level has been appropriated. Public regulation is still necessary because early development may foreclose the possibility that surrounding users will obtain the full enjoyment of their land.

Commercial and industrial development might initially be handled through conventional zoning techniques because of the special problems they present.[25] However, for residential development the function of the government should be to define the desired level of amenity primarily in terms of population density in a given area. To avoid the common suburban practice of using low-density zones to exclude the poor and minority groups, minimum-density levels might be established by the state.[26] A market in development rights would then be established, and developers could purchase the right to construct a certain number of units.[27] Conventional subdivision regulation would be maintained, and developers would have to meet high sanitation and traffic control standards in the design of their projects. Funds from the sale of development rights could be used by governmental units to finance their share of the improvements.

The establishment of an amenity level would involve decisions, taken through the political process, about the desired overall population density of an area and about areas which should be withdrawn from development. For example, development might be prohibited from flood plains and other open-space areas. Open land could be purchased from funds obtained by the sale of development rights. The establishment of a density ceiling is desirable so that early purchasers will have some certainty of the amenity level that will prevail after development of the area is completed. The unit allotments should be sizeable enough to encourage the development of large projects for these are easier to buffer from conflicting uses. A person who purchased the right to construct a given number of units could build whatever type of housing he desired. And, if he decided that the market demanded lower densities, he could sell his unused developed rights, perhaps to existing residents.

A complex problem raised by this proposal is the allocation of the density quotas between present and future developers. It could be argued that if all rights were available for immediate purchase, they might become concentrated in the hands of developers with less need for liquidity. The result would be to give these developers monopoly power to control construction and mortgage financing. Sharp price rises could also subsequently result if the supply were immediately allocated. Beyond this, the experience of the voluntary oil import quota program between 1957-59 indicates that the failure to provide for future entrants into the market creates pressures to increase the quotas and thus undermines the original objective of the program.[28]

A partial answer to these objections would be for the governmental unit to keep a supply of unit allotments in reserve for release if there is a temporary rise in demand.[29] However, the reserves should not be too great because one of the objectives of the proposed market allocation is to encourage coordinated development so that the character of an area will stabilize earlier than is the case with existing zoning. By and large, I think that the market will automatically solve the problem of newcomers. Either they will be rightfully excluded as the maximum number of units will have been built, or exisitng rights holders will find it profitable to sell. Moreover, the fact that the creation of a market in development rights will cause speculation is unobjectionable once the positive contributions of the speculator are appreciated.

The system proposed here would encourage the large speculator. The assembly of large blocks of land by speculators promotes the orderly development of urban areas by smoothing out fluctuations in prices and making large blocks of land available at a single time in response to market demands.[30] The successful speculator buys large blocks of land in advance of the demand for development and holds it until it is ready to be developed. "By acquiring land at the time when it is plentiful in relation to demand, the speculator raises its price and, by placing it on the market when it is scarce in terms of demand, he lowers its price."[31] These proposals would, however, operate to concentrate the housing construction industry. For example, a developer wishing to sell single-family homes might be unsuccessful unless he controlled a sufficient quantity of land to insure that the development would be buffered from higher density development in the surrounding area. This is desirable, for if development takes place in large units fewer external costs are imposed on surrounding property. The housing industry is one of the most fragmented in the country and this accounts, in large part, for the poor quality of housing construction, the unimaginative design of most residential projects, and the difficulty in accommodating different land uses. Larger developments would have the advantage of economies of scale and have more flexibility with regard to the aesthetic aspects of their projects.

It is assumed that these developments would be protected by restrictive covenant schemes. After a certain percentage of the fringe had been developed, the city might cancel any outstanding development rights and submit undeveloped land to the covenant scheme imposed on surrounding property. Further development would take place by the system for developed areas described earlier. Small-scale commercial development, such as gas stations and convenience shopping areas, could take place by this method.

The arguments sketched in this paper are tentative. Hopefully, however, they stimulate a fresh look at a regulatory system which no longer fulfills its original objective and has failed to develop a rationale for its continued existence.

Footnotes

1. See Davis and Kamien, "Externalities, Information, and Alternative Collective Action," in Joint Economic Committee, The Analysis and Evaluation of Public Expenditures: The PPB Systems, Vol. 1, p. 67, 77-86 (1969).
2. See Margolis, "Shadow Prices for Incorrect or Nonexistent Market Values," in Joint Economic Committee, The Analysis and Evaluation of Public Expenditures: The PPB System, Vol. 1, p. 533 (1969). Shadow prices are imputed prices to value public inputs and outputs. "The basic question asked by the analyst when he searches for a shadow price is: what would users of the public output be willing to pay?" Id. at 534.
3. See Cohen, "Dialogue on Private Property," 9 Rutgers Law Review 357 (1954).
4. See Hobhouse, Liberalism 38 (1964 paperback ed.).
5. Demsetz, "Some Aspects of Property Rights," 9 Journal of Law and Economics 61, 68 (1966).
6. The leading article is Philbrick, "Changing Conceptions of Property in Law," 86 University of Pennsylvania Law Review 691 (1938).
7. 67 Cal.2d 132, 60 Cal. Rptr. 377, 429 P.2d 889 (1967).
8. M. Scott, American City Planning Since 1890 121 (1969).
9. See M. Toll, Zoned American (1969).
10. This is, of course, a gross oversimplification of the concept, for not all externalities result in the inefficient allocation of resources. See Mishan, "The Postwar Literature on Externalities: An Interpretive Essay," 9 Journal of Economic Literature 1 (1971).
11. 3 Journal of Law and Economics 1 (1960).
12. ". . . a world in which all property rights are assigned and in which the cost of exchanging and policing property rights are [sic] zero." Demsetz, supra note 5, at 62.
13. In this context, bribe means only a payment by one party to another in return for a promise to forego or undertake some activity which would affect the person offering the payment.
14. Siegan, "Non-Zoning in Houston," 13 Journal of Law and Economics 71 (1970).
15. M. Olson, The Logic of Collective Action 34 (1968 paperback ed).
16. Id. at 35.
17. T. N. Tideman, Three Approaches to Improving Urban Land Use 47 (Unpublished Ph.D. Dissertation, Department of Economics, The University of Chicago, 1969). Mr. Tideman, now professor of economics at Harvard University, found that the probability of participation in a zoning hearing declines one-half every 79 feet. Ibid. A basic assumption of zoning has been that externalities are uniform in the sense that they will always be present in districts of the same classification. The Tideman thesis supports the contention that this assumption is not valid. See Crecine, Davis, and Jackson, "Urban Property Markets: Some Empirical Results and Their Implications for Municipal Zoning," 10 Journal of Law and Economics 79 (1967). For a more complete discussion of the implications of this research for zoning see Note, "Land-Use Control in Metropolitan Areas: The Failure of Zoning and a Proposed Alternative," 45 Southern California Law Review 355 (1971). The note parallels my own thinking in many respects.
18. See Crocker, "Property Rights and Transactions Costs: An Empirical Study," 14 Journal of Law and Economics 451, 463-64 (1971). See also Calabresi, "Transaction Costs, Resource Allocation, and Liability Rules—A Comment," 11 Journal of Law and Economics 67; and Demsetz, "When Does a Liability Rule Matter," 1 Journal of Legal Studies 29 (1972). Property rights should be assigned to the person who can best balance the benefits of

Toward A Revised Theory of Zoning

an activity against its costs, but zoning would seem to be a case, unlike air pollution, where the market will correct a wrong guess in the initial assignment of the right, because the localized nature of most land-use side effects makes negotiation among affected parties feasible. See Calabresi and Malamed, "Property Rules, Liability Rules, and Inalienability: One View of the Cathedral," 85 *Harvard Law Review* 1089, 1118 (1972).

19. Crocker, *supra* note 18, at 463.
20. Tideman, *supra* note 17, at 49.
21. C. Haar, *Land-Use Planning* 753 (2nd ed. 1971).
22. D. Mandelker, *The Zoning Dilemma* 53 (1971).
23. "[The economist] realizes that some of the most important costs attributable to doing one thing rather than another stem from the *foregone opportunities* that have to be sacrificed in doing this one thing. Thus, Robinson Crusoe pays no money to anyone, but realizes that the cost of picking raspberries can be thought of as the sacrificed amount of strawberries he might otherwise have picked with the same time and effort. This sacrifice of doing something else is called the 'opportunity cost.' " P. Samuelson, *Economics: An Introductory Analysis* 443 (7th ed. 1967).
24. Demsetz, *supra* note 5, at 68.
25. There is, however, a strong case for also removing zoning controls for these uses on the grounds that market will produce location choices which do not conflict with adjoining residential land. See Siegan, "The Houston Solution: The Case for Removing Public Land-Use Controls," 4 *Land-Use Controls Quarterly* 1, 3-4 (Summer, 1970).
26. *Cf.* Mandelker, "The Role of Housing and Metropolitan Development" in *Papers Submitted to Subcommittee on Housing Panels, House Committee on Banking and Currency*, 92nd Cong., 1st Sess. Part II, 785 (1971). Professor Mandelker argues that existing metropolitan distributions of land-use densities may be driving up the cost of land needed for low-income housing to the point where the cost of providing the housing becomes prohibitive either by the private market or under existing federal subsidy programs. He suggests that basic density allocations should be made by federal and state comprehensive land-use plans which would be administered by local units of government; local land-use planning would have to be consistent with regional land-use decisions taken by decision-making bodies with override power. Questions about density or amenity levels are, of course, political, for economics cannot tell us how much of a good we should produce. The decision about density levels involves, in part, a choice of how much of a public good is to be produced. Technical criteria such as the physical carrying capacity of the land and consumer willingness to pay for a given density level are highly relevant to the decision. However, the ultimate decision will not be based strictly on efficiency grounds because it will involve a judgment about how much amenity the public is entitled to have. Goods which are publicly produced for reasons other than market imperfections are called merit goods and are traditionally made through the political process. My disagreement with this analysis would be to suggest that reliance on a market would be a more efficient method of implementing a basic allocation decision.
27. For a cogent argument that market allocation of rights to use common resources within politically defined ceilings is the most efficient method of achieving the internalization of external costs, see J. H. Dales, *Pollution, Property, and Prices* (1968).
28. See Dan, "Implementation of Import Quotas: The Case of Oil," 14 *Journal of Law and Economics*, 1, 11-12 (1971).
29. *See* Dales, *supra* note 27, at 95-96.
30. Elias and Gillies, "Some Observations On the Role of Speculators and Speculation in Land Development," 12 *U.C.L.A. Law Review* 789 (1965). The advance allocation of densities should help to slow the sharply rising cost of raw land because low-density zoning "represents a major constriction on the efficient functioning of the market and can, in some circumstances, be the cause of large speculative profits in land. . ." Kamm, "Land Availability for Housing and Urban Growth." *Papers Submitted to Subcommittee on Housing Panels, supra* note 25, Part I, 263, 277.
31. Elias and Gillies, *supra* note 30, at 792.

Fasano and Frankland:

The Not-So-Quiet Revolution
In Land Use Control

Edward J. Sullivan

Edward Sullivan is the County Attorney for Washington County, Oregon. He prepared and argued the Fasano case, which is discussed in this article. Mr. Sullivan is a graduate of St. John's University, holds a master's from Portland State University, and his law degree from Willamette University.

Introduction

In the half-century or so since the advent of land use regulation in Oregon, the state had generally followed the same path as other states. A complete delegation of zoning power was given to cities and counties, and any problems which resulted were relegated to the courts.

Although the city of Portland was the first to attempt to regulate private land uses by a 1918 ordinance, the generally recognized date for such regulations was 1919 when the legislature conferred such power on all cities. The 1919 legislation typically centered on the zoning power of the municipality but added that such regulations be in accord with a "well-considered plan." The meaning of that phrase has never been interpreted by an appellate court in Oregon.

In 1947, the Oregon legislature gave to counties the power to zone. However, with the exception of interim zoning (which could last for a maximum of three years) county zoning regulations were required to "carry out" the comprehensive plan of the county. Thus, the comprehensive plan was a condition precedent for the exercise of the zoning power, save for interim zoning.

The status of land use law in Oregon from 1919 through 1973 is best described as chaotic. It seemed to change with the exigencies of the moment and reflected the difference between the city and county enabling legislation. The appellate courts of Oregon became increasingly concerned with the rights of applicants and opponents before zoning bodies and, even more so, to the standard by which the courts could judge land use applications. A substantial departure from the present system was required.

Until 1973, Oregon, and most other states, required little in the way of procedural fairness in zoning hearings. Such hearings were deemed "legislative" in character, and generally resulted in a clash between the applicant—who emphasized the benefit he was conferring upon the public in the form of an increased tax base and aesthetic perfection (as demonstrated by his architectural renderings) and the neighbors—who "didn't want apartments," feared effects of a new use in property values, and expected higher taxes if the proposal was granted.

In the middle stood the public official. Quite often he was torn between the need to add to the appraised value of the community by "upzoning" land on the one hand, and the political pressure by the neighbors on the other. The system was also conducive to political favors and corruption.

Quite often, contested cases resulted in shouting matches, emphasizing the personalities involved, rather than the appropriateness of the land use under consideration. The result was an atmosphere hardly conducive to decision-making and one which degraded the notion of planning in the popular mind.

Even more debilitating to the planning process was the very practical problem of how the court would review the zoning decisions of local governments. Most courts viewed zoning decisions as "legislative" acts, since they were so designated by local government (by use of an ordinance form), and passed by the local governing body. As such, these acts could be reviewed only for very narrow purposes—whether correct enactment procedure was followed and whether or not any constitutional rights were violated. The legislative reasoning behind such acts was not examined, and it remained for the unsuccessful party to negate every possible reason for sustaining the decision. This legal fiction, the so-called "presumption of validity" was necessary in the minds of the courts to avoid a separation of powers conflict.

On the other hand the courts were also concerned with the propriety of certain practices of zoning authorities and with a means of rectifying ill-considered decisions. Just as the court had dealt in terms of names in formulating the presumption of validity, it was forced to invent new terminology to deal with abuses of the zoning power. Thus, we find new terms in zoning such as "arbitrary and capricious" exercises of power, "spot zoning," and the "change or mistake rule"—the latter being that no amendments to the zoning maps were permitted in the absence of a physical change of circumstances in the neighborhood, or a mistake in the original zoning.

The result was to play one fiction against the other to achieve a desired result. If the courts desired to affirm a decision, they utilized the presumption of validity, stating that they would not interfere with the actions of another branch of government unless a constitutional violation was shown. If they desired to reverse the result, they could find such to be an "arbitrary or capricious" action. In Oregon, where the Supreme Court utilized the presumption of validity, decisions with respect to applications to change the land use on certain lands were nearly equally affirmed and reversed by the appellate courts.

It was against the background of this unacceptable state of affairs that the case of *Fasano v. Board of County Commissioners of Washington County*, 96 Or. Adv. Sh. 1059, _____ Or. _____, 507 P.2d 23 (1973) was decided.

Fasano—Low-Income Housing and the Presumption of Invalidity

In early 1970, the Board of County Commissioners of Washington County reversed the decision of its own planning commission and granted to A.G.S. Development Corporation a zone change from single family residential (minimum lot size 7,000 square feet per dwelling), to planned unit residential, to allow a mobile home park in an otherwise conventional single-family neighborhood. The densities allowed under existing and proposed zoning were about the same, so it is difficult to believe that the decision would have been challenged if a use other than a mobile home park were involved. The feelings of environmental, social, and economic degradation galvanized the neighborhood into action.

Certain nearby residents asked the state circuit court to review the record of the proceedings of the Board, and to reverse the allowance of the zone change. The circuit court did just that, relying on the "change or mistake rule" mentioned in recent Oregon Supreme Court decisions. The county in turn, believing that that rule ought to be reconsidered by the court, appealed the decision to the Oregon Court of Appeals.

The court of appeals affirmed the decision of the circuit court. It decided against the contention of the county that the comprehensive plan was the standard for zoning and rezoning rather than the "change or mistake rule," by stating that it would require both conformity to the comprehensive plan (which it took to be the zoning maps, a common judicial view) and adherence to the Supreme Court "change or mistake rule."

One course was left to the county—to seek review of the court of appeals decision by the Oregon Supreme Court. This review was not a matter of right, but of grace, and is sought by petition. Although relatively few petitions for review are granted, the state Supreme Court did so. Further, that court allowed additional briefs to be filed and allowed the motion of the League of Oregon Cities, Association of Oregon Counties, and the Oregon Chapter of the American Institute of Planners to intervene as parties *amicus curiae*.

The Supreme Court heard arguments on March 1, 1972. That fall, the court announced it desired re-argument on the matter, and allowed further briefs to be filed.

The points raised by the court relating to re-argument demonstrate its awareness of the issues involved. The court desired clarification of the relationship of the comprehensive plan to zoning, the presence of safeguards to prevent arbitrary rezoning, procedural requirements for rezoning hearings, and securing an adequate record below for the reviewing court.

A year and a day after the first arguments before it, the Oregon Supreme Court released its important opinion. It affirmed the result of the two lower courts, but did so for very different reasons.

Fasano—A New Standard of Judicial Review of Land Use Decisions

With the *Fasano* decision, the Oregon Supreme Court undertook to abandon previous fictions utilized in the review of local land use decisions. The court rejected both the "arbitrary and capricious" standard outright, and severely curtailed the use of the "change or mistake rule," rejecting it as the sole standard of review. The "spot zoning" terminology of previous decisions was curiously absent in *Fasano*.

Instead, the court went out of its way to emphasize the primacy of the comprehensive plan as the major standard by which local land use decisions were to be judged. The court carefully separated and explained the planning and zoning functions of local government, although it found these functions to be part of an integrated land use process. The court further elaborated that the function of zoning was to "carry out" the comprehensive plan.

Further, the court stated that in exercise of their zoning functions, cities and counties utilized powers delegated to them by the state. Hence, that exercise was conditioned upon compliance with the state enabling legislation and the standards therein.

The court then added two further requirements which have caused some confusion in local zoning administration: (1) the court stated that however much the proposed rezoning (and by implication all other exercises of the zoning power, such as special exceptions, conditional uses, variances, etc.) conformed to the comprehensive plan, the same would also have to fulfill a "public need." It would suggest that this means that the court desires a showing not only that the applicant receives a monetary gain from approval, but that the public has a need for the use in question; and, (2) the court added that it would also require a conscious evaluation by the land use authority of other available property for which such use is permissible, instead of flooding the market with such uses without any need to do so.

The court stated that it was probably subject to criticism, that the decision made the local zoning process too difficult, but found that the high stakes at issue justified such a posture.

Even more important for the state of zoning law were the pronouncements of the Oregon Supreme Court with respect to the nature of rezoning hearings.

The court stated that while the original zoning and major revisions thereof were legislative acts and the subject of a heavy presumption of validity, the nature of the rezoning process (and other permit-granting functions) in applying general policy embodied in the state zoning enabling legislation and the local comprehensive plan to specific situations partook more of an *adjudication* than legislature policy-making.

Thus, the court termed these functions as "quasi-judicial" and, from that characterization, drew several conclusions as to the quality of such hearings.

The burden of proof, as in judicial situations, was upon the applicant to prove each of the points noted in the last section. The court added that the more drastic the nature of the application over existing permissible land uses, the greater the burden of the applicant. Further, the court stated that parties in a rezoning (or other permit-granting) hearing were entitled to certain rights:

1. The right to notice and an opportunity to be heard (this right accrues in both legislative and quasi-judicial hearings);
2. The right to present and rebut evidence (presumably, this means the right to cross-examine opponents or their witnesses, possibly under oath);
3. The right to an impartial tribunal (the court elaborated that this meant a tribunal with no pre-hearing or *ex parte* contacts, a significant departure from existing practice; and,
4. The right to a record of the hearing and adequate findings (reasons) justifying the action of the land use authority. In this connection, the court found the county's reasons for rezoning too "superficial and conclusory" to uphold the same.

The changes in zoning practice before most zoning authorities were far-reaching and were aided by several pieces of legislation by the 1973 Oregon legislature to secure the rights of all parties in land use cases. The legislature added enabling legislation for a hearings officer, provided for conflict of interest standards, and required both cities and counties to adopt comprehensive plans.

Frankland—How High is a "Garden Apartment?"

The Oregon Supreme Court did not rest in its labors in 1973 with *Fasano*. It proceeded to decide another complex case, again on review from the Oregon Court of Appeals, *Frankland v. City of Lake Oswego*, 98 Adv. Sh. 519, ___ Or. ___, 517 P.2d 1042 (1973).

Roger Frankland and his wife bought a home in the unincorporated area of Multnomah County and found that the adjacent land had been bought by a developer and annexed to the city of Lake Oswego in return for a zoning classification as a PUD (Planned Unit Development). The portion next to the Franklands was sold to another developer who promised to place garden apartments thereon and showed some architectural renderings in support of his proposal.

While construction was underway, the Franklands stated that the building under construction was not the same as the one they believed would be built. After some discussions with, and hearings before, various agencies of the city, the Franklands and other neighbors brought suit against the city and certain of its officers and the developers to obtain the zone change and construction. As the Franklands could not afford a bond, construction on the site continued and the building, five stories in height, was occupied.

The circuit court heard the plaintiffs' case and then dismissed their suit, finding that the city properly rezoned the property and that the resulting apartment building was within that grant.

The Franklands appealed the decision to the Oregon Court of Appeals which reversed the circuit court decision, finding that the "change or mistake rule" applied and was not met by the city or the developers (this decision preceded the *Fasano* decision by the Supreme Court, and thus the old fiction was used). The court added that the final building was not in accordance with the building plan approved by the city. Lastly, the court found that procedural rules prevented the defendants from presenting any case at all to the circuit court, and so it remanded the case to the circuit court for appropriate relief, including payment of damages or demolition of the building.

This time, it was the turn of the developers to seek review by petition to the Oregon Supreme Court. That court took no action on the petition for more than a year while it decided *Fasano*, whereupon it granted review.

The decision which resulted was another attempt to instill rational rules into the zoning process. The Oregon Supreme Court did not address itself to the simple question of whether the pre-*Fasano* "change or mistake rule," or *Fasano* itself applied to the rezoning. Instead, it looked to the conformity of the finished structure with approved plans.

That court, placing photos of the architectural renderings and the final building in its opinion found the two inconsistent. Although there had been hearings held by the city on conformity of the building to the approved plan, the court found such hearings informal and without legal efficacy. The developer simply failed to build according to the approved plans and had damaged the plaintiffs, who had lost their view of Mt. Hood. The whole proceeding was clouded by the fact that the term "garden apartment" was not defined in the city ordinance.

The Supreme Court concluded that it would modify the court of appeals' decision to the extent that it allowed the defendants to put on their case as to whatever defenses they had alleged, but stated that if those defenses were not well-taken, the defendants could be made to pay damages or demolish the building.

Although the *Frankland* case has not been completed, several portions of the Supreme Court decision indicate changes in the way the courts will view developer vs. neighbor conflicts in the land use game.

In the first place, the court found that the neighbors were sufficiently damaged by the loss of their view to be able to maintain a suit to prevent construction of a building on adjacent property. The court stated that if damages were to be awarded, they would be measured by the differences in the market value of the Frankland home (and others) if the building had been constructed in accordance with the approved plan, and the existing market value. In short, the circuit court will be asked to determine the value of a view.

Secondly, the Supreme Court stressed its favorable impression of the Planned Unit Development concept, possibly to allay fears that this was a judicially suspect classification as a result of its decisions in *Fasano* and *Frankland*. The court stressed the need for such concepts to meet the needs created by urbanization and sprawl.

Thirdly, the opinion of the court, as in *Fasano*, emphasized the concern of the court for procedural fairness to all persons having an interest in the outcome of a zoning hearing—a far cry from the usual formal position of judicial abdication which characterizes most reviewing courts.

Conclusion

Both the *Fasano* and *Frankland* decisions leave some points unanswered, such as what is "public need" and "other available property," how close must one be to an illegal zoning act to collect damages, etc. But clearly, these two cases represent a new approach to land use regulation by the courts.

This new approach is geared more to the functions under consideration than the names attributed to those functions. Further, this approach expresses a due process requirement that hearings before zoning authorities be fairly conducted, and that procedures therein generally conform to those expected of courts or administrative tribunals. Finally, there is a warning to those who might build first and litigate the consequences later—that the result may be unacceptable to the judiciary.

In any case, there are some fresh new thoughts coming out of Oregon in the area of land use regulation, and the results may indeed be beneficial to this nation.

The Quiet Revolution

In Land Use Control

Fred P. Bosselman
and David L. Callies

Fred Bosselman is a partner in the firm of Ross, Hardies, O'Keefe, Babcock &
Parsons; Chicago, Illinois. He is the Associate Reporter for the American Law
Institute's Model Land Development Code, director of the Metropolitan Housing
and Planning Council of Chicago, co-author of The Quiet Revolution in Land
Use Control, The Taking Issue, *and* Exclusionary Zoning *[Praeger, 1973], and*
has served as a consultant to the President's Council on Environmental Quality,
the U.S. Environmental Protection Agency, the states of Florida and Virginia,
and the National Commission on Urban Problems. Mr. Bosselman is a graduate
of the University of Colorado and of Harvard Law School.

David Callies is an associate in the law firm of Ross, Hardies, O'Keefe, Babcock
& Parsons; Chicago, Illinois. He is a member of the Council of State Govern-
ments, Task Force on Natural Resources and Land Use Information and Tech-
nology, and was the Assistant State's Attorney for McHenry County, Illinois. Mr.
Callies is a graduate of DePauw University, and has a J.D. from the University of
Michigan Law School and a LL.M. from the University of Nottingham, England.

This article consists of two "chapters" and a postscript from the full 350+ page
report—by the same title—issued by the Council on Environmental Quality, in
1971. The remaining text, with specific case and legislative descriptions and
analyses, has not been reprinted here.

Foreword

[Editor's Note: the following is a portion of the foreword to the report (prepared for the
Council on Environmental Quality), signed by Russell E. Train—Chairman of CEQ—on
December 15, 1971.]

The Council on Environmental Quality commissioned this report on the innovative
land use laws of several States in order to learn how some of the most complex land use
issues are being addressed. We do not necessarily endorse any of the laws analyzed in the
Report, but we invite attention to them as examples of approaches States are taking to the
difficult problem of reallocating responsibilities between State and local government.
The progressive initiatives of several States are evidence that the great debate has begun,
that efforts are underway in widely separated areas of the country to broaden the community making decisions with respect to certain land use issues. Undoubtedly, matters of
purely local interest—for example, where to allow a gas station—should remain under
local control. Probably the great majority of land use decisions made by government are
properly local in effect.

However, as our society has become more complex it has become clear that some land
use determinations of one locality often have very important consequences for citizens in

other areas. It is these issues of greater than local significance in which State and regional involvement seems appropriate, even necessary, if the broader community affected by such decisions is to have some influence over them.

We are encouraged by the increasing concern in the States over these problems. We hope that this report will contribute to greater interest and familiarity with land use regulation, and that readers will share the urgency we feel with respect to land use as the most important environmental issue remaining substantially unaddressed as a matter of national policy.

Introduction

[Editor's Note: this section as well as the next two ("Key Issues" and "Postscript") are the first and last two chapters of the Report, in their entirety.]

This country is in the midst of a revolution in the way we regulate the use of our land. It is a peaceful revolution, conducted entirely within the law. It is a quiet revolution, and its supporters include both conservatives and liberals. It is a disorganized revolution, with no central cadre of leaders, but it is a revolution nonetheless.

The ancien regime being overthrown is the feudal system under which the entire pattern of land development has been controlled by thousands of individual local governments, each seeking to maximize its tax base and minimize its social problems, and caring less what happens to all the others.

The tools of the revolution are new laws taking a wide variety of forms but each sharing a common theme—the need to provide some degree of state or regional participation in the major decisions that affect the use of our increasingly limited supply of land. The function of this report is to discuss and analyze these new laws and to try to predict and perhaps influence the course of this "quiet revolution."

Land use controls developed very late in the history of the United States, primarily after the turn of the century. As experience in other countries has demonstrated, there is little to quicken interest in such controls if there is a super-abundance of land. During the first century of a nation in which a strong belief in the inviolability of private property rights was coupled with a largely agrarian economy, there was no impetus to control the use of land.

Land use controls in the United States have therefore logically developed against a backdrop of the emerging importance of the urban area as steadily receding western frontiers dwindled. As early as 1692, for example, a law was passed in Massachusetts Bay Colony forbidding "nuisance" industries from operating in any but certain districts designated for such uses by town officials, but even then the law was applied only to Boston, Salem, Charlestown, and other market towns and cities of the province—the urban areas of the day.

It was in the cities that it became apparent that regulations were needed to prevent one man's use of his land from depreciating the value of his neighbor's property. Those who were concerned about these issues called themselves city planners, and they viewed the use of land as an urban problem. Rudimentary ordinances regulating building height and land use appeared in Boston and Los Angeles around 1909. Then in the next decade many cities passed local ordinances dividing real estate into districts which permitted some uses and excluded others. This system of local "zoning," as it came to be known, provided planners and legislators with a process containing a wide range of political options with which to achieve a consensus of interests within the local community. After the Supreme Court gave its blessing in 1926 the issue became, what kind of restrictions and where?—rather than whether there should be restrictions at all.

The Quiet Revolution

From the beginning the state governments saw land use control as an urban problem. A Standard Zoning Enabling Act delegating the responsibility for zoning to the city governments was prepared by an advisory committee appointed by the then-Secretary of Commerce, Herbert Hoover, and variations of it were quickly adopted by most of the states. Through the 1940's and 1950's zoning techniques were refined: The number and kinds of zones increased; greater flexibility was introduced through open space ratios, floor plan ratios, and performance standards. Planned unit development—the uniting of compatible uses and relaxation of standard restrictions according to a development plan—was added to the arsenal of zoning devices.

The complexity of the new techniques cannot obscure the fact that local zoning remains essentially what it was from the beginning—simply a process by which the residents of a local community examine what people propose to do with their land and decide whether or not they will let them. The comprehensive planning envisioned by zoning's founders was never achieved, in part because the growing interrelatedness of our increasingly complex society makes it impossible for individual local governments to plan comprehensively, and in part because the physical consideration of land use, with which zoning was in theory designed to deal, frequently became submerged in petty local prejudices about who gets to live and work where.

The real problem is the structure of zoning itself, with its emphasis on very local control of land use by a dizzying multiplicity of local jurisdictions. While the Standard Act was a *state* enabling act, it was nonetheless an *enabling* act, directed at delegating land use control to the local level, historically at the city level where the problems which called zoning into being first arose. It has become increasingly apparent that the local zoning ordinance, virtually the sole means of land use control in the United States for over half a century, has proved woefully inadequate to combat a host of problems of statewide significance, social problems as well as problems involving environmental pollution and destruction of vital ecological systems, which threaten our very existence.

It is this realization that local zoning is inadequate to cope with problems that are statewide or regionwide in scope that has fueled the quiet revolution in land use control. A recognition of the inadequacies of local zoning must not, however, cause the values of citizen participation and local control, which local zoning so strongly emphasizes, to be submerged completely in some anonymous state bureaucracy. Although the governmental entities created by the states to deal with land use problems are statewide or regional rather than local in orientation, these innovations have never involved a total usurpation of local control, and have rarely constituted an attack on the integrity of the local zoning process. Even Hawaii's statewide system of land use controls, sometimes thought to vest exclusive authority over land use in the state, recognizes the importance of a major role for local governments.

The innovations wrought by the "quiet revolution" are not, by and large, the results of battles between local governments and states from which the states eventually emerge victorious. Rather, the innovations in most cases have resulted from a growing awareness on the part of both local communities and statewide interests that states, not local governments, are the only existing political entities capable of devising innovative techniques and governmental structures to solve problems such as pollution, destruction of fragile natural resources, the shortage of decent housing, and many other problems which are now widely recognized as simply beyond the capacity of local governments acting alone.

For example, Hawaii, Vermont, and Maine have each adopted a statewide land regulatory system, but the techniques of land use control employed by each of the three are markedly different. Other states have not adopted statewide land use controls, but have provided land use controls for "critical areas" of each state's environment. Thus Wisconsin protects shorelands around lakes and along waterways, while Massachusetts is one of the states that has adopted laws to protect its wetlands, and California has created a special agency to deal with the problems of San Francisco Bay.

Other innovative legislation focuses on key types of land development. The New England River Basin Commission, like other such commissions, attempts to control the placement of dams and similar structures that are determinative of development patterns within river basins. In Minnesota the Twin Cities Regional Council regulates development by controlling the location of sewers, airports and a variety of other key facilities. And Massachusetts has created a new state agency to ensure that housing can be located in accordance with statewide needs.

The following nine chapters each considers one of these recent innovative land regulatory systems in greater detail, based primarily on a review of the key statutes, regulations and decisions and on interviews with the administering officials and other groups affected by the legislation.

These nine land regulatory systems are only a sampling of the recent legislative activity in this area. Another chapter discusses in more summary fashion a number of other recent laws. The final chapter attempts to synthesize some of the key issues that run through all of the attempts to quietly revolutionize our land regulatory systems.

The nature of the innovations in land use regulation varies from state to state, and sometimes from one institution to another within a state. Some of the devices employed are old ones in novel juxtaposition. Others are entirely, imaginatively new in concept and design. But if there is a commonality it is a regional and land resource orientation that attempts to preserve and protect a vital resource—land—for the use of the region as a whole.

Key Issues in State Land Use Regulation

The administrators of all the programs covered in this report are sailing uncharted waters. Each day brings new problems that must be solved by the use of common sense interpretations of sketchy statutory guidelines. It should be no surprise, therefore, to learn that although the administrators find their work challenging and interesting, they also find themselves so occupied with immediate tasks that they have little time to spend contemplating the long range philosophy behind their work. Except in Hawaii, where there is now some reexamination of basic goals, the administrators are too busy to be reflective. If you ask them, "What are the key issues?" they are likely to respond —"finding time to review these 10 applications before midnight."

Given the youth of this legislation, and the charged-up atmosphere in which it is administered, it is not even easy for the outside observer to sit back and view it from a broader perspective. But the following six issues seem to recur throughout most of the states that have been affected by the quiet revolution.

(1) **Toward a New Concept of Land.** If one were to pinpoint any single predominant cause of the quiet revolution, it is a subtle but significant change in our very concept of the term "land," a concept that underlies our whole philosophy of land use regulation. "Land" means something quite different to us now than it meant to our grandfather's generation. Its new meaning is hard to define with precision, but it is not hard to illustrate the direction of the change.

247

The Quiet Revolution

Basically, we are drawing away from the 19th century idea that land's only function is to enable its owner to make money. One example of this change in attitude is that wetlands, which were once characterized as "useless," are now thought of as having "value." As we increasingly understand the science of ecology and the web of connections between the use of any particular piece of land and the impact on the environment as a whole, we increasingly see the need to protect wetlands and other areas that were formerly ignored.

This concern over the interrelatedness of land uses has led to a recognition of the need to deal with entire ecological systems rather than small segments of them. San Francisco Bay, Lake Tahoe, the Hackensack Meadowlands, Adirondack Park are now all seen as single entities rather than as a collection of governmental units.

The new attitude toward land can also be seen reflected in the increasing concern about its scarcity. Industries that in an earlier day seemed to have their choice of an unlimited supply of land now see land as a limiting factor. With some, such as the forest products industry, this recognition came early—with others, such as agriculture, it is just beginning in states like Hawaii and California.

The economically productive users of land are not the only ones who are increasingly recognizing its scarcity. Wilderness buffs have recognized this for some time. But now the large segment of Americans who just want to live in the country, and who once seemed to have a wide choice of location, now find their supply of land limited. The jet plane, and particularly the interstate highway network, have permitted millions of Americans to achieve their goal of "country living" on either a permanent or temporary basis, but they are finding that there isn't as much "country" to live in as there used to be. Their annoyance is reflected in the new legislation in Maine and Colorado.

The scarcity of land reflects both its increasing use and the increasing limitations put on its use by local governments. The problems of inner city dwellers seeking adequate housing seem impossible to solve unless we can overcome the scarcity of suburban land on which low and moderate-income dwellings can be built. The Massachusetts Zoning Appeals Act was passed in recognition of this scarcity.

Conservationists describe the changing attitude toward land by saying that land should be considered a *resource* rather than a *commodity*. But while this correctly indicates the direction of the change, it ignores the crucial importance of our constitutional right to own land and to buy and sell it freely. It is essential that land be treated as *both* a resource and a commodity. The right to move throughout the country and buy and sell land in the process is an essential element in the mobility and flexibility our society needs to adjust to the rapid changes of our times. Conservationists who view land only as a resource are ignoring the social and economic impact that would come with any massive restrictions on the free alienability of land. But land speculators who view land only as a commodity are ignoring the growing public realization that our finite supply of land can no longer be dealt with in the freewheeling ways of our frontier heritage.

The idea that land is a resource as well as a commodity may appear self-evident, but in the context of our traditions of land use regulation it is a highly novel concept. Our existing systems of land use regulation were created by dealers in real estate interested in maximizing the value of land as a commodity. Subdivision regulations which encouraged uniform lots fronting on public streets enabled land to be divided into tradable units. Traditional zoning ordinances with only a few use districts, each governed by relatively nondiscretionary regulations, attempted to give these lots some of the fungible qualities of corn futures or stock certificates, making it possible to determine in advance the specific type of use permitted on the land and providing quick shorthand labels for identifying various categories of land. Bulk and yard regulations created an envelope on each single lot which enabled the owner of that lot to build without further consideration of the relationship of his land to the land of his neighbors, thus assuring potential buyers of the land's usability. The highest goal of the system was to enable barkers to sell Florida lots in Grand Central Station.

The promoters of these land use regulations in the 1920's made no attempt to conserve land for particular purposes or to direct it into a specific use, but only sought to prevent land from being used in a manner that would depreciate the value of neighboring land. The traditional answer to the question, "Why regulate land use?" was "to maximize land values." To achieve this purpose they sought to restrict those uses of land that adversely affected the price of neighboring land by concentrating them in specific parts of the city.

Where development would not harm property values it went unregulated. Zoning permitted residential uses to be built in the most polluted industrial districts on the theory that any development which did not reduce the value of the surrounding land should not be prohibited. Land use regulation was limited to urban areas where the close proximity of land uses made it likely that the particular use of one man's land might reduce the value of another's, but there was no regulation of land outside urban areas where such a reduction in value was not likely to take place.

In a dynamic and mobile society such as ours, the ability to buy and sell land readily is an essential ingredient in the operation of the system, and the extent to which zoning and subdivision control have been adopted throughout the country testifies to the usefulness of these original concepts. The last 20 years, however, has seen increasing recognition that the purpose of land regulation should go beyond the protection of the commodity value of land. A realization is growing that important social and environmental goals require more specific controls on the use that may be made of scarce land resources.

This recognition is seen not only in the new state role in land use regulation, but in the actions of many local governments. Modern zoning ordinances typically rely less and less on pre-stated regulations and require developers to work with local administrative officials in designing a type of development that fits more closely into the specific circumstances of the surrounding neighborhood. Similarly, regulations tend to encourage larger scale development in which the various land uses are arranged and designed according to a comprehensive plan for the specific site, as opposed to the traditional lot-by-lot development under which individual lots were sold to individual purchasers who might develop each lot according to pre-established rules. More specialized use districts, which permit only those uses appropriate to a specific geographic area rather than some abstract category of uses such as M-1 or R-4, are also evidence of local governments' growing attempt to tailor land use regulations to local needs.

Most importantly, perhaps, numerous systems of local land use regulation are beginning to contain regulations that recognize land as a resource as well as a commodity. Exclusive agricultural and industrial zoning preserves land as a resource for these important uses. Regulations prohibiting topsoil removal or requiring common open space find their justification in the protection of land as a resource for recreation and beauty. Regulations which require that a specified percentage of dwelling units in each housing development be reserved for low-income groups are recognizing the importance of land as an essential resource for housing all elements of our society.

Recent years have seen a rapid increase in local zoning and subdivision regulation in relatively undeveloped areas. Here the concern is not that the use of land might injure immediate neighbors, but that it might impair the possibility of more desirable long-range land use patterns. Increasingly the question being asked is not only, "Will this use reduce the value of surrounding land?" but "Will this make the best use of our land resources?"

The clearest evidence, however, that there has been a change in the attitude toward why land should be regulated is in the legislation described in this report. The purposes sought to be achieved by the various bills are a far cry from the simple value-maximization concepts of early real estate interests. Hawaii seeks to conserve the land for agriculture and to preserve scenic beauty. In Tahoe and San Francisco the goal is to preserve the amenities of the area. Maine and Vermont are trying to protect the rural atmosphere of their states. Massachusetts wants to preserve some suburban land as a resource for low and moderate-income housing and to preserve wetlands as a resource for wildlife and other ecological values. In the Hackensack Meadows the goal of New Jersey is to utilize this centrally located land for the ideal combination of development and conservation purposes.

But the recognition of new purposes for regulating land should not and does not mean that the old concerns with land's value and salability should be ignored. On the contrary, the longer-range view expressed in the new land regulatory systems will enhance land values over the long run to a far greater degree than systems motivated primarily by a desire to increase immediate salability. The preservation of the amenities of San Francisco Bay is of tremendous economic value to all landowners in the Bay area. The preservation of the quality of Maine's lakes and coastline will be of great value to owners of property in those areas, not just today but for years to come. Today's broader view of land values recognizes that in the long run land values will reflect our ability to maintain a society in which people will want to own land, and this is the overall goal of the legislation now being enacted by the states.

(2) The Role of the State. Changes in a state's pattern of land use involve thousands of individual decisions—to drill a well, to widen a street, to build a power plant, to build a garage—the new patterns that result are the sum of all of these decisions, some major, others very minor. The state's goals can be achieved if only the major decisions can be regulated. One of the important issues in each state land regulatory system is to separate the major decisions from the minor so that state officials are not bogged down with gas station applications when they should be considering power plant sites, and so that irate homeowners do not have to go to the state capital to get permission to build a garage.

To succeed in solving this dilemma it is essential to avoid the classic bureaucratic trap. *Regulation is not desirable for its own sake.* Any system of land regulation imposes substantial costs. These include not only the costs borne by the taxpayers who pay the administrators' salaries and expenses, but the costs borne by the developers and eventually passed on to the consumer. Time is a particularly important cost to most land developers because heavy front-end expenses are usually paid with money borrowed at relatively high interest rates, which makes each additional day of delay a significant factor in increasing the cost.

The costs imposed on developers by land use regulations have a peculiarly regressive nature. Developers of expensive housing, for example, can much more easily absorb the cost of regulation than developers of housing designed for lower income groups. The cost of processing an application to build a mobile home park and a luxury apartment building may be approximately the same, but when considered as a percentage of the consumers' cost per unit, the costs loom much larger to the mobile home buyer.

Regulation has other inherent disadvantages. Any complex system of regulation has a natural tendency to reduce innovation. Minima become maxima. When regulators approve one design it creates a powerful incentive for other builders to use the same approach. The monotonous subdivision of the 1950's is being replaced by the monotonous planned unit development of the 1970's.

For these reasons, all of the states engaging in land use regulation have used some method of concentrating their energies on a limited number of important development decisions to avoid diffusing the state regulatory power too widely. A variety of methods are used: In the Twin Cities, regulation is concentrated on major capital improvements, such as airports and sewers. Both Vermont and Maine have attempted to define development subject to the state's jurisdiction in a way that excludes small-scale development and concentrates only on development of more significant size. Hawaii classifies development into four basic categories and (in theory at least) the state attempts to decide only the proper category applicable to a particular piece of land, leaving the details to be worked out by the counties.

The problem of isolating the types or areas of development that have a significant state or regional impact does not seem headed for an easy solution. Further experimentation with the various methods now in use in the states may discover increasingly better methods. But the need is apparent for some method of concentrating state efforts on major land use issues if the burdens of regulation are not to exceed its benefits. Those who cry for comprehensive regulation of all development by the state merely show that they have not thought through the problem.

(3) The Role of Local Government. Local regulation of land use has been in existence for many years in at least the urbanized portions of most states. These local systems of zoning and subdivision control have proven quite adequate for controlling many types of development, particularly small-scale development in urban areas. At a time of increasing demands for citizen participation and community control, the value of encouraging local decision-making wherever possible is obvious.

A common failing of most of the new state land regulatory systems is that they do not relate in a logical manner to the continuing need for local participation. Most of them tend to by-pass the existing system of local regulation and set up completely independent and unrelated systems. This requires the developer who is subject to both systems to go through two separate and distinct administrative processes, often doubling the time required and substantially increasing the costs required to obtain approval of the development proposal.

Most states have chosen to create duplicating procedures in order to eliminate the need to make any change in existing zoning and other regulatory systems. By leaving local zoning alone, the state reduces the number of potential enemies of new legislation. Moreover, in many states the motives behind the state land regulatory system were solely to *prohibit* development that would otherwise occur. To persons having this motive the duplication does not seem to be a problem because duplication can only operate to prevent and not to encourage development.

Not all of the states have accepted the idea of duplication. The Massachusetts Zoning Appeals Act explicitly rejects it; here the state system comes into play only as a means of reversing a decision of a local board. The Hawaii system also minimizes duplication; some of the major development proposals require action by both state and county agencies, but most ordinary development needs action by only one or the other.

As the states move toward more balanced systems of land use regulation that are not weighted exclusively toward the prevention of development, it will be increasingly necessary to merge both state and local regulations into a single system with specific roles for both state and local government in order to reduce the cost to the consumer and taxpayer of duplicate regulatory mechanisms.

(4) Regulation and Planning. Once government recognizes that land can be a resource to achieve many different goals, some method is needed to balance these various goals to see which uses of land will provide the greatest overall benefit. The operations of the Hawaiian Land Use Commission offer a good example of this balancing process. The Commission is constantly weighing the need for more housing against the need for agricultural land—the need to protect the views of the mountains against the need to attract jobs and tourists.

"Planning" can be defined as just this kind of balancing process. The Hawaiian Land Use Commission is engaged in "planning" although most of the Commissioners do not think of themselves as planners. Similarly, many of the other agencies discussed in this report are determining the best use of land by a planning process which measures alternative uses against the overall goals and policies of the state. In some cases these policies are clearly articulated and the process is consciously perceived as "planning," while in others it is not.

In Maine, for example, the statutory direction given to the Environmental Improvement Commission would also appear to preclude much balancing of conflicting goals. The statute directs the Board to insure maximum protection of the environment and does not provide any process by which countervailing development needs can be weighed. In practice, however, the Board utilizes a balancing process in deciding how far to press its jurisdiction.

Other statutes more explicitly instruct the administrator to consider a variety of goals. The Wisconsin Shorelands Act, although primarily oriented toward protecting the environmental values of the rivers and lakes, does recognize the need for some types of development. Similarly, the Massachusetts Zoning Appeals Act, although primarily oriented toward making land available for housing needs, also recognizes that it is important to protect health and safety and preserve open space.

Other statutes involve more sophisticated planning processes. In Vermont, although the present regulatory process is oriented primarily toward protection of environmental values, the planners are directed to prepare a plan that takes into consideration both environmental and socio-economic conditions. The Twin Cities Regional Council uses a comprehensive planning approach as a basis for the decisions assigned to it. Similarly, the Tahoe Regional Planning Agency and the Hackensack Meadowlands Development Commission are taking into consideration a wide variety of factors in preparing the plans on which their regulatory systems are based.

It seems clear that as state land regulatory systems evolve they will increasingly spawn better planning processes on which to base regulatory decisions. The Massachusetts Wetlands Act, for example, does not ask its administrators to balance the pros and cons of various uses of the wetlands. The legislature has presumably done this balancing itself and concluded that the goal of preserving the wetlands outweighs all other possible goals. Consequently, the administration of the Act can be said to involve a minimum of planning. But as it increasingly becomes recognized that other values are involved, it seems reasonable to assume that the state will institute a planning process that will take all values into consideration.

To see regulation as the predecessor of planning is not wholly logical. But Americans have rarely looked kindly on the idea of planning for its own sake, and have paid attention to planning only when it immediately affects decision-making. As a political matter, probably the most feasible method of moving towards a well-planned system of state land use regulation is to begin with a regulatory system that concentrates on a few goals that are generally perceived as important, and then to gradually expand the system by adding more comprehensive planning elements, as is being done in Vermont. To insist that the planning precede the regulation is probably to sacrifice feasibility on the altar of logic.

If the land regulatory systems are to be assisted by competent land use planning, it will require substantial redirection of current state planning efforts in many states. The Department of Housing and Urban Development has increasingly been directing the state's attention towards the management of state government programs, with the result that many states have been drifting away from the more comprehensive approach toward land use planning that was characteristic of the states in the 1930's. There is no reason why land use planning is inconsistent with budgetary and management planning, and if the state planning agencies are to perform a meaningful role in land use regulation, they must reassert their interest in comprehensive planning for land use. Unless the state planners divert at least a share of their attention toward land use issues, they may find that other more specialized agencies will have taken over, and the opportunity for a comprehensive approach will have been lost.

(5) Constitutional Limits on Regulation. One of the most important issues in any land regulatory system is the extent to which the use of land may be restricted without violating constitutional rights. Almost every state and local government that is trying to implement an environmentally-oriented land regulatory system finds itself plagued with constitutional doubts. The constitution prohibits the "taking" of property without payment of just compensation. Judicial interpretations of this clause have held that the regulation of property in a manner to severely limit its use may in some cases be interpreted as such a taking. These cases pose a constant problem to land use regulators.

Most land regulatory systems find a need to prevent all "use" of at least some portion of the land within their jurisdiction. Funds are not usually available to pay the owners of this land for the loss in speculative value to which they might claim to be entitled. The administrators therefore find themselves in the difficult position of either permitting uses that would be environmentally harmful or facing court challenges that may endanger the entire regulatory program.

This dilemma posed by the "taking" issue requires a creative legal response on the part of the regulatory agencies and their attorneys. A number of approaches are promising:

First, if one really studies the cases, the law on this subject has by no means been as bad as most people seem to assume. The Supreme Court of the United States has frequently upheld regulatory systems that prevent any development of a man's land if the regulation is essential to promote the public health or safety, and the preservation of a livable environment and a desirable ecological balance is in the long run clearly essential to the health of the nation. "Brandeis briefs" and expert ecological testimony, when combined with a sophisticated analysis of existing case law, can provide sound constitutional arguments for the validity of many regulatory measures that might otherwise be thought so restrictive as to require compensation.

Second, draftsmen of regulations need to make a careful analysis of the types of activities that may be allowed to take place on land without destroying environmental values. Too often regulations have taken the form of blanket prohibitions when a variety of activities could be permitted on the land without detracting from the values that the regulations are designed to protect.

Third, further exploration is needed to provide a sound legal rationale for setting off benefits created by the regulatory program against the losses caused by restrictions. A regulatory program that prohibits the filling of low-lying land in a flood plain, for example, may reduce the value of the portion of a man's land on which filling is prohibited, but it may substantially increase the value of the higher land by reducing the threat of flooding. Mechanisms by which these benefits can be set off against any losses can be very helpful in reducing the necessity of paying compensation.

Fourth, where compensation must be paid, new legal methods of relating the amount of compensation more exactly to the losses suffered should be devised. The government should not be forced to purchase the entire land if some lesser remedy provides equitable compensation. Compensation through the purchase of development rights, a year-to-year-interest or some type of easement should be considered.

This report is not the place to discuss in detail the many ramifications of the constitutional issue, and the many interesting approaches to it being undertaken around the country. Those who create systems of land regulation based on modern ecological knowledge should be aware of the constitutional issue, but should not be so afraid of it that they ignore the approaches that are available for working creatively within the constitutional limits.

(6) Choice of State Agency. The selection of the proper agency to exercise the state's role in land use regulation has not followed any uniform pattern. Three alternatives seem to be found in the existing legislation: line agencies of state government, independent state commissions, and state-created regional commissions.

Line agencies have been used primarily for systems of regulation that focus on a single purpose or a small number of purposes. Thus, both the Massachusetts Zoning Appeals Act, the Wisconsin Shoreland Protection program, and most wetlands acts are administered by line agencies. All of these programs have relatively specific goals that fall within the purview of an existing agency.

Where more comprehensive statewide land use regulation has been tried, independent state commissions have been chosen. Hawaii, Vermont and Maine have all used this model, and public attitudes in the three states would all seem to favor continuation of independent commissions for statewide land use regulation—existing state agencies are all thought to be too biased towards the existing programs they administer to do a fair job in balancing the full range of policies that go into these decisions. But independent commissions contribute to the fragmentation of executive authority at the state level.

The ideal approach from a textbook standpoint would be a new line agency directly under the governor, but in some states centralization of power in the governor is not popular. State planning agencies might serve a regulatory function, but in many states these agencies have paid little attention to land use matters.

Where the regulation is concentrated in a specific geographical area of the state, the states have generally chosen to set up independent commissions having a regional orientation. In some cases members of the commission are appointed by the governor. In other cases the local governments in the region exercise direct or indirect control in the selection of members of the commission. Some of the regional agencies have proven quite successful, but participation by the local governments in the selection of members seems likely to produce a strong pro-development bias because of the dependence of local governments on new development to produce tax revenues.

Selection of the appropriate agency to represent state or regional interests will undoubtedly vary with the specific conditions in each state at each particular time. Hopefully, the inter-agency bickering that accompanies so many programs of an interdisciplinary nature can be minimized.

Postscript: Future Directions

The great advantage of our federal system is that it facilitates experimentation. New state laws need not follow a single pattern but can search out many avenues for solutions.

To those seeking to decide what directions their state should take, assistance is promised by the various land use policy bills now pending before Congress. But these bills will provide only funds and basic guidelines, not detailed prescriptions.

Organizations such as the Council of State Governments and the American Society of Planning Officials are assembling resources to assist their members in finding creative new solutions for land use regulation. A study by Richard RuBino for the Council of State Governments, currently in preparation, will explore "The Emerging Role of States in Land Resource Management."

Also in process is a Model Land Development Code being prepared by the American Law Institute. Intended not as a uniform law but as a guide to the issues, the complete code is not likely to be ready until 1974, but tentative drafts of portions of it are available from the Institute at 4025 Chestnut Street, Philadelphia, Pennsylvania 19104.

But none of this assistance can replace good hard work at the state level—analyzing the issues and forging creative approaches. The reform of our land regulatory systems is a fascinating challenge that will continue to occupy us for many years to come.

Acknowledgements

When a report is based on literally hundreds of interviews it is impossible to single out individuals for the thanks they deserve. From Maine to Hawaii we were impressed with the willingness with which busy people spent their valuable time giving us their views about land use problems. Our associate Bill Eads was of invaluable assistance in the preparation of the preliminary draft of this report. Essential assistance was also provided by Bill Walsh, John Banta, Maxwell Davis, Michael Sawyier and Michael McCracken. And no one is happier to see its completion than Janet Janowski and Virginia Bertz who typed draft after draft with unfailing speed, precision and good humor. The advice and counsel of Boyd Gibbons and Bill Reilly of the Council on Environmental Quality shaped the scope and direction of the entire project. To them and to the members of the Council we owe our special thanks for their support.

The Taking Issue:

A Study of the Constitutional Limits

Fred P. Bosselman,
David Callies, and
John Banta

Fred Bosselman is a partner in the firm of Ross, Hardies, O'Keefe, Babcock & Parsons; Chicago, Illinois. He is the Associate Reporter for the American Law Institute's Model Land Development Code, director of the Metropolitan Housing and Planning Council of Chicago, co-author of The Quiet Revolution in Land Use Control, The Taking Issue, and Exclusionary Zoning [Praeger, 1973], and has served as a consultant to the President's Council on Environmental Quality, the U.S. Environmental Protection Agency, the states of Florida and Virginia, and the National Commission on Urban Problems. Mr. Bosselman is a graduate of the University of Colorado and of Harvard Law School.

David Callies is an associate in the law firm of Ross, Hardies, O'Keefe, Babcock & Parsons; Chicago, Illinois. He is a member of the Council of State Governments, Task Force on Natural Resources and Land Use Information and Technology, and was the Assistant State's Attorney for McHenry County, Illinois. Mr. Callies is a graduate of DePauw University, and has a J.D. from the University of Michigan Law School, and an LL.M. from the University of Nottingham, England.

John Banta is the staff attorney for the Conservation Foundation in Washington, D.C. He was an associate in the law firm of Ross, Hardies, O'Keefe, Babcock & Parsons; Chicago, Illinois. He is a graduate of Hiram College and has a law degree from Harvard Law School.

This article consists of several "chapters" from the full 329 page report—titled "The Taking Issue: A Study of the Constitutional Limits of Governmental Authority to Regulate the Use of Privately-owned Land Without Paying Compensation to the Owners"—issued by the Council on Environmental Quality, in 1973. The remaining text—chapters 1 through 16—has not been reprinted here.

Foreword

[Editor's Note: the following is a portion of the foreword to the report (prepared for the Council on Environmental Quality), signed by Russell E. Train—Chairman of CEQ—on July 9, 1973.]

Few subjects are more fraught with emotion and less understood than the rights of private property and the Constitutional limits to public control of those rights. If this is a highly charged emotional issue, it is no less serious a matter of national concern, as evidenced by the current debate over land use legislation in the Congress and in State legislatures throughout the country.

In a continuing effort to encourage informed public debate on land use reform, the Council commissioned the following study, "The Taking Issue." It is a natural sequel to the authors' earlier report to the Council entitled "The Quiet Revolution in Land Use Control," which examined a number of innovative State land use control initiatives. Since publication of "The Quiet Revolution . . . " a number of states have passed new land use legislation—Florida, California, New York and Oregon, for example—while others, such as Maryland, have confronted serious obstacles to such reforms. At the heart of most controversies over proposed State land use legislation is a fundamental legal question: What are the Constitutional limits to the control of private land? That is the issue which this report addresses. It offers an informative insight into the political and legal history of our Constitutional powers affecting land, the various court interpretations of those powers, and options open to future judicial and legislative action.

We are hopeful that this study of "The Taking Issue" will serve to clarify and inform public debate, in order that America's future can be better served by a more rational system of land use policies and controls.

Preface

This book has been written in response to the concern of the Council on Environmental Quality about the interrelationship between environmental quality and constitutional law. As the regulation of land use becomes an increasingly important component of programs for enhancing environmental quality the constitutional parameters within which land use regulation must operate become increasingly important.

Although land use regulation can raise issues under a variety of constitutional clauses this study focuses on the clause of the Fifth Amendment to the United States Constitution that poses by far the most significant restraint on the regulation of land use, the "taking clause": ". . . nor shall private property be taken for public use without just compensation."

This report traces the distinction between a valid regulation of the use of land and a "taking" that requires compensation, showing the history of the distinction and projecting probable future trends in this area of the law. The report is divided into four parts.

Part I presents an overview of current land use problems, showing the way in which the taking issue is affecting land use decisions in all parts of the country. It is entitled "The Pervasiveness of the Taking Issue."

Part II traces the concept of "taking" from its origins in Medieval England, down through British and Colonial American history, to the adoption of the "taking clause" in the United States Constitution. It follows the development of the taking clause through Supreme Court decisions of the Nineteenth Century to the major judicial expansions of the taking clause in the early Twentieth Century. This part is entitled "Taking and Regulation Through Seven and a Half Centuries."

Part III examines the current United States case law on the taking issue. The cases are analyzed from three different perspectives: 1) according to the similarity of their underlying facts; 2) according to certain general principles suggested by legal scholars; and 3) according to the date of decision. This Part is entitled "The Regulatory Taking in Current Law."

Part IV projects possible future trends in the interpretation of the taking clause as it affects the regulation of land use, and proposes a series of four alternative strategies for dealing with the issue, ranging from frontal attack to complete capitulation. This Part is entitled "The Future of the Taking Issue."

This study is an outgrowth of *The Quiet Revolution in Land Use Control*, an examination of new regulatory techniques which we wrote for the Council on Environmental Quality in 1971. Observation of these techniques in action convinced us of the importance of the taking issue. The reader is referred to that volume for more detailed background information on new types of land use regulation.

Introductory Note: A Constitutional Slice Through the Environment

"Each of these separate views of the environmental system is only a narrow slice through the complex whole. While each can illuminate some features of the whole system, the picture it yields is necessarily false to a degree. For in looking at one set of relationships we inevitably ignore a good deal of the rest; yet in the real world everything in the environment is connected to everything else." [Barry Commoner, *The Closing Circle*, p. 23 (1971).]

The complexity of environmental issues is notorious. Why, then, have we chosen to pay such close attention to a single point of law that we must examine over 700 years of legal history and analyze hundreds of court decisions? Is the issue really that important?

Just as the analysis of environmental problems demonstrates their interconnectedness, so the search for solutions also involves the fusing together of disparate elements. A solution must make economic sense, have political acceptability, avoid harmful side effects, allow efficient administration . . . and on and on. Solutions to environmental problems are like chains with many interconnected links.

The taking issue is the weak link in many of these chains. All over the country, as Part I demonstrates, attempts to solve environmental problems through land use regulation are threatened by the fear that they will be challenged in court as an unconstitutional taking of property without compensation.

When these challenges occur it is not enough to respond that everything is interconnected. While breadth of judicial vision is to be encouraged, response to the legal challenge must still be made in the framework of traditional legal concepts. This constitutional slice through the environment will be the field on which the battle is fought.

We do not claim that the strengthening of this one link is a quick cure for all environmental issues. Land use regulation is only one of many tools, suitable for some but not all environmental problems, and the chain of land use regulation has many other links, constitutional and otherwise. Nevertheless, if the challenge posed by the taking issue can be overcome we believe it will make a very significant impact on environmental quality.

If this book seems technical and detailed, it is because it is designed to assist government officials and attorneys who seek to fashion solutions to environmental problems. They are not seeking catchy cliches but detailed documentation from which they can work. That is what this book seeks to provide.

The Pervasiveness of the Taking Issue

North, east, south and west—debates over land use are heard in all parts of the country. And whenever problems are severe and strict regulations are suggested, the taking issue is likely to rear its head. Any new regulation brings charges by landowners and developers that their property is being taken without compensation.

The Taking Issue

One can appreciate the importance of the taking issue only when one sees the tremendous variety of disputes regarding the use of land which are affected by the taking issue: such varied programs as, e.g., wetlands protection, development timing, and historic preservation, all raise issues under the taking clause.

The nature of these issues is remarkably similar throughout the country. Although regional accents vary, the picture of new regulatory programs facing claims under the taking clause can be duplicated in almost every state of the union. A review of some of these current issues will provide an overview of the impact of the taking issue.

We were not surprised to find the taking clause a pervasive problem. We were surprised, after the hundreds of interviews that formed the basis of this Part I, to find the fear of the taking clause as powerful as it appears to be.

Many people seriously believe that the Constitution gives every man the right to do whatever he wants with his land. Foreign concepts like "environmental protection" and "zoning" were probably sneaked through by the Warren court!

Many more people recognize the validity of land use regulation in general, but believe that it may never be used to reduce the value of a man's land to the point where he can't make a profit on it. After all, what good is land if you can't make a profit on it.

The courts have never adopted either of these philosophies, as Part III demonstrates. Yet they are so influential with the thousands of local government officials who play the major role in regulating the use of land that these philosophies have an independent existence above and beyond the law.

The right to make money buying and selling land is a cherished American folkway, and one that cannot be lightly ignored. But in an increasingly crowded and polluted environment can we afford to continue circulating the myth that tells us that the taking clause protects this right of unrestricted use regardless of its impact on society? Obviously not, yet we must not let concern for the environment blind us to the fact that regulations have real economic impact on real people, and we must search for solutions that will take their interests into account.

Summary and Conclusions

The founding fathers placed in the Constitution the following words: ". . . nor shall private property be taken for public use without just compensation."[1] The application of this "taking clause" to land use regulation is the subject of this book.

Why do these twelve words deserve so much study? Because any system of land use regulation will work only if it satisfies each and every link in a chain of interconnected tests. It must be politically feasible; it must make sense economically; . . . and it must hold up in court. The taking issue is an important link in that chain, because if the courts find the system of regulation so severe that it constitutes a taking, the whole system collapses.

Our survey of land use problems around the country (Chapters 1-4) found that the similarities between the various sections of the country are greater than the differences. It is true that there are fewer land use problems in those states that are experiencing little growth pressure, and there are more problems in those states that have a particularly fragile environment. But throughout the country attempts are being made to regulate the use of land in new ways—and throughout the country these regulations are being influenced by concern over the taking issue.

Our strongest impression from this survey is that the fear of the taking issue is stronger than the taking clause itself. It is an American fable or myth that a man can use his land any way he pleases regardless of his neighbors. The myth survives, indeed thrives, even though unsupported by the pattern of court decisions. Thus, attempts to resolve land use controversies must deal not only with the law, but with the myth as well.

1. The History of the Taking Issue. How did a constitutional clause concerned with the *taking* of land become applicable to the *regulation* of land anyway? Originally it wasn't. The "taking" clause derived from the English nobles' fear of the King's seizures of land for his own use, a fear that was reflected in the Magna Carta: "No free man shall be deprived . . . of his freehold . . . unless by the lawful judgment of his peers and by the law of the land."[2]

But the use of land was being regulated—often very severely regulated—throughout English and early American history. Only around the turn of the Twentieth Century did judges and legal scholars popularize the notion that if regulation of the use of land became excessive, it could amount to the equivalent of a taking.

Chapter 5 sets out the early land use conflicts in medieval England. It discusses the various statutes and proclamations which attempted to control the growth and building of London and its environs, and highlights the movement towards the fencing of English common land between the Thirteenth and Seventeenth Centuries. Finally, the Chapter closes with a summary of the attitudes toward property of Coke and Blackstone—philosophies which affected property concepts carried to the New World.

Chapter 6 picks up the story in Colonial America. An examination and analysis of colonial regulations shows that the prevailing pattern of land use regulation was quite similar to that in England. Compensation was generally provided for physical takings of developed property, but literally hundreds of regulations of the use of land were enforced without any compensation to the landowner.

Nor was the issue of compensation for land use regulation raised either during the revolutionary period or in the drafting of the Constitution or Bill of Rights. Rather the draftsmen of the taking clause seem to have carried over the historic British concern over arbitrary seizure of land by the King—perhaps as reflected in seizures during the then recent revolutionary war—and to have applied that concern to actions of the new Federal Government.

The courts have insisted that the taking clause be strictly observed. Whenever the government has needed land for some public purpose it has either purchased the land on the open market or exercised the power of condemnation, paying the owner the fair market value of his land.

Court decisions during the entire first half of the Nineteenth Century (Chapter 7) find courts construing the taking clause strictly. To paraphrase a well-known commentator of the period writing in 1857, in order for an owner to be entitled to protection under the taking clause his property must have been actually taken in the physical sense of the word. No indirect or consequential damage, no matter how serious, warranted compensation.

The last half of the Nineteenth Century led to a certain ambivalence on the part of the courts, as the country's tremendous economic expansion inevitably produced conflicts with vested interests. Nonetheless, late in the Nineteenth Century the Supreme Court handed down cases such as *Powell v. Pennsylvania*[3] and *Mugler v. Kansas*[4] which denied compensation to the owners of business properties that became virtually valueless because of state regulatory statutes. These statutes were held to be valid police regulations, not takings of property within the meaning of the constitutional prohibition.

But Justice Holmes was soon to change the Court's direction, as Chapter 8 points out.

Only two years after *Mugler* v. *Kansas,* Holmes wrote from the bench of the Massachusetts Supreme Court in *Rideout* v. *Knox*[5] that the power of eminent domain (the power to acquire land) and the police power (the power to regulate land) differed only in degree and no clear line could be drawn between them. He continued to develop this philosophy in subsequent decisions and influenced a number of leading scholars of the period.

Then, in December of 1922, in the now famous case of *Pennsylvania Coal Company* v. *Mahon,* Holmes announced his famous rule: "The general rule at least is, that while property may be regulated to a certain extent, if regulation goes too far it will be recognized as a taking."[6]

When a diminution of property values reaches a certain magnitude, he said, a taking occurs. Thus, Holmes declared Pennsylvania's Kohler Act, passed to prevent coal mine subsidence from destroying whole towns, unconstitutional as an undue regulation of the property of the coal company.

Based on Holmes' reasoning the courts have continued to use a balancing test—a weighing of the public benefits of the regulation against the extent of loss of property values. The Supreme Court lost interest in the issue soon after *Pennsylvania Coal* and has refused to hear cases arising under the taking clause except in very rare instances. As a result, the application of the Court's balancing test has been left to the lower Federal Courts—and especially to the state courts, in which most land use regulation cases arise.

2. The State of the Current Law. Over the last fifty years the state courts have decided literally hundreds of cases, each of which determines whether the value of a particular land use regulation does or does not outweigh the loss of property value to a particular landowner. As might be expected, given the lack of leadership from a common central court, this mass of decisions has often been characterized as "chaotic." Since no state court feels itself particularly bound by the decisions of the courts of a different state, interpretations of the taking clause vary considerably.

Chapters 9, 10, and 11 look at these state court decisions from three different perspectives. Chapter 9 categorizes the cases in relation to various types of land use regulation that are involved. This classification is particularly useful for people concerned with specific regulations for such purposes as wetland protection, historic preservation, etc. In general this Chapter shows a general tendency of the courts to uphold well thought out regulations, though there are very few subjects on which one cannot find cases going both ways on very similar facts.

Chapter 10 reviews the legal literature on the relationship between land use regulation and the taking clause. Most of the scholars who have studied this subject have found that there are no universal principles which will consistently explain the results of the cases. Each case is decided on its own facts, as the courts frequently point out. Nevertheless, the commentators have found a few tendencies worth noting. The one most often described is the tendency of the courts to prefer regulations that control those uses of land that were treated as "nuisances" under the traditional common law.

Commentators have also tried to find some correlation between the amount that property values are reduced by a regulation and the willingness of the courts to find the regulation constitutional. For the most part, this attempt to find some numerical correlation appears not to have proven useful in predicting the outcome of future decisions.

A dramatic upsurge of concern over the environment took place in the late '60's and early '70's. We wondered whether this "new mood" would affect the judiciary, so we culled out the taking cases decided after January 1, 1970, and examined them separately in Chapter 11.

We discovered an interesting trend. Although the number of cases is still small, there is a strong tendency on the part of the courts to approve land use regulations if the purpose of the regulation is statewide or regional in nature rather than merely local. Although the courts are also supporting local land use regulations with a reasonable degree of consistency, they show an obvious preference for regulations having broad multi-purpose goals.

3. Strategies for the Future: The Importance of the Myth. The court decisions form only the visible surface of the law. Below the surface lies the myth of the taking clause—a powerful public perception of the clause as the embodiment of every man's right to buy and sell land for a profit. As the Task Force on Land Use and Urban Growth put it, "The popular impression of the takings clause may be even more out of date than some court opinions."[7]

Land use regulation is predominantly a function of local government—over ten thousand separate local governments, each exercising control over the land within its particular jurisdiction. Since the "myth" of the taking clause assumes that less can be regulated than the court decisions actually permit, many local governments fail to exercise their powers—or if they do, they back down easily when challenged. Other local governments despair of reaching any reasonable accommodation with landowners and decide to prohibit everything, leaving the issue up to the courts to resolve.

Why has the myth of the taking clause made land values so much more sacrosanct than a reading of the court decisions would actually suggest? We suspect a number of causes inherent in the structure of American local government.

The myth of the taking clause is inhibiting the sort of reasonable regulatory action that is needed to protect the environment while respecting the position of individual landowners. In weighing strategies to deal with the taking issue, therefore, we begin with awareness that a new legal doctrine will have little impact unless it filters down to where the action is. The law in this area is what local officials think it is. While it is important to establish sound legal principles, it is equally important to communicate these principles to the people who are making the decisions.

4. Strategies for Dealing with the Taking Issue: Experience, Not Logic. The taking clause has bedeviled some of our brightest and most lucid legal scholars. A number of excellent articles have appeared in our legal periodicals over the past ten years. We were impressed with the profound logic by which each author attempted to make sense out of the confused body of cases—at least until we read the next article in which a new author convincingly demolished the logic of his predecessor and expounded a new and even more convincing system of analysis.

We eventually came away with a sense of frustration, convinced that the world did not need one more analytically good, true and beautiful solution to the taking problem. Holmes' own observation that experience, not logic, governed the law, seemed most appropriate here.

We began by arraying five potential strategies for approaching the taking issue, ranging from one end of the spectrum to the other. Chapter 12 presents the argument that the courts should discard the idea that a regulation of the use of land can constitute a "taking." It suggests that the idea of a regulatory taking was a judicial fiction of the early 1900's, wholly inconsistent with the tradition of the founding fathers. It recommends a return to the strict construction of the taking clause in the manner in which it was originally conceived. Such an approach would subject land use regulations to the same standards of judicial review that now apply to other government regulations.

Chapter 13 proposes a less direct approach. It points out that many courts have apparently treated the idea of regulatory taking more as a hypothetical possibility than a real one. The Supreme Court of California, for example, appears unlikely to hold any regulation invalid under the taking clause. The United States Supreme Court itself (the last time it ruled on the issue) left some doubt whether any regulation could constitute a taking as long as the court was convinced that the public purpose served by the regulation was important. This suggests an emphasis on demonstrating the importance of the purpose behind land use regulations.

Chapter 14 discusses another approach to the taking issue, one that has been suggested by a number of commentators: the drafting of statutory standards to determine when compensation is required. Although the taking test is a constitutional one which is ultimately in the hands of the courts, the courts have generally accepted legislative determinations in similar situations.

The English have for years used a system of statutory standards for determining whether compensation must be paid to a person affected by a land use regulation. In general, compensation is paid only if the land is capable of "no reasonably beneficial use," under the regulation. But even then compensation is not paid if the regulation is designed to promote certain listed purposes (e.g., flood control, adequacy of sewerage services, etc.). Surprisingly, the British system appears to please both developer, administrator and environmentalist. It might be studied in more depth as a model for statutory standards to be adopted here.

The first three strategies have sought some change in the substantive law. Chapter 15 suggests that even if the existing law remains unchanged most land use regulations can survive attack in the courts if they are based on sound factual evidence and are carefully drafted. This Chapter discusses some examples to illustrate these points.

Finally, Chapter 16 explores the alternative of providing compensation whenever possible to foreclose attacks on land use regulations under the taking clause. It discusses various suggestions for systems of compensable regulations including the one newly proposed to the American Law Institute. It also points out the possibility of using massive land acquisition programs in lieu of regulation, but does not discuss this alternative extensively because the cost appears to make such a program impractical.

5. Evaluating the Strategies. Having examined a range of possible strategies we concluded that it was impossible to recommend one single strategy to deal with the taking issue. The taking issue represents an inevitable conflict between two valid and important interests; the need for a livable environment and the importance of private property rights. No magic words will make the conflict disappear.

A dramatic overruling of the *Pennsylvania Coal* case would help deflate the myth that now makes the taking clause so powerful. But courts would still evaluate regulations against their own standards of reasonableness, and if the purpose of the regulation appears doubtful the extent of individual losses will surely affect a judge's sense of what is reasonable.

Much can be accomplished by expanding the courts' awareness of the important purposes that lie behind land use regulations. Judges suspect that a parochial viewpoint motivates many local zoning decisions. This suspicion can often be allayed by showing that the regulation is consistent with an important policy that transcends local boundaries. The work of Professors Dunham, Sax and Van Alstyne is helpful in providing a framework for the necessary factual presentation.

We were impressed with the success of the British system of providing statutory standards to determine when compensation should be paid. Any system that seems to please developers, environmentalists and planning officials deserves further study. Experiments with similar systems deserve a trial in this country.

But in the long run the strategy that would contribute most to a more equitable resolution of the taking cases would be simply to spend more time in the drafting of regulations and the presentation of facts supporting—or opposing—them. Too often these regulations take the form of sweeping prohibitions and blanket indictments of all development simply because no one has taken the time to study the problem in depth and work out a reasonable compromise between the needs of the environment and the rights of the individuals.

Finally, state and local governments should undertake experiments with new methods to provide compensation to landowners. The system of compensable regulations proposed for the American Law Institute's Model Land Development Code is an example of such a system. Density transfer systems such as those proposed by Professor Costonis also may provide a way of furnishing landowners the equivalent of compensation.

We doubt that any of these strategies will provide an answer for all situations. It will be necessary to pick and choose a strategy or combination of strategies to deal with each set of problems as they arise. Only an approach that rejects the two extremes—stop-growth and full-speed-ahead—will provide a long range solution to the problems posed by the taking issue.

6. Highlights. In final summary, we were most struck by the following:

A. The taking clause is a serious problem wherever there is substantial pressure for urban growth, and particularly where the environment is sensitive.

B. The popular fear of the taking clause is an even more serious problem than actual court decisions.

C. There is little historical basis for the idea that a regulation of the use of land can constitute a taking of the land.

D. The most recent court decisions, those of the '70's, strongly support land use regulations based on overall state or regional goals—regulations of the type we discussed in *The Quiet Revolution in Land Use Control*.[8]

E. More thorough consideration should be given to the possibility of statutory standards to determine when compensation must be paid. The British have found their experience with such standards highly satisfactory.

F. Finally, there is a great deal that a good lawyer can do working within existing laws if he has access to good factual evidence and if he practices careful draftsmanship. These subjects deserve more detailed consideration in order to provide attorneys with the kind of expert assistance they need.

Acknowledgements

This work was made possible by a research grant from the Council on Environmental Quality. We would like to express our deepest appreciation to the members and staff of the Council, not only for their financial assistance but for the creative help in defining this project and analyzing its conclusions.

We would also like to acknowledge and express our appreciation to Stanley Katz, professor of Legal History at the University of Chicago Law School, J. F. Garner, Professor of Public Law at the University of Nottingham, Professor and Mrs. Albert Kiralfy, University of London, and Sir Desmond Heap, President of the Law Society, all of whom were of great assistance to us in developing the historical analysis in this report, but none of whom bears any blame for the conclusions derived therefrom. We would also like to express our appreciation to the London Library (St. James Square), the University of London's Institute for Advanced Legal Studies, and the Library of the House of Commons, for making their normally private facilities available to us.

The Taking Issue

Research assistance in the preparation of Part I was provided by Irene Holmes and Robert Snyder; in Part II by Victor Bass, James Deen, James Friedman, Norden Gilbert, Scott Reznick and Merideth Wright; in Part III by Donald Rickertsen, all students in law or history at the University of Chicago. Much of the historical research necessary for this report required examination of original sources and the help of these students proved particularly valuable.

Countless persons responded graciously to our inquiries about current problems under the taking issue that provided the material for Part I. Listing their names would be impossible but we are very thankful for their valuable assistance. The Task Force on Land Use and Urban Growth of the Citizens' Advisory Committee on Environmental Quality provided a very valuable sounding board for some of our ideas. We would like to express our appreciation to the chairman, Laurance Rockefeller, and to the executive director, William Reilly.

Finally, the study of English law necessary for this report was greatly aided by a travel and study grant from the Ford Foundation.

Footnotes

1. U.S. Constitution, Amendment V.
2. The Clause is sometimes called Article 39 because the original 1215 Magna Carta contained 63 articles, of which the above was Article 39. By 1225, the Charter consisted of 37 Articles as the original 63 were pared down and consolidated, of which the aforementioned was number 29.
3. 127 U.S. 393 (1922).
4. 123 U.S. 623, 8 S. Ct. 273 (1887).
5. 148 Mass. 368, 19 N.E. 390 (1889).
6. 260 U.S. at 415.
7. Citizens' Advisory Committee on Environmental Quality Task Force on Land Use and Urban Growth, *The Use of Land*, 147-148 (1973).
8. Fred Bosselman and David Callies, *The Quiet Revolution in Land Use Control* (1971).

The Taking Issue:

A Review*

Donald G. Hagman

Donald G. Hagman is professor of law at the University of California, Los Angeles. He is the author of numerous articles and books, includng Urban Planning and Land Development Control Law; Public Planning and Control of Urban and Land Development; and he is currently researching, under a HUD grant, the topic of "Windfalls For Wipeouts" [featured elsewhere in this volume]. Mr. Hagman is a graduate of Marquette University and holds a law degree from the University of Wisconsin and LL.M. from Harvard Law School.

This article is reprinted in full, with permission from 87 Harvard Law Review 482 (1973). Copyright 1973 by the Harvard Law Review Association.

As a sequel to their best selling The Quiet Revolution in Land Use Control,[1] Bosselman and Callies, with the addition of author Banta, have examined the toughest issue in land use control: the limitations on regulation of land imposed by the fifth amendment proscription, "nor shall private property be taken for public use without just compensation." While the book is addressed to the lawyers and government officials who must grapple with this difficult area of the law, the authors write so clearly that the book could be assigned as collateral reading in a high school civics class—and I intend that statement as a compliment.

As an initial observation, I might point out that the subject matter of the book is not accurately described by its title or by its subtitle. The description of the book on its title page is more helpful: "A Study of the Constitutional Limits of Governmental Authority to Regulate the Use of Privately-owned Land Without Paying Compensation to the Owners." That description is still misleading, however, since the constitutional discussion is almost exclusively limited to the "taking" clause. Due process is only briefly mentioned and equal protection is virtually ignored. Moreover, the book is not even about taking, insofar as that term is a synonym for eminent domain.

An introductory note indicates one motivation for writing the book. The authors stress that environmental management of land by regulation is done timorously today because of fear that the constitutionality of such regulation will be challenged in court.[2] A full exploration of the subject, therefore, might encourage environmental policymakers to strengthen land use controls by showing them that their fears are largely unfounded. There is more to this problem than the introductory note suggests. Some environmental policymakers use their fears of unconstitutionality as an excuse—they do not want to regulate severely, either because they are development oriented or because they believe it unfair. On the other hand, fears of invalidity do not always deter action. For example, it is now well documented that localities often use their land use control powers for exclusionary purposes. The courts have been rather rigorous in invalidating such practices in recent years.[3] Yet the practice continues because local government officials want ʌo continue, and they are not significantly dissuaded by potential judicial invalidation. They typically face only the risk of a lawsuit which may never be filed. If it is filed, they reason, it can be settled. If it is not settled, the local government risks only a finding of invalidity and the cost of financing the lawsuit.[4]

But there is another significant fear that has developed recently, one which is largely ignored by the authors. This is the fear that excessive zeal in regulation will lead to successful actions of inverse condemnation.[5] In such a suit, the successful plaintiff-landowner in effect forces the regulating government to purchase the regulated property. To be sure, unless the regulation is tantamount to physical possession or is done for the purpose of lowering acquisition costs, inverse condemnation actions are not likely to be successful. But the minimal prospect has made local government officials cautious because the stakes are high.

Another type of fear ignored by the authors derives from the possibility of civil rights actions alleging discriminatory regulation on the part of local government officials and subjecting those officials to personal liability.[6] If such officials are deterred from risking the public fisc, imagine their caution about risking an invasion of their personal finances, however slight the risk might be.

Pervasiveness and History

Part I of the book, "The Pervasiveness of the Taking Issue," demonstrates that a large number of states and localities have recently enacted environmentally conscious regulations which are quite rigorous but which also significantly depress values of privately held land. Whether such regulations have permeated the country is difficult to say. There surely are still some states, localities, and courts therein[7] where it is business as usual —the developers continue to hold sway. But it is doubtless true that there are considerably fewer areas where the land use development game of yesteryear can still be played under the old rules.

Part II of the book, entitled "Taking and Regulation Through Seven and a Half Centuries," begins with a chapter discussing the English heritage on taking and regulation. No doubt written largely by Callies,[8] the discussion is delightful and interesting. One must praise both a government agency that would publish a book containing such a scholarly discussion and a practicing lawyer who would undertake an assignment that could earn the envy of his academic colleagues. The chapter establishes the fact that severe, noncompensable regulation of land for the public benefit was permissible from the days of medieval England, despite the Magna Carta provision that "[n]o freeman shall be. . . deprived of his freehold . . . unless by the lawful judgment of his peers and by the law of the land." While that clause is a precursor of the taking clause, the relevance of English antecedents may be questioned. A footnote concedes that "technically of course the English nobles did not 'own' land in the same sense that we would use the term today" (p. 53 n.1).[9] The social, political, economic, and property law contexts were then considerably different. Just as a demonstration that American courts once tolerated slavery would not prove that racial segregation is valid today, a discussion of the Magna Carta may add little elucidation to the current taking problem.

American colonial history is examined next, and it is not surprising to find that severe land use control regulations were imposed which similarly were not found to result in a taking, despite the appearance by 1780 of compensation clauses in state constitutions. In fact, the authors point out that in the early period of colonization, payment was not always made when the government actually took undeveloped land, as distinguished from developed land (p. 85). I do not doubt it. Consider the argument of a landowner located ten miles from the nearest town who was blessed with a road across his land. It was his only access to civilization. Fairness did not require that he be compensated for the few feet of his land used for the road when the value of the remainder of his land probably increased a thousandfold. Indeed, it is monstrous today that a landowner who receives enormous benefits to his remaining land from a public facility should have to be paid for a small amount of land taken, yet in some states increases in value cannot be offset against the payment due for land taken.[10]

The rule permitting land use regulation without compensation lasted through centuries of Anglo-American law until 1922 when the United States Supreme Court decided *Pennsylvania Coal Co. v. Mahon.*[11] *The Taking Issue*'s authors give their view of the decision in the chapter subtitled "Holmes Rewrites the Constitution." In *Mahon*, a rigorous regulation of land use was invalidated as a taking. Holmes introduced a balancing test: regulation in the public interest can be held invalid if it deprives the property of too much value. Prior thereto, as the book nicely explains, it was the *kind* of action (physicial possession) which called for compensation. After *Mahon* the "difference between regulation and taking was a difference of *degree not kind*" (p. 134).

Current Legal Developments

Part III deals with post-*Mahon* confusion by describing the regulatory taking issue under current law. The authors begin with a chapter reviewing a number of classic situations in which judicial resolutions have fallen on both sides of the line between valid regulation and invalid taking. It is not surprising that these situations result, for the utilization of a balancing test seldom produces consistency. Moreover, while *Mahon* stated a new test, it did not overrule a batch of other Supreme Court decisions applying different tests.[12] It is often the utilization of one or some of those varying precedents, rather than the overpowering weight of any interest on the scale, which provides a court with an acceptable justification for its decision. The classic situations that continue to cause trouble for the courts are separately discussed in *The Taking Issue*: regulation of mining, flood prone areas, wetlands or estuarine areas, beach lands, open space in new subdivisions, population density and agricultural land, historic buildings or districts, signs and related unaesthetic development, and the phasing or timing of residential development.

The next chapter in Part III is imaginatively titled "Are Some Public Purposes More Public Than Others?" This chapter provides a useful service by citing and summarizing the works of the scholars who have tried to sort out the cases and define the line between takings and valid regulation of land use. In recent years Professors Dunham, Michelman, Sax, and Van Alstyne, the best property/land use/local government men in the country, have made noble efforts but have largely failed.[13]

The chapter points out one public purpose usually recognized as more public than others: the suppression of land uses regarded as nuisances or as nuisance-like. In these instances the courts are generally willing to allow very strict regulation, subscribing to the view that there is no property in a nuisance. An example of this situation is regulation requiring the boarding up or even the tearing down of a building when it is so deteriorated that it may fall on its occupants or passers-by. Cases involving regulation of flood prone areas have some nuisance-like aspects, too—the buildings in such areas float down-stream, clogging channels and destroying other public and private property. Even pres-ervation of historic districts can benefit from the nuisance precedents. It is surely a gross use of land for one property owner to build a garish new building for his own profit at the expense of all the other landowners in the area who are trying to preserve—albeit for their profit—a history for future generations.

This section of the chapter also discusses situations in which the courts do not regard public purposes as being very public; that is, the regulation appears to benefit a narrow segment of the public while its burden is primarily visited on another narrow segment. For example, land use controls used to protect the central business district by refusing permission to erect a suburban shopping center may raise judicial hostility.

The other subtitles in the "How Public?" chapter do not belong there. Rather than dealing with the "publicness" of the regulation, they describe other sorts of tests which the scholars have been able to identify. For instance, courts frequently invalidate regula-tions where eminent domain would customarily be used or where regulation is used to lower acquisition costs. Zoning for park use rather than acquiring the necessary land typifies the former; rezoning land from multiple family to agricultural use so as to lower its value when the governmental entity wants to acquire the site for an airport is an example of the latter. Another test, which the authors call "Suitability of the Regulation to the Nature of the Property," is described with reference to spot zoning cases and cases involving development in ecologically insensitive rural areas where a little land de-velopment could hardly be harmful. In these cases the courts have framed the test in terms of the rationality of the land use planning. If it does not make sense to restrain develop-ment or if one landowner is regulated and his neighbor is not, with no discernible difference between the two, the Constitution may support judicial intervention. The final test discussed is "The Extent of Loss in Land Values"—regulation is frequently invali-dated if there is no reasonable economic use left to property after the regulation. The above tests, of course, hardly represent airtight categories. If a city council were to rezone one parcel of land in a single-family residential area for a mortuary, the regulation might be held invalid as a taking of neighboring property on various grounds: near nuisance, benefiting one narrowly at the expense of another, irrational planning, or considerable loss to neighbors.

The Taking Issue next considers "Cases from the Seventies: A Quiet Judicial Revolu-tion." Focusing on these cases, the authors tentatively opine that courts are upholding stringent regulations designed to protect the environment or to slow or stop growth. The authors also conclude that the courts have been especially supportive of state and regional regulation, but less so with respect to local regulation. Both conclusions are sound.

Prior to the 1970's there was little state and regional regulation to sustain. But as such regulations have been enacted, they have been upheld. One reason may be that the integrity of the state or regional body is thought to be much greater than that of the local entity. Courts need not be as wary of regulation by a state or regional body as they should be of regulation by the Smallville City Council, which is more likely to be acting on behalf of a friendly real estate man or to protect the community from a public housing project, or for any of a number of reasons for which a group of neighbors takes advantage of a governmental unit and a boundary line to accomplish quasi-private purposes at the expense of the general public. Planners used to applaud the "liberal" courts which broadly upheld local land use regulations. But with the revelations that the exclusionary land use control cases have brought to public attention, it appears that these "liberal" courts were too deferential. Accordingly, some of the courts of Neanderthal repute now enjoy more respect. The presumption of validity of local land use controls is weaker and more courts are prepared to scrutinize the asserted justifications for these controls.[14] Thus, if one examines only cases involving *local* regulation of land use, the "quiet judicial revolution" is not so apparent, since the justifications are often rejected as mere trappings to hide an exclusionary or parochial motive. But to the extent that local regulations are primarily and legitimately designed to promote orderly growth or environmental protection, they are probably as likely to be upheld as have been regional and state regulations in recent years. It is because they can also look exclusionary and parochial that the results are mixed.

Five Governmental Strategies

Part IV of the book, "Governmental Strategies for Approaching the Taking Issue," offers five such strategies and makes a case for each. Unfortunately, the weaknesses of these strategies are only superficially discussed, and the authors do not state their preference. Given the opinions expressed in earlier sections of the book, that which is offered first, "The Strategy of Strict Construction," might be their preference. Under this strategy, the courts would simply stop invalidating regulations under the taking clause, returning to the pre-*Mahon* days. Such a result, the authors argue, would be consistent with the intent of the draftsmen of the clause. They explain away the *Mahon* decision as a rare aberration of one who is otherwise probably the most highly respected American judge in history.[15] They assert that Holmes' reasoning stemmed from his "Fascination with the 'Bundle of Sticks' " concept. Perhaps so. In *Mahon*, a regulation precluded the extraction of coal when further mining would lead to surface subsidence. The result was to destroy totally the value of the mineral right the Pennsylvania Coal Company owned in certain lands. Since the only "stick" of property the company had was totally taken, Holmes concluded that regulation was invalid. No doubt if the case had been brought by a landowner who owned many sticks in a bundle, the regulation would have been upheld because, under the Holmes balancing view, considerable economic use of the remaining sticks would have been possible.[16]

The Taking Issue's authors imply, however, that were it not for the presence of the separately owned mineral rights stick in *Mahon*, the regulation would have been sustained without the appearance of the upstart balancing test, and that test would never have become a gloss on the taking clause. I think that reasoning is defective. Holmes' opinion in *Mahon* can be read and has been read as *intending* to create a balancing test. The fact that the case came up in the context of a total taking of one separate stick does not mean that Holmes would necessarily have approved a regulation that took less than all the sticks in a bundle.

The stick construction strategy has one major advantage—it is simple. If the government proceeds by eminent domain, compensation is paid. If it proceeds by regulation, there is no compensation. But is society willing to trust government, particularly local government, to use regulation only when it ought to be used and eminent domain in all other situations? Budgetary constraints being what they are, it takes an exceedingly fair-minded government to spend money for what it can obtain by regulation.

The authors of *The Taking Issue* argue for strict construction on the ground that land regulation should be permissible to the same degree as regulation of other sorts of property, where the taking clause has not been much of a limitation to regulation despite significant diminutions in value. The distinction is an interesting one that I have often wondered about. Perhaps it can be justified on these grounds: land use controls seldom deal with basic, important issues of health and safety, as other regulations might; regulations of other property ordinarily do not have such drastic and direct effects on values; and such regulations do not have as precise locational effects as do land use controls, which may force particular property owners to serve the public interest without public expense.

The authors also argue that even under strict construction, all is not lost for the property owner, for "the full panoply of due process protections remains" (p. 253). The substantive due process test does not provide very full protection today, but its protection is weak in part because it overlaps protection conferred by the taking clause which the courts now utilize significantly. If the taking clause loses its vitality by adoption of the strict construction test, courts may reinvigorate the overlapping portion of the substantive due process test. Yet if that does happen, not much change in the protection presently afforded landowners would in fact be accomplished by the strict construction strategy.

The authors still favor continuation of the taking clause protection when a "real" taking occurs (p. 254), such as when a local government zones arid land for the growing of aquatic plants when it really wants to acquire it for a park. That is regulation for the purpose of lowering values for acquisition. Of course the government should not be able to escape payment of compensation in that kind of case. The problem is that courts ordinarily do not scrutinize motives, and clever governments can regulate in a way which allows them to accomplish their purpose with impunity.

The strict construction strategy is also deficient in that it is not something we can do by just deciding to do it. The legislatures and executive officials cannot decree that the taking clause will be limited to "real" takings and will not extend to government regulations. The courts, particularly the Supreme Court, must be persuaded to provide a new definition of the test; yet landowners have not been without victories before the present Court.[17]

The second strategy presented envisages an "Evolving Public Purpose." By concentrating on public rights and public benefits from nondevelopment of an ecologically important or sensitive area, it is possible to reason that any development could have nuisance-like qualities. In that case, ordinary development might be treated as would traditional nuisance-type development. When a court uses a balancing test, with the new ecological concerns weighted heavily, the public purpose "can virtually never be outbalanced by an individual's loss of property values" (p. 236).

Some courts have already been moved in the direction of the evolving public purpose strategy, and this movement will probably continue. It is difficult to argue against such a strategy, because society has in the past paid far too little attention to the environment. But there remains the nagging problem—if society wants to protect the environment, why haphazardly place the burden on particular property owners who, after all, bought before society changed the rules of the game?

The third strategy, "Statutory Limitations on Regulation," is responsive to suggestions by Professors Michelman and Van Alstyne that legislative bodies stop loading on the courts the duty of deciding when compensation is due and instead specify guidelines themselves. But one major disadvantage of this approach is that the legislatures may be more generous than constitutional provisions require. For example, the Uniform Relocation Assistance and Real Property Acquisition Policies Act of 1970[18] requires that compensation be paid in several situations where it is not constitutionally required. Similarly, many states have been forced[19] by the Highway Beautification Act of 1965 to compensate sign owners when signs are removed,[20] though it is generally constitutionally possible to do so without compensation under the police power. And since Congress passed the River and Harbor Act of 1970, law professors can no longer confound students with the old doctrine that the value of land attributable to the presence of a navigable stream is not property.[21]

In this connection the authors include a full discussion of the English system under which Parliament has prescribed when compensation will be paid, the courts having no constitution—let alone a taking clause—with which to invalidate regulation. The discussion indicates that Parliament has provided compensation for regulation in situations in which it is not available in America. And the Land Compensation Act,[22] passed in 1973 after years of study, has recently expanded the situations which require payment of compensation. The Taking Issue minimizes the English experience by suggesting that compensation is not often sought in England, but that may only be because the provisions dampen regulatory zeal in the first instance. While the legislative strategy might be the right one, there is little evidence that landowners would be any less protected from regulation under such a strategy.

The fourth strategy is "Sound Evidence and Careful Drafting." That strategy urges careful presentation of cases with "Brandeis" briefs, and the drafting of narrow regulations. The authors claim that such a strategy will lead to judicial breakthroughs and minimize adverse taking decisions. Of course the "good guys" have no monopoly on careful lawyering, but no one can seriously object to better presentation of cases from either side. Better drafting should also be encouraged, though it is sometimes difficult to tell the difference between good drafting and drafting which hides the real purpose in a maze of findings, purposes, and provisions without substance that are included solely to fool the courts.

The fifth and last strategy should not be considered the least; indeed, it is in part the strategy I am pursuing. The Taking Issue calls this alternative "Sidestepping the Taking Issue," that is, avoiding noncompensatory regulation. One of its substrategies is the concept of land acquisition—land banks and the like. This approach avoids the taking issue but, as the authors point out, is an expensive way of proceeding. Moreover, having participated in studies for the Public Land Law Review Commission, I am not persuaded that government in this country understands how to manage the land it already has, despite the fact that land banks in other countries have apparently worked out rather well.

Another substrategy presented for sidestepping the issue recounts the success governments have had in asserting a preexisting title to land, largely at the ocean shorelines. For example, in Gion v. City of Santa Cruz,[23] the California Supreme Court found that halfhearted efforts by owners of beachfront lands to keep trespassers off resulted in an implied dedication to the public. The result, unfortunately, has tended to be bigger, stronger fences and less access.

Eight pages are devoted to the substrategy that most interests me, called "Compensable Regulations." Most of the eight pages deal with compensable regulations in which the legislature or the court gives the regulating body an option of paying compensation at least to the extent necessary to remove the constitutional taint. For example, if rezoning a marsh from heavy industry to agricultural use would reduce values ninety percent, a payment of money might limit the loss to, say, fifty percent. A court might accept the regulation accompanied by a fifty percent reduction of values whereas the ninety percent reduction would be held invalid.

Less than half a page of this discussion is devoted to the work of John Costonis, who is my intellectual bedfellow concerning the taking issue. Costonis, an alumnus of the law firm where *The Taking Issue* was written, has used the days since he graduated to debug his "density transfer system."[24] Costonis' idea is that when strict regulation precludes development on a particular site, the owner should still be left with development rights, which could then be sold to owners who wish to make a more intensive use of their own property than would otherwise be permitted. For example, Costonis' first application of the technique is to historic buildings in central business districts. Rather than only regulating to preclude destruction of such a building, Costonis would require the owner of the historic building to maintain it, but would also allow that owner to sell his unused development rights to other owners who could then build more intensely than existing regulation would permit in areas where the city agrees more intensive development is possible. The essential feature of this technique is its concern for compensating the regulated landowner, out of funds paid by the landowner who benefits thereby.

Windfalls and [for] Wipeouts

My hoped-for contribution in this area will come from the work on my project, *Windfalls and Wipeouts.*[25] I have observed that owners of land who receive development permission or happen to be located next to a large public facility such as a transit station on a new subway line enjoy a large increase in value—a windfall. Generally speaking, under present law they keep this increment in value almost entirely for themselves, though it is conferred by public action. The public is treated unjustly in not sharing in part of this benefit. Meanwhile, others are "wiped out" because they are denied development permission or because development is permitted nearby which casts off externalities—as in the case of freeways, where the only "enjoyments" are noise, fumes, dirt, and frantic movement. It surely makes sense to recapture from those who have windfalls in order to be more generous to those who are wiped out. Costonis' density transfer scheme is one proposal we will be investigating, together with many others, such as zoning by eminent domain,[26] unearned increment taxes to fund undeserved decrements, and several other transfer devices which have been tried or discussed in this country and in Australia, Canada, England and New Zealand.

These latter techniques, I believe, are the answer to the taking issue which, as regulation becomes more and more rigorous, will more urgently demand a solution. With the new environmentally motivated regulation, the number and size of both windfalls and wipeouts have been magnified, making the injustice to the public and the individual landowners increasingly less tolerable.

Footnotes

The Taking Issue: An Analysis of the Constitutional Limits of Land Use Control. By Fred Bosselman, David Callies, and John Banta. Washington, D.C.: Council on Environmental Quality. 1973. $2.00 (paper). Mr. Bosselman is a partner and Mr. Callies and Mr. Banta are associates in the law firm of Ross, Hardies, O'Keefe, Babcock & Parsons, Chicago, Illinois.

1. F Bosselman & D. Callies, *The Quiet Revolution in Land Use Control* (1971).
2. Policymakers are reinforced in this view by "cold" lawyers who, though they serve public agencies, are often inclined to be overly cautious and raise the possibility of a constitutional challenge, even though the success of such a challenge is remote. See Letter from Richard S. Volpert to Joseph Guandolo, May 23, 1967, in Local Government Law Service Letter, November, 1967, at 35.
3. There are now hundreds of cases on the subject and almost as many law review articles. See, e.g., Annot., 48 A.L.R.3d 1210 (1973).

4. There is no risk that damages for civil rights violations will be assessed against the governmental entity, because a municipality is not a "person" within the meaning of the Civil Rights Act of 1871, 42 U.S.C. § 1983 (1970). See Monroe v. Pape, 365 U.S. 167 (1961). This limitation does not apply, however, to damage actions brought against the government officials as individuals.

5. See generally Beuscher, Some Tentative Notes on the Integration of Police Power and Eminent Domain by the Courts: So-called Inverse or Reverse Condemnation, 1968 Urban L. Ann. 1.

6. See, e.g., Harrison v. Brooks, 446 F.2d 404 (1st Cir. 1971).

7. The courts in the various states naturally differ on the level of rigor of regulations they will sustain. See, e.g., Cunningham, Zoning Law in Michigan and New Jersey: A Comparative Study, 63 Mich. L. Rev. 1171 (1965). The author indicates that what he calls "the 'lawyer's view' has generally prevailed in Michigan and the 'planner's view' has generally prevailed in New Jersey." Id. at 1172. Of course, a change in judicial personnel or attitudes can lead to a shift along what is actually a continuum.

8. David Callies studied English planning law at the University of Nottingham with John Garner, a prominent English planning lawyer, and has written about English law on several occasions. E.g., Callies, Positive Planning in England: A Survey, 4 Land-Use Controls Q., Spring, 1970, at 12; Garner & Callies, Planning Law in England and Wales and in the United States, 1 Anglo-Am. L. Rev. 292 (1972).

9. Instead of owning land, the nobles held it subject to feudal obligations.

10. The rules are described in Hagman, Special Benefits in Road Cases: Myths and Realities, 1964 Institute on Eminent Domain 135. The essential foolishness of compensating in such situations is ably discussed in Waite, Governmental Power and Private Property, 16 Cath. U.L. Rev. 283 (1967).

11. 260 U.S. 393 (1922).

12. See, e.g., Hadacheck v. Sebastian, 239 U.S. 394 (1914); Mugler v. Kansas, 123 U.S. 623 (1887).

13. See Dunham Griggs v. Allegheny County in Perspective: Thirty Years of Supreme Court Expropriation Law, 1962 Sup. Ct. Rev. 63; Michelman, Property, Utility and Fairness: Comments on the Ethical Foundations of "Just Compensation" Law, 80 Harv. L. Rev. 1165 (1967); Sax, Takings, Private Property and Public Rights, 81 Yale L.J. 149 (1971); Sax, Takings and the Police Power, 74 Yale L.J. 36 (1964); Van Alstyne, Taking or Damaging by Police Power : The Search for Inverse Condemnation Criteria, 44 So. Cal. L. Rev. 1 (1971). Extracts from the works of these and other authors plus relevant cases are the bulk of my Chapter 16 in D. Hagman, Public Planning and Control of Urban and Land Development (1973). See also D. Hagman, Urban Planning and Land Development Control Law §§ 178-82 (1971).

14. See Fasano v. Board of County Comm'rs, 507 P.2d 23 (Ore. 1973); Feiler, Metropolitanization and Land-Use Parochialism—Toward a Judicial Attitude, 69 Mich. L. Rev. 655 (1971).

15. This conclusion that Holmes was wrong in introducing a balancing test for land use regulations finds support in the prestigious report Task Force on Land Use and Urban Growth, Citizens' Advisory Committee on Environmental Quality, The Use of Land: A Citizens' Policy Guide to Urban Growth 173-75 (1973).

16. Cf. Goldblatt v. Town of Hempstead, 369 U.S. 590 (1962), the latest Supreme Court opinion on the question of what constitutes a taking. In Goldblatt, a regulation precluded the landowner from continuing his gravel pit operation. The landowner alleged a taking but lost his case because he failed to establish that the regulation prevented all other economic use of his property.

17. See, e.g., Salyer Land Co. v. Tulare Lake Basin Water Storage Dist., 410 U.S. 719 (1973) (voting franchise in a water district can be limited to landowners); Almota Farmers Elevator & Warehouse Co. v. United States, 409 U.S. 470 (1973) (expanding the measure of "just compensation").

18. Pub. L. No. 91-646, 84 Stat. 1894 (codified in scattered sections of 42 U.S.C.).

19. See, e.g., Lamm v. Volpe, 449 F.2d 1202 (10th Cir. 1971), cert. denied, 405 U.S. 1095 (1972).

20. See 23 U.S.C. § 131(g) (1970).

21. See 33 U.S.C. § 595a (1970). See also United States v. 967,905 Acres of Land, 447 F.2d 764 (8th Cir. 1971), cert. denied, 405 U.S. 974 (1972).

22. Land Compensation Act 1973, c. 26.

23. 2 Cal. 3d 29, 465 P.2d 50, 84 Cal. Rptr. 162 (1970).

24. J. Costonis, Space Adrift: Landmark Preservation and the Marketplace (1973); Costonis, The Chicago Plan: Incentive Zoning and the Preservation of Urban Landmarks, 85 Harv. L. Rev. 574 (1972); Costonis, Development Rights Transfer: An Exploratory Essay, 83 Yale L.J. 75 (1973).

25. Comprehensive Planning Research and Demonstration Project N. Calif. PD-13, U.S. Department of Housing and Urban Development, June 30, 1973. See also Wexler, Betterment Recovery: A Financial Proposal for Sounder Land Use Planning, 3 Yale Rev. L. & Social Action 192 (1973).

26. See Hagman, Implementation of Land Use Planning in the Political Process, in Land Use Planning 128, 133-39 (T. Box ed. 1972). Briefly, zoning by eminent domain involves utilization of special assessment techniques. When permitted uses are changed by zoning, the owner being deprived is considered as damaged under eminent domain. Others are benefited because the development pressure shifts to them. They are specially assessed for their benefit in order to pay those damaged.

Windfalls For Wipeouts:

A Preliminary Report

Donald G. Hagman

Donald G. Hagman is professor of law at the University of California, Los Angeles. He is the author of numerous articles and books, including "Urban Planning and Land Development Control Law," and "Public Planning and Control of Urban and Land Development"; he is currently researching, under a HUD grant, the topic of "Windfalls For Wipeouts." Mr. Hagman is a graduate of Marquette University and holds a law degree from the University of Wisconsin and an LL.M. from Harvard Law School.

The author wishes to acknowledge the financial assistance of the Office of the Assistant Secretary for Policy Development and Research, U.S. Department of Housing and Urban Development, Comprehensive Planning Research and Demonstration Project Grant No. Calif. PD-13 under Section 701(b) of the Housing Act of 1954, as amended.

This article's "official" subtitle, per Mr. Hagman, is "Betterment Recapture and Worsenment Mitigation Techniques as an Rx for a Healthy and Just Environmentalism." The paper–of which this article is a shorter, edited version–was presented at The Dennis O'Harrow Memorial Lecture (1974 National Planning Conference). The article is reprinted with permission of Planning, the magazine of the American Society of Planning Officials.

Introduction: Windfalls and Wipeouts Defined

"Windfalls for wipeouts" is only a catchy title for an ageless conundrum of equity —should the owners of real estate be able to keep increases in values caused by society rather than by themselves? And, on the other hand, should society be able to impose losses on the owners of real estate without paying damages?

Sadly, windfalls for wipeouts is not about the *equalized* redistribution of wealth from rich to poor. It is not social planning. This is "sadly" so because the more even distribution of wealth is still the priority planning need in America. In windfalls for wipeouts I am doing what so many friends have done who once fought the war on poverty. They are now fighting the war on environmental degradation. We thought we were interested in the poor, but we were only interested in being where the action is.

With that acknowledgement of guilt feelings, focus your attention more precisely on windfalls for wipeouts, which involves transfer payments among property owners. To own property, as Mason Gaffney colorfully[1] states, is to be rich. So windfalls for wipeouts can involve transfers among the rich. First, what is a windfall? It might be defined as did Pigou, the great English economist:

> accretions to the real value of people's property that are not in any degree due to efforts made, intelligence exercised, risks borne, or capital invested by them.[2]

Windfalls For Wipeouts

The definition is helpful. If property increases in value because he works or spends to improve it, a property owner does not have a windfall. He has no *real* windfall if property increases in price but not in value because of inflation.

Yet Pigou's definition is too broad. The acceptance of some risk and the investment of some capital is something all owners of property must do if there is to be private ownership of property. We might accept the proposition that the greater the risk, the more an owner is entitled to a windfall. We might also agree that the less equity capital invested (the less he has in it), the more unconscionable a large windfall becomes. But to go the full distance with Pigou would put us out of the windfall business—there would be none.

Pigou is right in including personal property in his definition, for that kind of property can enjoy a windfall. But almost all attempts to recapture windfall—or betterment or unearned increment, which are terms synonymous with windfall—have been limited to recapture of increases in the value of real estate. Partially that is so because of the greater social or public character society assigns to real estate. (Historically, the king owned the real i.e. the "royal" estate, and merely permitted its use in exchange for obligations to be rendered to him.)

Pigou's definition also does not distinguish between increases in value caused by government and those caused by the non-governmental community. For example, a parking lot may increase in value because a neighbor builds a department store or because government builds an office building next door. In either case, the owner of the parking lot may reap a windfall. Government can act in other ways. It can regulate and make one parking lot valuable by limiting others; it can tax and create windfalls. For example, one of the major results of a shift from a property tax to a tax only on land is that taxes on improved real estate would be much lower and would be capitalized into windfalls.

> Let's take an example. Jones is dumb; exercising no particular investment savvy, he buys a parcel of land in 1965 for $5,000. It is zoned for single family use. Today he sells it for $500,000 because: (1) a transit station for a new subway line has been opened on adjacent property, and (2) the property has been rezoned for 100 story skyscrapers. Without lifting a finger, Jones has had a $495,000 windfall. In a sense, government caused the windfall either because it built the transit station or because it rezoned, or both. But if the transit system had been privately built, Jones might have had the same windfall. And the rezoning, while a necessary condition to Jones' windfall, was not a sufficient condition. Property can be rezoned for more intensive use and not enjoy any windfall unless there is market demand for that use.

The point is that while one can conceptually separate governmentally caused windfalls from the non-governmental community caused windfalls, they are very hard to disentangle and measure. It can more certainly be said, however, that Jones' windfall in the example was not caused by Jones, so it may not be unfair to make him share it. The fact that drone Jones did little or nothing to earn his increase compared to those who work and sweat for their income is a reason why the adherents of windfall recapture regard the following [sign] as obscene: "One good real estate investment is worth a lifetime of labor."

A working definition of windfall, for purposes at least of considering whether some of it should be recaptured, might be the following: a windfall is a real increase in the value of real estate, except that primarily caused by the owner.

> Jones might not have been so fortunate. His parcel bought for $5,000 might now be worth $5 because: (1) the city acquired adjacent land for a garbage dump, (2) other adjacent property was zoned for 100 story high rise buildings, (3) Jones' property was downzoned to a conservation, historic and antiquities zone, one which permits any use therein which is consistent with the reason for its inclusion in the zone. In Jones' case, the property was downzoned because it was

discovered to be the only known habitat of the Hexibilibus, a rare insect. The market value of Hexibilibus site property, located between a garbage dump and a 100 story highrise, is $5.

Dumb Jones suffered a wipeout. Wipeouts are the opposite of windfalls. Should government or the community be able to wipeout Jones without paying any compensation? Fairness might require he be paid something. Fate decides whether Jones is a windfaller or a wipeoutee.

If it is worth considering that fairness requires at least partial windfall recapture and partial mitigation of wipeouts, it does not take much imagination to conclude that the concepts might be linked. Windfall recapture could fund wipeout mitigation: Windfalls For Wipeouts.

Why the Sudden Interest

While perhaps through jaundiced eye, I note a quickening of interest these days in the ageless windfalls and wipeouts problem. The heightened interest is not because governmental development is suddenly creating windfalls and wipeouts, for government development activity is down from the 50's and 60's. There are also fewer wipeouts resulting from the externalities of governmental development because that which occurs is being done more sensitively as a result of the National Environmental Policy Act of 1969 (NEPA)[3] and similar laws.

A modest increase of interest stems from non-objective factors. Society *feels* somewhat more strongly these days that windfall profits from speculation in land is wrong and that something should be done about it. Increasingly, people *believe* that the king can do wrong and should be more neighborly. And as we become more civilized, some matters once thought fair are recognized as unfair and the grossest cases are thought to need adjustment by a more equalized application of the laws.

But if those factors were the whole story, we would not be here today. We are here because there are wipeouts of unprecedented magnitude and frequency resulting from governmental regulation which is being upheld by the courts.

Consider, if we were not talking in this environmental decade of the 70's, that there would be neither NEPA, that environmental litigant's workhorse for land use delay and obfuscation, nor any of the state environmental policy acts (SEPAs), much more than toothless tigers in a number of states.[4] We would not have celebrated NEPA's first birthday with the Clean Air Amendments of 1970,[5] a companion environmental juggernaut, under which land use control is taken over in an absolutist fashion by the air pollution fraternity, with their implementation plans for transportation and indirect sources. Under the Clean Air Act, development can hardly occur where air is bad. But then it can hardly occur where air is good, either, due to the nondegradation rule.[6]

Stimulated by the young air pollution upstarts, the water pollution types muscled in on land use control under the Water Pollution Control Act Amendments of 1972.[7] That act has powerful effects on location and hence on land use through its prohibitions on point source discharge any worse than the best attainable, moratoria on sewer connections where governmental sewer disposal plants are not providing secondary treatment, and reliance on land use plans and controls to eliminate the non-point sources of pollution.

Even the noise pollution set have been trying to get into the land use control act under the Noise Control Act of 1972.[8] But they may be cranking up too late to have a major impact on land use.

Meanwhile, as the pollution types were attracting all the attention, HUD slipped through the Flood Disaster Protection Act of 1973, [9] as close to federal zoning of flood plains as one could come. Hooray for HUD—its about time that "old boy" federal source of succor for the traditional land use planners and controllers got a piece of the environmental action.

I call all these acts the *quiet federalization of land use controls.* It represents a far more revolutionary step than does the resumption of control powers by state and regional bodies.[10] That is not to say state and regional bodies have been quiescent.

> Tough state and regional controls have been enacted, many now financially assisted by another important federal statute, the Coastal Zone Management Act of 1972.[11] These state and regional acts apply from sea to polluted sea. Who could fail to mention California's Coastal Zone Conservation Act of 1972,[12] Vermont's Environmental Control Law of 1970,[13] New York's Adirondack Park Agency Act,[14] Maine's Site Location of Development Law,[15] New Jersey's Wetlands Act,[16] Florida's Environmental Land and Water Management Act,[17] and, with apologies for not acknowledging them specifically, the many other state and regional land use control laws which have made Hawaii's law[18] considerably less lonely since the decade began.

While not as glamorous a subject, it must be noted that the states in the 70's have not only enacted tough state and regional controls, they have also enabled or required localities to get tougher.

> Since the beginning of the 70's, for example, California has required every city and county to have a general plan, which must have several elements, including an open space element. These plans must be complete by a statutorily set date, and there must be zoning and open space zoning and subdivision control, which controls, as well as the construction of capital improvements, must be consistent with the plans.[19]

On their own, discovering that when there's a will there's a way, localities have been imaginatively using traditional controls in a tough new way.

> From the shores of St. Petersburg,[20] Florida, with its attempt to outdo Boco Raton's "cap" by fixing a population limit *less* than the number of people *already* in the city, to the hills of Petaluma,[21] California, where its building permit quota system made it better known than when it was only the chicken capital of the world, tough new regulations are omnipresent. Mention Rampao,[22] Fairfax County,[23] and dozens of other local governments across the nation and planners salivate while developers release adrenaline.

Obsequious to environmentalism, and made bold by the prestigious public policy arguments presented by the likes of the Reillys,[24] Bosselmans, Callies, and Bantas[25] of the world, the courts have generally been upholding these tough new regulations[26] that emanate from all levels and sub-departments of government. The courts are not about to risk destruction of human life as it is now known; judges too get the message.

The effect of all these tough regulations is a synergistic nightmare, a paralyzing mish mash. Windfalls and wipeouts abound, but the market is so confused with the numerous signals that it doesn't know where to jump; property and its value just lies there, quivering.

The babbling cacophony of these multitudinous governmental voices clearly produces a windfall in only two cases. Lawyers and planners have full employment. And when a landowner or a developer finally does vest a development permission good for a reasonable time period against the world, his monopoly position is considerable, his windfall can be recognized, and it is of unprecedented magnitude. But hard-to-recognize windfalls and wipeouts abound. If the national land use planning bill[27] passes, with its encouragement to states to "put it all together" or states otherwise do so, and development permission does begin to clearly settle on some and to clearly be denied to others, the windfall and wipeout inequities will be massively apparent rather than transparent.

The Need to Recapture Some Windfalls and Mitigate Wipeouts

So who cares that windfalls and wipeouts abound? I care, because I believe that a planning system which does not address the windfall and wipeout problem is perceived as basically inequitable and no planning system so perceived can survive.

Windfalls For Wipeouts

Secondly, I believe it results in bad planning. To explain, I enlist the aid of some foreign heavyweights in addition to my own observations. The foreigners are enlisted in part to illustrate that a major trouble with planning is not the particular kind of planning system used but that no system can work well unless the windfall and wipeout problem is addressed. Note that my foreign heavyweights are from the "WASP" countries (Australia, Canada, England, and New Zealand)—not from exotic lands whose social, political, value and land systems are dramatically different from our own.

R. Else-Mitchell—a distinguished Australian jurist—heads the Commonwealth of Australia's Commission of Inquiry into Land Tenures. In its first report in November 1973, the Commission noted that witnesses identified the "lottery" aspect of planning as one of its major defects. Who gets the goodies is essentially arbitrary, and the Australians conclude that increases in value from rezoning or other development permissions should accrue to the public sector rather than be a matter of private fortune. And they conclude the same principle should hold for a reduction in value resulting from a planning decision. Implementation of such principles, say the Australians, converts the chance of winning or losing millions of dollars by the decision of a governing body or by the stroke of a planner's pen to a system of greater social equity.

Second, the Australians say, whenever there is a prospect of private profit or loss from planning decisions, planning tends to be done in secret and there is cause for suspicion of manipulation for private ends. Pressures are exerted to make planning changes profitable for owners rather than in the public interest, and where decisions are necessarily arbitrary, such as in drawing a boundary line, pressures are almost irresistible. That is why, Americans might observe, that the planning system in America is the mother's milk of local government corruption.

Third, the Australians allege, since permissions to develop are scarce, when a landowner obtains one he is in a quasi-monopoly position and can be expected to seek monopoly profits, thus increasing land costs.

Fourth, the Australians, being highly influenced by Henry George, make his point: why should the community put in facilities that increase land values at its own expense and let landowners in the area capture the increased value? Surely the Australian observations are valid issues in America.

The foreword of R.W.B. Bryant's excellent 1972 Canadian book on "Land Private Property Public Control" includes a tribute to Dennis O'Harrow for stimulating thought or providing information or both. So it is highly appropriate in this lecture that Bryant be quoted:

> There can be no effective means of controlling land use and development unless the financial problem of betterment due to community action is tackled. Zoning from one use to another ought to be possible, without any of the financial arguments which so very frequently prevent any reasonable consideration of the rezoning on its merits and in relation to general community development. So often it is a kind of tug-of-war between different interests motivated by financial gain or the fear of financial loss. . . .some arrangements [must be] made whereby public authorities can decide the use of this or that piece of land. . .without having to worry about financial consequences either to the owner or the public purse.[28]

An English view comes from famous lips. Winston Churchill observed over fifty years ago:

> The landlord who happens to own a plot of land on the outskirts of a great city . . . watches the busy population around him making the city larger, richer, more convenient . . . and all the while sits still and does nothing.
>
> Roads are made, streets are made, services are improved . . . water is brought from reservoirs

279

a hundred miles off in the mountains—and all the while the landlord sits still. . . . To not one of those improvements does the land monopolist contribute, and yet by every one of them the value of his land is enhanced. . . At last the land becomes ripe for sale—that means that the price is too tempting to be resisted any longer.

. . . The greater the population around the land, the greater the injury the public has sustained by its protracted denial, the more inconvenience caused to everybody, the more serious the loss in economic strength and activity, the larger will be the profit of the landlord when the sale is finally accomplished. In fact, you may say that the unearned increment on the land is reaped by the land monopolist in exact proportion, not to the service, but to the disservice done.

. . . The municipality, wishing for broader streets, better houses, more healthy, decent scientifically planned towns, is made to pay more to get them in proportion as it has exerted itself to make past improvements. . . .[29]

J. Pope from New Zealand has thought briefly and pensively about "The Benefits of Betterment" in a 1970 article in *The New Zealand Law Journal*.[30] Observing that the New Zealand Town and Country Planning Act 1943, s. 44 requires compensation for downzoning, Pope asks the very good question—why not charge for rezoning for more intensive uses. He believes such a charge would prevent speculators from sitting on their planning permissions, would constitute a source of funds to replace reserve fund contributions (dedication and fees in lieu thereof, exactions on development permissions) and might be a source of general fund revenues. He also observes that betterment recapture could be forgiven to write down land cost for industrial users. No doubt that suggestion stems from a keen desire to industrialize New Zealand, but such a tax expenditure subsidy could be used for other purposes—for example, to lower land costs for low income housing.

To these observations of the impediments imposed and opportunities lost by the absence of a windfall recapture and wipeout mitigation system, I add my own:

1. The environmental movement will soon be dead. Environmentalists cannot expect a long-term, healthy environmental movement unless they address the wipeout problem. Increasingly, landowners and developers are no longer ho-humming their way to bankruptcy.
2. There is an unduly keen interest in public service by members of the real estate industry. The real estate industry should be represented on planning bodies. Society needs their expertise; but too many are there with private interests in public clothing.
3. There is no planning. Since planning decisions cause windfalls and wipeouts, dealing with narrow externalities problems is where the action is. That's not planning; that's too often neighborhood squabble resolution. Exhausted by neighborhood squabble resolving, there is no time for planning bodies to deal with the larger public interest —theoretically the duty our public planning bodies are paid and charged to do.
4. Plan-making invites its own destruction. A city plans and zones some areas for intensive development, others for unintensive use. It places infrastructure accordingly. The result, if there is any effect at all, is that land prices are lower in the area scheduled for unintensive use. Where does the intensive (e.g. multiple family) developer go to reap his windfall after obtaining a rezoning? To ask the question is to answer it.
5. Sprawl abounds. There is never enough money to acquire property for open space use. It is usually impossible (either politically or constitutionally or both) to regulate it so severely that no use is permitted. The compromise is regulation for unintensive use: a euphemism for sprawl.
6. "Horsetrading" is the order of the day. As will be clear in the next section, there are some "cottage industry" type windfall recapture devices that have grown in America.

Generically, they might be called exactions on development permission and are subject to considerable haggling between developers and planning bodies that confer development permissions. The standards on which the amount of the exaction depends are such as "what the traffic will bear," "whether the developer is from our town or an outsider," "the relative state of the local government fisc this month as compared with last," the "growth or non-growth proclivities of the body in power today as distinguished from tomorrow." The chances that such a system can be administered with fairness are remote to the point of nonexistence.

7. Rapacious development occurs. There is a cliche about that land should be treated as a resource rather than a commodity. Careful examination might find the phrase wanting, but taken at its face value it might be said to mean that more respect must be shown for the land and the public interest, both present and future. But in a system where windfalls and wipeouts increasingly abound, landownership and development becomes a higher risk venture. A way to minimize risk is to get in, do it, and get out. That is hardly consistent with a social goal that developers should treat land as a resource. When government is not concerned about wipeouts, it is tantamount to being for rapacious development, for that is how high risk free enterprise institutions must work. Large wipeout risks justify huge windfall gains. In a society willing to consider public ownership and development of land, as some suggest, it is somewhat anomalous that few consider the use of transfer payments to modify gains and losses in a way which will make the development industry more nearly approach the risk associated with public or quasi-public utilities.

Windfall Recapture-Wipeout Avoidance Techniques

There are many techniques which might be considered for windfall recapture, some for wipeout avoidance, some which accomplish both purposes. Consider windfall recapture first.

A. Windfall Recapture: (1) Recapturing Community Costs Associated with New Development. Windfall recapture techniques have been used in America to recapture public capital costs associated with private development. If public infrastructure is financed entirely by the community at large, the property receiving the benefit of that infrastructure reaps a windfall. By imposing the cost on the development itself, the windfall is reduced. In the twentieth century, five windfall recapture techniques of this sort have evolved.

During the early 1900's, until the Great Depression, the *special assessment* was the most heavily utilized windfall recapture device. In 1913, Los Angeles, Kansas City, Portland, and Oakland derived over 20 percent of their revenues from special assessments. Nationwide, cities derived about 7 percent of their revenues from special assessments in 1930.[31] They have been nowhere near that high since, but in 1971 did produce $598 million of revenues for state and local governments.[32] In their new book, Oldman and Schoettle indicate "A separate chapter on Special Assessments does not now appear justified to us...", but they do include 30 pages and indicate "the course of developments in the next few years may make such a chapter necessary."[33]

Perhaps Oldman and Schoettle believe that there is no inherent reason why special assessments could not be used to finance fixed rail mass transit, or freeways, or oversized sewers. There is nothing inherent in the concept which limits the special assessment to its usual roll, recapturing *costs* of *local* improvements. Nothing inherent precludes its use for recapturing benefits conferred by general improvements.[34]

Windfalls For Wipeouts

During the post-World War II development splurge, the special assessment was still under the depression-cast shroud of disfavor, and local government insisted increasingly on the *dedication and improvement of public facilities* as a condition for final acceptance of subdivisions. Such exactions are windfall recapture devices. No aspect of subdivision law is as heavily litigated, developers resisting strenuously as communities continually shrink the subsidy to private development. As early as 1949, the landmark case of *Ayres v. City of Los Angeles*[35] established that developers could even be required to dedicate and improve lands where a considerable portion of the benefit flowed to the general public.

The next mutation for imposing costs on new development flowed from the realization by communities that there were circumstances where *fees in lieu of dedication and improvement* would be appropriate. In a sense, this windfall recapture device was more like a special assessment; it is more like a charge, a tax—but paid in advance.

By the mid-60's, localities were also discovering that the exactions that worked so well on subdivision permissions could also be *utilized with other development permissions* such as variances, conditional use permits, rezonings—even building permits. Dedication, improvement, and fees in lieu thereof were imposed as conditions on other types of permissions.

Of course, the stage of evolution is not everywhere the same in this country; there are still some parts of the country where dedication and improvement exactions on subdivision approval is still novel. On the other hand, the increasing use of the devices mentioned is not novel in any of the WASP countries. All are trying to load more of the community infrastructure costs on new development.

The above story is so familiar to planners, it makes little sense to elaborate or cite authority. However, the most recent step in the evolution that began with special assessments is not yet so well known. In the middle of the 1960s, cities and subdivider-developers in California had in effect *bargained to an agreement* concerning the relative shares of the infrastructure subdividers would provide and the community would provide. The agreement, changing almost yearly, was in the form of a statute that the lobbyists for the two groups had been able to get out of the legislature. Similar statutes existed in almost every state. They were widely evaded by cities. The statutes told the cities what they could ask for by way of exactions for approving subdivisions; they did not say that subdivisions had to be approved. So a subdivider-developer either did what the city said or took his subdivision elsewhere.

But some being law-abiding, some cities sought to opt out of the pesky agreement represented by the statute by inventing what I call *development taxes*. In one of the shortest,[36] most obscure, underrated, and yet significant land use cases in the '70s, Associated Home Builders of Greater East Bay took on the City of Newark, California,[37] on its development tax and lost. Cal. Gov't Code §37101 permitted cities to license businesses, and the Newark City

> ordinance, concededly solely a revenue measure, imposes a tax upon the business of constructing dwellings. The measure of the tax is the number of bedrooms in the units to be constructed. It is required to be paid before the building permit is issued, and the fees received are to be deposited by the city in a "capital outlay fund." . . . Respondent [city] points to the relatively greater fire and police protection and street use required for residents [than for commercial and industrial uses].[38]

Perhaps the ordinance stated that the capital outlay fund proceeds had to be used to provide public services to the taxed properties, but the court makes no mention of the requirement.

The decision might well stand for the proposition that the revenues from the license tax are general revenues and could be used for any purpose. If the business of constructing dwellings can be licensed, so can the business of subdividing—the tax being measured by the number of lots or whatever and so on. The case might stand for the proposition that all public costs associated with the new development can be loaded on the new development itself. Perhaps it even means that if the property with a development permission is worth more than it was without the development permission, the tax can be as much as the difference.

In effect, the license tax could constitute a buy-in fee to existing community infrastructure. And why not? If I am prepared to say, as I am,[39] that a special assessment could constitutionally recoup up to all the benefit received, only the mechanism—not the economics—is changed by the latest device to accomplish that end. The City of Newark scheme has swept California. And as California goes in city planning control powers, so ultimately goes the nation.

But not yet. Arizona cities got wind of the California practice. Tempe collected $400,000 before the Arizona Supreme Court held the tax was invalid.[40] Nevada cities and developers entered into one of those statutory agreements over the use of the new device.[41] Having won in the trial courts in Florida, developers there are now girding for legal battles over the technique in the appellate courts.[42]

A. Windfall Recapture [cont.]: (2) Other Recapture Devices. *Capital gains taxes* are not traditionally thought of as windfall recapture devices. Capital gains are taxed because they are income, and as long as the United States has had an income tax, capital gains have been considered income. But a capital gains tax, especially where there is a heavier one on real estate than on other capital assets, can be a windfall recapture device. That it can so be considered is demonstrated by the English Conservative Party view, stated as early as 1967, that a special capital gains tax on land is the best way of recapturing betterment. But they dallied when they came to power, and the Conservative Government did not announce its decision to enact such a tax until December 17, 1973.[43]

So Vermont's Land Gains Tax[44] effective May 1, 1973, became the first capital gains tax specially on land to be adopted in the WASP countries. Motivated primarily by the desire to discourage speculation and development by out-of-staters, it was also touted as a windfall recapture device which would raise funds to permit lower taxation on open space lands, though as enacted the gains tax instead funds homeowner property tax relief. The tax has been found valid by a court.[45]

A very similar tax, The Property Speculation Tax Act of 1973,[46] was enacted in New Zealand—effective August 22, 1973—aimed at curbing land speculation. And as of April 9, 1974, a lien has been put on all property sold in the Province of Ontario, Canada pending passage of a 50 percent land speculation tax.[47] The legislation is motivated by rising land costs partly resulting from land speculation.

So far as can be discerned, the ideas for these two enacted and two formally proposed capital gains taxes on land were not exported from one jurisdiction to another. They arose spontaneously. That they did suggests the tax idea is well worth watching as a windfall recapture device.

Betterment levies or unearned increment taxes differ from capital gains taxes in one major respect—the tax is imposed not because the gain is income but because the increment is unearned. It belongs to the community because the community created the increment. Further, the grant of development permission or the start of development as well as a sale or transfer may be a taxable event. In the modern "WASP world," these betterment recapture devices date back to the 1909 Act,[48] regarded as the first English planning law. The concept was exported to the other [WASP] countries, save the United States. The contrast is of interest. Except for the United States, the other countries did not have early capital gains taxes. Some still do not. That the capital gains tax might be a surrogate for betterment recapture may suggest why no betterment recapture schemes were ever tried in America. In any event, commentaries on the 1909 English Act and those modeled on it, indicate that little if any betterment was actually ever recovered under these acts.

Returning to power in 1964, the Labor Government in England implemented a new experiment for recapturing betterment, the 1947 experiment in nationalization of development rights having been ended by the Conservative Government. The Land Commission Act of 1967[49] created a 40 percent betterment levy. The commission created by the Act was empowered to acquire land by compulsory purchase and that feature of the Act was its undoing, the Conservatives repealing it almost immediately upon their resumption of power in 1971.[50] The betterment levy experiment, however, is an interesting one for thorough review by fans of that kind of windfall recapture device.

The Australians were aware of the English Act. In 1970 the State of New South Wales adopted an unearned increment tax in designated areas that were declared developable.[51] Enacted to provide funds to pay for community-provided infrastructure and to hold down land prices, the Act became unpopular even with the Liberals (the more conservative party)—which had secured its adoption—and it was repealed late in 1973.[52] It was repealed because land prices, which are seemingly of greater concern in the other WASP countries than they are in America, kept rising, and the unearned increment tax was blamed for that result. The Australian experiment constitutes a good case study that supporters of unearned increment taxes should contemplate.

One would be hard put to classify a *transfer tax*, a sales tax on land transactions, as a windfall recapture device. Traditionally, the tax is due whether or not the property sold has increased in value since its acquisition. Nevertheless, transfer taxes are a potential source of revenue, used in all the WASP countries. In Florida, a 0.3 percent tax resulted in revenues of $88.5 million in 1972.[53] While that amount included transfer taxes on other property as well, it does not appear to include Florida's typical $.55/$500 of consideration tax the federal government used to impose which is now abandoned and has been picked up by states and localities. A New York State tax at that rate produced $6.8 million.[54] In Pennsylvania, both the state and localities levy a one percent tax which resulted in $40.5 million in revenues.[55] A one percent rate in California with no exemptions would have produced an estimated $172 million in 1970-71.[56]

With a little enforcement, the transfer tax can be made very difficult to evade because title cannot be recorded unless the tax is paid. And if the tax is limited to increases in value, the result might be a hybrid "Unearned Land Value Transfer Tax Law": the name selected for such a tax proposed in a California bill.[57]

Whoever is interested in windfall recapture must at some point acknowledge a tremendous debt to Henry George.[58] His prose about the right of the community to increased land value has made the *land value taxation* movement a potent one for reform. Yet while many accept the concept of the community's right to at least some part of the increment, land value taxation wins few converts. I have had the "course" and remain unconverted.[59] While the converts to land value taxation continue to sharpen their arguments and produce studies[60] that "demonstrate" the soundness of land value taxation, more neutral reviews from such as Australia,[61] California,[62] England,[63] and the United States[64] continue to be less enthusiastic. As a practical matter, land value taxation cannot be sold in the United States as a windfall recapture device.

B. Wipeout Avoidance. As indicated earlier, the main interest these days in windfalls and wipeouts stems from the frequency and magnitude of wipeouts. There are only a few wipeout avoidance techniques in the United States, partially because courts have traditionally invalidated land use regulations that excessively depress land values. *Invalidation* of governmental action is not a wipeout avoidance device within the scope of this article, for I wish to address situations where the government *can* act *if* the wipeout is mitigated by transfer payments.

Compensable regulations are one wipeout avoidance technique. Presently, land use regulations in America are either held valid or invalid. There may be a need for a mid-way course under which severe regulations can be upheld if some compensation is paid. The other WASP countries are generally more generous than are governments in the United States in compensating for wipeouts from regulation. In England, for example, if a planning permission is revoked or modified before building operations are complete, the developer is entitled to claim damages for expenditures in construction and in preparation therefor, and for loss or damage attributable to the revocation or modification.[65] In the United States, the law is black or white—either the developer has or has not vested a right. If vested, the development can be completed. If the right has not vested, the developer's losses are not covered by government.

Compensation is also payable in England if planning permission is refused or made conditional for development within the concept of existing use.[66] A landowner has no right to maintain an existing use in the United States. An existing use can be made non-conforming and can eventually be terminated without compensation. In England, a landowner regulated so that land is incapable of any reasonably beneficial use can require the purchase of his property.[67] In the United States, such a regulation would be held invalid, but all regulations are presumed to be valid by the courts and the landowner might well be paid in England for regulations that would be held valid by some courts in America. The English are also more generous in acquiring property affected by condemnation blight, or "planning blight" as the English call it.[68]

The American Law Institute's "Model Land Development Code"[69] at long last nearing completion—has provisions for compensable regulation.[70] Compensable regulation is one of the strategies recommended for consideration in "The Taking Issue."[71] A California bill provides for payment for losses in property values due to a rollback in zoning, but the compensation is limited to the amount of the previous year's property taxes.[72] The Local Government Relations Division, Executive Department, State of Oregon, has a land value adjustment proposal which provides for compensation if a rezoning depreciates values by more than twenty percent.[73]

Nuisance law is a vehicle for encouraging neighborliness. Landowners can be forced to mitigate wipeouts through damage payments. Nuisance law has not evolved much ever since society gave public land use controls a virtual monopoly over externality control. But persuasive articles suggest a larger role for nuisance law in resolving externalities among neighbors.[74]

Even the king has been found to do wrong. Particularly in airport cases, the governmental activity has been found so noisy as to constitute a nuisance.[75] However, after several years of study, the English have taken the most outstanding, recent step toward encouraging neighborliness by governmental land users and developers. Under the Land Compensation Act 1973,[76] the governmental builder of public works is made liable for nuisance-like effects flowing from the use of the works—effects such as noise, vibration, smell, fumes, smoke, and artificial lighting.[77] The landowner can recover for damages to property located near the public improvement. Part of the property need not be taken for the project in order to be entitled to the proximity damage payment. While the English program may be expensive, perhaps the cost will be no greater than the cost of environmental impact statements in the United States which, as distinguished from what the English have done, neither require nor pay government to be a good neighbor.

C. Windfalls for Wipeouts. In order to fund wipeout mitigation with windfall recapture, one or more of the above windfall recapture techniques could be coupled with one or more of the above wipeout mitigation techniques. It is also possible to handle both windfall recapture and wipeout avoidance with concepts that deal with both matters simultaneously. These are the windfalls for wipeouts techniques.

The *transferable development rights* (TDRs) concept is new, exciting, and indigenously American. Since the movers and shakers of the TDR movement have been assembled for The Alfred Bettman Symposium on "Transferable Development Rights: Promise or Pipedream?" [which followed this lecture at the May 1974 ASPO Conference], my TDR discussion will be brief. The basic idea is that a landowner whose development right on land is restricted can nevertheless be permitted to use that development right on other land which can be developed beyond what would ordinarily be permitted. Alternatively, the landowner may be permitted to sell the development right to someone else who can then develop other land to an intensity beyond what is ordinarily permitted. The landowner's wipeout is mitigated either by permitting him a windfall on other land or by permitting him to sell the development rights that have been taken.

Preliminary observations are that the scheme will not work unless the demand for land is greater than the supply; otherwise, the development rights will be worthless. Therefore, supply will likely have to be constrained by public land use controls. Second, deciding the geographical areas to which development rights can be reattached to land may involve considerable public decision-making effort. TDRs are not a windfall-wipeout device that can nearly administer itself through a medium of transfer payments. Third, TDRs come in several versions,[78] and refined versions of earlier simplex forms have become most complex, portending the need for a highly trained and large bureaucracy.

TDRs have been authorized and used in New York City,[79] where a trial court decision on their use was not favorable.[80] They have also been authorized for use in Los Angeles.[81] Of course, the number of areas considering authorizing TDR use are now legion.

Zoning by eminent domain is also a windfall for wipeout device which is as American as TDRs and may be an alternative. Rather than being new, however, it is almost sixty years young and may be ready for a comeback. I first "discovered" the technique while teaching at the University of Minnesota in 1966, for Minnesota then had and still has a statute which permits zoning by eminent domain.[82] Not until 1971 did I advocate its use in a speech[83] which was a primogeniture for my notions about windfalls for wipeouts. By that time a modern day application of the technique had been approved by the Missouri Supreme Court,[84] proving that the earlier Minnesota cases were still good law. The concept might be more fully called *"Zoning by Special Assessment Funded Eminent Domain."* (At least its acronymn, ZSAFED, is more descriptive than the neuter TDR, which might be confused as the name of a conglomerate or an airline.) ZSAFED rediscovered can be briefly described. It is based on the assumption that when some land is restricted and suffers a wipeout, other land somewhere enjoys an offsetting windfall. That is so because demand for land utilization is not affected by a change in the location of useable land; demand merely seeks a supply elsewhere.

> Example: assume A and B each own half of an unzoned island. It is decided to zone A's land for agriculture and B's land for urban development. That decision represents the use of a zoning concept but not zoning in its police power form, for the right to develop A's land for anything but agricultural uses is taken by *eminent domain*. As a result of the taking, A's land is damaged. But since B's land is benefited by the taking because the demand for urban development has now been shunted there, B is *specially assessed* up to the amount of benefit received. The resulting funds are used to pay off A's damages. Windfalls for wipeouts. A is happy; B is happy. If at a later date the island authorities decide to roll back zoning on B's land for open space, B will be paid damages funded by special assessments on C, D, and so forth who are subsequent owners of B's land and who receive benefits because of the roll back.

Conclusion

I have defined windfalls and wipeouts in this paper and suggested that their magnitude and frequency in this environmental age is substantial as compared with yesteryear. Therefore, society's sense of equity is highly tensed and the land use planning and control system is crumbling from the failure to deal with windfalls and wipeouts. A foreign correspondent who wishes to remain anonymous put it well:

> I am convinced that the twin bogies of compensation and betterment are the key to every reasonable and sensible approach to planning legislation. I never cease to be astonished by the amount of abortive effort which goes into drafting, redrafting and attempting to operate planning legislation without first of all having adequately dealt with these bogies.[85]

But hope is not lost, for the techniques described in the preceding section can be evolved for windfall recapture and wipeout mitigation purposes. There are also techniques such as *land banking* or *excess condemnation for purposes of recoupment* which are alternative techniques. I have not covered those alternatives partially because of a previous ASPO paper,[86] partially because I believe techniques less than public ownership should first be tried, and partially because I do not believe land banking and excess recoupment are techniques whose time has yet come.

Let us share information about windfalls for wipeouts. The Council on Planning Librarians will shortly be publishing our bibliography, which may be of help to you. I may have coined the phrase, but I do not feel proprietary about efforts to evolve windfall for wipeout techniques. Let me hear from you, and you will hear from me.

As I began this paper, I had intended to close by expressing my faith in the concept of windfalls for wipeouts, but also by describing some of the considerable difficulties that must be faced before techniques will be workable. I have mentioned some of those difficulties elsewhere,[87] but space has here run out. Further, one should also be prepared at some time to state the criteria for a workable windfalls for wipeouts system. But I am personally full of too many signals at this point in my consideration of techniques to more fully state the criteria or describe the technique that best meets them.

Footnotes

1. "Those looking for color first will want to read Dr. Mason Gaffney. . . ." O. Oldman & F. Schoettle, State and Local Taxes and Finance 386 (1974). Gaffney is not only a thoughtful economist but is one of few who writes as if he enjoys it.
2. A. Pigou, A Study in Public Finance 156 (3rd rev. ed. 1949).

Windfalls For Wipeouts

3. 42 U.S.C. § 4321 *et seq.*
4. Hagman, *NEPA's Progeny Inhabit the States—Were the Genes Defective?* 1974 Urban L. Ann. 3.
5. 42 U.S.C. § 1857 *et seq.* Mandelker & Rothschild, *The Role of Land-Use Controls in Combating Air Pollution Under the Clean Air Act of 1970,* 3 Ecology L.Q. 235 (1973).
6. Sierra Club v. Ruckelshaus, 344 F. Supp. 253 (D.C. 1972), affirmed by 4 to 4 decision, Fri v. Sierra Club, 412 U.S. 451 (1973).
7. 33 U.S.C. § 1251 *et seq.*
8. 42 U.S.C. § 4901 *et seq.*
9. 87 Stat. 975 (1973).
10. F. Bosselman & D. Callies, The Quiet Revolution in Land Use Control (1971).
11. 16 U.S.C. § 1451 *et seq.*, Mandelker & Sherry, *The National Coastal Zone Management Act of 1972,* 1974 Urban L. Ann. 119.
12. Cal. Public Resources C. § 27000 *et seq.*
13. 10 Vt. Stat. Ann. § 6001 *et seq.*
14. N.Y. Unconsol. L. § 800 *et seq.*
15. 38 Me. Rev. Stat. Ann. § 481 *et seq.*
16. N.J. Stat. Ann. § 13:9A-1 *et seq.*
17. 14 Fla. Stat. § 380 *et seq.*
18. Haw. Rev. Stat. § 205 *et seq.*
19. D. Hagman, Public Control of California Land Development §§ 2.20, 2.21, 2.29, 3.45c (1973). A 1974 supplement will be published shortly.
20. *St. Petersburg Council Votes to Cut Back Population,* The New York Times, Mar. 26, 1974.
21. Anyone can cite to the New York Times, but who can cite to *Does City Have Right to Limit Its Growth,* The Wichita [Kansas] Eagle, Nov. 20, 1973, at 4A. A longer description of the Petaluma Controversy is Hart, *The Petaluma Case,* Cry California, Spring 1974, at 6. As of this writing the oral bench opinion in Construction Industry Association of Sonoma County v. Petaluma, No. C-73-0663-LHB, U.S. Dist. Ct. N.D. Cal., Jan. 17, 1974, which held the Petaluma ordinance invalid, has not been issued in written form.
22. Freilich, *Golden v. Town of Ramapo: Establishing a New Dimension in American Planning Law,* 4 The urban Lawyer ix (1972).
23. Fairfax County, Va. Zoning Ordinance, Chapter 30, Art. XIX, §§ 30-19.1—30.19.2, added March 4, 1974, imposed a 16 month moratorium on development throughout the county.
24. William Reilly was executive director of the Task Force on Land Use and Urban Growth, Citizens' Advisory Committee on Environmental Quality, The Use of Land: A Citizens' Policy Guide to Urban Growth (1973).
25. F. Bosselman, D. Callies & J. Banta, The Taking Issue (1973); a summary of The Taking Issue is found in Hagman, *Book Review,* 87 Harv. L. Rev. 482 (1973).
26. Compare the first message from the U.S. Supreme Court in four decades, which is clear—a small group of neighbors, clothed with a governmental entity, can zone almost as they please. Village of Belle Terre v. Boraas, 42 U.S.L.W. 4475 (1974).
27. Land Use Planning Act of 1974, H.R. 10294, 93d Cong., 2d Sess.; Land Use Policy and Planning Assistance Act, S. 268, 93d Cong., 1st Sess.
28. 351-52.
29. As quoted in House and Home, Aug. 1960, at 126.
39. 273 (July 1970).
31. Tax Foundation, Inc., Special Assessments and Service Charges in Municipal Finance 7-10 (1970).
32. Bureau of the Census, U.S. Dept. of Commerce, Governmental Finances in 1970-71.
33. O. Oldman & F. Schoettle, State and Local Taxes and Finance 412 (1974).
34. See D. Hagman, Public Planning and Control of Urban and Land Development 791-804 (1973) for some possible applications of special assessments.
35. 34 Cal. 2d 31, 207 P.2d 1 (1949).
36. Two pages.
37. 18 Cal. App. 3d 107, 95 Cal. Rptr. 648 (1971).
38. *Id.* at 109-10, 95 Cal. Rptr. 650-51.
39. McCoy v. Union Elevated R.R. Co. 247 U.S. 354 (1917); Brand v. Union Elevated R.R. 238 U.S. 586 (1915) and Norwood v. Baker, 172 U.S. 269 (1898) are indirect authorities on the point. There is no case to my knowledge which clearly indicates that benefit recapture in excess of costs is either constitutional or unconstitutional.
40. Home Builders Ass'n. of Central Ariz., Inc. v. Riddel 109 Ariz. 404, 510 P.2d 376 (1973). The California case is not cited.
41. Nev. Rev. Stat. §278.2 *et seq.*
42. Scott, *Legal Notes,* Urban Land, Dec. 1973, at 21.
43. Parliament, Dec. 17, 1973, The Times, Dec. 18, 1973, at 5. The Conservative Government lost the Spring 1974 elections before the tax was enacted.
44. 32 V.S.A. § 10001 *et seq.*
45. Andrews v. Lathrop, _____Vt._____, 315 A.2d 860 (1974).
46. 1973, No. 18.
47. Letter from L. Russwurm to Donald Hagman, April 18, 1974.

Windfalls For Wipeouts

48. Housing, Town Planning, etc. Act, 1909, 9 Edw. 7, c.44 §58.
49. 1967 c. 1.
50. Land Commission (Dissolution) Act 1971, c. 18.
51. The Land Development Contribution Act, 1970, Act No. 24, The Land Contribution Management Act, 1970, Act No. 22.
52. Land Development Contribution Management (Amendment) Act, 1973, Act No. 75.
53. Advisory Commission on Intergovernmental Relations, Federal-State-Local Finances: Significant Features of Fiscal Federalism 236-37 (M-79, 1974).
54. Id.
55. Id.
56. Krebs, Real Estate Transfer Tax, in Assembly Select Committee on Open Space Lands, Funding for Acquisition of Open Space Lands: Three Approaches 16 (Oct. 1972).
57. Cal. A.B. No. 3698, introduced April 15, 1974 by Assemblyman Z'berg.
58. H. George, Our Land and Land Policy, 9 Works of Henry George 108 (1898).
59. Hagman, The Single Tax and Land-Use Planning: Henry George Updated, 12 UCLA L. Rev. 762 (1965).
60. The Land Institute, (England) Site Value Rating (1973).
61. Royal Commission of Inquiry into Rating, Valuation and Local Government Finance (New South Wales), Report 54-72 (1967).
62. Cal. Assembly Committee on Revenue and Taxation, Interim Activities: 1971, Introduction (1971).
63. The Future Shape of Local Government Finance, Cmnd. No. 4741, at 26-29 (1971).
64. Price Waterhouse & Co., A Study of the Effects of Real Estate Property Tax Incentive Programs Upon Property Rehabilitation and New Construction, HUD Contract H-1300 (1973).
65. Town and Country Planning Act 1971, c. 78, §§ 164-65.
66. Id. §169 and Sch. 8, Pt. II.
67. Id. §§180, 189, 190.
68. Hagman, Planning (Condemnation) Blight, Participation and Just Compensation: Anglo-American Comparisons, 4 Urban Lawyer 434 (1972).
69. Proposed Official Draft No. 1, Tentative Draft No. 6 and Appendix A (April 15, 1974).
70. See e.g. §§ 5-102, 5-106, 9-111(3).
71. F. Bosselman, D. Callies, J. Banta, The Taking Issue 266-83, 302-09 (1973).
72. Cal. A.B. No. 3698, introduced April 15, 1974 by Assemblyman Z'berg.
73. Letter from Russ Lucas to Donald Hagman, Feb. 8, 1974.
74. Ellickson, Alternatives to Zoning: Covenants, Nuisance Rules, and Fines as Land Use Controls, 40 U. Chi. L. Rev. 681 (1973).
75. Berger, The California Supreme Court—A Shield Against Governmental Overreaching. Nestle v. Santa Monica, 9 Cal. West L. Rev. 199 (1973).
76. c. 26.
77. For background see the white paper Development and Compensation—Putting People First, Cmnd. 5124 (1972).
78. Costonis, Development Rights Transfer: An Exploratory Essay, 83 Yale L.J. 75 (1973) is the latest published version of the ideas of the leading TDR theoretician. Rose, A Proposal for the Separation and Marketability of Development Rights as a Technique to Preserve Open Space, 2 Real L.J. 635 (1974) is the most recent comprehensive survey. A. Moore, Transferable Development Rights: An Idea Whose Time Has Come (1974), is a Fairfax County, Virginia supervisor and a leading advocate for TDRs at the local government level. Other participants in the TDR "movement" are cited in the above referenced materials.
79. New York City Planning Commission. Resolutions 224, 225, Dec. 7, 1972.
80. Fred F. French Investing Co., Inc. v. City of New York, N.Y. Sup. Ct., N.Y.C., Trial Term, pt. 13, Jan. 30, 1974, N.Y.L.J., Jan. 30, 1974.
81. Los Angeles, Cal., Ord. 145,043, Ordinance Establishing a Specific Plan for Westwood Village, Aug. 24, 1973.
82. Minn. Stat. Ann. §§462.12-462.17 dates back to 1915. It is printed in part in D. Hagman, Public Planning and Control of Urban and Land Development 802-04 (1973).
83. Summarized in Hagman, Implementation of Land Use Planning in the Political Process, Land Use Planning 128, 133 (T. Box ed. 1972).
84. City of Kansas City v. Kindle, 446 S.W.2d 807 (Mo. 1969), 22 Z.D. 53, Mandelker, Reporter's Comment to 22 Z.D. 53 (1970).
85. Letter from _____ to Donald Hagman, April 26, 1974.
86. Hagman, Public Acquisition and Disposal of Lands, in American Society of Planning Officials, Land-Use Policies (1970).
87. Hagman, Windfalls for Wipeouts, in The Good Earth of America: Planning Our Land Use (C. Harriss ed. 1974) forthcoming from the American Assembly to be published by Prentice-Hall.

Impact Taxes:

Unfair (Good Intentions Aside)

Jay Janis

Jay Janis is a principal in MGIC-Janis Properties, Inc., and related companies in the real estate, development, and mortgage banking fields. Having formerly served as executive assistant to Secretary Weaver of the U.S. Department of HUD (1966-69), he is chairman of the [Florida] Governor's Council on State Housing Goals. Mr. Janis is a graduate of Yale University. Prepared for State Government, published by Council of State Governments, Iron Works Pike, Lexington, Kentucky 40511.

Introduction

Communities experiencing rapid population growth are faced with a number of very real problems. Among them is the need to upgrade existing public services to accommodate an expanding population—at a time when operating and maintenance costs have reached all-time highs. The only solution is to raise additional revenues to pay for the stress that is being put on existing public services. The impact tax—which is charged to new construction only—is one method that more and more communities are considering to raise these revenues.

Surely on one level, the good intentions behind the impact tax approach—to upgrade community services in the face of rapid growth—are unquestioned. Certainly the impact tax approach at least accepts the inevitability of growth and attempts to provide a means for dealing with it by raising the funds to upgrade the needed services.[1] On another level, however, the impact tax approach is clearly a politician's dream. This is because the tax falls not on the existing constituency but rather on the new people who have not yet arrived in the community and can hardly protest. In any event, impact taxes are unfair; and, depending upon the method of assessment and the use of the funds, they may sometimes be illegal as well. To prove this contention, we must look at three questions which are at the heart of the impact tax issue:

1. Who should pay for "the costs of growth"—the new residents, the old residents, or both?
2. Where should the funds be used—for services and improvements *within* the new development or *throughout* the entire community?
3. On what basis should the impact tax be assessed—a flat amount per unit; an adjustable amount according to value; or an amount based on the density of the project?

Who should pay?

Because impact taxes usually consist of a "fee" added to the cost of a building permit for new construction, builders are seemingly the ones who pay the impact tax. But appearances are deceiving. Builders regard fees and taxes as part of the total cost of development—just like land, sewers, concrete, steel, lumber, overhead, or the cost of money. A profit is added to these costs, and the new figure becomes the selling price. So consumers, not builders, bear the cost of the impact tax in the price of their new homes or apartments. Therefore, the proper question to ask is whether the new residents who move to the community or the old (i.e. present) residents who live there should pay the costs of upgrading services. Or should both groups pay?

Many believe that the increased cost of services localities currently experience is the fault of new residents who have migrated to the community. The impact tax, which is assessed against new construction only, is regarded by the town fathers as a way to balance the scales. This kind of reasoning is faulty on several grounds. In the first place, the increased cost of services can be readily explained by other factors such as inflation, changes in age composition, rising living standards, and changes in life style. Moreover, in many cases, services were inadequate before the new residents arrived. Highways may have been in disrepair; bridges inadequate; schools too few and dilapidated; libraries virtually non-existent; and municipal sewer treatment plants antiquated. In such cases, the problem was there before the new residents arrived, and the old residents had been getting a free ride in past years by underpaying for services that the community needed. This was the fault of local elected officials who often lacked the courage to raise taxes. However, to tax only new residents now to make up for past deficiencies seems grossly unfair. Besides, since old residents did not pay an impact tax when they arrived in the community, why should new residents have to pay one? After all, old residents were once new residents.

Further, taxing new residents in this manner also raises the cost of their housing. This comes at a time when housing costs are already excessive in relation to the ability of most Americans to pay for it. Housing is increasingly being priced beyond the reach of even middle-income families. At the rate we are going in Florida, for instance, by 1985 more than 62% of all families coming into the state will be unable to find a home they can afford. And keep in mind that when the impact tax is added to the purchase price and becomes part of the mortgage, the homebuyer ends up paying triple the amount of the tax over the 30-year life of his loan.

The burden of increased housing costs, of course, falls hardest on low-income families. When it comes to finding housing they can afford, they have a much harder time than middle or upper-income families. Lower-income families will be forced either to pay a dangerously high portion of their income for housing or find housing (probably substandard at that) in already overcrowded urban ghettos. In most cases, the economics of the situation will dictate the latter course of action. So impact taxes have the added stigma of being exclusionary obligations upon old residents; therefore, services which directly benefit only new residents are normally paid for by new residents by requiring builders to provide such services within the boundaries of their own subdivision. These on-site improvements usually include sewer and water lines; roads; drainage facilities; and, in certain cases such as new communities, sites for parks, schools, and the like. Beyond that, a builder may be required to pay for off-site improvements—such as the extension of a sewer main to his subdivision far from existing development—when these facilities are for the exclusive use of new residents within his development and are provided by the community ahead of its capital improvement schedule. In other cases, special taxing districts may be created to tax the residents of a specific neighborhood for improvements such as street lighting or landscape maintenance which are made only in that neighborhood.

But it would be unfair to charge *just* the new residents for services which benefit the entire community. If the Broward County, Florida, impact tax charged to new residents had not been invalidated by the courts, it would have been used to pay for improving bridges and roads throughout the entire community. The inequities of this approach are clear: "Laws that command one group to pay for a benefit inuring to all people must be rejected . . . the fee must be paid by the people who receive the service—if all receive —all must pay . . . a portion of the people cannot be singled out for that which should be done by all . . . "[2] Moreover, in the rush to tax new residents, communities should not forget that new residents have the same right to move to a community as old residents have to be there. And once they arrive in the community, these new residents have the same rights as the old residents.

On what basis should the impact tax be assessed?

This is perhaps the most difficult question of all to answer. If a flat fee per unit is charged—say, $1,000 for every new unit—the result is a regressive tax which discriminates against lower-income families.

On the other hand, if a sliding fee is charged based on estimated value of the completed structure, the result is a higher tax on upper-income families which discriminates against this group. While from a social point of view a progressive tax may be fairer than a regressive tax, two inequities in this approach still remain: the first is that lower-income families generally require more services than higher-income families; and the second is that the higher property taxes paid by upper-income families more than offset the cost of services they require.[3] Therefore, charging upper-income families more than lower-income families appears doubly unfair.

A third method—and the worst by far—is to base the tax on the density of the project. The Broward County impact tax relied upon that approach. The impact tax on a single-family home on a two-acre estate would have been as little as $32 per unit, while the impact tax on a single condominium apartment unit in a large highrise would have been several thousand dollars. The effect of this tax would be the encouragement of extremely low-density development, which in turn would lead to under-utilization of land and, more important, to urban sprawl. Nothing could be more inimical to sound public policy than urban sprawl, the evils of which—in terms of excessive energy consumption, environmental degradation and the squandering of scarce resources—have been carefully documented in a study recently published by the Council on Environmental Quality ["Costs of Sprawl"—see Chapter 13 in Volume II].

Conclusion

Whichever direction local governments turn, they will find that impact taxes are unfair in one way or another. If the Florida Legislature should pass the enabling legislation suggested by Representative Boyd, local ordinances which are subsequently adopted pursuant to it will have to run the gauntlet of 5th and 14th Amendment challenges at the least. Many will not survive. Therefore, communities should study other alternatives to generate revenues for upgrading community services.

In the meantime, it would seem that the only fair way to cushion the impact of growth is for local governments to require builders to create better living environments with a full range of facilities provided within their developments. This means that local governments will need to become more demanding both with regard to the quality of projects they approve and the quantity of services which builders must provide.

At the same time, localities will have to upgrade the services they are providing to the community by raising the necessary taxes. This means that local politicians will have to bite the bullet and tell their constituents that the quality of life in their community depends upon their willingness to pay for it.

Footnotes

1. Occasionally communities purposely impose impact taxes so high that either building is made infeasible or only wealthy families can live in the community. In such cases impact taxes are prima facie unfair, but clearly that is not the intent of Representative Boyd's proposed statewide impact tax for Florida. His proposed legislation has several useful safeguards, and this article is directed not so much at the specifics of his bill as against impact taxes in general as they are being applied nationwide. Nonetheless, many of the arguments in this article are relevant to his bill.

2. Judge Arthur J. Franza (Janis Development Corp. v. City of Sunrise, Broward Co. Circuit Court, Florida, 1973).

Broward County Ordinance (73-2) dated May 7, 1973, provided for the "imposition of charges . . . for the purpose of providing funds for the expansion of existing county roads and bridges . . . and the construction of additional roads and bridges . . . to lessen traffic congestion (throughout Broward County) on the roads, streets, and highways thereof." The Ordinance imposed what is designated a "land use fee" progressively graduated in nature depending upon "density." Plaintiffs' argument was based on the following five points: Point I Broward County, as a non-charter county, possesses no inherent or constitutional powers under the Florida Constitution, 1968, authorizing or empowering it to enact and enforce Ordinance 73-2. Point II Broward County Ordinance 73-2, and the charges imposed thereunder, are not an exercise of any police power vested in Broward County, may not be held valid as such, and must be tested as an exercise of the power of taxation. Point III The charges imposed by Broward County Ordinance 73-2 cannot qualify as an assessment for benefit or special assessment, and said charges constitute an unconstitutional taking of property without due process of law or compensation. Point IV Under the terms of the Florida Constitution, Article VII, Sections 1 and 9 (1968), and existing general law, Broward County, Florida, and City of Sunrise are without authority to establish, assess, levy or impose a land use tax as set forth in Ordinance 73-2. Point V The provisions of Broward County Ordinance 73-2 are violative of the Fourteenth Amendment to the Constitution of The United States and Article 1, Section 9, of the Constitution of the State of Florida.

More specifically, although the Ordinance stated that the funds were to be used for improvements "serving the vicinity of the project in which the charges are collected," the plaintiffs pointed out that "the property assessed will not necessarily abut the improvements for which the assessment is spent. Under Section 5 (of the Ordinance) the improvement may be however far away the phrase ' . . . in the vicinity of . . . ' permits."

"Further, under Section 6 (of the Ordinance) setting forth trust fund restrictions, all that is guaranteed an assessed county property owner is that the funds will be spent in the unincorporated part of the county, or if used in a municipality, that the improvement will be of direct benefit to the unincorporated area of the county. There is no requirement that the improvement benefit the assessed property."

"Under Section 6 a city property owner who is assessed is assured only that the funds collected will be used in his municipality, or if used in some other municipality or the county, that the improvement will be of direct benefit to his municipality. There is no requirement that the improvement benefit the assessed property."

"Under the terms of Ordinance 73-2 and in keeping with the limitations set forth therein, the funds taken from a property owner by assessment may be used on an 'improvement' which is remote from his assessed property or which is actually detrimental to the value or use of his assessed property."

"The purported assessment under Ordinance 73-2 is not for, or even calculated to be for, a project bestowing some special benefit or enhancement of value of the assessed property. The most that can be said under the terms of the ordinance is that the ultimate project will benefit the public at large. The law of this state does not permit one person's property to be taken by special assessment to pay for benefits to the general public."

"In the application of Ordinance 73-2 to dwelling units the distinction between those assessed and those not assessed bears no relationship to either value or enhancement of same. For example, the owner of an existing structure pays no assessment even if the funds are spent on a project which directly doubles or triples the value of his land. The person who builds a new home must pay even if the funds are used for a project that is detrimental to his new home."

With regard to Point V concerning the constitutionality of the Ordinance, the plaintiffs contended that from both the point of view of the Fourteenth Amendment to the United States Constitution and the Florida Constitution " . . . it is clear that if the State is to classify for the purpose of imposing unequal burdens, then all persons similarly situated must be treated alike, and the classifications must be reasonable, not arbitrary, and the classifications must rest on some difference having a fair and substantial relation to the object of the act or ordinance."

"Further, as to excise taxes, the Supreme Court held in Volusia County Kennel Club v. Haggard, 73 So. 2d 884 (Fla. 1954), referring at page 888 to an earlier decision of the United States Supreme Court, that: 'The essence of the *Steward Dry Goods* decision is that the amount of the tax must bear a reasonable relation to the value of the thing taxed. If the tax is deemed a license tax, it must bear a reasonable relation to the value of the privilege obtained in return. If it is a gross receipts tax, it must bear a reasonable relation to the value of the gross receipts.' "

"Ordinance 73-2 must be tested against the foregoing constitutional principles."

"The purpose of Ordinance 73-2 is two-fold, though the purposes may be best described as primary and secondary, or even incidental. The primary purpose of the ordinance is to raise additional funds for the expansion of existing roads and bridges and construction of new roads and bridges in order to *lessen* traffic congestion."

"Though not expressly stated in the ordinance, a secondary purpose may be to retard the influx of new residents to Broward County, Florida."

"The former purpose is obviously a legitimate county goal. The latter purpose may, under emergency circumstances, be a legitimate county goal, though it is obviously contrary to the traditional rights and privileges of citizens of the country. It is, however, pertinent that nowhere in the ordinance is there any specific declaration that population limitation is a purpose of the ordinance, or that it has been legislatively found to be a purpose or a goal."

"Nevertheless, even if both of the purposes discussed above are good purposes, the commands of the Court in the above-quoted cases must be abided. As stated by the Court in *Volusia County Kennel Club v. Haggard*, 73 So.2d 884 (Fla. 1954) at page 886: '. . . *Even a good purpose must be accomplished in a lawful manner and it would be a dangerous doctrine to say that the government may or should ignore fundamental principles of the Constitution and the law in order to accomplish a good purpose.*' " [Emphasis by Court.]

"The first step in examination of Ordinance 73-2 is to consider the distinction, if any, between those who are taxed or charged and those who are not."

"Applying this examination to dwellings, the attempted classification is fairly simple. Owners of dwellings now in existence, and dwellings for which a building permit has been issued prior to the effective date of the ordinance, *are not* required to pay. Persons seeking building permits and certificates of occupancy for new dwellings, or new additions to existing dwellings, are required to pay."

"Thus, under the classifications of the ordinance, any person who seeks to construct a home on his vacant lot, to tear down his existing home and construct another on his presently occupied lot or to construct an addition to his present dwelling, must bear the tax or charge to expand existing roads and bridges and construct new roads and bridges."

"On the other hand, owners of existing dwellings will bear no such burden, even though such class obviously includes the vast majority of public road users."

"Plaintiffs respectfully submit that the imposition of the tax or charge on the limited class set forth above, in light of the object of the ordinance to finance public roads and bridges to be used by the larger class which is free from the tax or charge, is in violation of the constitutional principles set forth in the decisions of the Supreme Court quoted above."

"In this regard, it is noteworthy that a stated purpose of Ordinance 73-2 set forth in Section 2 thereof is *to lessen traffic congestion* on the streets and bridges. Thus, persons building new homes are being singled out to bear a substantial tax or charge to solve the *existing* inadequacy of streets and bridges, not merely any new traffic burden they may contribute to. Those who constitute the existing traffic problem, those who already own existing dwelling places, are spared the tax."

"Plaintiffs respectfully submit that this arbitrary attempted classification and imposition of burden constitutes a denial of due process of law and equal protection of law. Said attempted classification clearly falls within those condemned by the Supreme Court in *Seaboard Air Line v. Simon*, 56 Fla. 545, 47 So. 1001 (1908) wherein the Court stated at page 1005: '. . . But, under the decisions of the Supreme Court of this United States, where there appears to be no just basis for a classification adopted, and the regulation imposes a material burden upon a part only of a comprehensive class with reference to legal duties and obligations that pertain in substantially the same manner to all of the class, the classification is not in accord with the requirements of the constitution as to due process of law and the equal protection of the laws . . . ' "

"Plaintiffs urge that, particularly in light of the objectives of the ordinance to finance roads and bridges, the singling out of a small group including plaintiffs to bear a burden, the products of which will be enjoyed by all dwellers and all road users, cannot stand."

"The above-discussed constitutional infirmities would control and compel a finding of invalidity, even if Ordinance 73-2 imposed a flat unvarying charge on each person assessed. But it does not. Ordinance 73-2 imposes a progressive graduated tax or charge, and this graduation not only aggravates the above-discussed constitutional infirmity, but also renders Ordinance 73-2 inherently and internally unconstitutional in its application to those who are singled out to bear the burden."

"Stated alternatively, Ordinance 73-2, as a product of its graduated nature, attempts to create and impose unreasonable and arbitrary classifications among those who *are* required to pay, in violation of the constitutional principles set forth in the cases discussed above."

"This constitutional infirmity can best be demonstrated by considering the application of Ordinance 73-2 to various factual propositions."

"For example, under Ordinance 73-2, a new 1,000-square-foot dwelling built on a one-acre plot would be assessed at $9.56. However, a 1,000-square-foot condominium dwelling in a project containing 30 such units per acre would be assessed at $286.85. Thus, the tax or charge on one 1,000-square-foot dwelling is 30 times the tax or charge on another 1,000-square-foot dwelling."

"Viewed from another standpoint, the application of Ordinance 73-2 is equally unreasonable and arbitrary. A developer whose development consisted of a 15-acre tract with 30 one-half-acre lots each having a 3,000-square-foot home on it would be assessed and compelled to pay $172.11 for each 3,000-square-foot dwelling and $5,163.21 for the 30-unit project."

"However, a developer whose development of 30 dwelling units of 3,000-square-feet each was in the form of a highrise project with 30 units per acre would be assessed and compelled to pay $2,581.61 for each 3,000-square-foot dwelling and $77,448.30 for the 30-unit project."

"Viewed from the standpoint of the objective of Ordinance 73-2 to finance roads it is simply absurd and capricious to suggest that 30 families spread out over 15 acres create $5,163.21 worth of traffic or congestion, while 30 like families in a condominium project create $77,448.30 worth of traffic and congestion."

The case was heard in June, 1973, in The Circuit Court of The Seventeenth Judicial Circuit, and Judge Arthur Franza's decision was delivered on October 5, 1973. Pertinent excerpts are as follows:

"Common sense dictates that new construction has a tremendous impact on roads, all services and on the environment. But it is an aggravated impact, the origin already there. It is a total community problem, not a segregated ill produced by one industry."

"If we could wall our county and stop growth from outside, how do we stop it inside?"

"Must we equate the birth rate to the death rate. If we can't how do we expel or eliminate each other. By seniority of residence, or do we fall back on the Neanderthal rule of survival of the fittest[?]".

"Paper walls of ordinance around any city cannot endure. The moats of another century, the Alps, the Berlin Wall, the Great Wall of China, and the impregnable Maginot Line did not stand the test of time."

"Even if we did successfully build a wall and other communities followed suit, where would our children and their children go? This type wall does nothing more than separate the people from their inalienable rights under our Constitution."

"Our children may see the day that what is unconstitutional now may be constitutional then; but not now, not now, hopefully never."

"The problem really is not new dwellings per se, but new people. New people have all rights and obligations of resident people—no more, no less, in this America. They are citizens of the United States and they are all equal—no charge, no premium—equal! How long ago were we new people?"

"Obviously, the Broward County Commissioners are acutely aware of the problem, as are many other public officials. The people are certainly aware. The answer or cure does not lie with this ordinance however. The answer must be found elsewhere and it is there to be found. The state has begun."

"If government is zoning 7,000 units on 246 acres, it ought not to later cry congestion. Government itself is the primary cause of that which they now abhor."

"Laws that command one group of people to pay for a benefit inuring to all the people must be rejected. Every incidence that encroaches on our individual liberty or right must be struck down."

"The nomenclature of the monies attempted to be collected is 'fee.' In reality, it is a tax. Each consumer would be charged differing amounts as scheduled in the ordinance although each consumer's impact upon the community is approximately the same. A person adding to his home does not affect population impact, but he must pay. This schedule alone is repugnant to the 14th Amendment of equal protection under the law, because of its disparity of payment."

"The fee must have a reasonable relation to the services and, conversely, there must be a reasonable relation to the type and degree of service received to the amount of fee imposed."

"The fee must be paid by the people who receive the services. If all receive it, all must pay."

"A portion of the people cannot be singled out to do that which should be done by all."

"The areas of service to be rendered in the ordinance could bear no relation whatever to the area supposedly generating the fee. The area of service and the method to arrive at it are too vague and uncertain and bears no reasonable relation to the fee imposed or where it is to be used. Consequently, it is a tax."

"Therefore, when magnified through the eye of the 14th Amendment of the U.S. Constitution, Article VII, Sections 1 and 9, Article III, Section 2, of the Florida Constitution, Florida Statute 125 and case law, it is apparent that the subject ordinance does violate the basic concepts of constitutional safeguards."

Broward County has appealed the Circuit Court's decision to the Fourth District Court of Appeals (Broward County, Florida, et al. v. Janis Development Corporation, et al., Case Nos. 73-1239 and 74-306), and a decision on the appeal is expected shortly.

3. See Anthony Downs, Opening up the Suburbs (New Haven and London: Yale University Press, 1973), pp. 46-50; Ashley Economic Services, Inc., The Fiscal Impact of Growth (Newport Beach, California, 1974).

Regulating the Timing of Urban Development

Henry Fagin

Henry Fagin is a professor of administration in the Graduate School of Administration, as well as research administrator in the Public Policy Research Organization, at the University of California, Irvine. He was a professor of planning from 1962-1967 in the Department of Urban and Regional Planning at the University of Wisconsin, Madison, and a research professor in 1958 in the Department of Political Science, University of California, Berkeley. Mr. Fagin is a graduate of Columbia University's School of Architecture, and holds a master's degree from the school of Planning and Housing at Columbia.

Reprinted, with permission, from a symposium on "Land Planning in a Democracy," appearing in Law and Contemporary Problems (Vol. 20, No. 2, Spring, 1955), published by the Duke University School of Law, Durham, North Carolina. Copyright, 1955, by Duke University.

Introduction

Coordination, a major aspect of planning, involves *space* and *time*. Effective urban planning demands a simultaneous attention to both.

In the past half-century a static attempt at space coordination has become widespread. Its essence is expressed in certain dictionary definitions of the noun *plan*: "a representation drawn on a plane" or "a scheme of arrangement." The master plan, the comprehensive plan, the zoning plan frequently are interpreted as embodying an ideal and ultimate balance among districts of land classified as residential, commercial, and industrial. Since this conception deals with the *what* irrespective of the *when*, it represents what I term static space coordination.

A dynamic approach to space coordination is suggested by other dictionary definitions of *plan*: "a schematic program indicating parts in their arrangement," "a method of action." Here we shift from dealing mainly with ultimate categories and patterns of land use to considering the activities involved in urban development. This latter approach stresses the coordination of programs of action. It relates industrial, business, service, and residential construction activities; it coordinates the variety of activities that extend the urban transportation system; and it relates all these to the activities that utilize parcels of land.

The evolving demands on urban planning already have forced a shift in focus from the *map* to the program of action. The ultimate master plan map as the goal of planning is being replaced by a "planning process" conception in which the master plan is regarded as an open-ended sequence of plans describing at each successive point in time a desirable equilibrium among ever-changing activities. Any single map in the series represents a cross-section cut through the community at some critical instant in time—a concatenation little likely to be repeated at any other time. (One eminent city administrator now uses the term "forward programming" in place of "master planning.")

Neccessarily, this conception of urban planning involves coordination in time as well as space, of programs as well as land areas. Capital budget programming is a start, but deals only with a small portion of a large problem. *It is my belief that until the science of planning invents greatly improved methods for regulating the timing of urban development, many attempts at space coordination must continue to fail—master plans remaining unrealized, zoning ordinances ineffectual and rapidly obsolescing. Static space coordination is not merely inferior, it is impossible in a dynamic world.* [Emphasis added.]

Time Coordination

Coordination in time has two aspects. **Tempo,** the rate of urban development, is the first. The Borough of Mountain Lakes, New Jersey, which has acquired most of its remaining developable land and sells a limited number of building lots annually, is regulating the absolute tempo of its growth.

Moses Lake, a city in the state of Washington, makes the tempo conditional on certain future events. In the proposed Moses Lake "reclamation zone," certain lands may not be utilized for buildings until they have been filled in accordance with established grades. Already the city has refused to approve a subdivision plat for lands within one area subject to flooding.

The statutes of Washington empower a planning agency to disapprove a subdivision not in the *public interest.* According to Floyd M. Jennings, planning consultant to the Association of Washington Cities, this proviso "has not been adjudicated in the State of Washington, to the best of [his] knowledge. . . ." However, a number of cities have adopted subdivision ordinance provisions specifying that:

> Land, which the planning commission has found to be unsuitable for subdivision due to flooding, bad drainage, steep slopes, rock formations, or other features likely to be harmful to the safety, health, and general welfare of the future residents, and which the planning commission considers inappropriate for subdivision, shall not be subdivided unless adequate methods are formulated by the developer and approved by the city engineer.

Mr. Jennings writes that "None of these local experiences have been adjudicated by a Court of Record or by a lower court in this state."

Sequence is the second aspect of time coordination. It is exemplified in a zoning ordinance under active consideration in Clarkstown, New York. In this ordinance there will be an attempt to encourage growth around existing settlements before opening additional lands to intensive use.

To carry out this program, some areas, placed at first in one-acre residence districts, are designated on the new zoning map for change to the ⅓-acre district. Specific conditions must be found to exist before such changes will be made, but changes in these areas shall have priority over those in other areas. Thus, within the general reserve of two-acre and one-acre open land, certain districts will be available immediately for intensive development while other specifically designated and mapped areas will become available after the initial lands near full utilization. This will tend to bring about a planned sequence of land development at designed densities.

Existing measures affecting the timing of urban development appear to be motivated by a number of considerations—not all of them, to be sure, equally valid in social, economic or legal terms. For instance, acreage zoning and minimum-size dwelling regulations when carried to excess; obsolete building code requirements retained mainly to maintain a high local cost of new construction and thereby to discourage new tax burdens; controls over dwelling appearance which hamper large-scale or prefabricated building operations—all these tend to slow the rate of growth though they are intended primarily for other purposes.

Five Planning Bases for Timing Control

But there are at least five well-considered motivations for regulating the timing of urban development. These derive from the specific nature of modern community building activities and community requirements:

First, the need to economize on the costs of municipal facilities and services. These costs are strongly affected by the sequence in which the different areas of a municipality are developed. This matter involves the efficient provision of police and fire protection, schools, bus lines, streets and highways, utilities, and other important facilities. The sequence of building operations determines, for example, whether linear facilities such as pipes and streets will have to be extended inefficiently over long distances to serve scattered users or will be extended gradually to serve areas built in careful phase with efficient facility growth.

The order in which the parts of a large community are built affects both the initial expense of facilities and their costs of maintenance and operation. Large-scale builders like the Levitts place great emphasis in their construction operations on careful scheduling for the most economical possible sequence of development section by section. The proposed Clarkstown regulations discussed above are intended to reduce long-term municipal expenses.

Second, the need to retain municipal control over the eventual character of development. For example, the desired over-all future town pattern may require intensive development served by public sewer and water lines in an extensive valley at present remote from any utility lines. If there is no control over the timing of building, however, the area in question may be the early subject of a substantial amount of low-intensity construction served by individual wells and separate sewage disposal fields. The existence of this type of development may later make it impossible to convert the valley to the more intensive character required by the evolving municipal pattern, even though important community-wide reasons exist for doing so. In similar fashion, an important future industrial area may become so cut-up by scattered small-scale factories as to preclude its eventual development as a planned, coordinated industrial district when the time is ripe.

Third, the need to maintain a desirable degree of balance among various uses of land. For example, it is essential to the economic stability of certain municipalities which contain large areas of low-value homes that the service costs be offset by tax income from commercial and industrial ratables. In such places it is essential that new residential construction be timed in proper relation with business and industrial expansion.

Another sort of balance involves the subtle relationship of areas of varied character. The village of Hastings-on-Hudson in New York has a policy exercised through the zoning ordinance which regulates the timing of apartment construction in relation to the rate of one-family home building in accordance with a 15 to 85 ratio. Thus, for instance, whenever 85 new one-family dwellings have been built, the village may issue permits enabling 15 dwelling-units in apartment buildings. This regulation is intended to maintain what is locally felt to be a desirable predominance of one-family dwellings in a commuter village, but at the same time to make possible a necessary though smaller supply of rental apartments. The device makes the timing of one element conditional on the timing of another related element.

Fourth, the need to achieve greater detail and specificity in development regulation. The growing awareness of this need is evidenced by the trends in zoning towards increased use of special permit devices subject to detailed requirements and conditions and by the popularity of "designed-district" provisions.

In Great Britain a desire for greater sensitivity of controls led to the present system of development permissions instituted after country-wide public acquisition of "development rights." Local authorities may grant or withhold permission to build, according to the needs of a development plan. At least in the negative sense—that is being able to prevent development unless it accords with a municipally determined time schedule —the British regulations illustrate an application of control over timing to enable specific conformity with a detailed municipal plan. Under the British controls, for example, on a specific site in a developing area, permission for a store building may be denied on one day if the planning authority considers the construction premature, and at a later date permission may be granted.

There is, of course, a direct but generally unrecognized counterpart to this in the United States. Commonly, a municipality, petitioned to rezone a residential tract for a regional shopping center, refuses to do so when requested, but later decides the propitious moment has arrived and enacts the necessary amendment.

So long as zoning practice provided roomy districts, each with a capacity for more than the expected amount of pertinent development, the element of *time* was unimportant. With the current trend to specific changes for specific projects, however, timing has become an integral element in zoning administration. Occasionally, indeed, special zoning amendments and special use permits are so drawn as to become null and void after a specified period of time if construction has not commenced.

Fifth, the need to maintain a high quality of community services and facilities. This requires during periods of rapid building expansion that adequate intervals of time be assured for the assimilation of residential, business or industrial additions to the community.

When newcomers are added faster than municipal facilities and services can be increased, the resulting overloads on existing capacities cause a decline in the quality of services. Uncontrolled, this deterioration can result in seriously substandard levels of water supply, sewage and waste disposal, public school education, and public recreation. Moreover, if the rate of sudden and unanticipated shopping or industrial expansion outstrips the pace of highway improvement, residential streets may be flooded by excessive traffic seeking to by-pass congestion. (It is possible that adequate time for the *social* integration of incoming families represents a sixth legitimate basis for regulating community growth.)

Sands Point, New York, has adopted a means of partially regulating the rate of residential development to keep it in reasonable relationship with community facility and service capacities. In the Sands Point zoning ordinance, land subdivision is defined as a business use, permitted in residential districts only, on special permit. The village planning board in connection with its review of each subdivision is required to make a finding as to the village's capacity to absorb the proposed new lots. If deemed appropriate, the subdivision approval may be accompanied by a limitation on the number of lots for which building permits will be issued in any one year. The planning board is empowered at its discretion to limit building to 20 per cent of the approved lots in each of the ensuing five years.

Toward a More Solid Framework for Regulating the Timing of Urban Development

Motivated by the foregoing five planning bases for timing control, it is possible to design reasonable and workable regulations affecting both the sequence and the tempo of building operations. The following suggestion sketches one possible approach to such regulations.

Zones of Building Priority. Under the system of controls suggested here, the zoning map is derived from the series of land use maps that comprises the master plan sequence described above in the first section. It shows all lands in the specific use, density and bulk district designations determined appropriate by the local governing body. These designations embody the best current thinking as to the most desirable municipal pattern. Land for which a specific designation cannot yet reasonably be made is placed in a large-acreage "reserve district," from which portions are assigned to particular districts from time to time.

Superimposed on these basic districts, however, is an additional set of building sequence districts called *zones of building priority*; and these range from first priority to last priority through an appropriately numbered series. Building permit applications are granted in the order of the zones of building priority and within each such zone in the order of application dates.

The assignment of particular zones of building priority expresses the sequence of development most advantageous to the municipality for economizing on municipal costs and for securing the desired character of development—the first two bases above.

Regulating the Tempo of Building. The availability of building permits under the suggested controls is determined separately for each broad zoning classification—close and open type residence, business, manufacturing, etc. The number of permits available from time to time is derived from: findings as to the current balance among different types of development—basis number three, above; findings as to the status of specific private and public projects proposed to be encouraged by the municipality in the public interest—basis number four, above; and findings as to the current capacity to assimilate the proposed structures in view of the progress of municipal programs for facilities and services—basis number five, above.

A municipality exercising this system for regulating the timing of urban development should be obliged by statute to carry forward programs of municipal facility and service expansion reasonably related to development trends so as not to block the utilization of land but to expedite it in orderly fashion. A developer of land should have the opportunity of improving the building priority rating of his land by offering to construct off-site facilities and to provide services needed for proper development, but not yet feasible of municipal programming.

Undoubtedly, the institution of systematic controls over the timing of development will affect the market value of various parcels of land—some upward, some downward—but this has always been true of measures taken under the police power. Possibly, in certain municipalities each parcel of land in separate ownership on the effective starting date of the regulations will be considered entitled to one building permit irrespective of priority zone; and perhaps in rural areas building permits will be granted irrespective of priority zone in all applications involving very large lots—five or ten acres or more per structure.

Viewing the municipality in its entirety, the advantages of wisely exercised time regulation for shaping and achieving superior urban patterns will afford a greatly increased property value for the total of all land. After a period of readjustment, new value levels will reflect the real utility of the land, and ad valorem taxes will distribute the burdens of municipal service costs accordingly.

In occasional specific circumstances some form of compensation possibly will be warranted to offset individual losses. This may follow the Mountain Lakes precedent of municipal purchase at fair present market value; with respect to vacant tracts it may entail differential tax rates as between the different zones of building priority; it may involve a municipal option to buy agricultural land after a stated period of continued farming use; or it may involve adapting the British method—municipal purchase of development rights.

In general, however, the mass of mounting evidence eloquently argues that regulating the timing of urban development is a valid and necessary exercise of the police power. Such regulation not only is permissible in the legal sense but has become an urgent responsibility of municipal government needed to protect the very health, safety, and welfare of our rapidly growing suburban communities. In the light of planning theory as expounded in this paper and of the accumulated experiments of municipalities throughout the nation, it is clear that tempo and sequence zoning administered pursuant to soundly based municipal planning policy and in accordance with reasonable regulations will be powerful aids toward improving the quality of our communities.

CHAPTER FIVE

LIMITS TO GROWTH AND ZERO GROWTH

This chapter includes discussions and critiques of the concepts, issues, and impacts of the notions of "limits to growth" and "zero population or economic growth." These ideas were made popular in the environmental and planning-related literature of the late 1960s and early 1970s, by such persons as Ehrlich, Forrester, and Meadows. [For a brief summary of some of the literature, see the article by Michael Agelasto, in the last article of this chapter.]

In the first article, **Ross Macdonald** summarizes the basic problems commonly identified as part of the 'limits to growth' concept: "exponentially growing world population, depletion of non-renewable resources . . . , exponentially increasing pollution of the environment, marginal world food production, and the vast and probably increasing disparity in living standards between the citizens of rich and poor nations."

The author refers to one of the most widely-circulated reports of the 1970s: *The Limits to Growth*, by the Club of Rome. He identifies a number of faults of the report, but concludes that it has helped raise the consciousness of the public. "Whatever the defects and merits of the *Limits* book, it has done the world the very valuable service of emphasizing that continued growth strongly exacerbates world problems and that there are indeed definite limits to growth, no matter when the world will actually run up against them."

Larry Ruff, on the other hand, clearly is not satisifed with the *The Limits of Growth* volume; he castigates the work at length. [The reader may be interested in the fact that this review was selected for reprint from an issue of *Ecology Law Quarterly*.] The kindest words he levels—parallel to Macdonald's remarks in the previous article—are that "it will stir discussion and inspire work on both sides of the great debate . . . inevitably some good work on social systems will result . . . ."

The author's major criticism is summarized by the following: "What else can be said about a work which reduces the world to a handful of basic variables, invents a few interrelationships among these, makes some wild guesses about the form and magnitude of these interrelationships, grinds the whole thing through the electronic idiot, and then presents the little exercise as something 'so fundamental and general that we do not expect our broad conclusions to be substantially altered by further revisions.' "

Ruff finds himself faced with a difficult task: on which level to critique the book. He rejects one: to treat the report "as a serious scholarly piece" because it reveals "so many arbitrary assumptions, glaring omissions, and egregious oversimplications that a criticism along these lines could fill reams." (The author then proceeds to present several examples of what he considers to be invalid assumptions, etc.) He contents himself with with attempting to answer the question: "Is there any value in the kind of exercise carried out by *The Limits to Growth*, even if it is done less badly?"

Finding little use for the model which was used, Ruff is concerned that "clever packaging can turn scientific disaster into commercial success." The result is that the "existence of flashy, over-sold cures may distract the patient from seeking the tedious treatment that holds real promise of helping him . . . ."

Ruff himself tries to posit an answer to the "limits-to-growth" dilemma. "Although we will be unable to predict exactly where society will be a hundred years from now, if the social system is correctly structured we can be reasonably certain that society will be in a state which is acceptable to its members and better than any we could determine for them." [It should be noted that this optimistic forecast leaves Ruff open to the same type of criticism—posing conclusions which may be unfounded—that he levels against *The Limits to Growth.*]

In the article titled "A Blueprint For Survival"—published in **The Ecologist** magazine—a team of scientists predict that "if current trends are allowed to persist, the breakdown of society and the irreversible disruption of the life-support systems on this planet . . . are inevitable." (This statement, and the conclusions of that team, shortly predated the publication of the report of the Club of Rome.

The article states: "*Indefinite* growth of whatever type cannot be sustained by *finite* resources. This is the nub of the environmental predicament." It sees the casual regard for ecosystems as unacceptable, and ultimately, as destructive to humankind. But, it is alleged, man has "set himself the goal of reducing it to rubble in the shortest possible time." The authors then proceed to discuss various potential failures: of world food supplies, exhaustion of resources, and the collapse of society. [Some would see many of the conclusions as bordering on rhetoric and even gross overstatement at times, with solid observations interspersed throughout. But like much of the early 'doomsday' literature. statements of enormity seem to prevail.]

The article concludes with two sections titled, "Towards the Stable Society: Strategy for Change" and "The Goal." With a series of notable ideas (but using such verbose or confusing terms as antidisamenity legislation), the article nevertheless seems to have ignored many of the economic and social repercussions of its own suggestions. [Some of the proposals are non-pragmatic, and unlikely to bring any local or state decision-maker (who is not already persuaded) into agreement with this line of thinking.]

Back to back in *Ecology Law Quarterly* with the Ruff review (on *The Limits to Growth*) was **Jerome Muys** review of *The Doomsday Syndrome:* a book written in response to the criers of impending doom for this planet. John Maddox—the author *The Doomsday Syndrome*—feels that doomsday preaching may accomplish quite the opposite "of what its authors intend. Instead of alerting people to important problems, it may seriously undermine the capacity of the human race to look out for its survival." Five chapters of the book indict the claims of the doomsday prophets, in a manner which Muys calls "a scholarly, skillfully constructed 'lawyer's brief' attempting to blunt, if not wholly refute, the principal factual assumptions and exaggerations . . . ."

Much of the Muys review provides, in effect, a digest/synopsis version of the major ideas of the book, with scattered editorial comments. He states that several of the book's themes are "patently debating or briefing techniques, reflecting the kind of argumentative posturing so well known to lawyers, and cannot be taken seriously . . ." Yet, Maddox seems to make "a good case for his brief that society has within its power the ability to make the political decisions necessary to avoid doomsday."

A cogent observation by Muys, is that: "Maddox repeatedly finds it necessary to minimize the current environment predicament as a corollary to his call to arms for a determined response . . . . This is unfortunate, since it seems quite clear that both premises are true: environmental pollution *is* a threat to the global environment *and* strong institutional responses *are* essential."

There is an element here, says Muys, of "making mountains out of molehills. . . . Little harm has yet materialized from the doomsday syndrome diagnosed by Dr. Maddox. If anything, society appears to have responded to the 'extremist' cries of alarm relatively expeditiously . . . ."

But one is left to ruminate on a curious policy-making dilemma regarding global resource restrictions. It would seem unlikely that in the daily decision-making of a local official, the world's growth-saturation limits will be discussed; on the other hand, the establishment of a local limits method, such as large-lot zoning, may be proposed and debated at length. Such a change may impact heavily both on public planning decisions and on the mode and costs of land development undertaken in that particular jurisdiction.

Growth is not so much a product of grand global schemes, as it is the result of a series of local, incremental decisions.

Richard Zeckhauser identifies himself as the "defender of the out-of-fashion view that growth is not pernicious, but desirable." He summarizes his article's three basic sections as follows. "Ground Rules: Many objections to economic growth would vanish if appropriate terminologies were defined and ground rules established. Predictions: There is no convincing evidence that slowing growth would create a rosier present or future. Distribution of Welfare: An antigrowth policy would help some groups and hurt others, and there is no compelling argument that the groups it would help are more deserving than those it would harm."

The author sees as invalid the belief that there could be "a central decision-maker, using the investment rate as a throttle, . . . [to] ease us onto a Golden Age track." He finds the experience of government tampering with the economy in the past, as more likely to result in an "economy out of kilter, producing an entirely inappropriate mix of goods and services."

The major portion of the article concentrates on the effects of such policies on individual's welfare, the distributional effects of growth, the risks of economic growth, and issues "beyond the economic perspective." Zeckhauser touches on a number of the social side-effects which are discussed in the next several articles in this chapter; but as he correctly notes, "Social decline . . . is a fuzzy concept, difficult to observe, and . . . introduces a danger into the growth debate."

Roland McKean seeks to take a broad overview of "Growth vs. No-Growth." He does not think that "the most highly publicized costs of growth [as in *The Limits to Growth*] are by themselves so ruinous and unmanageable," because the political process will often provide partial (though not wholly satisfactory) responses to growing limits problems; likewise, the private sector will make some "automatic adjustments." "Thus, I assert . . . that a sensible scenario for the future portrays declines of wealth and a series of painful adjustments, including a leveling-off or decline of population, but not a sudden collapse of any kind." There will be some accompanying degree of environmental deterioration and use of exhaustible resources.

The author then poses a host of other side-effects of growth, many of which are not often discussed; he labels these "Poverty of the Spirit" problems: "pervasive control and ownership by government," a reduction in durable relationships due to a high degree of personal mobility, and a "decline of [desirable] customs and behavioral rules." He nevertheless admits that: "Perhaps growth has nothing to do with these phenomena . . . [but] I cannot help believing that continued growth will make it harder and harder for us to avoid interfering with each other, harder and harder for us to govern ourselves."

The article then addresses no-growth: a number of strategies for meeting/enforcing it, and the disadvantages of zero economic growth (the latter include those "inherently associated with a static as opposed to a dynamic economy, and some connected with the particular measures required to implement a ZEG policy"). This would include restricted choice of products (via central planning), drops in real income with little prospect for future increases, a somewhat static society, distributional conflicts and bitterness (individual as well as international), fewer changes in technology, lessened creativity, and even—"spiritual poverty."

McKean uses an intriguing analogy: no-growth is a ham-handed strategy akin to "reducing a city's power supply by 10 percent in order to reduce fires, accidental electrocutions, and atrocious movies." He instead prefers the strategy of "levying of externality-charges," taxing nonrenewable resources more heavily, and increasing research on energy/pollution/population control.

In the next article, the Chairman of the President's Council on Environmental Quality—**Russell Peterson**—strikes the chord that "Any program to limit population growth must be developed in harmony with human dignity and individual freedom." Following this truism however, is a statement that might present the analyst with some problems, "In turn, limiting population will enhance such dignity and freedom and help people everywhere to realize their highest potential." [The author seems to be drawing this conclusion from the fact that limits to population "means" everyone can be fed adequately. Very few of the repercussions of zero-growth are quite so simplistic or beneficial. In the next article, Klein for example, presents contrasting ideas and forebodings.]

The title of the article by **Rudolf Klein**, in "The Trouble With a Zero-Growth World," states that the perils of continued growth are "guaranteed to chill the spines . . . of agnostics," but at the same time "it is imperative to explore some of the implications of moving in this direction [of a nongrowth society]." The major theme of Klein, is that in fact there can be sketched "a scenario of social catastrophe in a nongrowth society to equal, in its horror, the scenario of ecological catastrophe in a growth society."

The author investigates one line of reasoning; that continued economic growth currently tends to blunt the "edge of conflict" of competing groups in society, some of which are trying to improve their position (housing, etc.). This in turn provides expectations in a "game in which everyone can win at least something." In the reverse—non-growth society is a zero-sum game. Thus, the author claims, it is possible that "the politics of compromise would be replaced by the politics of revolution." (This would become even worse in regard to international disparities, where the relative position of the United States—if frozen by nongrowth—might be unacceptable, and might be felt as tantamount to repudiating hope, condemning "a majority of the globe's inhabitants to permanent poverty."

On the other hand, this may not be the case at all if other assumptions are made, such as the creation of "a new political and social situation." But Klein sees both types of scenarios as rather naive, which "beg crucial questions about what is meant by a nongrowth society . . . ." The author addresses, for example, the idea of nongrowth from two perspectives: zero economic growth, and zero population growth. Moreover, he asks the critical question "how is . . . change to be controlled?" With control, says Klein, there is strong likelihood that growth management would "entail political friction" and would involve (unless there were absolute central control), a "manic-depressive pattern of economic management . . . ."

Though he finds many of the so-called extreme positions improbable, Klein nonetheless returns to an examination of why developing countries would not be particularly appreciative of nongrowth. Moreover, he suggests that "the stable society, in population and economic terms, might turn out to be, in political and military terms, a singularly unstable one." He believes however, that in a slowly-adjusting future, it is most likely that "societies of economic satiety" would first gradually emphasize nongrowth; in turn, these changes would "slowly percolate elsewhere" [to other countries] over a period of decades.

One major study—by the [U.S.] **Commission on Population Growth and the American Future**—addressed the issues of the "pervasive impact of population growth on every facet of American life . . . ." Disclaiming any "simple or immediate solutions," the Commission came to a series of findings and conclusions which are highlighted in this article. [The reader may be interested in referring to the multi-volumed study published by the Commission, for further data and a number of excellent research articles and commentaries.]

"No substantial benefits will result from the continued growth of our population . . ." the report finds, and there seems to be no "convincing economic argument for continued natural population growth." Recognizing that the "lead time is decades in length" in order to achieve population stabilization, the article points out that "it is necessary to face the issue now and come to deliberate and informed decisions about population problems—their burdens, their costs, their remedies."

The Commission's report deals with sometimes unpopular topics: "the control of reproduction . . . population growth for racial and ethnic minorities," illegal immigration, and so forth. It has recommendations with respect to birth control information, maternal and child care programs, equal opportunities in employment, national population distribution, increased comprehensive planning on the metropolitan and regional levels, subsidized housing, and planning for a stabilized national population. The article asserts that "the recommendations we propose are worthwhile for many reasons as well as appropriate to steering a prudent demographic course into a future filled with uncertainties." [When the Commission issued its report, it aroused a great deal of interest; in fact, the issuance of a film setting forth the findings of that Commission was even stifled for several months. The latter detail, while not necessarily important in and of itself, does indicate the resistence to the Report and to its conclusions that was briefly engendered.]

In a report written for the Commission on Population Growth and the American Future, **Lincoln Day** asks what a zero population growth rate portends for the United States . . . "to consider what might be expected, both demographically and socially, of a population that has ceased to grow." Day summarizes some of the demographic possibilities from other parts of the report (as background for his discussion of the social aspects—covering size of population, age structure, sex ratio, marital status, residence, mortality, fertility, and international and internal migration trends.

The author insists that there "are no one-to-one causal relationships between social patterns and a zero rate of population growth . . . . We must avoid lapsing into demographic determinism." With regard to health, for example, Day sees that it is possible but purely conjectural as to whether health needs will be any greater with an increasing percentage of the population consisting of older persons.

The article also covers the social consequences of potential changes in economic conditions (workforce, longevity of training, demand for certain types of products and consumer goods, investment capital); and it goes on to analyze status succession ("a reduction in opportunity" for promotions . . . particularly when retirement occurs at a later age, "a reduction in the levels of aspiration," and a change in the type of reward/ motivation for workers on-the-job). Other areas are the author's analyses of the status of women (lower fertility rates, lower marriage rates, and the need for greater opportunities for personal development); behavior (will societal/personal attitudes change, such as responsiveness to change and reform, political activism, etc.); and personality structure (fewer large families, alterations in birth order and personality development, "less privatism in child care," etc.). One example of the interrelationship of factors, is creativity ("Is creativity affected by the amount of competition? Is it a function of age, and if so, is the change in age structure associated with a stationary population likely to have any effect on the amount and kind of creativity in a society?").

Day concludes with ruminations on social security and public programs; as in previous sections, his findings seldom are stated conclusively. While probably giving little guidance to local planners, the approach nevertheless accomplishes one of the author's objectives to establish that "what is feared has less to do with the consequences of a zero rate of growth itself, than with the consequences of moving too rapidly onto unfamiliar demographic ground before social attitudes and institutions have had the chance to adjust to the new demands posed."

In the next article, **Wilbur Thompson** points out a number of the "Problems That Sprout in the Shadow of No-Growth."

Thompson suggests that: "The sincerity of any brief for the case of no-growth—the protection of the natural environment—is bound to be highly suspect when the protectors live sprawled over half- and full-acre lots, with two or more cars in every driveway, and when they make waste in the good old American way." He adds: "Any policy which permits the local inhabitants to hold their numbers in check simply so they can push their consumption per capita to the limit would seem to be more self-indulgent than environment-concerned."

The majority of the article focuses on the interrelationships between growth and access/opportunity for housing within a community or its market area. If we are to manage growth, then optimally, an urban area would "sort out and weigh the many benefits and costs associated with various rates of local growth and then move to control its own growth." However, he states that "we have much more to learn about these matters but, beyond that, there is little evidence that we are in a position to manage local growth in the social interest."

One of the primary reasons this inability exists, claims Thompson, is that various interest groups hold clout beyond their numbers. Some persons utilize the no-growth for other purposes than environmental protection concerns, and there are those who are under-represented or not represented at all in the debate (typically the renting poor who work, but do not live, in the community). Finally, the author suggests that localities begin to deal directly with the matter, "and control the job formation that generates that growth" . . . rather than to work backwards, and perhaps inequitably, by restraining residential development.

William Alonso views the rapid shift "from the traditional boosterism to a questioning and even an abhorrence of growth," and sees this as due at least in part to the "new Malthusian concern with the consequences of unlimited population growth . . . ." He heavily criticizes local growth control policies as "regressive and counterproductive in terms of social well-being."

For the author, the local debates over growth unfortunately almost inevitably are "based on the limited viewpoint of the municipal corporation, and thus miss many of the most important consequences, good and bad, for the real city" [which he defines as being "composed of people and their relations to each other, to their institutions, and to their physical environment," and not the formal governmental boundaries]. While Alonso points out that the local reactions against growth are understandable from the residents' limited perspectives, this balkanized resist-growth attitude of "local government encourages beggar-thy-neighbor strategies . . . [and] leads to the meanest forms of municipal mercantilism, ones which ignore more important consequences for people."

The article finds that: "Local policy affects primarily the intrametropolitan form and distribution of that development, and, if it is set by the selfish interests of the component municipalities, it does so inefficiently and unjustly." The author quite accurately concludes that "what is viewed as an issue of growth [or no-growth] at a lower level is an issue of distribution at the next higher level. Thus, growth decisions for each locality within a metropolitan area should be bargained out among all the components of the metropolis to insure that their effects on the futures of the other localities will be considered. This is necessary both for fairness and efficiency."

This theme will be reiterated time and again throughout this set . . . from Chapters 6 and 7 of Volume I, through much of Volume II, and in several of the Chapters of Volume III. It is a critical and recurrent issue.

Willard Johnson picks up on the effects of growth management on low income persons, in his article, "Should The Poor Buy No-Growth?" He questions whether the current "superindustrial society is going to be like the 'traditional society . . . [which has] historically, been bottom-heavy with poor people." Then he posits the crucial questions: "What is the proper response of the poor to the call for a return to a no-growth society? Should the poor buy no-growth?"

The answer, to Johnson, is self-evident; the question is nearly irrelevant, as the poor are not going to obtain what the rich won't "sell" or release. Thus, he feels, the answer lies in the fact that "it will take power to alter the direction of fundamental economic trends and patterns of resource utilization in the United States and in the world." (To couch the issue otherwise, the author claims, is only a "ruse.")

Johnson sees that while it is true that many of the poor are structured-in to our society (being "relatively impervious to the benefits of general economic progress"), nevertheless many of the rest can and do benefit somewhat from growth and increases in national productivity. But to arrive at any real solution, he believes we must see that "a lack of continued growth, without substantial change in national policies to facilitate the transfer of wealth and income through transfer payments, tax reform and job development, or vigorous antidiscrimination efforts would probably have disastrous consequences for blacks, and perhaps for the poor more generally." Johnson is convinced that relief is not in sight without the redistribution of wealth and income as a public policy goal and program.

No-growth offers little solace indeed, and yet at the same time the "pro-growthers" are not effective in convincing the poor and minorities that at least certain types of growth are vital or beneficial to their interests. Johnson then returns to his diagnosis of redistribution as the "answer" for the poor [the "managed growth" discussion seems to disappear], and presents an alternative which he feels holds out some hope for as much as 70 percent of the populace. The scheme will probably not find general acceptance, however, because of "pernicious attitudes and practices" regarding the welfare system and individuals' "dependency" on the public dole.

The author's theme that alliances between growth advocates and the poor, or between the middle class and the poor, may occur (and then lead to redistribution schemes) is interesting, liberal, and unfortunately, unconvincing. There is little in it for the controlled-/no- growther segment of the population to form that alliance . . . not at least as it is currently perceiving its own supposed self-interests.

In the last article, **Michael Agelasto** looks more directly at local managed growth strategies, and examines the "Equity Consideration in Controlled Growth Policies." He concludes that ultimately, "growth control policies will remain regressive . . . [unless] the 'haves' are willing to make the necessary trade-offs," and suggests that in a no-growth economy "the poor and their liberal advocates . . . should seek positive controls [as those outlined here] rather than argue for growth." Also, planners should examine proposed policies "both for regressive and equitable side-effects."

The author points out that there are differential impacts on various sub-groups of the poor (as the aged, the handicapped, etc.). [This suggests still another reason why it is perhaps almost impossible to obtain the type of political consensus suggested by Johnson in the previous article.] Agelasto then does a quick, but useful scan of the literature relating to the limits to growth issue . . . but concludes that both the growth and the no-growth citizen advocates are muddled and defensive in much of their thinking.

The article follows the thesis that "no-growth will become a reality for many communities; that even if growth were possible it would not necessarily help eradicate poverty; and that local communities attempting to control growth should do so in an equitable way." Agelasto then speaks to the techniques often utilized to control growth, noting that "most of the instrumentalities used by localities for controlling growth are regressive" . . . and makes the critical point that these instrumentalities "hurt the poor without substantially hurting others, and sometimes in fact make the rich better off." [While perhaps partly inaccurate, the statement's implicit conclusion is nonetheless valid: the disenfranchised, fragmented, body of the "poor" makes for an ineffectual and non-influential political animal indeed.]

In the section titled "Inner City Vs. Outer City" and "Positive Local Controls," many of the author's points are intriguing [but often problematic].

But then much of the field, when it attempts to propose "solutions" which are equitable and which serve the broad spectrum of the public interest, tends toward the "fair" but the naive. One is led, perhaps, to believe that these dilemmas cannot be viewed with any real optimism for the near future. This is a theme which underlies much of the work in the next two chapters [Chapters 6 and 7], which deal with the exclusionary effects of local land controls.

—RWS

The Problem
of Growth

and The Limits to Growth

J. Ross Macdonald

J. Ross Macdonald is Vice President of Corporate Research and Development at Texas Instruments, Inc. He is a member of the National Academy of Sciences and the National Academy of Engineering, Chairman of the Numerical Data Advisory Board of the National Research Council, and was Associate Physicist at Argonne National Laboratory. Mr. Macdonald is a graduate of Williams College; he holds a bachelor's and a master's of science from the Massachusetts Institute of Technology; and he has a Ph.D. of philosophy and a Ph.D. of science from Oxford University, England.

This article originally appeared in Research Management Journal *under a similar title, and is reprinted with permission from* Research Management Journal, *November, 1973.*

The question of the role of technology in world problems is both a difficult one and a vitally important one. Viewpoints can range between the extremes of technocratic optimism that technology alone can solve the major problems of the world, to the pessimistic Luddite view that technology is at best irrelevant to the solutions of these problems and may, in fact, be the root cause for many or all of them.

First what are some of these major problems? There is considerable agreement that among them should be numbered exponentially growing world population, depletion of non-renewable resources by exponentially growing industrial output, exponentially increasing pollution of the environment, marginal world food production, and the vast and probably increasing disparity in living standards between the citizens of rich and poor nations. The main problem is thus the approaching collision between continued growth of all kinds and the inevitably limited resources and carrying capacity of space-ship earth.

As most of you know, Dennis Meadows and his colleagues at the Massachusetts Institute of Technology published in 1972, with the support of the prestigious Club of Rome, a now famous report of their computerized world model in the book, *The Limits to Growth.* This model, which, it is emphasized, is preliminary, oversimplified, and unfinished, yields the result that growth will stop and the world economy catastrophically collapse in the next 40 to at most 100 years unless exponential growth of some of the main factors, such as population, stops occurring relatively soon. Meadows and his colleagues believe that there is still a short time remaining in which to alter the exponential growth trends and approach a condition of ecological and economic equilibrium.

The Problem of Growth

A major element in the results of the *Limits* study is the short time remaining before wholesale disaster comes according to this world model. That there must be a limit to growth is nothing new. Everyone knows that population will stop increasing, given even unlimited food and energy, before the point is reached that people are packed too close together to move. This is, if nothing else, a simple consequence of reproductive biology!

Meadows and Aurelio Peccei, the head of the Club of Rome, insist that their world model is designed for exploring the long-term dynamic properties of complex systems but is not intended as a forecasting model; thus, the M.I.T. research is explorative, not predictive. They, nevertheless, maintain that their conclusions, such as world collapse in 100 years or less, are meaningful, important, and should be taken seriously. The distinction they make here is too fine a one to mean much to me. When is prediction not prediction?

Many criticisms have been leveled against the *Limits* model, too many to discuss in detail here. Of particular importance seems to be the lack of a functioning price system in the model. In addition, there are no continuous increases in technology and productivity incorporated in the model structure, no adaptive learning, and no account taken of social and political factors. In spite of its complexity, the model is too simple, and no serious attempt to validate it has been made.

Dr. R. Golub, an English physicist who has studied the model and its results, believes that it represents an attempt to substitute mathematics for knowledge and computation for understanding. A danger in models of this kind is that they give a spurious appearance of precise knowledge of quantities and relationships and a false sense of confidence in their results. It has been well said, that in such a computerized approach there is less there than meets the eye.

In spite of statements by Meadows that the*Limits* model is preliminary and unfinished, the great publicity it has had and the authors' own assertions that its conclusions are meaningful and important have seemingly led too many people to believe that since its results follow from the model they should indeed be taken seriously. Although one should never lose sight of the crucial fact that a model is not the real world, the results of a model may sometimes be valid and important in the real world, nevertheless, even though their method of deduction, through the model, may be highly suspect.

In the *Limits* study, one has trouble avoiding the suspicion that "the model is the message." Meadows himself has emphasized that only about 0.1% of the data needed to construct a satisfactory world model is now available. It is, in fact, dangerous that the old computer adage, GIGO, standing for garbage in, garbage out, has evidently been reinterpreted by many to mean, in the context of the *Limits* study: garbage in, gospel out.

Whatever the defects and merits of the *Limits* book, it has done the world the very valuable service of emphasizing that continued growth strongly exacerbates world problems and that there are indeed definite limits to growth, no matter when the world will actually run up against them.

There are two main choices facing us. We can continue our present unrestricted growth until catastrophe comes, brought about by the limits imposed from the outside by nature and, as in the past, involving the four horsemen of the apocalypse: conquest, war, famine, and death. Alternatively, we can institute a program aimed at achieving a worldwide limitation to growth, in order to begin approaching a long-term viable equilibrium.

What can technology bring to the problem of limiting world growth? Dr. Peccei, perhaps speaking for the Club of Rome, leans to the pessimistic side. He believes that the "moral and cultural crises in human nature cannot be substantially cured by technological fixes or solutions or simplistic political or philanthropic arrangements between rich and poor." By implication he thus implies that technological solutions are simplistic. In a sense this is correct since even perfect technological solutions generally require governmental, political, economic, and social imperatives and changes for their successful implementation. Many of the most crucial world problems require for their solution widespread change in people and their attitudes. Such change, while it can be aided by technology, is far more difficult to achieve than is continued progress in technology alone.

On the perhaps more optimistic side we find Herman Kahn, the well-known designer of scenarios of possible futures. He believes that we already have sufficient technology to solve world problems and that during the next 100 years or so it will be applied well enough that world population will stabilize at a viable level of 15 to 30 billion people. To me this isn't really a happy view. I predict that all of us who are eating enough, or perhaps too much, today would find a world containing about 10-times more people than it now has most unpleasant, even if actually viable on a purely physical level.

Instead, I submit we need to design and realize a world that in some important sense maximizes and maintains the product of human quality and excellence by human quantity; a resultant I will denote by πw, since π is the usual symbol for a product. Clearly, neither the extreme of one Christ-like person as the sole world inhabitant nor 30 to 50 billion ape-like citizens of earth maximizes πw. Somewhere in between these extremes, at an overall population level which can be indefinitely maintained on earth, we should establish the maximum πw condition, that where all are able to approach maximum individual self-realization for the good of all. I grant you that this sounds suspiciously like πw in the sky by and by; yet I believe it is a realizable and noble goal.

Man must accept the responsibility of being the pilot of spaceship earth. Earthkeeping responsibilities and professions must be developed and institutionalized. Piloting goes poorly in the dark. We must not turn our backs on science and technology, which will continue to be needed to dispel the darkness of ignorance. Yet we must be vigilant to ensure that these unparalleled tools remain servants, not masters and are used to cut through problems rather than turning against us in our hands. The British biologist Peter Medawar has well said, "The bells that toll for mankind are attached to our own neck, and it must be our fault if they do not make a cheerful and harmonious sound."

Only in the last few decades have we really begun to understand that the most important goal of science must be to understand the physical world in order to understand and master ourselves rather than just to master the rest of nature. Mastery without wisdom is devilish rather than divine. I strongly believe we need a new and greater Copernican revolution where each individual gives up something of his view of being the center of the universe and perceives the true center in the hopes, aspirations, and realization of the potentialities of all mankind now and in the full future.

A final challenge has been well put by Carl Sandburg in *The People, Yes.* He said:

> The white man drew a small circle in the sand and told the red man, "This is what the Indian knows," and drawing a big circle around the small one, "This is what the white man knows." The Indian took the stick and swept an immense ring around both circles. "This is where the white man and the red man know nothing."

May I remind you that "science" is derived from the latin verb "to know?"

The Limits
to Growth:

A Review*

Larry E. Ruff

Larry Ruff is Program Officer at the Office of Resources and Environment, Ford Foundation. He formerly was director of the Washington Environmental Research Center, Environmental Protection Agency, and was an assistant professor of economics, University of California at San Diego. Dr. Ruff is a graduate of the California Institute of Technology and holds a doctorate from Stanford University.

This article—a digest of the original—is reprinted with permission, and originally appeared in Ecology Law Quarterly, volume 2, page 879, 1972, School of Law, University of California at Berkeley. The views are those of the author and do not necessarily reflect the views of The Ford Foundation or the U.S. Environmental Protection Agency.

Chutzpah! Incredible, outrageous *chutzpah!* What else can be said about a work which reduces the world to a handful of basic variables, invents a few interrelationships among these, makes some wild guesses about the form and magnitude of these interrelationships, grinds the whole thing through the electronic idiot, and then presents the little exercise as something "so fundamental and general that we do not expect our broad conclusions to be substantially altered by further revisions."[1] Now *that* is *chutzpah!*

The work at issue was sponsored by the Club of Rome's "Project on the Predicament of Mankind" and published with more fanfare than anything in recent years, with the possible exception of *The Pentagon Papers.* Over a period of twelve long months, a mathematical model was constructed which, in the humble view of the authors, revealed the "basic behavior modes"[2] of global society over longtime-horizons. When they found that the world they had created with such care always collapsed, either from pollution, resource exhaustion, overpopulation, or some combination of these, they rushed out to alert the oblivious world to the impending disaster. It is all more than a little reminiscent of an old story about a falling acorn, Chicken Little, and the sky.

The reviewer of *The Limits to Growth* is faced with a difficult choice, namely, on which level to criticize the work? There are several distinct and rich approaches available. The most tempting is to criticize the style and mode of presentation. Although such great fun that it cannot completely be resisted, this approach does not get to the real issues and is unbecoming to anyone who has not authored his own best-seller.

A second inviting level of criticism is to treat *The Limits to Growth* as a serious scholarly piece and to make more-or-less constructive comments about particular assumptions or parameter values used in the model. Even though most details of the model have been carefully confined to obscure manuscripts hidden in Cambridge desk drawers, the flow diagrams, graphs, and prose in *The Limits to Growth* reveal so many arbitrary assumptions, glaring omissions, and egregious oversimplifications that a criticism along these lines could fill reams. One could point out that neither "pollution" nor "nonrenewable resources" can be treated as a single, aggregate variable, or that it is absurd to make the birth rate a simple function of industrial output per capita and life expectancy. One could suggest that a model purporting to represent the world system might include a price variable or two, since there is occasional speculation that economic factors have something to do with the way the world operates; maybe it would be better to assume capital-output ratios, lifetimes of capital, fraction of land harvested, natural resources used per unit of output, etc., are determined somehow *inside* the world system rather than being set arbitrarily by some external power. One could raise a question about the assertion that it will be impossible within the next century to reduce the pollution per unit of industrial output to less than one-fourth of its present value, perhaps by pointing to United States plans to reduce this ratio to ten percent or less of present values for many major pollutants within the next decade or so; of course, reduction of this magnitude will require substantial investments in pollution control equipment and the authors have seen fit to preclude such investments from their model. One might suggest that future development patterns will be different from those in the past, that Brazilians in the year 2015 will not produce and consume the same way Americans did in 1870, even if their income level is the same. One could, in fact, suggest an equally realistic set of assumptions for the authors' model which would result in predictions of Utopia for the next century.

This line of criticism, which could be extended indefinitely, suffers from serious defects. For one thing, bringing The Limits to Growth into the arena of ordinary academic debate lends respectability to what is essentially an irresponsible work. More to the point, criticism of details implies acceptance of the basic method used in this study and diverts the discussion from a more fundamental question: Is there any value in the kind of exercise carried out by The Limits of Growth, even if it is done less badly? Since this question must be addressed in order to put the book in perspective, the criticism here will be directed toward the methods used by the Meadows' group and not at the details or style of Limits.

The Limits to Modeling

The basic analytical device of Limits is simulation modeling, in which the real system being modeled is defined in terms of "state variables" (e.g., population, capital stock, pollution levels, etc.) and relationships or "feedback loops" among them which determine how the state variables change from one time period to the next. Once the analyst decides which variables are important in his model, specifies exactly the structure of the feedback system, and selects the magnitude of the parameters, it is a straightforward exercise to crank out the "behavior modes" of the model as far into the future as desired; in fact, the process is so mechanical that it can be done even by a computer.

The process of setting up and running a simulation model is so logical and so mechanical that it is a natural for computer programmers and engineers. But, obviously, there is no magic in it which gives the systems analyst any special insight into human motivations, social processes, or institutions, or the evolution of the world social system over time. And the process is "dynamic" only in the trivial sense that one of the mathematical variables is called "time" and not at all in the truly fundamental sense that social values, institutions, and processes *change* over time. Each behavioral relation must be specified, each feedback loop identified, each parameter value selected before the computer can do its mechanical thing; and once the computer has begun, the future is absolutely determined, with no possibilities for change except those which have been anticipated and built into the model by the analyst.

Simulation modeling, then, is limited by the same thing that limits other methods of analyzing and predicting social events: our knowledge of social and physical processes. If we understand how these processes operate over several generations into the future and under new and unprecedented circumstances, then we are very wise indeed and we may, if we choose, display this wisdom in the form of a simulation model. But if we do not understand these things, then we had best be humble and refrain from making fools of ourselves by pretending to wisdom—in the form of a simulation model or in any other form. Models which summarize and integrate our limited knowledge, or which are designed to be tested by rigorous statistical techniques and thereby add to our limited knowledge are valuable and indispensable scientific tools. But models which try to hide our ignorance behind a facade of mathematical gimmickry or which imply that there is some clever substitute for understanding are dangerous toys.

How To Sell a Bad Model

Because of the inherent limitations in our understanding of the world, any effort to model global human society over a century or so is doomed to be a scientific failure. However, The Limits to Growth has demonstrated that clever packaging can turn scientific disaster into commercial success. Since there are likely to be many more such products on the market in the near future, it is worth alerting the potential customer to some of the likely packaging tricks he will encounter.

An extremely valuable device for the pusher of a bad model is the misuse of "sensitivity analysis." Sensitivity analysis is a standard procedure in modeling, in which the analyst varies assumptions in the model to determine which are most critical to the outcome. If small changes in some parameter value or in some structural feature of the model produce large changes in the behavior of the model, the conscientious analyst will alert his audience to be cautious in accepting his conclusions until they are confident that the critical assumptions are correct. The less conscientious analyst, on the other hand, will ignore the critical features of his model and will emphasize the unimportant ones, pointing out that large changes in *some* parameters have little effect suggesting that this proves his results are independent of the precise assumptions made throughout his model.

The Limits to Growth provides an extreme example of this technique. The model in *Limits* assumes that human society goes speeding drunkenly along until it plows head-on into a solid wall of resource exhaustion or pollution or starvation, with no anticipation of the wall and no braking action or change of direction. For example, the birth rate is assumed to be an increasing function of gross industrial output per capita with a lag of "a generation or two";[3] this results in a rapidly rising birth rate in a time of starvation and deprivation, as people keep having babies, because gross industrial output (not even consumption) was high during their grandparents' lifetimes.

The issue here is not the absurdity of this and similar features of the model—it is the critical nature of these features. Does The Limits to Growth alert us to these assumptions or investigate the effects of making birth rates a function of consumption or perhaps of *changes* in consumption, or shorten the lags involved and see how this affects the behavior of the model? No. It points with pride to the trivial fact that a society which is assumed to speed headlong into a wall does not much care exactly where that wall is! Double the initial stock of resources or change other external parameters and it makes no difference: the world rushes headlong to its preprogrammed doom. Therefore, say the authors, do not quibble about details of the model—they are all unimportant. It will be a long time, one hopes, before we are exposed to a more disingenuous use of sensitivity analysis to package a bad product.

Another device for giving an illusion of validity to a bad model is to demonstrate that the model "fits" past observed behavior of the system being modeled. Of course, the model should fit the observed world and an attempt to make it do so is the minimum effort at scientific validation which should be tolerated. It is perhaps noteworthy that The Limits to Growth makes only passing reference to how well the model fits the past observed behavior of the world. But a good fit does not prove anything about the validity of a model unless the model is "small" relative to the number and detail of real-world observations used. If the model is large and complex, with many unknown parameter values to be determined, while the number of real-world observations is small, it is a simple matter to choose the parameter values so that the model output fits the observations very closely and still have a large number of parameters which can be chosen to produce whatever future the analyst desires; in the simplest case, a straight line can be made to fit exactly a single point, and still have any desired slope. When a large model is "calibrated" or "validated" on a small body of data, a "good fit" means only that the analyst knows how to do his algebra; it says little about the validity of the model as a description of reality.

A particularly disarming sales pitch for the Meadows-type stuff is to admit most of the weakness mentioned above, but to argue that the present model "is the most useful model now available for dealing with problems far out on the space-time graph."[4] After all, runs this line, one must have some method of predicting the distant future if one is to make intelligent decisions; so we had better use the extant simulation model until we have a better one. It can't hurt and may even help.

There is something to this argument, of course, just as there is some truth to the analogous argument of the purveyor of patent medicines or cancer cures. But the dangers are also analogous. The existence of flashy, over-sold cures may distract the patient from seeking the tedious treatment that holds real promise of helping him; and the prospect of fame and fortune in the quick-cure market may divert resources from more productive uses. Before putting much effort into finding the best snake oil or world model, we had better be certain that snake oil or a world model is what we need for the problem at hand.

Is There Another Way?

The basic premise underlying most of the Limits-style activity is that the proper way to prepare for the distant future is to predict it. Having predicted it, we decide which features of it are undesirable and then take direct actions which, according to our predictive model, will eliminate the undesirable features of the future. For example, the authors assert:

> [A]ll of the "natural" constraints to population growth operate [by raising] the death rate. Any society wishing to avoid that result must take deliberate action to control the positive feedback loop—to reduce the birth rate.[5]

Ignoring how ridiculous the assertion is, the method is clear enough: predict the future; identify its undesirable features; take direct action to eliminate them.

If this were the proper way to deal with the distant future, we would be in serious trouble indeed. Our predictive methods are and always will be hopelessly inadequate. We have no way to evaluate the future for our great-grandchildren, and any attempt to change the future is as likely to make it worse as to make it better. There is an alternative, namely, to structure social institutions in such a way that the future largely takes care of itself. If the social system has the proper feedback and adjustment mechanisms built into it, if it provides incentives and opportunities for those most near the problems to look for and find solutions and to anticipate and to insure against the unknown future, then it will be able to adjust to the future as it unfolds, automatically making the proper adjustments along the way. Although we will be unable to predict exactly where society will be a hundred years from now, if the social system is correctly structured we can be reasonably certain that society will be in a state which is acceptable to its members and better than any we could determine for them. Unless we feel a compulsion to dictate to our great-grandchildren, we should desire nothing more.

The population example is instructive. We cannot know what population will be in eighty years. If we could know, we would not know whether it is too large or too small even in terms of our own preferences, because we cannot know what technological and economic conditions will be; and it would be presumptuous of us to judge for our great-grandchildren how they will feel about crowding, urbanization, etc. So how can we make a judgment that all-out efforts must be made to hold population at 1975 levels? We cannot. What we can do is to improve our understanding of what social processes determine population growth, what feedbacks are operating to adjust population levels to technical and economic circumstances and to the values of the society, whatever these may be. If we find weaknesses in the feedback structure then we can suggest policies for strengthening it. For example, perhaps parents do not bear enough of the social cost of children and should be made to do so. We might suggest changes which would strengthen this stabilizing feedback in the sytem, even though we have no idea how large future populations will be. The emphasis should be on improving the ability of the social system to adjust to, and not on refining our "best guess" about, the unknown and unknowable future.

This process must, of course, involve modeling of the social system as a means of integrating and testing our understanding. But if the analysts forget to turn off the computer some night and come in the next morning to find that their model has "predicted" disaster in ninety years, they will recognize that it is their model and not the world which is running amok. They will ask themselves what is wrong with their model that caused it to produce such an unlikely result and will go back to careful analysis of the real world as the best means of improving their model—not the other way around. If this sounds like a dull and tedious task compared to the exercise the Meadows' group went through, it is. Some acts are tough to follow.

The Limits to Chutzpah

All this discussion really misses the point, of course. The Limits to Growth should not be judged by ordinary scientific criteria because the book's analysis is on a different level—in fact, several different levels. On a scientific level, The Limits to Growth will be a success in the same sense that Piltdown Man was a scientific success—it will stir discussion and inspire work on both sides of the great debate about its validity. Although most of this induced effort will follow Limits and will, therefore, be misdirected, inevitably some good work on social systems will result and *Limits* will get enough credit to be called a success by its authors and sponsors.

On yet another level, *The Limits to Growth* is bound to be successful, because it joins *The Population Bomb*[6] and other doomsday works in a unique and enviable position. In effect, these works have looked ahead and seen that certain social adjustments are inevitable, have asserted that society is doomed because there is no chance that these adjustments will be made, and then have offered doomed society one small hope: if we take their advice, we can be saved. We must take drastic action to stop population growth, recycle resources, change consumption practices, develop new technology, make goods and capital last longer, change agricultural methods, control pollution, conserve energy, etc. Our only hope is to follow their prescriptions.

Like Balboa ordering the sun to go dark, these prophets are taking no great risks. They know or should know that the actions they command are nothing more than the adjustments a smooth-running society will make to changing circumstances. Birth rates are dropping, resources are recycled, consumption patterns are changing, and technology is being developed not because someone looked at a world model and realized that some parameter would have to be changed, but because the real world has built-in feedbacks and stabilizing forces which the prophets of doom, inadvertently or otherwise, neglected to include in their models. When society has successfully adjusted, they will step forward to take credit for showing us the way to salvation; and that will put them very near the limits to *chutzpah.*

Footnotes

*The Limits to Growth: A Report of the Club of Rome's Project on the Predicament of Mankind. By Donella H. Meadows, Dennis L. Meadows, Jorgen Randers, and William W. Behrens III. New York: Universe Books. 1972. $2.75 (paper).
1. D. H. Meadows, D. L. Meadows, J. Randers, & W. Behrens III, The Limits to Growth: A Report of the Club of Rome's Project on the Predicament of Mankind 22 (1972) [hereinafter cited as Meadows].
2. Id.
3. Meadows, supra note 1, at 117.
4. Id. at 21.
5. Id. at 159.
6. P. Ehrlich, The Population Bomb (1968).

A Blueprint For Survival:

Excerpts

The Ecologist

> *According to* The Ecologist *magazine: "This document was drawn up by a team of British scientists and philosophers professionally involved in the study of global environmental problems. The aim of their full report is to 'herald the dawn of a new age' in which 'Man will learn to live with the rest of Nature rather than against it.'"*

> *The article, by the same title, originally appeared in the January 1972 issue of* The Ecologist *(73 Kew Green; Richmond, Surrey; England), and is reprinted here with permission from the Houghton Mifflin Company, Boston, Massachusetts.*

Preface

This document has been drawn up by a small team of people, all of whom, in different capacities, are professionally involved in the study of global environmental problems. Four considerations have prompted us to do this:

1. An examination of the relevant information available has impressed upon us the extreme gravity of the global situation today. For, if current trends are allowed to persist, the breakdown of society and the irreversible disruption of the life-support systems on this planet, possibly by the end of the century, certainly within the lifetimes of our children, are inevitable.
2. Governments, and ours is no exception, are either refusing to face the relevant facts, or are briefing their scientists in such a way that their seriousness is played down. Whatever the reasons, no corrective measures of any consequence are being undertaken.
3. This situation has already prompted the formation of the Club of Rome, a group of scientists and industrialists from many countries, which is currently trying to persuade governments, industrial leaders and trade unions throughout the world to face these facts and to take appropriate action while there is yet time. It must now give rise to a national movement to act at a national level, and if need be to assume political status and contest the next general election. It is hoped that such an example will be emulated in other countries, thereby giving rise to an international movement, complementing the invaluable work being done by the Club of Rome.
4. Such a movement cannot hope to succeed unless it has previously formulated a new philosophy of life, whose goals can be achieved without destroying the environment, and a precise and comprehensive programme for bringing about the sort of society in which it can be implemented.

This we have tried to do, and our *Blueprint for Survival* heralds the formation of the *Movement For Survival* and, it is hoped, the dawn of a new age in which Man will learn to live with the rest of Nature rather than against it.

Introduction: The Need for Change

[*Editor's Note: this section of the "Blueprint" is reprinted in full—less the illustrations.*]

110. The principal defect of the industrial way of life with its ethos of expansion is that it is not sustainable. Its termination within the lifetime of someone born today is inevitable—unless it continues to be sustained for a while longer by an entrenched minority at the cost of imposing great suffering on the rest of mankind. We can be certain, however, that sooner or later it will end (only the precise time and circumstances are in doubt), and that it will do so in one of two ways: either against our will, in a succession of famines, epidemics, social crises and wars; or because we want it to—because we wish to create a society which will not impose hardship and cruelty upon our children—in a succession of thoughtful, humane and measured changes. We believe that a growing number of people are aware of this choice, and are more interested in our proposals for creating a sustainable society than in yet another recitation of the reasons why this should be done. We will therefore consider these reasons only briefly, reserving a fuller analysis for the four appendices which follow the *Blueprint* proper. [*Material omitted.*]

111. Radical change is both necessary and inevitable because the present increases in human numbers and *per capita* consumption, by disrupting ecosystems and depleting resources, are undermining the very foundations of survival. At present the world population of 3,600 million is increasing by 2 per cent per year (72 million), but this overall figure conceals crucially important differences between countries. The industrialised countries with one-third of the world population have annual growth rates of between 0.5 and 1.0 per cent; the undeveloped countries on the other hand, with two-thirds of the world population, have annual growth rates of between 2 and 3 per cent, and from 40 to 45 per cent of their populations is under 15. It is commonly overlooked that in countries with an unbalanced age structure of this kind the population will continue to increase for many years even after fertility has fallen to the replacement level. As the Population Council has pointed out: "If replacement is achieved in the developed world by 2000 and in the developing world by 2040, then the world's population will stabilise at nearly 15.5 billion (15,500 million) about a century hence, or well over four times the present size."

112. The *per capita* use of energy and raw materials also shows a sharp division between the developed and the undeveloped parts of the world. Both are increasing their use of these commodities, but consumption in the developed countries is so much higher that, even with their smaller share of the population, their consumption may well represent over 80 per cent of the world total. For the same reason, similar percentage increases are far more significant in the developed countries; to take one example, between 1957 and 1967 *per capita* steel consumption rose by 12 per cent in the US and by 41 per cent in India, but the actual increases (in kg per year) were from 568 to 634 and from 9.2 to 13 respectively. Nor is there any sign that an eventual end to economic growth is envisaged, and indeed industrial economies appear to break down if growth ceases or even slows, however high the absolute level of consumption. Even the US still aims at an annual growth of GNP of 4 per cent or more. Within this overall figure much higher growth rates occur for the use of particular resources, such as oil.

113. The combination of human numbers and *per capita* consumption has a considerable impact on the environment, in terms of both the resources we take from it and the pollutants we impose on it. A distinguished group of scientists, who came together for a

A Blueprint For Survival

"Study of Critical Environmental Problems" (SCEP) under the auspices of the Massachusetts Institute of Technology, state in their report the clear need for a means of measuring this impact, and have coined the term "ecological demand," which they define as "a summation of all man's demands on the environment, such as the extraction of resources and the return of wastes." Gross Domestic Product (GDP), which is population multiplied by material standard of living appears to provide the most convenient measure of ecological demand, and according to the UN *Statistical Yearbook* this is increasing annually by 5 to 6 per cent, or doubling every 13.5 years. If this trend should continue, then in the time taken for world population to double (which is estimated to be by just after the year 2000), total ecological demand will have increased by a factor of six. SCEP estimates that "such demand-producing activities as agriculture, mining and industry have global annual rates of increase of 3.5 per cent and 7 per cent respectively. An integrated rate of increase is estimated to be between 5 and 6 per cent per year, in comparison with an annual rate of population increase of only 2 per cent."

114. It should go without saying that the world cannot accommodate this continued increase in ecological demand. *Indefinite* growth of whatever type cannot be sustained by *finite* resources. This is the nub of the environmental predicament. It is still less possible to maintain indefinite *exponential* growth—and unfortunately the growth of ecological demand is proceeding exponentially (i.e. it is increasing geometrically, by compound interest).

115. The implications of exponential growth are not generally appreciated and are well worth considering. As Professor Forrester explains it,[1] ". . . pure exponential growth possesses the characteristic of behaving according to a 'doubling time.' Each fixed time interval shows a doubling of the relevant system variable. Exponential growth is treacherous and misleading. A system variable can continue through many doubling intervals without seeming to reach significant size. But then in one or two more doubling periods, still following the same law of exponential growth, it suddenly seems to become overwhelming."

116. Thus, supposing world petroleum reserves stood at 2,100 billion barrels, and supposing our rate of consumption was increasing by 6.9 per cent per year, then as can be seen from Figure 1, demand will exceed supply by the end of the century. What is significant, however, is not the speed at which such vast reserves can be depleted, but that as late as 1975 there will appear to be reserves fully ample enough to last for considerably longer. Such a situation can easily lull one into a false sense of security and the belief that a given growth rate can be sustained, if not indefinitely, as least for a good deal longer than is actually the case. [It is perhaps worth bearing in mind that the actual rate of petroleum consumption *is* increasing by 6.9 per cent per year, and according to the optimistic estimate of W. P. Ryman, Deputy Exploration Manager of the Standard Oil Company of New Jersey, world petroleum reserves (including deposits yet to be discovered) are about 2,100 billion barrels.] The same basic logic applies to the availability of any resource including land, and it is largely because of this particular dynamic of exponential growth that the environmental predicament has come upon us so suddenly, and why its solution requires urgent and radical measures, many of which run counter to values which, in our industrial society we have been taught to regard as fundamental.

117. If we allow the present growth rate to persist, total ecological demand will increase by a factor of 32 over the next 66 years—and there can be no serious person today willing to concede the possibility, or indeed the desirability, of our accommodating the pressures arising from such growth. For this can be done only at the cost of disrupting ecosystems and exhausting resources, which must lead to the failure of food supplies and the collapse of society. It is worth briefly considering each in turn.

Disruption of ecosystems

120. We depend for our survival on the predictability of ecological processes. If they were at all arbitrary, we would not know when to reap or sow, and we would be at the mercy of environmental whim. We could learn nothing about the rest of nature, advance no hypotheses, suggest no "laws." Fortunately, ecological processes are predictable, and although theirs is a relatively young discipline, ecologists have been able to formulate a number of important "laws," one of which in particular relates to environmental predictability: namely, that all ecosystems tend towards stability, and further than the more diverse and complex the ecosystem the more stable it is; that is, the more species there are, and the more they interrelate, the more stable is their environment. By stability is meant the ability to return to the original position after any change, instead of being forced into a totally different pattern—and hence predictability.

121. Unfortunately, we behave as if we knew nothing of the environment and had no conception of its predictability, treating it instead with scant and brutal regard as if it were an idiosyncratic and extremely stupid slave. We seem never to have reflected on the fact that a tropical rain forest supports innumerable insect species and yet is never devastated by them; that its rampant luxuriance is not contingent on our overflying it once a month and bombarding it with insecticides, herbicides, fungicides, and what-have-you. And yet we tremble over our wheatfields and cabbage patches with a desperate battery of synthetic chemicals, in an absurd attempt to impede the operation of the immutable "law" we have just mentioned—that all ecosystems tend towards stability, therefore diversity and complexity, therefore a growing number of different plant and animal species until a climax or optimal condition is achieved. If we were clever, we would recognise that successful long-term agriculture demands the achievement of an artificial climax, an imitation of the pre-existing ecosystem, so that the level of unwanted species could be controlled by those that did no harm to the crop-plants.

122. Instead we have put our money on pesticides, which although they have been effective, have been so only to a limited and now diminishing extent: according to SCEP, the 34 per cent increase in world food production from 1951 to 1966 required increased investments in nitrogenous fertilisers of 146 per cent and in pesticides of 300 per cent. At the same time they have created a number of serious problems, notably resistance—some 250 pest species are resistant to one group of pesticides or another, while many others require increased applications to keep their populations within manageable proportions—and the promotion of formerly innocuous species to pest proportions, because the predators that formerly kept them down have been destroyed. The spread of DDT and other organochlorines in the environment has resulted in alarming population declines among woodcock, grebes, various birds of prey and seabirds, and in a number of fish species, principally the sea trout. SCEP comments: "the oceans are an ultimate accumulation site of DDT and its residues. As much as 25 per cent of the DDT compounds produced to date may have been transferred to the sea. The amount in the marine biota is estimated to be in the order of less than 0.1 per cent of total production and has already produced a demonstrable impact upon the marine environment . . . The decline in productivity of marine food fish and the accumulation of levels of DDT in their tissues which are unacceptable to man can only be accelerated by DDT's continued release to the environment . . ."

123. There are half a million man-made chemicals in use today, yet we cannot predict the behaviour or properties of the greater part of them (either singly or in combination) once they are released into the environment. We know, however, that the combined effects of pollution and habitat destruction menace the survival of no less than 280 mammal, 350 bird, and 20,000 plant species. To those who regret these losses but greet them with the comment that the survival of *Homo sapiens* is surely more important than that of an eagle or a primrose, we repeat that *Homo sapiens* himself depends on the continued resilience of those ecological networks of which eagles and primroses are integral parts. We do not need to utterly destroy the ecosphere to bring catastrophe upon ourselves: all we have to do is to carry on as we are, clearing forests, "reclaiming" wetlands, and imposing sufficient quantities of pesticides, radioactive materials, plastics, sewage, and industrial wastes upon our air, water and land systems to make them inhospitable to the species on which their continued stability and integrity depend. Industrial man in the world today is like a bull in a china shop, with the single difference that a bull with half the information about the properties of china as we have about those of ecosystems would probably try and adapt its behaviour to its environment rather than the reverse. By contrast, *Homo sapiens industrialis* is determined that the china shop should adapt to him, and has therefore set himself the goal of reducing it to rubble in the shortest possible time.

Failure of food supplies

130. Increases in food production in the undeveloped world have barely kept abreast of population growth. Such increases as there have been are due not to higher productivity but to the opening up of new land for cultivation. Unfortunately this will not be possible for much longer: all the good land in the world is now being farmed, and according to the FAO[2], at present rates of expansion none of the marginal land that is left will be unfarmed by 1985—indeed some of the land now under cultivation has been so exhausted that it will have to be returned to permanent pasture.

131. For this reason, FAO's programme to feed the world depends on a programme of intensification, at the heart of which are the new high-yield varieties of wheat and rice. These are highly responsive to inorganic fertilisers and quick-maturing, so that up to ten times present yields can be obtained from them. Unfortunately, they are highly vulnerable to disease, and therefore require increased protection by pesticides, and of course they demand massive inputs of fertilisers (up to 27 times present ones). Not only will these disrupt local ecosystems, thereby jeopardising long-term productivity, but they force hard-pressed undeveloped nations to rely on the agro-chemical industries of the developed world.

132. Whatever their virtues and faults, the new genetic hybrids are not intended to solve the world food problem, but only to give us time to devise more permanent and realistic solutions. It is our view, however, that these hybrids are not the best means of doing this, since their use is likely to bring about a reduction in overall diversity, when the clear need is to develop an agriculture diverse enough to have long-term potential. We must beware of those "experts" who appear to advocate the transformation of the ecosphere into nothing more than a food-factory for man. The concept of a world consisting solely of man and a few favoured food plants is so ludicrously impracticable as to be seriously contemplated only by those who find solace in their own willful ignorance of the real world of biological diversity.

133. We in Britain must bear in mind that we depend on imports for half our food, and that we are unlikely to improve on this situation. The 150,000 acres which are lost from agriculture each year are about 70 per cent more productive than the average for all enclosed land[3], while we are already beginning to experience diminishing returns from the use of inorganic fertilisers. In the period 1964-9, applications of phosphates have gone up by 2 per cent, potash by 7 per cent, and nitrogen by 40 per cent[4], yet yields per acre of wheat, barley, lucerne and temporary grass have levelled off and are beginning to decline, while that of permanent grass has risen only slightly and may be levelling off[5]. As per capita food availability declines throughout the rest of the world, and it appears inevitable it will, we will find it progressively more difficult and expensive to meet our food requirements from abroad. The prospect of severe food shortages within the next thirty years is not so much a fantasy as that of the continued abundance promised us by so many of our politicians.

Exhaustion of resources

140. As we have seen, continued exponential growth of consumption of materials and energy is impossible. Present reserves of all but a few metals will be exhausted within 50 years, if consumption rates continue to grow as they are (see Figure 2). Obviously there will be new discoveries and advances in mining technology, but these are likely to provide us with only a limited stay of execution. Synthetics and substitutes are likely to be of little help, since they must be made from materials which themselves are in short supply; while the hoped-for availability of unlimited energy would not be the answer, since the problem is the ratio of useful metal to waste matter (which would have to be disposed of without disrupting ecosystems), not the need for cheap power. Indeed, the availability of unlimited power holds more of a threat than a promise, since energy use is inevitably polluting, and in addition we would ultimately have to face the problem of disposing of an intractable amount of waste heat.

Collapse of society

150. The developed nations consume such disproportionate amounts of protein, raw materials and fuels that unless they considerably reduce their consumption there is no hope of the undeveloped nations markedly improving their standards of living. This vast differential is a cause of much and growing discontent, made worse by our attempts at cultural uniformity on behalf of an expanding market economy. In the end, we are altering people's aspirations without providing the means for them to be satisfied. In the rush to industrialize we break up communities, so that the controls which formerly regulated behaviour are destroyed before alternatives can be provided. Urban drift is one result of this process, with a consequent rise in anti-social practices, crime, delinquency, and so on, which are so costly for society in terms both of money and of well-being.

151. At the same time, we are sowing the seeds of massive unemployment by increasing the ratio of capital to labour so that the provision of each job becomes ever more expensive. In a world of fast diminishing resources, we shall quickly come to the point when very great numbers of people will be thrown out of work, when the material compensations of urban life are either no longer available or prohibitively expensive, and consequently when whole sections of society will find good cause to express their considerable discontent in ways likely to be anything but pleasant for their fellows.

152. It is worth bearing in mind that the barriers between us and epidemics are not so strong as is commonly supposed. Not only is it increasingly difficult to control the vectors of disease, but it is more than probable that urban populations are being insidiously weakened by overall pollution levels, even when they are not high enough to be incriminated in any one illness. At the same time international mobility speeds the spread of disease. With this background, and at a time of widespread public demoralization, the collapse of vital social services such as power and sanitation, could easily provoke a series of epidemics—and we cannot say with confidence that we would be able to cope with them.

153. At times of great distress and social chaos, it is more than probable that governments will fall into the hands of reckless and unscrupulous elements, who will not hesitate to threaten neighbouring governments with attack, if they feel that they can wrest from them a larger share of the world's vanishing resources. Since a growing number of countries (an estimated 36 by 1980) will have nuclear power stations, and therefore sources of plutonium for nuclear warheads, the likelihood of a whole series of local (if not global) nuclear engagements is greatly increased.

Conclusion

160. A fuller discussion of ecosystems and their disruption, of social systems and their disruption, of population and food supply, and of resources and their depletion, can be found in Appendices A, B, C and D, respectively. [*Material omitted.*] There will be those who regard these accounts of the consequences of trying to accommodate present growth rates as fanciful. But the imaginative leap from the available scientific information to such predictions is negligible, compared with that required for those alternative predictions, laughably considered "optimistic," of a world of 10,000 to 15,000 million people, all with the same material standard of living as the US, on a concrete replica of this planet, the only moving parts being their machines and possibly themselves. Faced with inevitable change, we have to make decisions, and we must make these decisions *soberly* in the light of the best information, and not as if we were caricatures of the archetypal mad scientist.

161. By now it should be clear that the main problems of the environment do not arise from temporary and accidental malfunctions of existing economic and social systems. On the contrary, they are the warning signs of a profound incompatibility between deeply rooted beliefs in continuous growth and the dawning recognition of the earth as a space ship, limited in its resources and vulnerable to thoughtless mishandling. The nature of our response to these symptoms is crucial. If we refuse to recognise the cause of our trouble the result can only be increasing disillusion and growing strain upon the fragile institutions that maintain external peace and internal social cohesion. If, on the other hand, we can respond to this unprecedented challenge with informed and constructive action the rewards will be as great as the penalties for failure.

162. We are sufficiently aware of "political reality" to appreciate that many of the proposals we will make in the next chapter will be considered impracticable. However, we believe that if a strategy for survival is to have any chance of success, the solutions must be formulated in the light of the problems and not from a timorous and superficial understanding of what may or may not be immediately feasible. If we plan remedial action with our eyes on political rather than ecological reality, then very reasonably, very practicably, and very surely, we will muddle our way to extinction.

163. A measure of political reality is that government has yet to acknowledge the impending crisis. This is to some extent because it has given itself no machinery for looking at energy, resources, food, environmental disruption and social disruption as a whole, as part of a general, global pattern, preferring instead to deal with its many aspects as if they were self-contained analytical units. Lord Rothschild's Central Policy Review Staff in the Cabinet Office, which is the only body in government which might remedy the situation, appears not to think it worthwhile: at the moment at least, they are undertaking "no specific studies on the environment that would require an environmentalist or ecologist." There is a strong element of positive feedback here, in that there can be no appreciation of our predicament unless we view it in totality, and yet government can see no cause to do so unless it can be shown that such a predicament exists.

164. Possibly because government sees the world in fragments and not as a totality, it is difficult to detect in its actions or words any coherent general policy, although both major political parties appear to be mesmerised by two dominating notions: that economic expansion is essential for survival and is the best possible index of progress and well-being; and that unless solutions can be devised that do not threaten this notion, then the problems should not be regarded as existing. Unfortunately, government has an increasingly powerful incentive for continued expansion in the tendency for economic growth to create the need for more economic growth. This it does in six ways:

1. Firstly, the introduction of technological devices, i.e. the growth of the technosphere, can only occur to the detriment of the ecosphere, which means that it leads to the destruction of natural controls which must then be replaced by further technological ones. It is in this way that pesticides and artificial fertilisers create the need for yet more pesticides and artificial fertilisers.
2. Secondly, for various reasons, industrial growth, particularly in its earlier phases, promotes population growth. Even in its later phases, this can still occur at a high rate (0.5 per cent in the UK). Jobs must constantly be created for the additional people—not just any job, but those that are judged acceptable in terms of current values. This basically means that the capital outlay per person employed must be maintained, otherwise the level of "productivity" per man will fall, which is a determinant of both the "viability" of economic enterprise and of the "standard of living."
3. Thirdly, no government can hope to survive widespread and protracted unemployment, and without changing the basis of our industrial society, the only way government can prevent it is by stimulating economic growth.
4. Fourthly, business enterprises, whether state-owned or privately owned, tend to become self-perpetuating, which means that they require surpluses for further investment. This favours continued growth.
5. Fifthly, the success of a government and its ability to obtain support is to a large extent assessed in terms of its ability to increase the "standard of living" as measured by per capita gross national product (GNP).
6. Finally, confidence in the economy, which is basically a function of its ability to grow, must be maintained to ensure a healthy state of the stock market. Were confidence to fall, stock values would crash, drastically reducing the availability of capital for investment and hence further growth, which would lead to further unemployment. This would result in a further fall in stockmarket values and hence give rise to a positive-feedback chain-reaction, which under the existing order might well lead to social collapse.

For all these reasons, we can expect our government (whether Conservative or Labour) to encourage further increases in GNP regardless of the consequences, which in any case tame "experts" can be found to play down. It will curb growth only when public opinion demands such a move, in which case it will be politically expedient, and when a method is found for doing so without creating unemployment or excessive pressure on capital.

We believe this is possible only within the framework of a fully integrated plan.

165. The emphasis must be on integration. If we develop relatively clean technologies but do not end economic growths then sooner or later we will find ourselves with as great a pollution problem as before but without the means of tackling it. If we stablise our economies and husband our nonrenewable resources without stabilising our populations we will find we are no longer able to feed ourselves. As Forrester[1] and Meadows[6] convincingly make clear, daunting though an integrated programme may be, a piecemeal approach will cause more problems than it solves.

166. Our task is to create a society which is sustainable and which will give the fullest possible satisfaction to its members. Such a society by definition would depend not on expansion but on stability. This does not mean to say that it would be stagnant—indeed it could well afford more variety than does the state of uniformity at present being imposed by the pursuit of technological efficiency. We believe that the stable society, the achievement of which we shall discuss in the next chapter, as well as removing the sword of Damocles which hangs over the heads of future generations, is much more likely than the present one to bring the peace and fulfilment which hitherto have been regarded, sadly, as utopian.

Towards the Stable Society: Strategy for Change

[Editor's Note: this section of the "Blueprint" has been edited to include only several of the original paragraphs.]

210. The principal conditions of a stable society—one that to all intents and purposes can be sustained indefinitely while giving optimum satisfaction to its members—are:
(1) minimum disruption of ecological processes;
(2) maximum conservation of materials and energy—or an economy of stock rather than flow;
(3) a population in which recruitment equals loss; and
(4) a social system in which the individual can enjoy, rather than feel restricted by, the first three conditions.

211. The achievement of these four conditions will require controlled and well-orchestrated change on numerous fronts and this change will probably occur through seven operations:
(1) a control operation whereby environmental disruption is reduced as much as possible by technical means;
(2) a freeze operation, in which present trends are halted;
(3) a systemic substitution, by which the most dangerous components of these trends are replaced by technological substitutes, whose effect is less deleterious in the short-term, but over the long-term will be increasingly ineffective;
(4) systemic substitution, by which these technological substitutes are replaced by "natural" or self-regulating ones, i.e. those which either replicate or employ without undue disturbance the normal processes of the ecosphere, and are therefore likely to be sustainable over very long periods of time;
(5) the invention, promotion and application of alternative technologies which are energy and materials conservative, and which because they are designed for relatively "closed" economic communities are likely to disrupt ecological processes only minimally (e.g. intermediate technology);
(6) decentralisation of polity and economy at all levels, and the formation of com-

munities small enough to be reasonably self-regulating and self-supporting; and
(7) education for such communities.

212. As we shall see when we examine how our four conditions might be achieved, some changes will involve only a few of these operations, in others a number of the operations will be carried out almost simultaneously, and in others one will start well before another has ended. The usefulness of the operation-concept is simply to clarify the orchestration of change.

280. A cardinal assumption of this strategy is that it will not succeed without the most careful synchronisation and integration. We cannot say of a particular section of these proposals that it alone is acceptable, and therefore we will go ahead with it immediately but consider the rest later on! This section, therefore, is devoted to a schematic, annotated outline of how change might be orchestrated. It is necessarily unsophisticated and oversimplified, but we hope it will give some idea of how change in one quarter will aid change in the others.

281. Variables included in schematic outline:
(a) establishment of national population service
(b) introduction of raw materials, amortisation and power taxes; antidisamenity legislation; air, land and water quality targets; recycling grants; revised social accounting systems
(c) developed countries end commitment to persistent pesticides and subsidise similar move by undeveloped countries
(d) end of subsidies on inorganic fertilisers
(e) grants for use of organics and introduction of diversity
(f) emergency food programme for undeveloped countries
(g) progressive substitution of non-persistent for persistent pesticides
(h) integrated control research programme
(i) integrated control training programme
(j) substitution of integrated control for chemical control
(k) progressive introduction of diversified farming practices
(l) end of road building
(m) clearance of derelict land and beginning of renewal programme
(n) restrictions on private transport and subsidies for public transport
(o) development of rapid mass transit
(p) research into materials substitution
(q) development of alternative technologies
(r) decentralisation of industry: part one (redirection)
(s) decentralisation of industry: part two (development of community types)
(t) redistribution of government
(u) education research
(v) teacher training
(w) education
(x) experimental community
(y) domestic sewage to land
(z) target date for basic establishment of network of self-sufficient, self-regulating communities.

The Goal

[Editor's Note: this section of the "Blueprint" has been edited to include only several of the original paragraphs.]

311. There is every reason to suppose that the stable society would provide us with satisfactions that would more than compensate for those which, with the passing of the industrial state, it will become increasingly necessary to forgo.

353. Thus in many ways, the stable society, with its diversity of physical and social environments, would provide considerable scope for human skill and ingenuity.

354. Indeed, if we are capable of ensuring a relatively smooth transition to it, we can be optimistic about providing our children with a way of life psychologically, intellectually and aesthetically more satisfying than the present one. And we can be confident that it will be sustainable as ours cannot be, so that the legacy of despair we are about to leave them may at the last minute be changed to one of hope.

Acknowledgements

We would like to acknowledge the valuable comments contributed by Gerald Leach, The Rt. Rev. Hugh Montefiore, Brian Johnson and John Papworth. We are grateful to Potomac Associates, Washington DC, for permission to reproduce a graph from their forthcoming book The Limits of Growth by Dennis Meadows; to the MIT Press for permission to use a number of tables and to quote extensively from their book Man's Impact on the Global Environment, The Study of Critical Environmental Problems (SCEP); to Pemberton Books for permission to reproduce a graph from their book Population and Liberty by Jack Parsons; to Collier-MacMillan for permission to reproduce two tables from their book Too Many, by Georg Borgstrom; to Tom Stacey for permission to quote extensively from his book Can Britain Survive?, edited by E. Goldsmith. Parts of the Introduction and "Towards the Stable Society," notably those sections on stabilising the population and on creating a new social system, have been adapted from The Fall of Man by Robert Allen (to be published later this year by Allen Lane, The Penguin Press) by permission of author and publisher.

References

1. Jay Forrester. 1970. *World Dynamics*. Wright Allen Press, Cambridge, Mass.
2. FAO. 1969. *Provisional Indicative World Plan for Agriculture*. Rome
3. Stated by the Ministry of Agriculture to the Select Committee on Science and Technology. 1971. *Population of the United Kingdom*. HMSO, London.
4. Agricultural Advisory Council. 1971. *Modern Farming and the Soil*. HMSO, London.
5. Ministry of Agriculture (Statistics Division). 1970. *Output and utilisation of farm produce in the United Kingdom, 1968-9*. HMSO, London.
6. Dennis Meadows *et al.* 1972. *The Limits of Growth*. Club of Rome/MIT Press.

The Doomsday Syndrome:

A Review*

Jerome C. Muys

Jerome Muys is a partner in the Washington, D.C., law firm of Debevoise and Liberman. He is a member of the Council of the Natural Resources Law of the A.B.A., and an adjunct professor at the George Washington University Law Center. He was a visiting professor of law at the George Washington National Law Center, and served as assistant general counsel and chief of the legal staff of the Public Land Law Review Commission. Mr. Muys is a graduate of Princeton University and has a law degree from Stanford University.

This article—a digest of the original—is reprinted with permission, and originally appeared in Vol. 2 of the Ecology Law Quarterly, *page 867. Copyright 1972, School of Law, University of California at Berkeley.*

Dr. John Maddox, author of *The Doomsday Syndrome*, is a leading English scientist and the editor of *Nature* magazine. While his book is must reading for all environmentalists, what is readily apparent is that Dr. Maddox's treatise, despite his own professional background and its scientific thrust, is both in its structure and message really a book for lawyers.

The first sentence sets the tone. "This is not a scholarly work," Dr. Maddox tells us, "but a complaint."[1] The defendants are clearly identified: "the extremist wing of the environmental movement"—Paul Ehrlich, Barry Commoner, Rene Dubos,[2] the late Rachel Carson, and other proponents of the environmental apocalypse.[3] The actions for which Dr. Maddox seeks redress are the "calculated exaggeration [and] overstatement [which] is commonplace in the literature of doomsday."[4] The danger which the "prophets of doom" have caused, the complaint continues, are clear and present, namely

> that much of this gloomy foreboding about the immediate future will accomplish the opposite of what its authors intend. Instead of alerting people to important problems, it may seriously undermine the capacity of the human race to look out for its survival. The doomsday syndrome may in itself be as much a hazard as any of the conundrums which society has created for itself. . . . Paradoxically, the environmental message, at least in its crudest form, is self-defeating.[5]

The complaint's allegations about exaggeration and, in some cases, outright falsehoods by some environmentalists, will strike responsive chords in many experienced in the environmental movement here in the United States. Similarly, it is not difficult for anyone who has had the temerity to disagree on an issue with the national environmental establishment to empathize with Dr. Maddox's lament that "one of the distressing features of the present debate about the environment is the way in which it is supposed to be an argument between far-sighted people with the interests of humanity at heart and others who care not a tuppence for the future," aptly identified as a "false dichotomy [which] conceals a host of important issues."[6]

The Doomsday Syndrome

As any advocate knows, however, it is far easier, and often more effective, to paint the black hat on your opponent than to discuss the merits of his views. And, unfortunately, the white hat which some environmentalists would appropriate as their exclusive possession often seems to shade a somewhat darker heart. When one reflects upon how some of our leading environmental spokesmen have not hesitated to vilify those with whom they disagree, or upon how some wilderness lovers bitterly complain that they actually saw other human beings on the next ridge on their last outing, it brings understanding to Dostoyevsky's sad but insightful truth that many who loudly profess their love for humanity in the abstract often harbor a distaste for humans in particular. Dr. Maddox thus poses the moral dilemma of whether the objectives and achievements of the extremist environmentalists justify their means. He chooses not to answer the basic question, but instead suggests, unconvincingly it seems fair to say, that they really haven't accomplished very much.

The manifestations of the doomsday syndrome are set out in five chapters presenting a bill of particulars detailing and attacking what Dr. Maddox views as errors and exaggerations in various areas of concern: over-population, depletion of natural resources, famine, various kinds of ecological catastrophe, genetic engineering, and technological disruption of the delicate, interdependent balance between man and nature. Despite the author's disavowal of his treatise as a scholarly work, the bulk of the book is in fact taken up with a scholarly, skillfully constructed "lawyer's brief" attempting to blunt, if not wholly refute, the principal factual assumptions and exaggerations which are the foundation of the dire predictions of the "doomsday men."

It would be pretentious and foolhardy for this reviewer to attempt to assess the multifaceted scientific arguments which Dr. Maddox musters to counter the apocalyptic environmental message. However, the main thrust of his brief can be stated and an overall evaluation of its persuasiveness ventured.

"In the literature of doomsday," we are told, "the growth of the world's population is the most common theme, and indeed there is no precedent for the speed of growth in the past few decades."[7] In a chapter entitled "The Numbers Game," Dr. Maddox assures us, with a phalanx of statistics, historical Malthusian precedents for current fears, projections, trends, etc., that the "population explosion" is no more than a "damp squib."[8] Recognizing that it would be a great misfortune if the population grew to reach a point where the pressure on resources such as land became intolerable, he finds such an eventuality highly improbable, and offers the following sanguine assessment of the issue:

> What matters, therefore, is how a community decides to apportion resources between population growth and the other benefits which it might enjoy. Since there is no virtue in numbers as such, obviously it is prudent to grow as little as may be necessary. But there is nothing in demography nor in the record of the past few years to suggest that temporary lapses will bring catastrophe.[9]

The arguments mustered by Dr. Maddox in this chapter, both statistical and sociological, are quite persuasive. It should also be noted, moreover, that the United States Census Bureau has announced a substantial downward revision of its population estimates for the year 2000.[10]

"The End of the Lode" begins by reminding us that "in the proclamation of doomsday, one of the most common components is the assertion that the resources of the earth will prove to be inadequate in some sense or another."[11] Addressing predictions of world wide famine, Dr. Maddox asserts that "the truth is that food production in the world is now increasing much faster than the population . . . [and] should grow more quickly

The Doomsday Syndrome

than even the highest estimates of population growth."[12] The real problems we should be facing are, in his view, maldistribution of existing production, widespread under-nourishment flowing from unbalanced diets, how to further exploit existing knowledge and technology to increase productivity and food quality, and similar concerns. He concludes: "There is no doubt that the world could support 7,000 million people or even twice that number. The question is whether people will take the trouble to do so."[13] Again Dr. Maddox offers an impressive array of arguments, but their receptivity is dampened by current news accounts of increasingly serious drought and famine conditions in India and by reports from the United Nations' Food and Agriculture Organization that the "Green Revolution" (which helped spur recent agricultural productivity at a rate greater than population increases) is tapering off.

With respect to the current concern over an impending "energy crisis," Dr. Maddox eschews any serious effort to engage in the current fad over supply and demand projections for various fuels, commenting that "estimating the amounts of coal, petroleum and other fuels in the surface of the earth is like estimating the frequency of undetected murders."[14] Nevertheless, at current rates of consumption he concludes that there remains about a 135-year supply of petroleum, a 600-year supply of natural gas, coal reserves for 2,500 years, and oil shale for 40,000 years. Not surprisingly, then, we are assured that "talk of an absolute shortage of fuel is in other words unjustifiable."[15] Moreover, his feeling is that nuclear power will no doubt soon make any energy concerns moot, with the possibility that future developments may yield as much as the equivalent of 100 tons of coal from the hydrogen in a single bucket of water. "The important questions," we are admonished, "are to know just which kinds of fuel, at what prices, people will choose to use in the decades ahead."[16]

While one can agree with that view, it is startling for Dr. Maddox to tell the American consumer in the next breath that "energy is now more plentiful and cheaper than it has ever been," and that "there is no reason why it should not continue to become more plentiful and even cheaper. . . ."[17] Dr. Maddox is obviously far off base in that assertion. Although some consumer groups in the United States contend that our energy supplies *should* be more plentiful and cheaper than they are or promise to be in the near future, the obverse is all too painfully the apparent reality. Why this is so remains a matter of some dispute, and whether Congress or the responsible executive and regulatory agencies will make a meaningful effort to answer that question is problematical.

The author disposes of the concern over potential shortages of metallic minerals in a similar fashion, reiterating that the critical question is "the prices at which the metals and other minerals necessary to sustain modern industry will be available."[18] The current price support structure which led to the stockpiles of such minerals maintained by the United States, as well as the concern by source nations over the market impact of potential deep sea mineral development, seem to attest to the accuracy of Dr. Maddox's assessment of that particular supply picture.

In his chapter on the "Pollution Panic,"[19] Dr. Maddox takes on various matters of current public concern: the pesticides and insecticides controversy, possible climatic hazards from increasing carbon dioxide concentrations in the atmosphere, mercury poisoning, cyclamates, the SST, detergents, and similar issues. With respect to the DDT controversy, Dr. Maddox states his case as follows:

> The way in which Miss [Rachel] Carson drew attention to the misuses of DDT and the other persistent pesticides may have been a public service of a kind. The defect of *Silent Spring* is that it went much further and leveled complaints which were invalid at the time and which are, for

that matter, still invalid. The danger now is that too zealous an attack on DDT and related chemicals may deprive the world of important benefits.[20]

After characterizing a number of Miss Carson's points as "more definite" than they should be, "untrue," or "without foundation," Dr. Maddox concludes on a strong note:

> The truth is of course that there can never be as simple and uncomplicated a policy towards DDT, . . . or any other chemicals which may have useful functions in the practical world as Miss Rachel Carson . . . proclaim[s]. . . . The choice to be made is not that between unrestricted exploitation of a new technological device and outright self-denial. Instead, means must be found of gaining benefits at a cost which is acceptable to all concerned. It will not be easy to find ways of balancing the advantages to farmers of unrestricted use of pesticides against the disadvantages to, say, fishermen of contaminating estuaries, and the problem of evaluating the health of animals such as bald eagles to the population of North America is one that has not yet been tackled. But to bury all these difficulties beneath a popular belief that DDT and other pesticides are inherently malevolent and potentially calamitous is not merely an assault on reason but an act of intellectual cowardice.[21]

In response to the several concerns with possible climatic catastrophes resulting from various human endeavors, particularly the uncertain consequences likely to flow from increasing carbon dioxide in the atmosphere as a result of fossil fuel burning, Dr. Maddox asserts that "it is clear that the changes which have been observed are small and by no means irreversible."[22] He concedes, however, that "it is exceedingly difficult to make informed estimates of the likelihood of these developments," and argues that "the most urgent need is not for public anxiety nor even for a change in industrial practice but, rather, vigilance and a better scientific understanding of what happens in the atmosphere."[23] After surveying briefly the evidence on mercury pollution, Dr. Maddox asserts:

> [T]he chief lesson to be learned from this record of mercury contamination is that there is a need carefully to control the uses made of dangerous chemicals such as these but that, so far as can be told, no damage has been done by the small amounts of mercury likely to be present in the environment as a whole, [since] . . . the natural occurrence of mercury in the atmosphere and the oceans implies that people now and in the past have always been exposed to some of the material, which in turn suggests that sufficiently small quantities must be tolerable.[24]

The problems of increasing air and water pollution are viewed simply as matters of economics. Governments are challenged to "seek somehow to define in economic terms what constitutes the public good."[25] While Dr. Maddox believes that Lake Erie is far from "dead," he asserts that even if it is so viewed it can be resurrected for $1.3 billion if we feel strongly enough about it. He asks the now familiar question: how much are we willing to pay for clean air and water?

"Ecology Is A State of Mind" uses as a point of departure the truism that "the once humdrum word ecology has, in the past few years, become a rallying cry for the environmentalists."[26] Stating that "the essence of ecology is that different kinds of living things are interdependent,"[27] he reminds us that human beings are a vital part of the "web of life." For Dr. Maddox the overriding question is whether innovation will be detrimental to human beings, not to the ecosystem as a whole. Conceding that our relationship with plants and animals and the rest of the natural world is important, the author nevertheless warns that "one of the most immediate dangers, the long record of ecological mishap notwithstanding, is that too slavish a concern for what is thought to be ecology will inhibit people from taking prudent steps to safeguard the future of the human race."[28]

In the chapter on "Man Made Men," Dr. Maddox confronts the fears about much current biological research and its implications, characterized by the "persistent, awesome speculation . . . that it may help in due course to modify the nature of human beings."[29] His discussion ranges over the subjects of transplant surgery, artificial fertilization, and genetic engineering. This is perhaps his most lucid and scholarly chapter in surveying current scientific developments and potential. It is also his least persuasive. [T]he social hazards inherent in genetic engineering cannot be so summarily dismissed. The question is not simply whether "do-gooders" can ever be "malevolent," as Dr. Maddox suggests (although there must have been a few in the Third Reich), but must include the equally relevant concern whether they might become misguided or oblivious to the subtle implications of their work, even though well intentioned.

It is in his chapter entitled "Prosperity Is Possible" that Dr. Maddox, as scientist, takes the offensive against what he sees as the most paradoxical feature of the present discontent—"common disenchantment with science and all its works, especially technology."[30] To current concerns that modern technology may be becoming as much a curse as a blessing, Dr. Maddox replies that science and technology never promised us a rose garden: "[W]hat reason can there ever have been for supposing that technical innovations would always be an unmixed blessing?"[31] He touches base on all the familiar complaints: the failure of producers to bear the costs of environmental degradation (society can "internalize the externalities," but consumers will ultimately pay the bill); the environmental crisis signals the end of the private enterprise economic system (nonsense!); technology is an autonomous and uncontrollable juggernaut (Congress killed the SST, didn't it?); technology is dehumanizing (would you trade places with "a Victorian laborer or a latter-day peasant farmer on the Bay of Bengal?");[32] the mass media will become tools of oppressive governments ("Big Brother is a political animal, not a creation of technology");[33] computers may rob us of our freedom ("unrealistic or inordinately expensive");[34] cities are evil (blame city administrators, not technologists).

Perhaps it is because the subject is too close to home for a sensitive humanitarian scientist to face up to, but Dr. Maddox simply fails to acknowledge, let alone deal with, the very real problems posed by science and technology. His rebuttal here is unfortunately glib and superficial. It highlights the major shortcoming of our institutional arrangements for controlling and directing scientific research and technology, namely that it is very difficult to control technological innovations whose potential impact has never been adequately assessed.

Several themes recur in Dr. Maddox's complaint. A few are patently debating or briefing techniques, reflecting the kind of argumentative posturing so well known to lawyers, and cannot be taken seriously. For example, a common refrain is that 'things could always be (and indeed have been) worse." Just how this realization, assuming its validity in some instances, is any consolation is never explained. Consequently, one may strongly question whether "the most urgent need is that the environmentalists should recognize that the environment has been treated much more badly in the past than would now be permissible."[35] There is little solace in knowledge that previous insults to the environment have been even more gross than current depredations.

Another recurring contention is that "man's polluting efforts are dwarfed by what nature itself has done." We are admonished that "the threat of man-made catastrophe must also be measured against the possibility of natural catastrophe,"[36] since "in the long run . . . we shall all be dead."[37] Choosing as his yardstick a measure stopping just short of eternity (an exceedingly "long range" view for which he elsewhere repeatedly criticizes the "extremists"), Dr. Maddox is able to assert confidently that "on this scale, the self-destructive potential of terrestrial technology will be puny for a long time to come."[38] For purposes of comparison, we are told that the effect on the atmosphere from several volcanic eruptions over the last hundred years has probably exceeded that of several years of industrial activity. What we are to infer from such comparisons is not clearly stated, although again it appears to be that things could be worse. A more useful message would be that, given the uncontrollability of such natural impacts on our human environment, we should be exceedingly cautious in aggravating such natural threats by man-made assaults on that same environment. Is it not reasonable to proceed with great caution in those areas of human activity where we *can* exercise some control?

Beyond these briefing tactics, there are several substantive themes which pervade his work. A dominant theme is that "man will overcome," an optimistic view of the future rooted in the conviction that the past is prologue as far as the likely responses of social, legal, and governmental institutions to environmental threats are concerned. Thus he sums up his analysis of current predictions of environmental catastrophe with the observation that "the fallacy in all these generalizations is of course the supposition that the course of development of modern technology cannot be influenced by human beings."[39] Similarly, he concludes with respect to anticipated resources shortages:

> The trouble is that this prediction, like many others which are centered around emotive phrases such as "our plundered planet," is based on the assumption that the future will be like the present but more so. It makes no concession to the belief that with the passage of time, the human race will adapt to changes in the availability of raw materials much as it has done in the past two million years.[40]

Although he acknowledges that much of our current environmental plight is attributable to the complacence of previous generations, Dr. Maddox's review of historic and current responses to environmental and technological challenges makes a good case for his belief that society has within its power the ability to make the political decisions necessary to avoid doomsday. Hence he stresses that environmental pollution is "not so much a threat to the global environment, and the existence of the human race, as a demonstration of the need for the vigorous application of social instruments, laws and taxes, which are as old as society itself."[41] The weakness of this fundamental argument is that Dr. Maddox repeatedly finds it necessary to minimize the current environmental predicament as a corollary to his call to arms for a determined response to such problems through our social institutions. This is unfortunate, since it seems quite clear that both premises are true: environmental pollution *is* a threat to the global environment *and* strong institutional responses *are* essential.

Moreover, Dr. Maddox is convinced that "man will overcome" not by rejecting science and technology, but by controlling and utilizing them for positive, socially approved ends. In his view science and technology have become essential components of the resourcefulness and ingenuity which the human race must exercise if it is to continue to survive.[42] Correspondingly, he finds as one of the "abiding flaws" of the doomsday literature its denigration of the potential contribution of these "indispensable instruments" for continued survival.[43]

Dr. Maddox's complaint is perhaps weakest in its claim for damages. His principal fear seems to be that the exaggerations of the environmentalists, based as they are on demonstrably misleading assumptions, will produce a "cry wolf" reaction which will lull society into a do-nothing state. [H]e voices his concern that the environmental extremists will be wringing their hands and issuing condemnations when they should be utilizing existing social and legal institutions, and, where necessary, forging new ones, to deal with our environmental problems.

The Doomsday Syndrome

Recent events have also somewhat mooted Dr. Maddox's criticism. . . . [T]he national environmental organizations, which Dr. Maddox concedes have played a major role in the environmental movement in the United States, show distinct signs of shifting their focus from an essentially defensive, negative posture to one in which they hopefully may play a more positive role in the shaping of environmentally sound administrative and legislative decisions. They appear to be gradually coming to recognize that stopping project after project in court does not help make the difficult, balanced policy decisions which courts must necessarily remand to administrators or leave to Congress. Similarly, there appears to be some recognition that their energies can now be better directed toward sound planning techniques, balanced legislation, and reasonable administrative regulations, than in loudly denouncing "the polluters."

All in all, it would appear that little harm has yet materialized from the doomsday syndrome diagnosed by Dr. Maddox. If anything, society appears to have responded to the "extremist" cries of alarm relatively expeditiously and, on the whole, in the balanced fashion he advocates. Significantly, the last chapter of the book detailing recent legal and institutional developments seems almost wholly to undercut the central thesis of his work, suggesting that Dr. Maddox himself may be guilty of the same vice he attributes to the doomsday men, making mountains out of molehills. Indeed, in a paragraph only a few pages from the end of his book, Dr. Maddox seems to verge on recanting his central thesis:

> It is too soon to know what permanent effect the more extreme branches of the environmental movement will have had, but they have helped to dramatize a set of problems that might otherwise have been neglected. Public affairs are constantly refreshed by the challenges of those who ask that caricatures of the real world should be taken at their face value and the environmentalists deserve some credit for having pinpricked public administrations into actions that would not otherwise have been natural to them.[44]

But beyond the rightful quarrel of *The Doomsday Syndrome* with the tactics of some environmentalists, its disagreement with the reality, magnitude, and imminence of various environmental threats, and its call for action, not despair, in meeting such threats, the fundamental worry seems to be that preoccupation with remote environmental catastrophe will sidetrack concern and effort from more immediate, pressing social problems. Maddox is quite obviously a humanitarian expressing the very real apprehension that social justice may be delayed or denied by undue concern with what he views as largely speculative environmental threats:

> In advanced societies, machinery must be devised for the more equitable treatment of the poor and the disadvantaged. Urban life, although better than it used to be, can be improved. Even where medical care is excellent, ways need still to be discovered of preventing untimely death and unnecessary disease. And in less-developed societies, there are more primitive tasks to be undertaken. Nourishment is still too fitful. Schooling remains for many a luxury. Housing is shelter for some and a source of envy for others. The whole world knows, after what happened in Bengal in 1971, that Calcutta, for example, presents problems of race, poverty, disease, and freedom that affront and sometimes paralyze the conscience of industrialized societies. The question which the doomsday prophets pose for those who share their compassion for society is whether the energies of the human race should be spent on problems like these which, however difficult, can be solved or whether they should be spent on the avoidance of more distant trouble.[45]

Dr. Maddox leaves no doubt that, in his view, our energies ought to be directed to solving problems of a more immediate nature.

In conclusion, this lawyer's judgement on Dr. Maddox's complaint is:

(1) that it clearly will withstand a demurrer from environmental defendants;

(2) that his criticism of the tactics of some of the doomsday men, along with his chal-

lenges to their alleged exaggerations and undue concern over remote, hypothetical environmental threats, are properly for the jury, which is still out; and

(3) that his claims, if sustained, demonstrate only nominal damages at best.

But treating his complaint as an *amicus mundi* brief, it is commended to all concerned environmentalists as a reminder that their sincere dedication to halting further man-made environmental degradation should not be permitted to obscure the continuing, more immediate need to deal with widespread, age-old social injustices stemming from man's inhumanity to man.

Footnotes

* *The Doomsday Syndrome.* By John Maddox. New York: McGraw-Hill Book Co. 1972. Pp. vii, 293. $6.95.

1. J. Maddox, *The Doomsday Syndrome* at v. (1972).
2. One may seriously question whether Dr. Dubos is properly joined as a defendant, particularly in light of his recent address at the annual meeting of the American Association for the Advancement of Science which sounded essentially the same optimistic note with respect to our environmental difficulties as does *The Doomsday Syndrome.*
3. J. Maddox, *supra* note 1, at 30.
4. *Id.* at 19-20.
5. *Id.* at 3.
6. *Id.* at v.
7. *Id.* at 35.
8. *Id.* at 64.
9. *Id.* at 71.
10. N.Y. Times, Dec. 18, 1972, at 1, col. 1.
11. J. Maddox, *supra* note 1, at 75.
12. *Id.* at 82.
13. *Id.* at 93.
14. *Id.* at 99.
15. *Id.*
16. *Id.* at 99-100.
17. *Id.* at 101-02.
18. *Id.* at 105.
19. Panic about pollution is the most conspicuous part of the environmental crisis and has its roots in the fear, entirely justifiable in the 1950's, that nuclear radioactivity from weapons tests might cause genetic and other damage throughout the world. *Id.* at 113.
20. *Id.* at 127.
21. *Id.* at 137-38.
22. *Id.* at 142.
23. *Id.* at 138, 142.
24. *Id.* at 148-49.
25. *Id.* at 158.
26. *Id.* at 161.
27. *Id.* at 162.
28. *Id.* at 181.
29. *Id.* at 194.
30. *Id.* at 221.
31. *Id.* at 222.
32. *Id.* at 238.
33. *Id.* at 244.
34. *Id.* at 242.
35. *Id.* at 30.
36. *Id.* at 26.
37. *Id.* at 27.
38. *Id.* at 28.
39. *Id.* at 21.
40. *Id.* at 102.
41. *Id.* at 158.
42. *Id.* at 273.
43. *Id.* at 274.
44. J. Maddox, *supra* note 1, at 276.
45. *Id.* at 3-4.

The Risks
of Growth

Richard Zeckhauser

Richard Zeckhauser is a professor of political economy at the Kennedy School, Harvard University. He was previously an assistant and then an associate professor at the school. Mr. Zeckhauser is a graduate of Harvard, from which he also holds a Ph.D. in economics.

This article is reprinted by permission of Daedalus, *(Journal of the American Academy of Arts and Sciences, Boston, Mass., Fall 1973), The No-Growth Society. The version as it appears here is a digest (to approximately two-thirds) of the full original.*

Introduction

Economic growth, until recently a goal which elicited near universal agreement, now gets a bad press.[1] This decline in reputation was to be expected.

Little new has been added to the pro-growth argument, while the anti-forces have presented much new evidence. Advocates of growth retardation or arrest have surveyed the societal ills that have accompanied our recent years of growth, then extrapolated (perhaps a bit too quickly) from correlation to causality, and attributed them to the processes of growth. Furthermore, these advocates tell us, history reveals but a fraction of the dangers; they have peered into the future, and discerned that matters will become bleak indeed if we continue in the ways of growth.

In this essay I am cast as the defender of the out-of-fashion view that growth is not pernicious, but desirable. I shall make arguments in three areas.

1. **Ground Rules:** Many objections to economic growth would vanish if appropriate terminologies were defined and ground rules established.
2. **Predictions:** There is no convincing evidence that slowing growth would create a rosier present or future.
3. **Distribution of Welfare:** An antigrowth policy would help some groups and hurt others, and there is no compelling argument that the groups it would help are more deserving than those it would harm.

I conclude with a discussion of the risks of economic growth, and some significant qualifications regarding the restricted scope of my analysis.

Ground Rules

What we are discussing is growth of the total economic product. Appropriately defined, this is the total value to the individuals in a society of all the goods and services they consume, including not only the commodities traded on the market, but also those like congestion, health, leisure, and pollution which are not. Since nothing that people value economically is left out of this total economic product, we might label its growth "economic improvement."[2] Growth in GNP would not merit that label, for that measure has two shortcomings. First, it explicitly leaves out valued goods and services that are not traded on the market. Second, it includes intermediate market-traded goods, like defense and commutation expenditures, that are merely inputs to the production process rather than final contributors to economic welfare.

Recently, William Nordhaus and James Tobin have defined a statistic called the Measure of Economic Welfare (MEW)[3] that avoids these failings. Unfortunately, we have no experience with MEW statistics, and it is evident that, given our present lack of sophistication, many arbitrary decisions will be needed to compute them. The choice between MEW and GNP as guides to policy is a choice between an appropriate but insufficiently understood indicator and a biased but familiar and relatively unambiguous one. [*Material omitted.*]

I suggest that agreement on the following points would establish some ground rules for growth-rate discussions: A measure like MEW, such that its growth represents a true improvement, is the appropriate index of economic welfare. It is difficult, however, to compute an MEW index and well nigh impossible to assure its automatic maximization. Finally, the GNP, although its use is expedient, is a possible source of error.

Predictions

Accurate predictions are the foundation of robust policy judgments. A reasoned evaluation of the antigrowth argument requires that we determine the consequences of a policy of growth retardation. In a decentralized, predominately capitalistic society like our own, the growth rate is hardly a variable subject to control by central decision-makers. Rather, it is determined by a confluence of decisions by millions of citizens. Policy-makers can take a limited range of actions, and they can alter the incentives for action by others. Still, it would take an extraordinary piece of social engineering for them to create a no-growth society.

Perhaps those antigrowth advocates who propose that the government take direct action to slow the growth rate have been encouraged by the paradigm of neoclassical economics, which despite its long-standing attachment to little people making little decisions, has produced Big Brother growth models. In these models, a central decision-maker, using the investment rate as a throttle, can ease us onto a Golden Age track. In this world of graphs and equations, if the growth pace is too swift, a few adjustments in aggregate policy variables can put us on a slower course.

In the recent past, however, when growth was a sacred objective, we discovered that the government could actually do very little (at least with present knowledge of economic dynamics) to accelerate it. Boosts that were achieved, say with investment credits, in no way altered the basic structure of economic relations. The major effects they did achieve may simply have been transfusing growth from future booms back to present slumps. This implies that slowing growth by policy measures that were mere reversals of previous boosting efforts would be equally difficult. Effective short-range and long-run retardation would require experimentation with unaccustomed devices and procedures. [*Material omitted.*] Their effects are hard to predict. These policies might turn out to be more powerful than we expected, or they just might knock the economy out of kilter, producing an entirely inappropriate mix of goods and services. (When confronted with the antigrowth philosophy, even economists who normally cold shoulder the invisible hand are likely to experience stirrings of fondness for market-guided outcomes.)

What, then, can be the argument of those who favor slowing growth? First, they consider economic growth and MEW to be, in aggregate, negatively correlated. This proposition alone, however, does not lead to the conclusion that growth itself should be retarded, for it would be far preferable merely to discourage those components of economic growth that contribute negatively to MEW. Such people must also subscribe to the proposition that more refined procedures are too weak and that the best way to boost MEW is through a blunt curtailment of GNP growth. To establish these two propositions, however, an impressive body of evidence, or a series of logical arguments will have to be marshalled. Empirical data that have been gathered to date do not support the anti-growthites' view,[4] since decline is not yet upon us, but rather, they predict, just around the corner. These advocates of growth retardation would have us rely on the gloomy predictions of their analytic and computer models.

Let me turn to their darkest prophecy, that regarding exhaustible resources. [*Material omitted.*]

In their great devotion to natural resources, antigrowthmen have been relatively neglectful of the other factors of production: capital, labor and land. But growth can be achieved by increasing the inputs of these factors as well. How should we feel about using more of them in our productive processes? Our primary interest in capital derives from its interaction with people, an interaction which may be significant: witness the Lordstown linemen, the IBM executives, or the victims of auto accidents. But, for the most part, machines and buildings are machines and buildings, and we don't care how many of them are in existence.

Labor plays an interesting dual role. Population growth brings us increased labor input, but creates more claimants on the production process as well. Do more people each getting less (in terms of space as well as output) represent an improvement? This sounds like a theological question. It can be ducked for now, since our subject is economic growth, and we do not yet understand how economic growth influences population growth. If we did know, and if the relationship turned out to be strong, this might well dominate our thinking about economic growth.[5]

Land is the one factor of production that causes problems for the advocates of growth. Land has special structural properties. Short of filling the oceans, humans cannot manipulate the total stock of land, although they can affect its quality. More important for the present discussion, that stock has a utility independent of its productivity; the members of society, quite simply, care what landowners do with their asset. Given this externality, market forces alone will not provide an adequate guide to its optimal use. Economic growth, it would seem, could prove pernicious here in that it shifts the incentives for land use, probably to the detriment of the bulk of our citizens who enjoy scenic beauty and open space more than parking lots and shopping malls. Could this provide an argument for slowing growth? I don't think so. Measures like zoning, or taxes and subsidies on land use can go a long way toward assuring appropriate land use without creating as many harmful side effects as would slowing the growth process itself.

Economic Growth, the Distribution of Welfare, and Future Generations

The analysis thus far has been directed to the aggregate effects of growth. In a society that adheres to traditional liberal values, however, the appropriate way to evaluate growth policies, or any policies, is to examine their effects on the welfare of different individuals. Usually the choice of one policy over another benefits one individual or group more than another. Modern welfare economics, however, has provided us with the clear negative conclusion that we have no satisfactory procedure for weighing the interests of different individuals in order to arrive at an aggregate measure of welfare in our society: Benthamite utility calculations cannot be implemented. We could throw our hands up in despair or retreat to mysticism. But it seems more reasonable to list the consequences of different policies and to seek *ad hoc* procedures for evaluating the resulting lists.

It seems unequivocal that an individual's welfare is not solely determined by the bundle of goods and services he consumes. What matters very much, in addition, is his position vis-à-vis the others in his society with whom he can compare his condition. In order to compute the effects of economic growth on individual welfare, we certainly want to know how each individual is faring relative to his near and not-so-near neighbors. We would also like a comparison of his present status with the way things used to be. The fact that economic matters are getting better and better may make up for a relatively low position on the income totem pole; on the other hand, it may boost dissatisfaction by increasing expectations. (I would be uncomfortable trying to document my speculation that the first force predominates.)

When growth and distribution are discussed together, the usual concern is the welfare of different generations. From the standpoint of equity as well as the political exigencies of decision making, it seems equally important to identify the welfare of different income classes both at present and in the future. Consider the distributional implications of the stationary state, a limiting case of no growth. Assuming it could be achieved, it would allow very little room for departure from one's present position in the income distribution. And one's sons and daughters probably wouldn't be able to stray very far either.

The distributional effects of growth, on the other hand, are more difficult to predict. But we can say with some confidence that the types of societal changes that would come with growth would mix things up a bit. New skills and talents would become desirable; old ones would go out of style. Furthermore, the patronage-nepotism-old-boy system might lose some of its power when the old boys found their share of the market substantially diminished. Growth produces many gainers and, at least if relative position is important, many losers as well. The choice between growth and no-growth may depend on whether our concern is greater for the present or for the future poor, with the present poor being the natural advocates of growth. Let us examine, in turn, what retarding economic growth would do for the present poor and for future generations.

The ecology and antigrowth movements have many common objectives. This suggests that their members and major beneficiaries might come from the same classes. If, as is often alleged, the ecology movement has a middle and upper-class orientation, can the same bias be detected in its antigrowth offspring? Is the antigrowth movement founded on values that are particularly appealing to the upper strata of society? Are the areas of improvement it seeks those that our more privileged citizens are likely to value highly? Does it drain government funds from projects that would benefit the poor relatively more?

A look at the goals of the movement provides the answers. *Antigrowth promotes stability, insulation from rapid technological change, and acceptance of status quo living conditions. The most significant improvements it offers are in the physical environment.* [Emphasis added.] It would also protect us from certain societal disasters that would affect all members of society. If the movement were successful, however, it would eliminate the automatic revenue growth that is reaped by the federal government. New social legislation would be harder to secure, for it would have to out-wrestle old programs for funds.

A no-growth society would work most severely against the interests of the poorer members of society. [*Emphasis added.*] To improve their position, they would have to scrap over the fixed pile of societal resources; any absolute gain they achieved would be somebody else's absolute loss. If zero economic growth were imposed on the current structure of the American economy, Lester Thurow has calculated, "the distribution of family income would gradually grow more unequal, blacks would fall farther behind whites, and the share going to female earnings would fall below what it would otherwise be."[6] Not only would the poor lose the constant moving and shaking created by the natural economic processes of a growth-oriented society, but the political values of the more privileged classes would be likely to take a more conservative, perhaps even an oppressive turn. Traditionally, the increasing affluence of the lower strata of society has worked to the benefit of society as a whole, but in a no-growth society, any promotion of economic opportunities for the poor would work directly against the interests of the affluent.

Just as growth or no-growth affects politics, so politics can affect the type of growth we are likely to see. I argued above that we should evaluate the results of growth policies in terms of their effects on individuals. Growth is a people mixer. Though it may increase average welfare, it will also hurt some people. If the potential losers can foresee this, and if they can inhibit growth, then they will do so. Consider the advent of the automobile and the millions of jobs it created. [*Material omitted.*] A first dictum of pluralism is that small groups with heavy interests count more than large dispersed groups with small interests, even when the total interests of the latter are greater. Therefore the losers often exert a disproportionate influence in the political struggle. Where technological change is concerned, we would expect losers to be identified while gainers were not, a situation, I would argue, which tends to inhibit the types of technological change that would, on the whole, promote growth. Taken alone, this implies that we would be likely to have too little growth. Better seers than I would be needed to make confident predictions about the long-run distributional effects of this phenomenon. I would speculate though, that to succeed in preventing change, the identified potential losers would have to have significant power. Thus they would be unlikely to be among the underprivileged groups in the present society.

Future generations are most fortunate, at least from the standpoint of political argument. Their self-proclaimed supporters include both proponents and opponents of growth. The proponents argue that our only legacy to the future is the value of the capital stock we convey to them. Since, as Einstein has demonstrated to the skeptics, goods cannot be passed backwards through time, there is no way that future citizens can pay us. An increase in the capital stock we leave the people of the future must unambiguously increase their welfare. Antigrowthites who concentrate on economics may not consider a bountiful capital stock a boon. The difficulty they perceive relates to measurement. An increase in capital stock, as conventionally measured, may be accompanied by increases in environmental degradation and decreases in the levels of unexploited resources —undesirable movements which are not included in the definition of capital stock. The long-run picture the antigrowth forces perceive is particularly dreary. They confront us with a choice of suicides: drown in our refuse or perish when our resources run out.

I take a less alarmist view. The resources that are privately owned, as I have discussed above, provide no problem whatsoever. And we are improving our capabilities to place efficient rationing devices on the consumption of such commonly owned resources as ocean fish and environmental purity. Exacting prophecy is required to determine whether at some future time, growth in capital stock will or will not prove detrimental.

However, even in those areas where the problem is not one of prediction, we face extraordinarily difficult questions of a different sort. There can be no disagreement that other things being equal, our future citizens will be better off the cleaner the world into which they are born. Furthermore, we of the present can make sacrifices to preserve or at least to slow down the degradation of the environment. Even assuming that we had a universally accepted welfare meter and that we knew what made it go up and down, what should we sacrifice for our future brethren? In the liberal spirit, we are always interested in making transfers. But if historical trends can be extrapolated, our descendants will exceed us in material wealth. And even those members of the antigrowth lobby who would dispute this contention would not, I think, try to justify environmental preservation as a measure to improve the dynamic income distribution between us and our descendants.

Transfers to the future must be justified on grounds of efficiency; they should be made when, at a very small sacrifice to ourselves—a poorer generation—we can provide a big gain to the wealthier generations of the future.[7] We shouldn't dump garbage in the Grand Canyon, even though the money savings to our generation would more than offset our personal recreational loss. The losses to future citizens, after all, would be enormous. The decision here is easy, but it gets harder as the ratio of our savings to future loss narrows. Just what tradeoff rate in welfare should we require before we help the future at the expense of ourselves? How should we even address the question?[8] It's hard to know, but on the operational front two things seem clear: one to one is too low a ratio and, given a choice, present society as a whole would be less generous with its welfare than its antigrowth spokesmen would have it be. [Material omitted.]

The Risks of Economic Growth

The predictions of antigrowth forces have been shown to be unduly pessimistic. There is no dialectical force to the argument that economic growth must lead to a diminution in welfare. But the argument that growth, though good on average, raises the probability of various disastrous events, is more convincing. This makes it important to ask: What are the risks and dangers of unhindered economic growth?

In assessing these risks, it is useful to draw a distinction between those, like thalidomide deformation, that fall on individuals, and others, such as the melting of the polar icecaps, that affect society as a whole. Where individual risks are concerned, the economist's concept of *externality* provides the appropriate guide to policy. We do not want individuals imposing risks on others, particularly if those who must bear them will be unable to gain compensation for any losses they suffer either because they live at a far future time, or because casuality is difficult to prove, or because transaction costs make claims for suit uneconomic. Where personal gains (whether to a generation or an individual) can be secured by imposing risks on others, there is a natural tendency to take excessive risks. But what if actions risky to one or a few identified individuals hold out promise of great gain to others? In that case, the fact that there is no institutional framework for extracting compensation for conferred benefits is just as threatening. It will tend to prevent enough risks from being taken. In protecting some potential recipients of experimental treatment, for example, the FDA may have slowed the introduction of many beneficial drugs.

Some growth measures create risks for particular individuals; others generate more societal risks. If we are to formulate sensible policies, we must decide whether we prefer to see misfortunes suffered by a few people or by everyone at once. If misfortunes were universally shared, we would experience a more equal income distribution and, to the extent that relative income is important, less envy and more welfare. But this shared misfortune concept rules out the possibility of society as a whole having sufficient resources to compensate those who were unlucky. If significant redistribution were feasible, and could be agreed upon, then we should like risks to be more individual and less societal.

The societal risks of growth have had the more vocal opponents. We hear that we are going to run out of power, plunder our resources, ransack our genes, or push our society into disintegration. Some such potential crises have been dismissed above. Many others seem compelling and deserve study in much greater detail than is possible here. It seems best to concentrate here on what degree of risk we would like to see society as a whole assume. First, if there are no setbacks, we are not being risky enough. In order to reduce risk, we must sacrifice something else we value, perhaps even growth itself. When the price of that sacrifice gets too great (at the margin), we should live with the remaining risks. By way of analogy, economists point out that the ideal traffic safety program involves some traffic and some safety. We could, of course, have perfect safety merely by outlawing the automobile, but that would make travel more difficult.

If the strategy I propose were followed, economic growth would not proceed at a smooth exponential pace, but rather at variable speeds.[9] Once in a great while it might even go in reverse. Since times of sluggish contraction are more painful than equivalent periods of rapid expansion are pleasurable, we should sacrifice some speed of average growth to smooth out fluctuations. But the final result would still be an upward journey.

But what of the far future? We have no conception of the cumulative effects of our actions. There are too many things that could go wrong. When addressing this frequently heard concern, I suggest that one employ an expedient rule of thumb and simply ignore calculated dooms that are more than one hundred years away.[10] They have to take their place in line behind the many potential cataclysms that may intervene between now and then, the most apparent involving some form of warfare. If everything goes smoothly in the interim, the accelerating pace of scientific and technological progress will make our world and its problems almost unrecognizable a hundred years from now. It is hard to conceive of a growth-induced disaster that could not be averted or deflected by some significant scientific innovation. Indeed, nothing more than the successful exploitation of fusion energy would splash rosy paint on many black predictions of recent years. If growth and its risks are our concern, the foreseeable future should be our focus.

Beyond the Economic Perspective

If prescription for social policy is our goal, we should look for areas in which we can improve the present state of affairs. Now the neoclassical model of economics correctly tells us that if markets were everywhere perfect, we would not have to worry about growth or any of the other targets of social policy. The uncoordinated outcome would be efficient. But markets are hardly perfect. Flaws are particularly noticeable in markets for risky assets and capital, key ingredients to the whole growth process. This observation should forewarn us that something may go wrong.

The neoclassical model requires not only that we trade on perfect markets, but that we be utility isolationists and care not one bit about the welfare of others, nor about their decisions. However, where growth, its attractions and liabilities are concerned, no stipulation could be further from reality. In the short run, we may worry that a new factory

345

pollutes the clean air, a situation that an economist might label a static externality. And over the course of time, such matters can be even more consequential.

Henry Ford and other automotive pioneers gave an all-time boost to GNP by initiating mass production technology for automobiles. Our situation will never be the same. What would our society be like without automobiles? The question is mind boggling because virtually any answer must project a world so different from our own. Economic growth goes hand in hand with new products and new technologies, and these in turn produce changes in society and in its yardsticks for evaluating its own welfare. Here, too, we will need something more dynamic than the neoclassical paradigm which deals with a single society where tastes don't change.

From a policy standpoint, this discussion has focused primarily on economic welfare. In that limited domain, it is evident that slowing growth will not produce the optimal situation. But MEW and income distribution may not be all we care about. Religion, justice, independence, racial equality and brotherhood, the strength of the nuclear family, and sexual liberation are perhaps more important to our welfare.[11] If we could demonstrate an adverse causal relationship between economic growth and these social variables, we might wish to slow growth despite the economic consequences.

One of the nice things about economic growth is that it is observable and measurable. Social decline, on the other hand, is a fuzzy concept, difficult to observe, and not personal to the individual. This contrast introduces a danger into the growth debate. Where we are surely making progress, economically, progress can be documented. Where we may be backsliding, socially, we can hardly tell where we have been. If, in fact, growth is not in the best interest of society, economists should not be the ones to tell us, for economists are the gurus of growth, with the assignment to further it and guide it in profitable directions. The limited jurisdiction of economists, therefore, cannot support a very stimulating discussion on the merits of growth. It's time other tradesmen joined the debate.

Footnotes

1. My Kennedy School colleagues have provided me with helpful comments.
2. This terminology may seem to prejudge the issue. That is exactly what Thomas Schelling, who proposed it to me, intended.
3. W. Nordhaus and J. Tobin, "Is Growth Obsolete?" *Economic Growth* (New York: National Bureau of Economic Research, 1972). This piece provides an excellent scholarly survey of the growth-welfare relationship.
4. Nordhaus and Tobin ("Is Growth Obsolete?") indicate that economic growth has been accompanied by an increase in MEW. There is, of course, no logical reason why this pattern couldn't be broken in the future.
5. Our ignorance is reflected in the traditional economic assumption that population growth is an exogenous variable. In a very rough sort of a way, it seems that as we pass up the industrial development income ladder, children become more of a consumption and less of a production good. This in no way implies that more wealth would mean less population; we know very little about the long-run relation between income and demand for children.
6. Lester Thurow, "The Impact of Zero Economic Growth on Personal Incomes," mimeo, M.I.T., August 1972.
7. An adherent of the fixed-all-time-consumption-of-resources view of economic development would point out that at some point in the future, assuming humans continue to exist, per capita welfare will have to diminish. His decisions in providing for the future might depend on how much he thinks he will be benefiting our more affluent immediate descendants as opposed to the impoverished residents of the far future.
8. Some analysts might argue that the utility from altruistic behavior should be our guide, that if we get sufficient utility from providing for the future, then we should. This is the philosophy underlying some arguments that the social rate of discount should diverge from the interest rate we observe on the market. Starting from a very different philosophical basis, one could argue that the government is the custodian of the future and should take full account of any externalities that will befall it, even though compensation can never be charged. Acceptance of this point of view would lead to a high rate of transfer to the future. A third approach, similar in consequence to the second, would make intergeneration transfer decisions on the basis of a hypothetical

The Risks of Growth

contract that would have been agreed to by all future citizens standing behind a Rawlsian "veil of ignorance." The transfers would be equitable, because at the time the agreement was drawn, the parties would not know who would live when.

9. There is quite another source of variation. Technological advance is hardly the smooth exponential process posited in most economists' models. An invention like the transistor, which can provide a measurable boost for the total economy, may come along only once in a great while.

10. Economists' models, relying on unchanging assumptions, frequently show a decline, say, in income beyond some point t'. If this information is to be used for policy, it is important to know whether the real-time equivalent for t' is five, one hundred, or one million years.

11. A survey on this matter might not tell us much beyond identifying areas where consciousness is high. Perhaps people pay the most attention to the objective which they see as potentially most threatened. For example, when asked to name their most valuable consumption item, few individuals would select oxygen or water. Fortunately, for the present, neither seems likely to be taken away.

Growth vs.
No-Growth:
An Evaluation

Roland N. McKean

*Roland McKean is Commonwealth Professor of Economics at the University of
Virginia. He was a professor of economics at the University of California, Los
Angeles, from 1964 through 1968 and a research economist at the Rand Corporation in Santa Monica, California, from 1951-1964. Mr. McKean is a graduate of
the University of Chicago, and holds a master's and a doctorate in economics
from the University of Chicago.*

*This article is reprinted by permission of Daedalus, (Journal of the American
Academy of Arts and Sciences, Boston, Mass. Fall 1973), The No-Growth Society. The version as it appears here is a digest (to approximately two-thirds) of the
original.*

"Growth" is a harmless neutral concept meaning merely "a growing" or "an
increase."[1] If growth meant an increase in well-being in terms of an agreed-upon criterion
of well-being, it could hardly be opposed. Objections to growth must refer to the increase
of particular magnitudes—in population, GNP, or power consumption—that cause
negative growth of well-being according to some criterion. What is really objected to,
then, is *negative or uneconomic growth* according to certain concepts of social welfare.

Disagreement about these matters is bound to occur, because any kind of growth will
injure some individuals, and in the real world all injured persons will not be compensated. Moreover, even if they could be compensated, some might not like the outcome: in
any group decision, there is a basic value or criterion judgment about which members of
the group may disagree. To discuss costs or gains from any kind of growth or from
anything else, however, one must keep in mind a criterion that determines how costs and
gains are to be measured. In this paper I will use the concept of "economic efficiency,"
according to which gains (or costs) are priced at whatever individuals would voluntarily
pay, at the margin, to have (or avoid) them. This means accepting (or simulating) the
values that would emerge from a voluntary exchange system. One could substitute a
different criterion and, although similar phenomena would occur, the values attached to
them could differ.

Throughout the paper I will use the term "economic growth," as I believe most other
persons use it, to mean increases in GNP or some such indicator of aggregate final output.
In a sense this is a misuse of the word "economic," for growth would hardly be
economic—hardly an economical use of resources—if it entailed certain costs that were
not being counted (as is the case with GNP). It is convenient, however, to use the term
"economic growth" in this fashion, since this usage is widely accepted. Moreover, except
where I specifically mention population growth, my discussion will pertain to economic
growth.

Possible Interpretations of the Case for No-Growth

Let us examine alternative ways of interpreting the arguments in favor of retarded or zero growth. Critics of economic growth may mean that it constitutes two steps forward and one step back—that it has bad side effects which partly offset the good effects. In that event, it makes sense to see if reducing the bad effects can yield net gains. It would not make sense, however, simply to eliminate growth, for in these circumstances, one would sacrifice the two steps forward in order to avoid one step backward.

In this situation, most indexes of growth are misleading, of course, if they are mistaken for indexes of growth in welfare, for in terms of well-being they may reflect the two steps forward but little or none of the backsliding. Also, it might be noted that the distribution of benefits and injuries is not uniform. To recipients of benefits (perhaps the young and upwardly mobile), growth may seem lovely; while to the injured (among them the elderly or long-time residents who preferred their city when it was half its present size), economic growth may appear to be an undiluted evil.

Alternatively, critics of "economic growth" may mean that expansion of the economy has so many bad side effects that it really constitutes two steps forward and three steps back. As before, it would be sensible to try to reduce the steps backward as long as the effort yielded net gain. If reducing the bad side effects were too costly to be economical, however, it would be appropriate to stop the growth—in other words, to prevent the two steps forward in order to eliminate the three steps backward. Such a policy employs a meat axe instead of a scalpel, yet it is the best one can do when using the scalpel results in too many disadvantages.

It is possible, finally, that some opponents of growth believe its effects to be solely bad ones. In that case, stopping such growth would be an unambiguous improvement. I do not believe the consequences are so simple, however, and doubt that many other persons do.

Evaluating the Costs of Growth

Personally I do not think that the most highly publicized costs of growth are by themselves so ruinous and unmanageable.[2] Deterioration of the physical environment is unlikely to cause cataclysmic disaster; mainly it will bring about a declining level of material well-being.[3] The world will turn out to be less rich and sweet smelling than a few people for a few decades thought it was.

Realistic scenarios for the future would allow for the adjustments that even stubborn, stupid *Homo sapiens* can hardly avoid. To be sure, as far as forms of pollution are concerned, they result from the kinds of interdependencies in which individual action gets one almost nowhere. As Schelling has pointed out even more vividly than most,[4] individual decisions where negotiation costs are high (as they would be if we tried to hire each other to be less noisy) can trap societies in myriad and extremely persistent "nonoptimal" situations. Nonetheless, if the costs of inaction become high enough, some private agreements (to use soundproofing, for example) will seem worth the transaction costs, and government measures will appear to be worth the intervention costs. Similarly, as environmental quality deteriorates, people will, through voluntary contracts and the political process, divert their resources from material goods to environmental types of material well-being.

Admittedly, the political process, either within or among nations, does not respond in a timely or precise fashion,[5] but at least it provides gross responses to gross increases in the demand for public goods. These responses will be *truly* gross, though, if debate and adjustments are postponed until crises prompt government action.

In the private sector there will be many automatic adjustments. Prices, while they will not follow appropriate paths where resources are not owned privately, or markets do not exist, or prices are regulated, will eventually respond in a gross fashion even under these adverse conditions. These price changes will also help strike a balance between environmental quality and other forms of material wealth. Thus, I assert, along with numerous others,[6] that a sensible scenario for the future portrays declines of wealth and a series of painful adjustments, including a leveling off or decline of population, but not a sudden collapse of any kind.

The exhaustion of nonrenewable resources would bring about similar adjustments as we became poorer.[7] It would be an unlikely coincidence for technological advances to maintain per capita income indefinitely; economic growth will probably become negative someday. But all resources will not simultaneously and suddenly vanish without advance warning. Prices will rise, inducing people to shift to substitutes. Anticipating further price increases, speculators (that is, all of us) will find it profitable to store scarce materials, not for distant posterity but to apportion them out over a thirty- or forty-year period, and some would subsequently be kept for high-value uses over subsequent thirty- or forty-year periods. These apportionments will help make the process of getting poorer a matter of painful but not catastrophic adjustment.

These prospects raise in starkest form the question, "How much are we willing to sacrifice for posterity?" Clearly people will make enormous sacrifices for their children and grandchildren. They may also wish to put aside extra resources for the well-being of distant generations yet be unwilling to do so unless they are assured that others will also do so.[8] This free-rider difficulty raises the issue, "Can public policy promote economic efficiency (in terms of the wishes of the existing population) by extra conservation efforts?" Individual values on this point are difficult to discern. For most people the preferred compromise may be to profess, but not really demonstrate, concern about the distant future.

Population growth will, whenever extra persons add more to total social cost than they contribute,[9] reduce material well-being and accelerate environmental deterioration and the use of exhaustible resources. Here too, however, it is impossible for me to visualize a situation in which people, even acting individually, would fail completely to make adjustments as the negative marginal social product of people became larger and larger. Their adjustments would hardly be those which would be optimal in a hypothetical world of zero transaction costs and therefore zero free-rider difficulties, but there would be reductions in birth rates and increases in death rates as extra bodies produced less useful output and more undesirable consequences. Minor disasters might be involved in this process, but not sudden unprecedented madness or famine or plague. Nonetheless, the disadvantages of deliberately limiting population growth seem relatively small and hence the case for it is comparatively strong.

Growth and Poverty of the Spirit

Other possible side effects of growth, however, worry me as much as conventional forms of pollution and poverty. These other consequences produce or aggravate what might be called *poverty of the spirit*. They can be regarded as unconventional forms of pollution, since, analytically viewed, all side effects are similar to pollution:[10] they stem from overuse or suspected overuse[11] of some resource (with economic efficiency as the criterion) because the consent of the damaged parties is not bought. Thus, if our individual actions spread disease or despair, they use up people's health without purchase of their consent. The following external effects of growth, although we know little about them yet, may be as ominous as their threat to material well-being as such.

I believe that, from now on, many types of growth—in, for example, population, urban density, and material affluence—increase the probability of pervasive controls and ownership by government. The two extreme choices confronting people may be to accept an increasing degree of interference with each other, which is frustrating, or to vote for various majority-rule government restrictions, which are also frustrating. To be viable, behavioral rules have to be voluntarily accepted as a result of enlightened self-interest, and free-rider and other difficulties make it unlikely that such "social contracts" will evolve.[12]

I conclude that people will move in both of these directions but with much emphasis on the use of government, on coercive restrictions imposed by majority coalitions who object to particular spillovers. But majority rule, like any other political process, is a meat cleaver method of resolving conflicts. It leaves more people dissatisfied than would smoothly working markets (which are largely unavailable for resolving the conflicts under discussion because of transaction costs). Unresolved conflicts will become deeper and more numerous. The bargaining process in government will cost more and achieve less.

In short, government, as we allocate more and more burdens to its decision-making process, will become a more costly and embittering process. The simple increase in the number of alternatives confronting people puts them in conflict with each other more often. If transaction costs are low, conflict resolution by bargaining is comparatively easy. If such costs are high, however, the market offers little help. Thus the proliferation of conflicts *where transaction costs are high*, ulcer-generating in itself, increases the probability of an expanding and increasingly unpleasant role for government. Government seems, from the standpoint of each voter, to have enormous arbitrary power. The disgruntled citizen cannot turn to a competitor, and, as government grows, he feels a growing sense of impotence. Moreover, at best, the purchase and distribution of goods and services by government yield frustration, because almost no one, except the famous median voter on each issue, gets the amount or kind of defense or Medicare that he prefers for his tax dollar. Also, it should be remembered, the public goods themselves (defense or highways for example) inflict distressing external impacts without purchasing the consent of the damaged persons.[13]

Other more speculative impacts of population and economic growth may rob life in the future of much flavor and quality. With growth, there is pervasive change and perhaps a reduction in the probability of durable nonsuperficial relationships.[14] In a large and mobile population, for example, the chances of encountering or dealing with a person a second time and the chances of frequent or persistent dealings are comparatively small. If, on balance, the process of growth reduces the chances of having durable nonsuperficial relationships, this in itself is a considerable loss, for much of life is an almost pathetic search for such relationships.

More importantly, however, change and the impersonality of relationships may contribute to the decline of customs and behavioral rules which have, in the past, helped to reduce many external costs that people would otherwise have inflicted on each other.[15] At best there is a serious free-rider problem involved in people's decisions as to whether to be friendly or courteous, to take garbage cans to the rear of the house, to serve as witnesses, to refrain from making noise, and even to be honest. Through the centuries man developed ethical rules, and often enforced them by threats of retaliation, ostracism, and eternity in hell, to cope with various free-rider difficulties. Along with the decline of religion which threatened personal punishment and allowed no free riders, larger and more mobile societies suffer a decline in the possibilities of personal retaliation or ostracism, a decline which undermines behavioral codes and aggravates free-rider problems. In other words, growth tends to undermine the "social contracts" that are so important to the enforcement of amenity rights and the functioning of capitalism.

These observations are highly speculative, for many variables and uncertain relationships are involved. Furthermore, and this deserves emphasis, I am not suggesting that things were better under "Peter the Great;" on balance, life was probably dreadful for most people in most earlier eras, and at present it may be getting better every day, but this is irrelevant. The relevant question is this: if growth is not, or will not in the future be, a free lunch, are there policies that could make us better off in the decades ahead than we would otherwise be?

Another force helping to generate some of the above side effects as well as others is the rising value of time—in terms of real income that can be earned per hour—which results from economic growth. Increases in personal income influence a person's choice between work and leisure and his choices among leisure activities.[16] The extra income makes him able to afford more leisure and time-consuming activities, but the higher earnings per hour make such pursuits more expensive to him. This causes him to substitute relatively more productives uses of leisure time for those that yield constant results per hour. In many cases this "substitution effect" dominates the "income effect." Hence, as Linder has pointed out,[17] one often finds capital and other inputs being used to save time or make each hour more productive, and less time devoted to uses of time that cannot be made more productive. One observes more leisure activities involving television sets, cameras, automobiles, boats, and TV dinners, and fewer leisure activities using mainly a person's time. What concerns us here are the possible repercussions on others of these new choices by each individual. Thinking and decision making are among the uses of time that are becoming relatively expensive, so unless citizens gradually come to value these activities more, they may spend less time on them. Each of us has a stake, however, in getting other citizens to be well-informed, to think about issues, and to make decisions carefully.

Perhaps the impact of rising real incomes is offset by other developments, but this may be another way in which growth is aggravating the free-rider difficulties that plague the democratic process. Is growth pushing us more and more toward quick decisions, the acquisition of superficial information about numerous subjects, and centralization of effective power? If so, it may further increase the difficulty—the cost, that is—of governing ourselves. (Moreover, the costliness of time further exacerbates the problem of establishing nonsuperficial friendships.)

All of these effects seem as serious to me as the prospective decline in material well-being. People can apparently endure considerable poverty or physical hardship if struggling still yields slight improvements, and if they feel as though they can influence events somewhat. If struggle results in virtually no response, however, if events seem increasingly to be beyond the individual's control, then a deeper sort of poverty sets in than just the material sacrifices of having more pollution and fewer goods.

Also, to the extent that growth beyond some point does aggravate these spillovers, taking steps to check economic and population growth itself might be a more economical way of reducing the external costs than trying to alleviate the spillovers while reaping the desirable consequences of growth. In other words, it is conceivable that growth yields net disadvantages, yet that direct attacks on the disadvantages cost more than they gain. It is also conceivable, though, that by implementing a low-growth policy, government could alleviate the erosion of behavioral rules and the other spillovers described above.

It should be stressed that the relevant magnitudes are the marginal advantages and disadvantages of growth. Clearly, up to some point population and economic growth contributed more that they cost. Beyond some point, however, these forms of growth yield decreasing marginal returns, increasing marginal costs, and ultimately net marginal disadvantages. These net marginal disadvantages may climb rapidly as growth rates soar even if past growth has brought rich rewards.

To keep things in proportion, however, I must admit that attributing the above costs to economic growth is highly speculative. Other variables obviously contribute to the expanding role of government, the slump in respect for the individual, and the crumbling of useful traditions. Perhaps growth has nothing to do with these phenomena. My personal feeling, however, is that whether or not growth has played a significant role in the past, I cannot help believing that continued growth will make it harder and harder for us to avoid interfering with each other, harder and harder for us to govern ourselves.

Evaluating the Costs of No-Growth

We should now examine the principal costs of *stopping growth* and try to make some comparisons with alternative policies. Maybe growth will appear to be like democracy: the worst possible situation one can imagine—except for the alternatives. In the case of retarding population growth, apart from the difficulties of implementation, I cannot believe that the costs could be great. The consequences of settling for no more than four billion human beings on this planet, or 250 million in the United States, could hardly be catastrophic. If additional people still yield a positive net return at all, it is a modest one, and, at worst, limiting population would sacrifice a modest amount of material well-being. At some population level, externalities would make it economical to ask people to give up demands for large families in order to meet other intense demands.

The case is not quite so clear when one considers implementation, though here too I am comparatively optimistic regarding the retardation of population growth. On the whole I believe working toward low or zero population growth, if it does not come about naturally, would probably be worth the cost.

How would one set about stopping economic growth? Putting a legislative ceiling on the GNP would hardly affect anyone's behavior, since the GNP is merely the result of adding together various components that are determined by a host of variables. The only way to do anything would be to work on the variables that affect investment and consumption behavior. Establishing ceilings and controls on each industry's output would convert a private enterprise economy into a centrally planned one, thereby losing the coordination provided by markets. The result, I assert, would be clumsily inefficient, at least in terms of conventional criteria. If detailed central planning was the only way to achieve no-growth, I would chalk this up as an awesome cost of a no-growth policy.[18] Let us look, however, at other ways of reducing economic growth in a mixed economy.

Outputs could be reduced, though in a rather haphazard fashion, by measures short of detailed planning, such as limiting the work week to say thirty hours. Such a step would still require a lot of repugnant enforcement and loop-hole-plugging activities, perhaps even the monitoring of consumption and the use of leisure time. Furthermore, measures like limiting hours of work are extremely imprecise tools, which would cut back on many services that contribute little to pollution or depletion yet entail many of the disadvantages of central planning.

In my view the least unappealing type of mechanism would be to tax all output of goods for both consumption and investment, and devote the proceeds to environmental repair. With the objective of no-growth, the taxes and outlays would be adjusted to hold constant some such output indicator as GNP, and one would simply hope that the outcome yielded an appropriate amount of pollution and exhaustible resource use. But this whole technique of curtailing aggregate output is a rather clumsy way to reduce pollution and consumption of depletable resources.

Note how imprecise the linkage is between no-growth and these undesired effects. One could have no-growth of the GNP and still be polluting or using up energy sources at various rates. One's conclusion depends partly on how one measures growth, but practically any index will have only a loose connection with the increase in pollution or the consumption of exhaustible resources. As for the linkage between GNP and its undesired impacts, some forms of output are associated with high rates of pollution and depletion of nonrenewable resources; others are not.

If, however, we start regulating particular outputs, we're back in the business of detailed planning in order to do something other than just stop growth. If we start taxing particular outputs, we're trying to curtail the side effects rather than growth *per se* (which may turn out to look very sensible but which is not the topic at hand). Keeping in mind the imprecision of these linkages, let us consider the costs or disadvantages of tax expenditure programs that would prevent any increase in, say, the cumulative measure of consumption plus investment plus government expenditures for *goods* (as opposed to goods plus services).

Disadvantages of ZEG

There are several significant disadvantages of zero economic growth (ZEG): some inherently associated with a static as opposed to a dynamic economy, and some connected with the particular measures required to implement a ZEG policy. First and most obvious, the sacrificed consumption and investment would obviously have been desirable from the standpoint of existing persons. Also, some of the investment in durable facilities would have created returns for near future generations. Hence, if we stop economic growth to promote one set of objectives, we must give up the at least partially offsetting material benefits. In a free economy this would mean giving up not exactly what you and I personally visualize as frills but whatever consumers in general regarded as their least important purchases, presumably including quality and quantity in most categories of goods. In a planned economy, it would mean giving up, again not what you and I think of as frills, but whatever the planning establishment regarded as marginal. Below, I will argue that this sacrifice would be larger under a no-growth policy than under an alternative approach.

In the short run there would be transitional difficulties. The shock of taxes to prevent growth, though it would depend upon factors about which we know little, might be considerably greater than defense mobilization or demobilization, for the policy would throw most industries into readjustments. Unlike mobilization—which changes the composition of output—the no-growth policy would, in addition, stop investment and growth of total output. Accompanying this resource re-allocation would be a traumatic adjustment of attitudes as people were confronted, even gradually, with a drop in real income in comparison with their previous expectations, with the prospect of no future wage increases except perhaps for superior individual performance, and with the prospect of a relatively static society.

A more serious problem is that a no-growth policy would heighten distribution con-

Growth vs. No-Growth: An Evaluation

flicts within the nation and among nations. (Note, however, that if my earlier arguments are correct, no growth would reduce certain other conflicts attributed to growth.) Consider distribution conflicts within a nation. People resent it less when someone else gets a promotion or a higher income if they suffer only a comparative rather than an absolute loss. No-growth, however, might sharpen these conflicts and make it more difficult for politicians to encourage free entry into occupations and industries or to allow freely moving prices and rates of hire, more difficult for collective bargaining and government processes to work satisfactorily. British experience suggests that lack of growth may "produce as many and as unpleasant stresses on the social and political economy as industrial growth can impose on the ecological and natural resources of the globe."[19] No-growth may imply sharper distribution conflicts and the costs associated with them in terms of resources devoted to bargaining and conflict resolution and, perhaps more important, resources of the spirit squandered in anger, bitterness, and violence.

Conflicts among nations would be exacerbated for these as well as other reasons. If all nations did agree to retard economic growth, the underdeveloped nations would find it more difficult, whatever the agreed-upon formulae, to get ahead. Such countries would probably find the door forever closed to anything approaching the incomes enjoyed by the advanced countries. They would find it more difficult to bring about changes in resource allocation. But the conflict in interests is so sharp that it is hard to imagine worldwide agreement to limit growth. Suppose the U.S. pushes for an agreement to stop economic growth in order to reduce pollution and the use of exhaustible resources. It is difficult to imagine the underdeveloped nations agreeing to large sacrifices for the sake of the rest of the world, and, in view of the sensitivity of advanced nations about national security, one can hardly foresee their making large concessions. Without a worldwide agreement, however, the free-rider problem makes it hard to imagine unilateral or small-group action. What do these conflicting interests among nations signify for the costs of a no-growth policy? They imply that it would require tremendous negotiation costs and sacrifices of "national security" and "fairness among nations" to implement a no-growth policy. An alternative way to put the point is simply to say that the chances of any nation's adopting no-growth policies are slight.

Another speculative, yet perhaps important, consideration is the set of sacrifices entailed by having a more nearly static society. Under a no-growth policy, it would necessarily be less rewarding than before, in comparison with other activities, to search for changes in technology, to seek to identify changes in taste, or to shift resources. In short, changes, which may seem too attractive currently, would become less rewarding, relative to "housekeeping" and status-quo production, than at present. Initially there would be considerable re-allocation of resources in response to the new taxes and government programs. Investment in growth-promoting innovations would become relatively unattractive, however, since growth promotion would no longer be permitted. This might have some desirable consequences, such as reducing the adverse impacts of "future shock," but it would also have some deleterious ones. With fewer possibilities of change, people might feel they had less "adventure," less hope of discovering some larger purpose in life, less hope of something better ahead.

A closely related yet less speculative cost of the reduced rewards for change would be the weakening of incentives for producing knowledge and cultural diversity.[20] It would be possible, naturally, for some discovery and cultural innovations to occur, but study, research, new knowledge, and innovation would almost certainly be less rewarding than in a growing society, and fewer resources would be devoted to them. Although wages and rewards in general would be lower than in a growing economy, those available for growth-promoting activities would be especially affected. All in all, I am fairly confident that no-growth policies would reduce aggregate success in research and development and diminish the chances of solving particular technological problems or contributing to the well-being of posterity.

My biggest objection to a *no-growth policy*, however, is closely related to my principal apprehension concerning *unbridled growth*. I believe that measures to induce no-growth would likewise produce a government role that would intensify our "spiritual poverty." The taxes imposed to stop growth of consumption and investment would yield large revenues. The spending of these revenues in ways consistent with no-growth would, I have suggested, be better than detailed planning, but would nonetheless bring relatively large and discretionary government.

We cannot know for sure whether the revenues collected would exceed those involved in a more finely-tuned attack on pollution and resource exhaustion. For the reasons stated below, however, I believe that direct attacks on many of the side effects: (a) would yield more than they cost (in which case the blunt-instrument approach of checking growth is not the appropriate one, at least initially), and (b) would result in smaller government spending programs and less discretionary authority than a growth-reduction approach aimed at yielding the same abatements in pollution and resource depletion.

Given the variability of the input-output connections between growth and different forms of pollution, no-growth would leave the economy with too much of some forms and too little of others for its efficient operation. It is a ham-handed strategy somewhat like, to take an extreme analogy, reducing a city's power supply by 10 percent in order to reduce fires, accidental electrocutions, and atrocious movies; cutting down on power usage would eliminate some unknown quantities of these phenomena, but only by chance the appropriate ones.

An Alternative Policy

In my view the more economical approach to spillover abatement is probably to launch frontal attacks on the conventional externalities with the aim of reducing each form as long as the gains promise to exceed the costs. Moreover, it would often be economical to minimize the government's role, particularly its discretionary role, by using *price mechanisms*: effluent charges, liability reassignments (to fasten external costs on those activities that generate them), congestion fees, external-cost taxes on commonpool resources like fish, and other spillover charges.

These devices would be "fine tuning" compared to regulations or government-operated abatement programs. *The levying of externality-charges and the fixing of liabilities* on someone in the causal chain would probably use fewer resources and less government than would achieving the same amount of pollution abatement via growth reduction. In many instances, of course, transaction costs, such as those of collection and enforcement, would make it uneconomical to use such price mechanisms in the neat and complete manner in which they could be employed in a hypothetical zero-transaction-cost world.

Similarly, the logical straightforward thing to do about nonrenewable resources, if voters do want to preserve more for posterity, would be to *tax the use* of those particular resources. The size of such taxes could be adjusted by trial and error to yield the desired degree of deterrence, and the revenues could be used to reduce other taxes. To be realistic, however, a more effective means of doing something for posterity is probably to attempt to develop the fusion reactor and ways of tapping geothermal energy.

Economic growth as conventionally measured would be retarded by a combination of finely-tuned attacks on orthodox forms of *pollution*, plus conservation or research on *energy sources*, plus *population control*. While the benefits of growth would naturally be diminished, so would the "subtle" *external costs* because resulting reductions in affluence, the value of time,[21] and crowding would remove some of the pressures which may contribute to superficial relationships, the erosion of behavioral rules and ethical codes, government expansion, and other spillovers. These subtle spillovers may be important, and I don't like simply to accept whatever this policy would do to them. But the no-growth policy would also let them lie wherever no-growth dropped them. All I can say is that if further reductions in these effects appeared to be worth the cost, and if no-growth appeared to be the economical way to curtail them, then further reductions of growth might be considered.

Thus, I would expect highly undesirable effects either from untrammeled economic and population growth, or from government interventions to stop economic growth. As for population growth, I can visualize steps to retard or stop it that in my judgment promise more gains than costs. It is conceivable that the most economical means of conserving exhaustible resources and of relieving various forms of pollution is the meat-axe approach represented by a no-growth policy, but this seems improbable when one considers alternatives even in a crude and cursory fashion. The preferable course, it seems to me, would be to attack directly conventional forms of pollution and to tax the use of nonrenewable resources. This direct and more finely tuned approach would, of course, reduce growth and final output, as conventionally measured, thereby generating some of the costs and benefits attributed to no-growth. The by-product reduction of economic growth, in combination with zero population growth, would also diminish most of the subtle side effects discussed above, assuming that they are related to crowding, affluence, and material outputs. (Unfortunately, just as with a no-growth policy, these side effects might not be alleviated in the appropriate amounts.)[22]

Perhaps most importantly, this policy would keep government from being quite as large, pervasive, discretionary, quarrelsome, and costly as it would be under a no-growth policy. In comparison with such a direct attack on the difficulties, a zero economic growth goal seems a little like trying to eliminate the clouds in order to get better-lighted offices. It is not always an error to manipulate proxies, but I judge that it would be inefficient to do so in this instance.

Footnotes

1. The author is indebted, for support of research related to this subject, to NSF Grant 31400X to the Thomas Jefferson Center Foundation for studying the implications of different resource rights.
2. Many of the consequences are well portrayed by E. J. Mishan, *Technology and Growth: The Price We Pay* (New York: Praeger, 1969); Harold J. Barnett and Chandler Morse, *Scarcity and Growth*, Resources for the Future, Inc. (Baltimore: Johns Hopkins Press, 1963); and Harrison Brown, *The Challenge of Man's Future* (New York: Viking Press, 1954). Kenneth E. Boulding's work includes provocative discussions of many of these issues especially in "The Economics of the Coming Spaceship Earth," *Environmental Quality in a Growing Economy*, ed. H. Jarrett, Resources for the Future, Inc. (Baltimore: Johns Hopkins Press, 1966), pp. 3-14. Recently, such consequences have been publicized more widely by the book sponsored by the Club of Rome: D. L. Meadows, D. H. Meadows, J. Randers, and W. W. Behrens, *The Limits to Growth* (New York: Potomac Associates, 1972); and by Barbara Ward and René Dubos, *Only One Earth: The Care and Maintenance of a Small Planet*, a report

Growth vs. No-Growth: An Evaluation

commissioned for the United Nations Conference on the Human Environment (New York: W. W. Norton, 1972). W. Beckerman has provided useful criticism of such views in "Why We Need Economic Growth," *Lloyds Bank Review* (October 1971), 1-15.

3. Fred Singer, "Environmental Quality—When Does Growth Become Too Expensive?" *Is There an Optimal Level of Population?*, ed. S. Fred Singer (New York: McGraw-Hill, 1971), pp. 156-172.

4. Thomas C. Schelling, "On the Ecology of Micromotives," *Public Interest*, No. 25 (Fall 1971), 61-98. One of his many graphic summary statements is that often "the worst things in life are free."

5. For some factors that help explain government behavior, see Roland N. McKean, "Property Rights Within Government, and Devices to Increase Governmental Efficiency," *Southern Economic Journal*, 39 (October 1972), 177-186.

6. Fred Singer, "The Predicament of the Club of Rome" [a review of *The Limits to Growth*], EOS Transactions, American Geophysical Union, 53 (July 1972), 697-700, esp. 700; Rudolph Klein, "Growth and Its Enemies," *Commentary*, 53 (June 1972), 44. On the "Club of Rome Model" see also Allen Kneese and Ronald Ridker, "Predicament of Mankind" [a review of *The Limits to Growth*], *Washington Post*, March 2, 1972, pp. B1, B9.

7. For a variety of views, see especially the papers by Preston Cloud, Harrison Brown, Joseph L. Fisher, Alvin M. Weinberg and R. Philip Hammond, and Hans H. Landsberg in *Is There an Optimal Level of Population?*; and the essays in *Energy, Economic Growth, and the Environment*, ed. Sam H. Schurr, Resources for the Future, Inc. (Baltimore: Johns Hopkins Press, 1972).

8. This would imply a different "social rate of discount" from the one that emerges when the free-rider difficulty is taken as given. Also, of course, one may attach value to conservation if he does not accept economic efficiency as a criterion.

9. This depends, of course, on the stocks of land and capital, transaction costs, tastes, and one's criterion. For an excellent discussion, see Stephen Enke, "Economic Consequences of Rapid Population Growth," *Economic Journal*, 81 (December 1971), 800-811.

10. As E. J. Mishan has pointed out, the dumping of erotica into the environment creates spillover costs to some bystanders, using up at minimum their peace of mind without their consent—generating spillovers that are fully analogous to the effects of injecting pollutants into the atmosphere. "A Modest Proposal: Cleaning up Sex Pollution," *Harper's* (July 1972), 54-56.

11. Failure to produce external benefits that it would be efficient to produce can be regarded as an external cost, because it damages persons and overuses some resources in comparison with the state that could exist.

12. Roland N. McKean, "The Economics of Altruism, Trust, and Corporate Responsibility," to appear in a volume containing papers presented at the Russell Sage Conference on Altruism in March of 1972 (ed. E. S. Phelps).

13. Roland N. McKean, "Property Rights, Appropriability, and Externalities in Government," *Perspectives of Property*, ed. G. Wunderlich and W. L. Gibson, Jr. (Pennsylvania State University, Institute for Research on Land and Water Resources, 1972), pp. 32-55.

14. These points are related to some of those made in Alvin Toffler, *Future Shock* (New York: Random House, 1970).

15. McKean, "The Economics of Altruism, Trust, and Corporate Responsibility."

16. Gary S. Becker, "A Theory of the Allocation of Time," *Economic Journal* (September 1965), 493-517.

17. Staffan B. Linder, *The Harried Leisure Class* (New York: Columbia University Press, 1970).

18. Central planning of outputs and inputs seems to me vastly more difficult than the assignment and enforcement of new rights regarding one output that the "certificate plan" for population control implies.

19. Klein, "Growth and Its Enemies," p. 43.

20. We cannot claim to know much, however, about these causal connections. As Boulding once wrote, it is puzzling that the sudden growth of knowledge in the sixteenth century took place in Europe rather than in China, which was at that time ahead of Europe ("The Economics of the Coming Spaceship Earth," pp.8-9). But the explanation may lie in the cultural diversity and familiarity with differences that must have characterized Europe.

21. The Japanese have apparently tried (for different reasons) to attack even this variable in a direct fashion: levying fines on "supervisors who insist on working holidays and their normal days off," *Time*, August 21, 1972, p. 65. Personal income taxes, of course, also reduce the value of time to individuals.

22. It doesn't help much, but one can formulate the marginal conditions for appropriate policies regarding (1) those forms of pollution that can economically be attacked directly because transaction costs are low, and (2) those forms that should be attacked with various degrees of indirectness (because of collection, information, enforcement, or other transaction and intervention costs associated with relatively direct approaches). One would like to move in any of those directions as long as the marginal gains exceeded the marginal costs.

A Hierarchy of Needs—

In the Limiting of Growth

Russell W. Peterson

Russell Peterson is Chairman of the Council on Environmental Quality (CEQ). Formerly chairman of the executive committee of the National Commission on Critical Choices for America, he previously was Governor of Delaware, and was chairman of the National Advisory Commission on Criminal Justice, Standards, and Goals. Dr. Peterson is a graduate of the University of Wisconsin, from which he also holds a Ph.D. in chemistry.

This article is adapted from a speech delivered at the Symposium on Energy and Life, at Michigan State University, in March 1974.

Quality of Life: A Hierarchy

Each of us will, I am sure, define quality of life somewhat differently. I view it as a measure of one's success in the pursuit of happiness—success in the progressive satisfaction of a continuum of needs. Failure to fulfill one's needs leads to the frustration and hopelessness that account for much of the anger, fear, crime, violence and alienation that plague our society.

Abraham H. Maslow has provided an excellent analysis of this view. He describes a "hierarchy of needs" ranging from the basic needs of food, water, shelter, health, safety, love, and esteem to man's highest needs of self-fulfillment and self-actualization. Although each human being feels a need for all of these, his dominant goal at any time is the lowest unfulfilled need on his list. For example, until he has reasonably well satisfied his physiological requirements, such as food and water, he has little interest in safety or esteem. But once the most basic requirements are taken care of, his drive focuses on the next goal.

A person whose immediate goals are adequate food and shelter can find a good measure of happiness if he is able to work progressively toward those goals. On the other hand, the person with all of his basic needs gratified is miserable if he fails to achieve self-fulfillment. For it is the progressive movement toward the goal that counts. Once the goal is reached, it stops being a goal. One's continued happiness then depends on progressing toward the next goal in the hierarchy of needs.

All nations have citizens whose dominant needs range all along the spectrum. Some people are still struggling for food and shelter while others have obtained the highest fulfillment. In the developed nations such as ours the percentage of the very poor has been reduced to a low number, but in the other two-thirds of the world most of the people are still struggling for their most basic needs.

Since the dawn of the Industrial Revolution, the so-called developed nations have provided an ever-increasing percentage of their people with an abundance of food, drink, shelter, and material possessions. But as the basic needs were filled, people raised their sights to higher goals. This was especially true of young people from affluent homes, who never lacked the basics of life and so started from the beginning reaching for such higher goals as esteem and self-fulfillment. Seeing the society around them primarily motivated by the lower or material needs, many youth have found their idealism frustrated. They are demanding that we guide our future by something in addition to market signals.

Nearly all the growth in the United States economy today is in the service sector. It is said that the wave of the future is service, not production. Growth in the service industry has been criticized because it does not turn out "useful products." The error in this statement stems from our preconception that only material things are useful products.

If we view the quality of life as being determined by success in satisfying a continuum of needs, then it becomes necessary to measure productivity of economic, political and social institutions by something other than the production of goods and the GNP. As long as a high percentage of people were working to fulfill their basic needs, the GNP was pertinent. But today, when most people in our country have satisfied such needs, we now require additional measures to determine the effectiveness of our institutions in meeting our higher needs.

The fact that the public is increasingly unhappy with leaders in nearly all fields is probably caused by our harping on filling their old needs when it is new ones they want filled. This may explain why on one hand statistics show convincingly that the affluence of United States citizens as measured by GNP per capita is growing rapidly, but on the other hand many people are convinced that their quality of life is not as good as in the so-called "good old days."

Interdependency and Population Limits

Let's consider some of the factors that influence the quality of our lives. First, there is our escalating global interdependence. Over the years United States citizens have developed an independence, a self-sufficiency, a confidence that we could by ourselves accomplish anything. Now our Nation is undergoing the psychological shock of learning that it is increasingly dependent upon others. With an ever-expanding technology and growing economic strength, we developed the belief that we could control and dominate our environment. Now, more and more, we realize that we must learn to live in harmony with nature—not as its master, but as one element in a complex and interdependent life-supporting system.

We know that other species of life are vanishing from earth at an increasing rate, a clear warning that humanity too could become extinct. Miners used to take a bird with them into the mine to test the quality of their environment. When the bird expired, they knew it was time to get out. Test species on spaceship Earth are expiring. And we can't get out. The greatest threat to the future well-being of humanity is, in my opinion, population growth.

The solution of most of the major problems of mankind, such as malnourishment, disease, poor housing, unemployment, pollution, and the depletion of resources is dependent upon solving the population problem. The current world population is approximately 3.9 billion. It is increasing at an average annual rate of 2.0 percent, a rate which persisted during the 1960's in spite of the marked reduction in population growth in the developed nations.

To illustrate the impact of current population growth, let us consider the following.

> The developed nations with 1.1 billion today will continue to reduce their growth rate from today's 0.8 percent to zero by the year 2000. This is a reasonable possibility. But the developing nations, with 2.8 billion of the world's population will continue at their current 2.5 percent

growth rate. The result will be a global population of 6.7 billion in the year 2000 and 35 billion in 2074, one century from now.

In other words throughout all the centuries of history humanity has increased its number to 3.9 billion, but with the projected rate of growth—about 8 times that number or 31 billion would be added in the next century. At that time today's developing nations would have almost 97 percent of the world's population compared to 71 percent today.

The population problem is a world problem. No nation can solve it alone. All nations must do the job together.

We *can* and we *must* achieve zero population growth at an equilibrium level of 7.0 billion. *Nothing short of an intensive effort is justified.*

Any program to limit population growth must be developed in harmony with human dignity and individual freedom. In turn, limiting population will enhance such dignity and freedom and help people everywhere to realize their highest potential.

By limiting our numbers, we should be able to better feed the hundreds of millions of people who today fail to obtain their minimum caloric and nutritional requirements. The protein shortage is of crisis proportions and ranks well ahead of the oil crisis in many countries. The increasing number of protein-deficient nations and skyrocketing world trade in general are converting the world market for protein from a buyer's to a seller's market.

Some of the most affluent nations are now competing with poorer nations for grains which their citizens eat directly and which the affluent convert through animals, at ratios up to eight to one, into meat. The apparent leveling off in the world harvest of table grade fish adds to the mounting protein shortage.

The so-called "Green Revolution" markedly raised farm productivity in poor countries but at the same time led to millions of unemployed who fled to shanty towns around big cities where most of them ended up with less food and poorer shelter than they had on the farm.

The provision of adequate food for everyone is an urgent task. On one hand, we must provide more food for today's people in order to limit population growth; and on the other hand, as the population grows, it becomes more difficult to provide adequate food for everyone. Even with a limit of 7 billion people, the growth in the number of mouths to feed would be the greatest in the history of the world. Between 1973 and 2000 the increase would be 2.0 billion, a 51 percent gain in only 27 years. To feed them will be a staggering task indeed.

The Role of the U.S. Government

I believe the United States should dedicate itself to working within and through the United Nations to help limit the world's population to 7 billion and to help insure that everyone in present and future generations will have a healthful and satisfying diet. The two goals must go together. We will not realize one without doing the other.

The United States Government should encourage the maximum production of food in our country. We are well equipped in this area to make a major contribution to the world. We are currently following this course. In 1973-74, we will export twice as much wheat as we consume at home.

Economic Development: Conflict?

This brings me to another factor in the quality of our lives, economic development. For hundreds of centuries nearly all people were very poor. It wasn't until the Industrial

A Hierarchy of Needs

Revolution triggered spiraling economic activity that appreciable numbers of people began to realize a higher and higher material standard of living. The United States has led in providing the highest average level of goods and services per citizen with our Gross National Product or GNP/Capita—now, approximately $5,000. While it took about the last 200 years for the GNP per capita to increase ten-fold in constant dollars, the trend today indicates another ten-fold growth in just 30 to 40 years.

This projection has led to much concern about the long-range and worldwide implications of such growth. The book *Limits to Growth* has greatly intensified the worldwide debate on this subject. This work has been criticized on many fronts. It created a psychological shock by flashing an intellectual stone wall in front of many public and private managers and planners who are riding or steering our current political and economic juggernauts into the future.

In my opinion, all leaders should study the *Limits to Growth*. If all it does is make people aware of the significance of exponential growth, the certainty of limits to such growth given finite resources and the long delay between some decisions and their ultimate impact, it will have made a major contribution.

There are limits to some growth and not to others. To know which is which, and how to cope with each, is a mounting assignment for leaders everywhere. Leaders need to focus on the hierarchy of needs, find out where people are on that ladder of aspirations and then help them progressively climb to ever-higher rungs. (Some people are striving for a bowl of rice. And others want to compose a symphony, or fly like Jonathan Livingston Seagull.)

For a rapidly increasing percentage of people, living in harmony with nature is becoming a dominant need. In light of today's knowledge it is a nonfeasance to consider economic development without simultaneously considering its impact on the environment. Until recent years, such development has run roughshod over the environment. This has created critical problems primarily in the developed nations where industrial development has grown rapidly.

As the industrial economies flourish, they dig, scoop, and pump ever-increasing amounts of resources which nature has deposited in an orderly, neat and safe fashion; convert part of these resources to usable products; and then discard the non-usable portions immediately and the converted portions later in a disorderly, untidy, and frequently unsafe fashion in the air, water or land. As people become more affluent they manage to clean up and polish their immediate environment, but in doing so have contributed to messing up more remote areas. As the world gets more people, and more people become affluent, there are fewer and fewer remote areas in which to dig and to dump. Realization of this fact should help to get everyone to work to clean up our common planet.

Think about the pollution pressure we will face, even if we can reach the difficult goal of limiting the world's population to 7 billion. Neither the size of our planet nor our nonrenewable resources are going to increase. Yet there is much we can do.

In the United States, we should strengthen the effective program launched in 1970 with passage of the National Environmental Policy Act and the creation of the Council on Environmental Quality and the Environmental Protection Agency. These actions constitute a milestone in furthering the quality of life. They brought consideration of environmental factors into the same league with consideration of economic factors, permanently enshrining such consideration in the decision-making process of our Nation. Until NEPA was initiated, few realized, for example, the degree to which energy systems affect the environment. Converting fossil and nuclear fuels into energy leads to air pollution, water pollution, creation of solid wastes, land disruption and aesthetic degradation. The new conservation ethic brought on by the energy crisis will—if continued—do much to curb such pollution. But it will not solve the whole problem.

In a free market economy we can and should control pollution from economic activities by bringing the cost of such control to bear directly on the investment, cost and selling price relationship of business. Another step to clean up pollution would be a tax on discharges into the air and water. A further suggestion that merits serious consideration is to require businesses to collect, reclaim and appropriately dispose of all of their products once they have finished their service. Such a program would go a long way toward cleaning up litter, recovering valuable resources, placing the cost of disposing of solid waste on the product creating it and stimulating the design of products so as to facilitate resource recovery.

In 1950, when the GWP, the Gross World Product, reached its first trillion, there was little concern about pollution. Today environmental quality is receiving high priority throughout most of the world. This is because the prime cause of pollution, economic activity, has increased 3.5 times in just 23 years. The GWP is now $3.5 trillion. It will probably reach $12 trillion by 2000.

Eternal vigilance in fighting for environmental quality is a must. *Future economic development must guarantee protection of the environment.*

In considering the impending impact of economic growth on the environment, it is important to remember that the developing nations desperately need rapid economic development. This is necessary not only to provide a higher standard of living, but also to permit them to reach the socio-economic threshold that appears to be a prerequisite to stabilizing population growth. Even with a rapid growth in GNP per capita, such as 7 percent per year, the developing nations will, over the next several decades, have only a minor impact on pollution of the environment at least relative to that of the developed nations. By the year 2000 the combined GNP of the more affluent half of today's world will probably be about 10 times as high as that of the poorer half.

Thus, it is clear where the emphasis must be placed to keep the oncoming avalanche of economic development from despoiling the environment.

A Reaffirmation of Interdependence

Since we in the United States have been leading the way in economic development, it is up to us to lead the way also in demonstrating how economic development can be carried out while maintaining and furthering environmental quality. The growing interdependence of all of us on planet Earth and the need for us to plan and work together is clear. Accordingly, I will conclude by proposing that we celebrate our Nation's Bicentennial in 1976 with a new declaration—this time a *Declaration of Interdependence.*

> We the people of planet Earth with respect for the dignity of each human life, with concern for future generations, with growing appreciation of our relation to our environment, with recognition of limits to our resources and with need for adequate food, air, water, shelter, health, protection, justice and self-fulfillment, hereby declare our interdependence and resolve to work together in brotherhood and in harmony with our environment to enhance the quality of life everywhere.

The Trouble With A Zero-Growth World

Rudolf Klein

Rudolf Klein is Senior Fellow at the Center for Studies in Social Policy, in London. He was a member of the Medical Care Organization Unit at the London School of Hygiene and Chief Editorial Writer for The Observer. Mr. Klein holds a master's from Oxford University; he is the author of Social Policy and Public Expenditure *(1974) and* Complaints Against Doctors.

This article originally appeared in the June 2, 1974, issue of The New York Times Magazine: *1974 by The New York Times Company. Reprinted by permission.*

One of the dangers of swings in intellectual fashions is that ideas become accepted before their implications have begun to be explored, as yesterday's unconventional wisdom becomes transmuted into today's unquestioned orthodoxy. The success of the advocates of nongrowth in bringing about a mass conversion to their view is a case in point.

By now we all know what the physical world will look like by the year 2000 or so, assuming that nothing will change except that there will be more of everything. The picture of an overpopulated and overexploited world, with too many people competing for too little space, is guaranteed to chill the spines of even those agnostics who, like myself, remain skeptical about some of the more simple-minded predictions that have been made. If faith in growth—the identification of progress with rising material standards of living—is the original sin of Economic Man, then he no longer has any excuse for being unaware of the consequences if he does not repent soon. Just as the men and women of the Middle Ages were warned by the stained-glass images in their cathedrals of the results if they did not change their sinful ways, so today's congregations are being warned by the images on their television screens of the effects if they do not repent: The vision of a hell on this earth has replaced the medieval vision of a hell in the next world.

But if the arguments in favor of a nongrowth society deserve to be taken seriously, then it is imperative to explore some of the implications of moving in this direction. It is, of course, just possible that if—by some miracle—the United States were suddenly to decide to adopt a policy of nongrowth, this would simply freeze the existing social and political system in perpetuity—that the history of the future would be nothing but the rerun of the same old movie. This, however, is the least plausible of all the possible scenarios; it seems highly unlikely that it would be possible to introduce a revolutionary change in the economic basis of society without also affecting profoundly the social and political relationships of its members.

The trouble is that, precisely because nongrowth would mark a sharp break with our existing habits of thought and ways of doing things, a fundamental discontinuity in our historical experience, no one can predict what would happen—while prophesying what will happen if growth continues unchecked, in its present form, is all too easy. But if it is impossible to predict, it is essential to speculate. For the paradox is that while modern societies are beginning, if all too slowly and hesitantly, to learn how to cope with some of the consequences of growth (like dealing with pollution), they are utterly unprepared to deal with the effects of nongrowth. Yet these effects, particularly if they are unanticipated and undiscussed, could be shattering. It is not all that difficult to sketch out a scenario of social catastrophe in a nongrowth society to equal, in its horror, the scenario of ecological catastrophe in a growth society.

The starting point of such a doomsday scenario would be the Hobbesian assumption that politics in societies like the United States is about the allocation of resources. There are different groups—some ethnically defined, some economically defined—struggling to improve their position in society, as measured by their incomes, their housing, their access to education, job opportunities and so on. At present, economic growth tends to blunt the edge of this conflict. For everyone can expect to be better off next year than they were last year, even if their relative position does not change. Furthermore, it is possible for some groups actually to improve their relative position, without anyone actually being worse off in terms of hard cash. The competition for resources (social and financial) is therefore a game in which everyone can win at least something.

Now imagine the situation transformed by a decision to halt all economic growth. Immediately the competition for resources becomes a zero-sum game. One man's prize is another man's loss. If the blacks want to improve their share of desirable goods, it can only be at the expense of the whites. If the over-65's are to be given higher pensions, or improved medical services, it can only be at the expense of the working population or of the young.

From this, it would seem only too likely that the haves would man the barricades to defend their share of resources, against the have-nots. The politics of compromise would be replaced by the politics of revolution, because the have-nots would be forced to challenge the whole basis of society, and its distribution of wealth and power. For those who think that this distribution is wrong—and that most of the compromises are cosmetic anyway—this would be a welcome confrontation; not so, however, for those who take a more optimistic view of the possibilities of change in the existing society.

But the tensions created by nongrowth within a single political society like the United States would be compounded, more catastrophically still, within the international political community. For again, economic growth creates at least the possibility—even if in practice it has turned out to be illusory for some nations—of a general and continuing rise in standards of living. To abjure growth, by freezing the present situation, is thus to repudiate hope. It is to condemn a majority of the globe's inhabitants to permanent poverty unless (once again) the have-nots successfully manage to challenge the haves in order to bring about a redistribution of global resources in their own favor.

It is difficult to conceive such a challenge stopping short of war; perhaps the extreme form of this particular scenario would envisage China ultimately leading a coalition of the developing countries against the bourgeois superpowers, Russia and the United States. Given this kind of political doomsday assumption, not many of us would be left alive to witness the ecological disasters predicted by the antigrowth school; the problem of overpopulation would have been solved dramatically— unpleasantly but efficiently.

Like most speculations about the future, this doomsday scenario carries a contraband of undeclared assumptions in its baggage. It takes man to be an acquisitive, competitive and aggressive animal. It assumes a social ethic of work, struggle and achievement. Indeed this sort of political doomsday prediction is based on the same trick of argument as the ecological doomsday prophecy: it projects the present into the future, without allowing for the possibility that a changing situation will produce changing attitudes or policies and so falsify the forecasts.

If one reverses the assumptions, if one allows for the possibility that nongrowth will in itself create a new political and social situation, then it is possible to draw up a much more optimistic scenario at the opposite end of the spectrum of possible futures. This, I suspect, is what most advocates of nongrowth do, if only explicitly. In the optimistic scenario, competitive man is an aberration, the product of a society dedicated to growth, which stunts and distorts its members by generating artificial wants. From this point of view, the competition for limited resources is seen not as inevitable but as socially induced, a sign of the corruption brought about by tasting the apple of economic growth.

Given this approach, then, the repudiation of economic growth would in itself create the opportunity for a new kind of society to arise. This was, for instance, the view taken by one of the earliest advocates of nongrowth, John Stuart Mill, the English political philosopher, as long ago as 1848.

"I confess that I am not charmed with the ideal of life held out by those who think that the normal state of human beings is that of struggling to get on," Mill wrote, "that the trampling, crushing, elbowing, and treading on each other's heels, which form the existing type of social life, are the most desirable lot of humankind, or anything but the disagreeable symptoms of one of the phases of industrial progress." Instead, he thought, "the best state for human nature is that in which, while no one is poor, no one desires to be richer." And he concluded: "This condition of society, so greatly preferable to the present, is not only perfectly compatible with the stationary state, but, it would seem, more naturally allied with that state than with any other."

The stationary state of John Stuart Mill is the nongrowth society of today, and many of his views are reflected (if in less stately prose) in the writings of people as diverse as Marcuse or Galbraith. It is worth noting, though, that while Mill thought that the United States provided the most favorable conditions for the development of such a society —since the northern and middle states had "got rid of all social injustices and inequalities"—he was disappointed by the lack of progress in this direction: "All that these advantages seem to have done for them is that the life of the whole of one sex is devoted to dollar-hunting, and of the other to breeding dollar-hunters."

In his advocacy of the stationary state, Mill was, of course, drawing on a tradition as old as Western thought, a tradition which put the emphasis not on productive work but on reflective, artistic and other noneconomic activities—a point of view which also finds an echo in the works of Karl Marx when he contemplates the future of society after the disappearance of capitalism. In this perspective, it is the growth society which is the aberration—a temporary phenomenon of the past 500 years or so, against which must be set the thousands of years of history during which nongrowth was the norm. Thus nongrowth can be seen as a resolution of social and political tensions, rather than as their cause.

Stated in these deliberately crude and extreme terms, neither the pessimistic nor the optimistic scenario is particularly convincing. Both are rather like the naive scenarios fashionable in the early days of the hydrogen bomb, which postulated a simple antithesis between a universal nuclear holocaust or universal nuclear disarmament. They beg crucial questions about what is meant by a nongrowth society, about how such a society might evolve and about whether one is talking about a single nation-state like the United States or about the world community.

Nongrowth is a deceptively simple slogan. It would seem to imply a combination of zero population growth (Z.P.G.) and zero economic growth (Z.E.G.)—by which is usually meant, no further rise in the total population nor in such conventional indicators as the Gross National Product. This, in turn, would seem to suggest a rather unthreatening picture of a society continuing to enjoy its present standards of living which, in the case of the United States at any rate, are luxuriously high for the great majority. But, forgetting for a moment the international setting and making a start with the case of a single society like the United States, this particular intellectual ball of wool turns out to be a remarkable tangle which requires teasing out.

The first difficulty comes in trying to relate the two components of the stable society—Z.P.G. and Z.E.G.—to each other. If it is assumed that progress towards these two aims will proceed harmoniously in step, then it follows that no one's standards of living (as measured by per capita income) will fall—and the stable society appears as a well-cushioned resting place, a plausible setting for the optimistic scenario. But it is at least possible that economic growth might stop before population growth; indeed more than likely, since it is impossible to insure a stable population in the absence of compulsory abortion or euthanasia. If so, there would actually be a fall in per capita income. In turn, this would raise some exceedingly awkward questions as to whose income should be cut: the pessimistic, social and political cutthroat scenario would seem to be rather apposite in such an event.

Mancur Olson pointed out a further permutation in his introduction to the issue which *Daedalus*, Journal of the American Academy of Arts and Sciences, devoted to the subject of the No-Growth Society (compulsory reading for anyone interested in this subject). This was that it might be possible to combine a static economy with a falling population. In this case, there would actually be an increased income per capita, which would perhaps permit a superoptimistic scenario about a paradisiacal future combining affluence with ecological safety, social stability and social reform on behalf of deprived and under-privileged minorities.

But before jumping into this or into any other future, we should do well to ask a rather different sort of question: What are the social and political processes which will produce a stable society, as distinct from the social and political problems that may be created by the emergence of such a society? The two are obviously related, in that the circumstances of the birth are bound to affect subsequent developments. The discussion so far has, like most discussions of the nongrowth society, skirted round this issue; it has rather taken it for granted that there will be a collective social revelation, resulting in a collective social decision.

This, of course, is a nonsense belief, and it is precisely because this belief is widely held that much of the discussion about the stable society tends to have an element of religiosity about it, more concerned with spiritual conversion than practical realities. For the implications of even beginning to move toward a stable society are immense; political institutions would come under great pressure and social friction would grow.

This contention can easily be illustrated. To return to the first element in the equation of the stable society—zero population growth—there is no problem about this, only assuming that, by some instant process of education creating a generally shared consensus, all families in the United States will more or less keep to the required number of children (although there is obviously a little scope for variety, since some families may decide to have no children at all).

But what if they don't? What if some ethnic groups in the population keep to their ratio, while others exceed it? Would this be acceptable? Or would it be resisted since—in the long term—voting power tends to follow population size, and therefore differential ethnic population growths would imply a change in the ethnic balance of power? The idea of actually enforcing standard family sizes (as distinct from persuading people to accept voluntary limitation and introducing financial incentives designed to encourage such a development) tends to be widely resented, anyway. The idea that such a policy should be enforced on a discriminatory basis against a particular ethnic group would, surely, be equally widely resisted. It would introduce a particularly sensitive and divisive new issue into a political system which is already under strain in dealing with current social problems.

Difficulties of a different sort, but no less formidable, arise in the case of Z.E.G. It is implausible to assume that the present economy will remain as a mummified museum piece for perpetuity, that the United States will forever go on churning out the same number of cars, television sets, Ph.D.'s and garage mechanics. A stable society does not mean a frozen society, one hopes. But allowing for the possibility—indeed necessity—of change, how is such change to be controlled? For stability does imply control. It predicates that if Firm X (or University Y) produces too much in the way of goods, then Firm Z (or University W) will have to cut production back, if the total is not to be exceeded. It means that, if health and public services are to expand and improve in quality, the resources will have to be found by cutting other items of consumption.

The last point underlines the fact that progress from a growth to a stable society is also likely to mean progress from a society in which most of the decisions are taken by individuals or individual firms to a society where most of the decisions are taken collectively. It means (if we are really serious about Z.E.G.) more central control over the production and allocation of resources.

This is not necessarily a distressing prospect. Collective decision-making must not be confused with totalitarian decision-making, and it has indeed been argued by J. K. Galbraith and others that present-day American society offers the illusion rather than the reality of individual decision-making, since not only are these decisions affected by the brain-washing activities of Madison Avenue but take place in an economic and social environment controlled by the "techno-structure" of big business and government. But it would clearly impose extra burdens on existing political institutions.

As it is, there is already much debate about the adequacy of Congressional control over the executive and a widespread feeling that the present balance is unsatisfactory. However, progress towards Z.E.G. would demand a more powerful executive backed by a more all-embracing bureaucracy. In turn, this would imply yet a further shift in the balance between Congress and the executive—between accountability and centralized power— unless there was an accompanying change in the political institutions of the United States deliberately designed to meet this danger.

Collective decision-making also ought to be distinguished, though, from giving greater priority to collective services for society as a whole. On the whole, advocates of the stable society also tend to be advocates of the provision of more collective goods: more hospitals and fewer private cars, to encapsulate the standard argument. But while in a growing economy public and private affluence can go hand-in-hand, they part company in a stable society. The choice becomes sharpened in conditions of Z.E.G., and it certainly cannot be taken for granted that there would be a consensus in favor of allowing the rise in expenditure on health, education and pollution control to continue if this would actually mean a reduction in private consumption (it's all too easy to forget that measures designed to improve the environment or control pollution actually cost money, and therefore appear in the Gross National Product).

It is just possible—if one actually does believe Professor Galbraith's contention the people only want the gadgetry of modern technology because of the artificial pressures of the admen—that a collective decision would go in favor of more collective goods. However, it might be as well to consider seriously the possibility that the collective decision might be in favor of more private goods. If so, the result might paradoxically be more pollution and more political tension, since less would be spent on cleaning up the environment and on making the inner cities acceptable places in which to live. If this were the outcome, progress toward a stable society would actually increase social stress.

At this stage in the argument, however, it is necessary to reveal yet another concealed assumption. So far, I have tended to accept what might be called the social-engineering view of social change: that, given the political will and a little tinkering with the machinery of administration, it is practically possible to bring about certain desired changes. Only the self-evident difficulties of persuading a population to accept the personal implications of the general idea of Z.P.G. have been touched on so far.

But, in returning to Z.E.G., it is far from clear that in the present state of knowledge, it is actually possible to exercise the sort of precise, finger-tip control which is implied by the idea of nongrowth. The evidence, rather, appears to point in the opposite direction. But if, in fact, the economy continues to perform on a cyclical pattern, then it would seem—if Z.E.G. is to retain any meaning at all—that if by some unfortunate mishap the economy were to grow in one year, there would have to be a compensating fall in the following year. The manic-depressive pattern of economic management of recent decades might well be reinforced, with deeper and sharper recessions deliberately engineered to compensate for accidental growth—what might be called an economic abortion program. In turn, such a policy of economic management would once more entail political friction, deepening rather than narrowing divisions between the various economic, ethnic and social groups in American society.

All this may seem unnecessarily pessimistic, deliberately stressing the negative aspects of the evolution toward an American society based on nongrowth while neglecting the possibility of agreed and harmonious change. But the picture of possible futures painted so far appears positively cheerful and encouraging if the wider, global setting is also considered.

Again, there is a whole spectrum of scenarios, offering various mixes of gloom and optimism. For example, one possibility might be a unilateral decision by the United States to introduce no-growth in one country, on the reasonable enough argument that the American dream has been fulfilled in economic terms. Clearly such a conscious decision (always assuming that it is psychologically plausible and politically possible) would, in itself, tend to create that sense of dedication which would be required to cope with the problems so far discussed. Still, even this sort of ideological and economic isolationism would come under severe pressures. It would have to survive, for example, the spectacle of other countries—particularly in Western Europe—overtaking the United States in terms of per capita income.

In practice, though, it is difficult to take this particular scenario seriously. For even a unilateral American decision in favor of Z.E.G. has implications for the rest of the world.

No-growth in the United States means less growth elsewhere, given the nature of the world economy. In effect, therefore, the United States would be taking a paternalistic decision with damaging effect on much poorer nations (again, it's worth noting that, just as expenditure on improving the environment shows up in the national accounts, so does expenditure on foreign aid—and that both might be a casualty of Z.E.G.). Leaving aside the morality of such a course, it obviously has considerable implications for American foreign policy and the balance of power throughout the world. Economic isolationism implies political isolationism.

Abandoning this particular scenario, therefore, and accepting that the United States is inescapably a member of the global community, it then follows that the problems of a nongrowth society have to be considered in this wider context. The sorts of difficulties which have been discussed within the setting of a single country must now be translated in terms applicable to international society. Again, there are the problems of distribution—this time not as between ethnic groups and social classes, but as between different countries. Again, there are the problems of enforcing policy decisions—this time not in terms of strengthening the governmental machine of a single country but the mechanisms of international control. It hardly needs pointing out that while all the problems would be that much more severe, the means for tackling them are at present effectively nonexistent.

Indeed, what does the concept of a stable society imply when applied to the world community? Obviously the idea of Z.P.G. has even more urgency when applied on a global scale than in the case of a single country like the United States, since it is the soaring numbers in the underdeveloped and developing countries which help to per-petuate their poverty. Equally obviously, though, the difficulties of actually enforcing such a policy are compounded; indeed it is seen by some countries, notably by China, as a threat to their power.

But it is the idea of Z.E.G. on a global scale which is politically implausible. This would in effect mean condemning the majority of the world's population to poverty for the rest of time. But if this is a nonsense way of interpreting global Z.E.G., who is to decide which nations get how much? Who will ration out permission for growth? What are the standards—in terms of per capita income—which are going to be the upper limit of permissible growth?

Assuming that there would be no voluntary agreement, based on an international consensus, on points like these, the most likely outcome would be an attempt by the prosperous nations (whether capitalist or Communist) to enforce their policies on the rest of the world. In turn, such an attempt would be seen—and resisted—as an effort to make the world a pleasant place for the prosperous to live in, at the expense of the poor—a new form of colonial exploitation.

However, the developing countries might well decide to push for a redistribution of the global income in their own favor, using their control over what are going to become increasingly scarce natural resources like oil and various metals as their weapon. The "have" countries might actually be faced with the possibility of accepting a fall in their standards of living or engaging in an economic confrontation—possibly shading off into a military one—with the "have-nots." The stable society, in population and economic terms, might turn out to be, in political and military terms, a singularly unstable one.

The Trouble With A Zero-Growth World

In discussing the possibility of such developments, there is always the danger that one will be misunderstood to be predicting a particular outcome. This is far from being the intention of this article. For the only certain aspect of the future is that it will be a great deal more complex than the sort of simplified scenario that it is possible to construct. Futurology is useful only to the extent that it is seen as an intellectual game, creating an awareness of possibilities that might otherwise be ignored and stirring up discussion about what might otherwise be neglected policy options.

Indeed, by far the most plausible scenario does not involve anything even remotely resembling a deliberate policy decision to adopt a nongrowth policy, but a muddled, half-conscious drift—a gradual emphasis on new priorities, like trading economic growth for more leisure time, hesitantly and perhaps even inconsistently pursued over a period of decades as social values evolve. In this scenario, the change would first become apparent in the societies of economic satiety, like the United States, and slowly percolate elsewhere; conspicuous nonconsumption, on this reading of the situation, is the luxury of the well-to-do and the paradox may be that the acceptance of nongrowth in itself depends on the achievement of growth (just as population control seems to catch on only when it is seen as a way of increasing living standards).

Leaning on history, this scenario might then suggest that a society which had adopted the values of nongrowth would be introvert rather than extrovert, traditional rather than innovative. Whether it had settled for an egalitarian distribution of wealth or for the perpetuation of inequalities, it would be resistant to change, stressing social control as the inevitable counterpart of social stability. There would be little social mobility, since this tends to be a product of economic growth. There might well evolve a gerontocracy, with power going hand in hand with seniority, since it would no longer be open to the young to secede from existing organizations to start their own. The only frontiers that would be open for exploration would be those of artistic or spiritual activity.

The resemblance of the picture to medieval society in Western Europe is not accidental. For that was a society which was based on nongrowth, whose mold was indeed broken only when the Protestant ethic of economic achievement became the ideology of the newly developing capitalism. It would be absurd to push the parallel too far; a society which commands technological resources of infinite potential, but refrains from using them to their full limits to create extra economic wealth, cannot be equated with one which was ravaged by starvation and the plague. But perhaps it is worth remembering that building cathedrals can go hand in hand with burning heretics, that emphasizing spiritual rather than material values does not necessarily imply tolerance, that a sense of community may be achieved at the cost of accepting social hierarchy.

This is not to imply that nongrowth will, inevitably, bring about such a situation—any more than growth will, inevitably, bring about ecological disaster. It is to suggest, however, that nongrowth may carry certain social and political risks just as growth may carry certain ecological dangers, and that it may need a determined effort to avoid both.

Population Growth & the American Future:

Report Themes & Highlights

**Commission on Population Growth
and the American Future**

> *This article consists of a booklet titled "Themes and Highlights of the Final Report of the Commission on Population Growth and the American Future" (1972).*
>
> *The Commission's reports consist of seven volumes of papers and statements which provide significant research material for scholars, as well as concerned citizens.*
>
> *The "Themes and Highlights" booklet concludes: "This report represents the official views of the Commission, particularly as to the listed recommendations. Clearly, in the case of a Commission with such diverse membership, not every Commissioner subscribes in detail to every suggestion or statement of policy."*

Because of the pervasive impact of population growth on every facet of American life and its implications for the quality of life, the Commission has concluded that the time has come for the United States to adopt a deliberate population policy.

The United States today has a declining birthrate, low population density, enormous amounts of open space, and population leaving the central cities—but that does not eliminate the concern about population. This country, or any country, always has a "population problem" in the sense of achieving a proper balance between size, growth, and distribution on the one hand, and the quality of life to which its citizens aspire on the other.

Population issues involve virtually every aspect of our national life and hence any policies to deal with them must be correspondingly broad. But population policy is no substitute for social and economic planning and development. Successfully addressing the population problem requires that we also address our problems of poverty, sex discrimination, minority discrimination, careless exploitation of resources, environmental deterioration, and decaying cities.

The concern about population is as complex as it is consequential. There are no simple or immediate solutions. An attitude of indifference or complacency is unwarranted; so is the cry of early catastrophe and crisis.

In proposing this Commission to Congress in July 1969, President Nixon said:

> One of the most serious challenges to human destiny in the last third of this century will be the growth of the population. Whether man's response to that challenge will be a cause for pride or for despair in the year 2000 will depend very much on what we do today.

We have been asked to assess the impact that our growing population and changing patterns of settlement will have upon our government, economy, natural resources, and environment, and the various means by which our nation can achieve a population level properly suited for its resources and needs; and to make recommendations regarding a broad range of problems associated with population growth and its implications for America's future.

Our mandate is broad, reaching, in one way or another, into practically every aspect of American life. But, our perspective is population. Out of our deliberations have come major findings and recommendations that deserve careful consideration by this society and its government. Regardless of diverse approaches to the matter—whether one puts personal freedom or minority concerns or ecological balance at the center—the following points emerge.

Findings and Conclusions

The United States has a number of "population problems" that need close and continuous attention; two out of three Americans believe that the matter is "serious."

No substantial benefits will result from the continued growth of our population beyond that made almost unavoidable by the rapid growth of the past. On the contrary, it is our view that population growth of the current magnitude has aggravated many of the nation's problems and made their solution more difficult. The Commission believes that the gradual stabilization of population—bringing births into balance with deaths —would contribute significantly to the nation's ability to solve its problems, although such problems will not be solved by population stabilization alone. It would, however, enable our society to shift its focus increasingly from quantity to quality.

The nation has nothing to fear from a gradual approach to population stabilization. We have looked for, and have not found, any convincing economic argument for continued national population growth. The health of our economy does not depend on it, nor does the prosperity of business or the welfare of the average person. In fact, a reduction in the rate of population growth would bring important economic benefits, especially if the nation develops policies to take advantage of the opportunities for social and economic improvement that slower population growth would provide.

The Commission believes that slowing the rate of population growth would ease the problems facing the American government in the years ahead. Demands for governmental services will be less than they would be otherwise, and resources available for public support of education, health, and other governmental activities would be greater. However, it would be a serious error to read these conclusions as comforting and reassuring. Under the most optimistic assumptions, at least 50 million more people will be added to the United States population before the end of the century, increasing the demands on governmental services and making more difficult the achievement of a participatory political process responsive to contemporary conditions. More important, these added demands and complexities will fall on governmental structures and processes already severely burdened—many would say overburdened—by the problems facing the nation.

In this framework, we must face the fact that Americans have suddenly become a metropolitan people. In 1970, nearly 70 percent of the United States population was metropolitan—the figure will approach 85 percent by the year 2000. For better or for worse, we are in the process of becoming an almost totally urban society. Most metropolitan growth now results from natural increase, not migration. Thus, the trend toward bigness of metropolitan areas, if undesirable, cannot be substantially checked except as national growth is slowed or stopped.

Population Growth & the American Future

Migration is from low-income rural areas and abroad to metropolitan areas, from one metropolitan area to another, and from central cities to suburbs. Nearly 40 million or one in five Americans change homes each year. About one in 15, a total of 13 million, migrate across county lines. What is needed is guidance and assistance.

Along with the burgeoning urban problem is another of equal complexity and size: resources and the environment. Population growth is one of the major factors affecting the demand for resources and the impact on the environment in this country. From the standpoint of both resources and environment, considerable benefits would result over the next 30 to 50 years from a prompt reduction in our population growth. This conclusion emerges with particular clarity with regard to water, agricultural land, and outdoor recreation. Over this same period, we can, if we have to, solve the environmental and resource problems created by population growth, but we may not like some of the solutions. Continued growth incurs increasing risks, for we will be forced to adopt solutions to the consequences of growth before we understand their side effects.

Even a one-child difference in average family size makes an enormous difference over the decades. A century from now, with continued immigration, the two-child average would result in a population of 350 million, while growth at the three-child level would result in nearly a billion.

Demographic events have the quality of persisting over time—for example, the baby-boom generation born after World War II is still working its way through the age structure, with many repercussions. In view of its effect on the age distribution and the accommodations thus required, sharp shifts in most demographic trends are undesirable. Whether or not fluctuations occur, a slower average rate of population growth will result in an older age composition, with the problems of the aged in somewhat sharper relief.

It takes a long time to affect population growth rates in a democratically and ethically acceptable manner. Even with a two-child average from now on, it would take 60 years or so to achieve a nongrowing population. But precisely because the lead time is decades in length, it is necessary to face the issue now and come to deliberate and informed decisions about population problems—their burdens, their costs, their remedies.

Slowing population growth in this country is everyone's affair: All segments of the society should participate; all segments will benefit. The major contribution to growth now comes from the advantaged majority in our society. Because of their smaller number, our "have-not" groups—our racial and ethnic minorities—do not bear the primary responsibility for population growth, and inducing them to limit the number of children they have would not in itself stabilize our population. However, there are strong connections between high fertility and the economic and social problems that affect the 13 percent of our people who are poor. Therefore, we recognize that unless we address our racism and poverty, we will not be able to resolve the question of population growth for our racial and ethnic minorities. As deprived groups are brought into the educational, occupational, and residential mainstream, their fertility will probably decline to the level of the people already there.

In every society, there are norms of behavior that affect fertility, and every legal structure contains (usually inadvertent) regulations that encourage or discourage childbearing. As nearly as we can tell, the social and legal pressures in the United States, while present, are not particularly powerful one way or the other; but on balance, the pressure is probably toward childbearing.

There is a serious problem of unwanted fertility in this country. Making it easier to avoid unwanted childbearing will make a substantial contribution to the lives of the people involved as well as to slowing growth—and in any case, it is consistent with American values and desirable on that ground.

Illegal immigration is more troublesome than legal immigration, and is numerically substantial. As for legal immigration, that is indeed a contributor to population growth; but, for many people, traditional political, cultural, and humanitarian values outweigh demographic considerations.

Our population will stabilize as the American people challenge the traditional assumptions of growth and appreciate what is at stake, both for the individual family and the society at large. Zero population growth is best understood as an average accommodating small fluctuations and not as a fixed rate. The average of two children per family, which would yield zero growth over the long term, can be reached through many different combinations of proportions married and of different size families. Indeed, such diversity is itself highly desirable. And if our annual rates fall below the two-child average for some periods of time, we should not react with alarm, but rather should recognize that this will hasten the advent of stabilization.

We view population policy not as an end in itself, but as a means to facilitate the achievement of social goals desirable in their own right. Above all, the Commission wishes to emphasize that the objective of the policies we advocate is the enrichment of human life, not its restriction; that the control of reproduction, by assuring greater opportunity to each person, frees man to attain his individual dignity and reach his full potential. Recognizing that the great majority of parents desire to have the knowledge and the means to plan their families, the Commission believes that the resolution of population problems can and should be based on voluntary action determined by the individual's own best interest.

Policy Recommendations

In the light of its two years of deliberation and based on the substantial research it contracted, the Commission reached a number of conclusions and recommendations. These recommendations speak simultaneously to population issues and other social values important in their own right. In the broadest sense, the policies recommended aim at promoting desirable social conditions by increasing opportunities to exercise freedom of choice. At the same time, the result of such policies would be to slow population growth and hasten the advent of population stabilization. Their implementation depends to a considerable extent on the attainment of the necessary funds, organizational change, and research, the details of which are elaborated in the full text.

The Commission recommends:

In order to better prepare present and future generations to meet the challenges arising from population change, the federal government should enact a Population Education Act to assist school systems in establishing well-planned population education programs.

In order to maximize information and knowledge about human sexuality and its implications for the family, we should make sex education available through responsible community organizations, the media, and especially the schools; and similarly we should seek to improve the quality of education for parenthood throughout the society.

In order to improve the opportunities available for children, we should develop maternal and child health programs, provide adequate child-care arrangements for parents who wish to make use of them, eliminate discrimination against children born out of wedlock, and reform adoption laws.

In order to neutralize the legal, social, and institutional pressures that historically have encouraged childbearing, as well as to equalize opportunities generally, we should eliminate discrimination based on sex by adopting the proposed Equal Rights amendment to the Constitution.

In order to enable all Americans, regardless of age, marital status, or income, to avoid unwanted births and enhance their capacity to realize their own preferences in childbearing and family size, we should:

- Increase investment in the search for improved means by which individuals may control their own fertility.
- Extend subsidized family planning programs.
- Liberalize access to abortion services with the admonition that abortion not be considered a primary means of fertility control.
- Extend and improve the delivery of health services related to fertility—including prenatal and pediatric care, contraceptive services, voluntary sterilization, abortion, and the treatment of infertility—through public and private financing mechanisms.

In order to regulate the impact on population of migration from outside this country, we should not increase the present levels of legal immigration and we should stop illegal immigration.

In order to provide a framework for regional, state, and local planning and development, the federal government should develop a set of national population distribution guidelines.

In order to ease the problems created by population movement, we should develop programs for human resource development, counseling and assistance on worker relocation, and a growth center strategy to promote job opportunities in depressed areas.

In order to facilitate the accommodation of population movements, we need comprehensive planning on a metropolitan and regional scale which could be facilitated through greater public control over land use and the establishment of state and regional planning agencies and development corporations.

In order to increase freedom in choice of residential location, we should extend governmental provision of suburban housing for low- and moderate-income families and should take effective steps to promote genuinely free choice of housing within metropolitan areas on the part of racial and ethnic minorities.

In order to strengthen the basic statistics and research upon which all sound demographic, social, and economic policy must ultimately depend, the federal government should move promptly and boldly to implement specific improvements in these programs.

In order to improve the federal government's population-related programs and its capacity to evaluate the interaction between public policies, programs, and population, specific organizational changes should be made. These include the creation of a National Institute of Population Sciences within the National Institutes of Health, and an Office of Population Growth and Distribution within the Executive Office of the President.

And finally, this nation should welcome and plan for a stabilized population.

What matters ultimately is the impact of population growth upon the quality of American life; changes in population are merely the means to such a goal. Does this country want to continue to invest its resources simply in meeting more demands for more services, more classrooms, more hospitals, more housing, more roads, more everything . . . as the population continues to grow? Or should we concentrate our energies and resources on improving the quality of such services and extending them to those for whom such quality is at best a hope rather than a fact? The population problem is the problem of achieving, consistent with political and ethical standards, a lasting and constructive balance between numbers of people and an evolving definition of "the good life" in this country and the world.

We end as we began: Our country can no longer afford the uncritical acceptance of the population growth ethic. Given the whole trend of human history to the contrary, that is not an easy lesson to learn. The growth ethic seems to be so imprinted in human consciousness that it takes a deliberate effort of rationality and will to overcome it, but the effort now seems necessary. The recommendations we propose are worthwhile for many reasons as well as appropriate to steering a prudent demographic course into a future filled with uncertainties.

The Commission

CHAIRMAN: John D. Rockefeller 3rd; VICE CHAIRWOMAN: Grace Olivarez (Executive Director, Food for All, Inc.); VICE CHAIRMAN: Christian N. Ramsey, Jr., M.D. (President, The Institute for the Study of Health and Society); Joseph D. Beasley, M.D. (The Edward Wisner Professor of Public Health, Tulane University Medical Center); David E. Bell (Executive Vice President, The Ford Foundation); Bernard Berelson (President, The Population Council); Arnita Young Boswell (Associate Field Work Professor, School of Social Service Administration, University of Chicago); Margaret Bright (Professor, Dept. of Behavioral Sciences, and Professor, Dept. of Epidemiology—School of Hygiene and Public Health, The Johns Hopkins University); Marilyn Brant Chandler (Former Chairman of the Board, Otis Art Institute; Student, Volunteer); Paul B. Cornely, M.D. (Professor, Dept. of Community Health Practice, College of Medicine Howard University; and Assistant to the Executive Medical Officer Welfare and Retirement Fund, United Mine Workers of America); Alan Cranston (United States Senator, California); Lawrence A. Davis (President, Arkansas Agricultural, Mechanical & Normal College); Otis Dudley Duncan (Professor of Sociology, University of Michigan); John N. Erlenborn (United States Representative, 14th C. District of Illinois); Joan F. Flint (Housewife); R. V. Hansberger (Chairman and President, Boise Cascade Corporation); D. Gale Johnson (Chairman, Department of Economics, University of Chicago); John R. Meyer (President, National Bureau of Economic Research; Professor of Economics, Yale University); Bob Packwood (United States Senator, Oregon); James S. Rummonds (Student, Stanford School of Law); Stephen L. Salyer (Student, Davidson College); Howard D. Samuel (Vice President, Amalgamated Clothing Workers of America); James H. Scheuer (United States Representative, 22nd C. District of New York); and, George D. Woods (Director and Consultant, The First Boston Corporation).

The Staff

Executive Director: Charles F. Westoff; Deputy Director: Robert Parke, Jr.; Directors of Research: Sara Mills Mazie, Elliott R. Morss, A. E. Keir Nash, Ritchie H. Reed, and, Dianne Miller Wolman; Director of Policy Coordination: Carol Tucker Foreman; Assistant to the Chairman: David K. Lelewer; Director of Public Information: Gerald Lipson; General Counsel: Ben C. Fisher; Administrative Officer: Lois A. Brooks; Editorial Coordinator: Carol F. Donnelly; Press Officer: Rochelle Kutcher Green; Professional Staff: Gail E. Auslander, Phyllis Coghlan, Florence F. Einhorn, Duane S. Elgin, Dorothy Mann, Susan McIntosh, and, Steve W. Rawlings; Special Consultants: Daniel Callahan, Lenora T. Cartright, Robert F. Drury, Edgar M. Hoover, Frederick S. Jaffe, Peter A. Morrison, Ronald G. Ridker, Normay B. Ryder, and, Irene B. Taeuber; Support Staff: Mary Ann Ferguson, Mildred G. Herald, Kathryn E. Herron, Mac Arthur C. Jones, Kituria D. Littlejohn, Betty Marshall, Pearl R. Phillips, Diane O. Sergeant, Judith M. Stock, and, Mary C. Wilcher.

Social Consequences of ZPG—

in the U.S.

Lincoln H. Day

Lincoln H. Day is a senior fellow in the Department of Demography, the Australian National University. He was the chief of the Demographic and Social Statistics Branch, Statistical Office, United Nations and an associate professor with a joint appointment to the Department of Epidemiology and Public Health and to the Department of Sociology, at Yale University. Mr. Day is a graduate of Yale University and holds a doctorate of sociology from Columbia University.

This article—originally titled "The Social Consequences of a Zero Population Growth Rate in the United States"—appeared in Research Reports, Volume I, Demographic and Social Aspects of Population Growth [Charles F. Westoff and Robert Parke, Jr. (eds.)] of the Commission on Population Growth and the American Future (Washington, D.C.: Government Printing Office, 1972).

Introduction

It is by now a truism that the increase of human populations—in every country—must eventually cease. A rate of population increase that averages zero is no less essential to the survival of the human species than it is to the continued existence of all other living forms. The most obvious reason for this is the limits of both space and resources. But, while physical limits are the most obvious, it is doubtful that they are the most important of the ultimate constraints on human numerical increase. We need not resort to research on animals[1] to infer that numerical increase among humans has the potential to press against the limits of "social and psychic space" well in advance of reaching those of a more physical nature; and concomitantly, that it is in the complex, high energy-consumption, technologically advanced societies that these limits will be reached the most rapidly.

The precise point at which the pressure of numbers would become mortally destructive to a society depends on many different social and cultural factors, including the expectations and aspirations of the population concerning its way of life. But given the complexity of human interaction in modern urban societies, we can be sure that social chaos would occur well in advance of any simple shortage of food or standing room. Failure to perform one's social role in a minimally adequate manner—in response to a power breakdown, for example, or as with a strike of food deliverymen, railroad workers, teachers, or garbage collectors—can, in such societies, have drastic consequences for literally hundreds of thousands.

Nor are the narrower limits of social and psychic space in the highly developed societies to be found solely in their characteristically higher degree of specialization. It is also in these societies that one finds the possibility of a greater degree of impingement of the members upon one another: impingement, for example, in the form of noise, pollution, and diverse visual stimuli. All of these can have profound physical and psychological effects on the individual, however meaningless they may be from the standpoint of providing any real satisfaction of the psychic need for genuine interpersonal contact.[2]

Though human beings do seem capable of adjusting to (or even relishing) considerable amounts of physical crowding over short durations—as at sporting events, pop concerts, demonstrations, or in those "tests of survivability" in fallout shelters where the participants are supplied with ample food and water and know they will not be incarcerated indefinitely—evidence is accumulating that the unrelieved competition among strangers for limited personal and social space can have profoundly disorganizing effects on the social relationships and behaviors necessary to the orderly continuation of human society.[3] Difficulties are already arising in our urban areas in such fields as transportation, communication, social services, recreation, and waste disposal. These are but mild forms of what on a larger scale could reduce social viability—either through outright increases in mortality, social conflict over scarce values, or the spread of that state of apathy and withdrawal which Durkheim termed *anomie* (literally, normlessness).

Given, then, the absolute necessity—reinforced, surely, by the social and psychic desirability—of achieving a zero population growth rate, what does this portend for the future of the United States?

To note that a population's average growth rate must ultimately equal zero does not preclude the possibility that such a rate may be accompanied by considerable fluctuation in short-term rates, and, hence, in total numbers. Wide fluctuations in the short run seem, in fact, to have characterized the experience of nearly all populations until mankind's relatively recent achievement of extensive control over mortality.

In a population like that of the United States, however, which can control both fertility and mortality, it seems reasonable to suppose that annual fluctuations in population size and composition will eventually narrow so as to constitute what demographers term a "stationary" population (that is, a population with an unchanging age and sex distribution and a zero population growth rate). In reaching this conclusion, I am making both an assumption and a hypothesis. With respect to *mortality*, I am assuming continuation of past trends (that is, that extensive control will be maintained and that, as a consequence, there will be virtually no annual fluctuation in age- and sex-specific death rates). With respect to *fertility*, I am hypothesizing about the social conditions that underlie childbearing behavior: Those social conditions that would be most instrumental in contributing to an average growth rate of zero are unlikely to change rapidly enough to produce wide annual fluctuations in birth rates. Such social conditions include those determining the status of women, patterns of residence, the social and economic position of the aged, and the nature and duration of formal schooling and vocational training. These, I suggest, are not only primary determinants of fertility, but constitute a kind of social attribute that is not subject to major short-run swings, either in character or in level of intensity.[4]

One cannot, of course, rule out the possibility of changes in the timing of childbearing in response to unforeseen events of major proportions, such as war, economic depression, or large-scale natural catastrophe. But these would be exceptional occurrences; and in a population substantially controlling mortality and fertility, their impact on levels of childbearing in the longer run would probably be offset by the more stabilizing influence of the underlying social and cultural setting.

Thus, what is being posited here is a stationary fertility model. This is one of essentially four possible fertility models that could be discussed: the linear, random, cyclical, and stationary.

I have rejected the linear model as an impossibility, at least in the long run. I have also rejected the random model—partly because of its improbability, if not impossibility, but primarily because any assumption of a random pattern of fertility behavior would seem to preclude further discussion concerning either the pattern of such behavior or its consequences. I have also rejected the cyclical—not because it is impossible or even implausible, for it is neither of these, but because analysis of such a model, whatever the assumed pattern of cyclical variation, would seem to add little to our understanding of the likely consequences of a zero average growth rate. Also, for the reasons already noted, the stationary, not the cyclical, pattern would seem to have the greater ultimate likelihood of coming into being in a country like the United States.

There is, of course, scant likelihood that the United States will attain a stationary population in the near future. Surveys of norms expressed about family size continue to show an "ideal" in excess of the number needed for replacement.[5] Moreover, the current age distribution has a potential for growth for at least another two generations.[6] Thus, there is an ineluctible quality in a population's age structure that necessitates action in the present for the achievement of goals well into the future.

Nevertheless, it is, I think, of some practical importance to consider what might be expected, both demographically and socially, of a population that has ceased to grow; such a population would seem to be, after all, one of the prime goals of any comprehensive rational and humane social policy.[7] Because the demographic possibilities for the United States population are dealt with elsewhere in the Commission's reports, they will be merely summarized here in order to provide the background necessary to discuss the social consequences of a zero population growth rate.

Demographic Characteristics of a Stationary Population

Size. We do not know what size the population will be when it reaches a stationary condition. Certainly the numbers of Americans will increase substantially beyond the present level; but at what level these additions will cease, and whether the current period of increase will be followed by one of decrease, cannot be determined at the present time. I might note, however, that even though a decrease is possible, it does not seem very likely—certainly not for a long time into the future.

Age structure. Even if we do not know the size of the future stationary population, we do know it will be older—assuming a continuation of low mortality. It will have a median age of approximately 37 years, as against the present median of 28.[8] However defined (and these definitions are rather arbitrary), the proportion in school age will be lower, the proportions in working and retirement ages higher; the proportion in "dependent" ages (that is, school and retirement ages together) will be lower and that in "nondependent" ages higher.

Sex ratio. The sex ratio of such a population will show a slight, but slowly diminishing, excess of males over females up to about age 48.

Marital status. One consequence of this more egalitarian and stable sex ratio will be the absence of any "marriage squeeze." Where custom decrees, for example, that a groom should ideally be two years older than his bride, a 35 percent increase in births over the number two years earlier (which is what happened in the United States in 1947)[9] would result (assuming equal age-specific migration rates) in sex ratios of only 77 males per 100 females at what have been in this country the prime marriageable ages for women (20-24).[10] The result for some is a departure from the "ideal"; for others, postponement of marriage; and for still others, possibly no marriage at all. With an essentially stationary population, there would be no demographic pressure in any of these directions. With little annual variation in birth rates (and hence in numbers of births), sex ratios within the age groups socially defined as ready for marriage would remain constant and nearly equal.

Nonetheless, there is in such stability no necessary implication for the *pattern* of marriage. Marriage in a stationary population of the sort predicated could be virtually universal or limited to a relatively small proportion of the population; it could occur at an early age or at a late age, over a wide range of ages or within a very narrow one, once a lifetime or several times. There is nothing about a stationary population in itself that would foster any one pattern of marriage more than another. The only implication of a stationary population for the pattern of marriage is the absence of any *demographic* pressure to remain unmarried against one's will.

Residence. A stationary population would also not seem to require any particular distribution by residence. It could be primarily rural, primarily small urban, primarily metropolitan, or any mixture of the three. Urbanization is well developed in those countries with the lowest average growth rates over the past two decades; but, there is no uniformity among these countries in either the proportion of the population that is urban or the proportion of the urban population living in agglomerations of different sizes.[11]

However, the absence of any necessary relationship between a stationary population and its pattern of residence does not mean that each of these patterns has the same likelihood of occurrence. For the present, whatever happens to fertility, it seems unlikely that the United States will experience a return movement to farm and rural residence. Farming in this country has steadily become less a way of life and more a strictly commercial enterprise, with all that this signifies in terms of the substitution of capital for human labor, of the removal of economically marginal operators, and of the increased economic valuation of land—the latter acting as still a further incentive to the use of land for the most commercially rewarding purposes. We can probably also expect to see a continuation, for many more years, of the trend toward metropolitanization, though this could involve considerable variation in patterns of residence, especially with improvements in mass transit that would permit commuting over greater distances at no greater expenditure of time. It is important to remember, however, that continuation of these trends in the pattern of residence depends in no way upon whether fertility moves in a direction commensurate with attainment of a stationary population. The future geographical distribution of the population will not be a direct consequence of any movement in the direction of a zero population growth rate.

Mortality. Low mortality has already been assumed to be characteristic of the stationary population under discussion. However undesirable from a personal and social point of view, in a stationary American population of the future, there could continue to be higher mortality among certain occupational and disadvantaged groups, and, of course, among those whose life styles are characterized by heavy smoking, over-eating, lack of exercise, or aggressive driving. The main difference as regards mortality between the present situation and a stationary population is that, in the latter, death would occur about 50 percent more frequently at the mortality levels assumed in my calculations. This rise in the incidence of death would be the result of the higher proportions of the population in the age groups more exposed to the risk of dying. With death consequently a more frequent experience in people's lives, it might be more difficult to deny; one response to which could be development of sounder social supports than now exist for both the dying and the aggrieved.[12]

Fertility. The replacement-level pattern of fertility of a stationary population could rest on a variety of demographic conditions, between the one extreme in which childbearing was confined to a small group having very high fertility and the other in which there was nearly universal childbearing at the level of two children per woman. For example, among French women born in 1905-09, fertility at virtual replacement level was achieved with a considerable dispersion of parities, while the same result among Swedish women born in 1925-29 emerged from a much greater concentration.[13] There is nothing about a stationary population in itself that necessitates any particular distribution of birth parities. All that maintenance of a stationary population requires is that the number of births be equal to the number of deaths.

International migration. If a population is to remain stationary, any level of international migration would have to be compensated for by the rate of natural increase. A net annual gain of 300,000, for example, would have to result in that many fewer births, each year. And this does not take into consideration the fact that the age structure of migrant populations tends to be heavily concentrated in the young adult, child-bearing age groups, potentially making their increment to the population even greater. There are, of course, many determinants of the rate and direction of international migration, particularly government migration policies; but to the extent that demographic factors in the receiving country play a role, it seems reasonable to suppose that a stationary population—because of the constancy of its age composition, its labor force, and possibly its job market—would be both less likely to attract immigrants and less likely to produce emigrants.

Internal migration. There would appear to be much less certainty concerning internal migration. Though it is conceivable that present high rates of mobility could continue with a stationary population, this seems rather unlikely. For one thing, a limit to the number of people who can leave agriculture must soon be reached. For another, the trend to a stationary population would reduce incentives to migrate by permitting better, less hasty planning of land use and urban renewal; it would thus lead to fewer forced removals and presumably, to less dissatisfaction with one's housing and living conditions. A stationary population might also help reduce fluctuation in economic activity and, for that reason, result in less frequent moving about in search of, or because of, changes in conditions of employment. However, essentially the same general rates of internal migration have prevailed in the United States over the past quarter century, despite some rather substantial changes during that period in our age structure. This stability suggests that, whatever the effect of a stationary population on the amount and direction of internal migration, this effect will be mediated through a variety of nondemographic conditions. There is nothing, in itself, about a stationary population that would seem to necessitate any particular pattern of internal migration.

Social Consequences of a Stationary Population

What nondemographic conditions would flow from a stationary population is a matter for conjecture, not prediction. It is quite possible that, so far as conditions of life are concerned, the significance of any stationary population in this country will lie more in its sheer size than in the zero growth rate and stable age and sex distribution that actually define it as a stationary population. The addition over the next three decades of between three and four billion human beings to the world as a whole, and of some 70 to 100 million Americans to the United States alone, can be expected to bring changes scarcely imaginable in terms of our present perspectives. All we can do in discussing the social consequences of a stationary population is to speculate about what might happen to our present social arrangements if population growth and fluctuations in the age structure ceased to be elements in our social setting. However, many changes we cannot now foresee may well be more instrumental in shaping the outlines of life in a demographically stationary society than those changes selected for discussion.

Apart from the certainty of change en route to the stationary condition, there are no one-to-one causal relationships between social patterns and a zero rate of population growth. The range of possible consequences is very wide indeed. Life could be meager or bountiful, violent or peaceful, miserable or happy. A population's size and composition will set limits, but demographic conditions will not, except at the very extremes of overpopulation and underpopulation, be the ultimate determinants of the conditions of human life.

We must avoid lapsing into demographic determinism. A stationary population would only make the "good life" more attainable, it would not, in itself, produce it, though, ultimately, of course, a zero rate of growth is requisite to survival itself. Under any set of demographic conditions—again, short of the extremes—conditions of life will be more a consequence of institutional structures, social attitudes, and policies, than of any population characteristics as such.

Health. There is no better way to illustrate the complexity of the relationship between social conditions and demographic patterns than to consider the social consequences of an older age structure. One might suppose, first of all, that the demand for medical and hospital services, for old age homes and wheelchairs would necessarily increase with an aging of the population. But even here one can posit no one-to-one causal relationship. Much depends on habits of life prior to old age—on diet, exercise, and the intake of drugs, for instance. Much also depends on current conditions, such as the quality of the air and the level and intensity of environmental noise. Also involved is the degree of physical threat in the external environment, for though injury and disability from falls and accidents afflict the aged everywhere, societies apparently differ very substantially with respect to the frequency of such events. Societies also differ very considerably with respect to another set of conditions that affects the general well-being of the elderly: the level of physical threat from social violence.

Moreover, aging is as much a social and psychological process as a biological one. Given conditions that enabled older persons to remain active and useful, that did not rob them of status and livelihood, and that gave them a reasonable degree of predictability concerning the future, the older age distribution of a stationary population might well contain a smaller proportion of "aged" in a social, psychological, and possibly even physical sense than is now the case. In this country today, access to medical care remains costly; the decline of small-scale agriculture and small-scale business has simultaneously lessened the economic opportunities for older people and deprived them of status; pensions hardly compare with wages; and urban sprawl is combined with little opportunity for healthful exercise or for informal and chance encounters, and with a woefully inadequate system of public transportation.

This is not to deny the likelihood of a greater prevalence of chronic ailments and disabilities within a more aged population. But just how much greater this prevalence would be is extremely difficult to predict. The actual prevalence—and also, for that matter, the consequences for human behavior—of such infirmities is determined by so much more than age itself; further, more improvements may occur in medical and rehabilitative science and technology to reduce the prevalence or seriousness of certain conditions. Moreover, the number of infirm is itself difficult to ascertain with any degree of precision. If studies of prevalence within a national population are to be based on anything approaching a statistically reliable sample, it is necessary to study a rather sizable population, and, for financial and administrative reasons, to depend largely on self-reporting, not medical examination. Yet, self-reporting on such matters is subject to considerable error from a variety of sources—ranging from simple lapses of memory to differences in individual interpretation concerning the seriousness, or even existence, of a given affliction.[14]

A halt to population increase in conjunction with continued low mortality means that the proportion of people in the upper ages will be higher than it now is. But what this will signify concerning the health and vigor of the population is necessarily conjectural, this far in advance of the fact. Obviously, aging cannot be prevented; but *when* aging begins and *how* it manifests itself would seem to be explained far less by considerations of birthdays than of conditions of life.

Economic conditions. As in the case of health, a wide range of possible consequences applies also to the relationship between economic conditions and a stationary population. A different pattern of economic conditions might be worthwhile from the standpoint of the conservation of resources or the enhancement of the quality of life.[15] However, there is nothing in a stationary population itself that would inevitably be productive of any particular economic change or condition. Economic change, stability, or decline are all possible with a stationary population.[16] So also are economic activities that stress the private sector, and those emphasizing the public, those that would violate ecological relationships, and those that would not.

Because the economic conditions associated with various patterns of population increase are discussed elsewhere in the Commission's reports, I shall here only summarize what can be concluded concerning the more direct, and more specifically social, consequences of the economic conditions presumably associated with a stationary population.

There would, of course, be a lower proportion in the economically "dependent" ages. Concomitantly, the work force would be generally older and therefore, presumably, more experienced and skilled. Certain skills and experiences may be matters of universal value in an industrialized economy: discipline and a sense of time, for example. But in cases of rapid economic growth (a feature of which would be changes in the distribution of jobs by occupational category), it is just possible that the acquisition of certain skills and experiences could retard, rather than advance, adjustment to the demands of altered conditions. Older workers would conceivably have more to lose—economically, socially, and psychologically—by such changes. It is possible, though, that the economic effects of their inhibitions could be at least partially offset by the employment of currently "marginal" workers: students, the disabled, mothers of young children, or older women with little prior work experience.

What proportion of a stationary population would be in the working ages, and what proportion in the economically dependent ages is in part a matter of arbitrary definition. If we assume working ages to range from 18 to 65, the proportion in these ages would be eight percent higher in the envisaged stationary population than was actually the case in the United States in 1969. However, one could argue that a more appropriate delineation of the "dependent" ages would be those under 21 rather than 18, together with those 70 and over rather than 65 and over. This would take account, on the one hand, of the long period of schooling and training characteristic of modern industrial societies (whether or not this is functionally necessary). On the other, it would also provide for the fact that (1) a high-longevity population can be expected to retain its health and physical vigor to an older age and (2) older persons, for a variety of reasons, frequently wish to continue working.[17] There is nothing sacred about an arbitrary retirement age of 65. In many occupations in Sweden, for example, this age is 70. Using these 18-69 age limits would increase the proportion in the working ages by 13 percent over what it was in the United States in 1969.

So far as capital formation is concerned, we can again only speculate about what consequences might flow from a stationary population. The relationships seem to be merely possibilities, and ones frequently at cross-purposes. If business confidence is dependent upon a growing population, then a stationary population will, by definition, lessen such confidence and, presumably, the investment it would encourage. But business confidence has been low during periods of rapid population increase and, judging from Scandinavian experience, vice versa. As already noted, a stationary population does not preclude an expanding economy. Whether businessmen, in the face of a population that continued to be stationary, could persist in making their confidence dependent upon numerical increases is certainly questionable.

Compared with banks, insurance companies, and businesses themselves, individuals are of little importance as sources of capital.[18] They may, however, play a relatively greater role as a source of genuine "risk" capital. In such a case, so far as purely demographic conditions are concerned, the rate of capital formation will be more likely a response to purely local conditions, such as internal migration and unemployment rates, or even family size among the owners of capital.

Because age is associated with social position and income, and also, though to an undetermined extent, with health and stamina, the changed age structure in a stationary population will have repercussions for the nature of demand. One could, for example, reasonably expect an aging of the population to be conducive to a decline in the market for private automobiles and to an expansion in that for public transportation, to the extent that the private ownership and use of automobiles could continue to be permitted in a society of the population size and geographic distribution likely to be reached before a stationary condition is attained. Thus, a change in age structure of the sort envisaged should reduce somewhat the pressure to accommodate this ubiquitous symbol of private affluence and cause of public squalor. With a reduction of some 21 percent in the proportion of the population aged 15-25, there should be somewhat less support for further construction of roads and parking facilities. This would result in less loss of ratable properties condemned for such construction and less ruination of neighborhoods, both urban and rural[19]—though aggregate demand, because of population size, could, of course, remain quite high. A smaller proportion in those age groups for which the automobile seems to hold a special appeal, and a correspondingly higher proportion in those for which it is a positive nuisance, and also for which there would be a greater dependence on competing forms of transportation, should at least help to lessen the automobile's current social and ecological depredations.

Nonetheless, other demographic factors (particularly the sheer size of the population we can expect by the time this stationary condition is attained and the geographic distribution and internal migration rates of that population) would seem to be more important demographic determinants of market conditions than would the relatively slight changes in age structure accompanying the transition to a stationary population.

As for economies of scale, the size of any demographically defined market in the United States, quite apart from the possibilities inherent in trade, can itself be assumed to be large enough to permit any desirable economies of scale in the production of goods and services demanded by it. This country's much publicized "teenage market," for example, already comprises more people than are to be found in the entire populations of every European country save the United Kingdom, West Germany, Italy, France, Poland, and Spain; more than in any country in Africa, except Nigeria and the United Arab Republic; more than in any country of the Western Hemisphere outside Brazil, Mexico, and, of course, the United States.

But before we put too much emphasis on population, let us remember that the market significance of demographic factors will be slight in comparison with that of employment levels, income distribution, and the socialization of tastes and values through advertising, school, and the media of mass communication.[20] Again, it must be noted that the determinants of prime significance are social and cultural, not demographic. As such, they are capable of differing substantially among different peoples and of undergoing, in a growing economy, substantial change over time, whatever the demographic character of the society.

A stationary population could presumably permit more certainty in economic forecasting, particularly at the national and (to a lesser degree) regional levels. But if internal migration is high—and it could be, even with a stationary population—forecasting by local firms, with a local labor market or a local sales market, could continue to be a rather uncertain undertaking. A stationary population should also permit more accurate forecasting, particularly at the national and regional levels, with respect to provision of social services. But here, too, internal migration could continue to create difficulties for such forecasting at the local level.

With a stationary population there should be less tendency toward inflation. The smoother age distribution should result in less fluctuation, at least at the national and, possibly, regional levels, in demand for schooling, housing (originating in sudden swings in the rate of formation of new families and households), and jobs. The greater certainty in forecasting already referred to could result in less speculation, certainly in real estate but also in other business activity; for a stationary population would offer no specifically demographic encouragement to overcapitalization or to unwise investment on the assumption that a larger potential market, flowing inevitably from an increase in population, would somehow compensate for possible errors in judgment.

Yet the role of population in causing or preventing inflation must surely be minimal. Primary importance, at least under present kinds of conditions, lies first, in the decisions of government with respect to taxation, trade, the amount and direction of public expenditure, wage and price controls, forced savings and transfer payments for retirement, health, welfare, and recreation; and second, in the decisions of the larger businesses (and labor unions) concerning remuneration, postponed payment plans, the introduction of labor-saving devices and techniques, and investment. A population's characteristics and growth rate may set the limits to possible economic conditions, but the limits set are broad indeed.

Status succession. In any system in which power and position are determined at least in part by length of service, a stationary population enjoying low mortality is going to afford less opportunity for promotion. At the probabilities of death used in my calculations for this paper, a stationary population would have fully 90 percent as many males, and 95 percent as many females, at age 50 as at age 20. Contrasted with the present figures of 62 and 68 percent, respectively, this represents a considerable reduction in this particular kind of opportunity.

Whether a lower rate of social mobility is to be viewed with satisfaction or alarm is largely a matter of values; for, even now, success in this competitive struggle can be enjoyed by only a minority. Moreover, fluctuation in annual numbers of births has given some birth cohorts a decided advantage, and others a decided disadvantage, in such competition. Those Americans born in 1935, for example, have had only about 60 percent as many age peers to compete with for space in school, attention of teachers, and jobs and promotions as have those born in 1947, and only about half as many as will those born in 1962.[21]

One consequence of decreased status mobility could be a somewhat lower rate of internal migration, at least among the upper income groups, as fewer executives and professionals are moved about to "higher" positions, and fewer families change houses in response to "upward" (or "downward") movement. To the extent that this occurred, neighborhoods would become more demographically stable. Real estate speculators and salesmen might suffer a bit, in consequence, but housing could come to take a smaller share of one's income; and neighborhoods become less subject to movements of persons who, because of their anticipated transitional status, could afford to allow themselves little emotional attachment to their places of residence.

It is also possible that this shortage of opportunity for promotion could lead to more job-switching, including a higher tendency to go into business for oneself, on the (in this instance) false assumption that the structural limits to status mobility would be less constraining elsewhere. It is possible, too, that for a time there would be a heightened competitiveness in response to the diminished number of opportunities; but it seems unlikely that aspirations for higher position could be entertained for very long without some sort of positive reinforcement.

Competition on the basis of families rather than individuals might be reinforced through a greater participation in the labor force by women. This is already taking place and could increase with a reduction in fertility and extension of day-care facilities. Such competition would, of course, be more for income than for position or promotion; but in any society in which the status symbols were largely distributed through the market-place, any activity that tended to increase or maintain one's opportunities for participation in this marketplace would have its significance for the attainment of status.[22]

Another possibility is the adoption of more stringent retirement practices, to open up by fiat positions of power and prestige no longer created demographically. This might have some appeal if combined with a generous pension scheme and abundant alternative activities, such as small-scale farming or shopkeeping, as is to some extent the case, for example, in France. But there seems little chance that such alternatives could be developed very readily in the United States. The trend has, in fact, been very much in the opposite direction. Moreoever, the receptivity to such a program would seem to decrease as one moves up the occupational ladder to those in the very positions it would be most desirable to open up if faith in the possibility of promotion were to continue.[23] With (1) an absence of suitable alternative activities, (2) employment still apparently an important social and psychological activity for most workers—quite apart from its economic functions—and (3) higher proportion of the work force in the upper ages, it seems more likely that retirement would come at a later, rather than an earlier, age.

Ultimately, I should expect a reduction in the levels of aspiration, which—given a lower actual rate of social mobility—would be the more rational psychic response. I should also expect that, as the actuality of the situation became more widely recognized, and as alternatives that might tend to reinforce a system of competition (such as the employment of wives) were exhausted, this lesser amount of status mobility would increase emphasis on equality: equality, first, in basic services (e.g., health and welfare, environmental protection, public transportation), but eventually, in income itself. This would extend to society at large a practice already followed by labor unions—limiting competition among individuals of essentially the same economic position and the same (i.e., virtually nonexistent) opportunity for promotion.

Whether a decline in status-striving would necessarily delay the march toward "progress" (or some other similarly metaphysical concept) is at best a debatable point. Surely there is more to human motivation—even in the occupational sphere—that can be accounted for by the hope of invidious distinction. The satisfaction of doing a job well, the approbation of one's peers, the intrinsic interest one might have in certain activities, the quality of the on-the-job associations with one's fellow workers, for example, all figure in the motivation of a work force. To attain a given end, these types of motivating factors may have to play a more prominent role than they currently do; but, there seems no reason to doubt their capacity for taking up whatever slack might remain after the virtual disappearance of the, even now, limited opportunities for promotion.

If there is, indeed, a decline in competitiveness and in level of aspiration, one undoubted consequence will be a reduction in status frustration, for promotion can be socially disruptive and emotionally frustrating through creating aspirations where formerly there were none, and subordinates of those who were formerly peers. As Stouffer and his associates found in their classic American Soldier study, morale with respect to perceived opportunities would appear to be higher where promotions are few than where they are many.[24] Surely there are enormous emotional costs in any system, such as that in the United States today, that condemns a high proportion of its total work force to the self-defined category of occupational "failure." If the advent of a stationary population serves to reduce the incidence of such "failure," a case could certainly be made that this was a positive consequence of such demographic change.

The status of women. Changes in the status of women that might be associated with a stationary population are considered elsewhere in this report. As with each of the other areas touched upon here, the influence of demographic patterns on the life chances of women will be mediated through a complex of many social and cultural conditions. Suffice it to say, here, that the implications of a zero growth rate for the status of women would have to do mainly with lower average fertility. Whether or not attainment of a stationary population entails a change in the proportion marrying or in average age at marriage, it will, of necessity, reduce still further the number of women-years devoted to the bearing and rearing of children. This reduction could be spread evenly throughout the society, or concentrated within one segment as childbearing becomes the monopoly of another. There have always been adherents to the view that, ideally, childbearing would be the monopoly of a select few who are presumed—usually on genetic, or, more recently, psychological grounds—to be peculiarly qualified for this function. However, it appears likely that childbearing will continue to be undertaken by a large majority of the women of this society. But unless childbearing is postponed to a substantially higher age, the average duration of the "period of the empty nest" will inevitably be longer.

In the transition to a stationary population, some increase can probably be expected in the proportion of women remaining childless, either voluntarily (through greater access to the means of birth control) or involuntarily (as a consequence of infecundity associated with a later age at marriage). But given present patterns of fertility in this country, the reduction in child-centered activity within one's lifetime would seem likely to have the widest repercussions for that 50 percent of all women who, under current probabilities, would bear three or more children, and particularly the 25 percent who would bear four or more.[25]

What would be the consequences of exempting a higher proportion of women from activities involving reproduction and child care? Even the current pattern of fertility —which still is higher than that needed for replacement—has prompted recognition of the fact that women need to prepare themselves for playing a role other than, or in addition to, that connected with childrearing. As long as the small, nuclear family remains the primary social unit for reproduction and socialization, changing the role of the wife-mother will have important implications for the role of the husband-father, as well. Among other things, shortening the duration of women's obligations to children will increase the pressure on men to regard women as more than simply "helpmeets" and childrearers. It could also heighten the importance of the husband-wife relationship. Under present family and occupational patterns, men are likely to have a much wider range of contacts and experiences than do their wives—whose universe is often contrastingly bounded by home and shopping center. Unless women are presented with opportunities to continue their personal development within marriage, the longer period of childlessness could serve to emphasize this gulf. The necessity for such changes in attitudes, for increased opportunities for women, and for such facilities as day care, retraining programs, and public transportation to allow access to activities outside the home, can only be increased by the changes in patterns of childbearing associated with a stationary population.

Behavior. Among those who have on occasion succumbed to the temptations of demographic determinism, the main anxieties expressed about a stationary population concern its age structure. A well-known economist-demographer, for instance, avers that a society with the older age structure of a stationary population "would not be likely to be receptive to change and indeed would have a strong tendency towards nostalgia and conservatism."[26] And a French writer has characterized such a population as one of "old people ruminating over old ideas in old houses."[27]

As it happens, the cause of such concern is an age structure little different from the current age structures of Sweden and England and Wales—populations hardly characterized by rampant decrepitude. Table 1 shows the percentage age distributions of these two populations, in comparison with that of the hypothetical stationary population of the United States.

Social Consequences of ZPG

Table 1.—Percentage Distribution of Age in England and Wales, Sweden, and Hypothetical United States Populations

Age	1969 population of England and Wales (a)	1967 population of Sweden (b)	Hypothetical stationary population of U.S.[a] (c)	Ratios: (c)(a)	Ratios: (c)(b)
Under 10 years	16.55%	14.16%	13.71%	.83	.97
10-19 years	13.86	14.28	13.64	.98	.96
20-29 years	14.05	14.83	13.50	.96	.91
30-39 years	12.04	11.55	13.32	1.11	1.15
40-49 years	13.02	13.35	12.96	1.00	.97
50-59 years	11.94	13.06	12.09	1.01	.93
60-69 years	10.49	10.43	10.26	.98	.98
70 years and over	8.05	8.34	10.50	1.30	1.26
Total	100.00%	100.00%	99.98%		

[a] Derived from U.S. Dept. of Health, Education, and Welfare, Public Health Service, *Vital Statistics of the United States, 1967.*

Only in the oldest age category (70 and over) does the stationary population differ much from that of these two actual populations, and then only to the extent of 2.45 percentage points in the case of England and Wales, and 2.16 percentage points in the case of Sweden.

But is receptivity to change always desirable, and nostalgia and conservatism always undesirable? Would it not be more pertinent to ask: "Receptivity to what kinds of change? Nostalgia and conservatism about what?" And, for that matter, which "old ideas" in which "old houses"?

"Conservatism," "progressive," "reactionary," "radical" are spongy concepts, especially when removed from their specific referents. Were Hitler's youthful storm troopers "progressive"? Were the aged Townsendites "conservative"? And even if we know, as individuals, what we mean by these terms, can we assume that the "conservative" on one issue is going to be "conservative" on others as well, or—more germane to the present discussion—that these views, however categorized, are causally related to age? In terms of the demonstrated willingness to introduce changes in economic behavior, education, and the status of women, the world's most conservative societies are those with the youngest—not the oldest—populations. And this holds even when we consider only the adult portions of those populations.

Within our own society, a recent public opinion poll finds older women more willing than younger to remove legal restrictions on access to abortion.[28] Is this lesser receptivity to change? In 1968, the New Republic continued with its long-standing custom of rating congressmen on the basis of certain "key votes" during the previous session. On the 12 Senate votes selected, despite considerable overlap, "progressivism," as defined by this self-designated "liberal" magazine was, indeed, associated with "youth": The median age of those with no more than three "unfavorable" votes was four years younger than that of those with no more than three "favorable" votes. Yet, on the one issue of the 12 selected that reflects attitudes toward the Vietnam War, the "hawks" and "doves" had the same median age; and there was no difference between the two groups in distribution by age.[29] New Republic also analyzed the 80th Congress (1947-48), which probably separated the "liberals" from the "conservatives" more than any other Congress since World War II. Again, the ratings show a difference of four years between the median age of the "liberals" (those with no more than four "unfavorable" votes out of the 15 selected) and the "conservatives" (those with no more than four "favorable" votes).[30] But, this time, the relationship is reversed: It is the "liberals" who are older.

It is possible that a stationary—hence older— population would be less subject to fads, whether in clothing, grooming, the arts, recreation, or politics. Participating less in the mainstream of the society and being less completely socialized, still "in process" of development, younger persons seem to have fewer countervailing pressures toward conformity with adult (or other) patterns of thought and behavior. Add to this a high proportion of the population in these socially-defined "youthful" ages, and a substantial amount of disposable wealth in their pockets, and there is a further stimulus to fad in the incentive to exploit the greater liability of young people for economic or political gain. A reduction in the proportion in these youthful age groups would surely reduce this incentive, or, at the least, confine it to a smaller share of the total operation in business and politics.

But what is the determining factor in this greater lability of the "young"? Is it not social position, rather than age? To argue in terms of age is to commit a fallacy—the fallacy of misplaced emphasis—for the behavior of any group above the age of infancy is determined by its position in society, not its accumulation of years. To worry about the supposed behavioral consequences of an aging, or more aged, population is to divert attention from the real issue: how to incorporate a higher proportion of old people—given the inevitability of a cessation of population increase and the desirability of low mortality—into society in a socially and emotionally meaningful way.

Personality structure. If being an unwanted child or the parent of an unwanted child has any positive consequences for human personality, it has so far managed to elude both the researcher and the casual observer. The virtually total disappearance of unwanted children—unwanted at time of conception, at any rate—implied in this model of a stationary population can hardly fail to have at least some beneficial effect on the mental condition on the general public.[31]

But what about the consequences for personality of the implied changes in family size? Are there differences in personality associated with different orders of birth, or that arise as a consequence of different parent-child or sibling relationships originating in different family sizes? If there are such differences, any change in the distribution of family sizes will alter the distribution of personality types. The evidence on this, however, is at best equivocal; the studies of these relationships generally disregard such other possible factors in the formation of personality as contacts with persons outside one's family, social and cultural change, successive attainment of age-associated statuses, and cultural and subcultural differences.[32]

Knowing more about the relation between family size, birth order, and personality structure would seem of some interest from the point of view of family and school counseling and of understanding the factors underlying child development. But before we devote too much time and energy to the issue, two points should be emphasized: (1) The family is only one of many socializing influences; and, (2) the human stake in achieving a cessation of population increase, in combination with the likely persistence of a desire for parenthood among the great majority of the population, will outweigh in importance any possible negative associations turned up on this score by the psychologists. As with the prospect of a higher proportion of aged, the question is one of making the best of the situation, rather than of sacrificing more important values in a misguided effort to avoid a demonstrably lesser evil—if evil it even is, in this particular instance.

Surely there is a wider range of choice than that between avoiding the issue entirely and using it as an excuse for postponing major efforts to halt population increase. Should an association be found between, say, socialization in the small family and personality traits defined as undesirable, the prudent course would appear to be, not the restriction of childbearing to larger families, but the provision of more opportunities for children to enjoy close contact with their peers. One concomitant of a general reduction in family size might, in fact, be a lessening of the present degree of exclusiveness with regard to the care of one's children, and a correspondingly heightened receptivity to a more communal approach. This need not be limited to day-care centers, but could also take place on a private basis among individual families who could interchange and share children for extended periods of time. The current development of a more receptive attitude toward adoption would seem to indicate a changing attitude concerning the purely biological basis of parenthood, as would the rise of communal family living and of neighborhood arrangements to trade child care duties on an informal but regular basis. Less privatism in child care would fit into the particular requirements of a stationary population by freeing women from exclusive preoccupation with their own preschool youngsters. Simultaneously, it would offer them (and possibly men, too) the opportunity to enjoy a close relationship with children over a longer period of time than is possible when such relationships must be confined to one's own biological children. Less privatism in child care could, of course, further serve the requirements of a stationary population by helping to reduce the prevalence of any negative personality traits arising (and, as already noted, there is no proof that this occurs) from socialization prominently involving the small nuclear family.

Creativity. A personality trait deserving, perhaps, of more extended comment because of its presumed importance to society, and its presumed relationship to various attributes of a stationary population, is creativity. Is creativity affected by the amount of competition? Is it a function of age, and, if so, is the change in age structure associated with a stationary population likely to have any effect on the amount and kind of creativity in a society?

However one may define it, there is no denying that creativity takes many forms, pertains to a myriad of activities (by no means all of which are socially desirable), and is exceedingly difficult, if not impossible, to measure with any precision. No population anywhere would seem to lack at least the potential for creative thought and action in all areas of endeavor. But whether this potential is realized will depend ultimately upon the culture base: on values and norms, and prior development in language, the arts, science, and technology, for example. For every creation must be built not only upon the accumulation of what has gone before, but also on the happy combination of circumstances which afforded its creator the opportunity to exercise his special gifts.

The same holds for its acceptance: Whether a creation is incorporated into the rest of the culture will be determined less by its specific merits than by the current interests of the society and the supporting power of its culture base.[33] In certain areas of activity, that part of the culture base subsumed under the term "competition" can be a spur to creativity. But in other areas, it will be a hindrance, either by encouraging alternative activities or by so penalizing creative "failure" as to dissuade the potentially creative from undertaking a particular activity and making the effort necessary to become creative in it.

One may suppose three ways in which creativity might be related to chronological age: (1) There is a decline in energy, strength, endurance, and cognition presumably associated with growing older; (2) experience, which the aged would presumably have more of because of having lived longer, may be conducive to psychic inflexibility and to a lesser receptivity to new ideas; and (3) different social positions afford different levels of opportunity for creativity, and assignment to these positions (and the role expectations associated with them) is to at least some extent a function of age.

Unfortunately, the problems of defining and measuring creativity remain when one tries to assess the significance of age to this attribute. This has not kept the relationship from being the subject of several investigations, however. Problems of definition and measurement have been solved for purposes of these investigations by dealing only with those who have achieved some degree of eminence in the field under consideration. Such a procedure, however necessary for research purposes, excludes those more numerous—and possibly just as creative—individuals whose works, or names, did not find their way into the historical accounts.[34] But it is in their treatment of age itself that these studies are particularly remiss for our purposes here. To afford any meaningful conclusions, whatever the definition of creativity, analysis would have to relate to the population, in the statistical sense, "at risk." The need, as Zuckerman has pointed out in her study of scientific achievement, is for data "not on the proportion of contributors in each age but on the proportion of each age group making major contributions." Yet standardization by age in these studies is notoriously absent, with the result that we must "regard the findings on age and discovery with scepticism."[35]

If age is, indeed, related to creativity, it would seem to be so primarily because of its intermediate relationship to social position. One study of a small sample has found that younger scientists more frequently cite recent work.[36] But this may show less about their responsiveness to new ideas and, therefore, about the likelihood of their being creative, than it does about their present social position: More recently in graduate school, they would conceivably have been more recently in close association, as students, with individuals working at the frontiers of their disciplines and, for that reason, be more informed about the recent literature in the particular specialty on which they were writing. Or, they might, out of ignorance arising from inexperience, be giving the more recent citation for essentially the same findings reported on in an earlier publication—a phenomenon, tantamount to scholarly amnesia, to which the less codified social sciences would seem particularly prone.[37]

Social Consequences of ZPG

One feature of a stationary population that does seem to have some possible significance for creativity is the fact that the age structure of such a population will offer fewer promotions and, therefore, open up fewer administrative posts for those in any particular age group. A smaller proportion of the more experienced, and possibly more knowledgeable, among the population would thus be siphoned off into activities palpably less conducive to creativity—at least to creativity in fields other than administration. Therefore, it is just possible that an increase in creativity would ensue from the transition to a stationary population. Nonetheless, the prime determinant of the level and nature of this creativity would still be the total social and cultural environment. The demographic environment could do little more than set the stage.

Social security and public programs. Changes in the proportion of the population in different age groups, as well as changes in family size and the status of women, might well be reflected in the amount and type of social security provided in a stationary population. On the one hand, a stationary population (enjoying low mortality) will doubtless place a greater emphasis on social, as opposed to private, means for the support of the aged, infirm, and disabled. This will arise, in part, in the presumably greater political power of the older population—because of their relatively greater numbers—and in part in the substitution of a greater dependency of age for a lesser dependency of youth. Only a population with a youthful age distribution can effectively relegate support for the aged to the contributions of children and relatives. With an older age distribution and the lack of the extended-family household, there will be every incentive for the development of procedures for enabling (or, from another point of view, requiring) the aged to support themselves by means of forced savings—customarily in the form of social security payments during the years of peak earnings. This is likely to occur, whatever the material level of living; and it will probably continue along present lines of development in this country, regardless of changes in age structure. The transition to a stationary—and therefore older—population will thus merely reinforce a trend already well underway.

The transition to a stationary population may also be expected to reinforce certain trends with respect to programs specifically related to women. If women are to be able to combine motherhood with employment, schooling, or any other time-consuming activities outside the home, they will need maternity leaves, access to quality household help, and financial support for travel and various kinds of advanced training. A stationary population structure of the sort predicated here could encourage an assortment of programs for women that would make the childbearing period a less complete break with other periods in the life cycle. Many specific things could be done to accomplish this goal, including (1) increasing the availability of part-time work, (2) staggering working hours to make them more responsive to individual needs (a measure already being tried with apparent success by some European companies), and (3) permitting greater flexibility and variation, particularly concerning timing and age, in the requirements for obtaining educational degrees.

It is also conceivable that a society with a stationary population might put more emphasis on the quality of public services for children, perhaps as a way of husbanding its resources—by more substantially capitalizing for future productivity and relatively smaller proportion of the total population. With fewer children per family, and women tending increasingly to divide their time between home and outside interests, there would be greater pressure on the community to provide conditions conducive to both the safety and the earlier independence of children, conditions that would, in other words, free parents from the necessity of constantly hovering, chauffeuring, and supervising their progeny. Because many of the sorts of facilities that meet the needs of children (e.g., public transportation, safe places to walk, parks and plazas at which to meet one's friends, and even public toilets) are also conducive to the well-being of the aged, this convergence of interest might increase the probability that such changes would be introduced. The absence of peaks and troughs in the annual influx of births would also make such introduction easier, for there would be less need to withhold expenditure in anticipation of the future requirements of successively larger cohorts (even though continuation of high rates of internal mobility could still make planning along these lines an uncertain venture at the local level).

With a smaller average size of families and a possibly larger proportion of the population living alone, it seems likely that the general direction of public programs in the hypothesized stationary population would be toward the provision of more kinds of support for individuals at the various stages of the life cycle.

Conclusion

The purpose of this discussion has been to take a wide-range look at the possible social consequences related to a particular combination of demographic conditions—a population structure characterized by a zero average growth rate and an age structure remaining uniform from one year to the next. Two difficulties are encountered in such an effort: (1) the intellectual feat of trying to separate the likely consequences accruing to changes in *absolute* numbers from those that might be expected to relate to the specific demographic features under discussion (that is, the cessation of growth and stability of the proportion of the population in different age groups) and (2) the problem of giving proper consideration to all of the variables likely to come into play in the relation between changes in demographic structure and their associated social consequences.

With regard to the first difficulty, the inevitability of further expansion of the American population complicates the task of distinguishing the social consequences of a zero growth rate itself. Change in the absolute size of the American population—of the magnitude expected before growth subsides—will itself constitute a major determinant of social conditions, attitudes, and values. However, my concern here is with the consequences of a particular population structure, rather than with the impact of additional numbers on the American way of life. Therefore, I have, for the most part, left aside the effects of increasing size and dealt with the social implications of change in the growth rate, as though this change were to be superimposed upon a social context little different from what we know in the United States today.

Thus, the nature of my remarks is hypothetical rather than projective. What I have outlined here is essentially a hypothetical picture of what might happen were the United States to achieve a cessation of population increase and a stable age structure with all other factors held constant. While it may seem that I have indulged in a merely mechanical exercise, it is, I feel, worth doing if it has helped to dispel some of the fears that seem to arise whenever people contemplate life in a numerically stable society.

What I hope to have shown in this review is that what is feared has less to do with the consequences of a zero rate of growth itself, than with the consequences of moving too rapidly onto unfamiliar demographic ground before social attitudes and institutions have had the chance to adjust to the new demands posed. But, in the absence of substantial changes in fertility or the timing of childbearing, the pattern of past birth and death rates will delay transition to a stationary condition for at least another seven decades.[38] Thus, the more rational fear with respect to demographic change would appear to be that of the consequences of increase in size, rather than of any decline in the rate of population growth.

The second difficulty in making an analysis like this is simply that the complexity of the social fabric makes adequate treatment of all the possible interactions a superhuman task. What I have done here is to explore the possible consequences of the demographic changes predicated for a few of those specific areas of social life that it seems would be most intimately affected. I make no claims that my selection has been exhaustive.

Before concluding, I must point out that in hypothesizing a relationship between a given social condition and a stationary population, I do not mean to imply that the influence of one upon the other is necessarily in one direction only. Many of the sorts of changes mentioned here as possible social consequences of the stationary population can just as well be viewed as measures that would hasten the transition to such a population structure; in other words, they can be seen as determinants, as well as consequences, of a stationary population. Presumably, the sorts of social arrangements that would mesh with the requirements of a particular demographic structure would also be those conducive to moving a society's population characteristics toward such a structure.[39]

My conclusions can now be summed up in four sentences:
(1) A cessation of population increase is inevitable.
(2) A stationary population, at least in the United States, is likely.
(3) The consequences of any population structure will be as much a function of the social and cultural setting as of any particular configuration of demographic patterns.
(4) But to the extent that population structure is itself a determinant of social conditions, the concomitants of a stationary population are far more likely to be desirable than undesirable—both for the society and for the individual.

Footnotes

1. John B. Calhoun, "Population Density and Social Pathology," *Scientific American*, February 1962.
2. Lincoln H. Day and Alice Taylor Day, *Too Many Americans* (Boston: Houghton Mifflin, 1964), esp. chapter 3.
3. In this connection, see Edward F. Hall, *The Hidden Dimension* (Garden City: Doubleday, 1966), especially chapters 4-6, 13-14; John M. Darley and Bibb Latane, "When Will People Help in a Crisis?" *Psychology Today*, December 1968; and Albert Eide Parr, "The City as Habitat," *The Centennial Review*, Spring 1970.
4. Lincoln H. Day and Alice Taylor Day, "Family Size in Industrialized Countries: An Inquiry into the Social-Cultural Determinants of Levels of Childbearing," *Journal of Marriage and the Family*, May 1969.
5. Judith Blake, "Reproductive Motivation and Population Policy," *BioScience*, March 1, 1971, p. 216.
6. Tomas Frejka, "Reflections on the Demographic Conditions Needed to Establish a U.S. Stationary Population Growth," *Population Studies*, November 1968.
7. Lincoln H. Day and Alice Taylor Day, *Too Many Americans*, op. cit., Chapter 2, and Lincoln H. Day, "Concerning the Optimum Level of Population," in *Is There an Optimum Level of Population*, S. Fred Singer ed. (New York: McGraw-Hill, 1971).
8. Calculated from U.S. Dept. of Health, Education, and Welfare, Public Health Service, *Vital Statistics of the U.S. 1967*, Vol. II, *Mortality*, Part A, Section 5, Tables 5-2 and 5-3. These life tables for 1967 offer a slightly more favorable mortality schedule than do those for 1968, the most recent ones available.
9. Calculated from United Nations *Demographic Yearbook 1949-50*, Table 15.
10. Calculated from data in *Ibid.* and in U.S. Dept. of Health, Education, and Welfare, op. cit., Table 5-3.
11. United Nations, *Demographic Yearbook 1969*, Table 31, and United Nations, *Demographic Yearbook 1963*, Tables 6 and 32.
12. See, for example, Dael Wolfle, "Dying with Dignity," *Science*, June 19, 1970, p. 1403, and Geoffrey Gorer, *Death, Grief, and Mourning* (New York: Doubleday, 1967).
13. Lincoln H. Day and Alice Taylor Day, "Family Size in Industrialized Countries," op. cit., p. 243.
14. See, for example, U.S. Dept. of Health, Education, and Welfare, Public Health Service, *Vital and Health Statistics*, Series 2, No. 42, "Disability Components for an Index of Health," July 1971, pp. 23-26.
15. In this connection, see the excellent discussion in E. J. Mishan, *The Costs of Economic Growth* (London: Stables Press, 1967).

16. Lincoln H. Day, "A 'Young' Population Is Not Necessarily Good for a Nation or Its Business," *The New York Statistician,* January-February 1971.
17. A. J. Jaffe, "Men Prefer Not to Retire," *Industrial Gerontology,* Spring 1970.
18. Adolph A. Berle, Jr., *The Twentieth Century Capitalist Revolution* (New York: Harcourt Brace, 1954), pp. 37-40.
19. For a perceptive discussion of the consequences of the level of automobile usage in the United States today, see A. Q. Mowbray, *The Road to Ruin* (New York: Lippincott, 1969). Also see E. J. Mishan, *op. cit.,* especially chapter 8.
20. David M. Potter, *People of Plenty* (Chicago: University of Chicago Press, 1954), especially chapter 8.
21. Calculated from data in U.S. Bureau of the Census, Current Population Reports, Series P-25, No. 441, *Estimates of the Population of the United States, by Age, Race, and Sex: July 1, 1967 to July 1, 1969,* Table 1.
22. Lincoln H. Day, "Status Implications of the Employment of Married Women in the United States," *American Journal of Economics and Sociology,* June 1961.
23. A. J. Jaffe, *op. cit.*
24. Samuel A. Stouffer, *et al., The American Soldier* (Princeton: Princeton Univ. Press, 1949), Vol. I, pp. 250-258.
25. From data in United Nations, *Demographic Yearbook 1963,* Table 16.
26. A. J. Coale, "Should the United States Start a Campaign for Fewer Births?" *Population Index,* October-December, 1968.
27. Quoted in *ibid.*
28. Judith Blake, "Abortion and Public Opinion: The 1960-1970 Decade." *Science,* Feb. 12, 1971.
29. *New Republic,* Nov. 2, 1968; ages from *Who's Who in America, 1968.*
30. *New Republic,* Sept. 27, 1948; ages from *Congressional Directory, 1948.*
31. For an estimate of the number of unwanted births, see Larry Bumpass and Charles F. Westoff, "The 'Perfect Contraceptive' Population," *Science,* Sept. 18, 1970, and Norman B. Ryder and Charles F. Westoff, "Fertility Planning Status: United States, 1965," *Demography,* November 1969.
32. See, in this connection, Walter Toman, *Family Constellation: Its Effects on Personality and Social Behavior* (New York: Springer Publishing Co., 1969), especially pp. 251-256; and, for an example, Irving D. Harris, *The Promised Seed: A Comparative Study of Eminent First and Later Sons* (New York: Free Press of Glencoe, 1964), especially chapter 12.
33. For a more detailed discussion see Lincoln H. Day and Alice Taylor Day, *Too Many Americans, op. cit.,* pp. 189-196, 199-203.
34. Harriet Zuckerman, "Reflections on Age Stratification and the Codification of Scientific Knowledge" (paper presented at the meetings of the American Association for the Advancement of Science, December 28, 1970).
35. *Ibid.*
36. *Ibid.*
37. Pitirim Sorokin, *Fads and Foibles in Modern Sociology* (Chicago: Henry Regnery, 1965).
38. Tomas Frejka, *op. cit.*
39. Lincoln H. Day and Alice Taylor Day, "Family Size in Industrialized Countries," *op. cit.,* and William J. Goode, *World Revolution and Family Patterns* (New York: Free Press, 1963).
 * The views and opinions expressed in this paper are those of the author and do not necessarily represent those of the United Nations.

Problems That Sprout in the Shadow of No-Growth

Wilbur R. Thompson

Wilbur Thompson, economist and author of A Preface to Urban Economics, *is a part-time professor in the Department of Economics at Wayne State University, as well as professor of urban economics at the Medill School of Journalism, Northwestern University. He was chairman of the board of the Southwestern Michigan Transportation Authority. Dr. Thompson is a graduate of the School of Economics at Wayne State University, and holds both a master's and a doctorate in economics from the University of Michigan.*

This article is reprinted with permission, from the December 1973 AIA Journal of the American Institute of Architects; 1735 New York Avenue, N.W.; Washington, D.C.

If we ever did fully believe that raw growth was the universal solvent, we have been disabused of that naive notion for some time now. Today, almost as many places are trying to slow or stop growth as are seeking to promote it. Oregon has gained headlines over its invitation to come and visit but not, please, to come and stay, while in northern Mississippi, Tupelo, not to be distracted, still seeks "development" through growth and welcomes its steady influx of manufacturing plants, and nearby Corinth seeks to duplicate its "success."

Growth tightens the local labor market: good. There are considerable benefits bestowed by a) the process of growth and b) the larger size which is its inevitable consequence. It is appropriate to mention briefly a few of the more obvious benefits at the very beginning, both for perspective and also lest we forget. Raw growth in local job formation—of almost any kind and wage—acts to tighten the local labor market and serves thereby to raise and equalize incomes. The most able workers tend to be fully employed almost all of the time, and so it is primarily the less able who gain most as new jobs open up and as opportunities for upgrading improve. It is the lower income families who are most anxious to put a second earner to work, closing a little the income gap at the bottom.

But raw growth has even more to offer Tupelo, for with larger size the local economy becomes more diversified, and the local labor achieves greater balance and offers new opportunity. Winter seasonal demands for labor in some industries offset summer peaks in others, stabilizing employment. A variety of part-time work appears to fill the needs of the elderly, school-age youth, the handicapped and women with children at home. A rich mix of products and services generates demands for a wide range of skills and puts in place "occupational ladders" that give real meaning to on-the-job training as an alternative to formal schooling.

Finally, only with a much larger urban scale is Tupelo likely to provide the variety of

Problems That Sprout in the Shadow of No-Growth

professional work that makes it possible—probable—to offer *both* an educated husband and his educated wife suitable employment. The most critical resource of all, talent, is increasingly offered in "joint supply," both or neither. In short, those who would, in the name of environmental responsibility, slow or stop the growth of local employment and population must accept serious labor market and manpower planning responsibilities.

Growth tightens the local housing market: not so good. A local economy may generate vigorous growth in employment because it has fast-growing industries: the automobile industry in the 1920s, electronics and space industries in the '50s and '60s, and perhaps the health industry in the '70s and '80s. Or a local economy can flourish on a base of old industries by acquiring a larger and larger share of that which at the national level are slow-growing industries, such as for instance textiles and apparel in the Piedmont. In either case, the local prosperity stimulates heavy in-migration which, added to the natural increase in local population, outruns the sluggish increase in the stock of housing. The unusually tight local labor markets in the Piedmont are, for example, matched with even tighter housing markets. Most important, even if the newcomers are a cross section of all income classes (and not largely poor, as popular impression has it), the shortage will be most severe and persist the longest in low income housing.

The supply of high income housing can be appreciably increased in a single building period—a year or so—and the price rise here will tend to be modest and short-lived. But low income families live, by and large, in old houses that have filtered down from earlier owners, and at any given time the supply of 40- to 60-year-old houses is limited, virtually fixed in supply. (How would you increase the supply of 50-year-old houses!)

The very poor can, of course, make painful sacrifices in other spending and bid away a few 40-year-old dwellings from the near poor, who will release them only if they, in turn, can bid away an even greater number of 30-year-old units from the middle class. Remember that all income classes are growing in number and therefore the near-poor also needed more dwelling units, even before they released some to the poor. Under rapid local growth, every time a given income class passes down a few extra dwelling units (beyond the normal rate of filtering), it greatly intensifies the shortfall in its own normal supply. In other words, the filtering down of used housing can be accelerated under growth pressures but only slightly, and even then only at a very sharply increasing supply price for housing.

Housing shortages: a compromise of urban environmental policy. An acute shortage of good used housing is problem enough, but there is further cause for concern in the various market and political pressures engendered by that shortage. Recall that in 1945, we came out of the war with a critical shortage of housing in all price brackets. This huge backlog demand for housing, primarily traceable to five years of war but reinforced by a decade of depression that came before, confronted the nation with a difficult choice: produce as many houses as possible with the least delay, or put to practice the best in residential design. Our individual frustrations with postponed marriages, seemingly interminable periods of being doubled up with parents and other factors overwhelmed our modest interest in better communities, and so the construction industry responded speedily to market dictates with the "efficient" production of vast tracts of what later came to be called ticky-tack housing.

Nationally, our current rate of housing construction has slipped well below the projected "need" of 2.6 million units annually, and this gap has widened appreciably wherever the local rate of population growth and household formation exceeds to a large degree the national average rate of growth. Our currently mounting housing shortage surely threatens new harsh compromises with good practice in city building, especially in our most rapidly growing urban areas, precisely those places where most of our children will live.

Our new-found concern for the protection of the natural environment is threatened in rapidly urbanizing areas by local housing crises as surely as it is being shaken by the energy crisis. The shift from traditional suburban building practice to experimental forms, such as new towns, is burdened by their high "opportunity cost"—the larger number of standard housing units foregone, and the longer waiting period needed to "do it right."

Turning to another dimension of potential environmental damage, architectural critic Ada Louise Huxtable has, in commenting on the Forest Hills project in New York City, expressed concern that rapid growth puts heavy pressure on housing authorities to stick with familiar designs, and not innovate. But replicating highrise public housing projects can hardly be defended today in light of the recent Pruitt Igoe project demolition in St. Louis and the findings of the New York University study team led by Oscar Newman, which estimated crime rates in interior public spaces in 13- to 30-floor buildings at seven times the rate per 1,000 families found in three-floor walk-ups.

We just cannot afford, in social cost, to stick with familiar designs that spawn some of our most serious urban problems. Which would you rather have: delays in relieving housing shortages or environments that nurture crime? Growth has its price.

Housing shortages: a compromise of urban social policy. Rapid local growth and severe housing shortages could also force serious compromises in fundamental social policy, as reflected, for example, in the strength of our commitment to "social mixing." Those who oppose residential desegregation by income and race gain a much stronger bargaining position if the proponents of social mixing must also worry about an inadequate total supply of low income housing, wherever located. Affluent liberals will be hard put to hold their poor and black allies in line if white segregationists offer their political support for increased low income housing appropriations if the "mixers" will only drop their demands for mixing. To the poor, better housing *now* is likely to outweigh great moral heights to be gained down the line—the old "pie in the sky" internal tension of early unionism.

Again, housing allowances or rent supplements are currently much in favor as a less paternalistic way of moving the poor into better housing. In a slow-growing locality with a slack housing market, a high vacancy rate is protection against the risk of greatly inflating rents by simply handing out rent money—approaching low income housing problems solely from the demand side.

But under the heavy pressure of rapid growth and tight housing, rent supplements may solve only the financial problems of landlords; working instead to increase housing supplies would seem to go more to the root of the problem. When housing is in short supply across the board, direct public investment, as in public housing, or construction subsidies to elicit private investment may be less permissive but more efficient.

All in all, rapid local growth and a tight housing market would seem to threaten a host of national social policies and supportive city building practices that we faithfully preserve by dutifully transferring them from goals statement to goals statement ad infinitum.

Jobs or Housing: a Hobson's choice? Under vigorous growth, the marginal members of the local labor force find work and the distribution of income becomes less unequal, but these minimum-wage workers face a serious housing crunch which at least partly offsets

Problems That Sprout in the Shadow of No-Growth

their income gains. Much worse, those not in the labor force—the elderly, handicapped and female heads of households—suffer rent increases with no income offset. Local prosperity can impoverish some and in absolute terms, not just relative to others.

Seen in this light, it is irresponsible to promote local industrial expansion without coupling this action to a low income housing program that picks up the pieces. But we do it all the time.

The rough outlines of this hard tradeoff between full employment and good housing can be darkly seen in the results of some recent surveys. In a study for the National Academy of Sciences, Thomas Pettigrew calls our attention to a 1968 survey of Detroit blacks in which "three of the six chief perceived causes of race riots relate directly to housing: 'poor housing,' 'overcrowded living conditions,' and 'dirty neighborhoods.' " And "four of the seven issues considered by Miami blacks as 'big problems' for them involved housing." Both Detroit and Miami were, during the '60s, high growth areas, and the blacks are, of course, at the bottom of the housing ladder.

The focus sharpens when we compare the survey finding that "rural and small-city blacks reported far greater housing improvements than big-city blacks." (Slow-growing towns?)

One can, on the basis of other surveys of Detroit carried out by the Wayne State University Center for Urban Studies, make a reasonably convincing case that in the late '50s, a period of local stagnation beyond that of the nation, the problem of the poor was unemployment; and, in this boom year 1973, the local problem of the poor is housing. Growth or no-growth presents a Hobson's choice.

"Best" rate of growth: whose? Ideally, an urban area would, to the extent that it could, sort out and weigh the many benefits and costs associated with various rates of local growth and then move to control its own growth. Clearly, we have much more to learn about these matters but, beyond that, there is little evidence that we are in a position to manage local growth in the social interest.

Two serious complications come to mind:
1. We are not all of one mind on the "best" rate at which to grow.
2. The process of growth is a complex compound of unpredictable disequilibrating forces, as well as the more predictable equilibrating tendencies on which most economic theory rests.

Local policies designed to slow growth, favored by some, will be resisted by others who benefit from economic expansion. First, and most obvious, we have the local property owners who stand to make sizable capital gains from rising prices of land and buildings, not the least of which is that most numerous class, homeowners, whose gains are more than just "paper profits" to the degree that they are heavily mortgaged (i.e., have been "trading on the equity"). Perhaps next in importance are the owners of businesses serving the local market: bankers, retailers, real estate brokers and, of special interest, the local newspaper that molds public opinion.

Harder to evaluate, the marginal members of the labor force—the last hired and first fired—may not in themselves be a power to be reckoned with, all power to the people notwithstanding, but may in coalition with their champions, the old-line liberals, add a strong voice for local economic expansion.

Conversely, there are many whose interests are served by slow growth or even no-growth although, at least until recently, these groups seemed to be much less aware of their self-interests or perhaps just less vocal.

The group most vulnerable to the strains of rapid growth and the ones with probably the least political clout are renters who are not in the labor force, who have little if anything to gain from a tightening of the local labor market and who must rent in a tighter housing market. But they are joined today by a swelling number of amenity seekers: affluent residents living on out-of-town property income; wealthy, nonresident, second-home owners (so common in the northern New England states); and amateur ecologists, professional radicals and assorted new-style liberals, all much more articulate and knowledgeable about the nature and uses of political and economic power.

Faster growth: younger and prettier. The management of local growth is made even more difficult by the presence of "disequilibrating tendencies" not unlike those suggested by the old homilies "success breeds success" and "when it rains, it pours." Rapidly growing places are bright and clean and do attract more growth, just as declining places begin to wear out and look it, and are increasingly hard to sell to footloose business prospects.

Gene Clabes reported from Evansville that a major petroleum manufacturing corporation rejected that city as a location in part because its directors preferred a community that was growing at an annual rate of 2 to 3 percent (well above the national average rate), in sharp contrast to Evansville's .5 percent. If bigger is not better, newer is usually prettier.

Even in the large metropolitan areas that tend to grow at the national average rate there is a strong bias toward accommodating even the most rapid growth. A run-of-the-mill growth rate, such as the typical 14 percent of the 1960-70 period, becomes leveraged upward into a decennial rate of 100 to 200 percent in the suburbs and downward into 10 to 20 percent declines in central cities. As long as we permit and encourage simple (-minded?) centrifugal growth even in the largest urban areas, growth will strike these areas very unevenly, bringing all the problems of boom and bust. And those local governments most in charge of growth where it is occurring—the suburbs at the building frontier—are typically new, naive and weak, and see their own self-interest in rapid growth.

Suburban self-interest in growth lies not just in additions to tax base. More and more, we have all become sophisticated about the additional local expenditures required to service that growth. More subtle (and perhaps only dimly perceived) is the arithmetic of aging.

Suburbanites take pride in the fact that their environment is new and attractive, and they would like to remain young forever. But the only way that a community can continue to have, say, one-half of its housing less than 10 years old is for it to *double in size every 10 years.* (The reader is invited to work out the immutable arithmetic.) Not to grow that fast is to age, inexorably; and to age is usually to become poorer.

No given community can, of course, grow that fast for very long; annexation is not all that easy or open-ended. But this merely means that the baton must be passed from one "exhausted" suburb to another, each of which can remain young and affluent, temporarily, by maintaining a dizzying pace in new construction.

That is to say, with no effective regional government and with "untrammeled rights of private property," the basic metropolitan area growth decisions are made by the newest, youngest and most naive political subdivisions on the narrowest of grounds and, typically, "all systems are go."

No-growth: conservation or self-indulgence? The question of the day is: Can attractive communities choose, effectively, not to grow? A no-growth strategy begins typically with such tactics as denying building permits or delaying utility extensions into new residential subdivisions. While the effectiveness of these actions will undoubtedly vary with the

Problems That Sprout in the Shadow of No-Growth

circumstances—and our experience here is so limited that early predictions must be highly speculative and provisional—some of the more unpromising situations invite tentative comment or first reactions.

Suppressing residential construction in a place like Boulder, Colorado, seems destined to produce some unhappy side effects, unless handled with great care and sophistication. Located within easy commuting distance (30 miles) of the center of Denver, a metropolitan area growing at double the national average rate, favored by a beautiful mountain setting in an age of affluence, leisure and outdoor recreation, founded on the growth industry of higher education and drawing the typical research and development spinoffs, Boulder pursuing no-growth is like having four aces and trying to lose.

To try to slow local growth by slowing housing construction is to work backward. This seems, at least at first blush, to be analogous to containing inflation by capping it with price controls, without taking the supporting monetary and fiscal actions. A good guess is that local land values and house prices would rise sharply if the growth pressures were restrained for very long. Presumably nothing has changed the attractiveness of Boulder as a place to live. In fact, to the high bidders—the educated and affluent of the Denver area—this already favored place, now protected from invading hordes, could easily be even more attractive than before.

All in all, it is hard to avoid concluding that this, for some, primrose path avoids the pitfalls of growth by driving the poor out of town. This may not have been the proponents' intention but "the road to hell." And the "poor" could come to include college instructors with families bigger than their incomes.

The long-run outlook for this quick-and-dirty approach to growth control is no better. Why would the courts validate a tactic which holds the local population in check by rationing out the poor? How does this differ in effect from large-lot zoning and other land use devices that create all-high-income communities, devices that are being overturned one after another in a continuing series of court decisions?

The sincerity of any brief for the case of no-growth—the protection of the natural environment—is bound to be highly suspect when the protectors live sprawled over half- and full-acre lots, with two or more cars in every driveway, and when they make waste in the good old American way. Any policy which permits the local inhabitants to hold their numbers in check simply so they can push their consumption per capita to the limit would seem to be more self-indulgent than environment-concerned.

Still, one can imagine the "judge" responding more sympathetically to a community that came for the support of a no-growth policy that was:

1. founded on strong land use controls that looked with special favor on multiple dwellings and/or cluster development;
2. synchronized with a public transportation plan that reinforced low fare (or no fare) transit with selective automobile tolls and prohibitions;
3. designed to bring home and work to within walking or bicycling distance in many circumstances; and,
4. was, of course, financed so as to make ample provision for subsidized low income housing.

A serious agenda of good faith should precede the exercise of the power to deny admission to town, that is, to restrict the rights of others.

Instead of trying to control city size by restraining residential development, it seems much more logical and efficacious to go directly to the heart of the matter and control the job formation that generates that growth, to work from cause to effect. Returning to the example above, Boulder could choose instead to argue, before the State of Colorado, the case for decentralizing the University of Colorado, spinning off parts to other attractive sites.

This is not at all unrealistic; the medical school is already in Denver and community colleges have become nearly universal means of siphoning off excessive growth from main campuses. Such an action would be especially appropriate because Colorado has a big stake in the proper care and feeding of a strong center of research and development and graduate study. The greater Denver area is in competition with Minneapolis-St. Paul and Dallas-Fort Worth and other "nearby" regional capitals, and in that role it has need of a rich cultural and professional base as well as a pleasing natural environment.

ZPG: a silver (-plated) lining? One cannot fail to be tantalized by the thought that if growth is not the universal solvent, perhaps no-growth is that solvent. Clearly, if the local labor force and population do not increase, then we would not need to add more houses, on net. We would need only to feed into the filtering process enough new housing to provide for normal depreciation and replacements, plus whatever overall upgrading across the board we feel that we can, as a nation, afford. Housing would be inadequate only to the extent households were too poor to afford better quarters—problem enough without population growth adding to that inadequacy. No-growth would be a big step toward the solution of the housing problem.

But zero population growth, nationwide, might well substitute its own set of housing problems. Over the past 20 years, even supported by natural increases of 18 and 14 percent per decade, the population of many of our largest central cities (those that have been unable to grow by annexation) have declined by 10 to 15 percent per decade.

Would not the much sharper decline foreshadowed by ZPG threaten housing abandonments, declining tax bases and other pathologies of depopulation much more intensely than those with which these central cities are now struggling?

While careful discussion of the economics of central city depopulation must be left to others or for another time, offhand, it is well within the bounds of credibility that socially responsible policy at higher levels of government blended with sophisticated city management *could* turn even this problem into an opportunity. Zero population growth *could* open up and speed the recycling of the inner city. Just as the postwar population explosion and rural to urban exodus overloaded inner cities, the time may be near (and be coming faster than we ever anticipated) when we will be offered the opportunity to unload them and try again, for example, Harvey Perloff's in-town new towns. Better luck next time!

Urban Zero Population Growth

William Alonso

William Alonso is professor of planning at the University of California at Berkeley. He was an assistant and then an associate professor of city and regional planning at Harvard University. Mr. Alonso is a graduate of Harvard, from which he also holds a master's in city planning; in addition, he has a Ph.D. in regional sciences from the University of Pennsylvania.

This article is reprinted by permission of Daedalus, (Journal of the American Academy of Arts and Sciences, Boston, Mass. Fall 1973),The No-Growth Society. The version as it appears here is a digest (to approximately three-fourths) of the full original.

Introduction

It is remarkable how rapidly the fashion for American states and cities has shifted from the traditional boosterism to a questioning and even an abhorrence of growth. It is common to read in the newspapers that states such as Oregon, California, Vermont, and Maryland want to stop or limit their growth, as do cities such as San Francisco, Boulder, and countless suburbs.

Undoubtedly this has much to do with the new Malthusian concern with the consequences of unlimited population growth at national and world levels. Some seem to think that the place to start controlling the nation's population growth is at the level of their city, metropolis, or state. Others hope that, as the nation moves toward zero population growth (ZPG), so will their communities. Both these views are misleading half-truths.

Local policies to limit population are probably not very effective, and when they are effective they are regressive and counter-productive in terms of social well-being. They are seldom aimed at reducing local birthrates (except among those on welfare in big cities), but rather they are aimed at keeping outsiders out. Thus, what is locally perceived as a growth or no-growth policy in reality merely affects the geographic distribution of people and economic activity within some larger society such as the region or the nation.

Neither is it credible that, when and if the national rate of population growth moves toward zero, local populations will become stable. In the first place, natural increase (the excess of births over deaths) varies enormously from one area to another, so that as the national rate approached zero, many areas would fail to reproduce themselves while others would continue to grow by natural increase. In the second place, continued structural change in the economy is inevitable, with or without economic growth. Indeed, my impression is that such structural change would be deeper if conventionally defined economic growth were limited. Change in the economy would be mirrored in shifts in the location of economic activity and, accordingly, in population shifts. In short, a nationally stable population would be composed of many localities declining in population, many localities growing, and only some remaining stable.

Why should a city, a town, or a state prefer to stop its population growth? There are many conceivable reasons: growth might lower average income, or bring in poor people who do not mix comfortably with present residents; it might produce challenges to local social structure, or change life styles for the worse, or increase pollution and congestion, or overrun prized landscapes. These would be changes in the real city, which is composed of people and their relations to each other, to their institutions, and to their physical environment. But there is an unfortunate confusion which frequently overtakes the debate and which must be clarified at the outset. The word "city" is also used as the name of a municipal corporation which derives its income principally through taxation and, in exchange, provides certain services to the population. This corporate entity is only one of the elements of the *real* city. Yet very often debate and evaluation of advantages and disadvantages are based on the limited viewpoint of the municipal corporation, and thus miss many of the most important consequences, good and bad, for the real city.

A Suburb Says "No"

This confusion and some of its implications may be illustrated by a recent case in a wealthy metropolitan suburb where a substantial reserve of land was probably going to be placed on the market, and many thousands of new houses built. A consulting firm was retained, and it reported, after considerable analysis, that this would be very costly for the city. It remarked that it would be cheaper for the city to buy the land itself with money raised through the sale of municipal bonds. This report met an enthusiastic reception. It not only addressed the central preoccupation of local tax groups, it also confirmed the questioning of growth among local youth and cultivated older people, and it surprised and delighted environmentalists by showing that preserving the landscape made economic sense. So well did it match the concern of many people that its conclusions were widely quoted in the national press and are often cited as proving the case against growth.

But the case as presented confused the municipal corporation for the real city. The fiscal effects on the municipal corporation can be predicted very easily, and the consultant's diligence in gathering numbers was not really necessary. On the average, a new house has associated with it about two school-age children. The taxes it pays rarely cover even one child's school costs. It also imposes the costs of providing other municipal services, although these are small by comparison. Thus, in any such case, new houses are money losers for the municipal corporation. In this particular case it only made matters worse that, as a result of the current residents' wealth and love of learning, local schools were excellent and costs per child especially high. All of this was in spite of a market analysis which concluded that the average price of the new houses would be higher than the price of existing houses in that town. It is more common in similar cases for the new houses to be cheaper than the existing ones, and inhabited by people not as wealthy as the present inhabitants.

If we consider the real city of present residents, they would probably still be worse off, although the matter is not as clear. Some property values would rise; some merchants and other businessmen and their employees would profit; the small proportion of poor and minority in the city would have increased job opportunities and residential choices (and indeed they were the only ones to dissent from the nearly universal approval of the consultant's recommendations); the children of the upper middle class would meet a somewhat different group in school; some local businesses would more easily find certain types of labor; shopping and entertainment facilities might become more varied and extensive; and so forth. On the other hand, a lovely landscape would be largely filled up; congestion might increase; present residents would have to rub elbows with a slightly lower class and a broader ethnic group; there might be a slight increase in deviant behavior (on the part either of the newcomers or of present residents whose conduct might be redefined according to the more standard mores of the newcomers); and, of course, residents would pay higher taxes. It is quite likely that a full consideration of these effects would result in the same conclusion: buy the "insulation."

Who Is Choosing For Whom?

But there is yet a further consideration, which to my mind is conclusive. *What is the population of this city?* Is it only those living there now, or does it include those who would move in if they could? If we are speaking of a future community of which there are two alternative versions, it makes as much sense to consider the interests of *all* the people who would make up the expanded version, as to consider those of the original version. After all, even if growth is prevented, given the mobility of Americans, only a fraction of the future residents will consist of those living there now. The future majority will consist of newcomers, although they will be socially and economically similar to present residents. Who is choosing for whom?

If this seems abstract, the matter can be put another way. Suppose that growth is restricted. What happens to the people who would have moved in but could not? Obviously neither they nor their children cease to exist. They will find second-choice homes; their children will go to more run-of-the-mill schools and impose their costly presence on people who are less able to afford this added burden than the wealthy residents of the suburb in question. It would appear that they will be worse off, and so perhaps will the present residents of wherever they end up. The rub is that what seems from the local viewpoint an issue of *growth* is, in a larger framework, an issue of *distribution*, both in the social and in the geographic sense—not *whether* these people and their children shall exist, but *where* and *how*. In the abstract, the distribution problem could be solved if residents of the excluding locality made compensatory payments (a form of rent) to those whom they would exclude. But no feasible way of arranging for this suggests itself.

The point of the example is that the current balkanization of metropolitan areas into dozens and even hundreds of local governments encourages beggar-thy-neighbor strategies. Furthermore, confusing the muncipal corporation for the real city leads to the meanest forms of municipal mercantilism, ones which ignore more important consequences for people. Perhaps the most hopeful recent development on this matter, in spite of setbacks, is the emergence of a number of court opinions, of which *Serrano vs. Priest* was the first, that, under the equal protection principle, rule it unconstitutional to rely on property taxes for financing schools. If these decisions stand, their logic points to their application to other services and broader geographic areas. Hopefully, too, they will lessen the influence of base motives on the formulation of local population policies.

I cannot abandon the subject of local fiscal impacts, however, without making clear the abysmal state of knowledge in this area. [*Material omitted.*] The relatively few serious attempts to find out about these matters have run into grave theoretical, definitional, and data difficulties. Although some progress is being made through research, in the meantime debates and decisions are quite naturally based on shallow reasoning and spurious numerology. Some decisions will not wait.

Enforcing Growth Limitations

It is an open question whether a community can effectively enforce a choice to grow or not to grow, however it arrives at this choice. Until recently virtually every city in America tried to encourage growth by a variety of local actions and by seeking state and federal preferential treatment. Although there have been some dramatic successes, there have been very few. Indeed, there is now in this country, as in many others, a national policy of establishing growth centers for depressed regions, which by a variety of federal, state, and local actions, tries to induce rapid growth in selected small cities, but these programs have had very limited success.

It might appear to be easier to limit growth than to promote it, but this is not the case according to a rich experience of national policies in Europe and the socialist countries. Moscow, Paris, London, and Warsaw are among the centers where vigorous policies have been followed to contain and even reverse growth. The means at hand have often appeared foolproof, including not only the tax incentives and disincentives, subsidies, land use regulations, and other devices familiar in American experience, but also direct command over the location of jobs and people through state control over many enterprises, location and expansion permits for industry, residence permits, and job and housing assignments for people. Even so, these centers have continued to grow, although perhaps less than without these measures. These powerful tools have failed in the face of more powerful social and economic currents. Even in totally controlled societies power is not controlled monolithically, but distributed among the agencies of the state. In setting priorities and bargaining over specific decisions, the agencies charged with territorial distribution have not been able to count as much as the sectoral ones.

A locality in America may similarly choose to discourage growth either by making it hard for people to establish residence, or by discouraging the creation of jobs which would attract people. While a small independent city might succeed in this, it appears that a metropolitan area cannot. An industry or person excluded from one municipality will find a place in another within the metropolis. Overall metropolitan levels of population and employment are set largely by economic and demographic forces at national and international levels. *Local policy affects primarily the intrametropolitan form and distribution of that development, and, if it is set by the selfish interests of the component municipalities, it does so inefficiently and unjustly.* [Emphasis added.] A suburb may be able to keep population or industry out, but it can do so only by directing it to other suburbs or by keeping it cooped up in the central city.

Examine the normal instruments by which a municipality keeps people out. It may restrict the use of space, either absolutely through land reserves such as parks which keep everyone out, or through zoning which keeps out those who cannot afford large lots. Other devices of varying subtlety are available. It may refuse to accept subsidized housing. Or it may set high standards through building and related codes which raise the cost of housing. Or it may set very high standards for public services, especially schools, creating high local taxes that will discourage those who cannot afford them. Or it may maintain very poor schools, so that it is unattractive to the suburbanizing lower-middle class looking for the advancement of their children through education, but acceptable to those who can send their children to private schools. Or it may refuse to provide utilities for large-scale developments, but permit low density development by allowing septic tanks and water wells. Or it may keep out the jobs that would bring in new people, primarily potential industrial workers, by zoning, or by strong regulation of pollution, or by not allowing necessary infrastructure such as highway access.

It is clear that all of these instruments aimed at keeping people out tend to keep out those of lower income. In short, local population control policies are *regressive*. Thus what we see today, in city after city, and often at the state level, is a three-cornered political fight among: (a) the advocates of business and development, (b) the poor and working class and their liberal advocates, and (c) the environmentalists in alliance with no-growth people who are usually middle-class young or upper-middle class. This situation brings about strange alliances between, for instance, business groups and minority people, or ecologists and tax leagues. These same conflicts and contradictions are mirrored within many people who, traditional liberals, find themselves unable to reconcile their environmental interests with their concern for social equity.

Consequences of City Size

The difficulty of tracing and evaluating the consequences of particular developments has led many researchers to examine whether some conditions vary systematically with population size across the array of American metropolitan areas. It appears that education, pollution, and crime rise with population, while the indicators of physical and mental health are mixed. Many of these characteristics are two-edged and hard to interpret. The evidence is shallow, impressionistic, or nonexistent on some of the most vital questions such as those concerning social and economic mobility, tolerance of diversity, the rigidity and invidiousness of social hierarchy, feelings of alienation, ability to control one's fate, the situation of women, and privacy.

The effects of city size are clearest in economic areas. In the United States and other countries wages and per capita income rise rapidly and consistently with city size, even after taking into account their occupational and industrial composition. The cost of living and public costs also rise, but very little, so that real net income per capita improves markedly from smaller to bigger cities. This rise in income with urban size argues that bigger cities are more efficient engines of production, and this is confirmed by fragmentary data relating to value added or gross regional product. Furthermore, it seems that larger cities derive more of their products from innovative activities, from newer processes, and from generating, handling, and using information and ideas. Smaller cities tend to more established, routinized activities such as mass production manufacturing with well-established technologies. The system of cities is a dynamic one, spawning innovations and new activities at the top, which, as they mature, filter down to smaller and more provincial centers.

Furthermore, statistical analysis seems to show that the cost of living and of municipal services rises as a result not of increasing urban size as such, but of other factors, most notably high income itself. For instance, it is a popular belief that it is more costly to live in bigger cities. It comes as a surprise that, when equivalent levels of consumption in different areas are actually priced, there is very little cost increase in bigger cities. A clue to this apparent contradiction is provided by a recent poll which asked people how much money they thought a family of four would need to live modestly but comfortably in their areas. Their subjective estimates did increase rapidly with population size. It would seem that what size does is to raise levels of expectation as to what constitutes a modestly comfortable way of life. In bigger cities people expect more. This may be related to their dynamism and innovation.

Another misconception is that bigger metropoles suffer more severe income inequalities. In fact, the proportion of families below the poverty level decreases steadily as the size of the city increases, and indices of income distribution show that the general range of incomes remains about the same. It may be that, although the poor are proportionally fewer, the increase in their actual number and their concentration in certain districts make their situation both more visible and more troublesome in more populous areas, but this is a different matter.

Although they have been much discussed, general indicators of well-being or satisfaction are not available, and probably not possible. We do have, however, some social surveys of varying quality. The one that has received the widest publicity is a commercial poll which asked individuals whether they would prefer to live in farms, small towns, suburbs, or big cities. A majority, regardless of their present residence, said they would prefer to live in small towns. This finding has been used as supporting evidence for programs to disperse the national population. Yet one must be very wary of responses to such hypothetical questions when posed in the abstract, as in this case. It may well be that this expressed preference for small-town life is a romantic response, deeply rooted in traditional American imagery and more symbol than operational preference. What people say to an interviewer on the spur of the moment does not necessarily match what they would really do or what they really want.

Ideal Size and Borrowed Size

The idea that urban size matters carries with it a temptation to think that there may be a *best* size, and that, if this size were known, the ideal pattern of urbanization would be to create centers of that size until the entire urban population were accommodated. This is dangerous nonsense for at least four reasons. First, historic, economic, resource, and demographic circumstances vary greatly from city to city, so that a given size has sharply different implications in different places. Second, because different population groups have different preferences and interests, what might best serve one group might not suit another. Third, a change from one population size to another (or a holding steady) occurs at some concrete rate of growth or decline in real time, which in turn has important social, economic, and institutional consequences that affect different groups differently. Fourth, there is considerable evidence and some passable theory that the urban areas of a country are a system of interdependent elements and relations, so that a change in the size and the economic activities of Wichita affects in part those of Los Angeles.

The issue is one of finding the most satisfactory constellation of interacting sizes, not of finding a single best size. The idea of finding an ideal size to be repeated over and over is comparable to a musical theory that would find the most beautiful note and then compose a symphony by endless and exclusive repetition of that note.

The concept of a system of cities has many facets, but one of particular interest for our topic is the concept of *borrowed size*, whereby a small city or metropolitan area exhibits some of the characteristics of a larger one if it is near other population concentrations. A statistical measure called *population potential*, which measures the accessibility from a given location to other centers of population, behaves very much like population in statistical analysis. For instance, per capita income in a place is as strongly associated with this measure as with its actual population. This makes sense if one considers that the essential reason why income and population levels are associated is that population is a rough index of the number of opportunities for interaction available in that place. Similarly, population potential is an index of the opportunities for interaction with people in other places, and may be thought of as an index of borrowed size. Thus, because of their high population potential, small metropoles in megapolitan complexes, such as that on the Atlantic seaboard, have much higher incomes than independent metropoles of equivalent size. In simple terms, while they retain many of the advantages of smaller size, such as lower levels of congestion, they enjoy the advantages of larger size through their easy access to other centers. Their people can use the shopping and entertainment facilities of other cities to complement their own, their businessmen can share such facilities as warehousing and business services, and their labor markets enjoy a wider and more flexible range of demand and supply.

This phenomenon of borrowed size, with the hint that it is possible to have one's cake and eat it too, has not been sufficiently studied, in spite of the strong statistical evidence of its existence. It seems to account for the fact that in the large American megapolitan constellations, the smaller metropoles are growing more rapidly than the bigger ones. It is also quite visible, although virtually unstudied, in certain European urban patterns, such as those of Germany and the Low Countries, whose cities, quite small by our standards, apparently achieve sufficient scale for the functioning of a modern economy by borrowing size from one another. This phenomenon transforms the issue of the size and growth of a city by redefining it to include, in some degree, its neighbors.

Migration and Size Over Time

However, by studying the attributes of a cross section of urban sizes at one moment in time, one cannot draw reliable implications about what changes in size through time will do in any particular city. Unfortunately, little can be said about the consequences on a city of population growth, decline, or stability because the subject has been little studied. The absence of studies on the consequences of growth or no-growth cannot be blamed altogether on scholarly neglect. The difficulty is that the growth rates that have existed have included a substantial natural increase, so that a locality that has exhibited anything like zero population growth in the past decade has had a substantial net outmigration, of the order of 10 percent. An extreme case is McAllen-Pharr-Edinburg, Texas, which has held virtually stable in population through a natural increase of 25.8 percent and an outmigration of 25.4 percent. Since it is primarily the young who leave, this leads to a population with few young people and many old ones, and this, among other things, lowers the local birth rate and raises the death rate. Thus, Scranton, Pennsylvania, with a net outmigration of 20 percent for the past two decades, had a yearly rate of natural increase of only 0.16 percent in the 1960's. Such large rates of net outmigration occur only in distressed local economies, for, given the high rates of natural increase in the last decade, no reasonably prosperous area failed to grow by about 10 percent. Thus we have no instances for study which combine local zero population growth with economic well-being.

But the relation of migration to natural increase is more complicated than this suggests, and makes local population growth a more complex matter than national population growth. The key point is that, demographically, the United States is quite self-contained while urban areas are highly open systems. On the surface this does not seem to be so.

Urban Zero Population Growth

Currently the United States population is growing by 1.1 percent a year, and a fifth of this growth comes from abroad (much of it accounted for by returning Americans). Similarly, in the last decade, three-fourths of metropolitan growth was accounted for by natural increase and one-fourth by new arrivals.[1] But these figures for average net migration mask tremendous *cross-movements* of population. (As a rule of thumb, it takes ten migratory moves in and out of a metropolis to leave or take away one net migrant.)

Recent studies of these flows have made surprising findings of consequence for local population policies. Rates of inmigration are higher for prosperous places, but rates of outmigration do not appear to vary, except perhaps marginally, with local economic conditions. Instead, they depend primarily on the local proportion of young people. It seems that the young leave home in about equal numbers whether their home district is prosperous or distressed.[2] Thus, a policy which increases pay levels and the number of jobs in poor areas in an effort to retain the young may shift net migration from negative to positive, but it will do so by attracting more newcomers rather than by slowing down the exodus.

Conversely, if prosperous areas want to slow down arrivals, they could do so by making themselves ugly in economic terms. Their young would continue to leave, while inmigration would slow down or disappear, resulting in net outmigration. This, in turn, would gradually lower their rate of natural increase because the diminishing proportion of young people in their populations would lower the birth rate while the increasing age of the population would raise the death rate. Eventually, there would be few babies to grow into youth and leave, and the outmigration rate would slow down. This is, no doubt, a fanciful scenario. It amounts to choosing poverty, unemployment and old age. In brief, it amounts to choosing to be Scranton, and this is a choice that few will make. The alternative way of containing growth is by erecting barriers to migrants and this, as I have discussed, is likely to be ineffective; and if effective, it is regressive.

This example is based on the assumption that the local net reproduction rate would continue to be higher than a ZPG level.[3] To compensate for this, the age distribution for local ZPG would have to include far fewer young and far more older people than would a national ZPG situation. Even a metropolis which, through local family planning, achieved ZPG net reproduction rates might eventually maintain a balance of in- and outmigrants only if it were slightly less prosperous than the average. Otherwise, although it would have fewer births, it would also have fewer outmigrants, and would show a positive net migration since the potential pool of migrants from other places would be proportionately bigger than its own.

There is yet another paradox. I have focused the discussion thus far on the consequences and possibilities of local policies of population limitation, since this is the usual frame of reference, and I have obviously been negative about them. But examination of current patterns and trends persuades me that, whatever the difficulties of induced zero growth, it is quite possible that we will be faced in the 1980's with about eighty metropoles (central cities and their suburbs) which have spontaneously arrived at something near zero population growth. Whether this is good or bad, we have little understanding and experience of what such metropoles will be like. They will certainly be different from anything in our present experience, but we are ill-prepared to anticipate their problems and opportunities. The key difference will be that these will be reasonably prosperous places, whereas today only economically distressed ones show population stability.

This forecast is a chancy one, I realize, for two reasons. The first is that demographic forecasting has had an atrocious record. The second is that local forecasts are, of statistical necessity, much more prone to error than national forecasts. Nonetheless, I make this prognosis on the following basis [*Material omitted.*] This outmigration and variation in local rates of natural increase combined with a falling national rate point to the emergence of changes in quantity which amount to changes in quality. Whereas today any area that fails to grow or grows very little is poor and underemployed, should the birth rate continue to fall, we will have a new phenomenon: relatively prosperous areas which are stable in population, or which grow so little as not to matter.

What will such areas be like? They will have fewer young than today, and thus fewer children in school and a lighter fiscal burden. Economic evolution will be more by substitution than by adding new activities to existing ones, and may therefore involve more individual transitions. The burden of dependent aged will be greater. There will not be an appreciably greater continuity of population, since there will continue to be massive exchanges of the young with other areas. Two major sectors of the economy, construction and the education of children, will probably retrench.

Beyond this it is hard to see. It is possible that economic changes will be more of a shock because they will take the form of structural shifts rather than of adding on new activities. Possibly the young, being relatively scarce, will profit from accelerated social and economic mobility; but possibly the preponderance of old people and the limits on expansion will create a gerontracy. Possibly minorities will be frustrated, since there will not be new activities for them to move into and the old activities will be preempted. Possibly, however, they will benefit from lessened competition for the older housing stock which will permit them lesser per room densities together with lower rents.

Interconnected vs. Bar-the-Door Policies

Local policies for zero population growth ultimately run into the problem that ours is a highly interconnected society and economy. No state or city is an island, entire unto itself. Local policies may try to limit population by passing restrictive zoning, limiting housing permits, and the like. This is the I'm-all-right-Jack-and-bar-the-door version, much favored by suburbs, which forces out the young and is regressive. Local policies may try to curtail economic growth, but effective policies lead to unacceptable social and economic consequences. And a local policy of limiting births, which seems to me the most morally acceptable of these policies, will do little to reduce growth because the young from other places will inevitably arrive.

Because the nation is so interconnected, local population policies, whether for growth or no-growth, are usually an attempt at a mercantilistic beggaring of neighbors; however, because larger forces are operating in the system, they are likely to be ineffective. A hierarchy of levels is involved, so that what is viewed as an issue of *growth* at a lower level is an issue of *distribution* at the next higher level. Thus, growth decisions for each locality within a metropolitan area should be bargained out among all the components of the metropolis to insure that their effects on the futures of the other localities will be considered. This is necessary both for fairness and efficiency. If the objectives, plans and actions of diverse localities are inconsistent, they cannot all be right, and some will fail while others triumph. Only when these various growth considerations are viewed to-gether can it be seen whether they add up, where joint action can be more effective than unilateral action for achieving complementary objectives, and where negotiation and compensation are needed to reconcile diverging purposes and interests.

For much the same reasons the growth decisions of the various metropolitan areas and other regions should be based on state and national considerations. The task is again one of coordination and mediation, and as yet we have very little operational knowledge of how to go about it, either technically or politically. Yet this is the issue which has attracted considerable, if confused, attention under the rather misleading name of "national growth policy."

In any case it is clear that, although questions of local growth should be treated as questions of distribution at a higher level, we should avoid what is often done, setting as policy goals arbitrary demographic rates (no-growth or fast-growth) or particular geographic patterns of distribution (dispersal or concentration). These rates and patterns are not proper goals, although they may be important instruments for advancing the real goals of material efficiency, of equity and fairness, of ecological integrity, and of a high quality of life. They are used as goals because they are easy to grasp and they avoid the real questions which are hard. They are also used, I suspect, because they substitute what appears to be a technical objective for what is really a political matter of deciding how to balance alternative and often conflicting goals, and how to deal with costs and benefits which are very unevenly distributed.

"National growth policy" should more properly be called "national territorial distribution policy," and local growth policies *within* metropolitan areas should be thought of as elements in shaping the distribution of metropolitan growth. In neither case am I suggesting that the ideal would have the higher level dictate to the lower one. The interests of each collectivity and each governmental unit must be represented in the making of the higher level policy. One of the urgent and unresolved issues of our times is the need to evolve processes to give a voice in the making of important decisions to the relevant collectivities, be they corporations such as local governments, or other collectivities such as ethnic and other interest groups. But this is a larger matter than the subject of this paper.

Something like national zero population growth seems to be desirable, and we appear to be moving rapidly in that direction. But it is quite clear that even in a situation of national demographic stability, some localities will grow, some will shrink, and some will stay at about the same population. Through all this, vast cross-movements of population will continue, as will structural changes in the society and the economy. Many of today's problems will continue to exist, and some new ones will arise. We will not arrive at an eternally tranquil late afternoon.

Footnotes

1. It is startling to most people to learn that three-fifths of this net migration into metropolitan areas came from abroad, and only two-fifths from nonmetropolitan areas. Thus, nonmetropolitan net migration accounted for only one-tenth of metropolitan growth in the decade.
2. I must note that this is a topic of considerable scholarly debate at the moment. It is quite clear, at any rate, that local economic well-being matters far less than had been thought in determining the rate of leaving.
3. This would be a net reproduction rate of one which would mean that each generation would just replace itself if current birth and death rates were continued indefinitely in the absence of migration. Strictly speaking, however, net reproduction rates would have to be somewhat below the ZPG rate to accommodate immigrants from abroad.

Should The Poor Buy No-Growth?

Willard R. Johnson

Willard Johnson is a professor of Political Science in the political science department at the Massachusetts Institute of Technology. He is also a professor at the Fletcher School of Law and International Diplomacy, and was president of the Circle Inc.: a community economic development corporation in Boston. Dr. Johnson is a graduate of the University of California, Los Angeles; he holds a master's from the School of Advanced International Studies at Johns Hopkins University, and a doctorate in political science from Harvard University.

This article is reprinted by permission of Daedalus, Journal of the American Academy of Arts and Sciences, Boston, Mass. Fall 1973, The No-Growth Society. The version as it appears here is a digest (to approximately one-half) of the full original.

Introduction

No-growth societies—those that experience very little increase in population or per capita income or production—have, historically, been bottom-heavy with poor people. The so-called "traditional societies" are the only examples we know; they have emphasized ecological balance and man's accommodation to the forces of nature. Many people consider rapid expansion of production and reproduction to require some special (cultural if not racial) blessings such as the Protestant Ethic, the Spirit of Capitalism, and the Industrial Revolution.

Are we now to have a no-growth society composed of rich people or of some mixture of economic classes that includes a substantial number of rich people? The noted British socialist, Anthony Crosland, has stated that the current champions of the no-growth society

> are often kindly and dedicated people. But they are affluent; and fundamentally, though of course not consciously, they want to kick the ladder down behind them. They are militant mainly about threats to rural peace and wildlife and well loved beauty spots; but little concerned with the far more desperate problem of the urban environment in which 80 per cent of our citizens live.[1]

Is the superindustrial society going to be like the "traditional society"? Is such a society now, for the first time in history, to be the social condition of the wealthy instead of the poor? What is the proper response of the poor to the call for a return to a no-growth society? Should the poor buy no-growth?

In truth, practically nobody, rich or poor, argues for absolutely zero population or economic growth on a universal basis. Interests are not coherent in these matters any more than in most others. Changes in population and income are not always clearly related, certainly not in a consistently positive or negative way, and not in the same way for the aspiring as for the already affluent.

Should The Poor Buy No-Growth?

Rich people desire no population growth for the poor, but continued money growth for themselves and perhaps even for the poor if it does not dampen their own. The poor want to expand the ranks of the rich by at least their own number, but they do not want further income growth for the already rich. Some poor people think increases in their own numbers enhance their chances of becoming richer through political advantage in developed countries and through increased productive labor resources in developing countries. They may regard efforts to reduce their rates of population growth as motivated by genocidal or antidemocratic intentions. They may therefore prefer selective growth policies which favor growth in the numbers but not necessarily in the per capita wealth of the rich, and growth in the per capita wealth of the poor but not in their numbers.

In any case, the question of which policies the poor should prefer is irrelevant. The poor can't "buy" what the rich won't "sell," and the rich hoard all the really effective roles in determining the outcome of such policy debates. It will take *power* to alter the direction of fundamental economic trends and patterns of resource utilization in the United States and in the world.

No-Growth Defined

Population increase is not the real issue, however, at least not in America.[2] Our projected population profile suggests that the American population will double in about sixty years. While this will obviously put some strain on our resources, it will not overburden them. With only 6 percent of the world's population using perhaps 50 percent of its material resources, there is plenty of room for population growth in the United States.

A more important reason to control population growth would be to reduce the level of our resources utilization in order to permit the rest of the world to achieve a standard of living nearer to what current standards call decent. Nonetheless, many Americans are concerned that if we limit population increase to near the zero point, the present basically young U.S. population will grow older without replenishing the youth, and the society will come to resemble a Florida retirement colony.

There is evidence that American women no longer want to have more children than would permit the population to approach nearly zero growth.[3] It seems safe to say that the technology of preventing unwanted births will improve and that soon it will be safe and fairly painless, even morally, to reduce the rate of childbirth to the level desired by the women concerned. It may be that poorer women desire more children than richer ones,[4] or that, in any case, they desire more than the rich wish to see them have. Even so, population growth among the poor will not soon overburden our national resource base; it will, however, strain the resource base that those who control social policy allow to the poor.

Thus the real population issues to the poor are the incompatibility of their values and desires with those of the rich, and their lack of power to protect and satisfy their own values. With regard to the population of the domestic United States, though perhaps not to that of the world, it is a ruse to couch the issue in the language of population explosion or overburdened resources.

A definition of "no-growth" as zero increase in per capita net national product (NNP) is basically irrelevant to the real issues involved in the no-growth debate. There are a number of items that would augment per capita NNP that would also enhance the quality of life, even to the no-growth advocates. Indeed many of the controls that would be required to eliminate threats to ecological balance, controls which most no-growth advocates desire, involve money transactions, and thus contribute to an increased per capita NNP. Furthermore, as we assign money values to householding services, or increase our expenditures on education, keeping other things constant, we increase per capita NNP without putting any additional strain on ecological balance.

The real issue is to avoid the type of growth that threatens the future life of the human species and that hampers optimum satisfaction of human wants and needs. No-growth advocates do not arouse the concern of the poor as effectively as they might by calling for stable per capita net national product or even for zero population growth, when so many people still lack so much of what they want and need and of what their countrymen already have. It would be more relevant for them to emphasize the threatened depletion of resources fundamental to everybody's survival and health and to the survival of civilization itself—threats to life support systems and to ecological balance for the species.

Do the poor people in the United States or in the poor countries of the world have any special stake in defending against these threats that the richer populations do not have? Will they suffer sooner or to a greater extent? Are their survival resources any better or worse than those of the richer groups? These are questions well worth returning to.

Economic Growth and Elimination of Poverty

Can we really count on continued increases in per capita GNP or NNP to substantially reduce if not eliminate poverty in the United States? However indignant we might be over the fact that the owners and managers of Mobil Oil or General Motors will benefit more from growth than the poor, we might comfort ourselves if poverty were being eliminated, even if inequality were not. But there is no clear evidence that poverty is or can be eliminated as a consequence of the processes of general economic growth.

It is quite clear that the ranks of the poor have thinned recently during years of significant economic growth. It is not, however, that simple a matter. There have been some important fluctuations in the rate of poverty elimination; perhaps, despite economic growth, we are now entering a period of increasing numbers of poor. Structural features of the American economy cause the relationship between growth and the rate at which poverty is eliminated to produce different results at different times. Features of general growth that had a significant impact on poverty twenty years ago have much less today. Batchelder and several others[5] have noted that structured-in poverty will be increasingly difficult to eliminate.

Poverty is a feature built into the current American economy and social structure. It results from social, political and economic discrimination which thwarts needed investment in poor people.[6] Those most likely to be left out of the picture of general growth are blacks (except for young urban black families in the North in which both father and mother work), families headed by females, farm families, and the elderly. The poverty of these groups is relatively impervious to the benefits of general economic progress.[7] Economists are unable to agree as to the extent and reasons why these groups are isolated.

Improving the industrial structure, providing tight labor markets, and holding down inflation would be important public policy objectives in order to improve black incomes. However, economic growth has not and will not improve the situation very much, though recession may aggravate it considerably as it did between 1969 and 1970. Poverty seems to be built into our current social and economic structure. As Theodore Schultz has noted, our most important declines in poverty have been due to increases in income from labor, which are in turn due to increases in the demand for high skills and to the responsiveness of the labor force to this market situation. But blacks, agricultural workers, women, older people and workers in the South have generally been kicked out or held out of these labor markets.[8]

Growth, defined as rising per capita NNP, can have some positive effect on the incidence of poverty for some blacks, less so for whites. Lester Thurow, a leading analyst of measures of poverty, has determined that "General growth results in higher incomes for both blacks and whites," but the key element for blacks in this is the availability of jobs, especially of full-time jobs in the government service and industrial sectors.[9] These are the types of jobs that blacks have been able to get and to benefit from most fully. In the future, however, there is likely to be more flexibility in the service than in the industrial sector, especially if ecological balance becomes a more potent influence on our economic policies.

There are special implications here for the zero economic growth advocates. The industries in which blacks have a foothold and a potential for economic improvement are precisely those where we find the greatest ecological hazards. Blacks are particularly entrenched in the auto industry and many of the industries and services peripheral to it. Blacks constitute 23 percent of nonfarm, nonconstruction laborers.[10] Black workers form substantial contingents in industries which deal with chemicals, fabricated metals, primary metals, and nonelectrical machinery and transportation equipment. Industries like these are closely identified with the problems of poisoned lakes and streams, and with overuse of material resources, especially of nonrenewable resources such as petroleum, natural gas, and other fuels that will become increasingly important as energy sources in the future. Traffic problems, overcrowding, noise, and other invasions of psychic domains are also rooted in these industrial activities. Those whose predominant objectives are ecological may threaten economic progress for blacks as well as for great numbers of nonblack and nonminority poor.

An equally important if not more serious threat to these industries is the fact that the raw materials that feed them are close to exhaustion. This is particularly threatening to patterns of industry in the United States because we account for such high percentages of total world usage. The other way to relate per capita NNP and officially-defined poverty is to ask: Would a slackening of growth or a lack of growth especially hurt the poor? Would it wipe out the gains that have already been made? Certainly the periods of stagnation and decline in 1958, 1961-1962, and 1969-1970 have tended to do so. Especially among the black population there were income reversals in each of these periods.

The economic progress that poor people, especially blacks, made in the 1960's essentially ended with the Nixon Administration. The percentage of white and black families and individuals in poverty has remained virtually constant since 1968.[11] A lack of continued growth, without substantial change in national policies to facilitate the transfer of wealth and income through transfer payments, tax reform and job development, or vigorous antidiscrimination efforts would probably have disastrous consequences for blacks, and perhaps for the poor more generally.

It seems that the best we can hope for from recent economic trends is to reduce the number of people who live under conditions of abject poverty, below the level of income by which the Census Bureau officially defines poverty. But how long would we have to wait for those trends to eliminate poverty even at this unrealistically low level? Lowell Galloway, writing in 1965, attempted to strengthen the case for using growth as a tool to eliminate poverty.[12] Galloway concluded that growth could not eliminate poverty much below the 6 percent level. It is clear that the rate of poverty elimination is now virtually zero. Perhaps we have already reached Galloway's impervious hard core, but at 10 percent rather than 6.4 percent of all families. Poverty is going to continue to be a problem, even as officially defined, for more than another decade, despite projections of growth.

Relative Standards of Income and Wealth

We have discussed several concepts of poverty, all of them *absolute*, based, that is, on definite fixed budgets defined almost exclusively in terms of what it costs to meet certain selected needs. There are also *relativistic* concepts which define poverty in terms of the incomes of other groups. The absolutistic approach is akin to the legal concept of due process, a minimum standard to which everyone has a right, while the relativistic approach accords with the legal doctrine of equal protection or equity, which seeks to avoid extreme differences in the way the system deals with people.

The absolutistic is the less controversial of the two. Since we can predetermine consumption patterns and supply and calculate the cost of living, being poor or rich has, according to this standard, a precise and stable meaning. Ironically, however, a competitive free enterprise system that spurs individualism and egotism makes it harder, not easier, to ignore relative standing. People in our society, especially the poor, value keeping up with the Joneses. Thus it is perhaps more realistic to define poverty in relative terms that take into account the changes in income and expenditures patterns of the general society.

The most common relative standard of poverty is arbitrarily pegged at 50 percent of the median income. But, defined this way, poverty is less tractable than it is when defined by any but the most generous absolutistic standards. Here we are really talking about reducing income inequality.

Lack of progress emerges from a comparison of black and white median income. Patterns of distribution within each racial group have augmented the disparity between blacks and whites on the lower end of the income scale. In addition, the gap in absolute dollar figures is actually widening. Wealth inequalities may be a more significant factor in the no-growth debate than income inequalities: not only are they greater, but they also have long-range effects on income, and are likely to increase with growth. Furthermore, because of the power of wealth, they are less subject to change as a result of politics. Given the lack of strong redirecting forces in the economy, some growth probably gets absorbed into wealth: even the superrich can only spend so much on current consumption. This absorbed capital acts as a corrective, however, because, by limiting consumption, it dampens growth.

The disparities between white and black family wealth, or net family worth, are very stark. They have been calculated in a tentative fashion by Andrew Brimmer, who indicates an average gap of $16,214.[13] The disparities within the general society, ignoring racial differences, are even greater. While we have made some headway in reducing inequality since 1774, things have not changed very much in this century. The concentration of wealth has also been increasing.

In terms of the position of the poor in the no-growth debate, the type of wealth that is concentrated is more important than the degree of concentration. The superrich hold even larger portions of investment wealth than of general wealth, and it is investment wealth which directs the activities of productive corporations; which determines levels of expansion, job creation, prices, reinvestment, etc.; and which has such a profound effect on politics.

With this kind of concentrated economic power, perhaps it really doesn't matter whether the poor want to buy no-growth or not. The basic decisions are made by the superrich, and can only be moderated by political forces. To the relatively poor, the debate as it is currently argued ignores the real issues. Neither side can offer much relief, certainly not sufficient relief, without resorting to policies calling for a substantial redistribution of income, and perhaps of wealth as well.

Redistribution: Attitudes and Analyses

As we have seen, no trends allow us to predict in a clear-cut manner just when recent patterns of economic activity will eliminate poverty in the United States. Moreover, those debating growth or no-growth policies disagree about their implications for the poor. A decade of impressive economic growth but meager improvement in the poverty situation makes it an act of wisdom to side with Thurow, who asserts that "poverty cannot be eliminated without direct income transfers."[14] The real issue then is to determine the relationship between achieving effective income transfers and economic growth. Is it easier or harder to get redistribution with no growth as the goal of public policy or as the condition of the economy?

It is useful to distinguish the import of the no-growth debate as a debate or clash of values and preferences, from the implications of impending real limits to growth. Often the debate is argued as if both sides could assume the possibility of continued growth and thus dispute only the costs of such growth. The **"no-growthers"** point to the problems of continued growth: fouling of the atmosphere, dangers to health, offense to the senses, rising prices for scarce nonrenewable resources and the products that use them, crowding, ugliness, and loss of recreational resources and beauty spots.

The **"growthers"** point to the dangers of no-growth: the lack of improvement in economic well-being and the resultant increases in social turmoil among the poor as their convictions that they play in a zero sum game are confirmed; the increased rigidity and more forceful political control on the part of the superrich who neither wish nor feel the need to accept a more slender slice of the economic pie.

Stuart Chase has called this debate over growth an antagonism between partisans of the gross national product on the one hand and partisans of the quality of life on the other, between green-money men and green-earth men. Put this way, I again question whether either side has solace to offer the poor. The money men are holdovers from the days of what Charles Reich calls Consciousness II: a society which contains the seeds of its own destruction and will be replaced by Consciousness III. Consciousness III types are now busy organizing earth days and holding ecology marches; they would rather be honey-seekers than money-seekers, but then they can be both. The revolution they pursue is not likely to involve the partisans of the black revolution who find it hard to drop the concerns of Consciousness II, lest they leap-frog history altogether. The black and white youth of the counterculture quickly fell out with each other.

To be relevant to the needs of the poor, those who advocate growth will have to talk more specifically and effectively than they have to date about specific types and rates of growth that would alleviate the misery of the underclass. Merely saying that growth is good and has not done all it can do to eliminate poverty is not enough. On the other hand, they could take some of the heat off themselves by pointing out the failure of no-growth advocates to deal directly with the problems of the poor.

Should The Poor Buy No-Growth?

British economist E. J. Mishan, a no-growth advocate, is guilty of debating the issues in terms of values that, for all their humaneness, ignore the concerns of the poor. He challenges economic growth policies because he questions values deeply rooted in Western society. The trouble with growth, according to him, lies with the materialistic nature of a social order that piles up more and more material goods. He sees this as destructive to humane values and antithetical to human happiness. Growth, to him, is a potentially unbalanced, misdirected, and destructive force in itself. No doubt his concerns feed on a genuine consideration for the quality of life, but they seem to me mistaken about the contribution material goods can make to it.

John Kenneth Galbraith, sometimes counted in Mishan's camp on the growth question, is more concerned about the failure of the post-Keynesian synthesis on which we once relied, at least in terms of expectation, to harness growth to the interest of the general good, including the reduction of poverty. That synthesis coupled Keynes' policies for promoting high levels of employment and high rates of growth with Alfred Marshall's polices for allocating resources and distributing incomes in order to respond to social needs within a private, essentially market-oriented economy. The synthesis was effected by Paul Samuelson, who was not unconcerned about poverty and other socially disturbing imperfections in the economy, but who did not believe that a police state was required to protect advantage, or that fundamental redistribution of income and wealth was necessary to eliminate severe disadvantage.

Galbraith's analysis has revealed the failure of these assumptions to accord with reality. Monopolies did develop in the mature industrial societies, and are continuing to develop at an ever more rapid rate. Big business aided and abetted big government, and vice versa. Inflation became an overwhelming problem, even carrying over into periods of rising unemployment. Galbraith, like Mishan, now attacks economic growth itself; it doesn't work either as a goal or as a safety valve. An economy dominated by private decisions about consumption and production, he argues, tends to starve its public sectors.[15] The society's needs for long-term development, social betterment and general welfare get slighted in favor of luxuries and entertainment. It seems apparent today that big business can pretty much mold consumer tastes and spending patterns to its own needs.

Galbraith and Mishan call for a new synthesis, a reconstruction of economics, to move us toward more humane goals, and to permit us to analyze more realistically the obstacles to that movement. Perhaps they reject less the values growth produces than the values that produce growth.

At this point I should specify what I mean by redistribution, for there are several redistribution schemes, most of which promise great improvement, and it is quite possible to misunderstand their character and their promise. Initially we might, as a nation, choose simply to eliminate what is officially defined as poverty. We might also choose to transfer money directly only from the very richest of the population to the very poorest, rather than to spread the burden evenly among the nonpoor. More far-ranging proposals might reach substantially up into the ranks of those who find it virtually impossible to support their families adequately. These are not broken families, save perhaps in spirit. Heading these families, typically, is a working male, but, although they contain the clear majority of the country's population, they receive considerably less than a majority of the aggregate annual income.

Dr. Harold W. Watts of the University of Wisconsin proposed to the Democratic Party Platform hearings in St. Louis on June 17, 1972, one of the simplest plans yet advanced to aid not only the poor, but also the middle class that is under such financial stress. He proposed to replace the present public assistance and individual income tax programs, as well as all other means-tested programs with a "credit income tax" scheme. Each tax-payer would pay the same basic tax, at the rate of one third of all income received before the benefits derived from the redistribution scheme itself. There would be an additional 6⅔ percent surtax on income in surplus of $50,000, and still another 10 percent surtax on income in surplus of $100,000. Money would then be redistributed back to *everybody* on an equal footing, regardless of income. Each aged and disabled person would receive a payment of $1,560 a year, able-bodied adults eighteen to sixty-four would receive $1,320 a year, children ten to seventeen would receive $660, and younger ones $420. The modal family of four could not have an income less than $3,720. Such a family would break even, that is, receive back as much as it paid in taxes, at an annual income of $11,160. Work incentives would operate all along the road: any person earning $3.00 would keep $2.00 as long as his total income were less than $50,000 a year, and no person, however rich, would lose more than 50 percent of any dollar.

The impact such a scheme would have on the current distribution of income seems startling. Seventy percent of the entire population would benefit, ending up with more money than they did in 1970. The poorest 20 percent of the population would have 10 percent of the total final income, compared to between 7.7 and 7.9 percent in 1970. The next 50 percent of the population would enjoy an increase of 5 to 7 percent over their 1970 income. Perhaps equally important, in terms of the political feasibility of the scheme, the total revenue available to the government would *increase* by about $3 billion over that generated by the present system.[16]

With 70 percent of the populace, as well as the government, coming out ahead under such a scheme, why does it not command the support of the country? As Passell and Ross state, "On the face of it, there should be an easy solution to poverty in the United States. A redistribution of only 5 percent of the national income could bring every family up to a minimum $5,000 income." But they point to the fate of the President's Family Assistance Program as evidence that the idea of "explicit redistribution of income is still political anathema."[17]

Part of the handicap of such proposals is public confusion about their "costs." Such proposals involve taking money away from some people, perhaps from all income receivers at one stage or another of the operation. That which is taken away is popularly regarded as a cost. The confusion lies in the notion that it is a cost to "the country." Actually the money is taken from some people and given to others. It does not cost the country anything, except the quite limited expenses of the administrative system that supervises the transfers. The important question is whom does it cost? Watts' scheme costs only the 30 percent who receive the highest incomes, and them not very much. But there is an apparent inclination for most people to believe the extremely wealthy, who are in fact threatened, when they scream that the program would cost "the country" the nearly $44 billion in net losses that they themselves would suffer. Such "costs" should properly be measured against the costs of social control, the losses incurred through crime and social turmoil to the extent that it is rooted in poverty and needless deprivation, or even against the $40 to $45 billion that the present system transfers among our people with far less positive results.

Perhaps we have not touched on the deepest pitfall of all for redistribution programs, the attitudes held as much if not more fervently by the poor than by the rich: that to receive some direct benefit from a transfer system is to "get something for nothing" and to get something for nothing makes one "dependent" and therefore less than a man, certainly less than an American. It is one of the perversities of American life that only those who receive direct cash payments from government, not related to earnings from work, are considered dependent, and thus despicable; while those who receive services, benefits, and credits against costs they would otherwise pay, especially against taxes in the form of government guarantees, overruns, tax shelters, tax-free dividends, depreciation allowances, and the like, are considered independent, self-reliant embodiments of the work ethic. To add insult to injury, the welfare system has been designed and operated to ravish the family, degrade and deny the adult, and defeat the child.

What is the source of such pernicious attitudes and practices? Perhaps it is the insistent strain of individualism in American culture. The exaltation of self-help, self-development, and rags-to-riches hopes certainly seems to play a part. In a society where it is impossible to return to nature, and which cannot offer either enough work or enough pay for the work there is, one cannot sanely or justly assert the right to life without the right to the means for life.

These values of self-assertion and heroic individualism—each American making his own declaration of independence—are deemed to be a source not of pernicious outcomes, but of productivity. Productivity is considered perhaps the prime virtue; it defines the success of the individual and of the system; Eric Fromm takes it as the measure of virtue itself, although he charges the society that wishes to make people virtuous to make the unfolding and growth of every person the aim of all social and political activity. Instead, we have made it the prerequisite. Today productivity is preempted by technology, access to which is unequal. Virtue is assigned, then, only to those who control that access, a lessening proportion of the whole society. But people continue to live with their illusions, and thus to seek production, and the ordinary worker's growing sense of redundancy generates only vague anxieties. He will turn hardest against any initiative to distribute products to those who have lost or never gained any nexus with production at all.

This outlook fits more easily with overall economic growth than with no growth. Times of growth justify a faith in the availability and even the meaningfulness of work. No-growth threatens to awaken us to the prospect not simply of having less (which is not really necessary), but of being less, and without illusions.

Another cause is racism. However much one wishes to be able to discuss the sources of the failure of efforts at social justice in the United States without invoking that abused word, one cannot in this case. American political life is marvelously consistent in these matters. In American mythology the bottom of the social heap is defined by blackness, and thus, despite the fact that a majority of the poor, even a majority of the "dependent poor" are white, welfare and dependency are thought of as "black problems." Efforts to improve the lot of the poor and of those on welfare are popularly characterized as "more for the blacks." Anathema!

There are important differences in basic attitudes about welfare programs between the people of other industrial societies and Americans: they desire to spread the benefits and we to limit them; they see a sudden rise in the number of people drawing cash relief as a deficiency in their system of services while we blame the individual recipients; they seek to maximize the participation of the eligible and we to minimize it.

Limits to Growth, and Alliances

American prejudices are deeply rooted. They are not likely to be turned over by the weak commitment to the values that promote redistribution exhibited so far by prominent spokesmen for no-growth policies. For example, in the famous report of The Club of Rome Project on the Predicament of Mankind,[18] of the seven policy alternatives considered in simulating a condition of social equilibrium at "a decent living standard," only one related directly to the needs and conditions of the very poor elements of the world's population:

> Since the above policies alone would result in a rather low value of food per capita, some people would still be malnourished if the traditional inequalities of distribution persist. To avoid this situation, high value is placed on producing sufficient food for *all* people. Capital is therefore diverted to food production even if such an investment would be considered "uneconomic."[19]

The authors did not suggest any basic tampering with the distribution system itself. It is therefore an open question whether some people would not go hungry even if sufficient aggregate food production were achieved to supply all people.

The authors of the report did voice a concern about poverty and inequality and they devoted cogent but few words to attack "one of the most commonly accepted myths in our present society," namely, "the promise that a continuation of our present pattern of growth will lead to human equality." They demonstrated in the report that present patterns of population and capital growth are increasing the gap between rich and poor on a worldwide basis. They felt that "the ultimate result of a continued attempt to grow according to the present pattern will be a disastrous collapse."

They were most concerned about the general collapse they could foresee for industrial society, although presumably this would leave few pickings for any survivors. The compelling feature of the argument is not that it may be undesirable to continue present patterns of growth, but that it may be impossible to do so, and preserve society as we know it. The report is entitled, after all, *The Limits to Growth*. We may guess that, if the food resource limits are the first to be reached, then the developing countries would suffer first and perhaps most. If material resource limits are the first reached, the developed world would be hardest hit. But, either way, everybody would find the results disastrous.

These absolute limits of growth, at least for industrial society, may well be reached in less than a century and a half. If they are real, approaching them will hurt people in tangible ways. Fuel costs will mount until present patterns of industrial activity and even home heating are disrupted, businesses close, and people discover neighborliness or freeze. Mineral resources will be coveted more by producers and users alike, exacerbating international tensions and driving the prices of finished products even further out of the range of the poorer elements of society. Substitutes and the production innovations necessary to use them will be searched out, but there is some question whether these will be available on a general basis, or reserved for the wealthy elements or countries. Some nonsubstitutable resources will be exhausted and we will have to adjust our life styles to do without them.

Such changes and the forces they set in motion will perhaps make less credible the appeal so often made to growth itself as a way to bring economic improvements to the poor. *The social costs of continuing to deny the poor may then be such that those who pay them will be forced to take the question of direct redistribution of income, and perhaps of wealth, more seriously.* Present indications are, however, that improvements for the poor are likely to result not from a shift in attitude to one which values no-growth for itself, but rather from alliances between the very poor and the middle class. Both will have a direct interest in gaining a larger share of the economic pie, and together they would have the political power to wrest what they want and need from the superrich.

Footnotes

1. Mobil Oil Corporation, "Growth Is the Only Way America Will Ever Reduce Poverty," Advertisement, *New York Times*, April 13, 1972.
2. Glen C. Cain, "Issues in the Economics of a Population Policy in the United States," *American Economic Review*, 61, No. 2 (May 1971).
3. *Ibid.*
4. Paul R. Ehrlich and Anne H. Ehrlich, *Population, Resources and Environment: Issues in Human Ecology* (San Francisco: W. H. Freeman, 1972).
5. *SESBPUS*; Theodore W. Schultz, "Public Approaches to Minimize Poverty," *Poverty Amid Affluence*, ed. L. Fishman (New Haven, Conn.: Yale University Press, 1966).
6. *Ibid.*
7. Herman P. Miller, "Changes in the Number and Composition of the Poor," *Inequality and Poverty*, ed. Edward C. Budd (New York: Norton, 1968).
8. Schultz, "Public Approaches to Minimize Poverty," pp. 165-181.
9. Lester Thurow, ed., "Analyzing the American Income Distribution," *American Economic Review*, 60, No. 2 (May 1970), 261-269.
10. *SESBPUS*, p. 68.
11. *Ibid.*, pp. 38-39.
12. L. E. Galloway, "The Foundations of the 'War on Poverty,' " *American Economic Review*, 55, No. 1 (March 1965), 122-131.
13. Andrew F. Brimmer and Henry S. Terrell, "The Economic Potential of Black Capitalism," paper presented at the 82nd Annual Meeting of the American Economic Association (New York: December 1969).
14. Thurow, *Poverty and Discrimination*, p. 151.
15. J. K. Galbraith, *The Affluent Society* (New York: New American Library, 1970), Ch. 22.
16. Watts' calculations utilize Brookings Institution (Schultz) estimates for 1975. They assume a population of 214 million, total incomes of $1,046 billion, tax yield of $361 billion, less credits of $232 billion plus $18 billion in replaced public assistance programs. Total for government, $147 billion, as against present projections of $144 billion.
17. Peter Passell and Leonard Ross "Don't Knock the $2 Trillion Economy," *New York Times Sunday Magazine*, March 5, 1972, p. 70.
18. Donella H. Meadows, Dennis L. Meadows, Jorgen Randers, and William W. Brehrens, III, *The Limits to Growth*, A Report for the Club of Rome (New York: Universe Books, 1972).
19. *Ibid.*, p. 164.

No-Growth
And The Poor:

Equity Considerations in Controlled Growth Policies

Michael A. Agelasto, II

Michael Agelasto holds an AB degree from Columbia College. He has worked as a VISTA Volunteer, Director of a housing development corporation, and currently is a teaching assistant in the Department of City and Regional Planning, University of California, Berkeley from which he expects his MCP, in 1974. The author wishes to thank William Alonso, Jaime Biderman and William L. C. Wheaton for their helpful comments on earlier drafts.

This article basically is a partial reprint (with permission) of another by the same title, appearing in Planning Comment, Mark Cordray (ed.); double issue, Volume 9, Numbers 1 and 2, Spring 1973. A shorter and somewhat similar article titled "No Growth Can Help the Poor. . ." appeared in 1 Equilibrium 4 (October 1973).

Introduction

The federal government and numerous local governments have recently begun formulating growth and land use development policies. In the next few decades, many localities in the United States will experience a decline in growth as the nation itself approaches zero population growth. This local no-growth can take the form of a loss of population or a slow-down in economic activity (which may or may not result from a population decline). The decline in growth can be *spontaneous*—and legislation may be necessary to alter certain results of no-growth. Alternatively, no-growth can be induced by *legislative action*. This paper will focus on the latter type of growth control.

At present, several legislatures have initiated policies aimed at curtailing man's wasteful, unplanned use of the environment. But in their enthusiasm for controlling growth, supporters of this legislation have generally lost sight of the regressive effects of given policies on the poor. This paper will examine some equity concerns in controlled growth policies and will suggest provisions which might be included to ensure that controlled growth does not adversely affect the lower income population.

Beyond Definitions

The concept of equity has undergone basic definitional changes since it was first introduced in the Declaration of Independence. It started out as the right to *opportunity*—the principle that in the new American society the poor would be guaranteed the freedom of upward mobility and that others who had already made it would not deny them this right. The Fourteenth Amendment extended this legal right to all Americans.

But in the following century, equity became more concerned with the *result* than the opportunity. Whereas it was once thought that all horses should leave the gate together, it was now believed that all should finish together, or at least close to one another. The minimum wage, the guaranteed annual income, medicare and other welfare benefits reflect this change in definition. Equity is now measured by minimum criteria of success—levels of consumption or standard of living—rather than freedom of opportunity. Poverty is defined in many ways: in *absolute* terms (e.g., per capita income or wealth, above or below a given poverty level); in *relative* terms (e.g., a percent of mean per capita income, those who have fewer material goods than the rest and measures of income distribution, job stability or upward occupational mobility); or by use of a *surrogate* (ill-housed, suffering from hunger, etc.). Whatever the definition, it implicitly expresses the concern with results.

As we examine the effects of local growth legislation upon the poor, we also must necessarily consider the subgroups within the poor. Rates of economic growth may only slightly affect an old person whose life is determined by a fixed income—pension or social security. The working poor and youth, on the other hand, very much depend on the state of the local economy and the availability of jobs. To achieve a desired quality of life, they may resort to part time jobs or may have more than one member of the household working full time. The structured-in poor are those who are handicapped or who are not in the labor force because there are no jobs requiring their skills or those who must stay home to care for the children. They too are affected differently by growth. To a great extent they depend on transfer and welfare payments to obtain the standard of living afforded them by the rest of society. Therefore, generalizations that fail to take into account the differential impact of no-growth on subgroups within the poor are inadequate.

Roots of Growth Control

No-growth (the extreme form of controlled growth) has become a rather fashionable term of late. Its definition is left up to the user and rarely, it seems, do two users agree on meaning. Holding the antiposition, however, enables the no-growther to shift the burden of definition to his adversary—the proponent of growth—who is equally confused and ambiguous. Put on the defense, the advocate of growth is placed in the most difficult position of having to explain why he is in favor of more people (population growth), more GNP (economic growth), or more pollution (industrial growth).

What are the concerns of the no-growthers that cause them to question growth—a traditional value of American society? Two attitudes seem prevalent: the desire to prevent continued environmental deterioration, and the desire (conscious or not) to halt social mobility or minority groups.

To some, growth has put man on a collision course with the environment (Dansereau, 1970; Boulding, 1966; Daly, 1971; Ehrlich, 1970; Johnson and Hardesty, 1971). This awareness stems in part from Carson's *Silent Spring* (1962), through a plethora of save-the-earth books, and most recently reappears in Forrester (1971) and the Club of Rome's *The Limits to Growth* (Meadows et al., 1972). Presumably man's devotion to creating more of himself coupled with his appetite to consume more of nature are leading to his self-destruction. The evidence supporting this thesis, it is said, is apparent: sprawling "slurbs" infringing on the hinterland, and water and air polluted with man's waste. Some argue that the environmentalists are prophets of doom who do not show a clear, causal relationship between economic growth and environmental decay and understate the probability of future technological advances designed to clean up the environment (Klein, 1972). To others, the literature overstates future population increases and their effects on the environment (Ryder, 1972, Wattenberg, 1970). The argument in this debate—whether growth is desirable—is being defined and refined and no consensus has yet been reached (Murray, 1972).

The desire to stop social change is at times latent, but sometimes emotionally expressed (e.g., at local rezoning hearings). The fear is that economic growth provides for the upward mobility of minority groups by offering these "have-nots" various opportunities at the expense of the "haves." With the population expanding, more minorities are bound to achieve levels of income that allow them to "invade" more expensive residential communities and enjoy life styles previously known only to richer citizens (Alonso, 1973; Klein, 1972).

Quite naturally, a person desires to preserve for his personal use something he was lucky enough to find before others. One may locate a secluded public beach and convert it into private use for himself and a few friends. His motive to keep others out has not harmed anyone because those who do not yet know of the beach do not miss anything. These "first-come-first-served" are better off and no one has been made worse off. But as more and more people find out about the beach and demand to use it, the founder instinctively wants to protect his privacy. He might put up a fence or get the local authority to restrict the beach's use to those who live near it.

The individual himself has not intentionally harmed anyone. But when his action is added to similar actions by many other people, the result is regressive to a large part of the population, because it denies to the "have-nots" what the "haves" obtained by the fact they were there first. Thus, one man's innocently-held desire for privacy is among the reasons that one segment of society is withholding opportunities from another part of society (Schelling, 1971).

Man's inability to predict his future and control his destiny has worried him for centuries. He has often reacted by resisting change. More research is needed to determine the strength of the status-quo impulse among no-growth advocates.

Economic Growth: Poor People's Best Friend?

"Growth is the only way America will ever reduce poverty," reads a Mobil Oil advertisement. It's not surprising that corporations such as oil companies and building materials suppliers wish to sell this idea to the public. But, in fact, many individuals with genuine concern for the poor oppose controlled growth policies by reasoning that economic growth benefits the poor (Passell and Ross, 1972, 1973). Their argument runs that the bigger the economic pie, the more slices or crumbs that will fall to the poor. Implicit are the assumptions that: (a) the "poor" benefit as a group by a certain rate of economic growth; and (b) since the pie is larger, more people will be eating it. We questioned this first assumption in our discussion of subgroups within the poor. We now examine this second assumption.

Many factors are necessary for eliminating poverty. Economic growth is one only when the benefits are distributed in such a way as to improve the lot of the poor. A growing economy with an excess of unfilled jobs might cause employers to hire individuals they would otherwise consider unemployable. At the same time, the working poor will be able to find second jobs which will lift them out of poverty. Yet economic growth and labor's demand for higher wages may cause the employer to make more intensive use of capital. This results in automation. Those who had recently found jobs may now find that their skills are unneeded. Instead of hiring more cooks to fry the chicken, the restaurant buys an automatic chicken cooker and fires all the cooks it had just hired.

This "poverty in the wake of progress" phenomenon (Nelson, 1965, p. 4-5) does not lend itself to easy empirical testing. Nevertheless, several studies have shown that the "trickle down" theory is probably invalid for many poor, especially the structured-in poor (Anderson, 1964; Heistand, 1964). A more recent study has stated that a tight labor market and a booming economy by themselves do not benefit the minority poor. The study finds that the Mexican American poor in San Jose, California, appeared not to benefit from the rapid growth of that city from 1950-1970. In fact, if anything, they were made worse off (RAND, 1971). Yet studies like this have not been able to examine the progress over time of individual poor; the aggregate data does not tell the full story. For some time we have known that second and third generation poor become better off than those who first settled, but how much better off remains unknown. A tight labor market and growing economy appear to be pre-conditions for anti-poverty efforts aimed at the marginally employed and under-employed working poor. Manpower training programs, for example, experience greatest success when the program's "graduates" are immediately drawn into the labor force and given jobs.

A moderate rate of economic growth only slightly affects those poor who are not in the labor force. For them, employers would have to provide job training programs, drug rehabilitation centers, child care facilities and the like. It does not necessarily follow that moderate growth would be incentive enough to prompt employers to take on these tasks. For other poor—especially the elderly—employment opportunity makes no difference; transfer payments and other welfare aid is needed.

The main flaw in the growth-as-a-cure-for-poverty hypothesis is the absence of a national U.S. income redistribution policy. Arguably, in the 1960s, welfare payments and various other forms of federal and local aid provided for some redistribution of income; but the profits of economic growth for that period were not divided on an equal basis. A recent Department of Labor study supports this view and finds that incomes within the male labor force are in fact more unequal (*New York Times*, 1972). Clearly, one cannot rely solely on economic growth to eliminate poverty for Americans. Economic growth may have given some of the poor an opportunity, but it is not clear that it provided absolute benefits to many. *The poor and their liberal advocates would best spend their time seeking a redistribution policy in a growth economy or positive controls in a no-growth economy.*

How the Local Communities "Control" Growth

Our thesis thus far is that no-growth will become a reality for many communities; that even if growth were possible it would not necessarily help eradicate poverty; and that local communities attempting to control growth should do so in an equitable way. Here, we shall explore the standard instrumentalities used by localities to control population and territorial growth (which in some cases result in a decline in economic activity).

Although the motives for limiting growth among *individuals* are discernible, the reasons that *communities* choose to limit their size are less clear. The primary intent of most of the instrumentalities is land use regulation, with secondary effects of controlling growth or excluding certain social groups. Whether the secondary effects were in fact the primary intent is speculative, although sometimes suggested by the expectation of their results.

Almost intuitively, many communities are deciding that their present size is optimal. Rather than referring to the vast literature which discusses the advantages and disadvantages of certain city sizes and questions whether an optimal size is attainable or desirable (Alonso, 1970a,b; Richardson, 1972), community leaders have imposed certain restrictions which have a population limiting effect: (a) Exclusionary zoning and subdivision exactions; (b) Buying up land; (c) Staging growth—zoning and construction freezes; (d) Height, pollution and noise ordinances; (e) Voters' actions; (f) Refusal to extend city services; (g) Negative advertising; and, (h) Regional controls.

Controlling certain types of growth is nothing new. Many suburbs have legislated **exclusionary zoning** and imposed excessively costly subdivision exactions to prohibit the building of housing for the poor. Although courts have overturned zoning that discriminates racially, they have generally deferred to the legislatures on zoning that discriminates against low income people on an economic, non-racial basis. Exclusionary zoning, until it came under recent court attack, served as an effective tool for local communities wishing to exclude the poor (Babcock, 1966; Brooks, 1970; Dyke, 1972). Communities would zone undeveloped land into large lots which by decreasing the number of lots available for building would raise the cost of each. Other forms of exclusionary zoning include minimum building size, exclusion of multiple family dwellings, restrictions on the number of bedrooms, prohibition of mobile homes, and lot frontage requirements.

It is widely debated whether single family homes pay for themselves (Associated Home Builders of the East Bay, Inc., 1972; Gruen, 1972). Just considering the revenue from the property tax and cost of educating two children per household, cities realize costs exceed revenues. Feeling the fiscal crunch of having to provide more city services but being unable to float revenue bonds or increase real property taxes, municipalities resort to **exacting certain fees** from builders of new homes. These, which consist of building, sewer, gas and water permits, can easily add up to several thousand dollars. (San Jose recently enacted an additional construction tax of $114 to each new house, regardless of sales price, a figure which the city felt was equal to the cost of providing new services for that unit.) All these fees put new homes at sales prices above what many families could afford, and the municipality controls the growth of houses for lower income families.

A more expensive type of growth control is for the municipality to **purchase developable land** for recreation or for dormant open space. Employing this technique, Lincoln, Massachusetts, for example, was able to provide residents with 800 acres of land. This method seems to work best for communities that can afford it or, as in the case of Aspen, Colorado, have the proper enabling legislation to employ a variety of financing schemes. Many communities, like Palo Alto, California, are being told by consultants that it is cheaper to buy up land than have to provide the services if it were ever developed. Others dispute this claim, contending that the real revenue brought in by a single family home far exceeds the real estate taxes. The new occupants pay for local retail services and generate sales and gasoline taxes. Most cost-revenue studies, to date, fail to include these externalities and multiplier effects and do not state their assumptions clearly.

Other legislatures have tried to **stage growth** by freezing zoning, or limiting the issuance of building permits, or diverting population growth from existing centers to new towns. Petaluma, Calif., placed a ceiling of 500 building permits issued annually, stated that these had to be distributed evenly throughout the city and placed a moratorium on zoning until further policies could be developed. In order to avoid a court ruling this instrumentality exclusionary, Petaluma earmarked ten percent of these permits for low and moderate income housing. Similarly, Ramapo, New York, created a "phased growth" scheme that requires special permits for new development. Permits would be approved only if the subdivision already had existing services. In upholding the constitutionality of the ordinance, the court noted that it was not exclusionary because it included "provisions for low and moderate income housing on a large scale."

Height, pollution and noise controls are additional instrumentalities which may see increased use and acceptance. San Francisco was recently embroiled in a bitter controversy over the vertical shape of its downtown. Most of the opposition to new building came from residents who argued against the esthetic deterioration ("they block my view") and the "manhattanization" of the city's historic skyline (Brugmann, 1971). Builders, lenders, insurance companies, and construction trade unions argued that the city's economy (especially that of the building industry) needed new office buildings. Few, however, voiced concern over the thousands of service jobs—from janitorial to clerical—that were at stake for the low and moderate income residents, after the buildings were completed.

In order to prevent the continued destruction of the environment, **voters** in various states have created single purpose districts with jurisdiction over air, water, or sewerage quality. The advent of more levels of government means, in fact, more bodies with the ability to veto residential and commercial developments and the construction of permanent jobs that go with them. The San Francisco Bay area has 528 special purpose districts and many of these may cast vetoes or have the power to stall a development. The voters of Colorado voted down housing the 1974 Winter Olympics out of the fear that the increased economic activity would destroy the environment (Wren, 1973). "Don't Californicate Colorado" was the bumper-sticker slogan.

Communities are finding that another way to control growth is to **refuse to extend services**. Marin County, California, recently voted down a water bond, fully aware that the county's current residents needed new facilities but fearing that more services would attract new residents. Rich communities have long voted down school bond referendums out of the realization that many families can afford to send their children to private schools and anticipating that this vote would dissuade new residents who are poorer from appearing.

The governor of Oregon has initiated what is perhaps a new type of control: **negative advertising**. He has invited people to visit his state but not to stay. Just a few years ago, states were competing for population (which gives a state more Congressional representation), but now these same states seem to be saying: "We're a nice place to visit, but you wouldn't want to live here." Viewing the fiscal crunch, they in fact say: "We'd like your tax money, but not the costs of your children." To discourage further economic activity, Fort Lauderdale, Florida, closed down its publicity and advertising department, which it had funded for the past 19 years (last year's expenditure was over $580,000).

Finally, with the council of governments employing **regional controls**, municipalities band together to close their doors to outsiders. This development is based on the desire to control one's destiny but is also supported by a feeling of superiority and regionalism (what the Spanish call *patria chica*). A leader in this movement is the Association of Bay Area Governments (ABAG), the regional plan agency of the San Francisco 9-county region. What regional controls do is to take all the local controls and put them under one coordinator, hopefully producing a more efficient process. Centralization, however, is no guarantee of a more equitable product.

Inner City Vs. Outer City

It is clear from the above examples that most of the instrumentalities used by localities for controlling growth are regressive—*they hurt the poor without substantially hurting others, and sometimes in fact make the rich better off.* Most of our examples were taken from suburban communities where the concerns rested with the fear of over-population and environmental decay. Across the nation this conflict between the inner city and the outer city is played and replayed. Common to most metropolitan regions is a polarity in incomes, races and growth rates between the suburbs and core city. This supports the thesis that the no-growth suburbs can afford to give up something in order to obtain the environmental purity and population stability they desire. In other words, they should be willing to make a trade-off so that the instrumentalities they use are not regressive. Following this hypothesis: (a) The rich should be willing to pay for saving their environment. (b) Priority should be given to cleaning up the central city while environmental concerns are also directed toward saving suburban open space. (c) Economic growth not desired by the suburbs should be directed to central cities. (d) Public housing bonds should be included in bonds for open space to compensate the poor for increased suburban rents and land costs.

Concern over pollution has blinded many outer city dwellers to equity concerns. That the environment is seen as mainly a suburban issue (anti-sprawl) has caused some to label environmentalists "green bigots," who desire a green ring a la Ebenezer Howard to separate the white cities from the black city. But cleaning up the environment should be more important to the central cities, where smog and congestion affect daily living more than the prospect of another subdivision down the road affects outer city residents. In addition, the poor—since they are less mobile—are unable to escape environmental disamenities.

Industries and economic activity not desired by the suburbs should be redirected to the central city. Suburbs, however, should not be able to pick and choose—accepting non-nuisance industry while sending polluters to the core. Residential construction previously slated for suburban tracts should now go into city renewal and redevelopment. Thus, the symbiotic relationship of earlier decades would be restored and the suburbs will again acknowledge their dependence on the central city and forfeit their newly-gained self-sufficiency, growing independence and arrogance. Of late, the central-city/suburb symbiotic relationship has broken down into a parasitic one. The suburbs benefit from *borrowing size* from the core—taking advantage of city culture, shopping and employment, while refusing its disamenities and negative externalities (Alonso, 1973, p. 18).

Where down-zoning and other instrumentalities result in open space for suburbanites, higher level values and rents are usually felt by the lower income. Those wishing to leave the inner city for the outer city now find a move no longer possible. In order to balance the scale, the suburbs should accept the burden of housing their own ill-housed poor or pay the cities to house them. In the last decade, affluent suburbs have been losing their young and old (who can no longer afford to live there) to the inner city, where living costs are lower. Suburbs should start taking care of their own.

One way of making the trade-off is for the state to require public housing bonds (which always fail nowadays) be attached to open space referendums (which always pass). In this way, voters would be shown the direct relationship between requiring open space and subsequent increased housing costs. Illustrating the give-and-take by placing these inseparable issues on the ballot will prove educational as well. The suburbs who vote for open space but do not want public housing would be required, by state law, to transmit money representing the cost of public housing units to cities that do desire to build housing for the poor.

Recently, the issues of cleaning up the environment and bettering the lot of the poor have been placed in direct conflict. It is said that building homes for the poor or securing industrial employers will necessarily hurt the environment. Yet this is a *false dichotomy* into which both ecologists and advocates for the poor have fallen. The working poor suffer most from industrial pollution and live in neighborhoods affected most by environmental disamenities. Suburbanites are trying to avoid the same thing from happening to their communities. Ralph Nader contends that industry is purposely turning workers against environmentalists by threatening to cut back jobs if they are forced to curtail pollution. The environment should be cleaned up, but not at the expense of low-paying jobs. The equitable solution is not to abandon our drive against pollution; rather we must convince industry (perhaps with taxpayers' assistance) to employ more labor and capital in arresting pollution.

The need for compromise should not overshadow the interest-group politics of the situation. The poor and their advocates have been joined by unions, lenders, insurance companies, oil companies, and the like on some of these issues. These influentials have been moved not out of some altruistic motive, but rather by the possibility of using a good sub-issue (helping the poor) in their fight against the environmentalists. The poor should not be misled. How do their new supporters feel about building public housing in the suburbs? Do they lobby in Washington for a guaranteed annual income?

Many poor have little reason to support industry in its fight with the ecologists: for example, they are little affected by a plant locating in the suburbs, for they can expect only a small percentage of the jobs. In other words, the poor should choose their friends carefully and exact from big business certain things in exchange for cooperation on environmental issues. They might, for example, influence the building trades to accept more minority into their ranks. The poor nations are now finding they have "bargaining power" with developed countries that wish to locate their polluting industries in poor countries (Brown, 1973). It's time the U.S. poor define their "bargaining power" and make full use of it.

Those supporters of regional growth controls who live in the central city contend that the city has not benefited from recent growth. Citing crime statistics, loss of population and the loss of jobs for the working class, they say the situation cannot get much worse. Yet, since there is no *a priori* assurance that suburban communities in a controlled growth society would not continue to pick the types of growth—population and economic—they desire, controls to ensure equity are necessary. Otherwise, one can expect no-growth to be more regressive and less beneficial to the poor than even growth has been.

Positive Local Controls

We have examined some of the give-and-take necessary for developing an equitable no-growth policy. We noted above that many communities will be unable to influence their growth rate—that they will be shaped by no-growth. We are concerned here, however, with those communities which choose to induce no-growth through legislative acts. Therefore, we shall now look at *a pro-equity set of actions to ensure that local no-growth on the metropolitan scale does not unduly favor the wealthy at the expense of the poor.*

Among these actions are: (a) Regional tax base; (b) Revenue sharing; (c) Property tax; (d) Property tax alternatives; (e) Bonding power; (f) Industry; and, (g) Land Use Controls.

A **regional tax base** is currently used in the Minneapolis-St. Paul area. Forty per cent of the increased tax revenue generated by new commercial and industrial facilities located in the Twin Cities metropolitan area is shared among all local government units. This scheme, based on population, is weighted to give more money to those jurisdictions with lower assessed valuations. The use of the metropolitan area for the tax base rather than each locality which taxes for its specific needs considers the dynamic interrelatedness of the metropolis.

Federal **Revenue Sharing** ties into this concept. Localities will soon decide the use of revenue sharing money returned to them by the federal government. The uses of these funds are exceedingly important now that the Nixon Administration appears to be replacing more categorical grant programs with this local-option format. If localities choose to discontinue funding Great Society social programs like Model Cities, OEO, housing, employment and educational programs, the poor who benefit from these will inevitably suffer. A determination on the use of funds made at the regional level would hopefully eliminate the duplications and gaps that are so common in these programs today.

The prospect of the U.S. Supreme Court upholding the California *Serrano v. Priest* decision is questionable due to the recent *Rodriguez v. San Antonio* School District Supreme Court ruling, which held that education is not one of the rights guaranteed by the U.S. Constitution. The Court abstained from intervention into the system of local property taxation. One can speculate, however, as to what could have happened as an alternative to the **property tax**. Given the two usual types of taxes, highly progressive income taxes would be preferred over value added or sales taxes which tend to be highly regressive, proportionally hurting the poor more than others. The site valuation tax would replace the current taxation on buildings. This would curb speculation, especially premature subdivisions that have led to sprawl, by removing profit from speculation.

The **bonding power** of municipalities, where enabling legislation permits, could finance socially beneficial projects: e.g., public housing, job training centers, renewal projects. If these facilities were integrated into larger projects which pay taxes (such as putting a training center in an industrial park), tax revenues generated could help retire the bonds. Enabling legislation would have to provide that revenues would not go to school or other special assessment districts.

Communities that choose to control growth may do so by limiting **industry**. Pollution emission is one of a set of criteria used to determine which industry should be excluded. But it should not over-shadow other equally important criteria. A point system could be designed to give ratings to particular industries or firms under consideration. High ratings would go to that firm that will employ local residents rather than having to go outside the region to recruit workers. Industries that provide child care facilities or rehabilitation centers for the handicapped, drug addicts, veterans, or elderly would also receive favorable ratings.

Numerous **land control** instrumentalities have redistributive qualities. Many taxing mechanisms are sensitive to the fact that those who can pay should help pay for those who cannot. The costs incurred by the poor, for example, through down-zoning could be distributed among the general population in several ways. (a) Builders could be required to include housing for the poor in each subdivision; in lieu of this, they would contribute towards a city fund to purchase low income housing sites. (b) Subdivision exactions could be "doubly progressive." Different income subdivisions would be charged different rates for services dependent on the ability (sales price) of the house. The revenues generated could be used as transfer payments to the poor. (c) Covenants could be attached as a condition to subdivision map approval, requiring a certain number of an apartment building's units be sold or rented to families with incomes under a certain level. Such a covenant would run with the land so that successive owners of the development would be bound to it. (d) Density bonuses would require builders to provide units for the poor if they desired to increase the density of a project. In this case, the bonus has to be appetizing enough or the builder will settle for the lower density to avoid building for the poor. (e) Floating zones for public housing and other socially desirable developments could be established to facilitate legislative approval. (f) Since the scarcity of land is a concern, why not, rather than zoning for large lots, downzone so that all units must be built on lots of 6,000 square feet or less? (g) Finally, a quota for low income units could be made part of the general building permit quota of the controlled growth community. This distributive scheme, as the others, would have to meet constitutional requirements of due process and equal protection.

The old equity solutions that have sprung forth since the New Deal have often proven unsuccessful and counter intuitive. For example, liberals have long been fighting for the removal of exclusionary zoning. But if it were actually removed, contends one writer, the beneficiaries of the new policy would be low and moderate income whites living in the inner city who had been previously unable to leave the central city but who now find inexpensive housing stock in the suburbs. Racial segregation would be accentuated (Levy, 1972). Code enforcement is another example of a program designed to help the poor but which accomplished quite the opposite results. Rehabilitation and code enforcement programs tend either to raise the rents of the poor (as the landlord passes the costs of the repairs along to the tenants) or to show that the building is not worth repairing—forcing demolition and leaving the poor person without even a dilapidated house (Hartman et al., 1972).

Federal Growth Controls

While many argue that equity-based instrumentalities placed at the local level are most effective (Muth, 1969), others put their faith in the centralized federal government (Strong, 1971). This question aside, the federal government will, at the very least, be needed to play a coordinative role as various local, regional and state governments adopt controlled growth policies. Often local legislatures fail to realize the impact of their policies outside their jurisdiction; they confuse the municipal corporation for the "real city" (Alonso, 1973). The "real city" is dynamic and includes the present residents as well as people who *will* in-migrate in the future and others who *would* in-migrate if certain conditions were different. Since cities and regions that pursue isolationism would likely impose (often unintentionally) negative impacts on national efficiency and equity goals as well, the federal government would be needed to monitor no-growth policies.

The call for an American growth policy came with the insertion into the Housing and Urban Development Act of 1970 of a requirement that the President periodically report to Congress on national growth policy. The Ashley sub-committee hearings and papers that followed the release of the first White House report in 1972 brought to light a feeling among many that the President failed to address the issue (U.S. Congress, 1972a,b). To avoid future embarrassment, the White House, in preparation of its 1974 report, distributed to various executive departments a set of 135 questions aimed at defining national growth policy (Memorandum dated May 31, 1972 from John D. Erlichman re National Growth Policy). Nowhere was the question asked: how will such policies benefit or hurt the poor? For several years, the Jackson committee has also debated a national land use policy, and for the most part it also has avoided the equity question (U.S. Congress, 1971a, 1972b,c).

It has been argued elsewhere that the U.S. has an "implicit" growth policy achieved by its taxation, military spending, highway location and other policies (Alonso, 1971). Although certain branches in the federal government are surely aware of the second and third level effects of these implicit policies, no real attempt has yet been made to systematically examine them as a whole for equity considerations. This need is vital, yet we will concentrate here on **a variety of possible policies** whose primary effects would be equity: (a) Revenue sharing; (b) Federal development policies; (c) Direct federal involvement; and, (d) Population Control.

As stated above, local governments need guidelines to ensure that they make equitable use of **revenue sharing** funds. A highly improbable but very desirable formula for revenue sharing would be for the federal government to eliminate altogether federal income tax deductions for mortgage interest, depreciation, and local property taxes and instead share this increased revenue with localities based on each's amount of poverty.

It is important to examine **federal land development policies** for possible positive policies. With all the recent agitation over new towns, only a few writers have pointed out the inequitable and undesirable impacts they may have (Alonso, 1970c; Rodwin and Susskind, 1971, p. 10ff). New Towns are criticized for taking jobs away from the dying cities or for moving poor people away from areas where they have political clout. Even fewer writers have proposed alternative strategies. Among the innovative proposals are all-black new towns and working class industrial manpower communities (Galantay, 1968; Burton and Garn, 1972).

Historically, **direct involvement** has been the way that the federal government asserts its control in equity matters. But the Nixon Administration's "new federalism" appears to be scrapping this method. If we were to witness a political about-face, a suggested involvement would be for the federal government itself to build public housing. Using its sovereign immunity powers, the government could over-ride the numerous local controls that restrict the building of public housing in the suburbs. Or the federal government could provide an allowance or tax incentive to builders who ventured into high risk and high cost areas.

Finally, were the federal government to change its **population control policy** (current tax policy encourages large families), it could bribe the poor through money payments not to have children. Other forms of control that do not compensate the poor for relinquishing their right to propagation would be necessarily regressive.

Summary

In a growth economy, the poor and their liberal advocates would best spend their time seeking a redistribution policy. Conversely, in a no-growth economy, they should seek *positive* controls rather than argue for growth, which has not been proven conclusively to benefit the poor. A survey of current no-growth legislation indicates it generally hurts the poor, while having a neutral or even beneficial effect on the rich. This need not be so, for, as we have shown, numerous controls can have redistribution results.

Planners are often reminded to anticipate the effects of proposed policies before deciding which alternative is best. A policy should be *examined both for regressive and equitable side-effects*. Criticizing a policy is no substitute for offering a positive alternative; we have tried here to do both.

While in most cases, the central cities want their economy to expand, many suburbs, on the other hand, are content to stop growing. These interests *can* and *should* be reconciled through policies that redistribute both income and growth from the "haves" to the "have-nots." without making anyone, in absolute terms, worse off.

Fortunately, the no-growth issue has not yet reached many parts of the nation and planners have time to determine the following: (a) The extent of the anti-social change attitude among no-growth advocates; (b) Which industries offer jobs to the poor; (c) Equity consequences of implicit growth policies; and, (d) The feasibility of regional revenue sharing.

Whether controlled growth policies will be equitable depends to a large extent on the political climate. Policies, we have shown, can be equitable, but only when the "haves" are willing to make the necessary trade-offs. If not, growth control policies will remain regressive and continue to make the rich better off at the expense of the poor.

References

Alonso, William (1970a), "Economics of Urban Size," 26 *Papers of the Regional Science Association*.

_____, (1970b), "The Question of City Size and National Policy," Working Paper 125, Institute of Urban and Regional Development, University of California, Berkeley.

_____, (1970c), "What are New Towns for?," 7 *Urban Studies* (Feb.), pp. 37-55.

_____, (1971), "Problems, Purposes, and Implicit Policies for a National Strategy of Urbanization," Working Paper 158, Institute of Urban and Regional Development, University of California, Berkeley.

_____, (1973), "Urban Zero Population Growth," in *Daedalus*, "The No Growth Society," forthcoming.

Associated Home Builders of the Greater East Bay, Inc., (1972), *Growth Cost Revenue Studies*, Berkeley, 7 chapters.

Anderson, W. H. Locke (1964), "Trickling Down: The Relationship between Economic Growth and the Extent of Poverty Among American Families," 78 *Quarterly Journal of Economics* (Nov.), pp. 511-524.

Babcock, Richard (1966), *The Zoning Game*, Madison: University of Wisconsin Press, 202 p.

Boulding, Kenneth E. (1966), "The Economics of the Coming Spaceship Earth," in Johnson and Hardesty eds. (1971), pp. 58-68.

Brooks, Mary E. (1970), "Exclusionary Zoning," Planning Advisory Service Report No. 254, (Chicago: American Society of Planning Officials), 42 p.

Brooks, Harvey (1973), "The Technology of Zero Growth," in *Daedalus*, "The No Growth Society," forthcoming.

Brown, Lester R. (1973), "Rich Countries and Poor in a Finite, Interdependent World," in *Daedalus*, "The No Growth Society," forthcoming.

Brugmann, Bruce B. et al (1971), *The Ultimate Highrise*. San Francisco: San Francisco Bay Guardian Books, 255 p.

Burton, Richard P. and Garn, Harvey A. (1972), "The President's Report on National Growth, 1972: A Critique and Alternate Formulation" in U.S. Congress (1972a).

Carson, Rachel (1962), *Silent Spring*, Boston: Houghton-Mifflin Company, 368 p.

Daly, Herman E. (1971), "Toward a New Economics-Questioning Growth," in Johnson and Hardesty (1971), pp. 73-84.

Dansereau, Pierre ed. (1970), *Challenge for Survival*. New York: Columbia University Press, 235 p.
Dyke, James W., Jr. (1972), "The Use of Zoning Laws to Prevent Poor People from Moving into Suburbia," 16 *Howard Law Journal*, pp. 351-365.
Finkler, Earl, (1972), "No Growth as a Planning Alternative: A Preliminary Examination of an Emerging Issue," Planning Advisory Service Report No. 283, (Chicago: American Society of Planning Officials), 65 p.
Foley, Donald L. (1963), *Controlling London's Growth–Planning the Great Wen*, 1940-1960. Berkeley: University of California Press. 224 p.
Forrester, Jay W. (1971), *World Dynamics*. Cambridge, Mass.: Wright Allen Press.
Galantay, Erwin, (1968), "Black New Towns," in 49 *Progressive Architecture*, pp. 126-131.
Gruen Gruen & Associates (1972), *Impacts of Growth: An Analytical Framework and Fiscal Examples*. San Francisco, 194 p.
Hartman, Chester W. et al (1972), "Municipal Housing Code Enforcement and Low Income Tenants," unpublished report. Berkeley: Earl Warren Legal Institute.
Heistand, Dale L. (1964). *Economic Growth and Employment Opportunities for Minorities*. New York: Columbia University Press.
Johnson, Warren A. and Hardesty, John eds. (1971), *Economic Growth vs. the Environment*. Belmont, Ca.: Wadsworth Publishing Co. 201 p.
Klein, Rudolf (1972), "Growth and Its Enemies," in 53 *Commentary* (June) pp. 40-44.
Levy, John M. (1972), "Exclusionary Zoning: After the Walls Come Down," 38 *Planning*, (Aug.), pp. 158-160.
Meadows, Donella H. et al. (1972), *The Limits to Growth*. New York: Signet/New American Library, 207 p.
Murray, Bertram G., Jr. (1972) "Continuous Growth or No Growth? What the Ecologists can teach the Economists," *New York Times Magazine*, Dec. 10.
Muth, Richard F. (1969), *Cities and Housing: The Spatial Pattern of Urban Residential Land Use*. Chicago: University of Chicago Press.
Nelson, Richard R. (1965) *Economic Growth and Poverty*. Santa Monica: The RAND Corporation, P-3082, 13 p.
New York Times (1972), "Study Finds Incomes More Unequal," Dec. 27.
Passell, Peter and Ross, Leonard (1972), "Don't Knock the $2-Trillion Economy," *New York Times Magazine*, March 5.
———, (1973), *The Retreat from Riches: Affluence and Its Enemies*. New York: Viking Press.
RAND Corporation (1971), "Alternate Growth Strategies for San Jose: Initial Report of the Rand Urban Policy Analysis Project," Santa Monica: RAND. 111 p. Reprinted in U.S. Congress (1972a), pp. 151-267.
Richardson, Harry W. (1972), "Optimality in City Size, System of Cities and Urban Policy: A Skeptic's View," 9 *Urban Studies*, pp. 29-48.
Rodwin, Lloyd (1970), *Nation and Cities*, Boston: Houghton Mifflin. 395 p.
Rodwin, Lloyd and Susskind, Lawrence E. (1971), "New Communities and Urban Growth Strategies," paper originally entitled "Evaluating Alternative New Community Plans," presented to AIA Conference on New Communities, Washington, D.C. p.5.
Rybeck, Walter, (1969), "How the Property Tax Can be Modernized to Encourage Housing Construction, Rehabilitation and Repair," Washington, D.C.: The Urban Institute, photocopy.
Ryder, Norman B., (1973), "Two Cheers for ZPG," in *Daedalus*, "The No Growth Society," forthcoming.
Schelling, Thomas C. (1971), "On the Ecology of Micro-Motives," *Public Interest*, Fall, pp. 61-98.
U.S. Congress, (1971a), Senate Committee on Interior and Insular Affairs, Hearings on "National Land Use Policy," 92nd Congress, 1st Session.
———, (1972a), House Committee on Banking and Currency, "National Growth Policy" *Papers* submitted to Subcommittee on Housing, 92nd Congress, 2d Session.
———, (1972b), House Committee on Banking and Currency, "National Growth Policy" Hearings before Subcommittee on Housing, 92d Congress, 2d Session.
———, (1972c), Senate Committee on Interior and Insular Affairs, "Background Papers on Past and Pending Legislation and the Roles of the Executive Branch, Congress and the States in Land Use Policy and Planning," 92d Congress, 2d Session.
Strong, Ann L. (1971) in testimony, U.S. Congress (1971a), p. 347.
———, (1972) *Planned Urban Environments*. London: The Johns Hopkins Press. 406 p.
Wattenberg, Ben (1970), "The Nonsense Explosion," in *The New Republic*, April 4.
Wren, Christopher S. (1973), "I've Got Mine Jack—Environmentalism, Colorado Style," *New York Times Magazine*, March 11.

Bibliography Note

Michael Agelasto and Patricia Perry have prepared an exchange bibliography (No. 519) titled "The No-Growth Controversy" (January 1974), available from the Council of Planning Librarians. (Most of the excellent items are also included in the special bibliographies included in this book.)

CHAPTER SIX

ISSUES IN EXCLUSIONARY LAND USE

One of the most significant—and yet strikingly-neglected—areas of land use controls and growth management, is concerned with the various equity/social and discriminatory/exclusionary side-effects of local land use regulatory and planning systems.

Planning which takes into account "social" [including housing] needs is certainly one of the least well-developed disciplines of the planning "profession." Though social needs appears on nearly all municipal department checklists of items "to be considered," seldom does it play a central or predominant role in the development and administration of communities' comprehensive plans and land use controls.

Social planning—in terms of analyzing various exclusionary effects of the local systems—to the extent that it is undertaken at all, is usually handled minimally, and then, often only in terms of limited perspectives: (a) to meet some pressing needs of a narrow segment of a community's already-resident population, when such needs readily cannot be ignored due to deplorable conditions not politically tolerable, or because deteriorating sections of the municipality (such as delapidated housing and commercial structures) affect the municipality's economic self-interest; (b) to "salvage" strong land use and planning controls by "plugging in" [usually miniscule] low-income-housing-"program"-or-"bonus-system" elements . . . in order to allow the controls currently exercised or being planned to survive any potential legal challenges which might be based on claims of exclusion or discrimination.

This type of negative/preventive housing and social planning—many commentators would agree—borders on public-interest and general-welfare deception. Yet the profession seems to be doing little to rectify the situation by recommending methodologies and means of instituting appropriate public planning procedures, or by providing adequate guidance as to the equity considerations regarding use of the police powers. This type of professional education and information responsibility is badly needed.

The chapter begins with a comment and research bibliography by **Randall Scott**, who sees "locational segregation" in housing—occurring either in effect or by intent—as inevitably involving "severe curtailment of individual rights, freedoms, and constitutional guarantees." But this statement—while certainly a part of the basis for most court challenges dealing with exclusionary effects of land use practices—is one with which many [defendant] municipal attorneys might disagree; at least in terms of the facts of the case, and what constitutes invalid exclusion.

The author states his primary thesis as follows: "It is the assertion of this comment that where the powers of government have been used to effectuate discrimination or exclusion—albeit at times not altogether intentionally—then the resultant practices must be judged as unconstitutional, and measures must be taken to institute just and equitable housing and land use practices." The practices so identified, "which can lead to exclusionary/discriminatory results with respect to equitable opportunities in housing," are in chart form, so that the reader can make reference to "categories" of types of exclusionary practices.

It is suggested that most communities will seek to present "an entire litany of defenses" to "substantiate" the validity of their control efforts. One such subtle, and admittedly complicated, defense is the purposeful pursuit of "a course of minimal capital expenditures in the past." This is an excuse which is used, in turn, to obscure what Scott claims is the community's "affirmative obligation to meet new growth repercussions and housing needs which come at later stages in the evolution of that community."

The author asserts a second major thesis: that there should be, or must eventually develop, a "positive, affirmative responsibility of governments to recognize their duty to absorb a fair share of regional growth and housing needs; to plan and provide for the supportive municipal/public infrastructure; and to plan and regulate land use such that regional housing needs—in the broadest sense of the meaning of "housing," as more than mere physical shelter, are fairly and expeditiously met."

Scott concludes with a critical point . . . one with which other observers would split significantly as to its validity: that of the "regional" context of local, unilaterally-pursued planning and zoning. [This point, also made in the original AIP paper in 1972, has found some momentum in several courts recently. It is, however, not a widely-accepted principle.] The dilemma is restated as follows: "The issue inexorably returns to the question of whether a community has the unilateral right to determine its rate of growth and the housing which it will absorb if the exercise of that governmental authority has negative repercussions on the general welfare and on the meeting of [regional] housing needs."

One anti-exclusion article—relatively well-known due to its publication and dissemination by the American Society of Planning Officials [an effort bearing repetition and eventual expansion by/for the profession]—is that by **Daniel Lauber**, who was on the ASPO staff when the report was published in 1973. In the edited version which appears here, the author quotes an earlier, 1970 ASPO report: "Whatever the motive, if a locality's zoning action results in depriving minorities and low-income persons housing when there is a demonstrable need for such housing, it is considered exclusionary zoning." Lauber then states quite firmly for ASPO: "Due to the recognized invidious effects of exclusionary zoning on the welfare of individuals, communities, regions, and the nation as a whole, ASPO cannot countenance its use."

A prediction is made: "The developing litigation and cases indicate that unless exclusionary communities [which practice exclusion either intentionally or by effect] act affirmatively to meet their duty to ensure that persons of all income levels have access to decent housing within their boundaries, the courts, with a possible assist from state legislatures, will restrict or take away their power to zone locally." As yet, the courts have had only limited success, while the legislatures have not been overly anxious to restrict the use of local powers in order to promote social/equity issues. Instead, state legislatures have tended to intervene with local land use "prerogatives" only in very limited circumstances, such as to protect an environmentally-sensitive or "critical" land area(s).

The question of the exclusionary aspects of land use controls has been, unfortunately, almost universally ignored. This is a situation, and a problem, with which the authors in this chapter are concerned; the probability of finding acceptable and workable solutions, still seems low.

Lauber also proceeds to review the post-1970 litigation in the state and federal courts building on the discussion of pre-1970 litigation from the earlier ASPO report. [Lauber's specific case decision material has been omitted from these volumes; but included are the general principles, doctrines, and arguments which can be raised in

440

exclusionary zoning briefs: the material thus makes for a handy reference, short course on the legal issues, for planners and others.] The author closes with two, relatively hopeful conclusions regarding the courts. Perhaps overstated, they are partly qualified by Lauber's observation that the courts are but one avenue for providing answers. He believes that: "continuation of the past judicial approach will eventually result in all exclusionary provisions being struck down on a case-by-case basis. . . . [C]ombined with legislation and administrative procedures that support it, future court decisions can lead to a curtailment, if not complete elimination, of exclusionary zoning."

The difficulty is, however, that many courts are not sympathetic to affording this type of review, nor are they generally applying the legal doctrine in ways which would accomplish the desirable overall objective of effectively eliminating exclusionary land use practices. Moreover, clear and fully persuasive evidence of exclusionary effects —sufficient to bring the challenge under the cover of equal protection or other theories—may be difficult to establish and particularly determinations for local ordinances and planning.

In this area the courts—as well as the planning profession and public officials—must be educated and convinced of the relevance, weight, and veracity of arguments such as those presented in this chapter, if there is to be any reality to the belief that, in fact, exclusionary zoning can be curtailed.

In the third article, **Williams, Doughty, and Potter** discuss exclusionary practices, and note that there are conflicts between housing and other community values. Environmental values, according to the authors, consist of two main types: "basic environmental values" (such as critical or environmentally-sensitive lands) and the mere "maintenance of amenities." Thus, they conclude that: "if the only way to get the needed housing is by sacrificing this second type of environmental values, they will have to be sacrificed." The authors run into the dilemma of communities utilizing their police powers for purposes of exclusion, for protecting perceived "amenities," and for preserving some preconceptions of supposedly monolithic "community attitudes." Moreover, the article in effect suggests a major disagreement with a [later 1974] U.S. Supreme Court case: *Village of Belle Terre v. Boraas. (Belle Terre* is a decision which has been widely criticized for its dubious "reasoning" in regard to land use controls, and the probability that planners and others might be tempted to generalize that nearly "everything goes," given the over-broad holding of the court: "A quiet place where yards are wide, people few, and motor vehicles restricted are legitimate guidelines in a land use project [sic—actually, the community's underlying zoning ordinance and plan] addressed to family needs)."

The article outlines the basic goals, criteria, and strategies available to litigators . . . including the applicable doctrines and the remedies which ought to be considered during preparation of exclusion suits. For example, the article states that in order to fully understand 'housing needs,' "some mechanism will have to be devised which can estimate the total extent of such need"—a problem with which plaintiffs will have to deal, according to the author, if the courts are even to attempt to deal with these challenges. Moreover, in dealing with housing needs, "a realistic definition of housing must cover more than a single municipality. The housing market is regional or subregional in scope. . . ."

The authors ascertain that it is not very useful to pursue exclusion suits where the result is only "a decree and a rationale invalidating only one type of exclusionary control." They insist that: "such a suit must be designed to establish something akin to a regional process for housing, under judicial goading and continuing judicial supervision." [This comment in effect reiterates the jurisprudential difficulties noted earlier, such as delineating the "proper" judicial review function and its "appropriate" scope.]

The authors cite the arguments usually stated against broad judicial intervention, but still conclude that the courts should take an active role even if on an incremental, case-by-case basis. While the authors recognize that this may leave the judiciary open to criticism that it is "legislating," they find nevertheless that "this is not a normal situation. The problem is that the legislatures are presently paralyzed . . . it is not reasonable to expect legislatures to take the initiative . . . [nor is it] realistic to depend on the good faith reaction . . . [of these various agencies and other persons] in carrying out implementation."

Clearly, plaintiffs in such cases must undertake significant data research, must prepare the doctrinal development carefully, and must propose effective remedies. In the latter regard, both the school desegregation and the reapportionment lines of cases offer parallel examples for the courts in entering into this difficult—but perhaps necessarily judicial—political thicket. [In conjunction with the previous article by Lauber, these discussions of doctrine and judicial roles should be of interest and use to planners and public officials.]

Professors **Haar and Iatridis** raise a number of questions which are relevant to Williams' reflections regarding the appropriate place of the courts in dealing with questions of land use and exclusion. The first several pages of the article [edited from a recently published book] deal with exclusionary practices in general, and with typical "suburbia's life-style and its 'American Dream' . . . [consequently,] realistically, individuals at the local level cannot be expected to make their decisions readily on the basis of abstract values or public objectives, even though such imperatives flow from their duties to provide equal treatment to all under the Fourteenth Amendment. . . . [T]he problem is deeply embedded in the structure of our society and its social institutions."

A series of particularly pertinent questions are then levelled at the reader: significant issues which are both central to "abstract" jurisprudence, and yet are pragmatic in content: "What can the court say about legally enforced banning of economic classes and racial groups from the suburbs, and what can it say about states' rights overriding local ordinances? How directly can a judge probe into the motives of coordinate branches of government? And with what tools and expertise? . . . Court orders and decisions are important, but how far can they move ahead of accepted mores and traditions?" The testy issues continue: Are all of the interested parties to the exclusion conflict fairly represented in such suits? Can or should the court be an agent of change? How ably can an attorney—"even donning judicial robes"—cope with, and weigh, the needs, programs, plans, and a reasonable process of coordination and implementation for an entire region?

The article concludes, quite correctly, that there exists a major new area of research problems (and a need for careful study information): that "fresh perspectives on the role of the judiciary and of the separation of powers are in order."

The last articles in this chapter explain how two courts in New Jersey—a progressive judicial state in terms of exclusionary zoning doctrine—dealt with several exclusion challenges. The material has been inserted in these volumes even though it involves lower state court decisions, due to the unique manner in which the problem was addressed and resolved; the cases are instructive both as to the non-traditional analyses, and as to the non-necessity for courts or litigants to be limited by the "usual" manner for the judiciary to maneuver in such complex fields.

Judge Furman, of the Superior Court of New Jersey, revisits a case which has been before him twice in the last three years. In 1971, he found himself "plunged into a milieu" and into a decision where, of necessity, he "broke ground, out of conscience and out of conviction." In that decision, he made one of the most potentially influential findings [if adopted and followed as precedent] in recent exclusionary land use case law, with his statements relating to the concepts of the general welfare and of regional interests: "In pursuing the valid zoning purpose of a balanced community, a municipality must not ignore housing needs, that is, its fair proportion of the obligation to meet the housing needs of its own population and of the region. Housing needs are encompassed within the general welfare. The general welfare does not stop at each municipal boundary."

The above statement might well be subject to significant judicial and public policy debate in the years to come. In his second opinion [also reproduced in part at the end of his article], Furman clarifies two points in his 1971 decision: (a) what constitutes the "region" of and for evaluating housing needs; and, (b) what was and is the town's fair proportion of such needs (?).

Admitting that his decision constituted "a jump" in judicial thinking in this area, he says he nevertheless had to declare the town's ordinance to be invalid "because it failed to provide for the township's fair share of housing to meet the housing shortage. Whatever general welfare benefits might be served within the township by population limitations [the conceded objective], these were overridden and the general welfare, which does not stop at the Madison Township border, was in balance thwarted by exclusionary restrictions."

Noting that as a judge, he also has often quoted the old "shibboleths" that normally lead to upholding a municipality's activities as valid, in this case he found them to be unconvincing. He concludes as follows: "I submit that the issue has been recognized judicially and must persist: whether local zoning provides for each municipality's fair share of its region's new housing needs including new low and moderate income housing needs. I submit that zoning ordinances which fall palpably short of that standard, in the absence of special and overriding environmental and ecological factors, will be struck down by the court as unconstitutionally indefensible."

In still another New Jersey case—*Washington Township*—**Levin and Rose** were selected as expert aides to the court in drafting a plan as the basis for an order regarding an exclusionary community. The authors suggest that there are several important principles involved in this case: the concept of regional allocation; the need to combine the "skills of a planner and an attorney . . . in land use litigation"; and, the continuing attitude-equity conflict which "suggests the struggle over social and racial integration in the suburbs will be very long. It will not be simply and clearly resolved by court order; instead we are in for much more litigation involving costly, slow, technically sophisticated argumentation."

In *Washington Township*, Judge George Gelman was faced with a locality which obviously was seeking to "find a way around" an earlier court order. He thus had the choice of declaring the ordinance invalid; of determining "that the judicial branch is powerless to provide any relief"; or, of taking the course of "retain[ing] planning consultants to recommend the form of zoning relief appropriate under the circumstances— which would be a very novel approach. . . . " This use of a consultant lawyer/planner team, with the imposition of an order which depended upon the findings of these experts, has parallels in other areas of case law. But in terms of land use controls cases per se, this method might be both unusual, and worth the attention of jurists and litigators.

It would appear at least to have the advantage of providing expertise and assistance to the judge, who is of necessity, limited in his opportunities to study thoroughly issues and to formulate recommendations and orders. Moreover, the method certainly is a useful alternative, or a supplement, to the practice of having the prevailing side prepare proposed findings and orders for the court. [What continues to be absolutely necessary, of course, is for the judge not to bypass his own opportunity for independent evaluation of the case material and the information provided by the experts, before his final determination is made.]

Finally, the authors find that: "In our opinion, the courts and the legislatures will find it exceedingly difficult to reconcile the constitutionally protected freedom of movement with the protection and conservation of viable neighborhoods." Implicitly therefore, if the courts are to be brought into the forefront of handling these problems, they must be innovative, and must discover new modes of analysis and techniques for assistance . . . if they are to proceed at all capably through the morass of evidentiary and other problems in exclusionary litigation.

—**RWS**

Exclusion and Land Use:

A Comment and a Research Bibliography

Randall W. Scott

Randall Scott is editor of these volumes.

He wishes to acknowledge the significant assistance of Mr. William N. Myhre in aiding and checking the accuracy and completeness of the bibliography. Myhre, a ULI Research Intern for the summer of 1974, is a student in the joint graduate planning and law degree(s) program at the University of Pennsylvania.

This comment and bibliography appeared in a 1974 publication entitled "Fair Housing & Exclusionary Land Use," with the historical overview and summary of litigation [main article] by the National Committee Against Discrimination in Housing. (The publication is available for $3.50 [including postage] from NCDH, 1425 H Street, N.W., Washington, D.C. 20005.) This comment reflects, in part, a paper prepared for presentation to the American Institute of Planners Confer-In '72 and 1973 policy conference; a short version (on which this article is based) appeared in the October 1973 HUD Challenge magazine.

Introduction

America historically has been a nation pressed by the troubling issues of racial discrimination, unequal distribution of income, and major housing problems/inequities. But increasingly and most recently, this country has begun to see these difficulties reflected more and more in terms of various patterns of locational segregation and fragmentation, and in the loss of housing opportunities for certain groups within our society.

Locational segregation based on income levels and/or racial characteristics almost inevitably involves severe curtailment of individual rights, freedoms, and constitutional guarantees. It thus becomes insufficient to set the goal of a "decent" unit of housing for every American if the end result maintains or does little to discourage patterns of locational segregation. It is obvious that no longer may we be interested merely in "adequate" housing and in total numerical goals.

In the past, as planners and governmental officials we have been concerned primarily with projections of housing production, the quality of existing housing stock, and the cost-availability of housing units. Even with regard to the latter, we have tended to do or to accomplish relatively little—particularly where the political climate has dictated inaction (and especially since the cessation of the federal housing subsidy programs). But even so, most of these considerations have tended to neglect a primary factor of housing and social planning: the question of housing *location*.

Housing and Its Meaning/Impact

We are learning that housing, if placed in the proper context, means far more than "shelter" and its attendant physical facilities. It includes or involves:
- man's functioning and social well being;
- a living environment designed to take into account social, recreational, and ecological needs or factors;
- location in proximity to employment centers, with convenient, inexpensive, and efficient transportation to job markets;
- availability of adequate educational facilities;
- provision of municipal services on an equal basis (see the well-known "Shaw" case);
- easy access to commercial areas and entertainment centers;
- the right to live in the type of housing desired or affordable, without unreasonable restrictions imposed on the supply of such units (as apartments v. single-family); and,
- equality of opportunity, such that an individual's income level or race does not automatically preclude him from seeking or obtaining the housing that he needs, and in the community or area he chooses.

Thus when we speak of housing, we must recognize its repercussions on equity; equality; mobility—economic and social, as well as geographical; and the pursuit of individual life styles. Unfortunately in the past, these rights and guarantees have been interfered with or misshaped by local governments via exclusionary land use practices.

Underlying these practices have been several reinforcing strands of institutional development and power orientation that have helped produce the current inequality-in-housing-location dilemma. It is well-documented, for example, that there has been an accelerating pattern of higher income emigration from central cities; this, and such factors as land and transportation costs have tended to isolate lower income groups and to insulate the more mobile and well-to-do segments of the population.

Likewise, the evolution of the city has set a tone in many metropolitan areas from which suburbanites have sought escape. This has been reinforced by an attitude that outer-urban home-ownership is a desirable life style to which to aspire. In self-fulfilling prophecy, suburbia has become a haven from the city: a city which increasingly is being viewed as a caldron of the poor, the elderly, the minorities, and the underemployed.

Another issue involves the concepts of the powers, duties, and responsibilities of the various units of government—and primarily, in the interpretation and scope of the general police power. In relation to housing, this has been especially notable with respect to land use controls and planning regulations, which affect what historically had been the nearly sacrosanct privileges associated with private property.

And finally, we have retained to a large degree the concept of local self-government, where local governments have been delegated and have exercised the police power of the state to (supposedly) provide for and preserve the general welfare. As a result, we have seen the development of a set of fragmented and nearly autonomous local government units which exercise a full panoply of powers that profoundly affect land use and the provision of housing.

Unintentional Exclusion Still Unconstitutional?

In certain jurisdictions, this ideological heritage has coalesced into the syndrome of "an exclusionary suburb is a man's castle." It is the assertion of this comment that where the powers of government have been used to effectuate discrimination or exclusion —albeit at times not altogether intentionally—then the resultant practices must be judged as unconstitutional, and measures must be taken to institute just and equitable housing and land use policies.

The rubric "exclusionary land use practices" as used here involves a relatively wide spectrum of public and private stratagems which lead to unacceptable repercussions on housing opportunities. Many of the various factors which are capable of abuse are noted in a matrix in this article, for ease of conceptual reference. It should be noted that this list is based upon exclusionary results, and not simply by whether or not there was a pre-existing intent to exclude/discriminate.

At the same time, the matrix reflects the rather artificial distinctions which some public officials have made in the past (for example, most courts unfortunately have hesitated to find certain practices unconstitutional unless there have been the dual elements of "intent" and of "racial" discrimination). Occasionally some of the especially flagrant practices in the other five "categories" [besides race and intent] have been attacked and overturned. In such categories, however, generally the courts have found the cause and effect relationships more complex, and the practices have seemed to be intermingled with what superficially have appeared to be "sound" planning and public or private decision-making. Unless properly argued by plaintiffs, many courts thus have been reluctant to substitute judicial judgment for local "legislative" determinations.

As an example, multifamily housing frequently is excluded on the basis of sophisticated infrastructure justifications or environmental claims. This occurs most notably when a municipality insists that further development will not be allowed due to water and sewer facility limitations. In fact, the community actually may be avoiding the more painful problem of raising the revenues necessary to improve or expand the public services to required capacities, which is unjustifiable (as several state courts have noted) for it amounts to fiscal zoning: a mis-use of the police power, with pronounced exclusionary results.

Not infrequently, the very same exclusionary community will permit high-cost single-family housing—especially where the builder underwrites facility costs, the expense of which is passed on to the new home buyer—on the basis that the facilities can handle these small incremental increases, or that the fees obtained will "help pay the way." The effect of course, is to exclude low- and moderate-income families from housing in that community.

Practices Which Can Lead to Exclusionary/Discriminatory Results With Respect to Equitable Opportunities in Housing

Exclusion by INTENT— Purposeful Practices

Exclusion by EFFECT— Byproducts of Action

Racial

Civil rights and fair housing violations in sales, leasing, rentals, or advertising; block-busting.

Continued ghetto-area site selection and construction for public/subsidized housing.

Restrictive private covenants or informal agreements re housing and land use, to exclude minorities.

Referenda methods, or administrative refusals, regarding low-income housing development plans or projects.

Existing misconceptions and lack of understanding by the public regarding racial groups, and community/neighborhood consequences as property values, etc.; or outright hostility.

Corporate relocation to outlying areas which lack appropriate housing and transportation facilities (the impact is also felt by non-racial minority, low-income groups); the locating of governmental facilities without housing and employment "tie-ins" (given the commuting capabilities of the work force).

Growth

Building moratoria (variations on the no-growth, close-the-doors approach) where not absolutely essential.

Pursuance of unilateral slow-growth policies in planning, etc., in defiance of or without regional housing need determinations.

Refusal to provide adequate capacity or funding for municipal services, as sewage or water systems.

Issuance of building permits only for high-cost housing which produces high tax ratables and low costs.

Use of environmental excuses (where not clearly valid) to deny building permits, or to greatly limit densities.

Crisis-oriented moratoria, which occur due to lack of prior planning or unwillingness to undertake the expenditures required to correct facility deficiencies.

Lack of housing element in comprehensive planning process, resulting in inability to accommodate needs.

Non-use of funding availability (as Federal/State aids), or of savings due to operating efficiencies (as double school sessions).

Antiquated ordinances, codes, and regulations on local and state levels which effectively cause the market to respond inefficiently or inequitably to housing demand.

Economic

Exclusion by INTENT— Purposeful Practices

Unreasonable large-lot zoning.

Prohibition against multifamily dwellings.

Limitation on number of bedrooms.

Large floor space requirements.

Exorbitant fee-schedules or land dedication requirements.

Low-income housing permit or zoning refusals (see also racial by intent, above).

Exclusion by EFFECT— Byproducts of Action

Additive result of foregoing items effectively escalate costs of finished housing . . . including outmoded building codes, extravagant subdivision regulations, and non-use of efficient innovative design or land use approaches as PUD's, flexible zoning, etc.

Bureaucratic and administrative delays, and undue complexities in processing.

Miscellaneous: unequal municipal services; tax or methods to recover all "public" costs from the new home-buyers via "developer" fees; etc.

"Defenses" Need to be Examined

An entire litany of defenses has been heard from communities which seek to justify the exclusionary decisions at which they arrive. The most familiar involve the preferences of existing residents: preservation of the character of community; protection of property values; and the maintenance of homogeneity of housing types and styles.

A second set of justifications relates to widely held misconceptions about middle- and high-density development: the claims that open space and recreational space will be lost; that the designs will be unaesthetic and environmentally damaging; and that the new units will vastly generate more costs than revenues.

The third series revolves around predictions about the character of the potential residents: that more crime will occur; that the quality of the educational system will be reduced; and that there will be behavior patterns with which the already resident children should not be associated.

A fourth set of defenses poses presumed population and growth consequences: higher property taxes; pedestrian and vehicular congestion; insufficient school capacities; limited municipal financing capability, and inadequate municipal services. (But again it must be asserted that merely because a community has chosen a course of minimal capital expenditures in the past, this should not obscure its affirmative obligation to meet new growth repercussions and housing needs which come at later stages in the evolution of that community.)

Environmental concerns present a fifth set of objections, such as: already "over-burdened" treatment and water ecosystems (which points out the need for expanded federal and state financial assistance to eliminate this element from the exclusion-rationale); or that areas of ecological interest must be preserved in the natural state (a valid excuse capable of abuse; in this regard, a community not infrequently simply ignores development designs which show possible alternatives for reconciling housing needs with valid ecological concerns. A similar set of problems involves local determinations which have not taken into account building innovations, improved land use techniques, or time limitations: antiquated building codes; unrevised enabling legislation or land use classifications [thereby failing to reflect the changing needs and new technology]; and complex and lethargic administrative procedures in the application, hearing, permit or inspection stages [often purposefully utilized to delay or "shelve" development proposals.])

When and if these defenses are challenged in the courts, typically the community explains:

1. that it is operating within its authority under the state statutes for planning and zoning;
2. that it is exercising the police power in a way that is neither clearly arbitrary or capricious;
3. that the decisions made are within the legislative prerogative;
4. that in any event, the reasons for proceeding in the manner chosen are justifiable for the reasons cited [see the above litany]; and,
5. that the plaintiffs cannot demonstrate a clear abrogation of constitutional rights, and have not carried the burden of proof.

Nonetheless, such defenses must be carefully examined and the policies scrutinized for exclusionary results. If we are to find judicious and equitable solutions to the problems of locational segregation in housing, we must broaden our understanding of the inter-relationship between governmental authority and the proper exercise of that power for the general welfare of all citizens.

The General, and the Individual's, Welfare

While it is not surprising to find that a local citizenry will utilize its government to protect what it believes are correct impressions about property values, schools, tax rates, ad infinitum — if there are exclusionary results then there must be a finding that the abuse of governmental authority no longer will be tolerated . . . in the absence of compelling and overwhelming reasons to find otherwise. Land use controls and other related reg-ulatory devices must not serve to deny opportunities to particular segments or levels of society. Instead, it is essential that governmental authority be exercised for the general welfare of all citizens of the region and the state— and not merely to protect the interests of the "resident-elite" who have already arrived in a particular community or suburb.

The problems and issues must be considered and framed in terms of the rights, freedoms, and opportunities of all groups and of all citizens. The question on the other hand, is not one of complete uniformity for all persons, but rather whether any one community has a valid right: to exclude certain persons or to pursue exclusionary policies; to prohibit particular types of residential land uses; to enforce upon prospective residents a certain type or cost-level of housing; or to deny the meeting of regional housing needs because of narrow parochial interests or unilateral local government policies.

In 1926 in the *Euclid* v. *Ambler* case—one of a handful of zoning cases ever to reach the Supreme Court, it was stated "In the ordinance now under review, and all similar laws and regulations, must find their justification in some aspect of the police power, asserted for the public welfare." It is an underlying assertion of this comment that where land use practices have unconscionable exclusionary effects or results, they fail this public/ general welfare test: that in the words of the *Euclid* court, such practices would constitute cases where ". . . the general public interest would so far outweigh the interest of the municipality that the municipality would not be allowed to stand in the way."

It should be clear that where communities are allowed to follow unilateral exclusionary policies—in pursuance of seemingly valid planning ideals, and under the guise of the state police power—these practices severely and adversely affect the quantity, quality, cost, location, and equitable opportunities of decent housing in this country. In operation and total effect, exclusionary practices are detrimental both to individual rights and to the public interest and the general welfare—in contravention of State and Federal constitutions.

Affirmative Responsibilities of Local Governments

Government units must begin to acknowledge that the answer lies beyond the essentially negative obligation only to refrain from engaging in exclusion and discrimination. Rather, it must be a positive affirmative responsibility of governments to recognize their duty to absorb a fair share of regional growth and housing needs; to plan and provide for the supportive municipal/public infrastructure; and to plan and regulate land use such that regional housing needs—in the broadest sense—are fairly and expeditiously met.

Much of the doctrine surrounding the locational-exclusion problem is derived from litigation and court opinions; until just the past decade, many of the arguments were as yet poorly formulated, or were not recognized by the courts or legislatures. In 1965, the landmark case of *National Land and Investment Co.* v. *Easttown Board of Adjustment* found the Pennsylvania Supreme Court saying:

> The question posed is whether the township can stand in the way of the several forces which send our growing population into hither-to undeveloped areas in search of a comfortable place to live. We have concluded not. A zoning ordinance whose primary purpose is to prevent the entrance of newcomers in order to avoid future burdens, economic or otherwise, upon the administration of public services and facilities cannot be held valid . . . . Zoning is a tool in the hands of governmental bodies which . . . must not and cannot be used by those officials as an instrument by which they may shirk their responsibilities.

In a string of cases, Pennsylvania reiterated this position. In 1970 in *In re Girsh*, the court stated:

> . . . Township may not permissibly choose to only take as many people as can live in single-family housing, in effect freezing population near present levels . . . if Nether Providence is a logical place for development to take place, it should not be heard to say that it will not bear its rightful part of the burden.

And in *In re Kit-Mar Builders (1970)*, it was added: "It is not for any given township to say who may or may not live within its confines, while disregarding the interests of the entire area."

A number of victories were also won in the courts in New Jersey in the 1970s. Some of the most far-reaching decisions were in *Oakwood at Madison* v. *Township of Madison* and in *NAACP* v. *Township of Mount Laurel*, which suggest an expansion of the doctrine that a community must exercise its zoning powers in pursuit of the general welfare: clearly encompassing regional—and not just local—housing needs. Most recently—in the *Petaluma* case—a federal district court stated the following:

> It is appropriate to measure the potential effects that the exclusion practiced by Petaluma would have if it proliferated throughout the region itself. . . . [M]ay a municipality capable of support-ing a natural population expansion limit growth simply because it does not prefer to grow at the rate which would be dictated by prevailing market demand[?] It is our opinion that it may not. . . . A zoning regulation which has as its purpose the exclusion of additional residents in any degree is not a compelling governmental interest, nor is it one within the public welfare.

The court concluded by finding the town's plans and ordinances unconstitutional as being in violation of the right to travel. It retained jurisdiction for the purpose of scrutinizing later actions, appointing a special master to assist the court. The case now is on appeal.

Other Forums Must Take Responsibility

But the battle against exclusionary land use practices cannot be fought exclusively in the courtroom arena; the litigation process is not the only, nor even necessarily the best, or most effective, means of meeting the locational segregation dilemma. Various other methodologies have been attempted throughout the country. The most commonly cited is the Massachusetts Anti-Snob Zoning Law (Chapter 774) which permits appeals under certain conditions to a state board when local communities fail to approve comprehen-sive permits for low-income housing. In New York, the Urban Development Corporation approach has managed to weather most of the opposition and to achieve a modicum of success. In Pennsylvania, a novel opinion of the Attorney General provided for funding cut-offs of state recreational grants where communities engaged in exclusionary tactics. And in still other areas, state housing finance or development authorities have been instituted.

But as a minimum, it is herein suggested that *States* in the future take at least five steps:
(1) amend state enabling legislation to specifically prohibit exclusionary land use prac-tices by intent or effect by local communities;
(2) survey state land use and planning laws, including the forthcoming American Law Institute Model Land Development Code, and determine what revisions if any should be made to the state statutes;
(3) require that all communities make housing needs an express part of the comprehen-sive planning process;
(4) encourage the preparation of "social and economic impact statements" whenever major governmental decisions are proposed, to judge housing and other socio-economic effects (in addition to the usual physical-environmental impacts); and,
(5) require that the housing element in local community planning be designed to relate to regional low- and moderate-income housing and growth needs, in furtherance of the general welfare of the region and of the state.

Regional approaches have included the regional planning and review agency concept and the regional fair share plan, as in Dayton; both have enjoyed only limited success. If the regional concept is to be at all effective, the scope and procedure of review authority must be more clearly defined (including a plan for regional housing planning and review), and state and federal incentives/disincentives must legitimatize such regional review authority.

Unfortunately, there generally has been a lack of firm leadership emanating from either the State or the Federal levels; in part, this ambiguity reflects an unwillingness to live with the political consequences of intensified housing and planning requirements. Far too often, there has been a retreat from handling these issues in all but the most blatant cases of racial discrimination.

Philosophically, government appears unwilling to establish firm policy, guidance, and support relative to the equal opportunity/exclusion/discrimination issues in housing and land use, even though its potential arsenal for dealing with these problems is immense. (A-95 and 701 have been sparse beginnings in this direction.)

Since the first housing act in 1934, there has been evolving a thrust toward the development of a *national* housing policy: that of the mandated responsibility of government to provide adequate housing for all persons. Yet it has been shown time and again that exclusionary land use practices serve to frustrate the fulfillment of this national objective. As a first stage toward countering such practices, there must be developed a meaningful national urban growth policy, and a valid report on housing goals. If they are to be at all useful, these documents must not only recognize the scope of the exclusion problem, but must suggest alternative means for eliminating existing inequities. Eventual federal legislation must be backed by workable, effective administrative mechanisms —including adequate funding of planning, regional agencies, and municipal infrastructure facilities. To this must be added efficient and effective enforcement and disincentive methodologies.

Conclusion: Issues for the 70s

Two topics can be expected to occupy the attention of municipal and other governmental officials to an increasing extent. Both, for reasons previously cited, can tend to have widespread exclusionary effects—and therefore, must be carefully and constantly evaluated and monitored as to adverse effects on housing and land use.

The first problem area is that of environmental issues, where there is some danger of rhetoric becoming confused with valid planning—resulting in regulations and standards which unduly escalate the cost of homes, prohibit building, or become the basis of a refusal to accommodate growth needs. The real challenge is to recognize "actual" environmental dilemmas, and then to suggest wherever possible the mitigative socio-economic—as well as physical—policy actions/programs that must be undertaken.

The second major issue is the burgeoning "no-growth" or "slow-growth" movement, and the accompanying revolution in land use controls: including "phased growth" or "timed development" methodologies. It has been and will continue to become increasingly difficult to sift spurious objections from valid concerns, and proper land use regulation from unilateral discrimination and exclusion.

The issue inexorably returns to the question of whether a community has the unilateral right to determine its rate of growth and the housing which it will absorb if the exercise of that governmental authority has negative repercussions on the general welfare and on the meeting of housing needs.

Inevitably, the debate over exclusionary practices, housing, land use, growth, and the environment will be major focuses of government over at least the remainder of the decade. In turn, we must address the extremely difficult tasks of designing safeguards, guidelines, and mechanisms that will operate effectively to help ensure equitable and proper housing opportunities for all of our nation's residents and citizens.

Research Bibliography

Note to Reader:
Law review and other journal citations have the following format: the volume number precedes the title of the journal or the law review, the page number follows the title, and the year of publication is listed last.

Ackerman, Bruce L. "Integration for Subsidized Housing and the Question of Racial Occupancy Controls," 26 *Stanford Law Review* 245 (1974).

Adams, Robert B. "Minimum Lot Area Requirements in New York," 21 *Intramural Law Review of New York University* 24 (1965).

Adang, Peter J. "Snob Zoning: A Look at the Economic and Social Impact of Low Density Zoning," 15 *Syracuse Law Review* 507 (1964).

Advisory Commission on Intergovernmental Relations. *Urban and Rural America: Policies for Future Growth.* Washington, D.C.: Government Printing Office, 1968.

"Again—President Nixon Avoids the Hard Line on Forcing Housing Integration," *House & Home,* July 1971, p. 4.

Agelasto, Michael A., II. "No Growth and the Poor: Equity Considerations in Controlled Growth Policies," 9 *Planning Comment* 2 (Spring 1973).

Allen, H. William, III. "Restriction of Building Permits as a Means for Controlling the Rate of Community Development," 1969 *Urban Law Annual* 184 (1969).

Aloi, Frank and Arthur A. Goldberg. "Racial and Economic Exclusionary Zoning: The Beginning of the End?" 1971 *Urban Law Annual* 9 (1971).

Aloi, Frank A., Arthur A. Goldberg, and James M. White. "Racial and Economic Segregation by Zoning: Death Knell for Home Rule?" 1 *Toledo Law Review* 65 (1969).

Anderson, John. "Environmental Considerations: New Arguments for Large-Lot Zoning," 7 *Urban Law Annual* 370 (1974).

Anderson, Robert M. *American Law of Zoning: Zoning, Planning, Subdivision Control.* Rochester, New York: Lawyers Cooperative Publishing Company, 1968.

Anderson, Robert M. "Provincialism and the Public Interest," 5 *Federation Planning Information,* Report 1 (New Jersey Federation of Planning Officials, 1308 Wood Valley Rd., Mountainside, New Jersey; 1970).

"Another Theory of Residential Segregation," *Land Economics,* August 1971, p. 314.

"The Attack on Snob Zoning: Government Forces Move Against Land Use Controls that Shut Out the Less Affluent, Thwart Builders Already Hard-pressed to Meet Housing Demand," *Savings and Loan News,* November 1970, p. 30.

Aumente, Jerome. "Domestic Land Reform," *City,* January/February 1971, p. 56.

Babcock, Richard F. "The Courts Enter the Land Development Marketplace," *City,* January/February 1971, p. 64.

Babcock, Richard F. "*Sanbornton and Morales:* The Two Faces of 'Environment,'" 2 *Environmental Affairs* 758 (1973).

Babcock, Richard F. "Suburban Zoning, Housing and the Courts," 27 *The Record of the Association of the Bar of the City of New York* 230 (1972).

Babcock, Richard F. "A Watershed in Suburban Zoning," *HUD Challenge,* November 1972, p. 8.

Babcock, Richard F. *The Zoning Game: Municipal Practices and Policies.* Madison, Wisconsin: University of Wisconsin Press, 1966.

Babcock, Richard F. and Fred P. Bosselman. *Exclusionary Zoning: Land Use Regulation and Housing in the 1970s.* New York: Praeger Publishers, 1973.

Babcock, Richard F. and Fred P. Bosselman. "Suburban Zoning and the Apartment Boom," 111 *University of Pennsylvania Law Review* 1040 (1963).

Babcock, Richard F. and Clifford C. Weaver. "Exclusionary Suburban Zoning: One More Black Rebuff to the Latest Liberal Crusade," in *The Urban Scene in the Seventies.* James F. Blumstein and Eddie J. Martin, eds., Nashville, Tennessee: Vanderbilt University, 1974.

Bailey, Phyllis P. "Constitutional Law—Equal Protection—Zoning Ordinance Limiting Occupancy of Single Family Homes to Legal Families or Not More than Two Unrelated Persons Held Unconstitutional," 48 *Tulane Law Review* 412 (1974).

Bangs, Frank S., Jr., ed. *Land Use Law & Zoning Digest* (formerly, *Zoning Digest*). Periodical of the American Society of Planning Officials; monthly review of litigation and legislation. Chicago: ASPO.

Barr, MacDonald. *The Massachusetts Zoning Appeals Law: Lessons of the First Three Years.* Mimeographed. Submitted for Presentation at Confer-In '72, American Institute of Planners Annual Conference, Boston.

Bartke, Richard W. and Hilda R. Gage. "Mobile Homes: Zoning and Taxation," 55 *Cornell Law Review* 491 (1970).

Bass, G. Allen. "The Equal Protection Clause: A Single-edged Sword for the Gordian Knot of Exclusionary Zoning," 40 *University of Missouri-Kansas City Law Review* 24 (1971).

"The Battle for Apartments in Benign Suburbia: A Case of Judicial Lethargy," 59 *Northwestern University Law Review* 345 (1964).

"Battle to Open the Suburbs: New Attack on Zoning Laws," *U.S. News & World Report,* June 22, 1970, p. 39.

Exclusion and Land Use

"Battle of the Suburbs," *Newsweek*, November 15, 1971, p. 61.

Becker, David M. "Police Power and Minimum Lot Size Zoning—Part I: A Method of Analysis," 1969 *Washington University Law Quarterly* 263 (1969).

Bellman, Richard F. *Applicability of Employment Nondiscrimination Laws to Corporate Location and Relocation in Suburbia.* Mimeographed. Washington, D.C.: National Committee Against Discrimination in Housing, 1971.

Bellman, Richard F. *Summary of Recent Court Challenges to Exclusionary Land Use Practices.* Mimeographed. Washington, D.C.: National Committee Against Discrimination in Housing, 1972. (Supersedes 1971 version; later, superseded by NCDH and ULI publication, 1974. See NCDH and ULI, *Fair Housing*.)

Benoit, M. Deborah. "Expanding Protection Against Blockbusters Through the First Amendment," 7 *Urban Law Annual* 319 (1974).

Bergin, Thomas F. "Price-Exclusionary Zoning: A Social Analysis," 47 *St. John's Law Review* 1 (1972).

Bergman, Edward M. *Eliminating Zoning.* Cambridge, Massachusetts: Ballinger Publishing Co., 1974.

Bigham, W. Harold and C. Dent Bostick. "Exclusionary Zoning Practices: An Examination of the Current Controversy," 25 *Vanderbilt Law Review* 1111 (1972).

Black, Gilbert J. "Flight to Suburbia," *Commonweal*, January 21, 1972, p. 364.

Blank, Benson. "Time Control, Sequential Zoning: The Ramapo Case," 25 *Baylor Law Review* 318 (1973).

Blumrosen, Alfred W., et al. *Enforcing Fair Housing Laws: Apartments in White Suburbia.* Springfield, Virginia: National Technical Information Service, 1970.

Blumrosen, Alfred W. and James H. Blair, *Enforcing Equality in Housing and Employment Through State Civil Rights Laws.* Woodbridge, New Jersey: Appellate Printing Company, 1973.

Bonham, Gordon S. "Discrimination and Housing Quality," *Growth and Change*, October 1972, p. 26.

Bosselman, Fred P. "Can the Town of Ramapo Pass a Law to Bind the Rights of the Whole World?" 1 *Florida State University Law Review* 265 (1973).

Bowe, William J. "Regional Planning versus Decentralized Land-use Controls—Zoning for the Megalopolis," 18 *De Paul Law Review* 144 (1968).

Branfman, Eric J., Benjamin I. Cohen and David M. Trubek. "Measuring the Invisible Wall: Land Use Controls and the Residential Patterns of the Poor," 82 *The Yale Law Journal* 483 (1973).

"Breaking the Noose: Suburban Zoning and the Urban Crisis," 36 *Social Action* 3 (1970).

Brooks, Mary E. "Bills Introduced to Prohibit Exclusionary Zoning," *Planning*, May 1971, p. 63.

Brooks, Mary E. *Exclusionary Zoning.* Planning Advisory Service Report No. 254. Chicago: American Society of Planning Officials, 1970.

Brooks, Mary E. *Lower Income Housing: The Planners' Response.* Planning Advisory Service Report No. 282. Chicago: American Society of Planning Officials, 1972.

Brooks, Mary E. *Mandatory Dedication of Land or Fees-In-Lieu of Land for Parks and Schools.* Planning Advisory Service Report No. 266. Chicago: American Society of Planning Officials, 1971.

Brown, William H., Samuel C. Jackson and John H. Powell, Jr. *Open or Closed Suburb: Corporate Location and the Urban Crisis.* White Plains, New York: Suburban Action Institute, 1971.

Burchell, Robert W., David Listokin and George Sternlieb. *Open or Closed Communities? The Suburban Exclusionary Zoning Problem.* New Brunswick, New Jersey: Rutgers University Center for Urban Policy Research, forthcoming.

Business Week. Articles in March 28, 1970 (p. 168); July 11, 1970 (p. 61); April 17, 1971 (p. 60); etc.

Catz, Robert S. "Historical and Political Background of Federal Public Housing Programs," 50 *North Dakota Law Review* 25 (1973).

Chapman, Beth A. "The Constitutional Implications of a Restrictive Definition of Family in Zoning Ordinances," 17 *South Dakota Law Review* 203 (1972).

Charkoudian, Leon. "Massachusetts' Anti-Snob Zoning Law," *State Government: The Journal of State Affairs* [Council of State Governments], Spring 1972, p. 106.

City. Theme issue on the suburbs [the National Urban Coalition magazine]. January/February 1971.

"Civil Rights—Discrimination in Placement of Low-Rent Housing—Statute's Requirement that Locality's Governing Body Agree to Cooperate with HUD Used as a Shield to Protect Suburbs from Integration by Low Income Blacks," 2 *Fordham Law Journal* 349 (1974).

"Civil Rights—Remedies—In Remedying Discriminatory Local Administration of a Federally Funded Program, a Federal Court Should Not Order the Withholding of Funds from Another Program Not Found Discriminatory," 86 *Harvard Law Review* 427 (1972).

Clawson, Marion, ed. *Modernizing Urban Land Policy.* Papers presented at a Resources for the Future, Inc. Forum held in Washington, D.C., April 13-14, 1972. Baltimore: Johns Hopkins University Press, 1973.

Collier, Ettie. "Exclusionary Zoning and the Problem in *Black Jack*—a Denial of Housing to Whom?" 16 *St. Louis University Law Journal* 294 (1971).

Comarow, Avery. "It Pays to Stay When Blacks Move In—Contrary to a Pernicious Myth, Property Values in Integrated Areas Usually Keep Pace with Those in White Areas—and Sometimes Rise Faster," *Money*, November 1973, p. 62.

"Constitutional Law—Blockbusting—Antiblockbusting Section of the Civil Rights Act of 1968 Held not Violative of First Amendment. Finding of 'Group Pattern or Practice' Does Not Require a Showing of Conspiracy or Concerted Action," 2 *Fordham Urban Law Journal* 377 (1974).

"Constitutional Law—Due Process—Zoning—Suburban Township Zoning Ordinance Which does not Provide for Apartments as Permissible Residential Use Violates Due Process," 23 *Alabama Law Review* 157 (1970).

"Constitutional Law—Equal Protection Extended to Municipal Services—Possible Application to Exclusionary Zoning," 17 *New York Law Forum* 599 (1971).

"Constitutional Law—Equal Protection—Zoning—Snob Zoning: Must a Man's Home be a Castle?" 69 *Michigan Law Review* 339 (1970).

"Constitutional Law—Fair Housing Act of 1968—Antiblockbusting Provision Held to be a Valid Congressional Exercise of Thirteenth Amendment Enforcement Power," 7 *Indiana Law Review* 432 (1973).

"The Constitutionality of Local Zoning," 79 *Yale Law Journal* 896 (1970).

Cooney, Bernard J. "Suburban Apartment Zoning: Legality and Technique," 12 *Boston College Industrial and Commercial Law Review* 955 (1971).

The Council of State Governments. *A Place to Live: Housing Policy in the Seventies.* Lexington, Kentucky: The Council of State Governments, 1974.

County and Municipal Government Study Commission of the State of New Jersey. *Housing & Suburbs: Fiscal and Social Impact of Multifamily Housing.* Forthcoming 1974 [under HUD research contract N.J. PD-2].

Craig, Lois. "The Dayton Area's 'Fair Share' Housing Plan Enters the Implementation Phase," *City*, January/February 1972, p. 50.

Cunningham, Roger A. "Billboard Control Under the Highway Beautification Act of 1965," 71 *Michigan Law Review* 1295 (1973).

Cunningham, Roger A. "The Interrelationship Between Exclusionary Zoning and Exclusionary Subdivision Control—A Second Look," 6 *University of Michigan Journal of Law Reform* 290 (1973).

Cutler, Richard W. "Legal and Illegal Methods for Controlling Community Growth on the Urban Fringe," 1961 *Wisconsin Law Review* 370 (1961).

Cutler, Richard W. "Legality of Zoning to Exclude the Poor: A Preliminary Analysis of Evolving Law," 37 *Brooklyn Law Review* 483 (1971).

Daedalus. See Fall 1973 issue dealing with growth and no-growth issues. [Portions reprinted in *Management & Control of Growth*, Randall W. Scott, ed.]

Davidoff, Linda, Paul Davidoff and Neil N. Gold. "The Suburbs Have to Open Their Gates," *The New York Times Magazine*, November 7, 1971, p. 40.

Davidoff, Paul and Linda Davidoff. "Opening the Suburbs: Toward Inclusionary Land-Use Controls," 22 *Syracuse Law Review* 509 (1971).

Davidoff, Paul, Linda Davidoff and Neil N. Gold. "Suburban Action: Advocate Planning for an Open Society," 36 *Journal of the American Institute of Planners* 12 (1970).

Davidoff, Paul and Neil N. Gold. "Exclusionary Zoning," 1 *Yale Review of Law and Social Action* 56 (1970).

Davidoff, Paul and Linda Rosensweig. "Legislative Arena Also Moves Toward Increase in Minority Housing Opportunities in Suburbia," *AIP Newsletter*, July 1971, p. 14.

Davis, Mark S. "Standing to Challenge Housing Discrimination: The Limits of *Trafficante v. Metropolitan Life Ins. Co.*," 7 *Urban Law Annual* 311 (1974).

Dean, Charles. "Site Selection for Public Housing and the Expanded Equal Protection Concept," 7 *Urban Law Annual* 336 (1974).

"Developments in the Law of Equal Protection," 82 *Harvard Law Review* 1065 (1969).

Dietsch, Robert W. "Cracking the Suburbs," *New Republic*, September 5, 1970, p. 8.

"Discrimination in Employment and in Housing: Private Enforcement Provisions of the Civil Rights Acts of 1964 & 1968," 82 *Harvard Law Review* 834 (1969).

Donaldson, Scott. *The Suburban Myth.* New York: Columbia University Press, 1969.

Downs, Anthony. *Opening Up the Suburbs—An Urban Strategy for America.* New Haven, Connecticut: Yale University Press, 1973.

Dyke, James W., Jr. "Use of Zoning Laws to Prevent Poor People from Moving into Suburbia," 16 *Howard Law Journal* 351 (1971).

Eisen, Lloyd P. "Constitutional Law—Equal Protection—One-family Zoning Ordinances," 19 *New York Law Forum* 351 (1973).

Elliott, Donald H. and Norman Marcus. "From Euclid to Ramapo: New Directions in Land Development Controls," 1 *Hofstra Law Review* 56 (1973).

Ellis, Joseph M. "*Shapiro, Dandridge* and Residence Requirements in Public Housing," 1972 *Urban Law Annual* [School of Law—Washington University] 131 (1972).

"Equal Housing: Nixon Defines His Policy," *U.S. News & World Report*, June 21, 1971, p. 72.

Exclusion and Land Use

Equal Opportunity in Housing. Biweekly periodical. Englewood Cliffs, N.J.: Prentice-Hall, Inc. [in cooperation with the U.S. Department of Housing and Urban Development].

"Equal Protection and Exclusionary Zoning: *Boraas v. Village of Belle Terre,*" 60 *Virginia Law Review* 163 (1974).

"The Equal Protection Clause and Exclusionary Zoning After *Valtierra* and *Dandridge,*" 81 *Yale Law Journal* 61 (1971).

Erber, Ernest. *Jobs and Housing: A Study of Employment and Housing Opportunities for Racial Minorities in the Suburban Areas of the New York Metropolitan Region.* Mimeographed. Washington, D.C.: National Committee Against Discrimination in Housing, 1972.

Erber, Ernest and John P. Prior. *Housing Allocation Planning: An Annotated Bibliography,* Council of Planning Librarians Exchange Bibliography 547. March 1974.

Evans, Robert B. "Regional Land Use Control: The Stepping Stone Concept," 22 *Baylor Law Review* 1 (1970).

Ewald, Thomas R. "Public and Private Enforcement of Title VII of the Civil Rights Act of 1964—A Ten-Year Perspective," 7 *Urban Law Annual* 101 (1974).

"Exclusionary Practices—*Oakwood at Madison Inc. v. Township of Madison, N.J.,*" 23 *Zoning Digest* 421 (1971).

"Exclusionary Zoning and Equal Protection," 84 *Harvard Law Review* 1645 (1971).

"Fair Zoning is a 'Must,'" *The National Voter,* November/December 1970, p. 3.

Feiler, Michael H. "Metropolitanization and Land-use Parochialism—Toward a Judicial Attitude," 69 *Michigan Law Review* 655 (1971).

Fielding, Richard. "The Right to Travel: Another Constitutional Standard for Local Land Use Regulations," 39 *University of Chicago Law Review* 612 (1972).

Finch, Philip R. "Low-Income Housing in the Suburbs: The Problem of Exclusionary Zoning," 24 *University of Florida Law Review* 58 (1971).

Finkler, Earl. *Nongrowth as a Planning Alternative: A Preliminary Examination of an Emerging Issue.* Planning Advisory Service Report No. 283. Chicago: American Society of Planning Officials, 1972.

Finkler, Earl. *Nongrowth: A Review of the Literature.* Planning Advisory Service Report No. 289. Chicago: American Society of Planning Officials, 1973.

Fisher, Daniel F. "Constitutional Law: Equal Protection—an Emerging Standard of Review," 13 *Washburn Law Journal* 106 (1974).

Fisher, Gerald A. "General Public Interest vs. the Presumption of Zoning Ordinance Validity: A Debatable Question," 50 *Journal of Urban Law* 129 (1972).

Franklin, Herbert M. *Controlling Urban Growth—But for Whom? The Social Implications of Development Timing Controls.* Washington, D.C.: Potomac Institute, 1973.

Franklin, Herbert M. "Slow-Growth and the Law," *Housing and Development Reporter* [Bureau of National Affairs, Washington, D.C.], June 27, 1973, p. B-1.

Franklin, Herbert M. "Zoning Laws: Little Ordinances with Some Big Economic and Racial Ramifications," *Black Enterprise,* August 1972, p. 25.

Freilich, Robert H. "Editor's Comments—*Golden v. Town of Ramapo:* Establishing a New Dimension in American Planning Law," 4 *The Urban Lawyer* 404 (1972).

Freilich, Robert H., et al. *Freedom of Choice in Housing: The Impact of Restrictions in Kansas City Metropolitan Region.* Springfield, Virginia: National Technical Information Service, 1971.

Freilich, Robert H. and G. Allen Bass. "Exclusionary Zoning: Suggested Litigation Approaches," 3 *Urban Lawyer* 344 (1971).

Frieden, Bernard J. "Toward Equality of Urban Opportunity," 31 *Journal of the American Institute of Planners* 320 (1965).

Furman, David D. "Regional Housing Needs: 'Oakwood at Madison' ", in Scott, *Management & Control of Growth,* forthcoming 1974.

"Furor Over a Drive to Integrate the Suburbs," *U.S. News & World Report,* August 10, 1970, p. 23.

Galchus, Kenneth. "Property Values in an Integrated Neighborhood," *The Real Estate Appraiser,* November/December 1972, p. 15.

Geldon, Fred M. "Sensuous Market: an Analysis of School Finance and Exclusionary Zoning," 51 *Journal of Urban Law* 343 (1974).

Gladchun, Lawrence L. "Constitutional Law—Equal Protection—Zoning Ordinance Restricting Use of One-family Dwellings to No More than Two Unrelated Persons Unconstitutional," 51 *Journal of Urban Law* 307 (1973).

"Government Renews Pressure for Integrated Suburbs," *U.S. News & World Report,* June 28, 1971, p. 47.

"Government in the Suburbs—Housing Black Workers," *The New Republic,* July 17, 1971, p. 16.

Graham, Robert L. and Jason H. Kravitt. "The Evolution of Equal Protection—Education, Municipal Services and Wealth," 7 *Harvard Civil Rights—Civil Liberties Law Review* 103 (1972).

Grant, Drayton. "Constitutional Law—Equal Protection: Zoning for One-Family Dwellings so as to Exclude Voluntary Families is a Denial of Equal Protection, Tested Under the New More Intense Minimal Scrutiny," 40 Brooklyn Law Review 226 (1973).

Grier, George and Eunice Grier. Equality and Beyond: Housing Segregation and the Goals of the Great Society. Chicago: Quadrangle, 1966.

Groebe, William. "Exclusionary Land-use Techniques: Judicial Response and Legislative Initiative," 22 De Paul Law Review 388 (1972).

Guide to Practice Open Housing Law. Chicago: Leadership Council for Metropolitan Open Communities, 1974.

Haar, Charles M. " 'In Accordance with a Comprehensive Plan,' " 68 Harvard Law Review 1154 (1955).

Haar, Charles M. "Wayne Township: Zoning for Whom?—In Brief Reply," 67 Harvard Law Review 986 (1954).

Haar, Charles M. "Zoning for Minimum Standards: The Wayne Township Case," 66 Harvard Law Review 1051 (1953).

Haar, Charles M. and Demetrius S. Iatridis. Housing the Poor in Suburbia: Public Policy at the Grass Roots. Cambridge, Massachusetts: Ballinger Publishing Company, 1974.

Hodza, Richard. "Constitutionality of Minimum Sizes for Buildings and Lots," 15 Intramural Law Review of New York 83 (1960).

Hagman, Donald G. "The Single Tax and Land-Use Planning: Henry George Updated," 12 University of California Los Angeles Law Review 762 (1965).

Hagman, Donald G. "Urban Planning and Development—Race and Poverty—Past, Present, and Future," 46 Utah Law Review 46 (1971).

Hammer, Charles. "A Fresh Approach to Integrated Housing—Racially Changing Neighborhoods," The New Republic, September 15, 1973, p. 19.

Hartman, Chester W. "As White is to Suburbs," Civil Rights Digest, Spring 1970, p. 35.

Haworth, Edward E. and George Lefcoe. Federally Assisted Housing and Community Acceptance —A Developer's Handbook. Berkeley, California: Associated Home Builders, 1972.

Hecht, James L. Because It Is Right: Integration in Housing. Boston: Little, Brown & Co., Inc., 1970.

Hecht, James L. "Employers Join to Promote Open Housing," Harvard Business Review, July/August 1973, p. 14.

Henderson, Danny D. and J. Michael Walls. "Problems and Solutions in Exclusionary Zoning—Emphasis on Alabama," 4 Cumberland-Samford Law Review 105 (1973).

Hershman, Mendes (chairman). "Three Aspects of Zoning: Unincorporated Areas—Exclusionary Zoning—Conditional Zoning," 6 Real Property Probate and Trust Journal 178 (1971).

Heyman, Ira M. "Legal Assaults on Municipal Land Use Regulation," 5 Urban Lawyer 1 (1973).

Hirshon, Robert E. "Interrelationship Between Exclusionary Zoning and Exclusionary Subdivision Control," 5 University of Michigan Journal of Law Reform 351 (1971).

Holman, Michael S. "Removing the Bar of Exclusionary Zoning to a Decent Home," 32 Ohio State Law Journal 373 (1971).

Holmgren, Edward L. and Ernest Erber. "Fair Share Formulas," 4 HUD Challenge 22 (1973).

Jackson, Samuel C. "Attacking the Affluent Islands: A Legal Strategy for the 70s," 1971 Urban Law Annual 3 (1971).

Jewitt, Donald G. "Zoning—Lot Area Restrictions —Constitutionality of One-acre Requirement," 3 Villanova Law Review 115 (1957).

Johnson, Chester H. "Exclusionary Zoning: Damage Actions Under the Civil Rights Act," 1971 Law and Social Order 538 (1971).

Kaye, Terry L. "The Validity of Zoning an Entire Municipality Exclusively Residential," 7 Urban Law Annual 304 (1974).

"Keep Out. Suburban Zoning Laws Called Discriminatory to Negroes and Poor. Rules Bar Big Apartments, Call for Individual Homes that Bring Heavy Taxes," The Wall Street Journal, November 27, 1970, p. 1.

Kelson, Richard. "In re Appeal of Girsh: A Pig in the Parlor Instead of the Barnyard," 32 University of Pittsburgh Law Review 83 (1970).

King, A. Thomas and Peter Mieszkowski. "Racial Discrimination, Segregation and the Price of Housing," 81 Journal of Political Economy 590 (1973).

Kirby, Ronald, Frank de Leeuw and William Silverman. Residential Zoning and Equal Housing Opportunities: A Case Study in Black Jack, Missouri. Washington, D.C.: Urban Institute, 1972.

Klimberg, Toni. "Excluding the Commune from Suburbia: The Use of Zoning for Social Control," 23 Hastings Law Journal 1459 (1972).

Krasnowiecki, Jan. "Planned Unit Development: A Challenge to Established Theory and Practice of Land Use Control," 114 University of Pennsylvania Law Review 47 (1965).

Kristensen, Chris, John Levy and Tamar Savir. The Suburban Lock-Out Effect: Suburban Action Institute Research Report No. 1. Tarrytown, New York: Suburban Action Institute, 1971.

LaFontaine, Michael. "The Limits of Permissible Exclusion in Fiscal Zoning," 53 Boston University Law Review 453 (1973).

Exclusion and Land Use

Lamm, Richard D. and Steven A. G. Davison. "The Legal Control of Population Growth and Distribution in a Quality Environment: The Land Use Alternatives," 49 *Denver Law Journal* 1 (1972).

"Land Subdivision Regulation: Its Effects and Constitutionality," 41 *St. John's Law Review* 374 (1967).

Langendorf, Richard. "Residential Desegregation Potential," 35 *Journal of the American Institute of Planners* 90 (1969).

LaRussa, Dennis A. "Exclusionary Zoning: An Overview," 47 *Tulane Law Review* 1056 (1973).

Lauber, Daniel. *Recent Cases in Exclusionary Zoning*. Planning Advisory Service Report No. 292. Chicago: American Society of Planning Officials, 1973.

Law Center of the University of Southern California. *Potential Legal Arguments Available in Exclusionary Zoning Cases*. Mimeographed. Los Angeles: Law Center of the University of Southern California, 1970.

Lawson, Simpson. "Mr. Romney in St. Louis: The 'Real City' and Present Urban Realities," *City*, Summer 1972, p. 11.

Lazerow, Arthur S. "Discriminatory Zoning: Legal Battleground of the Seventies," 21 *American University Law Review* 157 (1971).

Le Blanc, Nancy E. "Race, Housing, and the Government," 26 *Vanderbilt Law Review* 487 (1973).

Lefcoe, George. "From Capitol Hill: The Impact of Civil Rights Litigation on HUD Policy," 4 *Urban Lawyer* 112 (1972).

Lefcoe, George. "The Public Housing Referendum Case, Zoning, and the Supreme Court," 59 *California Law Review* 1384 (1971).

"The Legal Significance of Cost Considerations in the Regulation of Apartments by Suburbs," 59 *Northwestern University Law Review* 413 (1964).

Levin, Melvin R. *Exploring Urban Problems*. Boston: The Urban Press, 1971.

Levy, John M. "Exclusionary Zoning: After the Walls Come Down," *Planning* [American Society of Planning Officials], August 1972, p. 158.

Lilley, William, III. "Housing Report: Courts Lead Revolutionary Trend Toward Desegregation of Residential Areas," *National Journal*, November 27, 1971, p. 2336.

Listokin, David. "Fair Share Housing Distribution: Will It Open the Suburbs to Apartment Development?" 2 *Real Estate Law Journal* 739 (1974).

"Local Government—City Size Limitations—Municipal Government Attempts to Curtail Growth May Violate Right to Travel," 60 *Georgetown Law Journal* 1363 (1972).

Long, Herman H. and Charles S. Johnson. *People vs. Property: Race Restrictive Covenants in Housing*. Nashville, Tennessee: Fisk University Press, 1947.

Lyon, Edwin L. "Exclusionary Zoning from a Regional Perspective," 1972 *Urban Law Annual* 239 (1972).

Mandelker, Daniel R. "Controlling Land Values in Areas of Rapid Urban Expansion," 12 *University of California Los Angeles Law Review* 734 (1965).

Mandelker, Daniel R. *The Zoning Dilemma: A Legal Strategy for Urban Change*. Indianapolis: Bobbs-Merrill, 1971.

Mann, Paul T. "Appeal of Girsh: A Judicial Requirement for Apartment Zoning," 24 *Southwestern Law Journal* 838 (1970).

Marciniak, Thaddeus. "Up the Down-Sliding Scale: *Boraas v. Village of Belle Terre*, and the Equal Protection Assault on Restrictive Definitions of 'Family' in Zoning Ordinances," 49 *Notre Dame Lawyer* 428 (1973).

Marcus, Norman. "Exclusionary Zoning: The Need for a Regional Planning Context," 16 *New York Law Forum* 732 (1970).

Masotti, Louis H. and Deborah Ellis Dennis. *Suburbs, Suburbia and Suburbanization: A Bibliography* (2nd ed.), Council of Planning Librarians Exchange Bibliography 524 and 525, February 1974.

Masotti, Louis H. and Jeffrey K. Hadden. *The Urbanization of the Suburbs*. Beverly Hills, California: Sage Publications, Inc., 1973.

Mayne, Wiley E., Jr. "The Responsibility of Local Zoning Authorities to Nonresident Indigents," 23 *Stanford Law Review* 774 (1971).

McGill, John R. "Substandard Lots and the Exception Clause—'Checker-Boarding' as a Means of Circumvention," 16 *Syracuse Law Review* 612 (1965).

McGrath, Joseph P. *Impact of Restrictive Zoning on Low and Moderate Income Families*. Mimeographed. Washington, D.C.: National Association of Home Builders, November 1970.

Mezey, Frederick C. "Beyond Exclusionary Zoning—A Practitioner's View of the New Zoning," 5 *Urban Lawyer* 56 (1973).

Michelman, Frank I. "The Advent of a Right to Housing: A Current Appraisal," 5 *Harvard Civil Rights—Civil Liberties Law Review* 207 (1970).

Michelman, Frank I. "Foreword: On Protecting the Poor Through the Fourteenth Amendment," 83 *Harvard Law Review* 7 (1060).

Minetz, Robert S. "Zoning Ordinances Which Restrict the Definition of a Family and Constitutional Considerations," 62 *Illinois Bar Journal* 38 (1973).

Mixon, John. "Jane Jacobs and the Law—Zoning for Diversity Examined," 62 *Northwestern University Law Review* 314 (1967).

Mogulof, Melvin B. "Interpretation: Regional Planning, Clearance, and Evaluation: A Look at the A-95 Process," 37 *Journal of The American Institute of Planners* 418 (November 1971).

Moskowitz, David H. "Standing of Future Residents in Exclusionary Zoning Cases," 6 Akron Law Review 189 (1973).

"Municipal Corporations—Zoning—Protection of Property Values Held Sufficient Justification for Total Exclusion of Trailer Camps," 17 Rutgers Law Review 659 (1963).

National Academy of Sciences, Advisory Committee to the Department of Housing and Urban Development. Freedom of Choice in Housing: Opportunities and Constraints. Report of the Social Science Panel, Division of Behavioral Sciences and the Recommendations of the Advisory Committee. Washington, D.C.: National Academy of Sciences, 1972.

National Association of Home Builders. Land Development Law for the Builder and His Attorney. Washington, D.C.: National Association of Home Builders, 1972.

National Commission on Urban Problems. Building the American City. Report of the Commission. Washington, D.C.: Government Printing Office, 1968.

National Committee Against Discrimination in Housing [NCDH]. The Impact of Housing Patterns on Job Opportunities. Washington, D.C.: NCDH, 1968.

National Committee Against Discrimination in Housing [NCDH]. Trends in Housing. NCDH periodical, various issues. Washington, D.C.: NCDH.

NCDH and ULI. Fair Housing and Exclusionary Land Use. Washington, D.C.: Urban Land Institute, 1974.

Nelson, Leonard M. "The Master Plan and Subdivision Control," 16 Maine Law Review 107 (1964).

"The New Jersey Judiciary's Response to Exclusionary Zoning," 25 Rutgers Law Review 172 (1970).

Newsweek. Articles in July 6, 1970 (p. 57); November 15, 1971 (p. 61); September 25, 1972 (p. 69); etc.

"A New Way to Integrate the Suburbs: Well-funded Organizations Help Blacks Finance Moves into White Areas," Business Week, March 28, 1970, p. 168.

Nilon, John W., Jr. "The Pennsylvania Supreme Court and Exclusionary Suburban Zoning: From Bilbar to Girsh—A Decade of Change," 16 Villanova Law Review 507 (1971).

"Nixon's Equal Housing Policy—Separating Racial from Economic Discrimination," Professional Builder, August 1971, p. 13.

Nolan, Val, Jr. and Frank E. Horack, Jr. "How Small a House? Zoning for Minimum Space Requirements," 67 Harvard Law Review 967 (1954).

"One Acre Minimum Lot Size Requirement in Zoning Ordinance Held to be Unconstitutional," 106 University of Pennsylvania Law Review 292 (1957).

Parkins, John A., Jr. "Judicial Attitudes Toward Multiple-Family Dwellings: A Reappraisal," 28 Washington and Lee Law Review 220 (1971).

Patterson, Jack. "Wall of Zoning: Suburban Racial and Economic Front," Commonweal, May 28, 1971, p. 283.

Pearlman, Daniel D. "State Housing Finance Agencies and the Myth of Low-Income Housing," 7 Clearinghouse Review 649 (1974).

"Pennsylvania High Court on Exclusionary Zoning," Planning [American Society of Planning Officials], June 1970, p. 70.

Phares, Donald. "Racial Transition and Residential Property Values," 5 Annals of Regional Science 152 (1971).

Potvin, D. Joseph. "Suburban Zoning Ordinances and Building Codes: Their Effect on Low and Moderate Income Housing," 45 Notre Dame Lawyer 123 (1969).

Pratter, Jerome. "Dispersed Subsidized Housing and Suburbia: Confrontation in Black Jack," Land-Use Controls Annual 1971. Chicago: American Society of Planning Officials, 1972.

President's Committee on Urban Housing. A Decent Home. Report of the President's Committee on Urban Housing. Washington, D.C.: Government Printing Office, 1969.

"The Pressure Builds for Open Housing: Suburbia's Discriminatory Codes are Coming Under Strong Legal Attack," Business Week, July 11, 1970, p. 61.

Rabin, Yale. Challenging Discriminatory Development Controls: Some Thoughts on Future Directions. Unpublished [cited in Lauber, Recent Cases . . .], November 20, 1970.

Rahenkamp, John. "Every Suburb Can Absorb a Share of the Low-Cost Housing," House and Home, May 1972, p. 60.

"Ramapo; Growth Controls; Comments on Golden" [by Sy J. Schulman, Robert Freilich, Randall W. Scott and Richard May, Jr.], 24 Zoning Digest 67 (1972).

"Ramapo Zoning Decision Assessed," NAHB Journal of Homebuilding [National Association of Home Builders], October 1972, p. 12.

Ranney, David C. "Regional Development and the Courts," 16 Syracuse Law Review 600 (1965).

Raymond and May Associates. Zoning Controversies in the Suburbs: Three Case Studies. Prepared for the Consideration of the National Commission on Urban Problems, Research Report No. 11. Washington, D.C.: Government Printing Office, 1968.

Reeb, Donald J. and James T. Kirk, Jr. Housing the Poor. New York: Praeger Publishers, 1973.

"Regional Impact of Zoning: A Suggested Approach," 114 University of Pennsylvania Law Review 1251 (1966).

Exclusion and Land Use

Reilly, William J. and S. J. Schulman. "The State Urban Development Corporation: New York's Innovation," 1 *Urban Lawyer* 129 (1969).

Reinstein, Robert J., with Gerald McFadden, Susan A. Feder and Robert E. Kerper, Jr. "A Case of Exclusionary Zoning," 46 *Temple Law Quarterly* 7 (1972).

Reitze, Arnold W., Jr. and Glenn L. Reitze. "Elitist Land Controls," *Environment*, April 1974, p. 2.

"Restrictive Zoning," *Planning* [American Society of Planning Officials], January, 1970, p. 12.

"The Right to Travel and its Application to Restrictive Housing Laws," 66 *Northwestern University Law Review* 635 (1971).

Rivkin, Malcolm D. "Three Hopeful Augurs of Suburban Change," *City*, January/February 1971, p. 65. [Reprinted in "Breaking Through the Suburban Barrier," *Urban Land*, May 1971, p. 9.]

Roisman, Florence W. "The Right to Public Housing," 39 *The George Washington Law Review* 691 (1971).

Rose, Jerome G. "The Courts and the Balanced Community: Recent Trends in New Jersey Zoning Law," 39 *Journal of the American Institute of Planners* 265 (1973).

Rosenhouse, Sharon and Edward J. Flynn. "The Power—The Danger: Zoning." Special Supplement to *The Record* [Hackensack, New Jersey], August 3, 1970.

Rubinowitz, Leonard S. "Exclusionary Zoning: A Wrong in Search of a Remedy," 6 *University of Michigan Journal of Law Reform* 625 (1973).

Ryan, Philip S. "Decent Housing as a Constitutional Right, 42 U.S.C. § 1983: Poor People's Remedy for Deprivation," 14 *Howard Law Journal* 338 (1968).

Sager, Lawrence G. "Exclusionary Zoning: Constitutional Limitations on the Power of Municipalities to Restrict the Use of Land," *Land Use Controls Annual 1972.* Chicago: American Society of Planning Officials, 1973.

Sager, Lawrence G. "Tight Little Islands: Exclusionary Zoning, Equal Protection, and the Indigent," 21 *Stanford Law Review* 767 (1969).

Saltman, Juliet Z. *Open Housing as a Social Movement.* Lexington, Massachusetts: Heath Lexington Books, 1971.

Sanoff, Henry, et al. "Changing Residential Racial Patterns," 4 *Urban and Social Change Review* 68 (1971).

Schechter, Alan H. "Impact of Open Housing Laws on Suburban Realtors," *Urban Affairs Quarterly*, June 1973, p. 439.

Schoenbrod, David S. "Large Lot Zoning," 78 *Yale Law Journal* 1418 (1969).

Schorr, Philip. "An Orchestrated Approach to Desegregating the Suburbs," *Real Estate Review*, Fall 1971, p. 61.

Schwartz, Barry. "*Joy v. Daniels*: Due Process and Quasi-Public Housing," 23 *Catholic University Law Review* 375 (1973).

Scott, John F. and Lois H. Scott. "They Are Not So much Anti-Negro as Pro-Middle Class," *The New York Times Magazine*, March 24, 1968, p. 46.

Scott, Randall W. "Exclusion and Land Use: A Comment and Research Bibliography," in *Management & Control of Growth* [See also in NCDH and ULI, *Fair Housing . . .*]. Washington, D.C.: Urban Land Institute, 1974.

Scott, Randall W. *Exclusionary Land Use Practices or Growth Policies and Exclusionary Zoning.* Mimeographed. American Institute of Planners, Confer-In '72, paper no. 22 [revised edition: 1973].

Scott, Randall W., ed. *Management & Control of Growth: Issues — Techniques — Problems — Trends.* 3 vols. Washington, D.C.: Urban Land Institute, 1974.

"Segregation and the Suburbs: Low-Income Housing, Zoning and the Fourteenth Amendment," 56 *Iowa Law Review* 1298 (1971).

Semer, Milton P. and Martin E. Sloane. "Equal Housing Opportunity and Individual Property Rights," 24 *Federal Bar Journal* 47 (1964).

Shaffer, Jay C. and Kenneth E. Meiser. "Exclusionary Use of the Planned Unit Development: Standards for Judicial Scrutiny," 8 *Harvard Civil Rights–Civil Liberties Law Review* 384 (1973).

Sherer, Samuel A. "Snob Zoning: Developments in Massachusetts and New Jersey," 7 *Harvard Journal on Legislation* 246 (1970).

Shields, Geoffrey and L. Sanford Spector. "Opening Up the Suburbs: Notes on a Movement for Social Change," 2 *Yale Review of Law and Social Action* 300 (1972).

Shipler, David K. "The Moral Dilemma of Zoning," *Nation*, August 3, 1970, p. 80.

Siegan, Bernard H. *Land Use Without Zoning.* Lexington, Massachusetts: D. C. Heath and Company, 1972.

Simon, Lawrence P., Jr. "Equal Protection in the Urban Environment: The Right to Equal Municipal Services," 46 *Tulane Law Review* 496 (1972).

Skipworth, Larry. "Plutocracy or Democracy in the Suburbs," *Planning Comment* [Department of City and Regional Planning, University of Pennsylvania], Winter-Fall 1971-1972, p. 8.

Sloane, Martin E. "The Housing Act of 1968: Best Yet—But Is It Enough?" 1 *Civil Rights Digest* 1 (1968).

Sloane, Martin E. "Housing Discrimination—The Response of the Law," 42 *North Carolina Law Review* 106 (1963).

Exclusion and Land Use

Sloane, Martin E. "One Year's Experience: Current and Potential Impact of the Housing Order," 32 *George Washington Law Review* 457 (1964).

Sloane, Martin E. and Monroe H. Freedman. "The Executive Order on Housing: The Constitutional Basis For What It Fails to Do," 9 *Howard Law Journal* 1 (1963).

Smith, James A., Jr. " 'Burning the House Down to Roast the Pig': Unrelated Individuals and Single Family Zoning's Blood Relation Criterion," 58 *Cornell Law Review* 138 (1972).

"State Police Power—Zoning—Validity of Ordinance Depends on Considerations of Regional, not Merely Local, General Welfare," 25 *Vanderbilt Law Review* 466 (1972).

Sternlieb, George et al. *Housing Development and Municipal Costs.* New Brunswick, New Jersey: Rutgers University Center for Urban Policy Research, 1973.

Sternlieb, George and Lynne B. Sagalyn, eds. *Housing, 1970-1971: An AMS Anthology.* New York: AMS Press, 1972.

Sternlieb, George and Lynne B. Sagalyn. *Zoning and Housing Costs: The Impact of Land-Use Controls on Housing Price.* New Brunswick, New Jersey: Center for Urban Policy Research, 1972.

Strong, Ann L. "Girsh and Kit-Mar: An Unlikely Route to Equal Opportunity in Housing," 22 *Zoning Digest* 100a (1970).

Struve, Guy Miller. "The Less-Restrictive-Alternative Principle and Economic Due Process," 80 *Harvard Law Review* 1463 (1967).

Suburban Action Institute. *A Study of Exclusion, Volumes I & II.* Prepared by SAI for the Department of Community Affairs, Commonwealth of Pennsylvania. December, 1973.

"Suburban Snobbery," *The New Republic,* June 26, 1971, p. 7.

Summerville, Jay A. "Zoning, Communes and Equal Protection," 1973 *Urban Law Annual* 319 (1973).

Sussna, Stephen S. "An Attempt at Realism—or Another Look at Exclusionary Zoning," in *Institute on Planning, Zoning, and Eminent Domain.* New York: Matthew Bender & Co., forthcoming 1974.

Sussna, Stephen S. "Court Battles Could Break Suburban Zoning Bottleneck," *Apartment Construction News,* June 1972, p. 14.

Sussna, Stephen S. "Place for the Poor in the Suburbs?" 88 *American City* 68 (1973).

Sussna, Stephen S. "Residential Densities: A Patchwork Placebo," 1 *Fordham Urban Law Journal* 127 (1972).

Symposium: "Apartments in Suburbia: Local Responsibility and Judicial Restraint," 59 *Northwestern University Law Review* 344 (1964). "The Battle for Apartments in Benign Suburbia: A Case of Judicial Lethargy," p. 345; "Aesthetic Control of Land Use: A House Built Upon the Sand?" p. 372; "Flexible Land Use Control: Herein of the Special Use," p. 394; "The Legal Significance of Cost Considerations in the Regulation of Apartments by Suburbs," p. 413.

Symposium: "Exclusionary Zoning," 22 *Syracuse Law Review* 465 (1971). Anderson, Robert M., "Introduction," p. 465; Williams, Norman, Jr. and Thomas Norman, "Exclusionary Land-Use Controls: The Case of North-Eastern New Jersey," p. 475; Davidoff, Paul and Linda Davidoff, "Opening the Suburbs: Toward Inclusionary Land-Use Controls," p. 509; Silkey, Robert F. and Lawrence Dickie, "A Survey of the Judicial Responses to Exclusionary Zoning," p. 537; Sandak, Jay H., "Exclusionary Zoning: A Legislative Approach," p. 583; George, Richard D., "Standing to Challenge Exclusionary Local Zoning Decisions: Restricted Access to State Courts and the Alternative Federal Forum," p. 598.

Symposium: "Land Planning and the Law: Emerging Policies and Techniques," 12 *University of California Los Angeles Law Review* 707 (1965). Dukeminier, Jesse, Jr., "Foreword: The Coming Search for Quality," p. 707; Weaver, Robert C., "National Land Policies—Historic and Emergent," p. 719; Mandelker, Daniel R., "Controlling Land Values in Areas of Rapid Urban Expansion," p. 734; Hagman, Donald G., "The Single Tax and Land-Use Planning: Henry George Updated," p. 762; Elias, C. E., Jr., and James Gillies, "Some Observations on the Role of Speculators and Speculation in Land Development," p. 789; Gunzburg, M. L., "Transportation Problems of the Megalopolitan," p. 800; Volpert, Robert S., "Creation and Maintenance of Open Space in Subdivisions: Another Approach," p. 830; Frieden, Bernard J., "The Legal Role in Urban Development," p. 856; Hirsch, Werner Z., "About Tomorrow's Urban America," p. 880; Bailey, Bruce R., "The Use and Abuse of Contract Zoning," p. 897; Smotkin, Harold J., "Subdivision Regulation and the Park Problem," p. 917; Tepper, Ronald and Bruce Toor, "Judicial Control Over Zoning Boards of Appeal: Suggestions for Reform," p. 937; Godbold, Wilford D., Jr., "*Coast Bank v. Minderhout* and the Reasonable Restraint on Alienation: Creature of Commercial Ambiguity," p. 954.

Exclusion and Land Use

Symposium: "Land Planning in a Democracy," 20 Law and Contemporary Problems 197 (1955). Kramer, Robert, "Foreword," p. 197; Johnson, Corwin W., "Constitutional Law and Community Planning," p. 199; Dukeminier, J. J., Jr., "Zoning for Aesthetic Objectives: A Reappraisal," p. 218; Fonoroff, Allen, "The Relationship of Zoning to Traffic-Generators," p. 238; Vladeck, William C., "Large Scale Developments and One House Zoning Controls," p. 255; Toll, Seymour I., "Zoning for Amenities," p. 266; Reps, John W., "Discretionary Powers of the Board of Zoning Appeals," p. 280; Fagin, Henry, "Regulating the Timing of Urban Development," p. 298; Norton, C. McKim, "Elimination of Incompatible Uses and Structures," p. 305; Williams, Norman, Jr., "Planning Law and Democratic Living," p. 317.

"Symposium—Land Use," 50 Iowa Law Review 243 (1965). Haar, Charles M., "Foreword," p. 243; Cribbet, John E., "Changing Concepts in the Law of Land Use," p. 245; Huber, Richard G., "Allocation of Rights in Land: Preliminary Considerations," p. 279; Barlowe, Raleigh, "Federal Programs for the Direction of Land Use," p. 337; Cunningham, Roger A., "Land-Use Control—The State and Local Programs," p. 367; Mann, Fred L., "Trends in the Use of Public Controls Affecting Agricultural Landownership in Europe and Great Britain," p. 458.

"Symposium: "Planned Unit Development," 114 University of Pennsylvania Law Review 3 (1965). Lloyd, Gerald W., "A Developer Looks at Planned Unit Development," p. 3; Hanke, Byron R., "Planned Unit Development and Land Use Intensity," p. 15; Krasnowiecki, Jan Z., "Planned Unit Development: A Challenge to Established Theory and Practice of Land Use Control," p. 47; Mandelker, Daniel R., "Reflections on the American System of Planning Controls: A Response to Professor Krasnowiecki," p. 98; Jay, L. S., K. D. Fines, and J. Furmage, "Village Planning in East Essex," p. 106; Craig, David W., "Planned Unit Development as Seen From City Hall," p. 127; Babcock, Richard F., "An Introduction to the Model Enabling Act for Planned Residential Development," p. 136; Babcock, Richard F., Jan Krasnowiecki, and David N. McBride, "The Model State Statute," p. 140.

Symposium: "Urban Housing and Planning," 20 Law and Contemporary Problems 351 (1955). Kramer, Robert, "Foreword," p. 351; Haar, Charles M., "The Master Plan: An Impermanent Constitution," p. 353; Siegel, Shirley A., "Relation of Planning and Zoning to Housing Policy and Law," p. 419; Slayton, William L., "Conservation of Existing Housing," p. 436; Dunham, Allison, "Private Enforcement of City Planning," p. 463; Smith, William C., "Municipal Economy and Land Use Restrictions," p. 481; Heap, Desmond, "New Developments in British Land Planning Law—1954 and After," p. 493; Cross, Harry M., "The Diminishing Fee," p. 517.

Symposium: "Zoning in Illinois," 1954 University of Illinois Law Forum 165 (1954). Cribbet, John E., "Foreword," p. 165; Mathews, Thomas A., "The Power to Zone in Illinois," p. 167; Babcock, Richard F., "Classification and Segregation Among Zoning Districts," p. 186; Dallstream, Andrew J. and Robert S. Hunt, "Variations, Exceptions and Special Uses," p. 213; Graham, Hugh J., Jr., "Legislative, Administrative and Judicial Procedure in Zoning," p. 242; Young, J. Nelson, "Airport Zoning," p. 261; Kneier, Charles M., "The Future of Zoning," p. 281.

Szita, Ellen. "Exclusionary Zoning in the Suburbs: The Case of New Canaan, Connecticut," Civil Rights Digest, Spring 1973, p. 3.

Taeuber, Karl E. "Effect of Income Redistribution on Racial Residential Segregation," 4 Urban Affairs Quarterly 5 (1968).

Thompson, Wilbur R. "Problems that Sprout in the Shadow of No-Growth," 60 AIA [American Institute of Architects] Journal 30 (1973).

Time. Articles in April 6, 1970 (p. 53); September 7, 1970 (p. 51); April 26, 1971 (p. 86); etc.

Toews, John C. "Validity Rules Concerning Zoning and Private Covenants: A Comparison and Critique," 39 Southern California Law Review 409 (1966).

Toll, Seymour I. Zoned American. New York: Grossman Publishers, 1969.

Totenberg, Nina. "Discriminating to End Discrimination," The New York Times Magazine, April 14, 1974, p. 9.

United States Commission on Civil Rights. Hearing Before United States Commission on Civil Rights: Hearing Held in Baltimore, Maryland, August 17-19, 1970. Washington, D.C.: Government Printing Office, 1970.

United States Commission on Civil Rights. Hearing Before United States Commission on Civil Rights: Hearing Held in Washington, D.C., June 14-17, 1971. Washington, D.C.: Government Printing Office, 1971.

United States Commission on Civil Rights. Land Use Control in Relation to Racial and Economic Integration. Staff Report. Washington, D.C.: United States Commission on Civil Rights, August 1973.

U.S. Congress. Papers [miscellaneous]. Submitted to the Subcommittee Housing Panels on Housing Production, Housing Demand, and Developing a Suitable Living Environment—House Committee on Banking and Currency. Washington, D.C.: Government Printing Office, 1971.

U.S. News and World Report. Articles in October 10, 1966 (p. 76); December 14, 1969 (p. 25); December 29, 1969 (p. 17); June 22, 1970 (p. 39); April 5, 1971 (p. 63); August 7, 1972 (p. 52); October 16, 1972 (p. 39); etc.

Urbanczyk, Stephen L. "Phased Zoning: Regulation of the Tempo and Sequence of Land Development," 26 *Stanford Law Review* 585 (1974).

"Validity of Municipal Law Barring Discrimination in Private Housing," 58 *Columbia Law Review* 728 (1958).

Van Dusen, Richard C. "Civil Rights and Housing," 5 *Urban Lawyer* 576 (1973).

Vaughn, Paul M. "Massachusetts Zoning Appeals Law: First Breach in the Exclusionary Wall," 54 *Boston University Law Review* 37 (1974).

Villa, Joyce Y. "*Golden v. Planning Board of Ramapo:* Time Phased Development Control Through Zoning Standards," 38 *Albany Law Review* 142 (1973).

Walsh, Kathleen M. *Zoning in the Suburbs: A Survey of the Component Elements of a Human Rights Issue.* New York: New York State Division of Human Rights, January 20, 1970.

Walsh, Robert E. "Are Local Zoning Bodies Required by the Constitution to Consider Regional Needs?" 3 *Connecticut Law Review* 244 (1971).

Washburn, Robert M. "Apartments in the Suburbs: In re Appeal of Joseph Girsh," 74 *Dickinson Law Review* 634 (1970).

Watson, Norman V. "Where Will Low-Income Families Live?" 3 *Real Estate Law Journal* 37 (1974).

Weaver, Robert C. *Dilemmas of Urban America.* Cambridge, Massachusetts: Harvard University Press, 1965.

Weinberg, Philip. "Regional Land-use Control: Prerequisite for Rational Planning," 46 *New York University Law Review* 786 (1971).

Wheeler, Steven M. "Regional Planning—Zoning—Minimum Lot Size and the General Welfare," 58 *Cornell Law Review* 1035 (1973).

Wike, Dan. "Welcome to the City of Black Jack, Missouri: Standing in an Exclusionary Zoning Case," 42 *University of Missouri at Kansas City Law Review* 227 (1973).

Williams, Norman, Jr. *American Planning Law: Land Use and the Police Power.* 5 vols. Chicago: Gallaghan & Co., 1974.

Williams, Norman, Jr. "Planning Law and Democratic Living," 20 *Law and Contemporary Problems* 317 (1955).

Williams, Norman, Jr. *The Structure of Urban Zoning.* New York: Buttenheim Publishing Corp., 1966.

Williams, Norman, Jr. "Three Systems of Land Use Controls," 25 *Rutgers Law Review* 80 (1970).

Williams, Norman, Jr., Tatyana Doughty and R. William Potter. "The Strategy on Exclusionary Zoning: Towards What Rationale and What Remedy?" *Land-Use Controls Annual 1972.* Chicago: American Society of Planning Officials, 1973.

Williams, Norman, Jr. and Thomas Norman. "Exclusionary Land-Use Controls: The Case of North-Eastern New Jersey," 22 *Syracuse Law Review* 475 (1971).

Williams, Norman, Jr. and Edward Wacks. "Segregation of Residential Areas Along Economic Lines: Lionshead Lake Revisited," 1969 *Wisconsin Law Review* 827 (1969).

Worden, Rolfe A. "Zoning—Townships—Complete Exclusion of Trailer Camps and Parks," 61 *Michigan Law Review* 1010 (1963).

Yanowitch, Michael H., et al. *Restrictive Zoning in Suburban Monroe County.* Mimeographed. Urban League of Rochester, Inc., New York, and Department of Housing and Urban Development, Washington, D.C., 1970.

"Zoning Against the Public Welfare: Judicial Limitations on Municipal Parochialism," 71 *Yale Law Journal* 720 (1962).

The Zoning and Planning Process in Baltimore County and Its Effect on Minority Group Residents. Mimeographed. A Report of the Maryland State Advisory Committee to the United States Commission on Civil Rights, March 1971.

Zoning Bulletin. Monthly publication: case abstracts. Boston: Quinlan Publishing Company.

"Zoning—Due Process—the Adjudicative Decision Inherent in Trace Rezoning Requires the Decision-Maker to Adhere to Standards of Minimal Due Process," 8 *Georgia Law Review* 254 (1973).

"Zoning Law—Growth Restrictions—Town Ordinance Conditioning Approval of Residential Subdivision Plan on the Availability of Necessary Municipal Services Held Valid," 1 *Fordham Urban Law Journal* 516 (1973).

"Zoning: Looking Beyond Municipal Borders," 1965 *Washington University Law Quarterly* 107 (1965).

"Zoning—Municipal Corporations—General Welfare as a Zoning Purpose Held to Encompass Local and Regional Housing Needs," 26 *Rutgers Law Review* 401 (1973).

"A Zoning Program for Phased Growth: Ramapo Township's Time Controls on Residential Development," 47 *New York University Law Review* 723 (1972).

Zuger, William P. "Exclusionary Zoning," 50 *North Dakota Law Review* 45 (1973).

Recent Cases in Exclusionary Zoning

Daniel Lauber

Daniel Lauber is a Research Associate for the American Society of Planning Officials (ASPO). Founded in 1934, ASPO is a nonprofit research and membership organization, concerned with issues and practices of land use planning. Mr. Lauber is a graduate of the University of Chicago, 1970, and holds an M.A. from the Department of Urban and Regional Planning of the University of Illinois, 1972.

This article is reprinted with the permission of the American Society of Planning Officials. It is a digest of an extensive, 33-page publication by the same title, published as an ASPO Planning Advisory Service Report, Number 292–June 1973. The full report, which includes expanded materials, is available for $6.00, prepaid, from ASPO; 1313 East Sixtieth Street; Chicago, Illinois 60637.

Motives and Techniques of Exclusionary Zoning

The number of legal challenges to exclusionary zoning has increased more than ten-fold since 1970 when ASPO last reported on the matter.[1] Imaginative new legislative, legal, and administrative approaches, both voluntary and involuntary, aimed at eliminating exclusionary zoning have been instituted. A review of the judicial and legislative events of the last three years indicates that current trends restricting the use of exclusionary devices will be intensified in this decade. However, the causes and deleterious effects of exclusionary zoning persist.

This report will update and expand on the earlier report and examine the legal status of the various exclusionary techniques. This report is directed to planners who do not necessarily possess a legal background. According to the 1970 PAS Report, "[w]hatever the motive, if a locality's zoning action results in denying minorities and low-income persons housing when there is a demonstrable need for such housing, it is considered exclusionary zoning."[2] The direct effect of such exclusionary practices is to deny low- and moderate-income persons access to housing and the critical social resources available outside the central city which could be used to improve their situation in life.[3] For example, such practices contribute directly to the inferior education lower-income children receive by confining them to what are generally conceded to be inferior and economically segregated inner-city schools.[4] Due to the disproportionately high number of blacks and Spanish-speaking Americans in the lower-income groups, this economic segregation is usually accompanied by racial segregation as well.

Similarly, the continuing migration of industrial and commercial establishments to outlying suburbs which exclude low- and moderate-income housing reduces the employment opportunities available to low- and moderate-income central city workers. Many workers are forced to make a choice: either commute as much as five hours a day at a cost of as much as $15 a week to a low-paying job in the suburbs or do without work altogether.[5] Between 1960 and 1970 the number of jobs in central cities decreased from 12 to 11 million, while jobs in the suburbs increased from 7 to 10 million. Sometime in this decade more people will be employed in the suburbs than in either the central cities or rural areas.[6] The number of reverse commuters increased by 72.7 per cent in the last decade to 1.46 million[7] even though transit schedules continued to favor incoming rather than outgoing commuters in peak hours. Also, suburban transportation is usually oriented toward residential areas, so the reverse commuter is hindered in his efforts to arrive easily at an industrial area.

Motivations for Exclusionary Zoning. Almost without exception, zoning in America has been a purely local function. Suburban zoning decisions are vested in governments whose interests are the needs and desires of their residents—most often the relatively wealthy and affluent—and not the needs of the moderate-income or the poor who live in the central city or less prestigious suburbs. The judicial attitude toward the review of land-use decisions has been one of deference to the judgement of local administrators and legislative bodies in zoning matters. In practice this deference has meant a broad tolerance of zoning decisions that bear any relationship to the public "health, safety, morals, or general welfare."[8] If a locality's decision is at all debatable, the courts have tended to affirm whatever choice the locality has made without investigating the motive for the choice or its secondary or tertiary effects. This judicial attitude has begun to change.

Most municipalities rely on the property tax as their main source of revenue. They assume that low- and moderate-cost apartments will cost more in services than they produce in revenue. Excluding this type of housing is thus excused as good economics. However, the St. Louis County Planning Department recently estimated the relative costs and revenues produced by developing a 132-unit apartment complex or single-family dwellings on the same 13-acre site. The agency found that building the apartment complex would result in a net surplus of revenue over service costs. Building single-family homes would result in a net loss. A more broad-based study by the North Central Texas Council of Governments found that the cities in the region which have the highest percentage of apartment units ". . . have enjoyed a slower rate of increase in per capita municipal expenditures for strict maintenance and for water and sewer." The study also concluded that those suburbs with the highest percentage of apartments were not necessarily the most densely populated. Between 1960 and 1970 "population density was found to bear no relationship to municipal expenditures for public safety, parks, recreation, and water and sewer service."[9] A number of studies have shown that garden apartments can produce greater revenue than educational costs.[10] The common assumption that low- and moderate-cost apartments and houses will necessarily generate less tax revenue than they will demand in service costs is clearly unwarranted.

There is a possibility that using the property tax for school financing may be modified as a result of recent judicial decisions which have forced legislative action. Courts in eight states have found their current property tax-based school financing systems to be unconstitutional. Although the United States Supreme Court refused earlier this year to declare a similar tax system in Texas violative of the federal constitution, its decision does not reverse those state court decisions based on equal protection provisions of state constitutions.[11] Many state agencies are now studying proposals for altering their traditional school financing systems.

Beyond the frequently claimed financial motivations for exclusion of low- and moderate-cost housing in the suburbs may lie other, more fundamental motives. Racial or economic prejudice are major reasons many communities enact exclusionary zoning ordinances. Simple snobbery or a desire to preserve the character of the community may be others. Frequently, communities may unconsciously exclude such housing. The suburbanite, though, should not be pictured as someone "callously self-seeking, snobbishly building barriers against the rights of others, incredibly insensitive to his obligations."[12] Whatever the motivation, the effect is still the same.

Exclusionary Zoning Practices. [*The original ASPO PAS Report discusses a number of methods used to exclude, by intent or by effect, certain classes of persons; this material is omitted.*]

Conclusion. Due to the recognized invidious effects of exclusionary zoning on the welfare of individuals, communities, regions, and the nation as a whole, ASPO cannot countenance its use. The developing litigation and cases indicate that unless exclusionary communities act affirmatively to meet their duty to ensure that persons of all income levels have access to decent housing within their boundaries, the courts, with a possible assist from state legislatures, will restrict or take away their power to zone locally.

The legality of these practices which have been tested in court will be examined in the next chapter. The possible attacks on exclusionary zoning are a mixture of legislative, administrative, and judicial strategies. The courts will probably function as the vanguard with the new legislative and administrative action occurring only after judicial decisions against exclusionary zoning are made. Even if new legislative or administrative regulation were adopted first, the courts would still play an essential role in the implementation and interpretation of these regulations.[13] In the chapters following, major federal and state court decisions dealing with exclusionary zoning practices will be examined and evaluated; major trends will be identified; and legislative and administrative approaches attacking exclusionary zoning will be described.

Review of Post-1970 Litigation

Federal Litigation. The judicial challenge to exclusionary zoning has been fought in both the federal and state courts. At the federal level, most challenges have been based on the due process clause or the equal protection clause of the Fourteenth Amendment to the United States Constitution.

1. **Fourteenth Amendment, U.S. Constitution:** . . . No State shall make or enforce any law which shall abridge the privileges or immunities of citizens of the United States;
2. **Due Process Clause:** nor shall any State deprive any person of life, liberty, or property, without due process of law;
3. **Equal Protection Clause:** nor deny to any person within its jurisdiction the equal protection of the laws.

Due process challenges can be divided into three types: (a) claims that ordinances promote illegitimate public objectives such as racial segregation; (b) claims that regulations use means not clearly related to objectives, which themselves are legitimate; and (c) claims that ordinances involve a taking of private property without just compensation.[14]

The purpose of zoning is to allow a municipality to regulate the use of private property in order to provide for the health, safety, morals, and general welfare of the public. To be upheld, a zoning ordinance must bear a substantial relation to these police power purposes and must not be unreasonable, arbitrary, or confiscatory.[15]

The equal protection argument was prompted by those zoning ordinances which operate more harshly on the poor than on others. Proponents of this argument have asserted that the equal protection clause places some limitations, not yet completely defined, on the power of states to enact laws treating different classes of individuals unequally. This argument has been used successfully in education, voting, and criminal process cases to strike down laws which, while not explicitly classifying people so as to discriminate between them, had the effect of discriminating between classes.[16] The United States Supreme Court has not yet specifically confronted the issue of whether that clause bars zoning laws which, by raising the price of property ownership, deprive the poor of access to a decent home, desirable neighborhoods, and a suitable living environment. Lower courts, however, have dealt more directly with this question.

Some legal scholars take the position that no governmental body may enact zoning ordinances that generally operate to confine the poor to the deteriorating central city. This conclusion derives from a view of equal protection which holds that laws which isolate the poor in a way that impairs their social mobility, even though based on *de facto* rather than *de jure* lines, are as invidious as those which discriminate according to race.[17]

The success of this line of argument is dependent upon the Supreme Court's treatment of income as a "suspect classification" or housing as a "fundamental interest." The U.S. Supreme Court will accord active review[18] to equal protection cases involving a suspect classification. To uphold a statute involving such a classification, there must be a close linkage between the classification and the statutory purpose it is meant to serve, and the public interests served by the statute must outweigh the private detriment caused by it. Any classification based on race is treated as a suspect classification and requires proof that there is some "overriding statutory purpose requiring the classification" in order to be upheld. In addition to carefully scrutinizing laws that classify people by race, courts have given special attention to classifications based on other factors such as alienage and, in some cases, illegitimacy. While the Court has said that discrimination based on wealth or property is "traditionally disfavored," its attitude toward such discrimination has actually been more equivocal than this statement would indicate. The strict standards of review applied to suspect classifications have been extended to cases in which a law treats people differently with respect to a fundamental interest. Without explicitly stating the standards that determine why certain interests have been identified as fundamental, the Supreme Court has accorded this treatment to cases involving voting rights and rights related to the criminal process.[19]

The Court will also accord active review status to cases in which a law treats people differently with respect to a fundamental interest. The limits of the equal protection doctrine are suggested in the Supreme Court's decision in *Dandridge* v. *Williams*[20] in which it stated that the category of fundamental interests would be limited to freedoms explicitly guaranteed by the Constitution. Under this approach, education, welfare, and housing would be excluded from future active review. Also, the ruling suggests that the suspect classification is limited to racial classifications.[21] These limits are further delineated in *Rodriguez* v. *San Antonio Independent School Board*[22] where Justice Powell, speaking for the 5 to 4 majority, rejected the lower court's decision that education is a fundamental right guaranteed by the Constitution against state interference and that state law using local property taxes to finance public schools had created a class of citizens based on wealth as "suspect" as those based on race.

Earlier, the Supreme Court had ruled in *Lindsey* v. *Normet*[23] that the:

> Constitution does not provide judicial remedies for every social and economic ill. We are unable to perceive in that document any constitutional guarantee to access to dwellings of a particular quality. . . . Absent constitutional mandate, the assurance of adequate housing . . . is a legislative not a judicial function.[24]

Recent Cases in Exclusionary Zoning

The *Dandridge* case forms a precedent which portends difficulties for any argument that wealth discrimination should be considered on the same footing as racial discrimination. The *Rodriguez* and *Lindsey* cases serve only to reinforce the fears initiated by *Dandridge*. Nevertheless, poverty and racial discrimination are sufficiently related to call for similar judicial treatment in certain cases.[25]

These recent rulings are the opposite of several early federal court decisions. Three of the four leading zoning cases in the 1920s—there have been none heard by the Supreme Court since—contained a rather explicit caveat. In response to allegations that the exclusion of apartments amounted to a form of economic segregation, these early opinions pointed out that new single-family houses were being built at that time within the reach of the lower-income groups.[26] If new single-family housing is beyond the reach of lower-income groups, the corollary of this opinion should outlaw the exclusion of housing, such as apartments, which would be within the financial grasp of these groups. In addition, *Village of Euclid v. Ambler Realty Company* offers the following possibility:

> It is not meant by this, however, to exclude the possibility of cases where the general public interest would so far outweigh the interest of the municipality that the municipality would not be allowed to stand in the way.[27]

When it finally comes, the decision drastically limiting the local power to exclude low- and moderate-income housing could be phrased, not as a new reading of the law, but as a return to principles enunciated in earlier court opinions.[28]

Two other cases have given opponents of exclusionary zoning reason to be optimistic. In *Edwards v. California*, the U.S. Supreme Court supported the argument that the poor have a constitutional right to move into any residential area of the state. Reasoning that a state may not isolate itself from the difficulties faced by other states, the Court refused to allow California to prevent indigents from moving into the state.[29] Twenty-eight years later the Court ruled that state residency requirements for receiving welfare payments were a denial of equal protection because population mobility is a constitutional right and any classification that restricts the right to travel cannot be upheld without a showing of compelling state interest.[30] Whether or not the present Supreme Court will apply that ruling to exclusionary zoning cases is, in light of the *Dandridge* decision, uncertain.

The direct attack on exclusionary zoning began in 1969, the year before ASPO's first report on the subject was issued.[31] Since then, final disposition has been made in the three federal court cases with which the report dealt. In addition, at least seven other such cases have been tried, with mixed success, at various levels in the federal judicial system.

[Extensive report materials omitted.]

State Court Decisions. While the federal court decisions have focused primarily on the question of racial discrimination, the state court decisions, particularly those of Pennsylvania and New Jersey, have tended to examine exclusionary zoning practices from a far broader perspective by focusing on the problem of regional growth and development. They appear to be developing a principle of intraregional mobility that encompasses more than the housing needs of racial minorities.[32] The decisions of these state courts show that some of them are becoming increasingly sensitive to the relationship between zoning practices and a wide range of contemporary problems such as education and employment and are willing to invalidate such ordinances and practices when they become too restrictive.

[The full ASPO report examines a number of decisions in the state courts of Pennsylvania, New Jersey, New York, and Michigan; material omitted.]

Challenges to Exclusionary Zoning

Evaluation of the Judicial Approach. There are several trends apparent in both the state and federal court decisions in challenges of exclusionary zoning practices.

1. Requirements of a large minimum lot size have generally been rejected as unrelated to the health, safety, or general welfare in particular applications. However, the concept has not been declared invalid per se.
2. The courts have ordered municipalities to plan for the housing needs of all their residents, particularly those in the lower- and middle-income brackets. Some courts have also ordered the implementation of these plans.
3. Challenges based upon the equal protection clauses of the U.S. Constitution and individual state constitutions have generally been successful. However, while the state courts have extended the equal protection argument to include discrimination on the basis of wealth as well as race, the federal courts have not.
4. The courts, particularly the state courts, have shown a growing awareness and understanding of the exclusionary effects and the social and economic consequences of an increasing number of zoning practices.

Federal Court Trends. In addition, the cases examined in the preceding chapter reflect several developing trends in the federal courts:

1. A referendum held on the questions of allowing the construction of public housing or zoning that would allow the construction of low- or moderate-cost housing may be constitutional even if the motive for holding the referendum is discriminatory.
2. However, actions by a local government, in response to discriminatory sentiments of its citizens, to prevent the construction of such housing are suspect and generally will not be allowed.
3. Challengers of exclusionary zoning, rather than having to prove an invidious motive, can look to the effect of land-use policies.
4. Scattered-site public housing located according to very specific formulas can be ordered by the court.
5. More generally: Under current federal legislation, the supremacy clause of the federal constitution probably will not be a successful weapon in the attack on exclusionary zoning practices. And, as a result of rulings by the Supreme Court,[33] housing is not a "fundamental interest." If it were, localities would have to justify restrictions on it by demonstrating some compelling interest.

State Court Trends. The state courts have been used more frequently as a forum to challenge exclusionary zoning practices. Unlike the federal bench, state courts have had to deal with zoning practices for decades. They know what is transpiring at the local level of government and understand how planning jargon can be used as a cover for prejudice. In addition, they appreciate the real limitations of any attempt by the judiciary to supervise a major restructuring of land-use policy.[34] Furthermore, many challenges to exclusionary zoning practices lack a substantial federal question needed to merit review by the federal courts, particularly the Supreme Court.

Trends in the state court rulings reflect their greater understanding of local zoning and planning practices.

1. Large minimum lot size requirements have been struck down as unrelated to the general welfare, health, or safety of the community and as an unreasonable use of the police power in violation of the due process and equal protection clauses of the

Fourteenth Amendment. However, they have not been declared unconstitutional per se.

2. Fiscal zoning has been rejected.
3. Minimum building cost requirements are illegal.
4. Minimum floor area requirements have been ruled illegal.
5. Limitations on the number of apartments that can be built annually are illegal in a growing number of states.
6. Cost-increasing variables have been rejected, although not ruled invalid per se.
7. Restrictions on the number of bedrooms in apartment units have generally been rejected, although not ruled invalid per se. The courts have ruled, however, that a municipality cannot restrict family size.
8. The burden of proof falls on the municipality that seeks to deny permits to allow mobile homes or apartments: in Michigan a zoning ordinance cannot stand when its primary purpose is to exclude a certain element of residential dwellers; mobile homes and apartments are afforded the status of "preferred use;" and, in Pennsylvania the burden of proof falls upon the municipality if it wishes to deny a permit for a special exception, as apartments are sometimes classified, or if it totally excludes, directly or by effect, a legitimate use such as multiple-family housing.
9. Courts are recognizing that apartments are not incompatible with single-family detached houses.
10. Virtually all state court rulings on exclusionary zoning have viewed the "general welfare" of enabling legislation to mean the general welfare of the regional rather than just the local population.
11. The major exception to this view is in New York where timed development, when not seen as exclusionary, was finally approved by the courts, and the "general welfare" was treated as that of only the local populace.
12. Local government has the duty to ensure housing for all its residents and potential residents. Courts have ordered local governments to make plans to accomplish these ends.
13. Discrimination on the basis of wealth in zoning ordinances violates principles of equal protection.
14. State courts have frequently stated explicitly that they will not countenance exclusionary zoning practices under any guise.

Judicial Approaches. Challengers to exclusionary zoning practices have generally followed one of two approaches. They have either challenged the validity of the law itself or the application of the law to the plaintiff's property. But these approaches have often failed. If one challenges a specific regulation and not the decision in regard to the particular fact situation, one may not win the case even if the court rules that the regulation is invalid. At great expense and time, Joseph Girsh got the Pennsylvania Supreme Court to declare that each community had to permit some apartments. A year later he still had not even begun to build his apartments. Nether Providence Township had rezoned other land for apartments and continued to deny Mr. Girsh his building permit. Girsh died, so the project never was built.[35]

There will probably be a tendency for new challenges to exclusionary zoning practices to attack the practices of some logical grouping of municipalities—a region, a county —rather than those of a single municipality. These legal challenges will continue to stress the regional nature of both the "general welfare" and housing needs. Such challenges may find success in a state like New Jersey where the lower courts have handled numerous exclusionary zoning cases. However, the comparatively inexperienced courts in other states may be more hostile to this approach until they develop a body of case law on the subject.

The problem in the judicial approach was succinctly recognized by New Jersey's Superior Court:

> The judiciary cannot be expected to alleviate a condition that definitely calls for legislative action from either the national or state governments. The courts can only meet each specific situation as it is presented, and while one community may have facts which justify court intervention, the relief will not necessarily be the same in all areas unless the factual content justifies intervention. . . .[36]

Other courts have since echoed this assessment.[37] If the United States Supreme Court were to find suburban zoning practice to be a denial of equal protection, even with the most sweeping language, only one case involving one parcel of land and one municipality will have been settled. The courts have a limited, but still essential role: to act as a predicate to legislative reform.[38]

The Legislative Approach. Legislative and administrative attempts to eliminate or overcome local exclusionary zoning practices can originate at several levels of government.

At the state level, legislation can be enacted to either prevent the use of exclusionary zoning practices in zoning ordinances or to overrule local ordinances and practices that are exclusionary. Opponents of exclusionary zoning have suggested that the states, at a minimum, take these four actions: (a) amend zoning and other municipal land-use power enabling legislation to specifically prohibit exclusionary land-use practices; (b) survey any existing exclusionary practices and outline corrective measures;[39] (c) require that housing needs be made an express part of all communities' comprehensive planning processes; and (d) require that the housing element in local planning be designed to relate to regional low- and moderate-income housing needs.[40]

In a law review article the Davidoffs call for the creation of a policy that explicitly rejects the notion that zoning should be based on income considerations except in a finding of special need.[41] They suggest seven proposals which are directed toward opening local communities to members of all classes and races who seek entry to them.[42]

[An extensive discussion of the Davidoffs' ideas is in the full ASPO PAS Report; material omitted.]

In addition to the Davidoffs' recommendations, further state enabling legislation should be enacted to provide assistance so that areawide planning and community development agencies can perform their regional housing functions. A comprehensive development guide and a community development program should be prepared and implemented at the state level concomitant with the development of similar instruments by local and regional jurisdictions throughout the state.[43] Without standards in state enabling legislation or some other statutory context within which regional housing needs can be allocated, such jurisdictions have no guide in making decisions about the distribution of land uses to meet regional needs.[44]

Just removing the statutory barriers and enacting positive enabling legislation will not guarantee the construction of low- and moderate-income housing near the jobs in the suburbs. Mary Nenno suggests other measures.[45]

[Material omitted.]

In addition, a state legislature could take advantage of its option to change its formula for allocation of "revenue sharing" funds for local distribution to grant increased funds to municipalities that have large numbers of low- and moderate-income residents. However, a realistic perspective must be maintained. There is little reason to expect any suburban and rural dominated state legislature to adopt such direct and explicit legislation.[46] Some states have instead pursued the second legislative approach and passed legislation which creates a state agency with power to preempt local governments' zoning authority.

Attempts have also been made at lower levels of government to foster the construction of low- and moderate-income housing in suburbs which exclude such housing.[47] Perhaps the most widely discussed is the regional housing dispersal plan adopted in 1970 by the Miami Valley Regional Planning Commission (Dayton, Ohio).[48]

Of ordinances enacted at the county level requiring a certain percentage of the total number of dwelling units to be devoted to lower-income households, the Fairfax County, Virginia, ordinance has received the most attention.[49] Land banking also offers the county or local government an opportunity to provide sites for low- and moderate-income housing.[50] Land banking involves the acquisition of developable land by a local government several years in advance of urbanization in order to guide urban development.

Although the federal role is in a state of flux and its future form unknown, federal subsidies must be forthcoming to support low- and moderate-income housing in the absence of state or local subsidy programs. Even with all exclusionary practices eliminated, low-income housing probably could not be built without subsidies. Equally important are the carrots the federal government can offer as incentives to recalcitrant communities to encourage them to cooperate with regional fair share programs. The A-95 review function accorded the Miami Valley Regional Planning Commission provides a potentially effective lever with which to gain the cooperation and participation of reluctant communities in the commission's fair share housing plan. But even the future of A-95 is cloudy. The Environmental Protection Agency has used funding disincentives to gain cooperation from localities. It has withdrawn funding from a major southern city by withdrawing certification, ordering a cutoff in funds, and recommending that other federal agencies take notice.[51]

In the past federal funds have subsidized much public improvement in suburban communities that practice exclusionary zoning. The very existence of these suburbs has been made possible by the construction of federally subsidized highways and the fortuitous locations of interchanges. Equally significant have been the subsidies for schools, open space, and community facilities. There is also the continuing role of FHA mortgage guarantees in the production of millions of suburban homes in communities from which low- and moderate-income minority groups are excluded by the discriminatory use of development controls as well as the federally assisted relocation of industrial firms from inner city renewal sites or highway rights-of-way to suburban locations beyond the reach of inner city job seekers.[52] What is needed is the commitment of the federal government to no longer subsidize in any manner, no matter how indirect it may seem, communities that practice exclusionary zoning.

Conclusion. No single approach challenging exclusionary zoning practices will eliminate them and guarantee a reduction in the economic and social dichotomies that now exist between central city and suburb or in the wide disparities in housing that currently exist between lower-income and higher-income groups. Continuation of the past judicial approach will eventually result in all exclusionary provisions being struck down on a case-by-case basis. Although courts in only three states—Michigan, New Jersey,

Pennsylvania—have handled many exclusionary zoning cases, their decisions will serve as precedents to courts in other states. But this approach could take a generation to succeed. If successful, the challenge posed in "pattern and practice" cases such as *Baylis* where plaintiffs ask the court to declare a number of exclusionary practices illegal throughout a state and order that inclusionary provisions be enacted in their place could bring about the elimination of exclusionary zoning practices somewhat sooner.

Changes in state zoning enabling legislation that prohibit the concept of exclusionary zoning and specific exclusionary practices would also contribute to a cessation of the use of such practices. However, continued surveillance of land-use regulations would be needed so that newly devised exclusionary practices could be prohibited. Until such changes in zoning enabling legislation are enacted and enforced, a statewide or several regional level public agencies with the power to preempt local zoning regulations found to be exclusionary should be created.

Yet the elimination of exclusionary zoning practices will not, by itself, guarantee that the suburbs will be open to the low- and moderate-income family. Incentives to encourage the inclusion of low- and moderate-income housing must be used.

Education of the population is an essential component of any effort to disperse low- and moderate-income housing into exclusionary communities. But the fears and ignorance that generate so much opposition to introducing this housing to the "better off" suburbs may be so entrenched that no program of education[53] could be effective. Here nothing succeeds like success. A successful low- or moderate-income scattered-site housing project will do more to relieve fears and anxieties about such housing than any attempt at community education.

The practice of exclusionary zoning can be reduced and eliminated by pursuing an assault on the judicial, legislative, and administrative fronts. By itself, a judicial decision will not end exclusionary practices. But combined with legislation and administrative procedures that support it, future court decisions can lead to a curtailment, if not complete elimination, of exclusionary zoning.

Footnotes

1. Mary Brooks, *Exclusionary Zoning,* Planning Advisory Service Report No. 254 (Chicago: ASPO, 1970), contains an overview of the subject as well as a review of pre-1971 litigation and legislation.
2. *Ibid.,* p. 3.
3. Note, "Exclusionary Zoning and Equal Protection," 84 *Harvard Law Review* 1645 (1971), at 1665.
4. For an excellent examination of more than 40 years of research on the educational and attitudinal effects of classroom segregation and integration, consult Meyer Weinberg, *Desegregation Research: An Appraisal* (Bloomington, Indiana: Phi Delta Kappa, 1968). The most widely discussed reports on the topic have been the two most comprehensive: U.S. Commission on Civil Rights, *Racial Isolation in the Public Schools* (Washington: U.S. Government Printing Office, 1967) and James Coleman, et al., *Equality of Educational Opportunity* (Washington: U.S. Department of Health, Education, and Welfare, 1966).
5. See Mollie Orshansky, "The Poor in City and Suburb, 1964," *Social Security Bulletin,* December 1966, pp. 29-30; and National Committee Against Discrimination in Housing, *The Impact of Housing Patterns on Job Opportunities* (Washington: National Committee Against Discrimination in Housing, 1968), p. 28.
6. Based on data contained in U.S. Bureau of the Census, *Census of Population: 1960.* Vol. 1, *Characteristics of the Population, Part 1, United States Summary* (Washington: U.S. Government Printing Office, 1964), p. 1-576; and U.S. Bureau of the Census, *Census of Population: 1970, General Social and Economic Characteristics, Final Report PC(1)-C1 United States Summary* (Washington: U.S. Government Printing Office, 1972), p. 1-415.
7. *Ibid.*
8. Lawrence Sager, "Exclusionary Zoning: Constitutional Limitations on the Power of Municipalities to Restrict the Use of Land." A paper prepared for panel and workshop discussion at the June 8-11, 1972, Biennial Conference, at the University of Colorado, Boulder, Colorado, p. 6. Lawrence Sager, New York University School of Law, 40 Washington Square South, New York, N.Y. 10012.

Recent Cases in Exclusionary Zoning

9. Randall W. Scott, *State and Urban Reporter*, November-December, 1972, p. 10.
10. Nassau County Planning Commission, *Apartments–Their Past and Future Impact on Suburban Living Patterns* (1963); Prince George's County Economic Development Committee, *A Study of Income Expenditures by Family Dwellings, 1963-1966*; "High-Rent Apartments in the Suburbs," *Urban Land*, October 1961; Dominic Del Guidice, "Cost-Revenue Implications of High-Rise Apartments," *Urban Land*, February, 1963. One report, James Pammel, *Apartments: Analysis of Multiple Family Dwellings, the Prospects and Recommendations for the City of Falls Church, Virginia* (January 1962), found that while garden apartments produce about the same deficit as do single-family houses, high-rise apartments produce a surplus of tax funds over expenditures. Apartments were found to produce more tax revenue than educational costs while the reverse was true for detached single-family dwellings in Vancouver, British Columbia: Planning and Property Department, "Supplementary Apartment Report" (Vancouver: The Corporation of the District of North Vancouver, B.C., April 1969).
11. *Rodriguez v. San Antonio Independent School District*, 337 F. Supp. 280 (W.D. Texas 1971), 41 *U.S. Law Week* 4407 (1973). School district financing cases are of particular interest to opponents of exclusionary zoning because they treat some of the same constitutional issues as do challenges to exclusionary zoning.
12. *Township of Willistown v. Chesterdale Farms, Inc.*, 300 A.2d 107 (Pennsylvania Cmwlth. 1973), at 114.
13. Larry Skipworth, "Plutocracy or Democracy in the Suburbs," *Planning Comment*, Winter-Fall, 1971-72, p. 8. Individual copies available for $2.50 from *Planning Comment*, Department of City and Regional Planning, University of Pennsylvania, 34th & Walnut Streets, Philadelphia, Pa. 19104.
14. Skipworth, p. 9.
15. *Ibid.*
16. Note 3, *supra* at 1649. The use of equal protection in this area is now believed to be restricted to racial classifications by the current Supreme Court interpretation.
17. *Ibid.*, p. 1650.
18. Active review means a more thorough examination of the facts of a case than is normally performed—"strict judicial scrutiny" according to the U.S. Supreme Court.
19. Note 3, *supra* at 1650-1652.
20. 397 U.S. 471 (1970).
21. Note 3, *supra* at 1652-1653.
22. 41 *U.S. Law Week* 4407 (1973).
23. 405 U.S. 56 (1972).
24. *Id.* at 74.
25. Note 3, *supra* at 1653.
26. *Miller v. Board of Public Works of Los Angeles*, 234 P. 381 (1925) *appeal dismissed*, 273 U.S. 781 (1927); *Brett v. Building Commissioner of Brookline*, 145 N.E. 269 (1924); *State Ex. rel. Twin City Building and Investment Company v. Houghton*, 174 N.W. 885 (1919), *rev'd. on rehearing*, 176 N.W. 159 (1920).
27. 272 U.S. 365 (1926) at 390.
28. George Sternlieb and Lynne Sagalyn, *Zoning and Housing Costs: The Impact of Land Use Controls on Housing Price* (New Brunswick, N.J.: Center for Urban Policy Research, 1972), p. 22.
29. 314 U.S. 160 (1941).
30. *Shapiro v. Thompson*, 394 U.S. 618 (1969).
31. For a discussion of the elements of the early court cases, see Brooks, *Exclusionary Zoning*, pp. 15-18.
32. David Heeter, "The Challenge to Exclusionary Zoning: Two Responses" (unpublished), p. 15.
33. *Lindsey v. Normet*, 405 U.S. 56 (1972); *Rodriguez v. San Antonio Independent School District*, 41 *U.S. Law Week* 4407 (1973).
34. Richard Babcock, "The Courts Enter the Land Development Marketplace," *City Magazine* (January-February 1971), p. 64.
35. Fred Bosselman, "Practical Application of Recent Zoning Decisions," in *Recent Decisions in Land and Municipal Law*, John Coutoure and John Wolhaupter, eds. (Washington: National Association of Home Builders, 1971), p. 8.
36. *Southern Burlington County NAACP v. Township of Mount Laurel*, 290 A.2d 465 (New Jersey Super. Ct. 1972), at 472.
37. In dismissing plaintiffs' request for sweeping relief including court orders requiring defendant municipalities to change their exclusionary zoning laws, Pennsylvania's Commonwealth Court ruled that plaintiffs lacked standing and repeatedly stated that granting of such relief by the court would "be a violation of the whole concept of separation of legislative and judicial branches of the government." *Commonwealth of Pennsylvania et al. v. County of Bucks et al.*, 302 A.2d 897 (Pennsylvania Cmwlth. 1973).
38. Babcock, p. 64.
39. These first two actions were among the reliefs sought in *Baylis*.
40. Randall W. Scott, "Exclusionary Land-Use Practices, or Growth Policies and Exclusionary Zoning." Submitted for presentation at Confer-In '72, American Institute of Planners Annual Conference, Boston, Paper No. 22, p. 13.
41. Paul and Linda Davidoff, "Opening the Suburbs: Toward Inclusionary Land-Use Controls," 22 *Syracuse Law Review* 509 (1971), at 525.
42. These proposals were introduced in greater detail in the New York Assembly by Assemblyman Franz Leichter. A.4947 New York Legislature Regular Session (1971). They were not enacted.

43. Mary Nenno, *Housing in Metropolitan Areas: Roles and Responsibilities of Five Key Actors* (Washington: National Association of Housing and Redevelopment Officials, 1973), p. 37.

44. Yale Rabin, "Challenging Discriminatory Development Controls: Some Thoughts on Future Directions," November 20, 1970 (unpublished), p. 6.

45. Nenno, p. 37.

46. The rural and suburban dominated Illinois General Assembly failed by 7 votes to give the required three-fifths majority needed to adopt a Workers Residential Rights Act (House Bill 709, 78th General Assembly, State of Illinois, 1973 and 1974) which embodied many of the Davidoffs' recommendations as well as potentially effective enforcement provisions. This act would have provided detailed standards in accordance with which a community that has experienced an increase in nonresidential building permits may adopt a low- and moderate-income housing development plan. In addition it provides state standards for such housing and sets forth formulae to determine if a community has met the minimum housing needs of low- and moderate-income workers.

47. Several of these efforts, in the implementation or discussion stages, are discussed in Mary Brooks, *Lower Income Housing* pp. 23-38.

48. Miami Valley Regional Planning Commission, *A Housing Plan for the Miami Valley Region—A Summary* (Dayton, Ohio, July 1970).

49. Proposed amendments to Chapter 30 (Zoning Ordinance) of the 1960 Code of the County of Fairfax, Virginia, requiring low- and moderate-income housing quota in the following districts: PHD, R-GC, RT-5, RTC-5, RT-10, RTC-10, RM-2, RM-2G, and RM-2M.

50. Carol Van Alstyne, ed., *Land Bank Handbook: Advance Acquisition of Sites for Low- and Moderate-Income Housing* (Greensboro, N.C.: Piedmont Triad Council of Governments, 1972).

51. Scott, p. 15.

52. Rabin, pp. 5-6.

53. See Brooks, *Lower Income Housing*, pp. 61-63.

Exclusionary Zoning Strategies:

Effective Lawsuit Goals & Criteria

Norman Williams, Jr.,
Tatyana Doughty, and
R. William Potter

Norman Williams is professor of urban planning and adjunct professor of law at Rutgers University; he is the author of the multi-volume work, Land Use and the Police Power. *He was previously executive director of the Governor's Advisory Commission on Transportation, New Jersey, and chief of the Office of Master Planning, New York City Department of City Planning. Mr. Williams is a graduate of Yale College, and holds a law degree from Yale University Law School.*

At the time of original publication [1972], Tatyana Doughty was a third-year student at Rutgers Law School and a member of the law review; she is a graduate of Bryn Mawr. R. William Potter was a third-year student at Rutgers and chairman of Rutgers Public Interest Research Group; he is a graduate of Princeton.

This article consists of a portion of an article originally titled "The Strategy On Exclusionary Zoning: Towards What Rationale and What Remedy?", published in the Land Use Controls Annual 1972 *(reprinted with permission of the American Society of Planning Officials).*

The question to be addressed is, what are the goals of an effective lawsuit against exclusionary zoning? What can such a lawsuit accomplish, and what should it try to accomplish? Moreover, what criteria should be used in deciding whether such a lawsuit is likely to be effective in reaching such goals?

Housing and Environmental Values

In litigation directed against exclusionary zoning there exists a potential conflict between housing needs and environmental values. The latter are of two kinds:
- Protecting basic environmental values; as, for example, preventing any development which would upset the ecological balance of an area.
- Maintaining the amenities of a pleasant low-density residential area.

As a general principle, if there is absolutely no way to avoid a conflict between the provision of needed housing and such environmental values, the need for housing must be given preference. However, somewhat different considerations are involved between the two types of environmental values. If a conflict should arise between housing and the critically important ecological values, a really serious question would be presented. Fortunately, in the present situation there is no reason why any conflict of this type need arise, if the strategy for the antiexclusionary litigation is thought through carefully in advance. As indicated above, the area available for residential development in the principal growth areas of New Jersey is large, and only a relatively small area is needed for the more intensive housing under discussion here.[27] There is therefore no reason whatever for precipitating a situation where the new, more intensive housing would be placed on an ecologically fragile site.[28]

As for the second type of environmental values, the protection of residential amenities involves considerations which are important, but not quite so commanding. The special amenities of low-density living—peace and quiet, freedom from heavy traffic, noise, and fumes, a rural or semirural appearance or "character"—depend upon the existence of a low-density pattern over a substantial area. In such areas, any more intensive use, including housing, can have a decided impact upon traffic generation and the street pattern and also upon the suburban "character."[29]

If the only way to get the needed housing is by sacrificing this second type of environmental values, they will have to be sacrificed. However, there is a good deal to be said for taking a little time to consider whether this is necessary.[30] While there may be times when it will be, the chances are this can be avoided or minimized.[31]

Goals

The goals of an antiexclusionary lawsuit may be stated simply:
- Such a suit should be designed to open up substantial areas of good residential land for more intensive housing, particularly for low- and moderate-income groups.
- On the assumption that there are opportunities for providing the needed housing without serious environmental damage, a lawsuit against exclusionary zoning should be pointed towards a rationale and a remedy which will make it possible to protect the ecological balance in the area, while ensuring provision of the needed housing. In addition, such a remedy should not cause more than a minimum of damage to those amenities in the residential environment which land-use controls are designed to protect.

In considering what type of lawsuit will be effective, it must be assumed that at least some towns will resort to every strategy to protect their present favored position.

Criteria

A lawsuit against exclusionary zoning can be expected to be effective if two critical elements—the legal rationale and the legal remedy—are designed quite specifically to ensure provision of the needed types of housing. This automatically rules out several types of lawsuits.
- First, if the result of a suit is simply to authorize residential development with smaller lot sizes or for luxury housing, it is likely that this will merely enable builders to increase their profits, instead of reducing the cost of housing.[32] Such a suit should not be expected to be of any help to lower-cost housing.
- Second, if such a suit is to open the way for the needed housing, some mechanism will have to be devised which can estimate the total extent of such need.
- Third, in the present metropolitan situation, a realistic definition of housing need must cover more than a single municipality. The housing market is regional or subregional in scope, for people tend to look for housing in various locations near their jobs. Furthermore, most of the new jobs are in outer or midsuburban locations, and those who most need good jobs live largely in the central cities. There is no way of

solving the major problems of these central cities, particularly for housing and recreation, within their present boundaries.[33] Thus, a substantial amount of out-migration may be expected. A realistic definition of housing need must therefore take into account the probable and desirable out-migration from such cities; that is to say, such a definition must focus upon regional needs. For these reasons there is simply no technically acceptable way to define the extent of housing need for a single municipality.[34] In contrast, the extent of the housing need for a larger area (a region or subregion) can be estimated, and such need can then be distributed among the municipalities according to various criteria. The choice of such criteria is a matter of the first importance and involves basic decisions on metropolitan growth policy. Several obvious possibilities come to mind at once: (1) the amount of in-commuting by low-paid workers; (2) the amount of existing inexpensive housing; and (3) the availability of: (a) more employment opportunities, present and future, including the extent of vacant land zoned for industry; (b) large areas of suitable terrain zoned for residence; (c) capacity in good schools, or bonding capacity to build more schools, or some other index of relative municipal wealth, such as assessed real property valuation per public school pupil; and (d) other public facilities, particularly sewers and mass transportation. Once such considerations are taken into account, it will be clear that some communities need and are appropriate for larger quantities of higher-density housing than others. Thus decisions as to the needed amount of housing will vary considerably among different communities.

- Fourth, since the suit is also intended to provide some protection for environmental amenities, the same mechanism used for determining housing needs can do so in two ways: by setting some upper limit to the needed housing, and by reviewing specific site proposals in the context of environmental considerations. That is to say, the remedy should open the way for rational consideration of both the total need for housing, particularly for less expensive housing, and the most appropriate locations for such housing.

- Finally, to state the obvious, a decree and a rationale invalidating only one type of exclusionary control will not advance things very far. A decree and a rationale limited in its effect to a single site will accomplish even less. Such a lawsuit should therefore be designed to avoid the prospect of repetitive litigation on the same or closely related issues.

Type of Lawsuit

These criteria point directly to the type of action to be brought.

- First, an effective lawsuit against exclusionary zoning should be brought against all the municipalities in an area of substantial size—in effect, a planning region or subregion.
- Second, such a suit should challenge the entire pattern of exclusionary controls in the area involved.
- Third, the plaintiffs should be chosen in such a way as to raise directly the question of regional need, including some present and potential in-commuters to work in the area, and perhaps also some of the central cities of the region.
- Fourth, the suit should aim towards a decree which would set up, under judicial supervision, a mechanism to determine the total need for housing, by income levels, on both a local and regional basis and to distribute the total regional need (in accordance with stated criteria) among local communities.

- Fifth, if the more intensive housing is to be fitted into the developing suburban pattern with a minimum of harm thereto, a mechanism must be available which would make it possible for the towns to consider the relative advantages of alternative locations. In other words, if an antiexclusionary zoning suit is to open the way to the most needed housing, while minimizing the potential environmental damage such a suit must be designed to establish something akin to a regional planning process for housing, under judicial goading and continuing judicial supervision.

The Judicial Function

It is in connection with the supervision of a mechanism to quantify and to distribute housing need that the most serious questions arise as to the scope of the judicial function. There is no technical difficulty in operating such a mechanism;[35] at least two counties are already doing so.[36] The more serious problem is whether the courts should step in to command and to supervise such a process on a large scale. If this seems like asking the courts to take on a difficult job, the short answer is that it is precisely that. On the other hand, the burden may not be any greater and in fact quite likely is less, than the burden of many uncoordinated law suits, challenging different devices as applied to different parcels of land. In the present metropolitan context, the judicial function is to translate broad constitutional or statutory principles into effective legal remedies. In other major areas of public policy, legislative and executive abdication has led to judicial control; this is almost a new definition of when the courts should step in. It is significant that a lower court in New Jersey has already issued a decree along these lines.[37]

The attack upon exclusionary zoning and the fashioning of an effective remedy involves many complex issues: the need for low-cost housing; the maintenance of pleasant residential neighborhoods; a broad variety of environmental and ecological issues; the validity of the present system of local financing for major public services; the adequacy of local public schools; and so on. In a normal situation, many of these questions would be appropriate for legislative solution; but this is not a normal situation. The problem is that the legislatures presently are paralyzed in dealing with such issues—for a simple reason. Suburban legislators play a dominant role in many legislatures. It is precisely those suburban areas for which the present system of governmental controls on land use serves to provide major benefits—not only zoning protection, but also an opportunity to improve the local tax base. The present local tax system encourages a suburban community actively to seek "good ratables" and to discourage "bad ratables," such as low-cost housing; in effect, the system provides a financial subsidy for those municipalities which adopt exclusionary zoning practices. In this situation, it is not reasonable to expect legislatures to take the initiative in abolishing such major benefits for their principal constituents.

In such a situation the judicial function therefore must have two aspects:

- The first is to distinguish basic rights—in this case, equality of access to housing, to a pleasant and healthful environment, and to good public services—from governmental interference directed explicitly against those with lower incomes.
- The second is to supervise the development and the implementation of remedies which will be genuinely effective in view of all the complex interrelationships indicated above.

It is in connection with the second function that the difficult questions arise. Fortunately this situation is not without persuasive precedent, for in two other analogous—and supremely important—situations during the last decade, the courts have successfully undertaken and carried out a similar role.

In connection with the reapportionment of legislatures, ever since *Baker v. Carr*[38] the courts have not only declared the general principle, but have also reviewed proposed legislative remedies, evaluated the practical problems involved, and approved (or disapproved) proposed solutions. In connection with the desegregation of public schools, the Supreme Court declared the general principle in *Brown v. Board of Education;*[39] but in the second *Brown*[40] decision, the Court wisely recognized the inevitable complexity of the problems involved in implementing the newly declared right and returned the problem to the lower courts with instructions to supervise the job of working it out.

The parallel between the problems of desegregation and reapportionment, and the problem of the termination of exclusionary land-use controls, is a close one. The case is persuasive that with exclusionary zoning the courts should follow the procedures set in those two earlier sets of precedents. Moreover, to do so in this type of situation will not provide a precedent for doing so in all sorts of other situations. In those few particularly important and special situations, judicial action can appropriately include both: (a) fashioning a remedy; and, (b) supervising its implementation. The criteria which will define and delimit these situations may be described as follows.

- The first and most essential element of the situation is that the legislature is paralyzed and unable to act—because an arrangement which violates basic rights of a substantial minority is eminently satisfactory to a large majority.
- Second, in these situations the implementation of the newly declared right requires some rather elaborate action by governmental agencies other than the court. Such implementation will often require complex reorganization of administrative (or even legislative) arrangements, where the importance of the declared right must be consistently balanced against other considerations—or against intransigent resistance, masked as other legitimate considerations. In such a situation those who are in charge of the machinery by which the right would normally be implemented are in reality adversary parties; for by implementing the right they would be losing what they regard as substantial personal advantages for themselves and their constituents: jobs for legislators facing reapportionment, segregated schools for segregationists, zoning protection and tax base enhancement in these zoning situations. It is therefore to be expected that many of them will react by resisting implementation—and the potential means of evasion are plentiful. To put the point bluntly, it is not realistic to depend on the good faith reaction of such people in carrying out implementation of the right.[41]
- Third, both the type and the amount of action required in implementation of the right may vary widely between different geographical situations. The point is obvious in connection with desegregation and reapportionment; in connection with zoning, a town with rapidly growing employment and large areas of vacant land zoned for industry is in a completely different situation from a remote rural township where there is almost no employment at all. Finally, in some instances what looks like the simple and obvious remedy may in fact accomplish nothing at all. For example, if the attention is focused upon the principle of lot size, a decree merely authorizing smaller lot sizes is likely to result merely in increased profits for the developer, rather than lower costs for consumers of housing. It is also likely to exacerbate efforts to preserve what environmentally valuable and ecologically fragile open space remains in the state.

The Basic Legal Theory

There are three possible legal theories upon which a lawsuit in this area, and the resulting decree, may be grounded:

- A constitutional decision based upon the equal protection clause; that is, a judicial declaration of equality of rights in access to housing and good residential land, as against overt governmental discrimination directed against those with lower incomes. This could be based upon either the federal or state constitutions.
- A new interpretation of the "general welfare" as including housing needs, at least in metropolitan areas, together with the notion that promotion of the "general welfare" is an affirmative criterion to which zoning laws must conform. This could be either a constitutional or a statutory concept.
- A further interpretation of the evolving constitutional doctrine of the right to travel and to settle in different parts of the country.

Equal Protection

The equal protection clause of the fourteenth amendment has been the principal instrument by which the law has proceeded against racial discrimination in connection with access to housing and to good residential land. On this basis the Supreme Court has outlawed racial zoning[42] and the enforcement of racial covenants[43] and has assisted in the demise of the alien land laws.[44] In these cases the emphasis upon racial discrimination was probably more important than the value judgment on the importance of housing, but the opinions make it clear that the Court regarded equal access to good housing and good residential land as a matter of serious importance. In more recent cases the Court has approached, but has not passed directly on, the question of whether there is a constitutional guarantee against the use of governmental power to limit access to housing on the basis of poverty.[45] A considerable legal literature has been produced on the Court's attitude toward this problem, focusing primarily on the question of how far the inverse presumption of validity—long recognized in due process-civil liberties cases[46]—should prevail in equal protection cases.[47]

This is not the place for a detailed review of this debate,[48] but a few points seem particularly worthy of mention.

- First, while recent Supreme Court opinions have enunciated some relevant principles, they are far from definitive. The Court's recent utterances indicate an ambivalent attitude—"a kind of free-floating anxiety about the problem of discrimination against the poor," as a recent commentator put it[49]—combined with a very real and thoroughly understandable concern over the potential implications of a broad ruling on the subject.[50]
- Second, commentators have been urging the Court to make a ruling on economic discrimination with respect to housing and have suggested various grounds upon which such a decision could be placed, without opening up too broad an area for future constitutional litigation. In these discussions, the commentators have emphasized some factors which are directly relevant to the question of exclusionary zoning. In particular, emphasis has been given to whether a given restriction may have the effect of blocking roads to social mobility and an escape from poverty, as for example by preventing equal opportunity in education and in employment.[51]
- There is also a serious question whether Supreme Court law is the place to look for the basic constitutional theory underlying a decision against exclusionary zoning. The

debate mentioned above has concentrated almost entirely on Supreme Court law; yet, with only one unimportant exception,[52] the Court has not decided a case on the use of the police power in planning law since 1928.[53] During the intervening forty-four years, the state courts have passed on nearly 10,000 such decisions, including a substantial number dealing with this particular issue, and there are a few important recent ones from lower federal courts.[54] It might, then, be worth examining the state decisions for a viable equal protection rationale—except for the fact that it is almost the accepted convention in American planning law that the precise legal basis for a constitutional decision is never mentioned.

General Welfare

Some of the recent decisions have suggested an alternative basic theory—quite an original one, as far as this field of law is concerned.[55] The Standard Zoning Enabling Act (still in effect in forty-six states) sets forth a list of the statutory goals of zoning, some broad and vague and some fairly specific; the former include a reference to promoting "the general welfare." The same phrase is also included in the standard list of nouns which are used to describe the bases for all public regulation under the police power. The "general welfare" is thus both a statutory and a constitutional concept in zoning. Under this theory, the general welfare requirement in the Standard Act is not merely an additional source of power, upon which additional restrictions (as for example aesthetic regulations) may be based, but is also an affirmative requirement to which all zoning restrictions must conform. If the notion of promoting the general welfare is to have any meaning in the context of contemporary metropolitan development, the provision of substantial new and inexpensive housing is clearly one of its most important aspects. In this context, it does not involve a major step—assuming appropriate plaintiffs are present who can raise the issue—to expand this notion of municipal responsibility to include a share of regional housing need. Under this theory, then, restrictions may be held not to conform to the general welfare requirement as set forth in the enabling law, or in general constitutional law.

The chief argument in favor of this approach is the traditional rule that, if a given lawsuit can be disposed of on narrow grounds, the courts will adopt this narrow ground rather than a broader one. More specifically, if a nonconstitutional basis is available, a constitutional ruling will not be made. Obviously, courts do not always follow this rule, and the use of a broader rationale may be somewhat more frequent when, as here, major legal issues are at stake.

There is a definite possibility that the courts may elect to use this narrower ground —that a zoning ordinance which stands in the way of better housing is *ultra-vires* the zoning enabling act—instead of addressing themselves to the constitutional issue of equal protection. The potential disadvantage in such a holding is obvious enough. The present exclusionary system has great advantages for those suburban areas which now hold the dominant power in the legislatures, and, if the courts attempt to abolish that system by a ruling based upon legislative intent, there is always the possibility that some statutory amendment may be passed to supersede such a ruling. A decision based upon this ground in effect involves a gamble that those benefiting from the present arrangements would not be able to think up and get passed a legislative amendment to give the exclusionary system at least a few more years of life. Such an amendment would probably set forth a legislative view that "the general welfare" should be interpreted in the parochial sense, i.e., with each municipality regarded as a separate unit—presumably with elaborate references to home rule and keeping government close to the people. Such action might not be too likely in a metropolitan state, but is far from inconceivable in others. If this should happen, in subsequent cases an antiexclusionary court would have to base the same ruling upon "the general welfare" as a constitutional concept, or shift to an equal protection rationale. It would be far better to settle the issue by invoking the constitutional ruling first.

Right to Travel

In another group of cases, the United States Supreme Court and some lower federal courts have been moving towards the establishment of a constitutional guarantee against local restrictions designed to prevent or discourage free interstate movement and also free movement within a state. For example, some thirty years ago the Court held invalid restrictions in California directed against the migration of "Okies" into that state.[56] More recently, an important decision[57] held that the long established one-year residency requirements adopted in many states as a prerequisite to receiving public welfare payments were invalid as an attempt to discourage interstate movement. Further, the decision held that the alleged state interest in protecting the state's finances against excessive demands for welfare was not a sufficient basis to justify such restrictions. The analogy to "fiscal zoning" is obvious. In addition, several lower federal courts have held invalid restrictions on access to public housing projects within individual communities, restricting these to local residents, on similar grounds.[58]

A ruling against exclusionary zoning, based primarily upon a right to interstate or intermunicipal travel, could have some serious consequences. In logic, such a decision would presumably preclude any arrangements which would set quantitative limits on the more intensive housing to be provided in any community. The principle may also have some perhaps unfortunate side effects. In the present rapidly changing situation, some suburban towns may be prepared to accept low- and/or moderate-cost housing, if they can be assured that priority will be given to solving their own greatest needs—that is, for their teachers and public employees.[59] It is of course true that such towns also have a broader responsibility to provide housing, and the existence of some housing with such a priority for local residents would of course not insulate such a community from a subsequent lawsuit based upon a share of regional need—but query whether it is antisocial for towns to take the initiative voluntarily to deal with their own problems first?

Conclusion re Legal Theories

The courts thus have a choice of alternative legal theories upon which to base the forthcoming decisions against exclusionary zoning. The long history of gradual progress against public and private discrimination in housing, phrased in racial terms, suggests a possible decision based upon broad equal protection grounds; and a decision on constitutional grounds is obviously less vulnerable to being undercut by legislatures stacked in favor of the beneficiaries of the present system. Yet in terms of the practical result, the choice of legal theories may not be too important. The two most likely possibilities —equal protection and general welfare—are both broad enough to provide essentially similar bases for more specific implementation looking toward providing the needed housing.

Nature and Extent of Municipal Responsibility

It seems probable that the basic legal theory of an antiexclusionary lawsuit will be based upon either equal protection or general welfare. As between these two, the choice of doctrine may not make a great deal of difference in the actual world, either on municipal action or on the type of housing produced. The next problem is to develop a legal rationale to implement that basic theory, in the context of the conflict between housing needs and suburban zoning restrictions. A review of the recent case law indicates that the courts have been developing two quite different rationales for a decision against exclusionary zoning, which might be referred to as "the Pennsylvania rationale" and "the sensible rationale." These two rationales differ widely in their implications for the future of metropolitan areas. This choice of a legal rationale on the nature and extent of municipal responsibility on housing is thus a matter of the first importance.

To start with, the "sensible" rationale, hereinafter referred to as the *first rationale*, has arisen primarily from cases involving a conflict between local land-use controls and federally sponsored inexpensive housing.[60] Under this rationale, any local community which invokes its planning and zoning powers is under an affirmative duty to use them on behalf of all groups of people in the community—not merely to provide for the rich, and perhaps also not merely for the poor, but for everybody. (There is a strong, though not always clearly expressed, flavor of equal protection doctrine in these opinions.) In most of the decisions to date, this rationale has focused directly upon a local need for housing within a municipality. The records in these cases made a clear showing of discrimination against local residents for economic and/or racial reasons, or at the least a quite conscious neglect of their needs. In any lawsuit which has been properly designed to raise the broader issue—that is, on the appropriate share of metropolitan housing needs for that town or towns—this rationale would presumably be expanded to include such needs.

Under the *second (Pennsylvania) rationale*, there is no clear definition of what is meant by "exclusionary zoning." Apparently it refers in a general way to a policy of resistance to more intensive land use and to suburban growth generally, and any fairly severe restrictions on new housing in a community are simply assumed to be exclusionary. Under this second rationale, a series of mechanical tests have been set up: at least one area must be open to multiple dwellings as of right, [61] no lot-size regulations shall require more than one acre, etc.[62] There is no attempt to guide the type of housing, the amount, or the locations; nor is there any indication of concern with providing for lower-income groups. The assumption apparently is that the interests of developers and of third-party non-beneficiaries are the same; if the former interests are satisfied, the latter will be too.[63]

The difference in actual results between these two rationales may be of major importance for the future structure of metropolitan areas. No one can predict the future with certainty, but in this situation it is not hard to foresee some of the probabilities. The essence of the first rationale is an affirmative duty to provide new housing. This necessarily implies a duty to provide whatever new housing is needed, which in turn requires, as a start, a determination in quantitative terms of the amount of new more intensive housing appropriate in each municipality. Such an approach thus goes far beyond approval of a specific site or project, and in fact is not likely to arise from a lawsuit where attention is focused upon a specific site or project. As indicated above, the major question here is whether the lawsuit has been framed so as to raise the question of regional housing needs, over and above purely local needs. An analysis and quantitative determination of local and regional housing needs will point to an increased need for low- and moderate-cost housing in almost all suburban towns.

- If such an approach were implemented, most suburban municipalities would then eventually tend to have a range of income levels, and so of housing types—with the proportions varying according to various criteria, including those suggested above.[64]
- Second, under these criteria, the appropriate amount of new more intensive housing would vary widely as between various townships. To take the obvious example, relatively more of such housing would be appropriate in a town located in a rapidly growing industrial area, with large vacant areas zoned for industry, and large amounts of dry flat land zoned for residence. Relatively less would be appropriate in a remote rural township with largely mountainous terrain, little employment, and not much prospect thereof.
- Third, under this approach the quantity of needed housing presumably would be determined by experts, working under the supervision of either a court or some regional agency. In this situation the municipalities would have no control over the quantity of new intensive housing; yet they would have the assurance that there would be some quantitative limit.[65] A decision to rezone some areas for such housing would therefore not necessarily result in opening up the entire township for the same kind of more intensive housing.
- Fourth, once an appropriate area of land[66] was made available for the needed housing, the municipality would retain a fairly free hand in zoning the remainder of its area.
- Finally, the local government could also exercise some control over decisions on the appropriate areas for the new housing. For example, it could guide such housing to nonecologically fragile areas, and to areas where the resulting traffic would not seriously disrupt the community's traffic pattern. On the other hand, the municipality would not have the power to restrict available locations unduly, nor to banish such housing to industrial districts. As far as exclusionary zoning is concerned, the test would then be whether enough land, somewhere in the municipality, was zoned for an appropriate density to make the new housing possible. If sufficient land is so zoned, it would not matter much—at least in equal protection or general welfare terms—what lot size, for example, was required in the most restrictive zoning district in town.[67]

Under the Pennsylvania rationale, metropolitan areas are likely to be very different. As that rationale has developed to date, many things are not clear, including its legal basis. The opinions appear to fluctuate back and forth between rationales based upon due process rights of the developer and equal protection for those excluded. In any event, every town would be required to permit some multiple dwellings, and no town could require lots over a certain size (perhaps one acre) anywhere.[68] The courts have indicated no interest in the income levels of the people served: in the leading Pennsylvania case on apartments, the proposed land use was clearly luxury housing, a high-rise multiple dwelling, and the opinion made it clear that to permit this would satisfy constitutional requirements. The probable results are not difficult to predict, especially under the present conditions of "fiscal zoning," i.e., before a basic change in the local real property tax system. The builders, free from many of the present restraints, could build what they most want to build, in a wide range of locations. It would hardly be argued seriously that what they most want to build is low-cost housing. This rationale is therefore likely to result in a substantial amount of expensive new housing for high-income people; that is, high-rise multiple dwellings, garden apartments, and townhouses, together with detached single-family housing on small lots.

Such new and more intensive housing would probably be concentrated largely in the prestige townships, where such housing is more readily salable—and where there are few poor people to upset things, and usually few jobs to attract such people. Moreover, no mechanism would exist for determining the quantities of such housing appropriate for various types of townships, and there would be no limit at all on the amount of such housing which could be built in a town. It is not clear to what extent the towns would have any locational control over such housing. One real possibility is that they could retain some control, so long as this control was phrased in terms of regulating building types and not density.[69] Under such a system, the decisions on the distribution of density would be made in effect by those developers who could obtain an option on land and were willing to sue.[70] In the absence of any public locational control, developers would be free to bid for any site which would appear to yield them substantial profits. It seems probable that the resulting serious environmental damage would be considerable; it seems practically certain that the gains in low- and moderate-cost housing would be negligible or nonexistent.

The differences between the results of the two rationales may be summarized in Table 1.

TABLE 1.

	First Rationale	Second (Pennsylvania) Rationale
On the occupants of the new more intensive house	A mix of various income groups	Mostly high income
On building types	A mix of building types	Perhaps the same, but with a much larger proportion of luxury housing, including single-family, detached houses on relatively small lots
On the treatment of different types of townships, in antiexclusionary litigation	The extent of responsibility for new housing would vary according to the amount of employment, and other criteria	No distinctions made between different townships
On what townships would grow fastest	Towns in industrial growth areas	The prestige townships
On control over the quantity of new more intensive housing	No local control—but there would be some assurance that a limit would exist	No public control at all
On the location of new intensive housing	Considerable local control	Little or no local control
Effect upon the local environment	Almost complete local control, to protect areas of special environmental value or ecological significance	Potentially devastating

From the viewpoint of the towns, especially the prestige towns, the choice is rather clear-cut. If the question comes up to them, would these towns rather accept some lower-income people among the new migrants, and retain some locational control over new housing? Or would these towns prefer to be assured that almost all new migrants are wealthy, but lose control over the amenities of their physical environment? Those with a sociological turn of mind will be looking forward with interest to the answer to this question.

Footnotes

27. See *supra* notes 16 and 17 and accompanying text. [[16] Aloi, Goldberg, & White, "Racial and Economic Segregation by Zoning: Death Knell for Home Rule?," 1969 *University of Toledo Law Review* 65; Becker,"Police Power and Minimum Lot Size Zoning," 1969 *Washington University Law Quarterly* 263;

Hagman, "Urban Planning and Development—Race and Poverty—Past, Present, and Future," 46 *Utah Law Review* 46 (1971); Sager, "Tight Little Islands: Exclusionary Zoning, Equal Protection, and the Indigent," 21 *Stanford Law Review* 767 (1969); "Symposium, Exclusionary Zoning," 22 *Syracuse Law Review* 465 (1971); Note, "Discriminatory Zoning: Legal Battleground of the Seventies," 21 American University Law Review 157 (1971); Note, "The Equal Protection Clause and Exclusionary Zoning after Valtierra and Dandridge," 81 *Yale Law Journal* 61 (1971); Note, "Exclusionary Zoning and Equal Protection," 84 *Harvard Law Review* 1645 (1971); Note, "Removing the Bar of Exclusionary Zoning to a Decent Home," 32 *Ohio State Law Journal* 373 (1971); Note, "Segregation and the Suburbs: Low-Income Housing, Zoning, and the Fourteenth Amendment," 56 *Iowa Law Review* 1298 (1971); Note, "The Responsibility of Local Zoning Authorities to Nonresident Indigents," 23 *Stanford Law Review* 774 (1971); Note, "The Constitutionality of Local Zoning," 79 *Yale Law Journal* 896 (1970); Note, "Snob Zoning: Developments in Massachusetts and New Jersey," 7 *Harvard Journal on Legislation* 246 (1970); Note, "Snob Zoning: Must a Man's Home Be a Castle?," 69 *Michigan Law Review* 339 (1970). [17] The Middlesex County Interim Master Plan, Vol. 20 (1968), estimates the unmet housing demand for low- and moderate-income households to be 23,605 units by 1975. Compare the finding in the ASPO study of zoning in Connecticut (American Society of Planning Officials, "New Directions in Connecticut Planning Legislation" at 189 [1967]), that the overall zoning pattern as mapped in that state did not provide enough capacity to take care of the anticipated population increase—but that rezoning only 6 per cent of the area then zoned for a half-acre or more, to permit a combination of single-family houses on 5,000-square-foot lots and garden apartments (at ten to the acre), would provide for doubling the state's present population, using the rezoned land alone.]

28. Unfortunately, we have to report that, after a detailed field inspection of the site involved in *Oakwood at Madison, Inc. v. Madison Township*, 117 N.J. Super. 11, 283, A.2d 353 (Law Div. 1972), the ecological problem at that site is more serious than was realized at the time the comment in 23 *Zoning Digest* 570 was written. South-Eastern Middlesex County and the adjacent area in Monmouth County depend primarily upon wells for water supply, and Burnt Fly Bog is an important recharge area for the ground-water system in that area. This bog covers an area of approximately 1,300 acres, extending across the county boundary. A recent single-family subdivision (built in 1968-69) has begun a residential incursion into the lowland of Burnt Fly Bog. The tract involved in *Oakwood at Madison*, covering 56.2 acres adjacent to the above-mentioned subdivison, represents a much deeper incursion extending 2,000 feet deeper into the center of Burnt Fly Bog. A far larger area, also adjacent and covering about 370 acres, almost all in the Bog, is in the ownership of the same or a related corporation. The proposed more intensive residential development in such an area would, of course, increase the run-off and bring a strong likelihood of incidental pollution with salt, oil, fertilizer, etc., directly into the surrounding recharge area. It was for this reason that in 1966 the two county planning boards made a joint declaration that the Bog should be publicly acquired and left untended, in its natural state. Because of the shortage of "Green Acres" funds, the contemplated public acquisition has been moving agonizingly slowly.

29. Like so many important things, this involves intangibles; essentially, the relationship between greenery and the mass of buildings plus attendant paved areas.

30. In the current metropolitan situation, those enjoying such values are at least as numerous, and perhaps considerably more numerous, than the lower-income groups who need new housing and a better environment so badly. Strategically it is not necessarily wise to ignore the majority.

31. *Cf. supra* notes 16 and 17.

32. *See supra* note 3. [[3] Although developers and lower-income groups both seek a more intensive use of land than current residents desire, their interests are not always synonymous. Developers, if given the choice, generally will build relatively high-income units and use any relaxation of zoning restrictions to reap greater profits. This would be of little benefit to the third-party nonbeneficiaries.]

33. Note the finding in the Kerner Report (Report of the National Advisory Commission on Civil Disorders, 1968, at 83) that the six principal complaints coming from the ghetto were as follows: police practices, unemployment, inadequate housing, inadequate education, poor recreation facilities, and the nonresponsive political mechanism. Four of these six problems would require land and public facilities for part of the solution, i.e., they would appropriately be dealt with in part through a planning program.

34. If a municipality is determined to make a try to define local housing needs, with some attention to regional needs, such an analysis could take into account such factors as the following:

(1) The existing supply of relatively inexpensive housing, less those dwelling units which are classified as substandard;

(2) The number of local residents (both households and unrelated individuals) with incomes below the poverty level, and below the minimum level which can afford new unsubsidized housing;

(3) As to the unrelated individuals, the extent to which such individuals would (in new housing) prefer to double up, or to continue living alone; and

(4) The number of nonresidents employed in the municipality, whose incomes are below the levels specified in (2) above, and the extent to which such persons would want to move into the community, if appropriate housing were available at prices they could afford.

Such an analysis would clearly be much better than nothing. However, it would not take into account the need for housing for nonresidents who might work in the community in the future; nor would it consider the relative desirability of the community as a place for the growth of employment or of more intensive housing.

35. Under such an arrangement, the judge, while retaining jurisdiction of the case, would appoint a special master with instructions to make a realistic estimate of total housing need by income categories, for the planning

subarea in question (or for a larger area), and to distribute the needed housing among the various townships, in accordance with stated criteria. If the townships decided to cooperate in such a study, they would have an opportunity to participate in the latter decisions—but not otherwise.

36. San Bernardino County Planning Department, "Government Subsidized Housing Distribution Model for Valley Portion San Bernardino County," (revised, January 20, 1972); Miami Valley Regional Planning Commission, Dayton, Ohio, "A Housing Plan for the Miami Valley Region," (April 1972). A recent ASPO study (Brooks, "Lower Income Housing: The Planners' Response," 1972) describes a substantial number of similar mechanisms which are now in various stages of development all over the country.

37. *Southern Burlington Co. NAACP v. Township of Mt. Laurel*, 1119 N.J. Super. 164, 290 A.2d 465 (Law Div. 1972).

38. 396 U.S. 186 (1962).

39. 347 U.S. 483 (1954).

40. 349 U.S. 294 (1955).

41. One lower New Jersey court has already taken upon itself the task of overseeing the implementation of just such an "affirmative plan" remedy. Judge Martino in *Southern Burlington County NAACP v. Township of Mount Laurel*, 119 N.J. Super. 164, 290 A.2d 465 (Law Div. 1972), after holding that Mt. Laurel's zoning ordinance unlawfully prevented plaintiffs from obtaining access to land suitable for the construction of government-subsidized housing expressly retained jurisdiction pending the development of a new ordinance consistent with the principles enunciated in his opinion. The decision is now before the New Jersey Supreme Court.

42. *Buchanan v. Warley*, 245 U.S. 60 (1917). *See also Monk v. City of Birmingham*, 87 F. Supp. 538 (1949), *aff'd.*, 185 F.2d 859 (1950), *cert. denied*, 341 U.S. 940 (1951).

43. *Shelley v. Kraemer*, 334 U.S. 1 (1948), *and see Barrows v. Jackson*, 346 U.S. 249 (1953); *see also Jones v. Alfred H. Mayer Co.*, 392 U.S. 409 (1968), which held that such discrimination even without state action is a "badge of slavery" within the purview of the thirteenth amendment; *Reitman v. Mulkey*, 387 U.S. 369 (1967), which held in effect that states owe their citizens protection against racial discrimination in sales of housing.

44. In *Sei Fujii v. California*, 217 P.2d 481 (Dist. Ct. App. 1950), *rehg. den.*, 218 p. 2d 595 (Dist. Ct. App. 1950), *aff'd.*, 38 Cal. 2d 718, 242 p.2d 617 (1952), *and Namba v. McCourt and Neuner*, 185 Ore. 579, 204 p.2d 569 (1949), the Supreme Courts of California and Oregon decided that, in the light of *Oyama v. California*, 332 U.S. 633 (1948) and other recent Supreme Court decisions, *Terrace v. Thompson*, 263 U.S. 197 (1923) and associated decisions should be regarded as overruled.

45. *Cf. Shapiro v. Thompson*. 394 U.S. 618 (1969); *Hunter v. Erickson*, 393 U.S. 385 (1969). Some analogy may be drawn to two lines of cases in which the Supreme Court has extended the equal protection clause to guarantee equal access to voting rights and procedural protections in criminal prosecutions are based upon an individual's ability to pay. *See, e.g., McDonald v. Board of Elections*, 394 U.S. 802 (1969); *Harper v. Virginia Board of Elections*, 383 U.S. 663 (1966); and *Williams v. Illinois*, 399 U.S. 235 (1970); *Douglas v. California*, 372 U.S. 353 (1963); *Griffin v. Illinois*, 351 U.S. 12 (1956). However, these cases have been distinguished from the problem of access to housing in that the right to vote and the right to due process in criminal prosecutions are "fundamental" constitutional guarantees whereas no such explicit right to be housed appears in the Constitution. *See generally* Michelman, "The Advent of a Right to Housing: A Current Appraisal," 5 *Harvard Civil Rights-Civil Liberties Law Review* 207 (1970). *But cf. Block v. Hirsh*, 256 U.S. 135, 156 (1921) (Holmes, J., dictum): "We submit that the due process right to life combined with the ninth amendment rights of all citizens, to an economic subsistence, guarantees citizens the right to equal housing."

46. *See United States v. Carolene Prods. Co.*, 304 U.S. 144, 152, n. 4 (1938). *See, e.g., Loving v. Virginia*, 388 U.S. 1 (1967); *Griswold v. Connecticut*, 381 U.S. 479 (1965); *McLaughlin v. Florida*, 379 U.S. 184 (1964). *See also* Lusky, "Minority Rights and the Public Interest," 52 *Yale Law Journal* 1 (1942); Note, "Judicial Review of the Administrative Exercise," 52 *Yale Law Journal* 168, and further articles collected at 175, n. 49. *See also* compilation of cases in concurrence of Mr. Justice Frankfurter in *Kovacs v. Cooper*, 336 U.S. 77, 90-94 (and comment of Mr. Justice Rutledge at 106); Note, "Presumption of Constitutionality not Applicable to Statutes Dealing with Civil Liberties," 40 *Columbia Law Review* 531 (1940); Richardson, "Freedom of Expression and the Function of Courts," 65 *Harvard Law Review* 1 2, n. 3,47-51 (1951); Kauper, "The First Ten Amendments," 37 *American Bar Association Journal* 717 (1951); Mason, "The Core of Free Government,1938-40; Mr. Justice Stone and the 'Preferred Freedoms,' " 65 *Yale Law Journal* 597 (1956); Cahn, "Fact—Skepticism and Fundamental Law," 33 *New York University Law Review* 1, 13-16 (1958); Frantz, "Two Kinds of Judicial Review," 19 *Lawyer's Guild Review* 75 (1959); McKay, "The Preference for Freedom," 34 *New York University Law Review* 1182 (1959).

47. The discussion on which presumption to adopt in equal protection cases has usually been focused upon one or both of two factors—(a) whether the basis of classification (e.g., poverty) is inherently suspect, as a racial classification certainly is, or (b) whether the interest involved (e.g., access to housing) is regarded as a "fundamental" right. In connection with the cases where the courts have approached this question of whether poverty is a suspect classification which cannot be used to deny housing as a fundamental interest, the courts and/or commentators have also emphasized two other criteria:

(1) whether the restriction involves active state intervention to create a barrier, or merely a limitation on the extent of some benefit conferred; and

(2) whether the right involved is one specifically mentioned in the Constitution.

The last is of course a purely mechanical criterion, with the implicit assumption that what is important in the late 20th century would surely not have escaped the attention of the Founding Fathers.

Exclusionary Zoning Strategies

48. See e.g., Lefcoe, "The Public Housing Referendum Case, Zoning and the Supreme Court," 59 California Law Review 1384 (1971); Michelman, "The Advent of a Right to Housing: A Current Appraisal," 5 Harvard Civil Rights-Civil Liberties Law Review 27 (1970); "The Supreme Court, 1968 Term, Foreward: On Protecting the Poor Through the Fourteenth Amendment," 83 Harvard Law Review 7 (1969); Sager, "Tight Little Islands: Exclusionary Zoning, Equal Protection, and the Indigent," 21 Stanford Law Review 767 (1969); Note, "The Equal Protection Clause and Exclusionary Zoning After Valtierra and Dandridge," 81 Yale Law Journal 91 (1971); Note, "Exclusionary Zoning and Equal Protection," 84 Harvard Law Review 1645 (1971); Note, "Segregation and the Suburbs: Low-Income Housing, Zoning, and the Fourteenth Amendment," 56 Iowa Law Review 1298 (1971); Note, "Snob Zoning: Must a Man's Home Be a Castle?," 51 Michigan Law Review 339 (1970).
49. Note, 84 Harvard Law Review 1645. However, in his dissent from the majority opinion in James v. Valtierra, 402 U.S. 137, at 144-45 (1971), Justice Marshall, joined by Justices Brennan and Blackmun, expressly stated the view that discrimination on the basis of poverty is a suspect classification: "It is far too late in the day to contend that the fourteenth amendment prohibits only racial discrimination; and to me, singling out the poor to bear a burden not placed on any other class of citizens tramples the values that the fourteenth amendment was designed to protect."
50. See James v. Valtierra, 402 U.S. 137 at 142 (1971); Compare 402 U.S. 137 at 144-45 (1971) (dissenting opinion); Dandridge v. Williams, 397 U.S. 471 (1970). See generally Note supra note 45 at 1652-62.
51. See generally Note, supra note 45 at 1662-66; Note, "The Equal Protection Clause and Exclusionary Zoning after Valtierra and Dandridge," 81 Yale Law Journal 61, 69-72 (1971).
52. Goldblatt v. Hempstead, 369 U.S. 590 (1962).
53. Nectow v. City of Cambridge, 277 U.S. 183 (1928).
54. See, e.g., Dailey v. City of Lawton, 425 F.2d 1037 (10th Cir. 1970), which affirmed the district court's injunction against municipal denial of a zone change and building permit for a privately sponsored low-income housing development; Southern Alameda Spanish-Speaking Org. v. Union City, 424 F.2d 291 (9th Cir. 1971) on remand, mem., Docket No. 51590 (N.D. Cal. July 31, 1970), which held invalid the annulment by referendum of a rezoning to permit a low-income housing project; Kennedy Park Homes Ass'n v. City of Lackawanna, 318 F. Supp. 669 (W.D.N.Y. 1970), aff'd. 436 F.2d 108 (2d Cir. 1970), cert. denied, 401 U.S. 1010 (1971), which invalidated the municipality's freeze on subdivision development mainly directed against a low-income housing project to be inhabited principally by blacks. But see Ranjel v. City of Lansing, 293 F.Supp. 301 (W. D. Mich. 1969), rev'd. 417 F.2d 321 (6th Circ. 1969), where the Court of Appeals reversed the District Court's grant of an injunction against a referendum on a zone change to allow construction of low-income townhouse units, on the ground that assertions that the referendum was racially motivated did not justify an injunction.
55. See, e.g., Oakwood at Madison, Inc. v. Township of Madison, 117 N.J. Super. 11, 283 A.2d 353 (Law Div. 1971). See generally, "Comment," 26 Rutgers Law Review 401 (1973).
56. Edwards v. California, 314 U.S. 160 (1941).
57. Shapiro v. Thompson, 394 U.S. 618 (1969).
58. See, e.g., Valenciano v. Bateman, 323 F. Supp. 600 (S. Ariz. 1971); King v. New Rochelle Municipal Housing Auth., 314 F. Supp. 427 (S.D.N.Y. 1970).
59. Compare Cameron v. Zoning Agent of Bellingham, 357 Mass. 314, 260 N.E.2d 143 (1970).
60. In Southern Alameda Spanish-Speaking Org. v. Union City, 424 F.2d 291 (9th Cir. 1970), which invalidated the annulment by referendum of a rezoning for more intensive low-cost housing, the court said at 295-96:

> Appellants' equal protection contentions, however, reach beyond purpose. They assert that the effect of the referendum is to deny decent housing and an integrated environment to low-income residents of Union City. If, apart from voter motive, the result of this zoning by referendum is discriminatory in this fashion, in our view a substantial constitutional question is presented.

> Surely, if the environmental benefits of land-use planning are to be enjoyed by a city and the quality of life of its residents is accordingly to be improved, the poor cannot be excluded from enjoyment of the benefits. Given the recognized importance of equal opportunities in housing, it may well be, as matter of law, that it is the responsibility of a city and its planning officials to see that the city's plan as initiated or as it develops accommodates the needs of its low-income families, who usually—if not always—are members of minority groups. It may be, as matter of fact, that Union City's plan, as it has emerged from the referendum, fails in this respect. These issues remain to be resolved.

> In Kennedy Park Homes Ass'n v. City of Lackawanna, 318 F. Supp. 669 (W.D.N.Y. 1970), which invalidated the municipality's refusal to approve a nonghetto housing development mainly for blacks, the court said at 697:

> The City officials in Lackawanna have the obligation to consider and plan for all of the citizens in the community. They have an obligation not only to plan for the sewer needs of the third ward citizens, but also the housing problem of the first. Industrial encroachment into former residential areas in the first ward which displaced people from their homes calls for as much attention as sewer backups in the third ward.

> The same theory is implicit in Justice Hall's famous dissent in Vickers v. Gloucester Tp., 37 N.J. 232, 252, 181 A.2d 129, 140 (1962) (especially in the observation that a growing township with large areas zoned for industry should find some area for mobile homes), and in his opinion for a unanimous court in De Simone v. Greater Englewood Housing Corp. No. 1, 56 N.J. 428, 267 A.2d 31 (1970, in dictum to the effect that municipal denial of a use variance for a low-income housing project "under the circumstances and proofs could not well be sustained." 56 N.J. at 443, 267 A.2d at 39.

61. *Appeal of Girsh*, 437 Pa. 237, 263 A.2d 395 (1970).

62. *Appeal of Kit-Mar Builders, Inc.*, 439 Pa. 466, 268 A. 2d 765 (1970).

63. *Compare* note 3, *supra*.

64. See section on "The Goals and Criteria for an Effective Lawsuit" p. 185, *infra*.

65. This limit would be subject to review from time to time by the same type of mechanism in light of the criteria indicated above.

66. Presumably with enough margin to provide for some choice of sites.

67. Whether a developer has a due-process argument in a large-acreage case is of course a different question.

68. *Appeal of Kit-Mar Builders, Inc.*, 439 Pa. 466, 268 A.2d 765 (1970); *Appeal of Girsh*, 437 Pa. 237, 263 A. 2d 395 (1970).

69. Note that building type zoning is better adapted than density zoning for the purpose of maintaining social and economic segregation.

70. The analogy to "floating zones" is obvious, except that in the case of such zones municipal consent is required.

Housing the Poor:

Exclusion and the Courts

Charles M. Haar and Demetrius S. Iatridis

Charles M. Haar is the Louis D. Brandeis Professor of Law at Harvard University. Formerly chairman of the Joint Center for Urban Studies, and previously the Assistant Secretary for Metropolitan Development at HUD, he is an author of numerous books and articles and a consultant/director (World Bank, Doxiadis Associates, etc.). Mr. Haar is a graduate of New York University, has a master's from the University of Wisconsin, and holds his degree from Harvard Law School.

Demetrius Iatridis is a professor of social planning at Boston College. He formerly was director of the Institute of Human Sciences at Boston College, and is an author of several research publications. Dr. Iatridis is a graduate of Washington and Jefferson College, has an M.S.W. from the University of Pittsburg, and holds his Ph.D. from Bryn Mawr.

This article consists of parts of several chapters from a book by Professors Haar and Iatridis: Housing the Poor in Suburbia *(Cambridge, Massachusetts: Ballinger ©1974). Reprinted with permission of the publisher.*

Suburbia: The Emerging Centerpiece

We are no longer an urban, but a suburban nation. Efforts to develop low- and moderate-income housing in the suburban communities reflect the perception that it is in those suburbs, not the cities, where the action is today. Empirical evidence suggests that the deep crisis of the American city, publicly declared, is rapidly expanding and emerging as a crisis of the suburb. In the decade 1960-1970, the population of the metropolitan areas increased by 19.8 percent—yet the cities themselves grew by only 3.9 percent, whereas the areas outside central cities grew by 15.9 percent.

The pursuit of happiness continues to lure millions of Americans each year into pulling up stakes and resettling elsewhere. Each person, each family, makes the decision to move in response to individually felt needs and individually sensed opportunities; yet, the millions of freely made, particular decisions aggregate into marked patterns of migration. In our time, the significant movement has been, first, out of rural areas and into cities and, most recently and most intensively, out of the cities and into the suburbs.

The reasons underlying this vast migration mingle motives of individuals with public policy. Men come together to live in cities, Aristotle reminds us, in order to live the good life. All the benefits of city life arise from the interdependency of the citizens; unfortunately, many of the ills that offend city dwellers also arise from that same interrelationship and from the congestion that accompanies it. The automobile, the availability of land, new economic or technological functions and building forms, all have helped disperse populations from the central city. Increasingly, urban spread seems to be the future pattern of settlement in the United States.

Housing the Poor

Many Americans recently have come to interpret the essential condition of urban life as a distasteful and dangerous interdependency. They have come to regard the poor and the black as pollutants; they have moved to the suburbs to find a purer environment and higher social status. For many, the suburb has become not only an escape valve from the conditions of the central city, but also a real or imaginary life-style, with distinct values, attitudes, and interests.

Once ensconced in their suburban havens, members of the white middle class have erected walls and moats to keep out the unwelcome features of the central city and to protect their suburban turf. One obstacle has worked more or less automatically: the high price of suburban housing. But that has not been a sufficient barricade to exclude every alien element, so suburban residents have at various times turned to more complex methods. Some have been privately created, such as gentlemen's agreements and restrictive covenants; these have been held to be invalid and unconstitutional, however, and in the end have been rendered illegal by such statutes as the Fair Housing Act of 1968. Other barriers have superseded these, taking the form of public laws and official rules —particularly zoning and other land-use regulations designed with exclusionary results in mind.

The suburbs have become, for at least two major reasons, the focus of massive efforts to satisfy the nation's housing shortage. The first reason is that national policies have approached the problem chiefly through the private enterprise system, with mortgage guarantees, incentives for home ownership, and encouragement of the home-building industries. These policies have affected the patterns of residency, because, as a general rule, housing has been built primarily for those groups who can afford to pay enough to allow the developer a reasonable margin of profit. The second reason is that most central cities have had little remaining land suitable and realistically priced for housing; moreover, employment and population have been increasing faster in suburbia than in the inner city. Developers have naturally been attracted in that direction.

Planning for Urban Growth

Public policies for regional and metropolitan development are not necessarily compatible with local grass-roots interests and values. This conflict is well-illustrated by several public issues, but it emerges with particular sharpness in the controversy over housing in the suburbs.

First, there is the question of where subsidized housing should be located. The inner city already has staggering concentrations of lower-income housing, high unemployment levels, and a scarcity of both land and quality services. It is in the interest of inner-city neighborhoods that low-income housing should be located elsewhere in the metropolis; this can provide an opportunity to upgrade the old neighborhoods and expand their socioeconomic structure. Meanwhile, the suburbs, where greater affluence prevails, reject lower-income housing and defy efforts to change their zoning ordinances. They want to control their socioeconomic environment and preserve the locally cherished values of low density, exclusiveness (racial and economic), reduced pollution, ample space, and pleasing aesthetics.

The second question to ask is how high density of low-income housing affects urban development policies. High concentrations of low-income housing in one location, particularly in the inner city, may cripple its capacity for absorption and its potential for development. The metropolitan area as a whole may also be affected. Will the central cities perhaps find themselves less and less able to cope with their problems? Reduced revenues due to the flight of the affluent to the suburbs, the increased cost and demand for municipal services for an inner-city population which has intense and special needs —these more recent difficulties increase the city's plight. By the same token, can the suburbs survive if the inner cities decline? Will suburban communities find themselves less and less able to cope with their own problems and destinies?

Third, both the central city and the suburbs stand to lose from the failure to adopt a metropolitan-wide approach. Revenues from property taxes have reached prohibitive heights in both places. Municipal expenses have increased rapidly merely to sustain levels of service delivery, and thus duplication and lack of coordination among metropolitan communities has become more wasteful and undesirable than ever. Public utilities throughout the metropolitan area face similar exigencies. Any attempt to exert significant public influence over the nature and location of metropolitan growth requires direct control of a significant part of the land, particularly at the peripheries. If most of the control over the metropolitan land area is left in private hands, with private ownership fragmented into thousands of small parcels, it becomes impossible to guide metropolitan or regional growth on any comprehensive basis. Transportation and sewer and water services, for instance, are directly dependent upon guided urban growth and location. A European example illustrates the possibilities. New growth areas in Stockholm are linked to downtown by subway, and feature high-density residential clusters around each station; huge shopping centers are built over each subway stop for the convenience of the pedestrian residents. In the United States, on the other hand, such developments evolve around the use of the automobile and near expressway interchanges. Whether the automobile or a fast mass-transportation system is to be the centerpiece of future urban trends, it is evident that rapid construction of new urban facilities to accommodate large-scale growth must be accomplished on what is initially vacant land, and it must take into account the metropolitan-wide development of transportation as well as other services.

There is a fourth consideration. Metropolitan-wide collaboration has never been easy. How should the scattering be arranged if the locus is to be the metropolitan area as a whole, and what criteria for the location of housing should be applied? Do metropolitan planning agencies and councils of governments have enough muscle to muster unified approaches?

Fifth, how should planners confront suburbia's life-style and its "American Dream"? And, conversely, how should they deal with the determination of certain minority groups to find local self-identity in the central-city neighborhoods? Social class consciousness, status, and race are so intricately interwoven that it is hard to separate them or ignore them in planning the growth of the metropolitan area, especially the siting of residences.

All these public policies, debated though they may be in the Congress and the state legislatures, cannot be grasped fully until they come to full view in the suburbs. The implications of the concrete elude us as we generalize. Yet, sharp and painful divisions also ensue. Realistically, individuals at the local level cannot be expected to make their decisions readily on the basis of abstract values or public objectives, even though such imperatives flow from their duties to provide equal treatment to all under the Fourteenth Amendment.

Surely the exclusion of certain groups from areas in which they would like to live is essentially unethical. Overcoming the new feudal view of suburban life, with its attendant enclaves and exclusionary moats, is the goal, based on a greater moral vision of society, that we have set out to find. But autonomous individuals remain unconvinced; and national policies must be unambiguous in order to be effective, because the problem is deeply embedded in the structure of our society and its social institutions.

Land Use Policies and Exclusion

Zoning ordinances and petitions for their change are invariably central to the controversies over subsidized housing; they are crucial in excluding families different from those already in residence, and they provide a key to the implementation of lower-income housing plans.

Land-use policies and zoning ordinances represent not merely decisions regarding land organization and physical planning, but also the issues of property rights, ecology, the public welfare, civil rights, and residential segregation. This has not always been recognized.

Direct public controls over land use are often truly employed as a means to insure that a community's land uses are properly situated in relation to one another, to stabilize and preserve property values, to enhance efficient municipal development, to exclude undesirable land uses and users—all, hopefully, contributing to the well-being of the inhabitants of the city, neighboring communities, and, indeed, the entire region. Yet nearly every land-use control entails some exclusion, even if indirectly, by raising the costs that the market would otherwise charge.

The potential for racial segregation to become a motive for legislative action was recognized (and put aside for consideration at some future, indeterminate time if the case could be established) by the first Supreme Court decision on the subject, which upheld the validity of comprehensive zoning in 1926. Fodder for sharp debate on both moral and constitutional grounds ever since that date, the exclusionary aspects of land-use controls have recently come to be recognized as a major roadblock to the implementation of national housing policies. Many believe that new zoning approaches to the use of suburban sites are among the most important changes that need to be made.

This underscores the crucial role of local-state relationships in the organization of space, over and above the traditional enabling legislation delegating to localities the power to control land uses. Several states, including Massachusetts and New York, have passed legislation or created agencies empowered to overturn local ordinances. What can the court say about legally enforced banning of economic classes and racial groups from the suburbs, and what can it say about states' rights overriding local ordinances? How directly can a judge probe into the motives of coordinate branches of government? And with what tools and expertise? Can the community's requirements for health, safety, and amenities be achieved without generating social and racial exclusion? Court orders and decisions are important. But how far can they move ahead of accepted mores and traditions?

Judges as Change Agents

Many of the concrete problems of housing the poor in suburbia are dumped willy-nilly into the laps of the courts. Can or should the judge become a change agent?

As early as *Euclid v. Ambler Realty Company,* the very first Supreme Court opinion upholding the zoning concept, the court stated:

> It is not meant by this, however, to exclude the possibility of cases where the general public interest would so far outweigh the interest of the municipality that the municipality would not be allowed to stand in the way.

But this flag, once hoisted by the Supreme Court, rallied few supporters in the judiciary.

In state court opinions throughout the 1960's, the trend was to brush away the question whether the maintenance of property values was an appropriate exercise of the zoning power, to avoid any review of intended (or unintended but inevitable) consequences of regulations that excluded selected groups or classes of people, and also to shy away from evaluating the overspill effects of local regulations on neighboring communities and the state. Despite growing sophistication about metropolitan networks, social cost-benefit accounting among local units of government, postures of presidential national commissions, exhortations by federal departments that suburbs should bear their "fair share" of the housing and welfare burdens, and the restlessness of minority groups and of central city mayors, few judges would grasp the thistle. Some *dicta* about the unreasonableness of large acreage zoning did appear. But, by and large, the quandary over the pattern of American settlements was left to other Alexander the Greats.

As students of a realistic jurisprudence, then, we can only applaud the willingness of recent decisions to isolate underlying factors. But as one attempts to grapple with the metropolitan zoning dilemma, at least two puzzles emerge, and in the curious way that paradoxes operate, they blunt initial reactions.

First, who are the true parties to the conflict? For behind the plaintiff, a man striving earnestly to earn a profit by putting a proposed use on his acreage, there march all the *amici*—the central cities which want to provide homes for their workers; federal officials, who believe that the housing, welfare, and education burdens are too heavy in the central cores; liberals, who wish to integrate suburban areas; mobile home manufacturers, seeking a mass market; and the poor—white and black—who find themselves locked into the central city. Quite an array, and seemingly all groups warranting protection by the judiciary. Yet, one must ask, how do these marchers get into the act? Or, as lawyers so picturesquely phrase it, where is their standing to sue? And, assuming their admittance, who speaks for them, asserts their interests, makes the reasoned elaboration of the case, presents testimony, provides the starting point for the judicial reasonings and conclusion, settles the terms of the final disposition? The courts, even though they provide the only local forum that does not depend upon the crisis constituency of political zones, cannot cope because they do not have before them all the parties who have a legitimate stake in the resolution. So, one difficulty with them as change agents is that the courts, under the present system, never get a chance to deal with all the interests that should intelligently be taken into account.

Second, even though he might be alerted to the inter-community struggle, how ably can a law school graduate—even donning judicial robes—cope with it? Where could the judge learn of the existence and contents of a physical plan for the entire region? How would he learn whether the burden (and who would define it?) of low-cost housing was being cast unfairly on one unit of the metropolitan area, and how could he measure and assess such unfairness or disproportion? How could he perceive, and then go on to weigh, the reasonableness of a process of coordination among municipalities which was intended to provide suitable sites for houses to meet the needs of various levels of society, measured in terms of income, age, or size of family? If no published comprehensive plan exists for the entire metropolitan area, one that has been democratically participated in, voted on, and adopted, from where could he assemble one? Where, with only two parties before him, could a judge acquire the relevant information about the metropolitan trends in population, housing, transportation, and land development?

The court may be cast in a novel role of drafting, in effect, a regional plan for the contending municipalities. It also requires re-examination of various governmental decisions in order to ascertain whether or not local enactments accord with a comprehensive trend. Hardly was this difficulty foreshadowed in the easier job the court undertook of validating an ordinance on regional grounds, involving a relatively simple decision as to whether there is territory available for a particular use within a region.

Above all, the court may find, as it becomes interjected into the troubling and difficult aspects of metropolitan relations, that it is the eye of the storm swirling over the central city—suburban conflict. The least democratic branch, yet it has a roving mandate to cover the whole state territory, and, as change agent, has a constitutional imperative to act when its jurisdiction is invoked.

Despite traditional avoidance of political questions, the freezing of the political process on the metropolitan level has forced the courts to intervene. The independent state judiciary can be said to be there precisely for that job: it cannot long tolerate provisions designed to permit as new residents only certain kinds of people or only those who can afford to live in certain types of preferred housing. The judiciary reminds us of another fundamental: unlike the philosopher, we cannot, once deciding that equities are about evenly balanced, silently steal away; the question demands resolution; one side must win, the other lose.

Some of the most revealing cases of the judge as change agent have occurred in the past few years. *Oakwood at Madison* represents a broad-ranging view of the courts as loosening up the arteries of the federal system. The *Mt. Laurel* case discusses the jurisprudential aspects of such an approach necessitated by the need for the dispersal of low-income housing. *Shaw* and its progeny should be related by you to the discussions dealing with municipal infrastructure, and the essential services for making urban living possible; if the equal-opportunity doctrine is extended from housing itself, the wide-ranging impact on suburbs and the metropolitan area could become one of the more engrossing issues of the 1970's.

Questions

1. *Enforcement and remedies*—The governing body or board of public works may provide by ordinance for the enforcement of the zoning article and of any ordinance or regulation made thereunder. In case any building or structure is erected, constructed, altered, repaired, converted, or maintained, or any building, structure or land is used in violation of this article or of any ordinance or other regulation made under authority conferred hereby, the proper local authorities of the municipality or any other interested party, in addition to other remedies, may institute any appropriate action or proceedings to prevent such unlawful erection, construction, reconstruction, alteration, repair, conversion, maintenance or use, to restrain, correct or abate such violation, to prevent the occupancy of said building, structure or land, or to prevent any illegal act, conduct, business or use in or about such premises.

"*Other interested party*" *persons included*—For purposes of the article to which this act is a supplement, the term "other interested party" in a criminal or quasicriminal proceeding shall include: (a) any citizen of the State of New Jersey: and (b) in the case of a civil proceeding in any court or in an administrative proceeding before a municipal agency, any person, whether residing within or without the municipality, whose right to use, acquire, or enjoy property is or may be affected by any action taken under the act to which this act is a supplement, or whose rights to use, acquire, or enjoy property under the act to which this act is a supplement, or under any other law of this State or of the

United States have been denied, violated or infringed by an action or a failure to act under the act to which this act is a supplement.

N.J. Stat. Ann. 40:55-47, 47.1 (Supp. 1970)—(See also Comment, Standing to Challenge Exclusionary Zoning Decisions, 22 Syracuse L. Rev. 598, 1971.)

2. What is the proper role of the courts in land-use planning policy questions that require the acquisition of special expertise and the balancing of complex societal interests? If the legislature, for example, is the more appropriate actor, what should a court do when the legislature refuses to act? Consider the Oakwood case in light of the failure of the New Jersey legislature in 1969 to enact the proposed Land-Use Planning and Development Law, supra, p. 357.

3. Precisely five months after the Oakwood decision, New Jersey Governor William T. Cahill delivered a special message to the legislature, saying in part:

> It must be apparent to members of this Legislature that the courts already have acted decisively in this area. Unless we act together to help open the way for needed housing, the courts will do it for us and will continue to move strongly in the direction of bypassing home rule by judicial process.

The Governor pointed out the decision in Oakwood and mentioned no fewer than seven significant challenges to local exclusionary zoning ordinances pending in the New Jersey Courts. (Special Message from Governor William T. Cahill to the New Jersey Legislature, New Horizons in Housing, March 27, 1972.)

Concluding Note

Exclusion, purposeful or otherwise, of low-income housing raises central questions regarding the courts and their interpretation of local autonomy to legislate land uses and therefore determine patterns of community life. With the advent of the poverty lawyer and the public interest law firm, there emerge new interpretations of the ancient common law and of the constitutional doctrines applicable to land-use controls. Fresh perspectives on the role of the judiciary and of the separation of powers are in order.

Recognition of the problem of exclusionary zoning has brought about changes on the legislative front in many states, with profound impact on intergovernmental relations. It also has brought the individual into court, and has raised novel issues of standing to sue and of the scope of judicial intervention and of the breadth of court decrees.

Uncertainty as to approval, plus the American belief that all problems are susceptible to some type of rational solution, have led to a bewildering blend of methods for dealing with the central city—suburban split and for implementing the national policy of "a decent home and a suitable living environment for every American family." They are being tested by traditional property and judicial concepts. Part of our job is to analyze the compromise point at which contending forces come to rest, and also to determine which of the many offerings holds the potentials of a fruitful settlement. John Rawls has concluded, "It would appear that we are bound to perform actions which bring about a greater good for others, whatever the cost to ourselves, provided that the sum of advantages altogether exceeds that of other acts open to us." Have the courts, at least, adopted this as a governing principle?

Regional Housing Needs:

Oakwood at Madison

David D. Furman

The Honorable David Furman is Judge of the Superior Court of New Jersey —Chancery Division (New Brunswick). He was formerly an associate in the firm Stryker, Tams & Horner of Newark, New Jersey, and attorney general for the state. Judge Furman is a graduate of Harvard College, and has a law degree from New York University.

Editor's Note: Judge Furman wrote the original trial court decision in Oakwood at Madison v. Township of Madison, 117 N.J. Super. 11, 283 A.2d 353 (1971). *After appeal but before a decision was rendered by the state supreme court —due to a change in the factual situation—Judge Furman was asked to render another decision re the changed circumstances, 320 A.2d 223 (1974). The case is now back in the state's highest court.*

Background: the Decision

Richard Babcock, in his penetrating and prophetic book *The Zoning Game*, published in 1966, forecast:

> The threat will be felt when the courts question the assumption that underpins the traditional interpretation of land-use statutes and ordinances; namely, that each corporate municipality, regardless of size, shape, or lack of responsibility for public services, is the repository of the general welfare.

Home rule was sacrosanct, each municipal zoning ordinance and zoning decision shielded by the presumption of validity, the philosophy of judges that state or county or regional control was anathema—harking back in New Jersey to Boss Frank Hague of Jersey City who said "I am the law," and consonant with the Jeffersonian doctrine that government is best which is closest to the people.

Into this milieu I was plunged in October, 1971, in the two week trial of *Oakwood at Madison v. Madison Township.* In the decision I broke ground, out of conscience and out of conviction, as follows:

> In pursuing the valid zoning purpose of a balanced community, a municipality must not ignore housing needs, that is, its fair proportion of the obligation to meet the housing needs of its own population and of the region. Housing needs are encompassed within the general welfare. The general welfare does not stop at each municipal boundary. Large areas of vacant and developable land should not be zoned, as Madison Township has, into such minimum lot sizes and with such other restrictions that regional as well as local housing needs are shunted aside.

The New Jersey Supreme Court has never decided the appeal in *Oakwood at Madison v. Madison Township.* A third oral argument is scheduled for September, 1974.

Meantime the township amended its zoning ordinance in some particulars. I presided at another trial in April of this year and rendered another decision striking down the zoning ordinance as amended in its entirety. I found that the advances towards moderate income housing opportunities were token and towards low income housing opportunities nil.

In the second opinion I attempted a clarification of two points possibly hazy in the first *Oakwood at Madison* opinion.

1. What is the region whose housing needs must be reasonably provided for by Madison Township?
2. What is Madison Township's fair proportion of the housing needs of its own population and of the region?

I defined the region as not coextensive with the county. Rather it is the area from which in view of available employment and transportation the population of Madison Township would be drawn in the absence of exclusionary zoning.

Without the rigidity of a mathematical formula I concluded that Madison Township's obligation to provide its fair proportion of the housing needs of its region would not be met unless its zoning ordinance provided the same proportion of low income housing capacity as its present low income population, that is, about 12% of its households with incomes under $7000 per year, and unless its zoning ordinance provided the same proportion of moderate income housing capacity as its present moderate income population, about 19% of its households with incomes between $7000 and $10,000 per year.

Why Madison Township?

Lawyers, newspaper reporters, fellow judges and others have asked me, "Why Madison Township?" or a variation of the question, "Why pick on Madison Township?" The simplest answer, of course, is that Madison Township in 1970 promulgated a zoning ordinance drastically curtailing housing opportunities, coincident in time with a desperate housing shortage in the county and region, which ordinance was attacked in my court as invalidly exclusionary by two developers and by six individuals, all of low income, representing as a class those who resided outside the township and had sought housing there unsuccessfully because of zoning restrictions.

Madison Township had overreached in its objective of population limitations. Of the vacant and developable land in all of Middlesex County, about 56,000 acres, Madison Township has 20% or about 11,000 acres. Yet those 11,000 acres were zoned in 1970 and rezoned under the 1973 amendments substantially to exclude all but the upper 10% of families and single persons in yearly income and with bedroom limitations and other provisions relating to multi-family housing substantially to exclude all but childless households or households with one child only.

Those of you whose familiarity with New Jersey is based upon the view out the windows of the Pennsylvania Railroad, now Penn Central, or the environs of Route 1, Route 22 or the New Jersey Turnpike may marvel that there is so much vacant and developable land in Madison Township, which is, after all, on Raritan Bay south of New Brunswick and Perth Amboy, within commuting range of New York City (15% of its wage earners work in New York City) and of industrial and urban northeast New Jersey.

But Madison Township's situation is not unique even in New Jersey and, I suppose, may be duplicated in many states. Historically it was a farming community. New Jersey earned its nickname "The Garden State" because Madison Township and communities like it supplied vegetables, fruits and other crops for the New York, Philadelphia and urban New Jersey markets, and during Prohibition, reputedly, the apple jack or "Jersey Lightning" for the speakeasies. After World War II everything changed. The soil had at best been marginal for farming. Advances in refrigeration and transportation brought vegetables and other crops into the city markets from remote states. Prohibition had been repealed. The housing pressures of an expanding population exploded on the Madison Townships of New Jersey. Madison's population upsurged from 7000 in 1950 to 48,000 in 1970; according to a township planning consultant it could hold in its 42 square miles a population of 200,000 without overcrowding. Much of the former farmland remains vacant and is held speculatively by developers and others. Faced with school and other improvement costs Madison's tax rate rose from one of the lowest in the county in 1950 to the highest in 1970.

This, then, is the profile of a township, its exclusionary approach to zoning in 1970, and the rebuff that exclusionary approach met in the Superior Court of New Jersey at the trial level. It would be unseemly and unfair for me to forecast the outcome of the appeal in the New Jersey Supreme Court.

Determining the Holding in the Case

I relied in my two *Oakwood at Madison* opinions on four precedents in the New Jersey Supreme Court. In the first year of the new court system under the 1947 Constitution, Chief Justice Vanderbilt—a nationally renowned figure—upheld a zoning ordinance excluding heavy industry anywhere in a municipality; but in his opinion, *Duffcon v. Cresskill*, 1 N.J. 509, he examined in specific detail the availability of industry within the same geographical region.

Later in *Fanale v. Hasbrouck Heights*, 26 N.J. 320, Chief Justice Weintraub—another nationally renowned figure—upheld a prohibition against new multi-family housing by zoning ordinance but noted: "There, of course, is no suggestion that the county is so developed that Hasbrouck Heights is the last hope for a solution." In zoning variance cases, *DeSimone*, 56 N.J. 428, and *Andrews*, 30 N.J. 245, the Supreme Court recognized that the serving of regional as well as local needs by, respectively, public multi-family housing and a parochial school were "special reasons" supporting zoning variances under the applicable New Jersey statute.

I concluded, and this of course, was a jump, that the Supreme Court would have recognized the general welfare of the region as overriding and would have struck down the Cresskill ordinance under review if there had not been adequate industry in the region and would have struck down the Hasbrouck Heights ordinance under review if there had not been adequate multi-family housing nearby.

As a parallel, finding desperate housing needs in the county and region, I held that the Madison Township zoning ordinance was invalid because it failed to provide for the township's fair share of housing to meet the housing shortage. Whatever general welfare benefits might be served within the township by population limitations (the conceded objective), these were overridden and the general welfare, which does not stop at the Madison Township border, was in balance thwarted by exclusionary zoning restrictions.

Arrayed against the authorities on which I founded some reliance is a significant statistic. Since 1959 the New Jersey Supreme Court has reviewed 18 zoning ordinances on the merits and upheld all but two. The two struck down involved, respectively: (a) a prohibition against landfill in a swampy area rendering the land unusable for any permitted private use, and (b) a prohibition against group rather than family rentals of seaside cottages. Compare the *Stony Brook* decision of the United States Supreme Court.

Among the zoning ordinances sustained by the New Jersey Supreme Court in the last 15 years were ones prohibiting trailer parks anywhere in a large, substantially undeveloped township—although previously allowed (Justice Hall vigorously dissented in one such case); prohibiting new residences in a light industrial zone; prohibiting drive-in restaurants; and prohibiting other than residential or agricultural uses on a major highway (except, of course, for pre-existing non-conforming uses)—despite almost no prior residential or agricultural development.

The shibboleths have been: (a) home rule; (b) the presumption of validity; (c) the judicial role is tightly circumscribed; (d) the court cannot pass upon the wisdom of a zoning ordinance; (e) the court cannot nullify the municipality's decision if the ordinance presents a debatable issue. I have often quoted them.

Will adherence to home rule serve the general welfare, which does not stop at each municipal border? Will adherence to home rule trap a disadvantaged population indefinitely in the ghettoes of the central cities?

Conclusion

I submit that the issue has been recognized judicially and must persist: whether local zoning provides for each municipality's fair share of its region's new housing needs including new low and moderate income housing needs. I submit that zoning ordinances which fall palpably short of that standard, in the absence of special and overriding environmental and ecological factors, will be struck down by the courts as constitutionally indefensible.

The 1974 Case Decision

Oakwood at Madison, Inc. v. Township of Madison, N.J., 320 A.2d 223 (1974).

FURMAN, J. S. C.

Madison Township amended its 1970 zoning ordinance, effective October 1, 1973, between the decision of this court holding the 1970 zoning ordinance invalid (reported in 117 N.J.Super. 11, 283 A.2d 353 (1971) and the resolution by the Supreme Court (certif. granted, 62 N.J. 185, 299 A.2d 720 (1972) of an appeal from that decision. The Supreme Court remanded to this court for a trial, retaining jurisdiction, in accordance with appellate procedural law that an appellate court determines the legal validity of the zoning ordinance in effect at that time. Tidewater Oil Co. v. Mayor, etc., Carteret, 44 N.J. 338, 341, 209 A.2d 105 (1965).

This court held in the earlier decision that:

> In pursuing the valid zoning purpose of a balanced community, a municipality must not ignore housing needs, that is, its fair proportion of the obligation to meet the housing needs of its own population and of the region. Housing needs are encompassed within the general welfare. The general welfare does not stop at each municipal boundary. Large areas of vacant and developable land should not be zoned, as Madison Township has, into such minimum lot sizes and with such other restrictions that regional as well as local housing needs are shunted aside. [at 20, 21, 283 A.2d at 358]

The precedents relied on include Chief Justice Vanderbilt's opinion in Duffcon Concrete Products v. Cresskill, 1 N.J. 509, 513, 64 A.2d 347 (1949), recognizing regional needs as a proper consideration in local zoning. A zoning ordinance prohibiting heavy industry anywhere within the municipality was sustained in Duffcon, but only under the circumstance that "in the same geographical region, there is present a concentration of industry in an area peculiarly adapted to industrial development and sufficiently large to accommodate such development for years to come . . ." [at 515, 64 A.2d at 351]

In Fanale v. Hasbrouck Heights, 26 N.J. 320, 139 A.2d 749 (1958), Chief Justice Weintraub, in upholding a prohibition by zoning ordinance against any new multi-family housing, noted:

> There, of course is no suggestion that the county is so developed that Hasbrouck Heights is the last hope for a solution, and hence we do not have the question whether under the existing statute the judiciary could resolve a crisis of that kind. [at 328-329, 139 A.2d at 754]

DeSimone v. Greater Englewood Housing Corp. No. 1, 56 N.J. 428, 442, 267 A.2d 31 (1970) and Andrews v. Ocean Co. Board of Adjustment, 30 N.J. 245, 251, 152 A.2d 580 (1959), recognized that the serving of regional as well as local needs by, respectively, public multi-family housing and a parochial school were "special reasons" supporting zoning variances under N.J.S.A. 40:55-39(d).

Regional Housing Needs

Presumptively, the Supreme Court would have recognized the general welfare as overriding and struck down the ordinances under review in *Duffcon* and in *Fanale* if, respectively, there had not been adequate industry or adequate multi-family housing nearby.

As a parallel, this court, finding desperate housing needs in the county and region, held that the Madison Township zoning ordinance was invalid because it failed to provide for the township's fair share of housing to meet the housing shortage. Whatever general welfare benefits might be served within the township by population limitations (the conceded objective), these were overridden and the general welfare in balance thwarted by exclusionary zoning restrictions against new low and moderate income housing.

Factually, a crisis in housing needs continues; most severe for those of low and moderate incomes, and a disadvantaged population remains trapped in the ghettoes of the central cities. The issue thus is whether the amended zoning ordinance of Madison Township provides for the township's fair share of new low and moderate income housing as well as of new high income housing.

Some preliminary clarifications may be appropriate. The region, the housing needs of which must be reasonably provided for by Madison Township, is in the view of this court, not coextensive with Middlesex County. Rather, it is the area from which, in view of available employment and transportation, the population of the township would be drawn, absent invalidly exclusionary zoning. Less than 1% of the Madison Township residents who are employed have their jobs within the township. But the township is bisected by arterial highways, including the Garden State Parkway, and by a commuter railroad with stations in adjoining municipalities. Access to employment even at some distance is practicable by automobile, bus and railroad. 50% of the work force is employed in Middlesex County, 15% in New York City, 10% in Essex County and the balance in nearby New Jersey counties, including 7% in Monmouth County to the south.

In determining the township's fair share of housing in all income ranges, the breakdown of population by yearly income according to the 1970 census is relevant. Only 12% of the township's households (both families and persons living alone) had incomes below $6627, 19% had incomes from $6627 to $9936, 24% had incomes from $9936 to $13,088, 27% had incomes from $13,088 to $19,236 and 18% had incomes above $19,236, as compared in each quintile to 20% of the State's households. Unquestionably, high costs of commutation to work have tended to reduce the township's proportion of low-income earners below that of nearby urban and industrial centers.

[Editor's Note: part of the middle portion of the opinion has been omitted here.]

Significantly, the township planner conceded that there is virtually no potential for low-income housing and no incentives in the ordinance or amendments to build low or moderate-income housing. He defined low income as up to $7000 a year, and moderate income as up to $10,000 a year.[1] In those categories, in his view, a family can afford to buy a dwelling at twice annual income or pay rent of about one-fourth annual income.

[Editor's Note: part of the middle and end portion of the opinion has been omitted here.]

Of the total 20,000 to 30,000 housing units which may be built in Madison Township under the 1970 zoning ordinance as amended, about 3500 at most would be within the reach of households with incomes of $10,000 a year, the upper limit of moderate incomes, and virtually none within the reach of households with incomes of $9000 a year or less. This contrasts with the present township population, approximating 12% low income and 19% moderate income. Of the vacant developable land in residential zones over 80% is zoned R40 and R80, only about 4% R7 and R10.

The zoning objective in 1970 of an elite community of high income families with few children is maintained by the 1973 amendments. The advances towards moderate-income housing opportunities are token, towards low-income housing opportunities nil.

The township asserts that because of high land and construction costs zoning for low-income single-family housing is impossible. Even without governmental subsidies, however, multi-family housing may be provided for low and moderate-income families. Incentives may be set, such as extra density for low and moderate-income units. Low and moderate-income single-family housing is an illusion on one and two-acre lots, a hope on 7500 to 15,000-square-foot lots.

Without the rigidity of a mathematical formula this court holds that Madison Township's obligation to provide its fair share of the housing needs of its region is not met unless its zoning ordinance approximates in additional housing unit capacity the same proportion of low-income housing as its present low-income population, about 12%, and the same proportion of moderate-income housing as its present moderate-income population, about 19%. The amended zoning ordinance under review falls palpably short and must be struck down in its entirety.

No opinion is rendered as to ecological and environmental factors apparently justifying the RP, R80 and to some extent R40 zones. The record on ecological and environmental factors was meager before the municipal authorities, but extensive depositions relevant to these subjects were stipulated into the record before this court. Concededly, ecological and environmental problems have no bearing except in Burnt Fly Bog, the Old Bridge sands, Raritan Bay beachfront, the salt marshes back of Raritan Bay and the four water courses running northwesterly through the township into South River. Ample land outside these areas is available, including specifically the AF districts and their environs and much of the R40, within which the township can meet its obligation to provide its fair share of its own and the region's housing.

Judgment for the plaintiffs.

Footnotes to the Opinion

1. The Director of County Planning estimated moderate income as up to $12,000 a year.

The 1971 Case Decision

Oakwood at Madison, Inc. v. Township of Madison, N.J., 283 A.2d 353 (1971).

FURMAN, J.S.C.

This prerogative writ action challenges the constitutionality of the Zoning Act, N.J.S.A. 40:55-30 et seq., and the validity under that act of the Madison Township zoning ordinance adopted on September 25, 1970. Plaintiffs are two developers, who own vacant and developable land in Madison Township, and six individuals, all with low income, representing as a class those who reside outside the township and have sought housing there unsuccessfully because of the newly adopted zoning restrictions, including one and two-acre minimum lot sizes.

Madison Township is 42 square miles in the southeast corner of Middlesex County, extending from Raritan Bay westward. In two decades of explosive growth from 1950 to 1970, paralleling the trend in the county and region, its population mounted from 7,366 to 48,715. Most of the new housing was single-family in developments on 15,000 square foot or smaller lots, and since 1965 multi-family in garden apartments. Reflecting school construction and other expanded costs of government, the real property tax rate increased from one of the lowest in 1950 to the highest in 1970 in the county.

Despite this population surge much of the township, approximately 30% of its land area, excluding Cheesequake State Park, is vacant and developable. A member of the planning firm which submitted a new master plan in May 1970 testified that the township could hold a population of 200,000 without overcrowding.

A new township administration in 1970 determined to curb population growth significantly and thus to stabilize the tax rate. The township was to "catch its breath," a phrase recurrent in the testimony. Because of exigencies of time arising from a court order in other litigation, the planning firm which was retained early in 1970 was given only two months within which to submit its proposal for a master plan. The deadline was met. The master plan proposal relied in part upon the studies of the township's previous planning consultant. It purported to represent a shift in approach, from explosive growth on a patchwork basis to orderly growth in densely developed areas and the preservation of open areas. The new planning firm's recommendations were followed, with three important exceptions discussed infra, in the ensuing zoning ordinance.

The attack on the constitutionality of the Zoning Act is novel. By way of background plaintiffs suggest that the purposes of zoning, which were enacted in 1928, a time of relatively static population, are not commensurate with the general welfare today, a time of rapid population expansion. Specifically plaintiffs contend that the declared zoning purposes are fatally defective, thwarting the general welfare, because they fail to encompass housing needs.

N.J.S.A. 40:55-32 is as follows:

> Such regulations shall be in accordance with a comprehensive plan and designed for one or more of the following purposes: to lessen congestion in the streets; secure safety from fire, flood, panic and other dangers; promote health, morals or the general welfare; provide adequate light and air; prevent the overcrowding of land or buildings; avoid undue concentration of population. Such regulations shall be made with reasonable consideration, among other things, to the character of the district and its peculiar suitability for particular uses, and with a view of conserving the value of property and encouraging the most appropriate use of land throughout such municipality.

The New Jersey Constitution (1947), Art. IV, § VI, par. 2, empowered the Legislature to enact a zoning enabling law authorizing municipalities to adopt zoning ordinances to regulate land uses. N.J.S.A. 40:55-30 et seq. was thereupon reenacted. The zoning enabling act is not immune from other constitutional requirements, including in conformity with the police power that it must be in reasonable furtherance of the public health, safety or general welfare. Fischer v. Bedminister Tp., 11 N.J. 194, 93 A.2d 378 (1952); Mansfield & Swett, Inc., v. West Orange, 120 N.J.L. 145, 198 A. 225 (Sup. Ct. 1938); cf. Ward v. Scott, 11 N.J. 117, 93 A.2d 385 (1952).

Provision for housing needs, local and regional, is not a specified purpose of zoning under N.J.S.A. 40:55-32, but promotion of the general welfare is. Although stated in the disjunctive as a zoning purpose, the general welfare must not be circumvented or flouted in municipal zoning. Harrington Glen, Inc. v. Mun. Bd. Adj. Bor. Leonia, 52 N.J. 22, 32, 243 A.2d 233 (1968); Roselle v. Wright, 21 N.J. 400, 410, 122 A.2d 506 (1956); Katobimar Realty Co. v. Webster 20 N.J. 114, 122, 123, 118 A.2d 824 (1955); Schmidt v. Board of Adjustment, Newark, 9 N.J. 405, 416, 88 A.2d 607 (1952); Gabe Collins Realty, Inc., v. Margate City, 112 N.J. Super. 341, 271 A.2d 430 (App. Div. 1970).

Thus, it cannot be maintained that the Legislature in the Zoning Act has empowered municipalities to defy the general welfare or to ignore housing needs, insofar as such needs are embraced within the general welfare. Whether provision for housing needs is or is not enumerated as a purpose of zoning appears to be a legislative, not a judicial, judgment. The challenge to the constitutionality of the Zoning Act is therefore dismissed.

Alternatively, plaintiffs contend that the township zoning ordinance is invalid because it fails to promote reasonably the legislative purposes of the Zoning Act in several provisions dealing with single and multi-family housing which are so essential that the entire ordinance should be struck down.

About 55% of the land area of the township is zoned R40 or R80. The R80 zone is new, the R40 zone expanded. Minimum lot size is one acre in R40 and two acres in R80. Minimum floor space is 1500 square feet in R40 and 1600 square feet in R80. According to the former township engineer, 80% of R40 (or about 5500 acres) and 30% of R80 (or about 2500 acres) is vacant and developable. Minimal acreage is vacant and developable in the R7, R10 and R20 zones. Since the 1930s there has not been a development on two-acre lots within the township. Since 1964 only one subdivision plan for one-acre lots has been proposed. Land and construction costs are such that the minimum purchase price in R40 would be $45,000 and in R80 $50,000. Only those with incomes in the top 10% of the nation and county could finance new housing in R40; an even smaller percentage in R80.

The multi-family zones, which are scattered through the township, are so restricted in land area that no more than 500 to 700 additional units can be built in all. Three or more bedroom units are not permitted. Two bedroom units must be limited to 20% of the total units in any apartment development. New units must not exceed 200 in any year.

Madison Township, among other municipalities, is encouraging new industry. Industry is moving into the county and region from the central cities. Population continues to expand rapidly. New housing is in short supply. Congestion is worsening under deplorable living conditions in the central cities, both of the county and nearby. The ghetto population to an increasing extent is trapped, unable to find or afford adequate housing in the suburbs because of restrictive zoning. See N.J.S.A. 55:16-2 (L. 1967, c. 112): "It is hereby declared that there is a severe housing shortage in the State.***"

The township concedes the invalidity of the limitation to 200 new multi-family units per year but defends all other provisions of the zoning ordinance which are challenged. Its contentions are that it is seeking a balanced community, encouraging high income and moderate income housing to balance its predominant low income housing, and protecting drainage systems where high density residential development might result in floods and surface drainage problems and interfere with and imperil underground water resources.

As recently stated by the Supreme Court in Harvard Enterprises, Inc., v. Bd. of Adj., Madison Tp., 56 N.J. 362, 266 A.2d 588 (1970), litigation arising out of prior zoning provisions in Madison Township:

> ***it should be noted that the judicial role in reviewing a zoning ordinance is tightly circumscribed. There is a strong presumption in favor of its validity, and the court cannot invalidate it, or any provision thereof, unless this presumption is overcome by a clear showing that it is arbitrary or unreasonable. [at 368, 266 A.2d at 592]

The underlying objective of the ordinance under attack was fiscal zoning, zoning as a device to avoid school construction and other governmental costs incident to population expansion. Housing needs of the region were not taken into consideration in its enactment, according to several members of the township council and planning board.

The three recommendations in the proposed master plan which were rejected by the township council and planning board all would have tended towards increased population and governmental services. The planning consultant advised no limitation on the number of bedrooms in multi-family apartment units, minimum floor spaces of 1100 square feet in the R40 zone and 1200 square feet in the R80 zone, and "floating zones" of high population density on less than half-acre minimum lots in any zone within the township but separated from each other, up to 100 houses in each floating zone.

Fiscal zoning per se is irrelevant to the statutory purposes of zoning. But the Supreme Court in Gruber v. Mayor, etc., Raritan Tp., 39 N.J. 1, 9, 186 A.2d 489 (1962) recognized that "alleviating the tax burden and the harmful school congestion" was a permissible zoning purpose if done reasonably and in furtherance of a comprehensive zoning plan. Gruber and the antecedent Newark, etc., Cream Co. v. Parsippany-Troy Hills Tp., 47 N.J. Super. 306, 135 A.2d 682 (Law Div. 1957), may be distinguished because they dealt with the pursuit of tax revenues through zoning for new industry, not the stabilization of the tax rate through zoning to exclude new low and moderate income housing.

In any event, the Madison Township zoning ordinance must stand or fall not as fiscal zoning. The test must be whether it promotes reasonably a balanced and well ordered plan for the entire municipality.

Several decisions have recognized balance within a municipality, which is in part undeveloped, as a valid zoning purpose. Kozesnik v. Montgomery Tp., 24 N.J. 154, 131 A.2d 1 (1957); Berdan v. Paterson, 1 N.J. 199, 205, 62 A.2d 680 (1948); Newark, etc., Cream Co. v. Parsippany-Troy Hills Tp., supra.

Fischer v. Bedminster Tp., supra is the leading New Jersey decision sustaining a large minimum lot size, five acres over 85% of the municipality. Its rationale does not apply. Chief Justice Vanderbilt rested his holding on "preserving the character of the community, maintaining the value of property therein and devoting the land throughout the township for its most appropriate use." The Madison Township zoning ordinance under attack has provided for one-acre and two-acre minimum lot sizes on largely vacant land, which as such has no established residential character or residential property values.

Other New Jersey decisions in favor of minimum lot requirements concern relatively small lot sizes in built-up communities. Bogert v. Washington Tp., 25 N.J. 57, 135 A.2d 1 (1957); Mountcrest Estates, Inc., v. Mayor, etc., Rockaway Tp , 96 N J. Super. 149, 232 A.2d 674 (App. Div. 1967); Clary v. Eatontown, 41 N.J. Super. 47, 124 A.2d 54 (App. Div. 1956).

On the other hand, the highest courts of Pennsylvania and Virginia have struck down two, three, and four-acre minimum lot requirements in undeveloped areas as invalid zoning, without reasonable relation to the general welfare. Appeal of Kit-Mar Builders, Inc., 439 Pa. 466, 268 A.2d 765 (Sup. Ct. 1970); National Land and Investment Co. v. Kohn, 419 Pa. 504, 215 A.2d 597 (Sup. Ct. 1965); Board of County Sup'rs of Fairfax County v. Carper, 200 Va. 653, 107 S.E.2d 390 (Sup. Ct. App. 1959).

The Pennsylvania Supreme Court commented in National Land:

> ***Four acre zoning represents Easttown's position that it does not desire to accommodate those who are pressing for admittance to the township unless such admittance will not create any additional burdens upon governmental functions and services. The question posed is whether the township can stand in the way of the natural forces which send our growing population into hitherto undeveloped areas in search of a comfortable

place to live. We have concluded not. A zoning ordinance whose primary purpose is to prevent the entrance of newcomers in order to avoid future burdens, economic and otherwise, upon the administration of public services and facilities cannot be held valid. [215 A.2d at 612.]

Minimum floor spaces by zoning were ruled valid in Lionshead Lake, Inc., v. Wayne Tp., 10 N.J. 165, 89 A.3d 693 (1952), an authority which is controlling if, in context with the entire challenged zoning ordinance, the minimum floor spaces of 1500 square feet in R40 and 1600 square feet in R80 serve the valid zoning purpose of a balanced community. See Nolan and Horack, "How Small A House?—Zoning for Mimimum Space Requirements," 67 Harv. L. Rev. 967 (1954), and Haar, "Zoning for Minimum Standards: The Wayne Township Case," 66 Harv. L. Rev. 1051 (1953).

In Madison Township's approach to the objective of balance, its attempted cure is a worse malady than whatever imbalance existed. About 8000 acres of land, apparently prime for low or moderate income housing development, have been taken out of the reach of 90% of the population, prohibitive in land and construction costs. The acreage available for multi-family apartments units is minuscule. Families with more than one child are barred from multi-family apartments because of the one and two bedroom restrictions, restrictions without any guise of a health or safety purpose.

The exclusionary approach in the ordinance under attack coincides in time with desperate housing needs in the county and region and expanding programs, federal and state, for subsidized housing for low income families.

Regional needs are a proper consideration in local zoning. DeSimone v. Greater Englewood Housing Corp. No. 1, 56 N.J. 428, 267 A.2d 31 (1970); Duffcon Concrete Products v. Cresskill, 1 N.J. 509, 513, 64 A.2d 347 (1949); Gartland v. Maywood, 45 N.J. Super. 1, 6, 131 A.2d 529 (App. Div. 1957); Molino v. Mayor, etc., Glassboro, 116 N.J. Super. 195, 204, 281 A.2d 401 (Law Div. 1971).

In pursuing the valid zoning purpose of a balanced community, a municipality must not ignore housing needs, that is, its fair proportion of the obligation to meet the housing needs of its own population and of the region. Housing needs are encompassed within the general welfare. The general welfare does not stop at each municipal boundary. Large areas of vacant and developable land should not be zoned, as Madison Township has, into such minimum lot sizes and with such other restrictions that regional as well as local housing needs are shunted aside. Vickers v. Tp. Com., Gloucester Tp., 37 N.J. 232, 181 A.2d 129 (1962), upholding a prohibition against trailer camps anywhere within a municipality, is not to the contrary.

The ordinance under attack must be held invalid because it fails to promote reasonably a balanced community in accordance with the general welfare, unless it is defensible on some other ground. Such other ground is urged, namely that low population density zoning provides protection against floods and other surface drainage problems and against diversion of water from an aquifer, an underground water resource.

Most of the R80 districts and a few of the R40 districts are along the course of four brooks running northwesterly through the township into South River. Deep Run, rising in Burnt Fly Bog, which is partially in the township, has overflowed its banks recurrently during heavy storms. Meadowland and woodland abut Matchaponix Brook, the western boundary of the township. Burnt Fly Bog, which is zoned R40 and R80, may be both an intake and a discharge area for the 45 square mile Englishtown aquifer.

Flood or drainage problems were not discussed in the proposed master plan of May 1970, in no specific detail in the studies of the previous planning consultant. There was no consideration in the record of alternative plans, such as retention basins. The common knowledge that impermeable surfaces, specifically roofs and streets, increase surface water run-off is insufficient to support the rezoning of substantially all vacant land in the township into one and two acre zones. Similarly, whether the Englishtown aquifer would be imperiled by the development of the Burnt Fly Bog area is a specialized hydrological subject.

Only engineering data and expert opinion and, it may be, ecological data and expert opinion could justify the ordinance under attack. These were lacking both in the legislative process and at the trial. The record fails to substantiate that safeguarding against flood and surface drainage problems and protection of the Englishtown aquifer would be reasonably advanced by the sweeping zoning revision into low population density districts along the four water courses and elsewhere or the exclusionary limitations on multi-family apartment units.

For all the foregoing reasons the Madison Township zoning ordinance of September 25, 1970 is held to be invalid in its entirety.

Suburban Land Use War:

Skirmish in Washington Township

Melvin R. Levin and
Jerome G. Rose

Melvin Levin is chairman of the graduate department of urban planning at Rutgers University. Formerly chairman of the Urban Institute of Boston University, he is author of Community and Regional Planning, Bureaucrats in Collision, *and* Exploring Urban Problems. *Dr. Levin is a graduate of the University of Chicago from which he also holds a Ph.D.*

Jerome Rose is a professor of urban planning at Rutgers University, and is editor-in-chief of the Real Estate Law Journal. *He is the author of* The Legal Advisor on Home Ownership, *and* Landlords and Tenants. . . . *Mr. Rose is a graduate of Cornell University and holds a law degree from Harvard.*

Introduction

During the Revolutionary War, New Jersey soldiers were famous for their extended and prolonged bouts of homesickness. Some historians have suggested that this malady was related to the Garden State's pattern of small yeoman farmers.Whatever the reason, New Jersey residents have long displayed a fierce attachment to their communities along with attenuated loyalties to their county and state.

It is possible that the bitter legal battles over local zoning practices now in progress in New Jersey are related to these deep community attachments. In addition, a combination of New Jersey's location in the path of expansion of the mammoth New York and Philadelphia metropolitan areas, and the advocacy efforts of the nearby Suburban Action Institute, have been critical factors in the eruption of large numbers of law suits instituted in New Jersey. Whatever the cause, it is apparent that a number of landmark land use cases have been launched in New Jersey. Names like *Mt. Laurel, Madison Township,* and *Mahwah* have attracted national attention as a result of law suits seeking to overturn their zoning ordinances as discriminatory and exclusionary.

Washington Township in Bergen County offers an example of a limited conflict in the "suburban land use war." [*Pascack Association, Ltd. v. Township of Washington,* New Jersey Superior Court Law Division Docket Nos. A-3790-72 and A-139-73 (1974).] The case involves the proposed intrusion of middle-income garden apartments into an affluent suburb. It does not, however, confront the hard-core problem of dispersing poor ghetto families into middle and upper-income suburbs. Nevertheless, the case is of broad interest in many respects:

- Resolution of the issues required the combined skills of a planner and an attorney, needed in an era of land use litigation.
- The case underscores the basic, unresolved problem of protecting and conserving viable communities and neighborhoods, while at the same time encouraging mobility and retention of lower-income people in the suburbs.

- It underscores the critical need for terminating the deadly practice of zoning by variance in favor of a rational allocation on a regional basis.
- The lengthy period of negotiation, appeals, and legal maneuvers, suggests the struggle over social and racial integration in suburbia will be very long. It will not be simply and clearly resolved by court order; instead we are in for much more litigation involving costly, slow, technically sophisticated argumentation.

Washington Township is a small, single-family residential community located in Bergen County, New Jersey. The Township has virtually no commercial development, no industry, and no multifamily dwellings. In 1970 the average value of an owner-occupied house in Washington Township was $37,600, compared to an average of $31,700 for a house in Bergen County as a whole. It is estimated that a minimum family income of $20,000 per year is needed to purchase a home in the Township. Only 3 percent of the land—approximately 100 acres—is available for development.

The case itself involved an action in which the owner of a 30-acre tract zoned for two-acre, single-family residences or office research use challenged the validity of the Township zoning ordinance, and appealed from the denial of a "use" variance to permit the construction of 520 garden apartment units on the site.

Court Order, Township Response

In January 1973, Judge George Gelman of the Superior Court, New Jersey, Law Division held that the then existing Washington Township zoning ordinance was invalid insofar as it had imposed a two-acre minimum lot size restriction on residential use on the subject property, and insofar as it failed to make provision for multifamily and/or rental housing within the municipality. He ordered the municipality to "proceed with reasonable promptness" to amend the ordinance and to make provision for multiple-family and/or rental housing.

Shortly thereafter, the Township amended its ordinance by providing for multifamily dwelling use, but on a site other than the property owned by the plaintiff. The amended ordinance of the Township also imposed numerous restrictions: A requirement that 70 percent of the dwelling units not have more than one bedroom, and the balance not more than two bedrooms; a minimum floor space requirement of 1,000 square feet for one-bedroom units and 1,200 square feet for two-bedroom units; a density limitation based on building heights, ranging from 6 units per acre for two-story buildings to 15 units per acre for four-story (elevator) buildings; and several other cost-raising requirements.

Most of the land in the district rezoned for multifamily and nonprofit uses was owned by the Township, the Young Men's Hebrew Association, and a fraternal order. In a subsequent proceeding, Judge Gelman noted that affidavits had been filed with the court "Which suggest that the rezoning of a large acreage which they chose for this purpose was not in good faith."

In his decision holding the Township zoning ordinance invalid, Judge Gelman summarized the basic issue—whether the Township of Washington can continue its zoning policy of excluding all multifamily and rental housing within its borders. "Can it, in other words, zone out people—including its own residents—who have a need for this type of housing, or is there a statutory requirement to provide as part of a comprehensive plan for a well-balanced community at least some area, however limited it must be under the circumstances present here, where such housing may be constructed?"

The Court Appoints "Advisers"

In October 1973, on the plaintiff's motion to have a judgment entered providing a judicial remedy in the still pending action—the plaintiff being unsatisfied with the Township's first "response"—Judge Gelman reviewed each of the three courses of action available to him: He could declare the zoning ordinance invalid and thereby make all vacant land in the Township available for multifamily use; he could determine that the judicial branch is powerless to provide any relief in zoning matters; or he could retain planning consultants to recommend the form of zoning relief appropriate under the circumstances—which would be a very novel approach for a court to take.

Judge Gelman chose the third alternative and appointed us as advisers to the court. Our report concluded that the Township's zoning amendment passed after the court's decision in January 1973, did not comply with the court order because that amendment did not serve the public need in the Township for multifamily housing.

The first public need we recognized was that of the young-married group, with total annual family income between $12,000 and $18,000. On the basis of current incomes and space requirements, it was indicated their current need is for rental housing in the range of $250 to $375 per month. If rental units in this price range are not provided within the confines of the Township, it was suggested that younger couples would be forced to look elsewhere for suitable housing.

The second category of public need in the Township was identified as the older couples, many of them with grown children living elsewhere. Older couples in the community often require small, easily maintained and reasonably-priced apartments in the area of $250 per month, assuming a retirement income of $10,000 to $12,000 per year. If such apartments are not available nearby, the alternatives for elderly, less affluent persons are to share housing with relatives or to sever ties with friends and the community and move elsewhere.

With no rental units available, it was clear that Washington Township, like many suburbs, geared its land use policies to one phase of the life cycle—child rearing—and, through persistent misuse of the zoning process, had created a backlog of demand for rental housing to serve portions of its own population.

Regional Need for Apartments

The failure of the Township to make provision for moderate-rental apartments would not be serious if such units were available elsewhere in the surrounding Pascack region. Such is not the case. Communities in the region and in other affluent New Jersey counties have enacted land use controls which effectively limit their regional role to serve as single-family residential dormitories for middle and upper-income families.

The community and the county planning board have accepted the designation of the eight-community Pascack Region delineated by the Bergen County Planning Board as the "region" of which Washington Township is a part. In 1970 the Pascack Region had a population of 72,000 and all of the member communities were low density, middle-to-upper income suburbs. (It may be noted parenthetically that in future litigation in other areas, the size and composition of service regions is likely to be a subject for considerable dispute.)

A 1970 report on housing needs by the county planning board concluded that the supply of rental housing available in the region and in the whole of Bergen County was insufficient to meet the demand largely because of the restrictive and exclusionary effect of municipal zoning ordinances: five of the eight municipalities in the region exclude *all* multifamily housing. Because of this exclusionary policy, a modest amount of rezoning for multifamily use in Washington Township, which is almost completely built up, would have a major impact in substantially increasing Bergen County's minuscular supply of land zoned for multifamily use. Apartments in almost any location in the region would be readily rentable.

It was cautioned, however, that locating large numbers of apartments in improper locations would, in the long run, compound rather than solve the region's development problems. It was appropriate to place sharp limits on the number and densities of apartment units constructed in the Township while encouraging apartment construction in regional, built-up urban centers which offer a range of shopping and services.

The proposed construction of garden apartments in Washington Township represents another example of the deadly practice of zoning by variance. In New Jersey as in other states, development has proceeded under a process known as "disjointed incrementalism." Construction occurs in response to successful developer initiatives to friendly zoning appeals boards.

Recognizing that the energy shortage and rising costs will accelerate trends to multifamily construction, we warned that if rezoning for apartment development takes place in a sporadic, *ad hoc* manner through developer initiatives to secure variances on such property as may come on the market, the result in the Pascack region and elsewhere may be more of the mangled land use pattern already existing. While recommending a decision to encourage a moderate amount of higher-density building in Washington Township as appropriate within the context of local, regional, and emerging national needs, we suggested restricting the number of such units to meet Township requirements. We underscored the need for greater numbers of apartments to be built elsewhere in the Pascack region around higher density commercial centers where transportation costs and fuel outlays can be minimized.

Specifically, it seems to be much more sensible to stimulate apartment development in and around commercial and service centers where young couples and older persons can walk to shops and services. All too often development has occurred where a sizable tract of low-cost land is available, leaving future residents and the community-at-large to shoulder the burden of increased transportation and servicing costs. In this particular case, if the Pascack Valley were a single unified community, Washington Township would be viewed as an outlying residential neighborhood suitable only for a restricted amount of high-density housing.

Advisers: Reshaping the Zoning Ordinance

A parcel other than the one owned by the plaintiff was designated for multifamily development in the zoning amendment of January 1973. We proposed that the site owned by the plaintiff be rezoned for multiple dwelling use.

The January 1973 amendment also imposed certain restrictions on apartment construction—restrictions the plaintiff charged would have a cumulative impact of increasing rental levels from 50 to 100 percent above the levels that would be required if the plaintiff's proposed variance were granted. We specifically disagreed with the ordinance requirement of 1,000 square feet of floor area and 1,200 square feet of floor area for one and two-bedroom apartments respectively and determined that these standards were "unduly restrictive." Instead, we supported the plaintiff's assertion that 800 and 1,000-square feet standards were more appropriate for one and two-bedroom units. In addition we found that the requirement of two full baths for two-bedroom units was excessively restrictive, as was the requirement that 70 percent of the units in a development must be one-bedroom apartments.

One of the other chief points at issue was density. The developer requested approval of 17 units to the acre for two-story garden apartment units, while the Township ordinance called for a maximum of 6 units to the acre for two-story development on the site which it had rezoned for multifamily use. We, as court advisers, recommended approval of up to 9 units to the acre as an appropriate density for a built-up, single-family community without a significant shopping and service area.

Another issue concerned the proportion of one bedroom versus two-bedroom units. In line with the practice in many suburbs, the township's zoning ordinance stipulated a maximum of 30 percent for one-bedroom units and 70 percent for two-bedroom units. We indicated in our report that we were opposed in principle to bedroom percentages that limit the availability of rental housing for larger families. However, we recommended, as a compromise, a prescription of 50 percent for one-bedroom and 50 percent for two-bedroom units. There is no absolute principle of planning theory to substantiate this particular prescription. We proposed it as a realistic compromise of conflicting interests.

Results of Suburban Resistance

Some suburbanites feared the apartments would result in higher property taxes; this mistaken attitude was laid to rest in our report. Analyzing the fiscal impact of apartment development on the Township, it was clear that most of the relatively few children living in apartments are of pre-kindergarten age. In contrast, most children residing in single-family houses are in the public school-age spectrum. From a cost-benefit standpoint, the largest municipal fiscal liability is clearly the four-bedroom, single-family dwelling, while one and two-bedroom apartments return a revenue surplus.

Concern over taxes is usually only the tip of the iceberg of the problem of opposition to apartment construction in the suburbs. Community apprehensions of apartment development revolve around social and racial issues. Recognizing that any substantial apartment house complex would constitute a major element in a small community, it was necessary to respond to the question as to why Washington Township should be singled out for an obligation not (yet) imposed on its neighbors.

Washington Township does not contain sizable industrial parks or major commercial installations and, therefore, does not benefit from tax receipts from major, nonresidential development. It is often argued that without such direct benefits a community has no obligation to provide rental housing. While there seems to be some justice in this argument, it ignores the obvious and not so obvious economic linkages among suburban communities and between suburbs and core cities.

The single-family suburb derives its economic sustenance from a labor force employed in either suburban offices and factories or in central cities. Thus, each suburban community receives economic benefits from the larger region of which it is a part and therefore must assume some responsibilities of and obligations to that region. The court agreed with our conclusions that such a regional responsibility exists.

Many suburban communities are apprehensive that apartments will attract "undesirable" people; that apartment buildings will fall into disrepair and become future slums or that they will inevitably lead to demands that a portion of the units or adjoining land be reserved for subsidized rental apartments for low-income families. Admitting there is no assurance that these fears are groundless, we nevertheless concluded that Washington Township can absorb a modest amount of middle-income apartment development without suffering damage to its social fabric or amenities.

The Hearing & the Court's 1974 Ruling

At the hearing preceding the court's ruling on our recommendations, the developer's representatives stressed the need for permitting high—15 to the acre—densities if rents were to be held to the $250-$300 monthly level. In our opinion, part of the reason for the developer's projected increase in rents was the high price he paid for the site. In a direct sense, the purchase price of the land and the developer's projected net returns were predicated on his assumption that he would be permitted to build at higher densities. Understandably, if this approval was not forthcoming and he was required to build at lower densities he would have to raise rent levels to achieve his original profit objective.

We believe that this is an illustration of an issue that will recur frequently. Many developers pay excessive prices for land based upon their expectation of being permitted to build at densities much higher than permitted under zoning existing at the time of purchase. If these expectations of higher densities are not realized, it becomes necessary for them to direct their development to a higher income market; for example, expensive condominiums or luxury apartments.

At the conclusion of our report to the Court, we stated that "The nation has learned through bitter experience that viable communities are precious, irreplaceable, and fragile. Fortunately, in Washington Township a reconciliation between modest change and protection of community values appears feasible."

After reviewing our report, the court ordered the township to issue to the plaintiff a building permit for multifamily, garden-type dwelling units at not less than 9 units per acre with the lower minimum floor area requirements we recommended. In addition, the court accepted our recommendation and reduced the zoning restriction on the proportion of one-bedroom units. The court's order also included the following provision: "The Township Planning Board shall be authorized to approve an application for site plan approval increasing the density of units per acre without the minimum floor area limitations hereinabove set forth upon a finding that such special requirements to residents of the age to 55 and above. . . ."

The Court then observed that consistent with the order, "The Township will have the opportunity, if it wishes, to assist a private developer in furnishing the type of housing needed by the community by increasing the density and eliminating other restrictions within the context of this order so as to make multifamily, residential-type dwelling units available to its citizens at a price which is more consistent with their ability to pay." This provision is directed at stimulating construction of efficiency apartments for senior citizens.

Conclusion

The Washington Township case is a microcosm of the kind of zoning battle now in progress across the nation. Because the issue in contention involved only a narrow portion of the income and class spectrum, a compromise was possible. A more difficult and complex issue arises when proposals for suburban rezoning would result in an influx of heavily subsidized, lower-income and welfare families, particularly if the newcomers are members of a racial minority.

The extent to which judicial determinations in exclusionary zoning cases will result in a more even socio-economic balance between central cities and the suburbs is uncertain. All that can be predicted at this time is another generation of litigation. In our opinion, the courts and the legislatures will find it exceedingly difficult to reconcile the constitutionally protected freedom of movement with the protection and conservation of viable neighborhoods.

CHAPTER SEVEN

EXCLUSION: PROPOSALS AND PRESCRIPTIONS

Professor Lawrence Sager accurately states the underlying theme of Chapter Six and Seven, when he writes: "the touchstone . . . [is] the question of a community's constitutional obligation to refrain from exclusionary zoning practices . . . [and] the constitutional imperative that land-use controls may not be applied in a fashion which substantially conflicts with the opportunity of low- and moderate-income persons to secure minimally adequate housing. . . . With zoning practices that in effect absolutely impose economic segregation, we have returned to the point at which the state directly effectuates housing discrimination. . . . The problem becomes, then, a matter of assessing the constitutional responsibility of a single municipality vis-a-vis housing needs which can only be measured on a regional basis." [Sager, "Exclusionary Zoning: Constituional Limitations on the Power of Municipalities to Restrict the Use of Land," in *ASPO Land Use Controls Annual 1972* (F. Bangs, ed., 1973).]

Similar messages that the practices and the effects of exclusion and discrimination are becoming imbedded in American society have been issued by numerous observers and study commissions over the past several years. One group—the **National Commission on Urban Problems**—carefully broached this subject in the context of the urban land conversion and public property management processes. With the issuance of its report in 1968 [the report of the "Douglas Commission"]—titled *Building the American City*—there was also a concurrent apex of concern with housing production and legislative programs which could deliver decent shelter to America's low- and moderate-income families. (Some of the Commission's work in fact directly influenced the 1968 Housing and Urban Development Act.)

The Commission's report has been edited here so as to present, in abbreviated form, the basic thrust of the Commission's activities and conclusions. Particularly stressed are the "black-letter" recommendations which are directly relevant to the problems of exclusionary land use controls and housing discrimination. (This report, and its substantiating and supplementary research papers, provide a veritable sourcebook on the nation's housing problems, and the private and public sector impediments to resolving such difficulties. The reader will wish to scrutinize the article and the conclusions presented here, and then turn perhaps to the full report and material for further data and explication.)

The anti-exclusionists extraordinaire—**Paul and Linda Davidoff**—lay a pungent indictment at the door of "affluent, powerful America [which] has an ugly side—racial and class hatred, violence, systematic injustice, and political repression. In the suburban residential communities of our metropolitan areas, the affluent and powerful segment of our society is enthroned."

"The future of our society as a whole, and of our cities in particular, rests with the suburbs." This statement is founded on the authors' belief that both individual rights and opportunities are damaged by current practices, and that the rebuilding of central cities cannot really occur until the pressure of the suburbs is relieved. [These assumptions may

515

provoke some contrary discussion as to the dynamics of urban economic forces.]

They then turn their attention to specific inclusionary land use techniques: defined as methods and controls designed ". . . to guarantee to residents of a state—or the nation—that local law derived from state police powers will not be employed to deny them access to residences within all parts of residential areas of local government units; to maximize local control over those aspects of land development that affect primarily the locality and its citizens." [With regard to the above two seemingly contradictory statements, the authors elaborate that the exercise of local powers should be sustained—but only with the qualification that "they meet the standards of *inclusiveness*."]

Noting several state devices for inclusion—such as the Massachusetts Anti-Snob Zoning Law and the New York State Urban Development Corporation—the Davidoffs make a number of proposals for inclusionary policies: termination of specific devices used by the community to exclude; conservation of municipal expenditures; housing for industrial workers; the establishment of a state urban growth fund to contribute to localities monies; to assist in supporting services and facilities for low- and moderate-income families [whose real estate taxes are insufficient to fully cover costs]; policies on government facilities location; elimination of abuses of the local property tax system, which effects exclusion including fiscal zoning; and, establishment of the right of regional (non-resident) persons to sue and to be heard regarding a particular locality's alleged exclusionary practices. With regard to this last point, during 1975 it can be expected that a number of state courts—and perhaps the United States Supreme Court—will address the issue of standing. The potential problem is that any such decision, in light of the predilections of the current court, could be as disadvantageous to anti-exclusionists as the *Belle Terre* case [as discussed in the Introduction to Chapter Six]. Such a case now might not fare as well as was hoped when the authors wrote this article, and implicitly suggests the probability of a favorable result if the court were to be given the opportunity to review an exclusionary zoning situation.

Lastly, one device dealt with at greater length is the local comprehensive planning process. The authors propose amending state enabling legislation to place various requirements on localities; one especially important idea is the implementation of the proposal that a "burden of analysis and evaluation should be placed on local planning agencies to assure that they have explicitly found that their community, in its public actions, will provide adequate shelter and environment for all economic classes and races. A plan for the fulfillment of such an 'open community standard' should be as important a part of the planning process as is the transportation plan or the land use plan."

For other potential mechanisms or techniques for inclusion—both public and private sector incentives/disincentives—the reader should refer to the materials in Chapters Six, Seven, and those in Volume III [of special interest are Royce Hanson's article on "Growth Control: The Role for Regionalism" and Francis Parker's analysis of "Regional Imperatives & Managed Growth"].

According to the research director of the National Committee Against Discrimination in Housing—**Ernest Erber**—there arose at approximately the beginning of this decade "a new challenge to the planning profession." This challenge consists of a need to develop adequate housing allocation planning, which evidenced itself primarily due to a growing perception of the problems involved with the "separation of population by income, reflected in concentration by race, and the consequent distortion of home/job relationships."

Seeing a need for "breakthroughs in concept, structure and function" of housing allocation planning, Erber believes there are required "new techniques for the quantification of housing need by dwelling unit type, size, and price, the staging of construction over time, and the location of units within the planning jurisdiction in relation to employment opportunities, infrastructure, vacant land, and transportation." Otherwise—one might infer—the concept of housing allocation may not be acceptable or operational in most communities around the country.

The author sees several phenomena which facilitated the emergence of allocation planning—including a factor which, curiously, has been both a hindrance and an encouragement to further development of housing allocation: "the resistance of outlying communities, whose citizens were intent upon protecting their perceived advantages against dilution expected to ensue from an influx of households of lower incomes and different ethnicity. This resistance was to be mollified by 'sharing the burden'; each suburban municipality would accept its 'fair share' of the poor—and ostensibly, the black." The record of success, however, is grim.

An idea is then presented which is critical to the future of housing allocation planning: the need for a shift from a concern with low-cost housing [most likely, publicly-subsidized] to the whole question of housing of all types and cost levels, and of growth, in a regional context. . . ."the implications of which have not yet been fully realized." Erber states that "allocation planning within this dimension [allocating all residential growth] is the same universe of metropolitan regional planning that contains the economic base, transportation, and the environment. Housing allocation limited to subsidized units cannot be properly related to these other basic regional components." [See the next article for discussion of the disadvantages—according to those authors—of the use of the "region" as a basis for analysis and remedies.]

The article closes with the poignantly discouraging observation (substantiated by 1974 and early 1975 events) that "housing allocation planning at the metropolitan regional level is as yet a tender shoot, however promising its potential. It should be nurtured by all Americans who are committed to maximizing choice in residential location, regardless of income or race."

Numerous anti-snob zoning litigators have suggested that the answers to exclusion somehow lie in utilizing the region as a remedial base. In their article, **Burchell, Listokin, and James** take on their designated "St. George dragon," and strive mightily to slay it. . . "this article argues that there are serious pitfalls to the regional remedy; the new broader territorial approach may in fact reinforce the status quo." The main point is that the remedy may in fact be a potential repository of *justifications* for exclusion: "exclusive suburban communities may turn more and more to the regional argument to defend exclusionary zoning ordinances."

The concise purpose and approach of the article is to describe the "emerging regional response to this controversy and discuss its theoretical deficiencies . . . focusing on employment growth versus housing production of an allegedly exclusionary zoned area." The first critical analytical factor is the definition of what constitutes the region under consideration . . . a concept [region] which the authors find to be overly elastic, and a poor yardstick of/for municipal responsibility. Moreover, as "the area upon which to assess housing needs expands, the ability to specify municipal regional responsibility diminishes." As a consequence therefore, regionalism conceivably could provide *substantiation* for the "existing social and housing stratification resulting from current exclusionary zoning practices rather than *reforming* the existing restrictive land use orientation."

Presenting one empirical analysis to demonstrate the validity of their conclusions, the authors note: "the point to be made is that to move to the regional level to determine a specific community's housing role is to dismiss the arguments about which most exclusionary zoning cases focus. On a regional base, both housing production and housing costs appear to be commensurate with both demonstrated need and ability to pay."

Summarized, this means that at the macro level, the micro disparities fold in and disappear, and the ability to present a legal challenge on the basis of exclusion may then become exceptionally difficult.

On the other hand, if the region as defined is decreased in size, then "preferred communities—the objects of most exclusionary zoning suits—demonstrate an increasing failure to provide housing at a cost which the family incomes of those locally employed can afford."

The authors perhaps appropriately conclude as follows: "All those who cry for the region as the minimal level of analysis: be prepared for the oft-times confounding results."

At the same time, the reader will want to bear in mind that this seemingly disparaging analysis of the utility of "region" should not be viewed as saying overly much, or as conclusively settling the issue. While it is clear—don't prepare a regional case if your data cannot substantiate your claims of exclusion, and be careful about relying on the theory of regional approaches and remedies—it might be worthwhile to ask some alternative questions.

Can the analysis be altered at all significantly by changing certain assumptions, such as those dealing with transportation access (cost and mode) to jobs? Are some classes —income or racial groups—effectively excluded by a lack of ability to utilize transportation, and obtain housing near employment centers? Isn't the regional context useful in showing disparate, and inequitable, service and employment opportunity levels? Isn't a growth-resistant community appropriately measured in a broad regional framework, to show the degree to which rational or efficient land use patterns may be distorted by local, unilateral actions? What about the arguments of regional cumulative impact, restriction of regional or intrastate mobility, rational or optimal land use patterns, or the existence of regional growth centers?

Some of the above questions are raised again—and debated further—in Chapter Nine: "The Approach of Petaluma, California," and in Chapter Ten (of Volume II). They illustrate perhaps, that though the "region" issue is one about which we should be wary, the concept of region is "not yet dead" . . . and in fact may still be enormously useful in the analysis and challenge of local exclusionary land use practices.

The chapter closes with an article which is an edited version of the 1974 report of the **United States Commission on Civil Rights.** Finding that the " 'white noose' of new suburban housing on the peripheries of decaying cities . . . is even more pronounced" than was the case in 1961, it also states that the documented problems require immediate recognition, or else "it is doubtful that any solution will be forthcoming."

The Commission sees that there are "dual causes of residential segregation —discrimination and low income." The overall lack of access to inexpensive housing is a product of income disparity, market forces, and "local practices which limit low-cost dwellings or exclude them altogether . . . with racial and economic motivations intertwined." This, the report says, is the "new racism of the seventies."

Furthermore, according to the Commission: "inadequate enforcement by Federal agencies and circumvention or, at best, lip service adherence by local authorities, builders, real estate agents, and others involved in the development of suburban communities have helped to perpetuate the systematic exclusion of minorities and low-income families." Turning its sharp criticism toward the executive branch, the Commission states: "although the Federal Government has recognized the suburban problem, it has done little to solve it. Neither HUD nor the Department of Justice has enforced existing antidiscrimination laws vigorously or effectively." The general conclusion is that the federal government must learn to proceed with "a determined effort to enforce Federal antidiscrimination laws . . . . While the time has long passed for assessing blame, it cannot be denied that Federal agencies share with local authorities, the housing industry, and its related professions a moral and legal responsibility for having created a problem which will never solve itself."

Stated without any mincing of words is the further conclusion that: "the Commission sees a dire need for a supervening authority over community land use control. One approach which the Commission recommends is the enactment by Congress of legislation establishing metropolitan-wide housing and community development agencies in every State. The agencies' purpose would be to guarantee the availability of housing at all income levels and without regard to race throughout the metropolitan area."

The Commission, having laid the accusations at the doors of what it sees as the culpable parties, proceeds to set forth a series of recommendations for action . . . for metropolitan-wide desegregation [ideas which merit special attention]; securing employment opportunities; federal enforcement efforts; and, national policy.

A closing statement is also made by the vice chairman of the Commission, Stephen Horn, who finds that we must fully understand the intertwined problems of discrimination and segregation in: (a) housing; (b) jobs/employment; and (c) education. "To speak of this interrelated trilogy has become almost trite, but the interrelationships are nevertheless true." It is obvious that the vice chairman is tired of what he views as the resistant or inertia-ridden public and private sectors, stating: "there is an immediate need to put the Federal Administration house in order . . ." and this likewise applies to the "developer, financier, and builder, local, State, and Federal officials, and tenant and homeowner alike." Otherwise, we will perpetuate, without careful consideration, "the tragic plight of millions of Americans whose only limit to access to suburban America in housing and jobs seems to be that the shade of their skin is less than lily white."

To those who are subject to *racial* discrimination, must be added America's *poor*. These poor [many of whom may also be disadvantageously affected by reason of their minority group status] are blocked off from much that this nation has to offer, and are locked into non-escape by such problems as inferior quality education, and the land use/housing/employment policies of recalcitrant suburbs and exclusive enclaves of middle-class America.

Finally, it should be stressed that we are entering an era when growth controls will affect more than racial groups and the lowest-income persons. If communities are allowed to proceed unilaterally to restrict absorption of future predicted growth simply to preserve the "current order of things"—and if this is done without any careful social and housing planning/consideration, as has been discussed in this and the preceding chapter—then the pressure will begin to reach upward into other levels of the income spectrum. Thus policies on growth, if mismanaged, could strike directly at a large portion of the American public . . . and indirectly on the general economy, on the costs of housing and transportation, and on the lifestyles of nearly all our citizens.

Whether these potential "cumulative side-effects" will be sufficient to cause political counter-pressures with regard to certain disadvantageous repercussions of growth controls, is debatable. However, given the usual spotty history of social reform and equity enforcement in this country, it is unfortunately not likely that the complex problems associated with growth management will provide much in the way of a lasting impetus for affirmative housing planning and inclusionary policies. Even though these dilemmas will be much-discussed, it is most likely there will be little action.

—RWS

Building the American City:

A Report [Summary]

**National Commission on
Urban Problems**

During 1967 and 1968, the [President's] National Commission on Urban Problems studied the problems and prospects of American housing, cities, regulatory and financing mechanisms, and so forth—presenting its findings in late 1968, in the well-known report: "Building the American City."

This article consists of selected portions of the full report (approximately 500 pages).

Letters of Transmittal

National Commission on Urban Problems
Washington, D.C., December 12, 1968.

Hon. Hubert H. Humphrey,
President of the Senate,
Hon. John W. McCormack,
Speaker of the House of Representatives,
House of Representatives, Washington, D.C.

Dear Sirs: I have the honor to transmit to you the unanimous report of the National Commission on Urban Problems. The Commission was appointed by the President on January 12, 1967, to carry out the purposes defined in section 301 of the Housing and Urban Development Act of 1965. The act calls for a report to be made to the House of Representatives and to the Senate of the United States.

The Commission has explored the subjects assigned to it with great care. It has conducted hearings in the central cities and suburbs of over 20 locations throughout the country. It received testimony from almost 350 witnesses. It has undertaken an extensive research program covering some 40 specific subjects. The members of this Commission, all private citizens, met for more than 70 working days and were extraordinarily faithful in their effort and attendance.

It is the earnest hope of the members of the Commission that this report will prove helpful to the President, to the Congress, to State and local governments, and to the American people in coping with a great domestic challenge.

Respectfully submitted on behalf of all the members of the Commission.

Faithfully yours,

Paul H. Douglas, *Chairman*

National Commission on Urban Problems,
Washington, D.C., December 12, 1968.

Hon. Lyndon B. Johnson,
President of the United States,
The White House, Washington, D.C.

Dear Mr. President: I have the honor to transmit to you the report of the National Commission on Urban Problems, established by your directive of January 12, 1967, to carry out the purposes defined by you and further elaborated in section 301 of the Housing and Urban Development Act of 1965.

The Commission has explored the subjects assigned to it with great care, has conducted hearings in locations throughout the country, has received testimony from almost 350 witnesses, and has undertaken extensive research on some 40 specific subjects.

It is the earnest hope of the members of the Commission that this report will prove helpful to you and to future administrations, to Congress, to State and local governments, and to the American people in coping with a great domestic challenge.

Respectfully submitted on behalf of the Commission.

Faithfully yours,

Paul H. Douglas, *Chairman*

Preface

President Lyndon B. Johnson in his message to Congress on March 2, 1965, called for the creation of a commission to study building codes, housing codes, zoning, local and Federal tax policies and development standards. He said such a commission could provide knowledge that would be useful in dealing with slums, urban growth, sprawl and blight, and to insure decent and durable housing. Congress approved his request and appropriated the funds to carry it out.

On January 12, 1967, President Johnson named the Chairman and members of the Commission and charged it to carry out the studies he and the Congress had requested. The President said the Commission's charter was twofold:

> *First:* to work with the Department of Housing and Urban Development and conduct a penetrating review of zoning, housing and building codes, taxation, and development standards. These processes have not kept pace with the times. Stunting growth and opportunity, they are the springboards from which many of the ills of urban life flow.

> *Second:* to recommend the solutions, particularly those ways in which the efforts of the Federal Government, private industry, and local communities can be marshaled to increase the supply of low-cost decent housing.

The congressional mandate was included as section 301 of the Housing and Urban Development Act of 1965. It described the purposes and needs for the study as follows.

> The Congress finds that the general welfare of the Nation requires that local authorities be encouraged and aided to prevent slums, blight, and sprawl, preserve natural beauty, and provide for decent, durable housing so that the goal of a decent home and a suitable living environment for every American family may be realized as soon as feasible. The Congress further finds that there is a need to study housing and building codes, zoning, tax policies, and development standards in order to determine how (1) local property owners and private enterprise can be encouraged to serve as large a part as they can of the total housing and building need, and (2) Federal, State, and local governmental assistance can be so directed as to place greater reliance on local property owners and private enterprise and enable them to serve a greater share of the total housing and building need.

521

Section 301 went on to direct a specific study of:

***the structure of (1) State and local urban and suburban housing and building laws, standards, codes, and regulations and their impact on housing and building costs, how they can be simplified, improved, and enforced, at the local level, and what methods might be adopted to promote more uniform building codes and the acceptance of technical innovations including new building practices and materials; (2) State and local zoning and land use laws, codes, and regulations, to find ways by which States and localities may improve and utilize them in order to obtain further growth and development; and (3) Federal, State, and local tax policies with respect to their effect on land and property cost and on incentives to build housing and make improvements in existing structures.

The Commission was directed to report to the President, to Congress, and to the Secretary of Housing and Urban Development by December 31, 1968.

While the congressional and presidential charges gave the broadest scope to the Commission's assignment, the Commission itself imposed certain limitations on itself to make its task manageable and to be able to concentrate on topics that were mentioned specifically in the charge and which have tended to be most neglected by scholars and public officials alike. Each of these major subjects could merit a Commission study in itself.

Generally excluded from the report are matters which have had recent intensive treatment by others, such as the public welfare system, education, riots and civil disorders, law enforcement, and transportation. This does not reflect any downgrading of the importance of these or other matters not dealt with, or not treated in depth. All of these topics are vital. The Commission stressed that the city must be viewed in terms of the entire urban area, in terms of all of its functions, and in terms of all of its people.

The Commission pursued several avenues in preparation for its report:

Inspections.—The Commission saw for itself the problems of the cities. The members visited the ghettos as well as the suburbs in 22 cities in every section of the country. It studied not only the critical areas, but also viewed the solutions that had been or were being applied.

Hearings.—The Commission also set up public hearings in these cities, listening to private citizens, professionals, and officials. People were asked to testify specifically on matters assigned to the Commission, but witnesses also were invited to give oral or written testimony on related matters which they considered urgent. The transcripts of the hearings have been published in five volumes.

Research.—The Commission staff and competent outside consultants engaged in many detailed research projects and studies, numbering over 40 in all, to establish a sound factual basis for the Commission's work. Many of these studies, because of their high quality and their timeliness, lent themselves to separate publications.

Meetings.—This was a working Commission. The members held meetings on more than 70 days to direct and review the research effort, and to frame recommendations for the specific problems that emerged.

The recommendations in the report all have majority approval of the Commission. Members frequently had differing viewpoints, but those who did not fully agree with the majority did not choose in most instances to register their differences in separate statements. The few such statements may be taken as a measure of the spirit in which the members worked. But the recommendations do represent the considered judgment of the Commission.

Because of the many subjects treated in the report, each Commission member obviously cannot be held personally responsible for every line or paragraph of the text. But the report does have general approval of the members. Their personal role in helping to rework the report through four major drafts indicated their involvement and also their dedication to the task.

Contents

[*Editor's Note: For the interest of the reader, the Table of Contents is reprinted below.*]

Introduction and Summary

- The anger of the slums is that of people disinherited from our society.
- From a cottonfield in the South, big cities look like the only chance left to the rural poor, but city slums become prisons for the disinherited when they arrive.
- Our big cities are hard up, costs of local government are skyrocketing, and representation for the poor in slums is almost nonexistent.
- Coping with metropolitan area problems is incredibly complex because of the proliferation of local governments, all with differing viewpoints, within those areas.
- Those most likely to live in substandard housing are the poor nonwhites who have big families and are renters. But they are not alone: a third of our affluent Nation cannot afford adequate, nonsubsidized housing today, despite great gains in our housing stock.
- Segregation has been a complex problem nagging at America for years. Foot dragging at all levels has not helped. The problem remains critical.
- Over the years accomplishments in subsidized housing have been extremely inadequate. The Nation in 30 years of public housing built fewer units than Congress, back in 1949, said were needed in the immediate next 6 years.
- Housing costs can be reduced if none of the many avenues for savings is dismissed as inconsequential. Add them all up and they promise to be substantial.
- Escalation of land prices adds an even bigger increment in the price of housing, and further explains the squeeze on low-income families seeking decent housing.
- Zoning was intended to control land development, but fiscal considerations often distort it, leading to economic and racial exclusion.
- Orderly urban growth can be the result of a political commitment on land-use decisions, who makes them and how they are made, plus the will to spend money on cities.
- Building code jurisdictions are thousands of little kingdoms, each having its own way: What goes in one town won't go in another—and for no good reason.
- Many places have no housing code. Those that do often do not enforce them properly. We need a new generation of housing codes embracing higher standards and tied in with environmental standards.
- To free the building industry, product manufacturers, planners, and the public from a hopeless maze of restrictions, we must develop a new system of codes and standards.
- No broad attack on housing problems can ignore the sticky, myth-ridden issue of restrictive practices. Needed: More labor efficiency coupled with job security.
- Cost-benefit ratios of the programs we suggest are mere bickering in light of our need for a real political commitment to solve our problems.
- Perhaps the characteristic phenomenon of American politics in the 1960's will someday be seen as the emergence of the city as a political issue.
- To do something about the urban crisis, as political commitment grows, we can start getting the rules changed: Revenue sharing, property tax modernization, Federal income tax revision. Tax incentives are not an efficient means to solve slum problems.
- The Commission believes in a larger role for the cities. We must improve local governments and then give them more money and more authority.
- The States are close enough to the people and yet enough removed from petty parochial interests to become major constructive forces in dealing with urban problems.

- The solutions we call for are a tall order, but they are in proportion to the enormity of the problems of our urban areas.

Recommendations

[*Editor's Note: Recommendations of the Commission were interspersed with the text in Parts II through VI. While many are relevant to the general scope of this anthology on growth management, only selected portions—as indicated—are reprinted here.*]

Recommendations from Part II: Housing Programs

[*Editor's Note: No "recommendations" were contained in Part I. All of Part II's recommendations are reprinted below.*]

Recommendation No. 1—Housing goals

The Commission believes that to meet America's housing needs we must build at least 2.0 to 2.25 million housing units a year. Of these, at least 500,000 units a year, exclusive of housing for the elderly, should house the poor and moderate-income families who at present costs and incomes cannot afford to rent or buy decent, safe and sanitary housing.

Recommendation No. 2—Annual Presidential housing message

The Commission recommends that in addition to long-range goals the President, in a separate annual housing message, which would parallel the Economic Report, State of the Union, and budget messages, propose specific housing construction goals to be achieved in the following fiscal year.

Recommendation No. 3—Relation to national economic policy

The Commission recommends that machinery be devised in the executive branch of the Government to insure that when basic economic decisions are made, their effects on housing construction and housing construction goals be clearly and deliberately considered. The Commission further recommends that the President and his Economic Advisers, the Federal Reserve Board, the Treasury Department, and other departments and major agencies of the Government, be required to state what effect any major change in economic policy (e.g., interest rate changes, tax reductions or increases, balance-of-payment proposals) would have on the successful building of the number of housing units set by the President in his annual housing construction goals message.

Recommendation No. 4—Reduction in the general level of interest rates

The Commission recommends that in the interest of meeting national housing goals, the Federal Government over the next decade strive to bring about a reduction in the general level of interest rates on indebtedness for housing.

Recommendation No. 5—Capital budget

The Commission recommends that a Federal capital budget be established in order that the most effective and least costly method of subsidizing housing, namely Federal grants or loans, can be used and amortized over the useful life of the asset.

Recommendation No. 6—Legislative authority should be sufficient to fund housing programs 3 years into the future

The Commission recommends that, in order to meet the national housing goals recommended by this Commission as well as those proposed by the President and adopted by the Congress, Congress authorize the Secretary of HUD to enter into contracts and obligations each year committing funds as obligations of the Federal Government to build housing and related projects for at least 3 years into the future without further authority from the Appropriations Committees.

Recommendation No. 7—Federal initiative to establish priority for needs

The Commission recommends that Congress amend the National Housing Act to change drastically the philosophy, methodology, and financial arrangements for Federal assistance in the provision of low-income housing, by adopting an active approach in dealing with localities.

Recommendation No. 8—Improved statistical data dealing with housing and other urban problems

The Commission recommends to the President and Congress that Federal statistical and research activities that bear upon social, economic, and governmental conditions in urban areas be maintained, expanded and improved. More specifically, we urge: that the Congress act favorably upon pending legislation to authorize a regular mid-decade census of population and housing; that adequate financing be provided for various federal censuses, surveys and research programs closely relevant to urban conditions and problems; that the Bureau of the Budget and various Federal statistical agencies improve and expand their programs for technical assistance to statistical offices of State and local governments; that the statistical and data collection activities of the Department of Housing and Urban Development be vastly expanded, with special reference to housing programs for the poor and near-poor and to the various conditions and facilities accompanying and surrounding low-cost housing, and that other appropriate Federal agencies act vigorously to develop needed new patterns of data classification and to close serious information gaps that now exist with regard to many aspects of public policy and effective government for urban areas.

Recommendation No. 9—Rewriting of Federal housing statutes

The Commission finds that Federal housing programs, although having accomplished much in transforming the United States into a nation of homeowners and in rendering some assistance to meet low- and moderate-income housing needs, presently (a) fall significantly short of optimum scale and quality and (b) constitute an increasingly complex administrative and financial maze of separate programs. The Commission suggests, therefore, that the time may be at hand for a rewriting of Federal housing statutes.

Recommendation No. 10—Simplifying programs and regulations

The Commission recommends that to the degree possible in the rewriting of the Housing Assistance Act and FHA legislation, housing assistance programs and their subsidies be consolidated, differences in the ceilings on profits to builders be rationalized, and minimum building standards between and among programs be made uniform.

Recommendation No. 11—State and local legislation to secure open housing

The Commission recommends (a) the enactment of open housing legislation by the 28 States not now having an open housing law; (b) the strengthening of the existing 22 State open housing laws; (c) the enactment of open housing ordinances by all cities and urban counties now without such ordinances; and (d) the vigorous enforcement of open housing legislation by all levels of government. The Commission considers legislative and administrative action proposed here and covering all residential dwelling units as the minimum legal, moral, and symbolic basis from which the Nation can proceed to attack the moral crises confronting urban America.

Recommendation No. 12—Federal requirements of local legislative and enforcement action

The Commission recommends that the Congress enact legislation to provide that all financial assistance programs (including grants, loans, and loan guarantees) administered by the Department of Housing and Urban Development be conditioned upon the existence within the local government area being served of an enforceable open occupancy ordinance, or in lieu thereof, enforceable State legislation providing for open occupancy.

Recommendation No. 13—Areawide housing plans and administration

The Commission recommends the enactment of State legislation to authorize carrying out the housing assistance function on a countywide basis both within and outside incorporated areas, and further to authorize and encourage the creation of multicounty housing agencies in those metropolitan areas covering more than a single county.

The Commission further recommends that States enact legislation creating or authorizing an instrumentality of the State to have the power of eminent domain; such power to be exercised for the purpose of building housing for families of low and moderate income in those municipalities or counties which have received Federal or State assistance for planning grants, urban renewal write-down, sewer or water projects or other programs, but which municipalities or counties have not used the land so subsidized for such purposes.

Recommendation No. 14—Elimination of local government rent supplement veto

The Commission recommends legislative action by the Congress to remove from the rent supplement program and the rent certificate program the requirement for approval by the governing body of the local political subdivision before such assistance can be provided.

Recommendation No. 15—"Extraterritorial" leasing by the city housing agencies

The Commission recommends that States amend their laws governing local housing agencies to permit, with specified safeguards, the leasing by such agencies of privately owned housing units anywhere in the metropolitan area.

Recommendation No. 16—Improvements in public housing policy and administration

The Commission recommends the inclusion of a number of improvements in public-housing legislation.

(a) Greater use of scattered sites

The Commission recommends that the Federal Government take steps to use, and to support, State and local use of a wide variety of sites feasible for housing purposes. This should include (without limitation to) parcels to vacant land within city borders, land owned by the Federal Government, dwellings on which VA and FHA mortgages have been foreclosed, abandoned sites reverting for delinquent taxes, urban renewal sites, and suburban land suitable for lease by city public housing authorities.

(b) Use 10 percent of units in 221 (d) (3) projects for low-income housing
(c) Removal of restrictions on amenities

The Commission recommends that in the rewritten legislation, all restrictions on amenities and accommodation standards now attached to housing assistance programs be dropped.

(d) Further encouragement to public housing tenants to purchase their units

The Commission recommends not only that residents of public-housing projects be permitted to purchase their units in single-family semidetached and other "suitable" structures but that they be encouraged to enter into cooperative ownership in multifamily structures as an alternative to eviction when income rises above eligibility limits. The Commission further recommends that the present experimental provision for contributions in kind or "sweat equity" be extended and enlarged.

(e) Interracial management staff

The Commission recommends that the management staffs of public housing developments be interracial, with the Secretary of HUD given discretion to make exceptions only for compelling reasons.

(f) Related commercial uses in public housing
(g) Provision of close cooperation between housing and social agencies in the community
(h) Increased governmental funds for family planning
(i) Removal of administrative regulations and legislative requirements which tend to restrict the number of units for large families
(j) Remove restrictive regulations which prevent architectural innovations in providing bedroom space for large, poor families
(k) Consideration of a 60-year mortgage for public housing units
(l) Improve the quality of life

Recommendation No. 17—Additional subsidy to reach the abject poor and the large poor family

The Commission recommends that Congress authorize a supplemental subsidy to enable the abject poor and large, low-income families to afford monthly rentals in low-rent public housing and other assisted programs.

Recommendation No. 18—Elimination of State and local referenda requirements for public housing and urban renewal projects

The Commission recommends that States eliminate or modify those requirements in public housing and urban renewal enabling legislation which call for submission of projects to popular referendum; if complete elimination is not found feasible, referenda should be required only when petitioned by a specified percentage of qualified voters.

Recommendation No. 19—Larger role for States

The Commission recommends that in the enactment of revised and simplified housing legislation, the Congress not only permit the present channeling of housing assistance funds directly to cities but also to particular States under certain conditions—to wit: where the State (a) provides for a statewide housing authority or other appropriate administrative machinery, and (b) provides from State funds a supplementary amount equal to at least half of the Federal assistance. Under such an arrangement, the qualifying State would receive its appropriate allotment of funds under a statewide housing assistance plan approved by the Secretary of the Department of Housing and Urban Development, following which the review and financing of local projects under the plan would be effected by the State, eliminating the present detailed time-consuming and frustrating Federal project reviews. The Commission emphasizes that this shift in intergovernmental relationships must be effected selectively as individual States demonstrate readiness to move vigorously in the field of housing assistance on both the program and fiscal fronts.

Recommendation No. 20—Federal Government—Builder of last resort

The Commission recommends that if, after a reasonable period of time, State and local action fails to make substantial progress toward meeting the needs for low- and moderate-income housing as determined by the Secretary of Housing and Urban Development, after consultation with the appropriate local officials, the Federal Government become the builder of last resort.

Recommendation No. 21—Consolidation of housing assistance activities

The Commission recommends that all low- and moderate-income housing assistance programs be administered by a single agency within the Department of Housing and Urban Development.

Recommendation No. 22—Removal of State constitutional barriers

The Commission recommends that each of the industrial or highly urbanized States remove existing constitutional and statutory barriers to involvement of private enterprise in efforts directed toward enlargement and revitalizing the economic and fiscal base of their major cities.

Recommendation No. 23—Establish programs of urban advisers

The Commission recommends the establishment of a program for urban advisers for the cities paralleling the county agent program established for rural families almost half a century ago.

Recommendation No. 24—Programing the urban renewal process

In line with the approach contained in the neighborhood development program enacted in title V of the Housing and Urban Development Act of 1968, the Commission not only recommends permitting urban renewal projects to be carried out in a series of annual undertakings not limited to a single area in accordance with the general plan, but also provision of Federal assistance for continuing local programing and planning not clearly provided in the new act.

Recommendation No. 25—Housing and other facilities for low-income Americans in urban renewal project areas

(a) Land for low-income housing

The Commission recommends that no urban-renewal project be approved by the Department of Housing and Urban Development unless it fits into an overall set of urban-renewal projects under which the rate of construction of low-income units for all of the projects meets or exceeds the rate at which they are removed. The Secretary should be authorized to waive this requirement where cities can demonstrate that they are meeting the objectives of housing low-income families through action under this or other public and private programs. An annual report of such waivers and the detailed proof on which they were based should be submitted to Congress.

(b) Attraction of commercial component to project

The Commission recommends that every effort be made within the nonresidential component to attract jobs and other establishments to be owned by residents of the project area.

(c) Replacement of low-cost housing demolished under Federal or federally aided programs

The Commission recommends that in addition to new housing being constructed to meet the low-income housing needs identified in this report, there be a specific linkage of urban renewal and other Federal or federally assisted programs involving demolition of residences, to Federal programs providing new housing in the areas affected, so that sufficient new housing available to low-income households (including but not limited to those displaced) is constructed in those areas to offset the market pressures created by the demolition of existing residences.

(d) Use of highway funds to replace low-income housing demolished for highway construction

The Commission recommends that highway funds be used to finance the construction of new housing for low-income households in a metropolitan area where demolition for highway construction reduces the supply of such housing, with the requirement that definite commitments to construct the new housing concerned be made before existing housing is demolished.

Recommendation No. 26—Reward for efficient performance

The Commission recommends that where cities demonstrate that they are meeting national housing and community development objectives, and where they have technically qualified and professionally competent staffs and have established good records of performance, Federal urban renewal assistance sufficient to support activities at a high level should be made without detailed and time-consuming reviews of proposed action and activities. Financial auditing and a general appraisal conducted at reasonable intervals can determine exact amounts of assistance due.

Recommendation No. 27—Funds for special programs

The Commission recommends that an additional sum amounting to from 1 to 5 percent of the Federal grant for a local program be made available in a contingency fund for program activities peculiar to the needs of the locality but not necessarily eligible under the detailed urban renewal regulations.

Recommendation No. 28—Long-term leasing of urban renewal land

The Commission recommends that urban renewal agencies not dispose of fee title to the land they acquire but that it be leased for a period ranging from 60 to 90 years, or a period equal to about one and one-half times the length of the mortgage on the property.

Recommendation No. 29—Extended relocation services

The Commission recommends that the fund allotment for each project allow for the provision of relocation, counseling, health services, and other social services to the residents of the area while demolition, new construction, and other renewal activities are proceeding and up to the time that residents are either satisfactorily relocated in another area or brought back to the project area after renewal has been completed.

Recommendation No. 30—Relocation housing

The Commission recommends that the Housing Act be amended to authorize the Secretary of Housing and Urban Development to provide loans and/or grants to communities for construction of new facilities and/or the acquisition of existing facilities to house families forced to be relocated as a result of public improvements and natural disasters.

Recommendation No. 31—Uniform and effective relocation policies

The Commission recommends that the Congress and State legislatures take action to make programs of acquisition and relocation both adequate and uniform for all programs which remove businessmen and residents, including tenants, in the course of land acquisition for public works programs.

(a) Uniform relocation policy and payments under Federal and federally aided programs

The Commission recommends the following features: (i) Federal legislation to provide for uniform relocation policies for all Federal and federally aided programs; (ii) allowance for compensation beyond fair market value for owner-occupants so they can purchase a similar home elsewhere without capital loss; (iii) provision of relocation adjustment payment paid either as a lump sum or over time for tenants who must pay higher rents because of relocation or who must move more than once; (iv) the requirements that adequate-quality housing be available for those displaced by any demolition before the demolition takes place and at prices they can reasonably afford; (v) the use of a specific center at the city or county level for all programs involving relocation; (vi) parallel State legislation to cover similar State or local public works programs; and (vii) authority for the use of mobile homes for interim relocation housing where required.

(b) Unified provision of services to those displaced

The Commission recommends that Congress allocate, through the Department of Housing and Urban Development, funds for the provision of all necessary services, both housing and social, to families and individuals being displaced.

(c) Improvement of relocation and displacement payments

The Commission recommends that the amount of payments made to those displaced and relocated from urban renewal projects be increased and related to household size.

(d) Direct GNMA mortgages in hardship cases

In order to meet the severe problem of lack of provision for the displaced family, the Commission recommends that the Government National Mortgage Association accept direct mortgage applications from families displaced by public action when local banking institutions place unusual financial requirements on such persons as a condition of granting the mortgage.

Recommendations from Part III:
Codes and Standards

Chapter on More Orderly Urban Development [Part III]

[Editor's Note: All of this chapter's recommendations are reprinted below.]
Recommendation No. 1—Enabling competent local governments to guide urban development effectively

The Commission recommends that State and Federal agencies take steps to assure that local governments bear primary responsibility for the guidance of urban development, and that they are capable of effectively performing this function.

Recommendation 1(a)—County or regional authority in small municipalities

The Commission recommends that State governments enact legislation granting to counties (or regional governments of general jurisdiction, where such governments exist) exclusive authority to exercise land-use control powers within small municipalities in metropolitan areas. Although conditions vary from State to State, it appears that municipalities within metropolitan areas should not have regulatory powers if (1) either their population is less than 25,000 or their area is less than 4 square miles, or (2) in the case of a municipality hereafter incorporated or not now exercising regulatory powers, their population is less than 50,000.

Recommendation 1(b)—State requirement of a local development guidance program

The Commission recommends that State governments enact legislation denying land-use regulatory powers, after a reasonable period of time, to local governments that lack a "development guidance program" as defined by State statute or administrative regulations made pursuant to such statute. Powers denied would be exercised by the State, regional, or county agencies as provided in the statute. The existence and enforcement by the States of such local development guidance program requirements should, after a reasonable period of time, be made a condition of State participation in the Federal 701 planning assistance program.

Recommendation 1(c)—Study of Government structure in relation to land-use controls

The Commission recommends that the Department of Housing and Urban Development require, as a condition of Federal 701 grants to States for local planning assistance, the submission of a comprehensive State study of (1) the allocation of planning and land-use control powers and other decisionmaking activities significantly affecting land use within metropolitan areas, (2) the need for regional decisionmaking or regional review of local decisions within such areas, (3) the need for State action to redistribute control powers, and (4) such other matters as may be required to assure more orderly urban development. Such study should be submitted within a reasonably short period after promulgation of the Secretary's requirements and should be published and distributed within the State. Revisions of such studies should be undertaken not less than every 5 years and should report progress made toward implementing recommendations contained in previous studies.

Recommendation 1(d)—Restructuring local planning and development responsibilities

The Commission recommends that State governments enact legislation authorizing but not requiring local governments to abolish local planning boards as traditionally constituted.

Recommendation 1(e)—State recognition of local land-use controls

The Commission recommends that State governments enact legislation granting to large units of local government the same regulatory power over the actions of State and other public agencies that they have over those of private developers.

Recommendation No. 2—Establishment of State agency for development planning and review

The Commission recommends that each State create a State agency for planning and development guidance directly responsible to the Governor. The agency should exercise three types of functions: (1) research and technical assistance to localities in land-use planning and control; (2) the preparation of State and regional land-use plans and policies and (3) adjudication and supervision of decisions by State and local agencies affecting land use.

Recommendation No. 3—Assuring greater choice in the location of housing

The Commission recommends that governments at all levels adopt policies and implementing techniques for expanding the choice of persons of all income levels in the selection of their homes.

Recommendation 3(a)—Assurance by local governments of housing variety

The Commission recommends that State governments amend State planning and zoning enabling acts to include as one of the purposes of the zoning power the provision of adequate sites for housing persons of all income levels and to require that governments exercising the zoning power prepare plans showing how the community proposes to carry out such objectives in accordance with county or regional housing plans, so that within the region as a whole adequate provision of sites for all income levels is made.

Recommendation 3(b)—Multicounty or regional housing plans

The Commission further recommends that State governments enact legislation requiring that multicounty or regional planning agencies prepare and maintain housing plans intended to assure that sites are available within each metropolitan area for development of new housing of all kinds and at all price levels. In the absence of a politically responsible multicounty or metropolitan-wide unit, the State should approve such housing plans for each metropolitan area.

Recommendation 3(c)—Collection of regional housing data

The Commission recommends that State governments enact legislation directing State or regional planning agencies to prepare and maintain, on a periodic basis, data on the general availability of housing and housing sites for persons of various income levels. The commission further recommends that the Congress provide financial aid to the States to assist them in carrying out these functions.

Recommendation 3(d)—Public acquisition of housing sites

The Commission recommends that State governments enact legislation authorizing State, regional, and local agencies to acquire land for present or future use or disposition to provide sites for low- and moderate-income housing.

Recommendation 3(e)—Establishment of State policy on housing near employment centers

The Commission recommends that the States adopt resolutions making it official State policy to encourage the provision of housing for employees of all income levels in areas reasonably close to places of employment.

Recommendation 3(f)—Establishment of Federal policy on housing near employment centers

The Commission recommends that the Congress amend the Housing Act to assert, as a matter of national policy, the desirability of providing for housing of employees of all income levels in areas reasonably close to places of employment, and that immediate executive action be taken to assure the availability of housing sites around new Federal installations.

Recommendation 3(g)—Facilitating court challenges to zoning actions

The Commission recommends that the Justice Department conduct research into the constitutionality (under the Federal Constitution) of various forms of exclusionary zoning—e.g., large-lot and minimum house-size zoning—and serve as amicus curiae in actions brought by aggrieved parties challenging such actions where they are considered by the Department to be unconstitutional.

The Commission further recommends that Congress enact legislation granting standing in the Federal courts to local governments whose citizens are aggrieved by exclusionary land-use regulations of other governments for the purpose of challenging the constitutionality of such requirements.

Recommendation No. 4—Unified planning and design of new neighborhoods

The Commission recommends that States enact legislation enabling localities to encourage unified planning and design of new neighborhoods and to prevent wasteful and unattractive scattered development. Specifically, the Commission proposes the following actions:

Recommendation 4(a)—Restriction of development through holding zones

The Commission recommends that State governments enable local governments to establish holding zones in order to postpone urban development in areas that are inappropriate for development within the next 3 to 5 years. Local governments should be authorized to limit development within such zones to houses on very large lots (e.g., 10 to 20 acres), agriculture, and open space uses. The State legislation should require that localities review holding zone designations at least every 5 years.

Recommendation 4(b)—Regulatory process for planned unit development

The Commission recommends that State governments enact enabling legislation for, and local governments adopt, provisions establishing a regulatory process for planned unit developments. Such legislation should authorize provisions to vary according to the size of projects (e.g., to permit high-rise buildings or light industry only in projects of more than a specified size).

Recommendation 4(c)—State authorization for planned development districts

The Commission recommends that State governments enact legislation enabling local governments to classify undeveloped land in planned development districts within which development would be allowed to occur only at a specified minimum scale. Such statutes should make clear that such minimums could be sufficiently large as to allow only development which created its own environment.

Recommendation 4(d)—Public assistance for land assembly

The Commission recommends that State governments enact legislation authorizing local governments of general jurisdiction to use the eminent domain power for the assembly of land needed for large planned-unit developments. Such legislation should include a procedure whereby such power can be used to assist private developers to assemble land for approved development. Any such assistance should be conditioned on the conformity of the project with regional plans intended to assure the availability of housing for low- and moderate-income families, and otherwise to insure that the powers are exercised in the public interest.

Recommendation No. 5—Assuring fairness and equality of treatment in the application of standards

The Commission recommends that State governments enact legislation establishing clear policies as to the allocation of various costs between developers and local governments. Such legislation should specify the kinds of improvements and facilities for which private developers may be required to bear the costs and the manner in which such obligations may be satisfied, and local governments should not be permitted to deviate from such State policies. As a minimum the legislation should require that developers provide local streets and utilities and dedicate land (or make payments in lieu of dedication) for rights-of-way, utilities, open space, recreation, parks, and schools, provided that such facilities will directly benefit the development and be readily accessible to it.

Recommendation No. 6—Strengthening development controls in developed areas

The Commission recommends that States and localities take action to encourage new development in deteriorating built-up areas and to protect built-up areas which now provide a satisfactory living environment and whose protection is in keeping with local plans. Specifically, the Commission proposes the following actions:

Recommendation 6(a)—Authorization of planned unit developments in built-up areas

State legislation authorizing the use of planned unit development provisions by localities should extend to situations in which land is assembled in built-up areas, allowing developers the option of obtaining planned unit development review.

Recommendation 6(b)—More effective powers and guidelines regarding variances, rezonings, and nonconforming uses

The Commission recommends that the States enact legislation authorizing local governments (1) to impose substantive limitations on the power of boards of appeal to grant variances; (2) to provide effective procedures and aids for the elimination of deleterious nonconforming uses which adversely affect the environment, and (3) to establish formal rezoning policies as a guide to decisions on individual rezonings.

Recommendation No. 7—Use of land purchase and compensative techniques for development control

The Commission recommends that States and localities with the assistance of the Federal Government, use public land purchase and compensation techniques for the control of development in situations where such approaches would accomplish better results than traditional police power regulations.

Recommendation 7(a)—Compensative regulation

The Commission recommends that the States enact legislation enabling property-owners to compel the purchase of property rights by regulating governments when regulations (or certain types of regulations specified by the statute) would constitute an unconstitutional "taking" of property without just compensation. Land so purchased would then be placed in a public reserve of urban land for present or future disposal and use in accordance with approved plans.

Recommendation 7(b)—State authorization for land banking

The Commission recommends that State governments enact legislation enabling State and/or local development authorities or agencies of general purpose governments to acquire land in advance of development for the following purposes: (a) assuring the continuing availability of sites needed for development; (b) controlling the timing, location, type, and scale of development; (c) preventing urban sprawl; and (d) reserving to the public gains in land values resulting from the action of government in promoting and servicing development. At a minimum, such legislation should authorize the acquisition of land surrounding highway interchanges. At such times as development of such land is deemed to be appropriate and in the interests of the region, such land could be sold or leased at no less than its fair market value for private development in accordance with approved plans. Wherever feasible, long-term leases should be the preferred method of disposing of any public land, and lease terms should be set so as to permit reassembly of properties for future replanning and development. Legislation should specify a maximum period that such land may be held by the public before lease or sale.

Recommendation 7(c)—Provision of Federal assistance for land acquisition

The Commission recommends that the Congress enact legislation establishing a Federal revolving fund to facilitate the purchase of land by local governments in owner-initiated compensation proceedings and as part of direct-purchase programs, with the Federal contribution to be returned to the fund upon disposition of the property. Furthermore, the Congress should enact legislation authorizing the Department of Transportation to assist States in acquiring land surrounding federally assisted highway interchanges.

Chapter on Building Codes [Part III]

[Editor's Note: Only part of the chapter's recommendations are reprinted below.]
Recommendation No. 2(a)—Use of Federal influence to curb restrictive building code provisions

The Commission recommends amendment of congressional authorizations for water and sewer and other appropriate facility grants to provide as a condition of eligibility for such grants that building codes in communities receiving such grant assistance shall not be more restrictive than nationally recognized model code standards and subsequently the building code standards to be developed by the National Institute of Building Sciences.

Recommendation No. 2(b)—Formulation of building code standards for rehabilitation housing

The Commission recommends that Congress authorize the Secretary of Housing and Urban Development to develop model standards to be incorporated in local building codes with special reference to the rehabilitation of existing housing.

Recommendation No. 2(c)—Eliminating unnecessary variations in Federal construction standards

The Commission recommends that the President initiate vigorous action to review the variations in standards used by Federal agencies in direct Federal construction, standards based upon nationally recognized current model codes, and subsequently the standards to be developed by the National Institute of Building Sciences.

Recommendation No. 3—Adoption of State building codes and mandating building code uniformity in metropolitan areas

The Commission recommends the enactment of State legislation providing for the adoption of State building codes dealing with human occupancy, conforming to nationally recognized model code standards developed and/or approved by the proposed National Institute of Building Sciences recommended earlier. We further recommend that such State legislation provide that within 1 year following the adoption of the State code, the provisions of such code shall be applicable without modification throughout each metropolitan area of the State which fails to adopt such nationally recognized standards.

Chapter on Housing Codes [Part III]

[Editor's Note: Only part of the chapter's recommendations are reprinted below.]

Improved administration

Recommendation No. 2—Housing code administration

The Commission recommends a wide range of actions to improve housing code administration at all levels of government.

(a) Goal and Guideline Formulation

The Commission recommends that the local housing code administration agency formulate a set of goals and guidelines for determining its functions and programs and request formal adoption by the local governing body.

(b) Establishment of neighborhood improvement and housing services agency

The Commission recommends that each large city (or urban county, as appropriate) establish a neighborhood improvement and housing services agency, with responsibility for: *(a)* neighborhood improvement and housing rehabilitation; *(b)* housing inspection, code enforcement and related services; and *(c)* housing information. The neighborhood improvement and housing services agency should provide a full array of informational, counseling, technical advisory, inspectional, and enforcement housing services to owners and tenants and to public and private agencies and individuals responsible for the planning, development and maintenance of housing and neighborhood facilities. These services should be locally financed but should receive State and Federal grants for specified services as appropriate.

(c) Establishment of citywide program of neighborhood improvement and housing maintenance

The Commission recommends as a major program strategy (whether or not the agency recommended above has yet been created) the establishment by localities of a systematic, citywide program of neighborhood improvement and housing maintenance (including code compliance through intensive administration backed up by vigorous enforcement) tied closely to an overall cooperative effort to improve the city's physical and human resources.

(d) Wide variety of code enforcement sanctions and remedies

The Commission recommends that State and local governments should: (1) Enhance the effectiveness of their enforcement effort by adopting a broad variety of newer sanctions and remedies, shifting from criminal prosecutions alone to an emphasis on the use of a variety of newer civil procedures, such as a shift of emphasis to include the use of civil penalties, the use of equitable remedies, such as injunctions and receiverships, the use of municipal repair remedies with recovery of cost through the imposition of liens, and, where warranted by the volume of cases, the establishment of a civil housing court; (2) strengthen the legal remedies presently used, by the establishment of housing courts where warranted and by improving the application of the criminal process through use of presentencing investigations, suspended sentences or sentences of probation, so as to accomplish correction of conditions through the use of that process to the extent possible.

Federal Policy

Recommendation No. 3—Acceptance of housing codes in Federal policy

The Commission recommends that a wide range of existing Federal policies and activities impinging on housing code administration be specifically modified, and that new policies and activities be established to recognize and support the basic concept of housing codes; namely, that they establish minimum acceptable standards for every dwelling.

(a) Definition of "substandard housing"

The Commission proposes that the term "substandard housing" be used henceforth to mean any dwelling unit in which there is substantial departure from accepted minimum standard housing code provisions, as such provisions have been upheld by the courts including the Supreme Court of the United States, and recommends that all branches of all levels of government, particularly the executive branch of the Federal Government, and most particularly the Department of Housing and Urban Development and the Bureau of the Census, use this meaning in their programs, reports and other activities.

(b) Recognition in national housing policy

The Commission recommends that the congressional declaration of national housing policy contained in section 2 of the Housing Act of 1949 explicitly recognize, among other factors, the enforcement of minimum standard housing codes as the means of accomplishing a large proportion of "the elimination of substandard and other inadequate housing" which is required by "the general welfare and security of the Nation and the health and living standards of its people."

(c) Survey of housing quality

The Commission recommends that the Secretary of Commerce initiate within the Bureau of the Census a periodic survey of housing quality throughout the United States as measured by conformance with acceptable state or local minimum standard housing codes using data supplied and personnel employed by local and State housing code administration agencies as may be feasible under local conditions, supplemented as necessary by direct census data.

Recommendations from Part IV: Government Structure, Finance, and Taxation

[*Editor's Note: Only a portion of Part IV's various chapters' recommendations are reprinted below.*]

Chapter on Government Structure

Recommendation No. 1—Machinery for structural change—A road to local self-determination

The Commission recommends that State governments promptly set up effective machinery to improve local government structure in present and prospective metropolitan areas. As a minimum, each State should:

(a) Assign to an existing or newly-created State agency a specific mandate to: (1) analyze existing conditions and problems of governmental organization in metropolitan areas; (2) prepare proposals for appropriate State constitutional and legislative changes; (3) aid official local commissions established in particular areas to develop governmental reorganization plans; and (4) provide special technical assistance to local governments in areas where reorganization plans are adopted, to help insure an orderly transition to the revised system.

(b) Provide procedures for the establishment of temporary local commissions to appraise and prepare explicit recommendations concerning governmental structure in particular areas; require that such commissions be set up for each metropolitan area, and that they prepare and publish their findings and recommendations within some specified interval; and provide funds to finance the work of such local commissions.

(c) Provide workable procedures for prompt official action upon recommendations for restructuring of local government that are developed by local commissions for particular areas, with adoption either: (1) by State legislative action, subject to cancellation before the effective date by local referendum; or (2) directly by local referendum, with the results in either case determined by a majority vote of the entire area affected.

Recommendation No. 2—Improvement of local government arrangements

To encourage intensive reexamination, and, where found desirable, the improvement of local government arrangement in major urban areas, the Commission recommends:

(a) That Congress promptly adopt legislation under which, beginning 5 years after its enactment, the eligibility of local governments in any metropolitan area to participate in Federal grant programs would be contingent upon there having been completed, within the preceding 10-year period, a comprehensive official study of local government structure within the area, carried out either directly by the State or States concerned or by a public agency authorized by State law to carry out such a study, and including the publication of findings and recommendations; and

(b) That Congress promptly amend section 701 of the Housing Act of 1954 so as specifically to authorize Federal aid under that section for the financing of official studies of governmental structure in metropolitan or major urban areas that are undertaken by State agencies or in accordance with State authorizing laws.

Recommendation No. 3—Actions by State governments

The Commission urges that the State governments take the earliest possible action, by legislation or, if necessary, by the amendment of their constitutions to—

(a) Authorize and help finance effective councils of local governments in present and prospective metropolitan areas;

(b) Permit counties to provide urban-type services through subordinate "service areas" with appropriate means of financing, where this is a feasible alternative to independent special districts;

(c) Eliminate provisions requiring numerous independent elective county officials which diffuse responsibility and prevent effective control by county governing boards.

(d) Eliminate onerous tax and debt limits which so impair the capability of municipal and county governments as to stimulate the creation of separate special district units;

(e) Review and revise laws concerning special districts to facilitate their merger, dissolution, or "taking over" in appropriate cases by county or municipal governments;

(f) Enforce minimum-size standards for proposed new municipalities, at least within present and prospective metropolitan areas; and

(g) Provide flexible procedures for annexation of territory by municipalities, intermunicipal mergers, and functional transfers between municipalities and counties.

Chapter on Urban Services

Recommendation No. 1—Accelerate improvement in poor neighborhoods by providing adequate city services

The Commission urges the governing bodies and key administrative officials of cities, urban counties, and major school districts (a) to examine intensively the relative quality of the services and facilities they provide to neighborhoods of differing economic and social characteristics; (b) to develop, publicize, and apply standards designed to assure equity on this score, and especially to insure that the particular needs of low-income neighborhoods are fully recognized and served; and (c) to move as rapidly and vigorously as possible to remedy deficiencies in public services and facilities that contribute to neighborhood deterioration.

We urge unions of municipal employees and members of professional groups to accept, with appropriate safeguards, the principle of compensation differentials among neighborhoods in order to achieve these objectives. Finally, we recommend that the States, through their urban affairs agencies or otherwise, encourage and assist urban local governments in these efforts.

Recommendation No. 2—Decentralization of municipal services to neighborhood city halls

The Commission proposes that large city governments take prompt and affirmative steps to decentralize appropriate municipal services to the neighborhood level, and to establish channels of communication with neighborhood residents.

Chapter on Federal Taxation & Housing

Recommendation No. 1—U.S. Treasury study

The Commission recommends that the President direct the Treasury Department to make an intensive analysis and submit explicit findings and recommendations concerning tax law changes best suited to provide materially more favorable treatment for investment in new residential construction (including major rehabilitation) than for other forms of real estate investment.

Recommendation No. 2—Tax incentives for upkeep of older rental housing

The Commission recommends that the Internal Revenue Code be amended to provide specific incentives for adequate maintenance and rehabilitation of rental residential property by allowing, within appropriate limits, for especially generous tax treatment of investor-owners' expenditures for these purposes with respect to structures of more than some specified age, such as 30 or 40 years.

Recommendation No. 3—Tax incentives for low- and moderate-income housing investment

The Commission recommends prompt revision of the Federal income tax laws to provide increased incentives for investment in low- and moderate-income housing, relative to other real estate investment, where such housing is governmentally subsidized and involves a legal limit upon the allowable return on investors' equity capital. Specifically, we propose that the Internal Revenue Code be amended to provide especially favorable treatment (whether through preferential depreciation allowances or through investment credits) for investments made under governmentally aided limited-profit programs for the construction and rehabilitation of low- and moderate-income housing.

National Commission on Urban Problems

Paul H. Douglas, *Chairman*, Washington, D.C.; David L. Baker, Garden Grove, California; Hugo Black, Jr., Miami, Florida; Lewis Davis, New York, New York; John De Grove, Boca Raton, Florida; Anthony Downs, Chicago, Illinois; Ezra Ehrenkrantz, San Francisco, California; Alex Feinberg, Camden, New Jersey; Jeh V. Johnson, Poughkeepsie, New York; John Lyons, St. Louis, Missouri; Richard W. O'Neill, New York, New York; Richard Ravitch, New York, New York; Carl E. Sanders, Atlanta, Georgia; Mrs. Chloethiel Woodard Smith, Washington, D.C.; Tom J. Vandergriff, Arlington, Texas; and Coleman Woodbury, Madison, Wisconsin.

Commission Staff

Executive Director: Howard E. Shuman; Associate and Assistant Directors: Allen D. Manvel, Walter Rybeck, Stanley D. Heckman, Walter L. Smart, Oscar Sutermeister, John H. Noble, Arthur S. Goldman, David M. Pellish, Frank T. DeStefano, Richard K. Guenther, Gordon E. Howard; Administrative Officer: Mrs. Jane Carey Enger; Special Consultants: William G. Colman, Erwin Knoll; Editorial and Research Assistants: Mrs. Marion Massen, David Engel, Miss Sone A. Takahara, Mrs. Ellen Kelly, Miss Hope Marindin, Joseph L. Falkson, Ray Hay; Staff Assistants: Mrs. Rose Marie Allen, Mrs. Mary Carlsen, Miss Juanita Cornelius, William F.

Building the American City

Glacken, Mrs. Eleanor A. Golden, Miss Catherine Hartigan, Mrs. Anne Healy, Miss Caroline Hinton, Willie Howell, Mrs. Anita Mintz, Mrs. Louise Pompeo, Miss Jane Powers, Mrs. Donna Prijatelj, Mrs. Mimi Ross, Miss Betty J. Sinclair, Mrs. Margaret Stein, Mrs. Nancy Stewart, Mrs Patty Tirana, Mrs. Norine Thompson, Mrs. Elena Van Meter, Mrs. Jo Ann Williams, Miss Mary Helen Woods, Miss Ellen Zachariasen, and Miss Jane Zinsmeister.

Opening the Suburbs:

Toward Inclusionary Controls

Paul Davidoff
and Linda Davidoff

Paul Davidoff is director of the Suburban Action Institute. He was previously director of the Urban Planning Program at Hunter College, and a lecturer at Princeton University and at Yale University. Mr. Davidoff is a graduate of Allegheny College and holds a master's from the University of Pennsylvania, from which he also holds a law degree.

Linda Davidoff is a lecturer in urban planning at State University of New York, Purchase, New York. She is also a planning consultant, a Democratic state committeewoman in New York, and vice-chairperson of the New York State New Democratic Coalition. Mrs. Davidoff is a graduate of Radcliffe College, and holds a master's from the University of Pennsylvania.

This article originally appeared under the title: "Opening the Suburbs: Toward Inclusionary Land Use Controls." It is a digest of the original, and is reprinted with permission from 22 Syracuse Law Review 510 (1971).

Introduction

Affluent, powerful America has an ugly side—racial and class hatred, violence, systematic injustice, and political repression. In the suburban residential communities of our metropolitan areas, the affluent and powerful segment of society is enthroned; in slums and ghettos of our aging cities live the powerless—the poor, the black, and the aged.

To an extent previously undreamed of in America, the wall which separates slum and suburb has become thick, high and impenetrable. Legal institutions have been devised so that the laws of suburban communities which control the use of the community's land and resources have become the servants of race and class separatism. In the 1960's, the term "apartheid" began to be used to describe the *de jure*, as well as the *de facto* methods employed to separate rich communities from poor, to protect rich Americans and their children from contact with poor and even middle-class Americans and their children; and to separate black Americans from white Americans. In the 1960's and 1970's suburban America has become the dominant community style of our nation. From an urban nation we have become predominantly a suburban one,[1] and this shift of population and of life style has helped to sharpen the race and class cleavages among us.

Will the suburbs remain an exclusive preserve for middle- and upper-middle-income families, or will they become open and available for citizens of all incomes and races? The answer to this question is of interest to residents of both the suburbs and the slums. Inherent in this dilemma is whether minority citizens, as well as moderate- and low-income families, will be allowed to enjoy the attractive qualities which are characteristic of suburbia. Furthermore, and perhaps more importantly, will our society destroy the existing barriers which separate our citizenry, or will a garrison state emerge wherein force will be exerted in order to repress any revolt by the black and the poor?

The question whether the suburbs will be open or will remain exclusive preserves is also the precondition to the question: Can our cities be saved from decay? In the overcrowded central city ghettos, no significant progress toward providing jobs, erasing social pathology, or tearing down decayed buildings and replacing them with new ones can be achieved until the pressure of overcrowding in the city ghettos can be relieved. This is the lesson of 15 years of urban renewal.

America's suburbs contain almost all of the vacant developable residential land within metropolitan areas.[2] Housing mobility must be increased in order to relieve central cities of the impossible burden of providing adequate housing with the limited available resources. This may be accomplished through changes in local land use controls combined with the infusion of new funds and new forms of aid from the federal government to permit the construction of vast amounts of moderate-income housing outside the central cities.

The bulk of the new jobs being created in the nation are located in the suburbs; this is particularly true of blue collar jobs.[3] The suggested construction of large scale development in the suburbs for moderate- and low-income families is not a recommendation for the demise of cities or for the dispersal of central city populations. Rather, it reflects a belief that only through the development of housing opportunities near the jobs in the suburbs, will it be possible to relieve the central cities of the pressures which prevent the successful rehabilitation and rebuilding of neighborhoods and structures.

The purpose of the suggested development of suburban resources is not to concentrate jobs and housing solely in the suburbs. Rather, it is an endeavor in accord with the recommendations of the Kerner Commission,[4] to offer opportunities throughout metropolitan areas which would present to residents of ghetto communities a choice—either to remain where they are or to move to other locations.

The ghetto is a condition created by social, political, and economic limitations on the opportunities of a class of the population; it is not a place, but a social condition. It should be possible to conceive programs which would end the limits to opportunities for ghetto residents and allow for the redevelopment of the place now called the ghetto to meet the needs of its residents. But in the absence of such programs, which could exploit suburban resources, it would be impossible to enable present ghetto populations wishing to remain where they now live to rebuild their communities according to acceptable standards.

Therefore, the future of our society as a whole, and of our cities in particular, rests with the suburbs. As long as our nation continues to show large-scale population movement from the countryside to the metropolitan areas, the exclusionary policies of the suburbs will continue to bottle up larger and larger concentrations of our poor people and minority-group families in the central cities. As long as this division between rich and poor, black and white, is perpetuated in the geographic divisions of our metropolitan areas, social tensions in our nation will continue to mount.

Exploration of the Problem

[*Editor's Note: extensive material relating to the history, goals, purposes, and use/abuse of zoning is omitted here.*]

Toward Inclusionary Land Use Controls

The objective of revising land use regulations is to assure that community health, safety, and amenity requirements can be achieved without producing the racial and social class isolation that has resulted from present practices, especially zoning. It is proper for a civilized urban community to seek to separate disharmonious land activities. It also seems appropriate for intelligent citizens to try to conserve scarce municipal expenditures and to plan for efficient forms of urban growth. However, the propriety of continued employment of the police power to regulate private behavior for the well-being of the local government must be questioned. Of greatest urgency is ending the use of the police power through zoning to achieve economic and racial segregation.

There is presently a period of growing public recognition of the abuses that have been perpetrated in the name of community planning and amenity through zoning and other land use controls. Within a year or two the United States Supreme Court will be asked to review the constitutionality of zoning devices which prevent large numbers of the population from gaining access to residence within suburban communities. The Supreme Court may be asked to review not only the specific exclusionary zoning practices but also to reconsider the general approval of zoning which it granted more than 40 years ago in the *Village of Euclid v. Ambler Realty Co.*[36] decision.

This article will leave open the question of whether zoning should be replaced entirely or only altered significantly. What is quite clear is that this very powerful mechanism of land development control must cease operating to deprive large portions of the population of the opportunity to share in the development of decent suburban environments. The standard that should guide a rethinking of zoning, and land use control in general, is that of *inclusion*.

Inclusionary Controls: Objectives and Questions. The objectives toward which land development policies should strive are: (1) To guarantee to residents of a state—or the nation—that local law derived from state police powers will not be employed to deny them access to residences within all parts of residential areas of local government units. (2) To maximize local control over those aspects of land development that affect primarily the locality and its citizens.

1. **Access to All Residential Land.** The theory that all parts of a municipality's residential land must be available to all sectors of the population is premised on the belief that public laws cannot be used to create race or income class zones either by direction or indirection, except upon the finding of a special need by a particular class.[37] In the discussions concerning both housing and land development policy, special treatment for low-, moderate-, middle-, and upper-income classes has been propounded. The law has recognized for some time the propriety of setting aside land to meet the housing needs of low-, moderate-, and middle-income families. Housing for such classes has been authorized by the public when the private sector cannot meet the demand. A more difficult case arises when discussion turns to whether the public should sponsor upper-income housing, because the need for public intervention to assist the class is significantly less apparent. Nevertheless, some students of American housing subsidies have shown that the upper-income classes are the major beneficiaries of public resource distribution. For example, the Secretary of the Department of Housing and Urban Development, George Romney, has been among a host of critics who have observed that the internal revenue system, with its income tax credits for mortgage

interest payments and for local real estate taxes, bestows considerably greater rewards upon upper-income homeowners than the public's many housing programs bestow on low- and moderate-income families.[38]

The federal urban renewal program has also been castigated for its strong tendencies to provide new housing units for middle- and upper-income families while at the same time forcing residents of slums to be relocated in other slums in order to make way for the development of luxury housing.[39] In a society more attuned to social equity than to preservation of property investments, stronger attacks upon this particular form of redistribution might be successful. Some have justified the fact that certain areas of metropolitan regions have been limited to families which could afford housing on large tracts, on the ground that upper-income families have the same right as other income groups to secure a portion of the residential turf.

Even if one were to accept the notion that upper-income groups deserve a special domain protected by the public, it might, nevertheless, seem equitable to propose that the land set aside for an income group should be proportional to their representation in the population. Today, very large proportions (in the New York region, 90 percent of all vacant land is zoned for single-family residential use) of vacant land is reserved for building lots of relatively large size.[40] In eight counties of New Jersey, 82 percent of developable vacant land is zoned for lots of one-half acre or more.[41] In a portion of Connecticut close to New York City (the Southwestern region), 77.6 percent of vacant residential land is zoned for lots of one acre or more.[42] Houses built on lots of one-fourth acre or more are selling for a minimum of $25,000 in the New York region today; houses built on lots of one-half acre or more are selling for more than $30,000 in New Jersey; houses built on lots of an acre or more are selling for over $45,000 in Southwestern Connecticut. At these prices, perhaps 25 percent of the population, earning $12,500 or more, can afford to buy houses built on this land.[43] Therefore, under current zoning practices, public law is being used to preserve perhaps 80 percent of the vacant residential land in metropolitan areas for the use of perhaps 25 percent of the population. And, if in fact most of this housing is available to families with incomes above $20,000, then less than 10 percent of all families can compete for it.[44] Our proposal is to create a policy that is explicit in rejecting the notion that zoning should be based on income considerations except on a finding of special need. It would provide that communities have the obligation to demonstrate in their comprehensive plans, and in their use of police power, that all classes of the population might find housing or land on which housing could be constructed in all sectors of the community.

2. **Existing Legislation to Counter Exclusionary Zoning.** Legislation to counter the effects of exclusionary zoning has already been passed in two states, Massachusetts and New York, and is being considered in a number of others. It is interesting to note, however, that both the Massachusetts and the New York statutes leave intact the underlying structure of exclusionary zoning, while providing that certain specific tracts of land in suburban areas can be exempted from the exclusionary pattern.

The Massachusetts approach—The "Anti-Snob Zoning" law of Massachusetts,[45] enacted in 1969, provides that at least 0.3 percent of the vacant residential land of a community must be made available for development each year for a period of five years upon application by eligible nonprofit or limited-profit housing sponsors for zoning changes. The law creates a special state zoning board of appeals which rules on the propriety of refusals by local jurisdictions to permit nonprofit or limited-profit sponsors to proceed with development plans. Where the commission finds that a local jurisdiction has failed to make land available under the law, it is empowered to issue a state permit, overriding local authorities, for the construction to proceed. Aside from difficulties with the enforcement of the statute, the fundamental problem with the Massachusetts law is its tacit approval of the continuation of exclusionary practices in the 98.5 percent of vacant developable land which will be unaffected by the statute. (After five years, a maximum of 1.5 percent of a community's land could be developed for low- and moderate-cost housing under the statute's provisions.) The law does not come to grips with the constitutional questions raised by exclusionary practices, and it does nothing to reduce the inflation of land prices in the suburbs that is caused by the reservation of most vacant land for high-cost development. The practical effects of the Massachusetts law are still to be determined; preliminary assessments of its effectiveness require caution in following its example.[46]

The New York approach—The Urban Development Corporation of New York [hereinafter referred to as UDC], created by the legislature in April, 1968 (in the urgent atmosphere that followed the death of Martin Luther King, Jr.), was granted the power to override local zoning and subdivision laws where they conflicted with UDC findings that a certain site was appropriate for low- or moderate-cost housing.[47] In the more than two years since its creation, however, the political constraints operating within the State Legislature have reasserted themselves, and the UDC has not acted to override exclusionary local zoning. Instead, it has worked with local governments, almost entirely in central-city jurisdictions, to undertake housing and renewal programs to benefit the citizens of those jurisdictions.[48] If the UDC would join in a case attacking the discriminatory aspects of zoning empowered by the state zoning enabling legislation, overriding local zoning could be made unnecessary. It might be argued that where the UDC uses its powers to override local zoning, the state agency is in fact accepting discriminatory zoning within a town and merely setting it aside on a particular tract of land. If successful in a constitutional attack against exclusionary practices, the UDC could make possible a situation in New York in which the purposes for which it was created could be achieved, not only through its efforts, but with the assistance of all the public and private entities concerned with the rapid development of decent housing for all residents of the state.

Neither the Massachusetts nor the New York advances in coping with local reluctance to participate in solutions to state housing problems are sufficient. They fail to create means for the private market to participate fully in the construction of housing for moderate as well as higher income groups. Further, they make it difficult for sponsors of publicly assisted low- and moderate-income housing to freely choose the locations in a community where they wish to construct housing units. Both the New York and Massachusetts approaches are tolerant of the existing structure of private-interest control of public law; they do little more than create possibilities for small islands of exception to the general rule. These exceptions are the 0.3 percent of vacant land made available for low- and moderate-income housing under the Massachusetts Act and the thus far unused power of the Urban Development Corporation to override local zoning on particular tracts of land. The only acceptable correctives to the patterns of segregation created by public law are those that entirely eliminate them. In order to solve the housing problem and to create housing choices for all classes in all areas of a state or region, it is necessary to maximize the choices open to housing consumers and developers within statewide safeguards.

3. **Local Home Rule.** Many of those who argue for maintenance of the present system of zoning assert that any diminution of the power of a locality to determine the proper density of residential development, or the type of housing units permitted, would represent a serious invasion of home rule powers. Local government is important. The growth of public demand for community participation in urban decision-making, and the popularity of the notion of federal revenue sharing, indicate that decentralization and local control should be bolstered, not weakened, in the area of land use controls. The important point to be made here is that it is possible to create a system of land use controls which enables communities to determine their own land development patterns, *provided they meet the standards of inclusiveness.* Having met such standards and having demonstrated that the community provides opportunity throughout its area for all segments of the population, there need be no outside forces threatening to regulate local land use. These threats do exist under the UDC formula and under the state appeals board created by the Massachusetts "Anti-Snob" Zoning Act.

Proposals for Inclusionary Policies. The following proposals are directed toward creating local communities open to members of all classes and races who seek entry to them.[49]

1. **Comprehensive Planning is Inclusionary Planning.** Throughout almost the entire history of zoning, local zoning ordinances have been required by statute to be "in accordance with a comprehensive plan." In one of the most interesting decisions dealing with that language, Justice Weintraub of the New Jersey Supreme Court stated that the minimum elements of such a plan connote "an integrated product of a rational process and [that] 'comprehensive' requires something beyond a piecemeal approach, both to be revealed by the ordinance considered in relation to the physical facts and the purposes authorized [by the New Jersey planning statutes]."[50] The difficulty with this definition is that zoning comporting with this standard has permitted comprehensive racial and economic segregation to be practiced in New Jersey as well as in most of the other states. If the state is to prohibit local zoning from creating racial segregation, it must directly mandate a new form of behavior. The requirements for this are specific demands for *inclusionary* practices, to be included in the language of state planning and zoning enabling laws. The comprehensive plan for zoning should be defined to mean a plan which makes provision throughout residential zones and nonresidential zones (in which residences are permitted) for housing types and densities which will not prohibit the development of low- and moderate-income housing. This provision should specifically prohibit zoning practices which would segregate income or racial groups to specific zones or specific parts of a community. Similar requirements should be established for comprehensive or master planning to be carried out by public planning agencies. A burden of analysis and evaluation should be placed on local planning agencies to assure that they have explicitly found that their community, in its public actions, will provide adequate shelter and environment for all economic classes and races. A plan for the fulfillment of such an "open community standard" should be as important a part of the planning process as is the transportation plan or the land use plan.

2. **Termination of Specific Discriminatory Devices. (a)** It should be a matter of state policy that no locality can exclude multi-family development from any of the zones in which it permits residential development. Such a conclusion is based upon findings that multi-family housing (housing including two or more dwelling units) represents a relatively inexpensive form of housing,[51] and upon the recognition that many families

prefer multi-family occupancy to single-family occupancy, as well as upon the recognition that multi-family structures can be constructed to the highest standards of contemporary aesthetic judgment, as in Reston, Virginia and Columbia, Maryland. **(b)** It should also be a matter of state public policy that no locality can establish a minimum habitable floor area requirement for a dwelling unit which sets a standard higher than the minimum established for the state by a state public health director. Variations in local minimum floor areas have no possible justification on health or safety grounds. **(c)** The next policy proposal is, perhaps, the most difficult to enact. It seems quite clear that there is no basis in police power concepts for distinguishing among types of residential uses. If that particular power to discriminate among types of residential uses is removed, then distinctions between residential zones must be based on factors related to the intensity of development, e.g., population density, floor area development, or percentage of lot covered by the structure. Regardless of the standard selected, it must be employed in a non-discriminatory fashion. This will have the greatest impact, today, on suburban residential lot area requirements. (But it should be noted, tangentially, that it would also affect city zoning where high density zoning is employed to attract luxury builders and to exclude low-income families.) The minimum lot size requirements for purposes of assuring public health and safety should be established by state health and building officials. In all probability this would lead to a situation in which no lot size greater than one acre would be required. One of the most apparently well-justified excuses which exclusionary towns have used in rejected pleas for higher density residential development has been the claimed absence of public water and sewer facilities. There is a good deal of what common law lawyers refer to as *chutzpah* behind this argument. Towns which have the obligation to serve the needs of citizens have effectively prohibited citizens from entering their communities by arguing a lack of facilities. To circumvent this, developers should be permitted, with state health and building officials' approval, to build at higher densities where they can reasonably construct adequate water and sewer facilities to meet the needs of the future residents of their developments. It would be useful to have a state urban growth fund available to assist in the payment of required facilities in circumstances where the proposed development was to provide publicly assisted low- and moderate-income housing.

3. **Conservation of Municipal Expenditures.** As a matter of policy it should be within the police power to zone for purposes of conserving municipal expenditures, provided that the purpose may be achieved only in circumstances where the effect of the controls employed is to enlarge, rather than limit, economic access to residence within the community. Efficiency in government should result in reduced taxes and reduced costs of living within a community.

4. **Housing for Industrial Workers.** It should also be a matter of public policy that no land within a community may be rezoned for industrial or commercial expansion without there first being made a finding that sufficient vacant housing at moderate cost and rental levels, or vacant residential land upon which such housing could be constructed, is available for housing all of the workers associated with the proposed new industrial or commercial development. In the absence of a positive finding, a locality should be required to rezone sufficient residential land to meet the housing needs of the potential workers as a precondition to rezoning for the industrial or commercial development. The housing to be provided for the workers must be constructed at prices within the economic means of the expected labor force.

5. **The Right of Regional Residents to Sue and to be Heard.** The State of New Jersey a year ago enacted legislation empowering nonresidents of a community to have standing to litigate against local zoning restrictions injurious to them.[52] This important action granted to excluded persons, such as central city residents, a right to contest suburban communities' discriminatory policies. In addition to this right, it should also be a matter of public policy that nonresidents who are affected by the issue should have a right to be heard at local zoning hearings.

6. **Urban Growth Fund.** Taking away communities' rights to exclude low- and moderate-income families will produce a potential for increased fiscal burdens on the affected communities. For this reason, and because the provision of housing for low- and moderate-income families will greatly assist states in solving their housing problems, states should create "urban growth funds" which could contribute toward the development of suburban services and facilities for which low- and moderate-income families' real estate taxes are incapable of paying for fully.

7. **Government Facilities Location.** It should be a matter of policy that government facilities, federal, state, or local, should be located in areas that have an adequate supply of housing for all of the people employed at that facility. Such state policies could be modeled after the "Federal Government Facilities Location Act" introduced by Senator Ribicoff in December, 1970.[53] Adoption of such a policy would make it impossible for communities to construct state-supported hospitals or schools, for example, where those who teach or work at the school would be unable to find housing within their means in the community where they work.

A Concluding Note on Prescriptions. The proposals offered in this section deal directly with the conditions which create, by public law, patterns of economic and racial segregation. It is suggested that legislative bodies must either voluntarily adopt standards to prevent continuation of these discriminatory practices, or they will be required to do so as a result of judicial decision.[54]

However, the proposals which have just been offered are really only deterrents to present abuses; they do not speak to the important issue of which kind of controls are needed to assure high standards of amenity in open communities. Planners, lawyers, urbanists and others are confronted with an important task. They must reconsider the propriety of maintaining zoning as the primary control over land development. It may be that zoning is the best land use control possible and that, without its discriminatory features, it could operate effectively to protect the quality of urban development. But zoning has also shown great weaknesses as a legal and planning device. It may be time to ask if there is not a better means.

It is also necessary to consider the fact that the very worst features of exclusionary zoning blossomed after racially restrictive covenants were struck down in *Shelley v. Kraemer*.[55] Those of us who oppose efforts to exclude minorities from developing areas would be well advised to think of the new game the discriminators will think up after exclusionary zoning is knocked down.

A Special Note on Those Now Residing in Acreage Zones. Many of the fears expressed by suburbanites when discussing the issue of eliminating exclusionary zoning revolve about the protection which would be offered to residents of already developed tracts of land. Thus, families living on lots of one or two acres fear new land use controls would permit neighbors to subdivide their acreage parcels into plots of one-fourth acres or less.

An analysis of the suburban land supply reveals that it would be unnecessary to require that existing developed land be made subject to re-subdivision at much higher densities.

This is the case because of the existence of vast amounts of vacant land in the suburbs. At least for the foreseeable future, families residing in developed tracts can be provided with the protection they seek. Where land has been developed at a certain density under an existing zoning regulation, that density should be maintained in the future, until good reasons for changing it are asserted. Thus, if a tract of land is now zoned for two-acre development and divided into two-acre parcels, and if exclusionary zoning, including two-acre zoning, is struck down or prohibited by legislation, existing development should still be protected as a permitted non-conforming use. However, in a developed tract containing a parcel of vacant land three or four times as large as the minimum lot size under the old zoning, that vacant parcel should be developable in conformance with the new zoning standard.

A Note About a Non-zoning Factor Contributing Strongly to Exclusionary Practices. A discussion of the changes required to stop local exclusionary practices would be incomplete if it failed to consider the impact of the local fiscal system on suburban behavior. A significant motivation for employing devices which deny moderate- and low-income families access to the suburbs is the operation of a local tax—in almost all communities, a real property tax. Many suburbanites are caught in the game of exclusion, not because of hatred of, or prejudice against the excluded, but out of a real economic self-interest in preserving a relatively low local tax rate. (This reason also provides a screen for those who do hate or fear the excluded.) The present system of raising revenues for local services relies heavily upon a local system which taxes real property. There are two major problems with such a system. The first is that wealth in real property is an outmoded system for judging one's ability to pay. For persons with steady or declining incomes, the real property tax can be grossly unrelated to their ability to pay. Recent studies suggest that such a tax is often highly regressive.[56] The second problem with the system is that it is local. It automatically requires local residents to judge potential residents in terms of their ability to pay their own way. This is particularly true where, as in most suburbs, the costs of providing new services and facilities in order to meet the needs of growing populations are extremely high. In fact, it would not matter whether the local tax was one based upon property, sales, or income: local residents would, for their own financial purposes, seek out newcomers who could pay at least as much to the community as it costs the community to service them.

"Fiscal zoning" is an outgrowth of a system requiring localities to rely heavily upon their own property wealth for revenue purposes. Its use has been in assisting communities with increasing their relative taxing wealth by zoning out undesirable uses and people; nevertheless, it has not eliminated the significant differences which exist between the taxing abilities of rich and poor communities.

Local real property taxation has resulted in significant differences in the ability of local government units to provide services for their residents. This situation has been felt most strongly in the area of education. [*Editor's Note: material omitted.*]

Any realistic study of the means for eliminating segregationist tendencies in the suburban use of public law must recognize the need for reform of the local tax system. [*Editor's Note: material omitted.*]

Movements for inclusionary land use controls and for reform of the tax system must develop simultaneously. There are many potential allies in the movement for more equitable land use controls once the tax system is changed.

It may well be that those who assert a belief in change, subject to the condition that the tax system be altered, would find another excuse if the tax system did change. It is certainly the case that there are opponents of a broadening of the social mix of their communities. But one of the advantages of ridding the debate about land controls of the fiscal issue is that it would rob discrimination of a cloak to hide behind. New disguises may be found, but it does seem better to isolate and explicate the discriminatory practices in the law in order to eliminate them.

Advocates of inclusionary practices are sometimes told that they should wait until the tax system is changed before they start pressing their fight to end zoning segregation. That would be a mistake. The racial and economic practices carried out through local zoning have great harmful effects on the excluded population and on the social and economic health of metropolitan regions and the nation. The struggle to dissolve exclusionary practices should not be made dependent upon the possible outcome of other issues; it should be carried forward now.

Footnotes

*The authors wish to acknowledge the helpful assistance in the development of this article offered by Tamar Savir and Lois Thompson.
1. 1960 Census of Population and Preliminary 1970 Reports.
2. Report of President's Comm. on Urban Housing, A Decent Home, 139-40 (The Kaiser Report 1969).
3. National Comm. Against Discrimination in Housing, The Impact of Housing Patterns on Job Opportunities 21 et seq. (1968).
4. Report of the National Advisory Comm'n on Civil Disorders (1968).
36. Supra note 13 [Village of Euclid v. Ambler Realty Co., 272 U.S. 365 (1926)].
37. See Sager, Tight Little Islands: Exclusionary Zoning, Equal Protection, and the Indigent, 21 Stan. L. Rev. 767 (1969) for a discussion of "substantive equal protection."
38. Transcript of remarks made by Secretary of Housing and Urban Development Romney at the dedication of a new Federal National Mortgage Association building, Oct. 23, 1969:
    The (middle income) people had public policy helping them and meeting their housing needs, both from the standpoint of mortgage policy as well as tax policy—the ability of those who have a mortgage to deduct their interest payments from their income tax return has resulted in the middle income families of this country meeting their housing needs without being aware of the fact that they were the beneficiaries of public policies which to an extent subsidized them in meeting their housing needs.
    . . .The people who have benefited by national housing policies in the main are not even aware that they had any help from public sources and that they tend to resent the idea that public money is being used, their tax money—and I hear the rattling of taxpayers here—being used to help the disadvantaged and the minority groups to meet their housing needs.
39. See Urban Renewal: The Record and the Controversy 291 et seq. (J. Wilson ed. 1966) for a classic discussion of relocation in urban renewal.
40. Supra note 5, at 214-15 [See Report of The National Comm'n on Urban Problems to the Congress and to the President of the United States, Building the American City, H.R. Doc. No. 91-34, 91st Cong., 1st Sess. 213-14 (1969) for a discussion of the economic impact of large-lot zoning.]
41. These figures were developed by the Division of State and Regional Planning, Department of Community Affairs, New Jersey and quoted in A Blueprint for Housing in New Jersey, Special Message by Governor William T. Cahill, Dec. 7, 1970.
42. South Western Regional Planning Agency, Zoning: Technical Report 3, at 22 (1967).
43. See text at 525 for discussion of income and housing prices.
44. Bureau of the Census, U.S. Dep't of Commerce, Current Population Reports, Series P-60, No. 66 (1969).
45. Mass. Ann. Laws ch. 40B, § 20 (1970 Supp.).
46. E. See, Massachusetts Zoning Appeals Act; Current Status, Aug. 3, 1970 (unpublished memorandum prepared in connection with a research and development project undertaken by Ross, Hardies, O'Keefe, Babcock, McDougald, and Parsons, for the Dep't of Housing and Urban Development).
47. N.Y. Unconsol. Laws §§ 6251-85 (McKinney 1968).
48. For a preliminary assessment of U.D.C.'s role, see Reilly & Schulman, The State Urban Development Corp.: New York's Innovation, 1 The Urban Lawyer 129-46 (1969).
49. The proposals set forth in general terms here have been introduced in greater detail in the New York Assembly Assemblyman Franz Leichter. A. 4947 N.Y. Leg. Reg. Sess. (1971).

50. Kozesnik v. Township of Montgomery, 24 N.J. 154, 166, 131 A.2d 1, 7 (1957). *See also* Haar, *In Accordance with a Comprehensive Plan*, 68 Harv. L. Rev. 1154 (1955).
51. *Supra* note 5, at 215 [See note 40, above].
52. N.J. Code Ann. Tit. 40, § 55-47 (Supp. 1970).
53. S. 4546, 91st Cong., 2nd Sess. (1970).
54. We believe that the developing case law in this area supports our view that the courts will strike down the exclusionary practices we have identified. For an excellent discussion of recent cases and the prospects for judicial action in the future, *see* City, Jan./Feb. 1971, at 58. We are particularly impressed with the implications of Governor Cahill's warning to the New Jersey Legislature. After reviewing the developing case law and the nature of restrictive zoning practices in New Jersey, the Governor told the Legislature:

    These decisions and other cases presently pending in the courts of this State and Nation have led knowledgeable attorneys to freely predict that large acreage and large square foot requirements, along with absolute prohibition against apartment construction, will soon be held violative of the Constitution and outside the scope of planning and zoning officials. It seems to me, therefore, that the message should be loud and clear. We must undertake corrective measures now if we are to insure the maintenance of controls in the hands of local officials.

    Special Message, *supra* note 41, at 15.
55. 334 U.S. 1 (1948).
56. R. Netzer, Economics of the Property Tax (1966).

Metropolitan Housing:

Allocation Planning

Ernest Erber

Ernest Erber is director of research and program planning for the National Committee Against Discrimination in Housing (NCDH), of Washington, D.C. A member of the American Institute of Planners, he formerly was area director for the Regional Plan Association of New York and executive director of the Passaic Valley Plan Association in New Jersey.

This article appeared in the April 1974 issue of Urban Land *(Urban Land Institute), and is based in part on an exchange bibliography (#547) by Mr. Erber and Mr. John P. Prior (Research Analyst at NCDH), from the Council of Planning Librarians.*

Commentary

Rich and poor have always lived in housing that reflected different income levels. When the housing market was free from governmental constraints, rich and poor often lived in close proximity, even if on separate blocks in small islands of similar quality. However, local veto power over subsidized housing and zoning, used to exclude people from a community on the basis of income, have made the residential location of low income households a subject of public policy. The result was increasing geographic separation based on income. From intermingled islands of similar households, the political process reshuffled the metropolitan populations into vast continents of social uniformity, with the sharpest contrast between the inner city and the affluent suburb.

By the end of the 1950s, large developments of tract houses for average income families, typified by Levittown, New York, were rapidly becoming the exception. By the end of the 1960s, zoning had made them all but impossible. Builders found the market for one-family homes shrinking to those in the upper levels of the income pyramid. Those priced out of the one-family market stimulated demand for rental units. However, since suburban towns of major metropolitan areas resisted rezoning for apartments, housing starts declined to historic lows.

The slack was taken up in 1970-72 with a spectacular increase in subsidized construction, mainly pursuant to Section 236 of the 1968 Housing Act. These units were concentrated in central cities because suburban jurisdictions resisted rezoning land to accommodate households of low or moderate income. Meanwhile, studies by the National Committee Against Discrimination in Housing, Inc. (NCDH) and others had documented the incomparably greater growth of job opportunities in the suburbs compared to the central city, especially jobs that matched the predominant skills of the social groups for whom subsidized housing was intended. The growing separation of population by income, reflected in concentration by race, and the consequent distortion of home/job relationships, gave impetus in 1970 to studies of possible solutions designed to allocate subsidized housing to suburban locations.

Metropolitan Housing

This was a new challenge to the planning profession. The extension of land use and density planning to allocation of housing by income of prospective occupants required new techniques for the quantification of housing need by dwelling unit type, size, and price, the staging of construction over time, and the location of units within the planning jurisdiction in relation to employment opportunities, infrastructure, vacant land, and transportation. Although the techniques had to be designed from scratch, they followed the familiar planning formula of relating the parts to the whole and to each other to meet standards of functional feasibility.

The central concept in allocation has as its antecedent the planners' time-honored projection of population, and its accommodation within given jurisdictions. Its application required translating residentially zoned acres into numbers of dwelling units of appropriate types and price levels; translating population into households of specified characteristics; and designing relevant criteria to guide their allocation to the indicated subareas of the overall planning jurisdiction.

The staff of the Dayton, Ohio area's Miami Valley Regional Planning Commission was the first to move beyond studies and formulate a subsidized housing allocation plan. Its adoption by the commission in September, 1970, requiring the approval of constituents that consisted of five counties and thirty municipalities, marked a major breakthrough. This demonstration of success in selling planned allocation to suburban governments did much to encourage other regional planning agencies to try to emulate Dayton. In less than three years, over twenty-five other planning agencies published housing allocation plans, a number of which have been adopted by their respective constituents and are being implemented. Among the latter that have received national recognition are the plans in the Washington, Denver, and Minneapolis metropolitan areas and San Bernardino County, California.

The rapid progress of housing allocation planning was made possible by several concurrent phenomena that set the stage. The background was the metropolitan transformation during the fifties and sixties, which replaced the traditional symbiotic relationship of central cities to their suburban peripheries with a new type of human settlement pattern, characterized by low density spread of residential, commercial, and industrial uses sustained by highway-borne, motorized transportation.

This new outer city (mislabeled suburbia) acted as a magnet upon the central city's middle and higher income households, and upon much of its economic base, leaving behind poverty, blight, and fiscal debility, all accentuated by growing minority racial concentration. The location of subsidized housing for low and moderate income families mainly in the inner city had the effect of hastening and perpetuating the socio-economic cleavage between the central city and the new urbanization beyond its borders. The racial consequences were unmistakable. It became increasingly clear that the trend was toward central cities that would be poor, black, and bankrupt, surrounded by new forms of urban settlement that would be relatively affluent, white, and fiscally viable.

Planning which sought to reverse this trend had to overcome the resistance of outlying communities, whose citizens were intent upon protecting their perceived advantages against dilution expected to ensue from an influx of households of lower incomes and different ethnicity. This resistance was to be mollified by "sharing the burden"; each suburban municipality would accept its "fair share" of the poor—and ostensibly, the black.

The second phenomenon that facilitated the emergence of housing allocation planning was the rapid spread and increased sophistication of metropolitan regional planning in the sixties. In an attempt to cope with the metropolitan explosion, regional planning was accelerated by federal promotion; metropolitan agencies achieved leverage through funding and grant application review authority (A-95). Projection of population and planning for its distribution has always been an exercise that played a more prominent role in metropolitan regional planning than in local planning because of the former's preoccupation with the rational incorporation of growth areas into the overall metropolitan fabric. Experience had, therefore, prepared and predisposed regional planners to respond to the challenge of applying planning methodology to housing unit allocation, especially since it centered largely on achieving a balance between central city and outer communities.

The third phenomenon pressing toward planned housing allocation was the nation's confrontation with its historic and unsolved problems of race and poverty during the 1960s. The federal government declared a "war on poverty" and adopted far-reaching civil rights laws affecting employment, education, and housing. The Secretary of the Department of Housing and Urban Development was directed by Title VIII of the Civil Rights Act of 1968 to take affirmative action to end discrimination in housing, soon to be interpreted by federal courts as a ban upon use of federal funds to build housing where it extends or perpetuates racial concentration. *Shannon* v. *HUD*, 436 F.2d 809 (3rd Cir. 1970).

In its circulars and more specifically orally, HUD's directives to agencies preparing plans with federal funds granted under Section 701 of the Housing Act pointed toward metropolitan allocation plans as the proper way to satisfy the law's "housing element" requirements. In 1972, HUD released its site selection criteria which graded proposed subsidized housing projects according to its potential for meeting area housing needs, avoiding minority residential concentrations, reducing minority residential concentrations, improving non-white employment opportunities, contributing to orderly growth, and conserving natural resources. The above standards became essential features of the allocation plans for Pueblo, Colorado, and Los Angeles, Sacramento, Santa Clara, and Ventura counties in California. In Santa Clara, planners published a manual which identifies available subsidized construction sites meeting HUD standards. (HUD abruptly dropped its pressure for metropolitan housing allocation planning early in 1973 when termination of federal housing subsidy programs subverted the workability of allocation plans.)

Housing allocation criteria and techniques have become more sophisticated as each new plan sought to improve upon preceding ones. Improvement efforts have been directed mainly to the following aspects:

- from limiting allocation to subsidized housing to inclusion of the total housing supply;
- from reliance upon largely mathematically determined "shares" to criteria that reflect metropolitan diversity in resources and opportunities;
- from a minimally essential data base to highly sophisticated and comprehensive information;
- from relatively short-range to long-range allocation planning; and
- from implementation limited to promotion of subsidized housing within each community's quota to efforts to influence each community's zoning for residential growth in keeping with the allocation plan.

The transition of allocation planning from "fair share" concepts for subsidized housing to allocating all residential growth through local zoning marks a quantum leap, the implications of which have not yet been fully realized. Allocation planning within this dimension is the same universe of metropolitan regional planning that contains the economic base, transportation, and the environment. Housing allocation limited to subsidized units cannot be properly related to these other basic regional components. The allocation of the total projected housing need is especially relevant to environmental planning. It provides a basis for overcoming the juxtaposition of housing needs against environmental considerations. Such a relationship between housing and environment at the metropolitan regional scale can produce the only ecological criteria acceptable on the basis of human needs.

The contemporary literature of housing allocation planning represents a first generation effort, telescoped into a brief three years of experience. The first tentative theoretical formulations are already in the process of being revised and strengthened on the basis of growing experience. Much more needs to be done in allocation planning theory. This, in turn, is dependent upon broadening and deepening allocation practice to feed back new findings and insights.

The success of this approach is dependent upon a willingness of public officials, taxpayers, environmentalists, minority spokesmen, homebuilders, and others to give it a fair trial. Homebuilders have generally not been receptive to metropolitan housing plans. Their avowed reason: it adds "another level of governmental approvals for housing" and has "been short on results." The first objection is not valid and the second one, premature.

Housing allocation plans set minimum, not maximum, quotas for local jurisdictions. They require each constitutent municipality to take steps to facilitate housing construction to meet assigned goals. Metropolitan planning agencies in Dayton, Rochester, and probably other places have helped builders by identifying locations for subsidized housing and documenting their requests for rezoning. The homebuilders' attitude toward metropolitan housing plans is in apparent contradiction to their sensible proposal that the 1968 Housing Act's ten-year goal of 26 million dwelling units be made meaningful by subdividing it into quotas for each of the states, with a requirement that each state allocate goals to its various local governments.

Unfortunately, it is true that housing allocation plans have not been translated into a significant number of dwelling units. This criticism becomes meaningless when examined in the light of the circumstances under which allocation plans came into being and are being implemented. Reluctant and resistant municipalities within each planning constituency continued to drag their feet, while the flow of federal funds for housing was turned off just when most of the plans were going into effect. Regional sewer moratoriums, triggered by termination of federal funding, have stymied implementation of housing plans in some metropolitan areas, such as Washington, D.C. Despite these obstacles, successes have been achieved: subsidized housing for moderate-income families, occupied also by low-income families receiving rent supplements, do stand on the ground in suburban locations only because an allocation plan existed.

However, results measured in housing starts are less important at this early stage than breakthroughs in concept, structure, and function. Housing allocation planning at the metropolitan regional level is as yet a tender shoot, however promising its potential. It should be nurtured by all Americans who are committed to maximizing choice in residential location, regardless of income or race.

It should also be nurtured by employers who value rational metropolitan distribution of the labor force in relation to employment opportunities. Lastly, it deserves the support, if only out of self-interest, of land developers and homebuilders whose business prospers when they can build housing and communities for the large group of people in the lower strata of the income pyramid.

Bibliography

[Editor's Note: these items are drawn from an annotated bibliography published by the Council of Planning Librarians: Exchange Bibliography 547 (March 1974).]

Allocation Plans

1. Cleveland City Planning Commission. *Housing Summary and Recommended Policy Statement*, Cleveland, June 1970.
2. Miami Valley Regional Planning Commission. *A Housing Plan for the Miami Valley Region*, Dayton, July 1970.
3. Middlesex County Planning Board. *Interim Master Plan*, New Brunswick, September 1970.
4. Dade County Planning Department. *Housing in the Metropolitan Plan*, Miami, September 1970.
5. Dayton City Planning Board. *Housing Opportunities: Policies for the Dispersal of Low and Moderate Income Housing*, Dayton, December 1970.
6. San Francisco Department of City Planning. *The Comprehensive Plan—Residence*, San Francisco, April 1971.
7. Genesee—Finger Lakes Regional Planning Board. *Housing: Regional Analysis and Program*, Rochester, June 1971.
8. Metropolitan Washington Council of Governments. *Fair Share Housing Formula*, Washington, January 1972.
9. San Bernardino County Planning Department. *Government Subsidized Distribution Model for Valley Portion, San Bernardino County*, San Bernardino, January 1972.
10. Los Angeles County Regional Planning Commission. *Preliminary Housing Element*, Los Angeles, April 1972.
11. Pueblo Area Council of Governments. *Pueblo Housing Element*, Pueblo, June 1972.
12. West Piedmont District Planning Commission. *Preliminary Housing Plan*, Martinsville, June 1972.
13. Southeastern Wisconsin Regional Planning Commission. *A Short Range Action Program for Southeastern Wisconsin*, Waukesha, June 1972.
14. Planning Policy Committee of Santa Clara County. *Site Selection Standards for Assisted Housing*, San Jose, 1972.
15. Planning Policy Committee of Santa Clara County. *Production Objectives for Assisted Housing*, San Jose, August 1972.
16. Sacramento Regional Area Planning Commission. *An Approach to the Distribution of Low and Moderate Income Housing*, Sacramento, August 1972.
17. Monroe County Planning Council. *Housing: A Challenge for Monroe County*, Rochester, November 1972.
18. Denver Regional Council of Governments. *A Regional Housing Plan: Policies and Their Implementation*, Denver, December 1972.
19. Ventura County Planning Department. *Housing Distribution Model*, Ventura, December 1972.
20. Delaware Valley Regional Planning Commission. *Fact Sheet: Housing Allocation Plan*, Philadelphia, March 1973.
21. Miami Valley Regional Planning Commission. *The Miami Valley Region's Housing Plan*, Dayton, March 1973.
22. Jacksonville Community Renewal Program. *A Housing Distribution Model for Jacksonville, Florida*, Working Paper #13, Jacksonville, April 1973.
23. Baltimore Area Housing Advisory Council. *A Housing Plan for the Baltimore Region*, Baltimore, May 1973.
24. East-West Gateway Coordinating Council. *Final Draft: Regional Housing Plan for St. Louis Metropolitan Area*, St. Louis, May 1973.
25. Metropolitan Council of the Twin Cities Area. *Housing: Plan, Policy, Program*, Minneapolis, June 1973.
26. Cuyahoga Metropolitan Housing Authority. *Study Reflecting Need in Cuyahoga County for Public Housing and Proposed Production Plan*, Cleveland, June 1973.
27. Northwest Arkansas Regional Planning Commission. *1973 Housing Element*, Springdale, June 1973.
28. Regional Housing Coalition. *An Interim Plan for Balanced Distribution of Housing Opportunities for Northeast Illinois*, Chicago, October 1973.
29. Toledo Regional Housing Coalition and Toledo Metropolitan Council of Governments. *A "Fair Share" Housing Allocation Plan for the Toledo Metropolitan Area*, Toledo, 1973.

Methodologies Useful in Housing Allocation

30. Hammer, Greene, Siler Associates. *The Housing Element for State, Regional and Local Planning Agencies*, (2 vols), Washington, D.C.: Hammer, Greene, Siler Associates, June 1971.
31. James, Franklin J. and James W. Hughes. *Economic Growth and Residential Patterns: A Methodological Investigation*, New Brunswick: Center for Urban Policy Research, 1972.

32. Nenno, Mary K. *Housing in Metropolitan Areas: Roles and Responsibilities of Five Key Factors*, Washington, D.C.: National Association of Housing and Redevelopment Officials, 1973.
33. Smith, Wallace F. *Housing Market Data from Census Materials: A Study of the Bay Area*, Berkeley: Univeristy of California Institute of Business and Economic Research, 1963.
34. United States Department of Housing and Urban Development. Federal Housing Administration. Economic and Market Analysis Division. *FHA Techniques in Housing Market Analysis*, rev. ed., Washington, D.C.: U. S. Government Printing Office, 1970.
35. University of Pennsylvania Institute of Public Policy Analysis. *Standards for Housing in Suburban Communities Based Upon Zoning for Work*, Philadelphia: Fels Center of Government, 1971.
36. Univeristy of Pennsylvania Institute of Public Policy Analysis. *Standards for Suburban Housing Mix: Bucks County, Pennsylvania*, Philadelphia: Fels Center of Government, 1972.

Commentaries and Critiques

37. Bertsch, Dale F. and Ann N. Shafor. "A Regional Housing Plan. The Miami Valley Regional Planning Commission Experience," *Planner Notebook*, I, April 1971.
38. Brooks, Mary E. *Low Income Housing: The Planners Response*, Chicago: American Society of Planning Officials, 1972.
39. Holmgren, Edward L. and Ernest Erber. "Fair Share Formulas," *HUD Challenge*, IV, April 1973, pp. 22-25.
40. Metropolitan Washington Housing and Planning Association. *Housing Needs of Montgomery County's Projected 90,000 New Workers*, Rockville, Maryland: Montgomery County Department of Community and Economic Development, 1972.
41. National Committee Against Discrimination in Housing. *Jobs and Housing: A Study of Employment and Housing Opportunities for Racial Minorities in Suburban Areas of the New York Metropolitan Region*, New York: 1970.
42. National Committee Against Discrimination in Housing. *Trends in Housing*, XVL (No. 2-3), 1972.
43. Rahenkamp, John. "Every Suburb Can Absorb a Share of the Low Cost Housing," *House and Home Magazine*, 40, May 1972, pp. 60-62.
44. Southern California Association of Governments. *A Technical Study of Housing Allocation Models*, Los Angeles: Southern California Association of Governments, May 1973.
45. Southern California Association of Governments. *An Elected Official's Guide to Selected Housing Allocation Models*, Los Angeles: Southern California Association of Governments, May 1973.

Legal Opinions Relevant to Allocation

46. *Daley v. City of Lawton, Oklahoma*, 425 F. 2d 1037 (10th Cir. 1970); and *Kennedy Park Homes Association, Inc. v. City of Lackawanna, New York*, 318 F. Supp. 669 (W.D.N.Y. aff'd., 436 F.2d 108 (2nd Cir. 1970), cert. denied, 401 U.S. 1010 (1971).
47. *Southern Alameda Spanish-Speaking Organization (SASSO) v. City of Union City, California*, 424 F. 2d 291 (9th Cir. 1970).
48. *Southern Burlington County NAACP v. Township of Mt. Laurel*, 119 N.J. Super. 164 (Superior Ct., 1972).
49. *Brookhaven Housing Coalition v. Kunzig*, 341 F. Supp. 1026, _____ F. Supp. _____ (E.D. N.Y. 1972), notice of appeal filed September 15, 1972.
50. *Shannon v. HUD*, 436 F. 2d 809 (3rd Cir. 1970); *Banks v. Perk*, 341 F. Supp. 1175 (N.D. Ohio, 1972); and *Gautreaux v. Chicago Housing Authority*, 296 F. Supp. 907, 304 F. Supp. 736 (N.D. Ill. 1967), aff'd as to program of relief, 436 F. 2d 306 (7th Cir. 1970) cert. denied, 402 U.S. 992 (1971).
51. *Crow v. Brown*, 332 F. Supp. 382 (N.D. Ga. 1971) aff'd per curiam, 457 F. 2d 788 (5th Cir. 1972).
52. *Mahaley v. CMHA*, 342 F. Supp. 250 (N.D. Ohio 1972).
53. *Oakwood at Madison v. Tp. of Madison*, 117, N.J., Super. 11 (Superior Ct. 1971).

Legislation and Regulation Relevant to Allocation

54. *1968 Civil Rights Act*, Title VIII.
55. *Demonstration Cities and Metropolitan Development Act* (1966).
56. Title IV, *Intergovernmental Cooperation Act of 1968*.
57. Office of Management and Budget. *Circular A-95*. (October 1, 1969).
58. *Executive Order 11512* (February 27, 1970).
59. United States Department of Labor. Office of Federal Contract Compliance. *Revised Order 4*. (February 5, 1970).
60. *HUD Site Selection Criteria* (February 1972).
61. *HUD Affirmative Fair Housing Marketing* (February 25, 1972).

Exclusionary Zoning:

Pitfalls of the Regional Remedy

**Robert W. Burchell, David Listokin
and Franklin J. James**

Dr. Burchell is associate research professor at the Center for Urban Policy Research at Rutgers University. He is also an urban planner and project manager at the Center, and an author/editor of numerous articles and monographs. Dr. Burchell is a graduate of the U.S. Coast Guard Academy, and received his master's and doctorate in urban planning from Rutgers University.

Franklin J. James is research associate at the Center for Urban Policy Research, Rutgers University. He was formerly research assistant at the National Bureau of Economic Research, New York City, and adjunct assistant professor, Brown University (Providence, Rhode Island). Dr. James is a graduate of the University of Georgia and is a Ph.D. candidate at Columbia University.

David Listokin is research associate at the Center for Urban Policy Research, Rutgers University. He was formerly an instructor at Rutgers University. Mr. Listokin is a graduate of Brooklyn College and holds a master's from Rutgers University, where he is also a Ph.D. candidate.

Introduction

Few issues in recent years have aroused as much criticism as exclusionary zoning.[1] It has been accused of producing a cornucopia of social evils, e.g., denying blacks suburban employment opportunities, intensifying inner-city school segregation, jointly reinforcing and furthering the social, racial and cultural schism of American society.[2]

Underlying much of the strictures against restrictive municipal land use controls is the belief local zoning prerogatives based on parochial considerations are untenable in a complex urbanized world. Many social scientists and litigants have advocated a regional approach to zoning in order to take broader needs and forces into consideration in anti-restrictive land use suits.[3] Their arguments have been incorporated in several recent judicial decisions[4] and regionalism is increasingly being viewed as the "St. George," slayer of the exclusionary zoning "dragon."

Such elation is premature. *This article argues that there are serious pitfalls to the regional remedy; the new broader territorial approach may in fact reinforce the status quo.* Exclusive suburban communities may turn more and more to the regional argument to defend exclusionary zoning ordinances.

This is no idle fear as this article will demonstrate. First, it discusses the actors in the exclusionary zoning drama and their justifications. Next it describes the emerging regional response to this controversy and discusses its theoretical deficiencies. These drawbacks will be empirically demonstrated in later sections, focusing on employment growth versus housing production of an allegedly exclusionary zoned area. The article focuses heavily on this job-housing ratio because one of the most severe alleged consequences of suburban restrictive land use is the retardation of moderately priced home building in an area of job expansion.

The Argument: Exclusionary Zoning

Exclusionary zoning has been defined mostly in terms of its impact on the poor. Lawrence Sager of the American Civil Liberties Union, for example, defined exclusionary zoning as zoning that raises the price of residential access to a particular area and thereby denies access to members of low-income groups.[5] Similarly, Norman Williams of Rutgers University described exclusionary zoning as those land use controls which appear to interfere seriously with the availability of low- and moderate-income housing where it is needed.[6]

The case law has zeroed in on specific local zoning practices, i.e., minimum building size, minimum lot size, minimum frontages, or limitations placed on multifamily development, as being part and parcel of the exclusionary zoning problem.

The defendants in legal action are local governmental bodies typified as "white suburban enclaves":

> (This community) symbolizes the sickness, the racism that exists throughout the land . . . It's getting to be the rich suburbs versus the rest of the state as far as education goes; it's wrong for the state to allow such discrepancies to exist . . .[7]

The answer has been:

> Why should any thinking and intelligent person welcome increased tax burdens upon himself and a reduction in the worth of his home.
>
> This is what he has sweated and toiled against: substandard zoning, low income housing, and other governmental subsidy programs that take bread from his pocket. This is not racism or moral irresponsibility, this is common sense upon his part.
>
> Most of the affluent suburbanites that I know are having difficulty in keeping their heads above the water of financial difficulty.
>
> Won't these and other gentlemen understand that our views are not racist or moral irresponsibility, but only our American heritage of striving to keep a decent, respectable way of life.[8]

The plaintiffs are the impoverished, and, as victims of municipal zoning restriction, are affected in a variety of ways. Allegedly they must face the deleterious byproducts of the inner city environment, i.e., decaying capital plant and the realities of decreasing public safety:

> A closed suburb (through exclusionary zoning) has and will continue to have a serious effect upon life in our nation. This condition is largely responsible for the continuation of a pattern of inner city racial ghettos and slums.[9]

Restrictive zoning is also accused of denying employment opportunities to those who need them most—the poor:

> Because low cost housing is not widely available in the suburbs (as a result of exclusionary zoning) many inner city workers are confronted with the choice of commuting to work—the expense and inconvenience of which may be prohibitive—or doing without work altogether.[10]

Finally the inability to participate in the suburban lifestyle denies excluded groups the advantages of both improved housing and local living environment, e.g., education:

> The Coleman report concluded that a major determinant of education quality is the socioeconomic background of the student body . . . . Since the central city's increasing racial and social homogenization can be at least partially attributed to exclusionary zoning, such land use has multiplied the problems implicit in educating inner city youths.[11]

The Issue: Adequate and Locally Available Housing

Examination of the literature and the pattern of communities selected for potential legal sanction indicates that a major determinant for the challenge of exclusionary zoning appears to be disregard for the housing needs of those who will be employed locally:

> It should also be a matter of public policy that no land within a community may be rezoned for industrial or commercial expansion without there first being made a finding that sufficient vacant housing at moderate cost and rental levels, or vacant residential land upon which such housing could be constructed, is available for housing all of the workers associated with the proposed new industrial or commercial development. In the absence of a positive finding, a locality should be required to rezone sufficient residential land to meet the housing needs of the potential workers as a precondition to rezoning for the industrial or commercial development. The housing to be provided for the workers must be constructed at prices within the economic means of the expected labor force.[12]

Concern regarding the availability of adequate housing lies near the heart of virtually all recent discussions of restrictive land use problems. The feeling is common that suburban housing is in such short supply as to produce a housing crisis. The notion of this suburban housing crisis rests on two facts.[13] First, job growth is most rapid in suburban areas, particularly in industries such as manufacturing or trade which employ substantial numbers of relatively unskilled workers. Second, new housing being constructed in suburban areas is often far too expensive to house these workers. A conclusion typically drawn from these two facts is that great shortages of low and middle income housing must exist in suburbs, and that the shortage must become more acute as time goes by. Some observers believe this shortage is sufficiently great to deny low income workers the job opportunities of the suburbs, and perhaps capable of producing labor shortages for suburban employers which will become severe enough to choke off future growth.

The particular plight of black Americans, and other minorities subjected to housing discrimination, has also been emphasized. Members of these groups earn generally low incomes, and thus are subject to the same forces for exclusion from suburban living as are other low income workers. In addition, the fact of color often bounds their housing choices within established ghetto areas in major cities. It has been pointed out, for instance,[14] that well-to-do black households are no more likely to live in suburban areas than are comparatively poor whites.[15]

Belief in the suburban housing shortage has so permeated popular thought that it is now often the basis for governmental housing policies to "open up" the suburbs to low income families and to minorities. These policies in many cases threaten to change radically many established institutions of state and local governments, ranging from the power of local communities to design land use controls on the basis of local priorities[16] to the overhaul of local fiscal structures in order to lessen or eliminate local reliance on the property tax.[17] As a result, it is crucial to develop a better grasp of the reality of the suburban housing problem.

The Response: Regionalism

Many of the solutions posed to the exclusionary zoning problem cast the recognition of the needs of the "region" as a minimum base from which to proceed.[18] One of the most influential law review articles on restrictive zoning [The author of the article, Lawrence Sager, noted in a footnote that while the regional argument could be used to attack local exclusionary zoning it had often been perversely used to defend local restrictive practices.], for example, argued that:

A finer problem worthy of mention here is the tension between the authority vested in the municipality to regulate its domain and regional considerations that extend well beyond the municipality's boundaries. The problems of the supply and desirability of low-cost housing that may be caused by exclusionary zoning will often be subject to full evaluation only within a regional frame of reference. On the other hand, municipalities have frequently claimed responsibility only for sound planning of their own bailiwick. The issue, then, is whether the local unit bears constitutional burdens the origins of which encompass broader circumstances. There is some precedent for expanding the responsibility of the municipality, that is, for reading the notion of a rational policy to include consideration of attributes of the world beyond the locality's borders. This approach is sensible in the normal land use context; it is essential as regards intelligent appraisal of the social harm deriving from exclusionary zoning.[19]

Another article concluded that:

If the concept of regional general welfare gains a wide acceptance, it may provide opponents of exclusionary zoning with the legal weapon they have been seeking to mount a successful challenge to the validity of such laws.[20]

Focus on regionalism has pervaded many leading court decisions striking down local exclusionary zoning policies. The Pennsylvania *Kit Mar*[21] decision, for example, declared large lot zoning unconstitutional because:

The implications of our decision in *National Land* is that communities must deal with the problems of population growth. They may not refuse to confront the future by adopting zoning regulations that effectively restrict populations to near present levels. It is not for any given township to say who may or may not live within its confines, while disregarding the interests of the entire area.[22]

Similar arguments are found in the *Girsh*,[23] *Madison*[24] cases among others.

This reversal from local to more inclusive land use considerations has long been advocated as the only rational, long term strategy possible in an urbanizing society. With reference to exclusionary zoning the evolving focus on regionalism is increasingly being viewed as bringing to an end the alleged adverse social practice.

But this latter view is premature and overly sanguine; the regional approach to considering land use decisions may *support* rather than attack existing restrictive practices. The most common application of regional considerations to local land use controls has involved a three step procedure:

1. First, an appropriate housing region has been defined encompassing the areas under challenge, and other relevant housing supply areas;
2. Second, the housing needs of households working and living in this region are approximated and compared with actually and potentially available housing supplies; and,
3. Third, disparities are identified, and responsibility for eliminating or ameliorating them allocated to the challenged areas through some explicit notion of fair share.

The regional definition is the key to the success of this entire approach. Most housing regions defined under this procedure will be quite heterogeneous. Because all workers and families live somewhere, if a region is defined too generously, few disparities between housing supply and housing consumption of working and resident households will be found. If the region is parsimoniously delimited, tradeoffs by households between worktrip length and housing costs will be inappropriately proscribed.

Furthermore, the regional approach to the identification and control of exclusionary zoning applies a very elastic yardstick. The supply of housing at any point in time is the result of construction cumulating over a very substantial time period. In many areas, much of this construction will have occurred prior to the widespread application of land-use controls; more recent construction of housing particularly for low or moderate income households need not be fairly or efficiently distributed among municipalities. Exclusionary communities surrounded by municipalities enforcing relatively open zoning ordinances may potentially be treated much differently than exactly similar communities surrounded by exclusionary neighbors. The regional approach may allow the concept of fair share too narrow an orbit; thus regional analysis may beg the question of the fairness of the historical distribution of housing for low or moderate income housing.

There are precedents validating these concerns. The courts, for example, while traditionally ignoring extraterritorial effects of local zoning ordinances have sometimes embraced regionalism to uphold the constitutionality of exclusionary municipal land use controls. The *Lionshead Lake*[25] decisions, for example, as analyzed by Charles Haar, perversely used the term region to endorse a minimum floor space ordinance.[26]

Richard Babcock[27] has similarly noticed the judiciary sometimes turning to the regional argument for justifying local restrictive practices. Babcock cites *Duffcon*[28] and *Valley View*[29] as cases which, although they exemplify a recognition of the term "region," are actually detrimental to regional planning and support "the traditional view of only looking to the municipality to determine suitability of a particular land use."[30] In both cases, sufficient land was available in adjacent municipalities to satisfy regional needs, though not within the confines of the municipalities under question.

As the area upon which to assess housing need expands, the ability to specify municipal regional responsibility diminishes. Regionalism may justify the existing social and housing stratification resulting from current exclusionary zoning practices rather than reforming the existing restrictive land use orientation. This scenario is demonstrated by first discussing how a regional housing market can be defined and then empirically showing that an area cited as an archetype of exclusionary zoning practice and the site of many antirestrictive land use suites come off "clean" when viewed from this regional *Weltanschaung.*

What is the Definition of a Region?

As one traces the literature it immediately becomes apparent that the definition of a region is not only difficult to derive, but, in addition, its designation usually pertains specifically to the subject matter of study. A water supply region may differ from a housing market delineation and both may depart significantly from areas joined by similar energy needs.

Obviously the definitional choice will depend on the emphasis of the discipline brought to bear upon it. Thus, geographers would emphasize *physical* similarities in defining a region while economists would stress *economic* interdependence. The wide range of focus and emphasis has been noted, among many others, by Walter Isard, who observed that:

> Any selection of a set of regions for specific nongeneral research must be related to the problems to be studied.[31]

A similar opinion was expressed in Vincent Ostrom's observation that:

> The definition of the scope of any particular region will vary with each set of functions being considered.[32]

As a result, the definition of housing market regions for the purpose of examining exclusionary zoning cannot be expected to conveniently follow pre-existing regional delimitations made for other purposes. Regional definition with all its problems will in many cases have to be customized for the job at hand.

Housing Substitutability and Regional Delineation. The Federal Housing Administration has defined a housing market region or area as the geographic entity within which non-farm dwelling units are in mutual competition.[33] Similarly, Ernest and Robert Fisher have noted that:

> The extent of a (housing-real estate) market is defined by the area over which units in the standing stock are assumed to be substituted for one another.[34]

And an almost identical definition was suggested by Charles Abrams, who referred to a housing market area as:

> The geographic area within which dwelling units are closely substitutable for one another—that is which contain all the units that are likely to be considered potential housing accommodations by the resident population.[35]

However, there are no hard and fast rules for determining whether or not housing units are in fact competing with one another. The FHA, for example, has admitted that:

> A technique is not available to determine the exact points at which specific dwelling units are just beyond the range of competition with other units so that the precise limits can be established for delineating the housing market area.[36]

Even the definition of competition is quite fuzzy. William Grigsby has pointed out that in fact all housing units within a metropolitan area are linked directly or indirectly in a competition matrix.[37] As a result, the competition guideline alone offers definite guidance only at the metropolitan level.

Journey to Work as an Element of Regional Housing Delineations. There is widespread consensus that the length of the journey to work has a major influence on the purchase or rental of a dwelling unit and thus the definition of a housing region. One study, for example, noted that the most important determinant of the individual's locational choice is the travel or distance from his income earning function, i.e., job or business.[38] Similarly, the FHA has observed that the location of actual and prospective employment centers and the availability of transportation facilities are among the major considerations in the location choice of the working population.[39] And Ernest and Robert Fisher,[40] as well as Charles Abrams[41] have concurred that the most important factor in analyzing a local housing market is indeed the journey to work.

In a recent leading case on exclusionary zoning in New Jersey,[42] the presiding judge spoke directly to the question of region with respect to housing. In defining the region, the housing needs of which must be met by the Township, the court said that the region is not coextensive with the county.

> Rather it is the area from which in view of available employment and transportation, the population of the township would be drawn absent invalid exclusionary zoning.[43]

Empirical support for the above contentions can be found in a 1964 survey conducted by Michigan University's Survey Research Center.[44] Of the sample population studied, 56 percent said that living close to the head of the household's place of work was *important;* of this group more than one-half felt this to be a *very important* factor in deciding where to live (Exhibit 1). In terms of specific groups, the accessibility to head of household's workplace was rated as an important consideration by more than 60 percent of both single respondents and childless couples; almost 60 percent of female married respondents, and more than half of the male married respondents (Exhibit 2).

EXHIBIT 1
IMPORTANCE OF BEING CLOSE TO ONE'S PLACE OF WORK
(Results in Percentages)

At the time of the most recent move being close to head's (of household) place of work was:

Respondent Group	Very Important (%)	Somewhat Important (%)	Made No Difference Not Important (%)	Total (%)	Number of Responses
All	32	24	44	100	370
Single; married without children	44	17	39	100	143
Married with children	24	30	46	100	213
Male married	27	25	48	100	143
Female married	33	26	41	100	150

Source: John Lansing and Eva Mueller, with Nancy Barth, *Residential Location and Urban Mobility* (Ann Arbor, Mich.: Survey Research Center, Institute for Social Research, The University of Michigan, 1964), p. 41.

EXHIBIT 2
JOURNEY-TO-WORK TIME LIMITS OF RECENT MOVERS
(Results in Percentages)

Travel Time (in minutes)	Limits Given by Those Who Moved Recently Who Had Established Commuting Time Limits (%)	Actual Time Spent Getting to Work by All Those who Moved Recently (%)
1-4	*	1
5-9	5	12
10-14	7	12
15-19	20	20
20-29	14	17
30-44	42	23
45-59	6	9
60 or more	6	6
TOTAL (%)	100	100
Median	32 min.	23 min.
Number of journeys to work	119	312

* Less than one-half of one percent.
Source: John Lansing, *Residential Location and Urban Mobility: The Second Wave of Interviews* (University of Michigan, Survey Research Center, 1966).

Other surveys have revealed similar findings. A 1967 survey conducted by the *Oakland Tribune*,[45] for example, indicated that nearness to work was the single most important consideration in selecting housing.

The importance of the worktrip in determining household location decisions offers the key element for defining the criterion of mutual competition of housing units, so that it can be employed for delimiting regions. By developing planning standards for reasonable work-trip lengths and/or cost, regions may be delineated in part on the basis of travel times at peak morning and evening worktrip periods.

How Far the Journey to Work? The determination of planning standards for worktrips is largely judgmental. Two basic ingredients in coming up with such a standard are the times and distances people actually travel, and the verbalized preferences of people regarding worktrip length.

The literature reveals that most people do not wish to travel more than about one-half hour to their job. A Michigan University study,[46] for example, revealed that half (median) of the families surveyed considered 32 minutes the maximum time they wished to travel. (The exact findings of this study are indicated in Exhibit 2.) Similarly, 77 percent of the respondents in a 1967 Oakland newspaper[47] survey expressed their unwillingness to commute more than 30 minutes to work; almost one-fifth were unwilling to travel more than 15 minutes.

These survey results do not appear to be unique to their locations. A survey conducted by the Rutgers University Center for Urban Policy Research[48] has shown, however, that for New Jersey residents the average journey to work was approximately eight miles. (Exhibit 3). Translated to commuting times for this area, this is approximately 20 minutes. Moreover, this New Jersey survey focused on the worktrips of middle and lower income households. Only families in single-family homes and townhouses costing around $35,000 or less were included, and residents of garden and highrise apartments were substantially over-represented.

EXHIBIT 3
JOURNEY-TO-WORK DISTANCES OF NEW JERSEY RESIDENTS
(1973)

Commuting Distance (in 5 mile rings)	N	Percent	Cumulative Percent
1	793	34.0	34.0
2	646	27.7	61.7
3	276	11.8	73.5
4	103	4.4	77.9
5	75	3.2	81.1
6	42	1.8	82.9
7	79	3.4	86.3
8	58	2.5	88.8
9	143	6.1	94.9
10	63	2.7	97.6
11	56	2.4	100.0
TOTAL	2,334	100.0	

Source: George Sternlieb, et al. Housing Development and Municipal Costs (New Brunswick, N.J.: Rutgers University Center for Urban Policy Research, 1973).

The following case study will delineate a housing market region according to the FHA's definition of a housing market—i.e., as one in which units are mutually competitive. Mutually competitive units are those units sharing certain features important to the consumer—e.g., cost, number of bedrooms, quality of local schools, etc. The key variable is the distance to work; other things being equal, a housing consumer will seek the best accommodation available within a reasonable commuting distance to his job.

Designation of the Housing Region. Using gauges of both desired and actual journeys to work, a 30-minute journey-to-work trip will be employed to delineate the housing region. The center of the designated housing region is the group of four communities accused of effecting exclusionary zoning [see footnote 1]. The range and location of housing choice is defined by travel time from this center by automobile during peak hours of morning and evening employment commute (7:00-9:00 A.M. and 4:30-6:30 P.M.). The private automobile commute was selected as indicative of the limits of the designated housing region, as mass transit facilities serving suburban areas typically are minimal. The physical boundaries of the automobile commute is a function of the quality, location and levels of usage of highways, expressways and roads within the region. These boundaries were determined by actually traveling both to and from the four communities (during morning and evening rush hours) on the major roads servicing the region. These test commutes revealed that the housing region of which these communities are a part, defined principally by the criteria of journey to work is a five county area, including the parent county in which the communities are located as well as four adjacent counties. Exhibit 4 depicts the locations of the designated housing region, its constituent counties and the four communities classified as exclusionary zoned.

EXHIBIT 4

THE DESIGNATED HOUSING REGION
(AS DETERMINED BY 30 MINUTE JOURNEY TO WORK)

Source: Center for Urban Policy Research, Spring 1974.

Empirical Analysis: Regional Housing Need and Satisfaction

Jobs have grown more rapidly than housing opportunities in many suburban communities. This disparity has led to the charge that suburbs have a special obligation to supplement this deficiency of housing. This report examines the provision of housing within allegedly exclusionary zoned communities relative to the needs of employees that have been attracted there. The performance of these communities in providing housing will be examined in the context of the housing region in which they participate.

To guide the reader through the empirical analysis, its structure will be summarized. Initially job growth and housing production are compared in the following areas: the five constituent counties of the designated housing region, within the primary county, and finally within the four communities themselves.

To set the scene, a comparison by county (within the designated housing region) of job growth versus housing production ensues. [Job growth at the county level was estimated using a variety of sources presented in James and Hughes, *Modeling State Growth: New Jersey 1980.* Job growth at the municipal level is determined by summing the reported male employment levels of all new, relocating or expanding facilities within the five county area. While this covered employment data is limited to larger manufacturing firms who report such information a conversion factor was employed to gain an estimate of total employment. Housing production is estimated using 1970 census data.] Subsequently those communities that attracted new manufacturing employers from 1960 to 1970 will be identified, and their housing production examined. Additionally municipalities have been classified as either primarily blue or white collar (in terms of occupation of residents) in order to compare the housing-job performance of each of these two types of communities. [Communities were classified blue or white collar according to significant differences from the mean of each county on the following key variables: Blue Collar Employment (craftsmen, foremen, operatives and laborers), House Value, Family Income, Housing Constructed Prior to 1940.]

The analysis which follows contains the following definitions and abbreviations:

1. *Designated housing region*—An area centering upon the midpoint of the four "exclusionary zoned" communities and delimited by a 30-minute journey to work trip outward from this node. Times are calculated during prime commuting hours via automobile along major thoroughfares within the region. If a majority of the county may be entered via the 30-minute journey to work criterion the whole county is included within the region.

2. *Primary county*—The county jurisdiction in the New York Metropolitan Area in which the four exclusionary zoned communities are located.

3. *Exclusionary zoned communities*—Four communities whose land use controls are alleged to prevent those of modest income from living within the community's bounds. Typically there is an absence of available land zoned for multifamily use, single family homes must be constructed on one or two acres and the minimum building size is in excess of 1,200 sq. ft.

4. $\dfrac{T.D.U.}{Total\,Emp.}$ —Net gain in occupied dwelling units in the area specified divided by the total 1960-1970 net gain in the area's employment.

5. $\dfrac{T.D.U.}{Male}$ —Net gain in occupied dwelling units in the area specified divided by the total 1960-1970 net gain in the area's male employment.

EXHIBIT 5

HOUSING AND JOB GROWTH IN THE DESIGNATED HOUSING REGION BETWEEN 1960 AND 1970, FOR THE REGION AND ITS CONSTITUENT COUNTIES

	Net Additional Occupied Dwelling Units (T.D.U.)	Housing Produced[1]: 1960-1970					Total Employment: Net Gain[2]			Ratios			
		Percent Increase	Net Additional Occupied Single-Family Units (S.F.D.U.)	Percent Increase	Net Additional Occupied Multi-Family Units (M.D.U.)	Percent Increase	Total	% Male of Total	Male	$\frac{T.D.U.}{Male}$	$\frac{M.D.U.}{Male}$	$\frac{T.D.U.}{Total\ Emp.}$	$\frac{M.D.U.}{T.D.U.}$
Primary County	49,047	20.7	11,608	5.7	37,439	53.0	124,160	63	78,221	.63	.48	.40	.76
Adjacent County "A"	38,853	46.2	22,269	15.0	16,584	145.4	45,421	67	30,432	1.28	.54	.86	-.43
Adjacent County "B"	21,288	22.2	6,774	3.6	14,514	19.9	33,393	69	23,041	.92	.63	.64	-.68
Adjacent County "C"	11,688	36.9	8,811	4.1	2,877	18.5	14,100	66	9,306	1.26	.31	-.83	-.25
Adjacent County "D"	25,660	65.7	15,074	40.0	10,586	139.7	28,200	61	18,612	1.38	.57	.91	.41
Designated Housing Region	146,536		64,536		82,000		245,274		159,612	.92	.51	.60	.56

Sources:
1. U.S. Census of Housing, 1960-1970, Year Round Housing Units.
2. James and Hughes, *Modeling State Growth: New Jersey 1980,* CUPR, 1973 and the
3. New York Dept. of Labor.

6. $\dfrac{M.D.U.}{Male}$ —Net gain in occupied, multifamily dwelling units (2 or more) in the area specified by the total 1960-1970 net gain in the area's male employment.

The analysis which follows will examine housing production versus job growth and housing cost versus household income of employees at various area levels. The point to be made is that to move to the regional level to determine a specific community's housing role is to dismiss the arguments about which most exclusionary zoning cases focus. On a regional base both housing production and housing costs appear to be commensurate with both demonstrated need and ability to pay. To pursue this point first overall housing production will be analyzed; then housing cost.

Housing Production Versus Job Growth Within the Delineated Region. Exhibit 5 details the housing and job growth of the designated housing region and its constituent counties in the last decade. Employment from 1960 to 1970 increased by 159,612 male jobs and housing units increased by 146,536 or 0.92 dwelling units per male job. (The rationale for such focus on male jobs is that males frequently are the primary wage earner in a given household). [The relationship of job growth to growth in numbers of employed heads of households is discussed in more detail in James and Hughes (Modeling State Growth: New Jersey 1980). The approximately correct rule of thumb is that each additional job can be translated into .75 additional employed heads of households.] Employing this comparison it appears evident that the five county regional delineation appears to truly represent a housing market as supply and demand are on a par. If this were not true, as much doubt would be cast on the definition of region as on the adequacy of housing market operation.

Usually, multi-family units can be afforded by a broader spectrum of income groups than is the case for single family homes. As the exhibit makes clear, fully 56 percent of net additional occupied housing units produced in the five county region were in multi-unit structures. The multi-family housing/job growth ratio ($\dfrac{M.D.U.}{Male}$ ratio) is .51. The significance of this figure for the availability of housing for workers will be addressed below.

The $\dfrac{T.D.U.}{Male}$, $\dfrac{M.D.U.}{Male}$ and other ratios differ considerably between the five constituent counties of the designated housing region. In the region as a whole, housing construction was much more geographically dispersed than was job growth. Almost two-thirds of total job growth in the region occurred in the primary county, while two-thirds of net housing increase occurred in the four adjacent counties.

Despite the fact that the overall housing increase was greatest in the primary county, its housing production was smallest relative to job growth ($\dfrac{T.D.U.}{Male}$ of .60). Three of the four adjacent counties within the region produced 1.3 additional housing units for each additional male job and much of this housing production may be available for workers holding jobs in the primary county.

While housing growth in the primary county was a relatively small portion of overall job growth in the county production of multi-family units was twice as great as in any other county. In this county three out of four net additions to occupied housing were in multi-family structures. The ratio of growth in multi-family units to job growth ($\dfrac{M.D.U.}{Male}$) showed surprisingly little variation among constituent counties of the region. Multi-family units tend to be a more relevant measure of housing availability for workers, as will be discussed below. Again, there seems to be every indication of a normally operating housing market.

Housing Production in Blue Versus White Collar Designated Communities. Communities in each of the five study counties are quite heterogeneous in terms of housing cost and age, and the occupation and incomes of residents. In order to gain insight into general differences in housing production among various types of communities, municipalities were divided into two groups on the basis of their job growth, and the characteristics of their housing stock and population in 1970. Each of these housing and population characteristics was employed to divide communities into: (a) communities with older, less costly housing, and relatively low median family incomes and high incidence of resident workers in blue collar occupations; and (b) all other municipalities. The first group is termed blue-collar municipalities, and the second, white collar municipalities.

In addition, communities of both types were further divided into those which received at least one major [a major facility is an establishment employing 20 or more persons] new or relocating manufacturing or warehousing establishment during the 1960s (termed employer attracting communities); and those which did not. The study region spanned two states, and the data necessary for these breakdowns were only available in the three study counties of one of the states. Exhibit 6 presents information on job and housing growth in employer attracting communities in the three county region. These employer attracting communities are divided in the exhibit into blue and white collar groups.

Virtually all net job growth in this abbreviated three-county region occurred in employer attracting communities in the three county region. In the two subsidiary counties (Adjacent counties A and B), communities which did not attract major new employers actually suffered a slight overall job loss during the sixties. Growth in occupied housing units was spread more evenly within each county; almost 30 percent of net housing growth in each county

EXHIBIT 6

HOUSING AND JOB GROWTH IN EMPLOYER ATTRACTING MUNICIPALITIES
BETWEEN 1960 AND 1970 FOR THE REGION AND ITS CONSTITUENT COUNTIES

	Housing Produced[1]: 1960-1970			Employment: Net Gain[2]		Ratios			
	Total Dwelling Units (T.D.U.)	Single-family (S.F.D.U.)	Multifamily (M.D.U.)	Total	Male	$\frac{T.D.U.}{Male}$	$\frac{M.D.U.}{Male}$	$\frac{T.D.U.}{Total\ Emp.}$	$\frac{M.D.U.}{T.D.U.}$
White Collar									
Primary County	22,407	9,861	12,546	66,777	42,070	.53	.29	.34	.56
Adjacent County "A"	20,840	11,741	9,126	30,892	20,800	.99	.44	.66	.30
Adjacent County "B"	8,617	3,745	4,422	21,003	12,812	.63	.35	.39	.36
Designated Housing Region*	51,414	25,320	26,094	118,672	75,682	.68	.34	.43	.51
Blue Collar									
Primary County	16,682	(3,787)**	20,469	49,789	31,367	.53	.65	.33	1.20
Adjacent County "A"	4,101	557	3,654	18,100	11,700	.35	.31	.23	.63
Adjacent County "B"	6,053	(2,097)	8,150	15,361	9,343	.65	.87	.39	1.27
Designated Housing Region*	26,836	(5,437)	32,273	83,205	52,410	.51	.61	.32	1.20

Notes:

*Region diminished by two counties due to data unavailability—region spans two states—employment data maintained at state level in one state was of insufficient detail to make the comparison.

Data adjusted to estimate total employment.

Numbers and percents may not add due to rounding.

**Parentheses indicate a decrease in particular units specified.

Sources:

1. U.S. Census of Housing, 1960-1970 (covers only communities to which employment has been attracted).

2. N.J. Dept. of Labor, Covered Employment Data (Adjusted to estimate total employment). See Appendix One.

occurred in municipalities which did not attract major new employers. As a result, the ratio of housing growth to growth in the number of jobs held by males ($\frac{T.D.U.}{Male}$) was much lower in employer attracting communities (.65) than in the region as a whole (.92). As in the designated region as a whole, in each county housing growth was more dispersed than was job growth.

The exhibit also demonstrates that suburban outmigration of firms to outlying white collar areas is not the monolithic employer choice popularized by sociological texts. Four out of every ten new jobs were located in blue collar suburbs. In concert with demand, more multi-family housing has been built in these blue collar communities than in white collar areas. Six additional multi-family units were built in blue collar areas for every 10 additional male workers. Only 3 such units were built per 10 male workers in white collar areas.

Numbers of single-family homes actually declined in these employer attracting blue collar communities. All growth in these homes was concentrated in white collar areas. Overall, white collar communities provided relatively more housing for each male job attracted than did their blue collar neighbors; the housing production/male job ratio ($\frac{T.D.U.}{Male}$) is .68 for white collar employment attracting communities and .51 for blue collar equivalents. However, new housing in white collar areas is largely comprised of one-family homes.

Thus there are significant differences among suburban communities in their housing production response to job growth. A number of both blue and white collar suburban municipalities in each county of the region experienced negligible job growth, yet provided significant quantities of additional housing units. Blue collar communities experienced substantial job growth, and all net housing growth in these municipalities was made up of units in multi-family structures. Sixty percent of job growth occurred in white collar communities. These white collar communities provided more additional housing units per additional male jobs than did blue collar areas. However, the bulk of these additional units were one-family homes. The forces producing this differentiation are not well understood, but it appears likely that to attribute all of it to exclusionary zoning would be an oversimplification.

The "Exclusionary Zoned" Communities. Where do the four communities fit into the overall picture? Each are white collar areas, of course; two of the four have experienced rapid job growth; and they are located in the primary county. Exhibit 7 summarizes their combined housing production performance relative to the primary county and the designated housing region as a whole.

The actual housing performance of the four communities as described in the Exhibit stands in sharp contrast to their initial characterization above. The $\frac{T.D.U.}{Male}$ ratio is as high in the four communities as in the designated housing region, and far higher than in the primary county; and multi-family units were constructed at the same pace in the four communities as in other white collar areas of the primary county, though multi-family units comprised a much smaller proportion of overall housing growth in the four communities than in the designated housing region, or even in other white collar communities in the primary county. When the four communities are compared with other white collar communities in the primary county, it is clear that this does not result from a lower rate of multi-family units relative to job growth, but rather a somewhat higher rate of construction of one-family homes.

EXHIBIT 7
THE HOUSING PRODUCTION RATIOS OF THE FOUR "EXCLUSIONARY" COMMUNITIES

	$\frac{T.D.U.}{Male}$	$\frac{M.D.U.}{Male}$	$\frac{M.D.U.}{T.D.U.}$
Four Communities Primary County	.92	.27	.29
White Collar Areas	.53	.29	.56
Total	.63	.48	.76
Designated Housing Region	.92	.51	.56

In summary, within the designated region, housing is produced on a par with the number of jobs attracted. This is not a surprising finding but rather is typical of the results that can be expected from the application of similar analysis to other areas, and a verification that the regional description adopted here is both a workable and reasonable one.

Further, communities differ systematically in their housing production performance. Housing development is more dispersed than job growth within each county and in the designated housing region as a whole. Communities and counties which attracted major new employers typically do not provide sufficient housing for new workers, and thus the failure of a specific community or group of communities to do so need not indicate the effect of exclusionary zoning per se. Rather, this may result from more basic forces affecting the operation of metropolitan housing markets. Finally, the characteristics of new housing differs considerably among communities of different types. Multi-family units comprise a much higher portion of new construction in what we have termed blue collar areas than in white collar areas, and this may reflect basic differences in the features of the community more than exclusionary zoning per se.

The Question of Housing Cost

In this section, the previous analysis is extended by examining whether employees in the exclusionary zoned communities, as well as the county and regional demarcations which have been described above, can afford available housing. In order to guide the reader through the analysis, its structure will be briefly described. Initially housing costs in the areas under study are analyzed. Subsequently the minimum family incomes needed to afford available housing is calculated. Finally, minimum family incomes necessary to afford local housing are compared to family incomes in the areas under study to determine whether local employees are financially able to purchase local housing.

Housing Costs. Exhibit 8 lists the median rents of new multi-family rental housing coming on-stream within the area over the period 1960 to 1970. Rents are presented for three [similar information was not available for the other two counties, for the reasons discussed] of the five constituent counties of the designated housing region as well as for the four allegedly exclusionary zoned communities. Median rents are presented for new housing units in both blue and white collar municipalities, where appropriate. This exhibit illustrates a number of trends. Blue collar communities in all of the areas have considerably lower cost rental housing than is the case for white collar locales. As an illustration, rental housing in the primary county's white collar communities costs over 30 percent more than in blue collar areas. In an adjacent county there is a 27 percent blue-white collar housing cost disparity. For the designated housing region as a whole, rental housing in white collar communities is 13 percent more expensive than in blue collar locales. Focusing on the four town area we see that the median 1970 rental level of local multi-family housing constructed from 1960 to 1970 was $195. The latter figure is 5 percent higher than the median rental level of housing construction in all other white collar areas and 18 percent higher than blue collar areas of the designated housing region. However, it is lower than the median rents of new multi-family units in other white collar communities of the primary county.

EXHIBIT 8
MEDIAN RENT OF NEW MULTI-FAMILY HOUSING (1960-1970) TO MEDIAN SURVEYED INCOME
(DEFLATED TO 1965) WITHIN THE DESIGNATED HOUSING REGION

	Median Rent of New Multi-Family Construction (1960-1970)		Required Family Income to Afford Rental Housing		Median Family Income of Surveyed Employees* (Deflated to 1965)		Surveyed Income / Required Income	
	White	Blue	White	Blue	White	Blue	White	Blue
Primary County	225	173	10,800	8,304	10,500	12,410	.97	1.49
Adjacent County "A"	166	169	7,968	8,112	10,763	9,083	1.35	1.12
Adjacent County "B"	183	144	8,784	6,912	10,508	11,396	1.20	1.65
Designated Housing Region	186	165	8,928	7,920	10,858	11,945	1.34	1.51
Exclusionary Zoned Communities	195		9,360	—	12,600	—	1.35	—

Note: *Mid-year of new construction period.
Source: U.S. Census of Housing 1970.

Exclusionary Zoning

Exhibit 9 lists median values of *new single family construction* from 1960 to 1970 in the designated housing region and the four "exclusionary zoned" communities. It is quite apparent that blue collar communities in most areas had considerably lower cost housing produced than was the case for white collar locales. The housing in the primary county's white collar communities cost almost one-third more than housing in its blue collar areas. In three of the four adjacent counties single family housing constructed in white collar communities varied from 17 to 37 percent higher than similar housing constructed in blue collar locales. For the designated housing region as a whole, new single family housing in white collar communities averaged 29 percent more expensive than in blue collar communities. For the alleged exclusionary zoned communities the median value of local single family housing constructed from 1960 to 1970 was $50,417. This latter figure is considerably higher than the median value of housing constructed in both the blue ($31,531) and white collar ($44,196) communities of the designated housing region yet only slightly higher than the $48,479 median value of new construction in white collar communities of the primary county.

Exhibit 10 lists the average sale price of both new and used housing sold during 1971 in the areas under examination. Comparing this exhibit to the former one we see that resale housing in white collar areas in 1971 is 20 percent less expensive than new single family housing constructed over the period 1960-1970. For blue collar areas resale and new single family housing do not evidence the significant cost separations found in white collar communities.

Threshold Income. Using basic real estate "rules of thumb" it is possible to calculate household income necessary to afford the median housing costs described above. [This calculation for single family housing consists of taking the median house value, subtracting from it the estimated downpayment (20 percent) to obtain the mortgage value. The monthly debt retirement for a thirty year mortgage at current interest rates is estimated as 1 percent of the total mortgage value (includes taxes and insurance). With this figure an annual "housing expense" is obtained. The income allocated to housing is estimated to be 20 percent or one-fifth of the total family income. Other sources indicate that 25 percent of the family's income should be allocated to housing but this includes monthly operating costs such as gas, electricity, etc. not included on our side of the expense ledger. For rental housing median *contract* rent is multiplied by five to obtain necessary monthly earnings and then by twelve for an annual figure.] This analysis is completed for the three types of housing offered locally: multi-family rental units and both resale and new single family units.

For the rental units (Exhibit 8) threshold incomes range from $8,800 to $11,000 for employment attracting white collar communities of the designated housing region; for blue collar areas the range is $6,900 to $8,300. For the "exclusionary zoned" communities rental housing is affordable by only those whose family income exceeds $9,400.

For single family resale housing (Exhibit 10) the incomes necessary to afford such housing range from $17,000 to $19,300 in white collar areas and from $12,500 to $16,100 in blue collar areas. For the communities claimed as exclusionary zoned the figure is $24,426. These latter income figures (adjusting slightly for year differences) are *double* the incomes necessary for rental units.

New single family construction adds a further increment in cost (Exhibit 9). For white collar areas of the designated housing region the increment is 15 percent, for blue collar areas 10 percent. The differential between *new* and used single family housing in the "exclusionary zoned" area is by no means as large.

Family Income. The next step of the analysis is to examine the family income of employees whose place of work is located in the areas under analysis. [Family income of employees in new, relocating and expanding firms in the areas was analyzed. This data was obtained through survey of such employees. The survey was undertaken in 1972 so it would not be valid to compare these incomes to the median values of new housing construction between 1960 and 1970 (in order to calculate threshold income). Consequently the surveyed employee family income was adjusted to reflect the time differential of the comparison. These incomes are also listed in Exhibits 9, 10 and 11. Family incomes of workers employed in both the blue and white collar areas varied slightly between the constituent counties of the designated housing region from approximately $14,000 to $16,000 in white collar areas and from $12,000 to $16,000 in blue collar communities. The means for the designated housing region for blue and white collar locales differed by approximately $1,000 annually; $15,700 in blue collar communities and $14,700 in white collar communities.' There were also pay differentials between firms located in the blue and white collar areas in the *same* county; firms locating in blue collar areas pay employees *more* than those to the white collar group in the eastern constituent counties and less in the western counties.

How do these incomes compare to the threshold incomes previously discussed? Again viewing Exhibits 8, 9 and 10, it may be seen that for *rental housing, actual income exceeds threshold income by 35 to 50 percent for white and blue collar areas respectively;* the exclusionary zoned area similarly reflects the regional experience. In other words, rental housing additions *within the region (one out of every two units produced) are well within the price range of the workers who have been attracted there;* a similar finding is evident for the four "exclusionary zoned" communities. [James has found similar conclusions for the distribution as well as the median. See footnote 13.]

When one moves from rental housing to resale housing (Exhibit 11) and finally to new housing (Exhibit 10) the ability to afford such housing in suburban areas by the workers attracted there decreases significantly. Under conventional standards only *resale* housing in blue collar areas can be afforded by those employed there. The price of resale single family housing in white collar communities exceeds working families' ability to pay by 27 percent and 21 and 49 percent gaps respectively for *new* housing in blue and white collar communities. The white collar disparities are equally or more evident in the exclusionary zoned communities under study.

In sum, as for the case of numbers of housing units, when the area of analysis decreases,

EXHIBIT 9

MEDIAN VALUE OF NEW SINGLE FAMILY HOUSING (1960-1970) TO MEDIAN SURVEYED INCOME (DEFLATED TO 1965) WITHIN THE DESIGNATED HOUSING REGION

	Median Value of New Construction (1960-1970)		Required Family Income to Afford Housing		Median Income of Surveyed Employees* (Deflated to 1965)		Surveyed Income / Required Income	
	White	Blue	White	Blue	White	Blue	White	Blue
Primary County	48,479	33,936	23,270	16,290	10,500	12,410	.45	.76
Adjacent County "A"	41,774	30,624	20,050	14,700	10,763	9,083	.54	.52
Adjacent County "B"	41,384	34,470	19,864	16,545	10,508	11,396	.53	.69
Adjacent County "C"	25,623	23,878	12,299	11,461	12,316	10,374	1.0	.91
Adjacent County "D"	47,217	29,857	22,621	14,331	11,137	N/A	.49	N/A
Designated Housing Region	44,196	31,531	21,215	15,135	10,858	11,945	.51	.79
Exclusionary Zoned Communities	50,417		24,198		12,600		.52	
Community #1	47,685		22,890		12,600		.55	

Note: *Mid-year of new construction coming on stream.

EXHIBIT 10

AVERAGE SALE OF SINGLE FAMILY HOUSING (1971) TO MEDIAN SURVEYED INCOME (DEFLATED TO 1971) WITHIN THE DESIGNATED HOUSING REGION

	1971 Average Sale		Required Family Income To Afford Housing		Median Income of Surveyed Employees (1972)		Surveyed Income / Required Income	
	White	Blue	White	Blue	White	Blue	White	Blue
Primary County	40,310	33,590	19,349	16,123	13,410	15,848	.70	.98
Adjacent County "A"	36,670	29,730	14,270	17,602	13,745	11,560	.96	.66
Adjacent County "B"	35,380	26,040	16,982	12,499	13,420	14,553	.80	1.16
Designated Housing Region*	38,620	29,320	18,538	14,074	13,466	15,356	.73	1.10
Exclusionary Zoned Communities	50,880		24,426		16,100		.66	
Community #1	42,400		20,352		16,100		.80	

Note: *Two counties were not included because 1971 Average Sale Price was available for only the New Jersey counties of the primary housing market.
Sources: N.J. Dept. of Community Affairs, and CUPR Survey of Relocating Firms.

preferred communities—the objects of most exclusionary zoning suits—demonstrate an increasing failure to provide housing at a cost which the family incomes of those locally employed can afford. Most employees holding jobs in the four exclusive communities cannot afford to live there. The case is clear. There is an insufficient number of multi-family units being constructed and both new and used single family units are far out of reach.

However, the picture is less exclusionary for the primary county as a whole. Rental units in most areas can be afforded by the incomes of most workers; used single family housing is accessible in blue collar areas; and new single family housing is still out of reach in many places.

Finally at the level of the designated housing region the cost partitions of the new housing provided appears to parallel the income requirements of those attracted there with the exceptions of new single family housing which is on the average only 10-20 percent above worker ability to pay. For the five county region as a whole, the housing market appears to be satisfactorily meeting the housing needs of workers.

Conclusion

The obvious conclusion drawn here both in terms of housing numbers and housing price is that a housing region properly defined is exactly that. People are housed according to ability to pay in a fairly regular fashion. For those who cannot afford new or resale single family housing in white collar communities similar housing is available in communities of less stature. For those who cannot afford to own single family housing, multi-family housing in significant quantity is available.

New single family housing is expensive in both blue and white collar areas and only in the former is used, single family housing noticeably cheaper than the newer variety. This may be in turn a surrogate for age of structure and a realistic appraisal of the environment of an area contributing to the sustained competitiveness of an aging housing stock within a "good" area.

Rental housing appears to be affordable by those of more modest income. This is true regardless of community stature. Rental multifamily housing is significantly cheaper than owned single family housing in all communities under study at all levels of investigation.

Epilogue

If one of these "exclusionary zoned" communities is viewed from the local perspective, it indeed fails to provide a form of housing that would serve the needs of those of modest income. Yet if close examination is made, these communities are usually building upper income housing at a pace which meets the needs of those of upper income viewed from a regional perspective, while other communities—for instance the blue collar communities identified in this analysis—provide housing for middle income and lower income workers.

Thus if we move from local appraisal of the condition surrounding local zoning to that of the region, the localities under scrutiny inevitably will secure a more favorable position. All those who cry for the region as the minimal level of analysis: be prepared for the oft-times confounding results. Haar, Babcock—ten years later—should be listened to. This type of analysis is much more likely to raise questions concerning the actual operation of suburban housing markets than provide easy guidelines for ameliorative policy.

Footnotes

1. This article is based on a larger study by the authors. See Robert W. Burchell, David Listokin and George Sternlieb, *Open or Closed Communities? The Suburban Exclusionary Zoning Problem.* (New Brunswick, New Jersey: Rutgers University, Center for Urban Policy Research, 1975).
2. See Lawrence Sager, "Tight Little Islands: Exclusionary Zoning, Equal Protection and the Indigent," *Stanford Law Review,* Vol. 4 (1970): Mary Brooks, "Exclusionary Zoning," *ASPO Report No. 254* (February 1970); "The New Jersey Judiciary's Response to Exclusionary Zoning," *Rutgers University Law Review,* Vol. 25 (1970). For an extensive review see David Listokin, et. al., *Exclusionary Zoning: A Review of Literature,* prepared for Council of Planning Librarians.
3. National Commission on Urban Problems, *Building the American City* (Government Printing Office, 1968); Norman Marcus, "Exclusionary Zoning: The Need for a Regional Planning Content," *New York Law Forum,* Vol. 16 (1970).
4. See for example, *National Land and Investment Co. v. Easttown Township Board of Adjustment,* 419 Pa. 504, 215 A.2d 597 (1965); *In Re Appeal of Girsh,* 437 Pa. 237, 263 A.2d 395 (1970).
5. Sager, see footnote 2 at p. 793.
6. Norman Williams and Thomas Norman, "Exclusionary Land Use Control: The Case of North Eastern New Jersey," *Syracuse Law Review,* Vol. 22 (1970-71), p. 478.
7. "Apartments in Mahwah," *Bergen (New Jersey) Record,* March 11, 1971; "Mahwah Dubbed Symbol of Racism in Suburbia," *Ridgewood* [*New Jersey*] *News,* January, 1971.
8. "Racism in Mahwah is Denied," (Letter to the Editor) *Bergen* [*New Jersey*] *Record,* March 2, 1971.
9. Frank Aloi, Arthur Goldberg and James White, "Racial and Economic Segregation by Zoning: Death Knoll for Home Rule," *University of Toledo Law Review,* Vol. 1 (1969).
10. Notes—"Exclusionary Zoning and Equal Protection," *Harvard University Law Review,* Vol. 84 (1971), pp. 1663-1664.
11. George Sternlieb and David Listokin, "Zoning—Exclusionary Zoning: State of the Art, Strategies for the Future" (Report prepared for HUD Housing Review Task Force, No. 4, June 1973, processed).
12. Sager, see footnote 2 at p. 793.
13. For an in-depth analysis, see Franklin James, "Can Suburbs House Suburban Workers in New Jersey," in Thomas Norman, ed., *New Jersey Trends* (New Brunswick, New Jersey: Institute for Environmental Studies, Rutgers University, 1974).
14. John Kain, "Theories of Residential Location and Realities of Race," in John Kain, ed., *The NBER Urban Simulation Model, Vol. II* (New York: National Bureau of Economic Research, 1969, processed).
15. It is clear that minority workers face much different problems in penetrating the suburbs than do low income workers in general, and the discussion of the particular problems of racial segregation should be examined separately from the general question of exclusion on the basis of income. They will not be discussed in this paper.
16. For an extensive analysis of such trends see Fred Bosselman and David Callies, *The Quiet Revolution in Land Use Control* (Washington, D.C.: Council on Environmental Quality, 1971).
17. Much of the housing-zoning literature assumes that local fiscal pressures are one of the major precipitating factors of exclusionary zoning. See David Listokin, ed. *Land Use Controls: Present Problems, Future Reform,* (New Brunswick, N.J.: Center for Urban Policy Research, Rutgers University, 1974). For countervailing analysis, see Franklin James and Oliver Duane Windsor, "Local Land Use Controls in New Jersey: Their Effects on Housing Costs and Community Fiscal Advantage," Paper submitted to AIP Conference, 1974 (Denver, Colorado).
18. Thomas O'Keefe, "Time Controls on Land Use: Prophylactic Law for Planners," *Cornell Law Review,* Vol. 57 (1972) p. 834. A regional approach to reforming land use has also been the strategy of many fair share housing distribution plans. See Mary Brooks, "Lower Income Housing: The Planners' Response," *ASPO Report No. 282* (July-August, 1972); David Listokin, "Fair Share Housing Distributions: Will it Open the Suburbs to Apartment Development," *Real Estate Law Journal,* Vol. 2 (1974).
19. Sager, see footnote 2 at 793.
20. "State Police Power—Zoning—Validity of Local Ordinance Depends on Considerations of Regional, Not Merely Local, General Welfare," *Vanderbilt Law Review,* Vol. 25 (1972), p. 472.
21. *Appeal of Kit-Mar Builders, Inc.* 439 Pa. 466, 268 A.2d 765 (1970).
22. *Ibid.,* 439 Pa. 474-75, 268 A.2d 768-69 (1970).
23. See footnote 4.
24. *Ibid.*
25. *Lionshead Lake, Inc. v. Township of Wayne,* 10 N.J. 165, 89 A.2d 693 (1952).
26. Charles Haar, "Zoning for Minimum Standards: The Wayne Township Case," *Harvard Law Review,* Vol. 66 (1953). Noted in Sager, footnote 2.
27. Richard Babcock, *The Zoning Game* (Madison: University of Wisconsin Press, 1966), p. 178.
28. *Duffcon Concrete Products v. Borough of Cresskill* 1 N.J. 509, 64 A.2d 347 (1949).
29. *Valley View Village, Inc., v. Proffett,* 221 F.2d 412 (6th Cir. 1955).
30. Edwin Lyon, "Exclusionary Zoning From a Regional Perspective," *Urban Law Annual* (1972) pp. 240-241.
31. Walter Isard, "Regional Science, The Concept of Region and Regional Structure" in Regional Science Association, *Papers and Proceedings,* Vol. 2 (1956), p. 19.

32. Vincent Ostrom, "The Political Dimension of Regional Analysis," in Regional Science Association, *Papers and Proceedings*, Vol. 2 (1956) p. 86. See also, Howard Odum and Harry Moore, *American Regionalism* (Gloucester, Mass.: Peter Smith, 1966).
33. Department of Housing and Urban Development, FHA Economic and Market Analyses Division, *FHA Techniques of Housing Market Analysis* (Washington, D.C.: Government Printing Office).
34. Ernest and Robert Fisher, *Urban Real Estate* (New York: Henry Holt, 1954) p. 223.
35. Charles Abrams, *The Language of Cities* (New York: Viking, 1971).
36. See footnote 33 at p. 4.
37. William C. Grigsby, *Housing Markets and Public Policy* (Philadelphia: University of Pennsylvania Press, 1963). See also Chester Rapkin, Louis Winnick and David Blank, *Housing Market Analysis: A Study of Theory and Methods* (Washington, D.C.: Housing and Home Finance Agency, 1953), p. 9.
38. David Blank and Louis Winnick, "The Structure of the Housing Market," *Quarterly Journal of Economics* (1953) p. 107.
39. See footnote 33 at p. 12.
40. See footnote 34 at p. 225.
41. See footnote 35 at p. 142.
42. *Oakwood at Madison, Inc. v. Township of Madison* (L-7502-70 P.W. 1974).
43. *Ibid.*
44. John Lansing and Eva Mueller, with Nancy Barth, *Residential Location and Urban Mobility* (Ann Arbor, Mich.: Survey Research Center, Institute for Social Research, University of Michigan, 1964) p. 41.
45. *The Sunday Tribune*, May 28, 1967. Cited in Association of Bay Area Governments, *Regional Housing Study Supplemental Report RA-4*, October 1969, p. 26.
46. John Lansing, *Residential Location and Urban Mobility: The Second Wave of Interviews* (Ann Arbor, Mich.: Survey Research Center, Institute for Social Research, University of Michigan, 1966) p. 75.
47. See footnote 45.
48. George Sternlieb, *et al., Housing Development and Municipal Costs* (New Brunswick, N.J.: Center for Urban Policy Research, Rutgers University, 1973).

Equal Opportunity in Suburbia:

A Report [Summary]

**United States Commission
on Civil Rights**

The United States Commission on Civil Rights is a temporary, independent, bipartisan agency established by the Congress in 1957 to: ● *Investigate complaints alleging denial of the right to vote by reason of race, color, religion, sex, or national origin, or by reason of fraudulent practices;* ● *Study and collect information concerning legal developments constituting a denial of equal protection of the laws under the Constitution because of race, color, religion, sex, or national origin, or in the administration of justice;* ● *Appraise Federal laws and policies with respect to the denial of equal protection of the laws because of race, color, religion, sex, or national origin, or in the administration of justice;* ● *Serve as a national clearinghouse for information concerning denials of equal protection of the laws because of race, color, religion, sex, or national origin; and* ● *Submit reports, findings, and recommendations to the President and the Congress.*

This article consists of selected portions of the full report (72 + pages), issued by the U.S. Commission on Civil Rights in July 1974.

Letter of Transmittal

THE PRESIDENT
THE PRESIDENT OF THE SENATE
THE SPEAKER OF THE HOUSE OF REPRESENTATIVES

SIRS:

The U.S. Commission on Civil Rights presents this report to you pursuant to Public Law 85—315 as amended.

This report is the product of an extensive study of racial isolation in this Nation's metropolitan areas—a study of why this pattern of isolation has occurred, how it is crippling the growth and prosperity of our cities, and how it can be arrested and reversed. Information was gathered through Commission hearings in St. Louis, Baltimore, and Washington, D.C., and factfinding meetings of State Advisory Committees in those cities and in Boston, Phoenix, and Milwaukee.

With prompt and effective action by both the legislative and executive branches of Government, the problems identified by the study can be solved to the advantage of city and suburb alike. We therefore urge your consideration both of the facts presented and the Commission's recommendations for corrective action.

Respectfully,

Arthur S. Flemming,* Chairman

Stephen Horn, Vice Chairman
Frankie M. Freeman
Maurice B. Mitchell**
Robert S. Rankin
Manuel Ruiz, Jr.
John A. Buggs, Staff Director
 * Not a member of the Commission during preparation of this report.
** Resigned from the Commission as of March 21, 1974.

Preface

More than a decade ago, this Commission noted the development of a "white noose" of new suburban housing on the peripheries of decaying cities with an "ever-increasing concentration of non-whites in racial ghettoes" [U.S. Commission on Civil Rights, 1961 Report: Housing 1 (1961).] Today that pattern is even more pronounced. The exodus of affluent whites from the cities has continued unabated, along with the large-scale movement of jobs and wealth. The new suburbs have enjoyed an era of unparalleled prosperity, while the central cities have strained to answer growing demands for services for the urban poor and, ironically, suburban commuters.

In 1969, the Commission decided to conduct a study of metropolitan area development and its social and economic impact on urban minorities. In public hearings in St. Louis, Baltimore, and Washington, D.C., between January 1970 and June 1971, the Commission documented the problem with the testimony of more than 150 witnesses—from welfare mothers to Cabinet secretaries, from public housing tenants to corporation presidents. Further testimony was gathered by the Commission's State Advisory Committees in those cities and in Boston, Milwaukee, and Phoenix.

This report is the result of that investigation. It includes both findings of fact and recommendations for action. Its purpose is not to single out for criticism any particular individuals, organizations, agencies, or communities, but to analyze this metropolitan pattern of racial polarization from its causes to its consequences.

By the time of publication, some of the facts contained in the report will undoubtedly need updating. Court cases challenging both government and private actions in a number of directly related or peripheral matters are currently pending in several jurisdictions; and the Federal Government's own housing programs are at best in a state of flux.

Nevertheless, the problems documented herein are long-lived, profound, and complex. Their solution will not be simple. But without an immediate recognition of their impact, it is doubtful that any solution will be forthcoming.

Contents

[Editor's Note: For the interest of the reader, the Table of Contents basically reprinted below.]

Racial and Economic Polarization Today

An Individual Perspective

To many, the problems of the inner city are known only as images flashing through the window of a moving car. To Larman Williams, his wife and children, they were a way of life:

> I guess mainly, where we were, we were dissatisfied with the facilities, we were dissatisfied with the clientele in and around the block. There was high crime in the area, in the neighborhood and on the block, there were attacks on neighbors. One lady across the street was hit on the head with a hatchet, robbed, murdered. Down the street from me on the left a lady was raped and was found the next morning in the nude. And people were prostituting all around and under us and in the apartment, that kind of stuff.
>
> My child was chased from school through an alley by someone, some man who was trying to seduce her. And for all of those reasons I just was afraid to come home to find my family maybe dead or my child raped, or just afraid.[1]

Williams, a high school assistant principal, testified at the January 1970 hearing of the United States Commission on Civil Rights in St. Louis, Missouri. Williams was not alone in his feelings. Inner-city residents at a series of Commission hearings testified about the crime, decayed housing, inferior schools, inadequate municipal services, and lack of jobs—about the dark streets lined with rotted houses in which they had to make their homes and raise their children.

In another sense, however, Larman Williams was fortunate in that his job and economic position enabled him to consider moving away from the conditions that so troubled him. It took a year of looking to find the right house, in suburban Ferguson, Missouri. But it was not enough that Williams was an able and willing buyer. Williams is black and Ferguson was virtually all white.

Only when his white pastor intervened was Williams even able to see the interior of the house.

> [We] took the name off of the sign and called the real estate people and of course they didn't call us back at that time. So [my pastor] asked me if I would mind if he would look into it and get the price of the house and all of [the] details that we would want to know, and I told him I wouldn't, and he got this information. And I said, "Well, that sounds good; I think we can handle that price and that kind of a thing."

Williams' pastor went to the owner of the home and told him he knew of a person who wanted to buy the house:

> . . . And the owner said that he didn't mind but his neighbors were not in the mood for selling to black people . . .
>
> My pastor went and knocked on their doors and he got them together and they had a caucus and a prayer meeting and decided that it was only the right thing to do, to sell to a black person.
>
> And then the person, the owner, called the real estate people and they came and got in contact with me and we made the transaction from there.[2]

It would not be difficult for Larman Williams to understand why the black population of St. Louis County in 1970 was only 4.1 percent and why the black population of St. Louis City was 43.7.[3]

Thousands today are not as fortunate as the Williams family. They remain in the ghettos of St. Louis, Baltimore, and Washington, D.C., in the "barrio" of Phoenix, and in the centers of dozens of other American cities. Many do not freely choose to live in these conditions. But they are trapped. They are poor. They are members of a minority group. Too often, they are poor because they are members of a minority group.

The National Perspective

The decade of the 1960s was one of increasing suburbanization of whites in metropolitan areas and of increasing concentration of blacks within central cities—in short, of increasing racial separation. Between 1960 and 1970 the white central-city population in metropolitan areas having a population of 500,000 or more declined by 1.9 million people, while the comparable black population increased by 2.8 million. The suburban rings of these same metropolitan areas had a white population increase of 12.5 million and a black population increase of only 0.8 million.[4] In terms of percentage changes, the increase in the black share of the central city population was 2¼ times as great as the increase in the black share of total metropolitan population in these areas.[5] Moreover, in 10 of the 34 metropolitan areas having a population of one million or more, the percentage of black suburban residents stayed the same or declined between 1960 and 1970.[6]

We cannot expect these patterns to reverse themselves on their own. If metropolitan population is projected to the year 2000, the percentage of whites living in central cities drops from about 40 percent in 1970 to approximately 25 percent in 2000; the change for blacks is from 79 percent in 1970 to between 70.1 and 74.8 percent.[7]

Equal Opportunity in Suburbia

As testimony before the Commission showed, this picture of racial separation in metropolitan residential patterns persists for two main reasons: past and present discrimination in the sale and rental of housing and because of the lower income of blacks and other minority group members.

While housing discrimination is not practiced as frequently or as openly as it was before such discrimination was outlawed, it is still accurate to describe most metropolitan areas as having two housing markets—one for whites and one for blacks. Even if discriminatory practices were ended, special effort would be needed to overcome residential patterns established by decades of discrimination.

Lower income also puts racial and ethnic minorities at a competitive disadvantage in the housing market. In 1969, according to Census Bureau statistics, nearly one-third of the Nation's blacks had incomes below the poverty level,[8] compared with one-tenth of the country's whites. The median family income for all black families in 1969 was $5,999, nearly 40 percent less than the median white family income of $9,794.[9]

The dual causes of residential segregation—discrimination and low income—must be looked at together, since they reinforce each other. For blacks to have incomes equal to whites would not in and of itself solve the problem. This would only lower the percentage of black metropolitan residents who live in central cities (in areas of one million or more population) from 81.1 to 78.4.[10]

At every income level whites are more likely than blacks to live in suburbia. In 1970, 85.5 percent of black metropolitan families earning less than $4,000 lived in the central city, as compared with 46.4 percent of white families in the same income range. In the $4,000 to $10,000 income range, 82.5 percent of the black families and 41.6 percent of the white families lived in the central city. For families with an annual income of $10,000 or more, the central city figures are 76.8 percent black and 30.9 percent white.[11]

But income is not irrelevant. Many white suburbanites bought their houses at a time when prices were significantly lower. Today the supply of inexpensive suburban housing is insufficient for even those black purchasers or renters whose income is comparable to that of whites.

To a great extent, the income disparity is also the result of discrimination. Inferior education has been offered to minority group members, with access to higher education often blocked. Even when a comparable education has been achieved, discrimination in employment prevents minority group members from converting their education to income as successfully as do whites.

The lack of inexpensive housing in suburbia is not only the result of market forces but also of local practices which limit low-cost dwellings or exclude them altogether. The motivation behind these restrictions is complex, with racial and economic motivations intertwined. The exclusion of low- and moderate-income housing not only assures open space, uncrowded schools and streets, and more favorable tax revenues; it also excludes low-income families. And this exclusion is disproportionately severe for blacks and other "undesirable" minorities because of their higher incidence of poverty. A witness at an open meeting conducted by the Commission's District of Columbia Advisory Committee in May 1970 described the all too common situation in Montgomery County, Maryland:

> Housing in Montgomery County is almost nonexistent for the black people who work for the Federal Government because, by and large, those people who work for the Federal Government are the lower paid employees. The [median] housing in Montgomery County last year, the new construction, sold for [about] $40,000, and anyone that earns $15,000 or less cannot afford to

buy a house today in Montgomery County. And I know very, very few black people who earn $15,000 a year.[12]

This economic-racial exclusion may well be called the racism of the 1970s. Coupled with vestiges of the more open racism of the past, it furnishes an explanation for the picture portrayed by the census figures, an image of a suburban "white noose" encircling a black inner city. As George Laurent, a witness at the Commission's Baltimore hearing, stated:

> [T]here are three reasons that blacks do not live in suburbia or in predominantly white sections of the cities: one, they don't want to live there; two, they can't afford it; and three, discrimination. By far the last is the most important.[13]

As already noted, reasons two and three are often closely related.

For a country as large and varied as the United States, it is hard to make generalizations which will be valid throughout. Thus this report is more relevant to older, generally northeastern or midwestern metropolitan areas with a substantial minority population than it is to others. The study of St. Louis and Baltimore leads to many conclusions that one can reasonably believe will apply to Detroit or Pittsburgh but not without modification to some newer metropolitan areas in the West and South.[14]

Generalizations about "the central city" or "the suburbs" also hide a great deal of diversity. Residents of the many prosperous neighborhoods which continue to exist in central cities can legitimately disclaim any assertion that their neighborhoods suffer from deteriorating housing or are losing jobs. Suburbs, too, come in all kinds—older, working-class suburbs, majority black suburbs, small towns until recently beyond the influence of the metropolitan area.[15]

Nevertheless, when all the exceptions and the diversity are taken into account, a clear pattern of differences between central cities and suburbs, between minority group neighborhoods and white neighborhoods, remains.

Conclusion

Despite a plethora of far-reaching remedial legislation, a dual housing market continues today in most metropolitan areas across the United States. Inadequate enforcement by Federal agencies and circumvention or, at best, lip-service adherence by local authorities, builders, real estate agents, and others involved in the development of suburban communities have helped to perpetuate the systematic exclusion of minorities and low-income families. The result has been the growth of overwhelmingly white, largely affluent suburbs, and the concurrent deterioration of central cities, overburdened by inordinately large and constantly increasing percentages of poor and minority residents.

The 1970 census shows a 94.3 percent white suburban population in metropolitan areas of 500,000 or more residents. In the same areas, the black population of the central city increased in 10 years from 18 to almost 24 percent.

Two of the sectors hardest hit by the extensive residential segregation which has accompanied rapid metropolitan growth have been education and employment. School desegregation has been thwarted and the separate school systems in the city and its surrounding suburbs are by no means equal. Although the central cities face more difficult education problems than the middle- and upper-income suburbs, they are forced by other economic considerations to spend proportionally less on schools and special programs. The city's cultural institutions and police, fire, and sanitation departments are just a handful of the competitors for its dwindling tax revenues. Ironically, suburbanites who visit or work in the city benefit from these city services, but the suburbs offer no reciprocal benefits to excluded urban minorities. Suburbanites, therefore, enjoy the best of both worlds, at the expense of the city dweller.

The urban employment picture has also been damaged by the lack of foresight or equitable planning in suburban growth. Major employers, including the Federal Government, have relocated thousands of jobs in suburban areas without consideration for the housing or transportation needs of low-income or minority employees. The testimony of numerous witnesses—employers as well as employees and unemployed —evidenced the fact that job opportunities in suburbia go unfilled while unemployment rolls in the central city grow longer. Costly, time-consuming, and otherwise inadequate transportation between city and suburb has proven no substitute for the opportunity to live reasonably close to one's place of employment.

The problem stems in large part from local zoning powers. While wooing industrial plants to suburban communities, local authorities have simultaneously applied land use controls to exclude or tightly limit low-cost homes and apartments. In some areas, existing black residential neighborhoods have been rezoned commercial to force their dissolution. Municipal veto power over rent supplement housing is another mighty weapon in the zoning arsenal. Because the exercise of these local powers affects other parts of the metropolitan area, the Commission sees a dire need for a supervening authority over community land use control.

One approach which the Commission recommends is the enactment by Congress of legislation establishing metropolitan-wide housing and community development agencies in every State. The agencies' purpose would be to guarantee the availability of housing at all income levels and without regard to race throughout the metropolitan area. (Details of that proposal are included in the recommendations.)

The Commission's other recommendations are addressed to the executive branch. Although the Federal Government has recognized the suburban problem, it has done little to solve it. Neither HUD nor the Department of Justice has enforced existing antidiscrimination laws vigorously or effectively. The housing section of the Justice Department's Civil Rights Division, which is responsible for enforcement of the Title VIII antidiscrimination provisions, has only 25 lawyers to handle what is supposed to be a nationwide effort. In 1971, HUD promulgated "affirmative marketing guidelines" requiring developers of new FHA subdivisions and multifamily projects to adopt affirmative programs, including the hiring of minority sales and rental agents, to assure the marketing of housing to all races. But the regulations established no mechanism to guarantee that such plans will actually be carried out.

Unless the Federal Government undertakes a determined effort to enforce Federal antidiscrimination laws, city-suburban polarization will continue and the cycle of urban poverty will perpetuate itself uninterrupted and unabated. While the time has long passed for assessing blame, it cannot be denied that Federal agencies share with local authorities, the housing industry, and its related professions a moral and legal responsibility for having created a problem which will never solve itself. The task now is to employ the tools suggested, and to make better use of the tools at hand, to break the suburban "noose" and put an end to America's increasing racial polarization.

Findings

1. Minorities, particularly blacks, have been largely excluded from the development of the Nation's suburban areas.

2. This exclusion was created primarily by explicit discrimination in the sale and rental of housing.

3. This exclusion is perpetuated today by both racial and economic discrimination. Economic discrimination is often intentionally directed at, and falls most heavily upon, minorities whose incomes generally are significantly below the national average.

4. Suburbanization has been accompanied by the movement of the affluent, primarily white population to the outer rings of the country's metropolitan areas, the so-called "white nooses" that now mark the point at which the city limits end and suburbia begins. Central cities often have been left racially and economically isolated and financially deprived. This process also has:

   a. prompted a movement of business and industry to suburbia—a movement which frequently results in minorities being excluded from suburban job opportunities, owing to their inaccessibility;

   b. caused cities increasingly to find themselves without financial resources to meet the needs and demands of their residents;

   c. led to decreasing economic resources in the city and a concomitant inability to devote sufficient resources to school financing;

   d. resulted in the continued growth of racially segregated school systems in metropolitan areas.

5. Since the bulk of new housing is being constructed in suburban areas, the exclusion of minorities from the suburbs diminishes their housing alternatives and often forces minorities to live in substandard inner city housing.

6. The private sector has been a major contributor to this racial and ethnic polarization.

   a. Private real estate practices continue to reinforce the existing dual housing market—an exclusionary device based upon racial and economic prejudice and aimed at minorities. Among these practices are steering, failure to admit sufficient black brokers to white real estate boards, control of listings, and reluctance of brokers to establish affirmative marketing procedures.

   b. Many financial institutions, such as banks and mortgage lenders, have discouraged integrated community development both by restrictive practices and by lack of affirmative programs in granting loans to minorities who desire housing in suburban areas.

   c. The homebuilding industry, on the whole, has not made an adequate attempt to market housing in a nondiscriminatory manner.

   d. Corporation officials generally have failed to consider the effect of corporate site selection upon low- and moderate-income employees, a practice which often results in disproportionately reducing minority employment.

7. Suburban governments have acted almost exclusively in their own economic interests, often to the detriment of the central city and of the metropolitan area as a whole. Such devices as exclusionary zoning, failure to enact or enforce fair housing ordinances, and failure to utilize Federal housing assistance programs have been the mechanisms for preserving insular suburban interests. Thus, white homeowners

often were able to purchase moderately-priced suburban homes in the 1940s and 1950s when such housing was denied to minorities. Today, this exclusionary pattern is perpetuated by those communities which seek to keep out further moderate-income development through these devices.

8. Past policies of the Federal Government, which openly encouraged racial separation, were instrumental in establishing today's patterns of racial polarization. Present policies of racial neutrality or of encouraging racial integration have failed to alter racially separate patterns.

9. Present Federal programs often are administered so as to continue rather than reduce racial segregation.

   a. Although Federal-aid highway programs have facilitated the movement of jobs and housing to the suburbs, responsible Federal highway officials have failed to use the leverage of their massive trust fund monies to alter exclusionary housing patterns in suburbs.

   b. Federal programs involving housing loans and guarantees are creating even more widespread housing segregation, rather than promoting equal housing opportunities.

   c. The Federal Government has failed to require that Federal contractors consider the availability of nondiscriminatory low-income housing for their employees prior to selecting a site for a new facility.

   d. In selecting sites for Federal facilities, the Federal Government only recently has begun to give priority to communities with an adequate supply of nondiscriminatory housing for Federal employees.

10. Despite its past responsibility for today's racial polarization, the Federal Government has failed to take adequate measures to enforce fair housing laws.

    a. The Department of Justice, whose function is limited in the enforcement of Title VIII, has been handicapped by inadequate staffing. The Justice Department has failed to take a sufficiently active role in coordinating Title VI enforcement among Federal agencies.

    b. The Department of Housing and Urban Development has been similarly understaffed and confined in its activities to answering complaints. Until recently, HUD did not conduct systematic reviews of HUD-funded programs for compliance with Title VI of the Civil Rights Act of 1964. Further, HUD has failed to use its own programs adequately to promote fair housing, as required by Title VIII of the Civil Rights Act of 1968.

Recommendations

1. Metropolitan-Wide Residential Desegregation

Congress should enact legislation aimed at facilitating free housing choice throughout metropolitan areas for people of all income levels on a nondiscriminatory basis, thereby reducing racial polarization. This legislation should provide for the following requirements and conditions:

a. Establishment of Metropolitan Housing and Community Development Agencies—Each State should be required, as a precondition to the receipt of future Federal housing and community development grants, to establish, within 1 year, several metropolitan housing and community development agencies in each metropolitan area within its borders or to create a single State metropolitan housing and community development agency with statewide authority. Funds should be provided to the State to finance the planning, establishment, and operation of these agencies.

b. *Representation on Metropolitan Housing and Community Development Agencies*—Each political jurisdiction in a metropolitan area should be represented on a metropolitan housing and community development agency. Such representation should be based on population, with provisions for representation by minorities and economically disadvantaged groups.

c. *Powers and Duties of Metropolitan Housing and Community Development Agencies*—

(1) Develop within 3 years a plan governing the location of housing at all income levels throughout the metropolitan area. Among the criteria which the plan must satisfy should be the following:

(a) Housing at various prices and rents will be readily accessible to centers of employment.

(b) There will be adequate transportation and community facilities.

(c) The plan will broaden the range of housing choice for families of all income levels on a nondiscriminatory basis.

(d) The plan will facilitate school desegregation.

(e) The plan will assure against placing a disproportionate share of lower-income housing in any single jurisdiction or group of jurisdictions.

HUD should be directed to review and approve each plan to determine consistency with the legislative criteria and feasibility in achieving them.

(2) The location of all housing—nonsubsidized as well as subsidized, conventionally financed as well as FHA or VA—should be subject to the metropolitan housing and community development agency plan.

(3) Metropolitan housing and community development agencies should be granted power to override various local and State laws and regulations, such as large-lot zoning ordinances, minimum-square-footage requirements, and building codes, which impede implementation of the plan.

(4) Metropolitan housing and community development agencies should be authorized to provide housing pursuant to the metropolitan plan. They should be expressly authorized to act as local public housing authorities and should be made eligible for participation in federally-subsidized housing programs, as well as market-priced housing programs, both FHA/VA and conventionally financed. It should be specified that metropolitan housing and community development agencies may provide such housing only to the extent that the traditional housing producers (local public housing authorities, builders, nonprofit sponsors, etc.) are not doing so.

(5) Applications for funds under various community development programs which have housing implications, such as those administered by the Department of Transportation, the Department of Health, Education, and Welfare, and the Environmental Protection Agency, as well as the Department of Housing and Urban Development [for example, the highway program of DOT, 23 USC § 109; water and sewer program of HUD, 42 USC §3101 *as amended* (Supp. V, 1965-1969), and open space program of HUD, 42 USC §1500 *as amended* (Supp. V, 1965-1969)], should be subject to approval by the metropolitan housing and community development agency for consistency with the metropolitan plan. Such approval should be made subject to review by the Department of Housing and Urban Development.

d. *Reimbursement Costs.*—Funds should be provided to reimburse local jurisdictions, including central cities, for added costs, such as those involved in financing education for the increased number of children of low- and moderate-income housing in the community resulting from implementation of the metropolitan plan. Local jurisdictions claiming such reimbursement should be required to provide a detailed accounting of the amount of increased cost and how it has been incurred. This could be accomplished through extension of existing Federal programs which give financing aid to educational agencies which have sudden and substantial increases in pupils because of Federal action (example: Public Law 81-874, impact aid).

e. *Affirmative Marketing*—Builders and developers of all housing—unsubsidized as well as subsidized, conventionally financed as well as FHA or VA—should be required to develop affirmative marketing plans for minority homeseekers and submit them to the agency. These plans should include the establishment of numerical goals for minority residence, based upon a realistic evaluation of minority housing need at different income levels.

f. *Housing Information Centers*—Each metropolitan housing and community development agency should establish offices readily accessible to neighborhoods with a high proportion of minority or lower-income households to provide information concerning the location of housing covering a wide range of income levels.

g. *The local approval provisions governing the public housing and rent supplement program should be eliminated*—Continuing veto power at the local level could thwart the new agency's purpose.

2. Securing Employment Opportunities

The Office of Federal Contract Compliance should require contractors and subcontractors as a condition of eligibility for Federal contracts, to demonstrate the adequacy of nondiscriminatory low- and moderate-income housing, in the communities in which they are located or propose to relocate, to meet current and prospective employee needs. In the event the supply of such housing is not adequate, contractors and subcontractors should be required to submit affirmative action plans, including firm commitments from local government officials, housing industry representatives, and civic leaders, that will assure an adequate supply of such housing within a reasonable time following execution of the contract. Failure to carry out the assurance should be made grounds for cancellation of the contract and ineligibility for future Government contracts.

3. Federal Enforcement Efforts

a. *Department of Justice*—The Civil Rights Division of the Department of Justice should increase its housing section staff and initiate more actions directed against restrictive land use practices and other forms of systematic denial of equal housing opportunity. The Department of Justice also should require all Federal agencies subject to Title VI of the Civil Rights Act of 1964 to adopt strengthened and uniform regulations.

b. *Department of Housing and Urban Development*—As the leader of the entire Federal fair housing effort, the Department of Housing and Urban Development should employ an adequate fair housing staff, expand programs to provide funding for groups working in the area of fair housing, and conduct increased reviews, including community-wide reviews, of the impact of its programs upon racial concentration.

c. *Federal Financial Regulatory Agencies*—All Federal financial regulatory agencies should require that supervised mortgage lending institutions take affirmative action to implement the prohibition against discrimination in mortgage financing in Title VIII of the Civil Rights Act of 1968. The agencies should require the maintenance of racial and ethnic data on rejected and approved mortgage loan applications to enable examiners to determine compliance with Title VIII. They should also require mortgage lending institutions to include nondiscrimination clauses in their contracts with builders and developers.

4. National Policy

In addition to the foregoing, the Commission recommends the adoption of a national public policy designed to promote racial integration of neighborhoods throughout the United States. To implement such a national public policy, the Congress should enact and the President should approve legislation designed to provide suitable subsidies, either through property tax abatements, income tax deductions, direct payments, or other such inducements to individuals and families of all races who voluntarily purchase homes in areas that will accomplish such an objective.

Additional Statement

By Vice Chairman Stephen Horn

For a decade congressional hearings, Presidential commissions, and scholarly studies have delineated the plight of minority Americans as they have sought access to the burgeoning suburbs which increasingly surround our deteriorating central cities. The latest volume in this literature by the United States Commission on Civil Rights is testimony that what needs to be done has not been done.

In addition to the recommendations which my colleagues and I have made, at least two further points need emphasis. First, there is an immediate need to put the Federal administrative house in order if national policies which relate to adequate education, employment, and housing for our people are to be implemented effectively. To speak of this interrelated trilogy has become almost trite, but the interrelationships are nevertheless true.

Our hearings in St. Louis, Baltimore, Washington, D.C., and elsewhere are replete with evidence of the failure of both intra-agency and interagency coordination to achieve the goal of decent schooling, a paying job, and sufficient shelter for the low-income and minority citizen. If these real human problems are to be addressed by President, Cabinet officer, bureau chief, and civil servant, I would suggest that as a start they begin by reading portions of the transcript of the *Washington Hearing* held June 14-17, 1971 (see pages 153-155; 251-254; 306-307; 322-325; 341-345; 359-361; and 368-369, among others). There and in earlier hearings was revealed a trial of delay and inertia which confronts developer, financier, and builder; local, State, and Federal officials; and tenant and homeowner alike.

It is obvious that too often there is great resistance to proposals for increased Federal coordination from some vested interests in congressional subcommittees, the private sector, and the Federal bureaucracy itself. But if the interrelations which must be addressed are to be defined and resolved so that houses and apartments can be built for those who are economically and culturally deprived, then casual Federal coordination must be replaced by vigorous Federal coordination in both Washington and the field.

The President's instincts were correct early in 1973 when he sought to designate a particular Cabinet officer to coordinate the activities of several departmental colleagues in related areas. There is also a need for a White House presence in the field so that Federal activities in a region can be brought together in accord with the President's policies. Congress should provide the President with sufficient authority to reorganize and bring together related functions which now exist in various departments and agencies so that he can do the job which the American people have elected him to do.

The second point which needs emphasis is that as we consider the tragic plight of millions of Americans whose only limit to access to suburban America in housing and jobs too often seems to be that the shade of their skin is less than lily white, we must also add another factor: the problems of simply being poor and lacking the cultural background and family impetus to secure an education with which one can attempt to get a job and earn the money to acquire adequate housing.

Testimony was received by the Commission that in the Miami Valley region of Ohio the major migration was by Appalachian whites, not blacks, and that it was more difficult to place the former than the latter [*Washington Hearing* at 24]. Because of family pride and a lack of emphasis on problems of class as well as race, often the rural-oriented Appalachian white found it more difficult to secure aid than did the more urban-oriented black [*Id.* at 33].

These problems of race and class were noted by the former mayor of Cleveland, Carl B. Stokes, who recalled the "great and fearsome resistance" when he sought " to put low-income housing into the white areas" of Cleveland.

He added a point which is often overlooked: ". . . I faced not only resistance but some of the most personal vilification not one degree less, and in some respects much more, when I went to put low-income housing for black families in the middle-income black areas in Cleveland" [Id. at 214]. The latter was clearly a case of "class" not "racial" discrimination.

It is time that the Federal Government and Americans generally face up to the need for economic and class desegregation in schools, jobs, and housing. In our zest to make up for the oversight of two centuries with regard to racial, color, and now sexual discrimination, we have ignored for too long the enormity of this task and the difficulties in achieving progress in school, employment, and housing desegregation if we do not recognize all the discriminatory factors which exist. The attempts to view the whole picture of economic and class discrimination have been few and have usually met with the same opposition as attempts at racial desegregation [See D. Hubert, Class. . . and the Classroom: The Duluth (Minnesota) Experience, Saturday Review, May 27, 1972, at 49, 55-58]. It is essential that we face up to this problem.

Acknowledgements

The Commission is indebted to the following staff members and former staff members who participated in conducting this project and in the preparation of this report: Paul Alexander, Ann E. Allen, George C. Bradley, Stephen C. Brown, Sophie C. Eilperin, Charles A. Ericksen, Lawrence B. Glick, Howard A. Glickstein, Martha B. Grey, Peter W. Gross, Hedy A. Harris, David H. Hunter, Lorraine W. Jackson, Othello T. Jones, Karen J. Krueger, Michele A. Macon, Carol J. McCabe, Leona Marx, Philip Montez, John H. Powell, Jr., C. Anita Prout, Everett J. Santos, Jacob Schlitt, Martin E. Sloane, Conrad P. Smith, John C. Ulfelder, Brenda A. Watts, Carole A. Williams, Jacques E. Wilmore.

Footnotes

1. Hearing Before the U.S. Commission on Civil Rights, St. Louis, Missouri, 301 (1970) (hereafter referred to as St. Louis Hearing).
2. Id. at 302.
3. Id. at 460.
4. Statement of Dr. George H. Brown, director, Bureau of the Census, U.S. Department of Commerce, Hearing Before the U.S. Commission on Civil Rights, Washington, D.C., table 1.5 at 531 (1971) (hereafter referred to as Washington Hearing).
5. Based on table 5, id. at 539.
6. Table 8, id. at 542-559.
7. Bureau of the Census, U.S. Department of Commerce, Population Inside and Outside Central Cities by Race: 2000, in Washington Hearing at 1087. These figures are not predictions, but projections of present trends based on various characteristics of the population and on alternative demographic assumptions.
8. U.S. Department of Labor, Black Americans 14 (1971).
9. Id.
10. Statement of Dr. George H. Brown, director, Bureau of the Census, U.S. Department of Commerce, Washington Hearing at 528. The National Commission on Urban Problems wrote in its report Building the American City (1968) (hereafter referred to as Douglas Commission Report) at 52:
    The suburban ring has a majority of the residents of the metropolitan area. It also has less than its proportionate share of the poor, and only 5 percent of American nonwhites . . . . The suburbs, however, contain nearly half the white metropolitan poor—a figure which suggests that the suburbs discriminate more on the basis of race than on the basis of economic status.
11. Washington Hearing at 527-528. These figures are for metropolitan areas having a population of one million or more.
12. Testimony of Charles Mahone, Transcript of Open Meeting Before the District of Columbia Advisory Committee to the U.S. Commission on Civil Rights 45 (May 14, 1970) (hereafter referred to as D.C. SAC Transcript).
13. Hearing Before the U.S. Commission on Civil Rights, Baltimore, Maryland, 108 (1970) (hereafter referred to as Baltimore Hearing).
14. W. B. Neenan, Political Economy of Urban Areas 16 (1972).
15. See R. Farley, The Changing Distribution of Negroes within Metropolitan Areas: The Emergence of Black Suburbs, 75 Am. J. 512 (1970); Suburbia: The New American Plurality, Time Magazine, March 15, 1971, at 14.